T0390308

Eastern Africa Series

KAMBA PROVERBS
FROM EASTERN KENYA

Eastern Africa Series

Women's Land Rights & Privatization in Eastern Africa
BIRGIT ENGLERT
& ELIZABETH DALEY (EDS)

War & the Politics of Identity in Ethiopia
KJETIL TRONVOLL

Moving People in Ethiopia
ALULA PANKHURST
& FRANÇOIS PIGUET (EDS)

Living Terraces in Ethiopia
ELIZABETH E. WATSON

Eritrea
GAIM KIBREAB

Borders & Borderlands as Resources in the Horn of Africa
DEREJE FEYISSA
& MARKUS VIRGIL HOEHNE (EDS)

After the Comprehensive Peace Agreement in Sudan
ELKE GRAWERT (ED.)

Land, Governance, Conflict & the Nuba of Sudan
GUMA KUNDA KOMEY

Ethiopia
JOHN MARKAKIS

Resurrecting Cannibals
HEIKE BEHREND

Pastoralism & Politics in Northern Kenya & Southern Ethiopia
GÜNTHER SCHLEE
& ABDULLAHI A. SHONGOLO

Islam & Ethnicity in Northern Kenya & Southern Ethiopia
GÜNTHER SCHLEE
with ABDULLAHI A. SHONGOLO

Foundations of an African Civilisation
DAVID W. PHILLIPSON

Regional Integration, Identity & Citizenship in the Greater Horn of Africa
KIDANE MENGISTEAB
& REDIE BEREKETEAB (EDS)

Dealing with Government in South Sudan
CHERRY LEONARDI

The Quest for Socialist Utopia
BAHRU ZEWDE

Disrupting Territories
JÖRG GERTEL, RICHARD ROTTENBURG
& SANDRA CALKINS (EDS)

The African Garrison State
KJETIL TRONVOLL
& DANIEL R. MEKONNEN

The State of Post-conflict Reconstruction
NASEEM BADIEY

Gender, Home & Identity
KATARZYNA GRABSKA

Remaking Mutirikwi
JOOST FONTEIN

Lost Nationalism
ELENA VEZZADINI

The Oromo & the Christian Kingdom of Ethiopia
MOHAMMED HASSEN

Darfur
CHRIS VAUGHAN

The Eritrean National Service
GAIM KIBREAB

Ploughing New Ground
GETNET BEKELE

Hawks & Doves in Sudan's Armed Conflict
SUAD M. E. MUSA

Ethiopian Warriorhood
TSEHAI BERHANE-SELASSIE

Land, Migration & Belonging
JOSEPH MUJERE

Land Tenure Security
SVEIN EGE (ED.)

Tanzanian Development
DAVID POTTS (ED.)

Nairobi in the Making
CONSTANCE SMITH

The Crisis of Democratization in the Greater Horn of Africa
KIDANE MENGISTEAB (ED.)

The Mission of Apolo Kivebulaya
EMMA WILD-WOOD

The Struggle for Land & Justice in Kenya
AMBREENA MANJI

Imperialism & Development
NICHOLAS WESTCOTT

*Kamba Proverbs from Eastern Kenya**
JEREMIAH M. KITUNDA

*Sports & Modernity in Late Imperial Ethiopia**
KATRIN BROMBER

* forthcoming

Kamba Proverbs from Eastern Kenya

Sources, Origins, and History

JEREMIAH M. KITUNDA

JAMES CURREY

James Currey
is an imprint of Boydell & Brewer Ltd
PO Box 9, Woodbridge, Suffolk IP12 3DF (GB)
www.jamescurrey.com

and of

Boydell & Brewer Inc.
668 Mt Hope Avenue, Rochester, NY 14620-2731 (US)
www.boydellandbrewer.com

© Jeremiah M. Kitunda 2021

First published in hardback 2021

The right of Jeremiah M. Kitunda to be identified as
the author of this work has been asserted in accordance with
sections 77 and 78 of the Copyright, Designs and Patents Act 1988

All Rights Reserved. Except as permitted under current legislation
no part of this work may be photocopied, stored in a retrieval system,
published, performed in public, adapted, broadcast, transmitted,
recorded or reproduced in any form or by any means, without the
prior permission of the copyright owner

The publisher has no responsibility for the continued existence or accuracy
of URLs for external or third-party internet websites referred to in this book,
and does not guarantee that any content on such websites is, or will remain,
accurate or appropriate

British Library Cataloguing in Publication Data
A catalogue record for this book is available from the British Library

ISBN 978-1-84701-280-7 (James Currey hardback)

This publication is printed on acid-free paper

Dedication

To the pioneer of the history of Ũkamba, Professor Kennell Jackson: *Mũndũ mũnene aumawa na ũkewa,* 'An elder is mocked through a story.' If there are imperfections in your pioneering work, we critique your underestimation of Kamba antiquity with humility.

To Professor Steven Feierman for your pioneering study on the antiquity of the Kamba Diaspora in Tanzania: *Kĩĩma mũtumĩa wona ekaĩle kamumbo, kĩvĩsĩ kiivona kĩlĩsĩte muumo kathaku,* 'A mountain an elder can see while sitting on a stool, a boy cannot see while perching on the pinnacle of a fig tree.' Not from the lofty mountains of Usambara but from the bellies of the Pangani ravines did you see Kamba antiquity stretching to the horizon.

To my parents, Agnes Kalũnda Kĩtũnda and Joseph Kĩtũnda Mũtava for instilling wisdom and fortitude. To my ancestors Mũtava wa Mũtũa wa Kyaũlũ wa Kĩvaa wa Tusya Ũteme and Mũkua Manzĩ na Kĩthango as well as my maternal ancestors Mũli wa Maĩthya wa Syĩngĩ. Thank you for passing down these proverbs to my generation.

To my grandmothers Nzembi mwĩĩtu wa Ĩlivĩ wa Kitonga and maternal grandmother, Mũmbi mwĩĩtu wa Kasũva for bequeathing me a special collection of *nthimo sya ĩvia yaũthia* – proverbs of the grindstone. Many evenings I sat close to you as you ground millet between two stones (*ĩvia na nzio*), singing songs that were full of proverbs, and so grinding those proverbs into my memory. I will forever sing your songs in proverbs.

Finally, to all Akamba. I hope this collection of your ancestors' wit and wisdom will help you renew your loci and locus in the twenty-first century.

Contents

Note on Translation and Orthography — ix
Acknowledgements — xi
Chronology — xiii
Map of Kenya showing location of Ũkamba — xvi

Part I: Introduction
1. Introduction — 3

Part II: The Natural World
2. Atmosphere and Biosphere — 13
3. Wild Plants — 27
4. Wild Game — 42
5. Wild Birds — 58
6. Predators and Vermin — 71
7. Insects in Kamba History — 93
8. Amphibians and Reptiles — 107

Part III: Kamba at Home
9. Farm, Hearth, and Home — 119
10. Crops and Other Plants — 150
11. Domesticated Animals — 169
12. Men and Masculinity — 206
13. Women and Motherhood — 228
14. Children and Adulthood — 250

Part IV: Kamba Society

15. Place Names and Ethnic Names	271
16. Beliefs, Rituals, and Cosmology	291
17. Wealth and Poverty	302
18. Cuisine and Consumption	314
19. Health, Healing, and the Body	334
20. Trade, Markets, and Industries	354
21. Politics, Conflict, and Peacemaking	397
Select Bibliography	433
Index	443

Note on Translation and Orthography

A note on Kamba orthography and translation is important for comprehending Kamba proverbs. It is also helpful to comment on how the term Kamba is used in the book. Kĩkamba is the language of the Akamba people and that word will be used in reference to the language. In the Western world, the anglicized version, Kamba, is used to refer to the people, culture, and language. In the book, Kamba will refer to the people or culture. This term is used with or without the definite article (depending on nuance). The people reside in the Eastern Kenya region that they call Ũkamba. The term Ũkambanĩ refers to those inside the land of Kamba.

In translating Kĩkamba proverbs into English, I have tried to be as literal as possible, but when a literal translation into English would obscure rather than clarify the meaning, I have opted for a dynamic equivalence, or paraphrase, to capture the general sense. Such divergences are explained in the commentary. These proverbs are written in Kĩkamba orthography followed by a literal translation. Tone marks will reliably guide the reader to the correct pronunciation of the written text, which in turn will aid comprehension.

Kĩkamba employs seventeen letters of the alphabet (a, c, e, ĩ, i, k, l, m, o, s, t, ũ, u, v, w, y, and z) with a few variations across dialects. The letters /I/ and /U/ are split into two accents. The letter /I/ is split into two sounds: /Ĩ/ produces sounds like *it* in English. The second /i/ sounds like the letter /e/ in English, as in the word *eat*, for instance. It is imperative to distinguish the letter /i/ from /ĩ/ and the letter /u/ from /ũ/. The diacritical in the letters I and U make an extremely important difference in pronunciation, comprehension, meaning, and interpretation of words. These tiny differences affect comprehension of written proverbs. If /u/ is used instead of /ũ/ or the letter /i/ instead of /ĩ/, for instance, Kamba speakers will not comprehend the proverbs at all, or only partially. This again strengthens the need to render proverbs as they are spoken and collected from the field. As Bartlett Whiting noted, 'Proverbs owe their birth not to the pen, but to the tongue, their appeal is not to the eye but to the ear.'[1] Therefore, their proper meanings are found in their original dialects. For that reason, each proverb is presented the way it was spoken and collected, leaving the dialects intact. Thus, proverbs collected from Mwingi are rendered in a way that other dialects may consider unusual Kĩkamba. A proverb like *Sere ndwĩ serasya*, 'A clattering sound does not produce itself', will sound unusual to Kĩkamba speakers in Machakos. Likewise, the Kitui Kamba will find it hard to understand a proverb like: *Mũtuma kĩnene e matako makwothea*, 'Whoever weaves a big basket has thighs for twining.' The word *matako* in Machakos means thighs but in Kitui it means buttocks. Kamba women twine threads on their thighs, not on their buttocks.

The consonant /b/ must be preceded by the letter /m/ to form a word, and the letters /d/ and /g/ must be preceded by the letter /n/ to form a word. The letter /h/ must be preceded by /t/ to form a word. In some cases in the book, /nz/ and /nth/ are used interchangeably, the latter representing Kitui dialects, and the former Machakos dialects. For example, *nzakame* in Kitui and *Nthakame* (blood) in Machakos.

The Machakos dialect codified by missionaries in the early 1900s does not use the letters /c/ and /r/. Moreover, it does not use the letter /g/ without /n/ before it. In the dialects of Kitui and the diaspora, these letters are used freely. They have to be used in recording, translating, and presenting proverbs, lest the proverbs lose their meaning and flavour. Remarkably, between the 1840s and 1890s, missionaries and ethnographers used this language – the Kitui and diasporic dialects as 'standard Kĩkamba'. The first vocabularies and dictionaries were based on dialects spoken in coastal Kenya and the Mpwapwa region of central Tanzania. It was not until the African Inland Mission took the lead in the robust study and publication of Kĩkamba from the 1930s that the Machakos dialect(s) came to be adopted for written Kĩkamba. The choice of the Machakos dialect(s) to serve as the standard for Kĩkamba was based on two facts both unrelated to any linguistic convention: first, its proximity to missionary stations and to the seats of imperial power in Machakos and colonial power in Nairobi; and second, the assumption that all Kamba evolved from Machakos before they spread to Kitui and the diaspora. Twentieth-century linguists gradually accepted the Machakos dialect merely for convenience as the 'standard form' of Kĩkamba.

---

[1] Bartlett Jere Whiting, *Proverbs in the Earlier English Drama* (Cambridge: Harvard University Press, 1938), xi.

Acknowledgements

This book is a result of many years of labour and for that reason incurred many debts from many people and institutions. Special thanks go to Appalachian State University for a faculty travel fund that financed research for this book. I am also deeply grateful to my colleagues at Appalachian State University for their support and invaluable comments on the draft chapters of this book. Topping this list are Ralph Lentz II, Michael Behrent, René Horst, Cameron Gokee, and Sheila Phipps. Outside Appalachian State, I am grateful to Professor Paul Custer, Tim Parsons, and Myles Osborne for reading draft manuscripts very critically, to Tony Bly for reading parts of the draft and to Dr Vincent Kituku for helping to analyse the Kamba proverbs. These colleagues offered substantial comments and corrections on various drafts of the manuscript. Without the immense effort, time, and commitment of Professor W. Scott Jessee this book would not have taken its current shape. I greatly thank Scott for patiently reading with a keen eye all the drafts of the manuscript.

Several graduate students deserve sincere acknowledgement for diverse roles in the preparation of the manuscript. I am grateful to Thomas McLamb for sketching the map, Josie Brown and Sarah Shartzer for their vital roles in organizing the data for the manuscript. Several interviewees deserve special thanks because they were my real teachers and mentors in the journey of writing this book. Mũsumbĩ Mũsilũ wa Mũvuvi of Kasilũnĩ tops the list of my informants. Mũsumbĩ combined several qualities that made him an outstanding informant capable of contextualizing most proverbs. From his collection of songs, I mined numerous proverbs analysed here.

My college best friend at the University of Nairobi, Nicodemus Mũasa Mũinde and his family extended invaluable hospitality during my research. Nicodemus connected me with a chain of well-informed elders within the Kabati and Wĩnzyei areas in Kitui. The most outstanding contact in this group was his grandmother, Mrs Nzũla wa Nzũmbĩ, singer and political campaigner. Thoroughly familiar with the history of Ũkamba, she helped navigate the proverbs of Central Kitui. From her songs I also extracted considerable new proverbs.

I recall with pleasure the assistance rendered to me by Joseph Mboya Mwanzĩa from Nũũ, Eliya Mwoki wa Manda from Maaĩ, Kĩlonzi Nzou and Mũsili Mũnũve of the Kenya Prisons (Kĩtui), and numerous Kamba residents of Nairobi. They supplied me with multiple proverbs and explained their meanings and origins.

I also want to thank social media groups of Kamba youth whose focus on exchanging proverbs via radio, YouTube, WhatsApp, and Facebook, spurred my interest in collecting and publishing Kamba proverbs. These groups greatly informed and enriched my collection. Special mention is due to Mutĩsya wa Mbatha alias Mutĩsya Wa Ngai aka Kyuo Kya Ngoso of Mumbunĩ (Machakos). Mbatha, a journalist and cultural enthusiast, has coined numerous axiomatic statements that are now recognized as *nthimo* – proverbs. I thank him for also inviting me to several social media groups whose regional diversity helped access views from different parts of my study area.

Great thanks to my relatives, well-wishers, teachers, and classmates for their moral support during the challenging years of my pre-college education. Exceptional thanks go to the Kyuso District officer Ali Alim Salim and his secretary Mr Julius Malonza (1983–87) and then Mwingĩ North Member of Parliament Honorable Stephen Kalonzo Musyoka, Chandaria Foundation, and the Lions Club of Thika, for their priceless support for my secondary and high-school education. At the University of Nairobi, I will be forever grateful for the help and mentorship that I received from Dr David Sperling, Dr Henry Mutoro, Dr Godfrey Muriuki, and Father Thomas MacDonald of the University of Nairobi Chaplaincy. I finally want to thank my wife Beatrice Mũeni and our boys Thomas Ndoto, Alan Kĩvaa, Aaron Nzengũ, and Caleb Mainga for their patience during the writing of this book. In short, I owe the success of this work to the above-mentioned people and institutions. I only own the errors and shortfalls of it.

Chronology

Antiquity and Monsoon Exchange Era 1000–500 BCE	The Kamba Bantu ancestors settled in East Africa according to archaeological and linguistic studies (Fourshey, 2018).
500 BCE–500 CE	The Kamba split from Nyamwezi in central Tanzania and migrate towards Kilimanjaro. Loquats and bananas reached East Africa from Asia (according to Maddox, 2006).
500 CE–600 CE	According to traditions, twenty-five Kamba families migrated from Kilimanjaro northwards through Taitaland to Ũkamba. They practised farming, apiculture, gathering, hunting, and herding.
600–700	Dispersal from Machakos into Kitui, Mount Kenya, Coast, Mount Kilimanjaro, and Mainland Tanzania. Development of the Kĩnana trade system. Asian Muslims settle on the coast and increase trade with the inland (Maddox, 2006).
Islamic Era 700–1497 800–1000	Al-Masudi (1975) describes the presence of the Kamba along the coast. Expansion of the kĩng'ang'a/kĩnana trade system into regional and long-distance trade. Asian chicken, sugarcane, and narcotic plants reach East Africa (Maddox, 2006).
1100–1300	Intensified cultivation of millet, cowpeas, pigeon peas, loquats, bananas, and sugarcane as well as intensified ivory trade with the coast and Ethiopia. The Kamba invade the Tanzanian Coast and establish dynasties across Tanzania (Feierman, 1974).

1300–1500	Immigrant Mũsei arriving on Ũseri plains from Ũkamba lay the foundation of the Marangu Chiefdom of the Chaga. The Kamba engaged in counter-raids with the Kilwa Sultanate, according to Ibn Battuta (Dunn, 1986). In April 1498, Vasco da Gama anchors at Mombasa port.
Vascon Exchange Era 1500–1800	Portuguese occupation of East Africa coast disrupts coastal trade, but stimulates expansion of inland trade (Maddox, 2006).
1600–1800	The Kamba acquires tobacco, maize, cassava, pawpaw, and sweet potatoes from the New World. Expansion of the Kwavi pastoralists to East Africa stimulating the Kamba political and social reorganization. Development of *mbenge* settlement patterns and political militarism developed in response to Kwavi raids (Ambler, 1988; Maddox, 2006).
Imperial Era 1800–1900	European imperialism grows, coinciding with ecological catastrophes in East Africa. The Kamba herdsmen, traders, and ecological refugees settle in parts of the coast and Tanzania.
1820–1830	British and French officers record the Kamba residents and traders along the coast.
1844–1859	Pioneer missionaries reach Ũkamba and the diasporic settlements across Tanzania. The first Kamba dictionaries and histories are written. The Kamba trade stretches from Ethiopia to the coast (Krapf, 1860).
1860–1889	Extensive documentation of the Kamba lifeways. Acquisition of more plants from around the world through imperial commerce.
Colonial Era 1889–1963	British administration of Kenya leads to increased ethnographic data, European material culture and lifestyles.

1914–1944	The Kamba enlist in the British imperial army, police force, and private security services. Droughts, famines, overcrowding, and colonial policies shatter traditional economies. Automobiles, donkeys, cats, horses, new breeds of cattle, dogs, chickens, and more plants reach Ũkamba. Towns, roads, clothes, markets, utensils, Western education and religions appear.
Independence and modernity 1963–1999	Modern schooling, European dress, radio, and modern building styles evident in Ũkamba, which forms part of the eastern province of Kenya.
Rise of social media 2000–2020	With political and technological changes, mobile phones, television, radio, vernacular magazines, the internet, and social media become stomping grounds for proverbs.

Map of Kenya showing location of Ũkamba. Credit: Thomas McLamb.

Part I

Introduction

1
Introduction

Proverbs are not simply relics of the past that provide entertainment and linguistic fun. As part of oral tradition, they contain historical and anthropological knowledge often missing from conventional sources. As condensed history, they assist in the reconstruction of the manners, characteristics, and worldviews of societies. They encode micro-histories concealed within their phraseology that provide unique historical information and pedagogical examples in ways that textual data cannot. Their origins can be traced through content analysis to reveal the historical and cultural contexts within which they were created and used.

This book presents a collection of two thousand proverbs of the Kamba of Eastern Kenya. It explores the proverbs as legitimate subjects of history, historical source material, and pedagogical tools, as well as conflict management tools. It draws from archival, herbaria, and museum data, oral interviews, as well as published sources of ethnographers, missionaries, pre-independence and post-independence collectors. The book traces the origins of each proverb within the cultural context of its appearance and later use.

The Kamba proverbs have defied modernity. Although their original meanings might have changed as modern generations apply them to their altered circumstances, in both urban and rural areas Kamba conversations are coloured with proverbs. The rise of social media in the early 2000s rejuvenated the use of proverbs among young Kamba despite their engagement with commerce and modernity or urban residence. As they acquired mobile phones and internet access, they exchanged proverbs via social media. Proverbial inferences can reveal vital information missing in conventional histories. They suggest that the Kamba were involved with the outside world in four successive periods of East African history: the *Monsoon Exchange era* from the age of the Roman Empire through the Islamic era to the end of 1497; the *Vascon Exchange era* from 1498 to 1799; the age of European imperialism and colonialism from about 1800 to the 1960s; and the era of independence since 1963.

The Kamba proverbs can redress this 'silencing the past' as relations of power came to shape sources, archives, narration, and a new corpus.[1] They provide an archive of social dynamics in the *lived* past. They can undercut colonial and postcolonial narratives developed from written records and state-sponsored oral traditions in several ways: they can be made by anyone with a knack for observation and turn of phrase; they become mental archives shared among everyone from schoolchildren to elders; they frame the past through storytelling.

Proverbs convey a 'thicker' description of the cultural practices and beliefs surrounding past people, places, and things, inspiring us to picture houses and artefacts so often turned up during archaeological fieldwork. Revealing the cultural and historical context of the proverbs is key to the pursuit of the history of Ũkamba and East Africa. Engagement with proverbs reveals new historical methods, and source materials that can facilitate research into multiple subjects in a manner that textual data cannot.[2]

Much of the existing literature tends to be ahistorical and largely the product of the colonial project whose interest was confined primarily to missionary work and colonial administration, as a path into the African mindset, making subject peoples easier to control. The respective prefaces of the works of ethnographers and colonial administrators' publications reveal that Europeans collected African proverbs as tools for fine tuning indirect rule.[3]

This study focuses on the historical contexts of the proverbs, examining proverbs along the lines suggested by Dwight Marvin and Oyekan Owomoyela, who leave no doubt that the age of proverbs can be estimated with considerable accuracy.[4] This can be done through content analysis, a method that reveals the approximate age of proverbs once historical markers within them are identified.[5] In 2005, Owomoyela analysed more than five thousand Yoruba proverbs and traced their history to their specific date or to a general period of creation, demonstrating that proverbs could be historicized. Nowadays, the etymology

---

[1] Michel-Rolph Trouillot, *Silencing the Past* (New York: Beacon Press, 1995), passim.
[2] Leroy Vail and Landeg White, *Power and the Praise Poem* (New York: James Currey, 1992), 319–20; Wolfgang Mieder, *African Proverb Scholarship* (Colorado Springs: African Proverbs Project, 1994), 5–6.
[3] Ferdinand Walser, *Luganda Proverbs* (Berlin: Reimer, 1982); Gerhard Lindblom, *Notes on Kamba Grammar* (Uppsala: Appelbergs Boktrykeri Aktiebolag, 1926); Emma Farnsworth, *A Kamba Grammar* (Nairobi: AIM, 1957).
[4] Dwight Marvin, *The Antiquity of Proverbs* (New York: G.P. Putnam, 1922), passim; Oyekan Owomoyela, *Yoruba Proverbs* (Lincoln: University of Nebraska Press, 2005), passim.
[5] George Gerbner, et al. (eds), *The Analysis of Communication Content* (New York: Wiley, 1969), 103.

of multiple English proverbs appears on websites. Researchers can scrutinize such accessible sources to get the point here: the history of proverbs is easy to excavate.[6] However, some have hidden historical markers requiring analysis of the content to date. Others have no historical markers at all. It is a mistake to assume that the earliest known record of a saying indicates its origin.

There are misconceptions that proverbs cannot be traced. They were 'utterances of unknown philosophers, the fragments of historic records, the attributed responses to precolonial oracles or the accepted lessons of forgotten myths and fables'.[7] Such assumptions rest on the definition of proverbs as static relics of the past, created in primordial times with creation ceasing thereafter. The truth is that proverbs emerge, grow over time and place; they age out and die as new ones are created and replace the old maxims.

In an increasingly homogenized world the task of collecting undocumented proverbs is ever more urgent, because as Kenyan ethnic groups assimilate to the broader society they are losing domains, speakers, and proverbial lore. This is clear in the loss of their oral art and proverbs at a rate of 60 per cent per generation.[8]

To the Kamba, proverbs are terse expressions with something withheld. This paradoxical structure of proverbs – as bearers of historical information and as floating signifiers – suggests a novel kind of dialogical reading. *Nthimo nĩ ndeto nthime na ndeto nzave. Na ĩngĩ nthimo nĩ ndeto sya ũkanio, ũthuthyo na ũthekya*, meaning proverbs are measured, weighed, and condensed statements for audiences and purposes of warning, encouragement, and amusement. *Nthimo* are passed through generations and endlessly created for admonition, encouragement, and amusement as well as to teach historical lessons, highlight good morals, and instil social values. All are familiar in all parts of Ũkambanĩ and constitute one of the subtle discursive links binding the Kamba.

Most proverbs employ introductory phrases that help determine the antiquity of a proverb, such as *Mũkamba wa tene aisye*, 'the ancient Mũkamba said', or *Mũkamba wa tene*, referring to ancestors who cannot even be listed in a genealogy. Another is *Mũkamba mũkw'ũ aisye*, 'The dead Kamba said', to mark the oldest proverbs whose originators cannot be traced. The second oldest class of proverbs, known to have been propounded by someone who can be remembered but remains nameless, is introduced by *Ve mũtumĩa wasyaa*, 'There was an old man who used to say'. The third class contains the original author's name as

[6] Owomoyela, *Yoruba*, 26–9; Durotoye Adeleke, 'Yoruba Proverbs as Historical Records', *Proverbium* 26 (2009): 19–48.
[7] Marvin, *Antiquity*, 35–107.
[8] Gerard Wanjohi, *Under One Roof* (Nairobi: Paulines Publications Africa, 2001), 1–6.

Matĩ wa Syũi asyaa, 'Matĩ wa Syũi used to say'. With proverbs attributed to an author, it becomes difficult to determine whether it is a fresh formulation or simply reused and attributed to speakers such as Matĩ wa Syũi. Singers and poets often reinvigorated proverbs in public, or simply employed them to season and popularize their works. Sometime speakers hide the name of the singer and say *Ve ngũi yainie yasya*, 'There was a musician who sang and spoke.' Other speakers quote parents and grandparents, as in *ũmau ambĩiye* or *ũmau ambĩyaa or andavisye*, 'my grandfather told me'.

These introductory phrases (such as *Ve ngũi yainie yasya* ... and so on) within proverbs reveal that some are recent enough for their sources to be found, while others emerged many centuries ago and the memory of the sources are lost. Each generation creates its own proverbs, adding to earlier ones to suit their needs in changing cultural and environmental circumstances. Often, they refer to new religions, plants, animals, and pathogens, encounters with other cultures, or the occurrence of environmental and economic changes. Each proverb carries a miniature history in its phrasing, hence revealing its own history. Researchers can correlate this information with general historical knowledge to approximate the date of creation.

Oral interviews constitute another method of determining the age of proverbs. Contrary to the prevailing assumption that Africans do not care about the origins of proverbs, my interviewees readily cited the first person and place they heard the proverb. They relished discussing the age of proverbs using content analysis and phraseology.

History of the Kamba proverbs

The history of collecting Kamba proverbs began in 1911, when the pioneering Swedish ethnographer Gerhard Lindblom (known to the Kamba as *Mũtya Ĩtumo* – one who captured a spear) collected fifty-three proverbs of immense historical value. Lindblom provided English translations and brief explanations of the meaning of each.[9] While Lindblom's work remains an outstanding source of Kamba proverbs, inaccuracies in translation, cultural misinterpretation, and the use of Swedish phonetic notation makes the book extremely difficult for readers. Even Kamba readers rely on the English translation due to the difficulty of Lindblom's style. These fifty-three proverbs, coming from a generation of old men born between 1800 and 1840, provide a case in point that proverbs can be historicized. We know that they existed by 1900. That Lindblom's informants had heard these proverbs as children lends credence to a conclusion that most circulated in the 1700s. If the

---

[9] Gerhard Lindblom, *African Wanderings* (Stockholm: Bonnier, 1914), 28–9.

informants heard them from their grandparents, such grandparents must have been at least sixty years old by the early 1800s, thus born in the Vascon era and earlier. This is one way of digging out the history of proverbs.

Thereafter, collection of proverbs progressed in six phases over a century. Proverbs collected between 1939 and 1952 was the work of the missionary Emma Farnsworth under the auspices of the African Inland Mission (hereafter the AIM) – a colonial mission enterprise. In 1952, Farnsworth published eighty-one proverbs in *A Kamba Grammar* based on the dialect of central Machakos. Half-way through the book, Farnsworth declared, 'No translation will be given for the remaining proverbs'; forty-one of these have been translated here for the first time. Farnsworth's collection came from both men and women of a specific place, Central Machakos, largely urbanized, Westernized, and Christianized.[10] These aspects affect the quality and structure of her collection compared to that of Lindblom's, which came from across Ũkamba from traditional Kamba men only. Farnsworth's collection reflects not only the AIM missionary sentiments, but also the cultural and historical experiences of central Machakos. All these limitations must be kept in mind. Nonetheless, Farnsworth's informants could recall historical events as far back as 1800 and the proverbs that refer to events dating back to the 1800s can help historians gauge the events as predating the Vascon era.

Afterwards, the mantle passed to an emergent class of educated and urbanized Christian Kamba men who graduated from Kenyan mission schools and universities outside Kenya. From 1952 to 1962, this emergent class of Kamba elites collected proverbs with objectives and methods utterly different from those of either Lindblom or Farnsworth. They were in their late twenties when they published their novels and storybooks with sprinklings of childhood proverbs.

Their collections celebrate the glorious past of the Kamba trade, hunting, honey-search, cattle-rustling expeditions, and subtle social interactions between the Kamba and their ecological settings. Some collectors defended traditions while others openly advocated for European lifestyles. The new generation of the Kamba elites pushed for the abandonment of Kamba traditions in pursuit of a 'more progressive *Mūsūngū* culture', 'modernity'. Sprinklings of proverbs appeared in Kamba grammars, novels, and storybooks. David Mwandia was perhaps the earliest Mũkamba to publish something pertinent to Kamba proverbs. His *Kilovoo* published in 1952 and *Kũsoma Kwa Kelĩ* published in 1957 featured four proverbs.[11] John Mbiti used proverbs in 1954 when

---

[10] Farnsworth, *Grammar*, 65.
[11] David Mwandia, *Kilovoo* (London: Eagle Press, 1952); David Mwandia, *Kũsoma Kwa Kelĩ* (London: McMillan, 1958), 14–47; William Stanner, 'The Kitui

he published *Mutunga na Ngewa yake,* the first indication that Kamba proverbs could feature in literary works. Mbiti has published poetry, storybooks, and other scholarly texts with multiple proverbs from central Kitui over a period of sixty-five years.[12] In 1962, David Kimilu published 247 proverbs in *Mūkamba Wa W'o,* the largest collection in a single publication, which have remained untranslated. Kimilu decried the declining interest of his generation in the culture and proverbial wisdom of their society.

The pre-independence generation's audience were expatriates. They also hoped to reach a population of readers that would emerge as literacy surged in foreseen decades. Generally, the purpose of writing at that time was to entertain younger generations and instil a desire for ancient Kīkamba stories, tales, and proverbs.[13] The authors recognized the vital functions of proverbs in introductions and conclusions to oral narratives, as was the practice with their storytellers. However, untranslated the proverbs would be of limited access. The publications of Farnsworth, Kimilu, and Mailu would have benefited a broader readership if translated into English and edited.

From 1963 to 1999 journalists and scholars systematically collected proverbs covering various themes, mainly about the precolonial era. In 1966, John Mbiti's *Akamba Stories* included proverbs.[14] The following year, Blanche Watuma's *Kūsoma kwa Katatū* continued from where Mwandia had left off.[15] David Mailu, on the Voice of Kenya, recited Kīkamba poems full of proverbs on national radio. In 1972, he published these poems and proverbs in an anthology, *Kī Kyambonie,* untranslated and now out of print. This little book contained proverbs from a corner of Machakos only rarely researched.[16] In 1990, Mwīkali Kīeti and Peter Coughlin published *Barking, You'll be Eaten*, with several new proverbs translated into English and accurately analysed. Significantly it was the first product of a collaboration between a Kamba author and a Western scholar. The complementary quality of the research and presentation is immense.[17]

Kamba Market, 1938–1939', *Ethnology* 8(2) (April 1969), 125–38; David Kimilu, *Mūkamba wa w'o* (Nairobi: Kenya Literature Bureau, 1962); Roy Mutisya, *Kīkamba Proverbs and Idioms* (Nairobi: Roma Publishers, 2002).

[12] John Mbiti, *Mutunga na Ngewa yake* (Nairobi: East Africa Literature Bureau, 1954).

[13] James Mūīmi, *Ngewa ya Syana* (Nairobi: Mowa Publishers, 1981).

[14] John Mbiti, *Akamba Stories* (Nairobi: Oxford University Press, 1983).

[15] Blanche Watuma and L.K. Mwaniki, *Kūsoma kwa Katatū* (Nairobi: Rabbit Books, 1989); Blanche Watuma, *Mūkamba na Syīthīo Syake* (Nairobi: Sengani Publishers, 2011), 51.

[16] David Mailu, *Kīkyambonie: Kīkamba Nthimo* (Nairobi: Combs Books, 1972).

[17] Mwīkali Kīeti and Peter Coughlin, *Barking, You'll be Eaten! The Wisdom of Kamba Oral Literature* (Nairobi: Phoenix Publishers, 1990).

Since 2000 there has been a surge of publications with collections of proverbs by both scholars and non-academic authors. In 2002, Roy Mutisya published 350 proverbs and 200 idioms in *Kĩkamba Proverbs and Idioms: Nthimo sya Kĩkamba na Myasyo*. Hailing from the Tiva River area of Kitui, he included new proverbs from southern Kitui. He was the first to gather a collection of proverbs and idioms in a single publication and distinguished between the two.[18] In 2006, John Mwau published a well-designed dictionary. Its value lay in the fact that since the first Kĩĩkamba–English dictionary by Johannes Krapf in 1850, none of the numerous dictionaries covered Kamba proverbs. Besides names of Kamba clans, and months of the year, the dictionary contains some 445 Kamba proverbs.[19]

Kamba Proverbs from Eastern Kenya examines two thousand proverbs gathered since childhood, pulled from childhood memory, peers in education, public conversations, social media, radio, songs, published sources, and fieldwork. Originally, before my goal became more scholarly, I simply wanted to learn Kamba wisdom. Inspiration came from the African Proverb project, which called for renewed collection and publication of African proverbs.[20]

Fieldwork, including oral interviews, provided the bulk of my Kamba proverbs. As a native speaker of Kĩkamba, my access to the subtle spoken registers and hence the full richness of meaning of the language is considerable. In the Ngomenĩ ward of Kitui County where I grew up, my childhood was full of proverbs. Most evenings, my great-grandfather habitually summoned us to the *thome*, a large open circular outdoor hearth. On the authority of his towering age over even our octogenarian grandparents, among whom we children were comfortably sandwiched, my centenarian great-grandfather lectured about changes over time in Ũkamba, including Kamba customs, lifestyles, and history, framed always in proverbs. He sprinkled more proverbs into the plot and ended with another in his conclusion. Therefore, this study is in part based on personal experience and a collection of one thousand proverbs that I had assembled even before formal research.

After collecting thousands of proverbs, I investigated the origins, cultural context, meaning, and application of each. I used content analysis of each proverb for approximate dating, although often interviewees were able to date proverbs based on what they had heard from their grandparents. However, I was suspicious when interviewees

---

[18] Roy Mutisya, *Kĩkamba Proverbs and Idioms* (Nairobi: Roma Publishers, 2002).
[19] John Mwau, *Kĩkamba Dictionary: Kĩkamba–English: Kĩkamba–Kĩkamba: English–Kĩkamba* (Nairobi: Mwau, JH, 2006).
[20] http://www.bu.edu/africa/alp/index1/african-proverbs-project/#:~:text=In%20the%20African%20Proverbs%20Project,Africa%20and%20Swahili%20from%20Tanzania. Accessed 23 May 2021.

associated the origin of a proverb to a specific singer, poet, or speaker. Cross-examining such claims with information drawn from different sources proved that the proverbs often had older historical precedents.

Since 2002, Kamba proverbs have appeared in newspapers, on Facebook, Twitter, websites, and virtually all other media. Yet nothing will ever replace fieldwork and interviews as research techniques. Appeals through the internet yielded dismal results compared to what I gathered from travelling and meeting people on buses and taxis; in homes, villages, work places, and schools. Additionally, music, public speeches, and poetry presentations via YouTube, radio, and television programmes contained proverbs. However, there are some shortcomings of these sources. Social media collections can be repetitive, misspelled, mistranslated, nearly incomprehensible, and above all very unstable, disappearing without warning. Traditional oral transmissions are certainly more stable. This can be assessed through personal experience. Proverbs that I heard as a child were repeated and interpreted in the same way decades later when I launched formal research.

A review of archived information, published collections, and the broader literature on proverbs helped contextualize the data and underscored connections with earlier research. Over the last eighty-five years, various researchers have collected Kamba proverbs at different times without consulting earlier collections. In this book, no proverb is directly or indirectly repeated. The sources of proverbs that have been published are cited, but collections from the field are not.

Part II

The Natural World

2
Atmosphere and Biosphere

1. *Ĩlata ya mbua ti ĩlata ya sua.*[1] **Rain's footprint is not the sun's footprint.**
Kamba believed that if the sun was extremely hot during the dry season it was a sign for heavy rain at the end of the season. Then the rain had to stop and give the sun its chance to brood the crops in order to ripen. The footsteps of the two were different – while the sun can wither plant life, rain could destroy or nourish crops.

2. *Kana kaketũũa thano kambĩĩaa ũkolotya mbuanĩ.* **A child who gets diarrhoea during the dry season begins farting during the rainy season.**
Diarrhoea was common during the rainy season due to contaminated water. Numerous proverbs used diarrhoea as a symbol of things to come. Thus, this ancient proverb means that future events can be detected by observing certain signs.[2]

3. *Katu nĩ ka mbua.*[3] **A little cloud signals rain.**
This proverb emerged during the first millennium era with the rise of farming. Farmers were keen to observe rain patterns. Whenever Kamba saw clouds they knew that rain would soon follow. It means certain things can be predicted through observation. The second interpretation is that the only useful cloud is the one bearing rain. Here, the meaning would be to stop pursuing ventures that will not bring profit at the end.

4. *Kwakya kũte katu.* **It is a cloudless dawn.**
This is an old expression of 'the writing is on the wall' or 'your goose is cooked'. It alludes to daybreaks in Ũkamba that often start out with clear skies. This clearness symbolizes clarity, openness, and the end of all problems.

---

[1] Mwau, *Dictionary*, 647.
[2] Mwau, *Dictionary*, 666.
[3] Farnsworth, *Grammar*, 133; Mwau, *Dictionary*, 649.

5. *Mũthenya wĩ mbua ndwĩ matu.*[4] **The day rain will fall has no clouds.**
This adage points to the unpredictability of things. The Kamba made close observations and concluded that weather was hardly predictable. While certain clouds may indicate an impending rainfall, a day with clear skies in the morning can turn rainy in the afternoon. The proverb has multiple implications: while predictability is still guaranteed, there are things that are abrupt and unpredictable.

6. *Matukũ oonthe ti wa sikũkũ.* **Not all days are holidays.**
This axiom emerged after independence, before which the term *sikũ kũũ* – Swahili for the great day or holiday – was not used. Since independence, the Kenyan government has established twelve national holidays during which people rest and revel. The proverb means multiple things, including life is not always about good things.

7. *Matukũ ma kĩng'ei nĩ mwonza.* **The days of a thief are seven.**
Emerging from the Vascon era, this means a thief can only conceal his tricks for a while before being caught and punished through embarrassment, banishment, fines, or death, as detailed in Douglas Penwill's *Kamba Customary Law*. The adage may not involve theft per se, but broadly means that every wrongdoing forever has a tragic end.

8. *Ndyĩsũvaa ũtukũ kweteele ũkya nĩyonee nthĩ.* **I do not beg the night while the dawn is coming.**
An ancient expression of protest against the meanness of a miser. This is another way of saying that alternatives do exist if only some little effort is made to find them.

9. *Ũkaema ona mbũi nziũ mũthenya ona ũtukũ ndũmyona.* **If you cannot see a black goat during the day, you cannot see it at night.**
If one cannot see in broad daylight, how much less in darkness? This is a deeply figurative statement open to manifold interpretations and applications. If one cannot accomplish simple things at the opportune time, they cannot achieve anything in difficult times.

10. *Ũthũku ũkaa na sua ndũkemene.* **Misfortune comes with the sun, don't hate yourself.**
Tribulation is not permanent, it arrives one day and a solution is found the next day. Dating from antiquity, the proverb encourages listeners to persevere in spite of challenges, for bad days are fewer than good days.

---

[4] Kimilu, *Mũkamba*, 117.

11. *Ũseo nĩ kĩla mũthenya ũthũku nĩ mũthenya o ũmwe.* **Goodness is daily, evil only a day.**
This ancient axiom emphasized that people should not focus on misfortunes only. There are many good but unappreciated things occurring in life. Even though bad things are the most challenging, good days outnumber bad ones.

12. *Yumaatatũ ndĩtũaa yumaa no yĩĩsaa ĩvika.* **Monday does not last; Friday also comes.**
This maxim is localized to northern Kitui where the Swahili way of counting days of the week is employed. It means corrupt officials should be warned that the electorate in the next elections will penalize them heavily.

13. *Kyetho kya yũlũ kĩtũaa.* **The heavenly spring is not permanent.**
This maxim was said during the sowing season as a warning to farmers to sow quickly because the rain can stop at any time. It emerged towards the end of the first millennium when the Kamba began to cultivate the plains of Ũkamba where rain was unreliable.

14. *Mbua ndĩkĩlaw'a metho.* **No one can see beyond the rain.**
This is an observation from early farming during the first millennium, when rain is falling one cannot see far as if rain covers the whole earth. In the same way the future is unknowable.

15. *Mbua ndĩ kĩthuma.* **Rain has no hide.**
The key to comprehending this adage is *Kĩthuma*, an animal hide used as a tent in precolonial times. While the hide protected the family from wind and sun, heavy rain could make the skin soft enough to collapse, exposing people to the downpour, hence the literal meaning of the adage. The deeper meaning, however, is that there are unstoppable things. Honorable Chief Kitonga, Member of Parliament for Kitui East, popularized this axiom when he used it as a political slogan in the 1970s.

16. *Mbua ndyasyaa.*[5] **Rain does not fail.**
While the literal meaning may be that rain does not lead to loss, it implies that farmers do not toil in vain. When it rains, farmers are rewarded. These proverbs encourage farmers in a drought-prone terrain to persist even when prospects of harvest are poor. Farmers have unwavering faith in rain.

---

[5] Kimilu, *Mũkamba*, 116.

17. *Mbua ya ĩmantha ti ĩmwe.*[6] **There is more than one rain for searching for wealth.**
This encourages someone determined to triumph over failure arguing that rain (and so new life, new opportunities) will follow, but at the rain's pace, and on its terms. Thus, it argues for patience – one's work should be undertaken in harmony with, and under the tutelage of, a chance that is ultimately benevolent and life-affirming.

18. *Mbua ya ũnyenyeũ ndĩvandĩawa.* **Mist rain is not fit for sowing.**
The Kamba differentiated types of precipitation, each good for distinct activities. Mist rainfall, which could not support farming, was the least desirable. The proverb has been used in diverse fields, from politics to development programmes and marital relationships. In a political poem from which this proverb was collected, the speaker meant that the candidate elected previously was a passing cloud. Even though the candidate had won, the politician's ability to initiate development was doubtful. The statement has historical precedents back to antiquity.

19. *Mbua ya nundu ndĩkyesaa.* **Mist rain never ends.**
Observably, mist rain persisted longer than actual rain in Ũkambanĩ, but it was not useful to farming. Emerging from the Monsoon era of agricultural intensification, this multi-variation proverb was used by patriarchs cautioning family members to beware of a person who might entice them into companionship but whose intentions are suspect.

20. *Mbua ĩkĩlea kua ĩetae mũumbĩ.* **Fog precedes the failure of rain.**[7]
Emerging from the Monsoon era, this proverb means when rain is reluctant to fall it brings fog instead. One who is not willing to do something brings up fake excuses.

21. *Mbua yũlea kua ĩkwatasya ũkũngi.*[8] **When the rain fails to fall, it blames the wind.**
First recorded by Lindblom in 1911, this ancient adage has appeared in many publications, often with variations. The Kamba observed that whenever strong winds drove clouds away, the rain failed. The rain (humans) exonerates itself by blaming the wind (an excuse).[9]

---

[6] Vincent Kituku, *East African Folktales* (Little Rock: August House Publishers, 1997), 74.
[7] Mwau, *Dictionary*, 655; Mutisya, *Proverbs*, 19.
[8] Gerhard Lindblom, *Kamba Riddles, Proverbs and Songs* (Uppsala: Appelbergs Boktryckeri Aktiebolag, 1934), 32; Kimilu, *Mũkamba*, 116; Mutisya, *Proverbs*, 118.
[9] Mutisya, *Proverbs*, 19.

22. *Mŭndŭ awetae mbua yaamuĩa.* **People should mention rain that beat them.**
East Africans were fond of telling about how much rain they endure. This ancient axiom means people can only talk about the intensity of rain they have experienced. By extension, one must talk about things that they know well.

23. *Ndŭkasuke mbua thaano.* **Do not slander rain during the dry season.**
This Monsoon-era proverb reflects how much the Kamba revered rain. It means do not commit avoidable errors. It also warns people against speaking ill of people who may show up soon. Doing so is like talking about the rain during the dry season, knowing very well that the rainy season will surely come.

24. *Ũtaathi nĩ wa mbua.*[10] **The rainbow portends rain.**
This ancient proverb uses the rainbow as an analogy for signs helping to predict the future. The Kamba believed that the rainbow was an indicator that the rain had stopped and it would not resume any time soon.

25. *Ũmanyaa kwĩ mbua nĩkwona ũtisi mbee wa Kolyanza.* **It will rain when you see lightning beyond Kolyanza.**
In Kitui, rains from March to May approach from the east over the Indian Ocean and are announced by lightning called *Kolyanza*. Whenever lightning appeared in the east, rain was guaranteed to follow. The Kamba used this phenomenon as a commentary for things predictable through behavioural patterns. Since this lightning is not seen in Machakos, the use of this proverb was limited to Kitui, indicating its creation during the Islamic period when the Kamba settled there.

26. *Vai mbua ĩte ũmuu.*[11] **There is no rain that has no mosquitoes.**
This proverb emerged in the early 1900s in newly mosquito-infested areas. With construction of dams, bridges, and culverts across rivers the landscape changed in favour of mosquitoes. Every rainy season the Kamba witnessed outbreaks of mosquitoes in such areas, hence the proverb. It means every object or person has some defects.

27. *Vai mbua ĩtakya.* **No rain lasts forever.**
Emerging from antiquity, this points to the fact that rain downpour in Ũkamba is usually overwhelming and often destructive, but it does not

---

[10] Mwau, *Dictionary*, 669.
[11] Vincent Kituku, *Sukulu Ĩte Ngũta: The School Without Walls Where Lessons Begin* (Boise: Vincent Kituku, 1997), 64.

last long, hence the proverb. This means, as Kituku put it, no project has endless benefits since business fluctuates like rain.[12]

28. *Ndũkaume ngwa ũtavika ĩtunĩ.* **Do not mock thunder if you cannot reach the sky.**
During hail storms old women hurled insults at thunder to drive it away. Insults did not silence the thunder because none could reach its source in the sky, hence the proverb. It means do not compete with a greater force. Stay within your level.

29. *Ndũkaũmange sua ĩtanathũa.*[13] **Do not ever mock the sun before sunset.**
Although easily seen as a stern warning against insulting authority, this proverb implies that one should never give up before death. Keep learning and do not shelve any project before you understand why it cannot work. It also warns against ruling out an ability of others to excel.

30. *Nzũũ syaema ũsyaa syaisye sua yĩĩ ĩvyũ mũno.* **When pigeon peas failed to bear pods, they said the sun was too hot.**
This is about lame excuses. The sun is vital for photosynthesis and ripening of crops. However, its scorching heat often destroys crops. This proverb appeared shortly after cultivation of pigeon peas intensified across Ũkamba during the Monsoon era. It encourages people to be realistic and refrain from lame excuses.

31. *Sua yoomya ũkatho ngoow'a nĩ mbua.*[14] **If the sun dries it up, the rain resuscitates.**
This emerged among farmers in antiquity in which they observed that the scorching sun subdued the vegetable world. Nevertheless, rain had cooling and peaceful effects. It means therefore that while some people might bring chaos and pain in society, peacemakers ought to heal the afflicted.

32. *Syathama thaano, itũngawa nĩ mbua.*[15] **When they migrate during the dry season, they return in the rainy season.**
During the dry season, birds and animals migrate to water sources far from settlements. They return to their favourite abodes after the rain, hence the proverb from the Monsoon era. Plants are also suppressed until the rains arrive. In the same manner, if a man leaves his home

---

[12] Kituku, *Sukulu*, 64.
[13] Kituku, *Sukulu*, 63.
[14] Mwau, *Dictionary*, 668.
[15] Lindblom, *Riddles*, 36.

during the dry season in search of work, food, or water, he is likely to return to cultivate his farm during the rainy season. The proverb is said of a person who has committed a crime and is obliged to flee his village only to return home when the affair blows over.

33. *Syatwaawa nĩ ũseve itũngawa nĩ ndutani.* **When wind blows them away, cyclones bring them back.**
During the dry season wind consistently blows south to north clearing foliage, but cyclones strike from north to south. Sometimes valuables are blown into people's compounds. This proverb urges listeners to invest where they will reap great profits.[16]

34. *Sua ĩyetelaa Mũsili.* **The sun does not wait for a judge.**
Even though the judge is all powerful, the sun will still set and never wait for him to deliberate a case if he is late. The sun was the most important of all celestial bodies, and there are several proverbs associated with it. Other variants appear in the literature.[17]

35. *Wamanthĩa suanĩ ĩĩa munyĩnĩ.* **If you toil in the sun, eat in the shade.**
Livelihood in precolonial days was earned during the day in intense heat. Obviously, one could not eat a meal under such conditions. Food was consumed in the shade. The maxim means enjoy your labour for you cannot continue handling yourself as a poor man when you have grown rich.

36. *Mũumbĩ ndwathawa kĩĩma.* **Mist is not shown the mountain.**
This ancient proverb emerged out of observation that the mist always settles on the mountain top. Since the final destination of the mist is the mountain, it is obvious that it will move towards the mountain. There is no point in telling the obvious. This means that one in need knows where to get the resources they need. An expert knows what to do and there is no need to teach him. Just as weeds require no sowing and weeding there are natural occurrences that require no human intervention.[18]

37. *No syĩĩma itakomanaa.*[19] **Only mountains fail to meet.**
This proverb indicates there are impossible things in life. While mountains do not meet, there is always a chance for people to meet as they move about the earth.

---

[16] Kimilu, *Mũkamba*, 118; Mutisya, *Proverbs*, 23.
[17] Mwau, *Dictionary*, 648.
[18] Kimilu, *Mũkamba*, 117; Mutisya, *Proverbs*, 55; Mwau, *Dictionary*, 661.
[19] Kituku, *Sukulu*, 38; Mwau, *Dictionary*, 649.

38. *Vai kĩĩma kĩsinda ĩnyũũ nzeve.*[20] **There is no hill with more air than the nose.**
This originated from mountain-dwelling Kamba during the first millennium. Among its multiple applications, it cautions someone not to compare themselves with others. People have different talents and ways of accomplishing the same goals.

39. *Vayĩ kĩĩma kĩkĩlĩtye kĩngĩ makanza.* **No one mountain has more lizards than another.**
This emerged during the first millennium as Kamba occupied Ũkamba highlands. Each hill, mountain, or rocky terrain features varieties of lizards such that it is hard to determine which place has more lizards than the other. This is a warning not to underestimate other peoples' strength for we may be of equal strength.

40. *Vayĩ kĩĩma ndakomba.* **I can mock any mountain.**
This saying was popularized in the early 2000s by competing musicians claiming they could challenge any singer in performance. This ancient proverb suggests that the speaker is strong enough to take on existing champions.

41. *Vayĩ kalĩma katalĩsĩka.* **There is no hill that cannot be climbed.**
Knowing the challenges of climbing mountains, the Kamba believed that all mountains could be climbed to the peak. The first Kenyan to climb to the top of Mount Kenya was a Kamba Second World War veteran named Joseph Munyao on the eve of independence. The proverb originated with mountain dwellers in Mboonĩ hills from the first millennium. Mountains and hills symbolized challenges in Kamba lore. This proverb therefore means there is no life challenge that cannot be overcome.

42. *Ve syĩĩma syĩ mbevo.* **There are mountains that are cold.**
This ancient maxim emerged from the observation that some hills are warm while others are cold. However, this is not literal, but a discourse about male–female relationships. Usually a cold mountain refers to a woman who cannot sexually satisfy despite her beauty or fulsome body.

43. *Kĩlaa kũmwe kwĩ ngongo.* **Jump! Some places have gullies.**
This ancient proverb helps historians understand landscape change in Ũkambanĩ. Gullies emerged when the Kamba intensified farming while keeping large herds and flocks on slopping grounds during the

---

[20] Kituku, *Sukulu*, 65.

nineteenth and twentieth centuries. This proverb emerged around that period.[21]

44. *Kĩkalo kya nthĩ kĩnene kyeteelasya mwene mbuta.* **Lassitude breeds depravation.**
This adage has appeared in publications in variations that appear to be wrong.[22] The saying came out of long-distance expeditions of the Vascon era. If one rests for too long, he exposes himself to robbery. On the other hand, if one wants something but does not act promptly, that opportunity often goes to someone else.

45. *Kya nthĩ kiĩ mwene.* **Something on the ground has no owner.**
This old proverb means anything found on the ground belongs to the finder. Alternately, in farming, cultivated crops belong to the cultivator even if cultivated on someone else's land.

46. *Ũsĩ ũatĩaa kyanda.*[23] **The river follows the valley depression.**
During the rain, new rivers form where there was a previous depression. The meaning of this old maxim is that young people follow the examples of elders in order to succeed.

47. *Ũsĩ ũtũlĩlaa vala vavũthũ.* **A river bursts its bank at its weakest point.**
Observation of nature applied to life as the weak and the poor are always blamed for the mistakes of the rich and the powerful. In environmental politics, for instance, conservationists blame ordinary citizens for environmental ruin.[24]

48. *Mũtũa kĩthamanĩ kya ũsĩ esaa ũtwaawa nĩ ũsĩ.* **Whoever dwells on a river island eventually drowns in the floods.**
This refers to settlements people made upon riverine islands. Since the islands were vulnerable to floods, they were often washed away with their inhabitants. Most island dwellers were farmers, leading to the conclusion that the proverb emerged during the first millennium.

---

[21] James McCann, *Green Land, Brown Land, Black Land: An Environmental History of Africa* (London: Heinemann, 1999); John Mbiti and Mutua Mulonzya (eds), *Ngaeka Waeka: Myali ya Kiikamba/ Kikamba Poems* (Nairobi: Akamba Cultural Trust, 2010), 99.
[22] Farnsworth, *Grammar*, 82; Blanche Watuma, *Kũsoma kwa Katatũ*, 67; Watuma, *Syĩthĩo*, 53; Mutisya, *Proverbs*, 2.
[23] Mwau, *Dictionary*, 669.
[24] KNA: DC/KTI/5/1/1 Soil Erosion and Utilization in the Ũkamba (Kitui) Reserve by Colin Maher, Agricultural Officer, September 1937.

49. *Mũingi wa ũsĩ ndathanaa.*[25] **One crossing a river does not issue commands.**
The migrant Kamba confronted rivers along the way and immediately they reached Ũkamba. People crossing rivers during high floods were not sure of their safety and thus did not command others, or make promises when they started wading. Thus, hope, anticipation, and speculation are not reliable strategies.

50. *Kasĩla kakaa konekaa mũthenya sua yaĩte.* **A path to be obscured is seen in broad sunlight.**
During the rainy season, paths are overgrown and develop dew by dawn but never during the day. Nature forced people to abandon now impassable paths, which became infested with snakes. This means that things bound to go wrong often show obvious signs quite early.[26]

51. *Myũnthĩ ĩthwĩwe nĩ kũkya.* **Days are hurt by dawn.**
This has multiple interpretations. One is that time never ceases; days come and go regardless of human procrastination. These are statements to encourage people going through difficult challenges; they emerged between the late nineteenth century and the end of colonialism.

52. *Wĩsĩ kenda ndwaa kũmĩa.* **You know up to nine, but never go to ten.**
This adage also alludes to the ancient Kamba counting system. The maxim came into use in the eighteenth century. Knowing up to number nine symbolizes shallow knowledge. Once things get into tens they become more solid and serious. The maxim was said in fierce contest to warn the opponents that they knew little about the character of the speaker.

53. *Waĩĩ kenda nũkũmĩe.* **If it was nine, make it ten.**
As Mwau has shown, precolonial Kamba counting counted from one to ten in a different way than today with *Ĩkũmi*, 'ten', symbolizing completeness. The axiom, which emerged during the twentieth century, means let fate complete its course.

54. *Ndunia nĩkeũkaa.* **The world changes.**
Emerging from the twentieth century when usage of Swahili *dunia*, 'world', became common in Kĩkamba implies that things can change unexpectedly. Do not be surprised if the weak become heroes.

---

[25] Mwau, *Dictionary*, 656.
[26] Mutisya, *Proverbs*, 10.

55. *Mwaka ti mũng'ong'oo.* **The year is not long.**
There is surely an end to everything. This is an ancient axiom of hope and encouragement during periods of hardship. It emerged during the lean days of the nineteenth century.

56. *Kĩvindu kya ũtukũ kĩsanasya na kaũndũ kaula i mbiti.* **Night-time darkness comes with something, as hyenas said.**
This ancient proverb points to dangers lurking in darkness. One tale features a group of hyenas that visited a rich man's homestead disguised as guests to steal he-goats and women. As they carried out their evil designs in pitch darkness they sang a song containing this proverb. The proverb means danger lurks in darkness. Be careful.

57. *Kĩwe kya ũtukũ nokyo kya mũthenya.* **A nightly whisper is the same as a day whisper.**
This proverb has multiple interpretations and applications. A whisper remains constant day or night, even with a change in location. One interpretation is that what is done under the cover of darkness can be revealed in broad daylight.

58. *Kũtingwa ũtukũ ũtakesaa.* **However long a night may seem, the dawn will break.**
The Kamba prefer day to night. While the unpleasant night may be long, dawn is always expected. This ancient axiom means nothing is permanent. It is close to 'This too shall pass.'[27]

59. *Mũthi na ũtukũ esaa kũthi mũthenya.* **He who travels at night eventually travels in broad daylight.**
The night was meant for resting and was dangerous and evil. The axiom thus means that certain habits are addictive. Even when done in deep secrecy, eventually such secrets become public knowledge – to the doer's great embarrassment. This proverb emerged in the precolonial period.

60. *Mũthi na ũtukũ ndathelaa malanga.* **A nocturnal person never lacks scars.**
Night was for secrets, evil, and dangers. Walking in the darkness exposed one to all kinds of dangers ranging from injury from stumps on the ground to snakebites to attacks by wild animals and thugs.

---

[27] Mwau, *Dictionary*, 652; John Mbiti, *Weteelete Ndakusaa* (Nairobi: Vide-Muwa Publishers, 2012), 166; David Mũsila, *Seasons of Hope* (Nairobi: Maneeshmedia, 2019), 30.

61. *Ũtukũ ndũtumaa nzele.*[28] Calabash bowls are not repaired at night.
Emerging from the Monsoon era, this adage alludes to the practice of sewing up broken calabash bowls. When a gourd vessel cracked it was expertly sewn back together using fibre and beeswax, a process only possible in daylight. The truth was that things have to be done in their right context and time. Nowadays, with artificial lighting, this statement is no longer true, demonstrating that truth in proverbs is temporal, geographical, situational, or circumstantial. Since 1900, speakers replaced the word *nzele* (bowl) with *ngũa* (clothes) to fit the vision of later generations.

62. *Ũtukũ nĩ mwaasa ũthamaa na ngovi.* The night is long, elephants migrate in the course of it.
Elephants were said to migrate at night when it was cooler and their only threat – humans – were asleep. Emerging during the Vascon era, the proverb means that there are many great things that happen at night. Take care.

63. *Ũtukũ ndũkalaatawa nĩ kwĩng'utha.*[29] Night cannot be rushed to dawn by folding up oneself.
This alludes to the cold nights where people without proper bedding had to fold themselves up to maximize warmth, yearning for daybreak to come with the warm sun. Such action does not make the cold night pass any faster. The proverb implies that time is fixed, one must find strategic ways to fit into it. One cannot constrain time.

64. *Ũtukũ wĩ matũ na nyũmba nĩ ngunga.* The night has ears and the house is a cave.
This ancient axiom warns listeners against speaking about others in the safety of their house at night as someone might be listening. The house is the safest place to speak of delicate matters. However, while a cave might be safe for speaking secrets it has echoes that can be overheard just as in a house.

65. *Mũeni akomaa kũla kũtakomawa.*[30] A stranger sleeps where no one sleeps.
There are multiple proverbs relating to guests, foreigners, and travellers, all expressing the same theme: home is best. Traditionally, the Kamba lodged guests in grain stores or outside on a mat, sometimes

---

[28] Kimilu, *Mũkamba*, 118; Mbiti, *Ngaeka*, 13.
[29] Mailu, *Kĩkyambonie*, 27.
[30] Farnsworth, *Grammar*, 127.

without blankets. These unpleasant circumstances led to proverbs praising homes but demeaning alien places.

66. *Vatakomwa vakomeawa nduka.* **Darkness leads to bedding down in unpleasant places.**
This adage with multiple variations originated with the Monsoon-era Kamba long-distance travels. The travellers were often obliged to lodge in unpleasant places as proceeding in darkness was riskier. It means some alternatives are taken when nothing else works.[31]

67. *Kathima kala kaluĩlasya nĩ kaiyĩĩawa.* **The trickling well is often fenced.**
From antiquity to the late twentieth century, water was common to all if flowing from springs. Water holes were, however, individually owned and fenced off against other people's livestock from as early as the Vascon era.[32] The axiom dating back to that period means a good person ought to be rewarded.

68. *Kĩthima kĩnaema mbiti kĩitonyeka nĩ ngũũe.* **A pig cannot manage a well that defeated the hyena.**
Matters defeating a strong person are not for the weak. The well symbolizes a difficult person while the hyena and pig respectively represent the tough and the weak. This proverb emerged during the Islamic era, when the Kamba expanded into drier plains and dug wells.

69. *Kĩla ũkĩa mũthenya kĩkakwĩthĩa nyũmba ũtukũ.* **What you fear during the day will come into your bedroom at night.**
This is a mother-to-son axiom. Mothers had occasional conversations about life with their sons, all covered with a flurry of proverbs not easy for outsiders to understand. In this proverb, the mother is persuading the son to get married. Even if afraid to say he was ready to marry, sexual desire will overwhelm him at night.

70. *Mwĩw'a ũthuasya ũla ũtonyetwe.*[33] **A thorn causes the pricked person to limp.**
Dating from antiquity this implies that no one can feel another's pain. This is specifically said of a man whose wife has deserted him. The departure of a wife inflicts suffering on the husband, which is compared to limping.

---

[31] Farnsworth, *Grammar*, 87; Mwau, *Dictionary*, 670.
[32] KNA: DC/MKS/4/10 Machakos District Political Record Book 1930–1938.
[33] Lindblom, *Riddles*, 33.

71. Ũkambonia kũũ kũte mwĩw'a. You will show me a leg without a thorn.
The proverb emerged out of the thorny landscape of Ũkamba in the Monsoon era, where herdsmen were vulnerable to thorns piercing their legs. When a person was pierced, they sought the assistance of a companion to take the thorn out. If there is no thorn, stop whining.

72. Ũla mũtine nĩ mwĩw'a nĩwe wĩsĩ vala ve kĩsemei. One pricked by a thorn knows where the *Acacia nilotica* tree is.
Whenever one was pricked by a thorn, the preferred thorn tree to dig the other out of the flesh was the *kĩsemei* tree (*Acacia nilotica*) as it was sturdy enough for this purpose. The symbolic meaning of this ancient axiom is that as need arises people know the right solution.

73. Ũtee wa nthongo vayaa nyeki nziũ. Beside a spring there is always green grass.
Grass was vital for its diverse roles in the social and economic evolution of Kamba society. This proverb encodes a language suggesting its coinage when grass for livestock was becoming scarce. The actual meaning is that different types of resources must be sought. Someone with resources is useful in a village.

74. Vayĩ mwando mũvĩte nĩ sua. There is no green millet flour that has missed the sun.
This proverb inspires hope when uttered but also can spell doom when rendered as *Mwando waku nĩwavĩtiwe nĩ sua*, 'Your green millet flour has missed the sun.' Both refer to pearl millet, the traditional staple crop of the Vascon-era Kamba. While millet may have been domesticated in West Africa thousands of years ago it did not become popular in Ũkamba until the Vascon era, precisely the time of the emergence of this proverb.[34]

75. Vayĩ ndia ĩtang'alw'a nĩ sua.[35] There is no pond the sun cannot dry up.
This precolonial maxim emerged in Ũkamba where water pans dry up when the rains subside, unlike the Kamba experience of their migration there. Observably, any wetland was at risk once exposed to the sun – just as with humans, the strong eventually weaken over time.

---

[34] Patrick Maundu, *Traditional Food Plants of Kenya* (Nairobi: National Museums of Kenya, 1999), 125; National Research Council, *Lost Crops of Africa*. Vol. 1 (Washington: National Academy Press, 1996).
[35] Kimilu, *Mũkamba*, 118.

3
Wild Plants

76. *Anakavĩte ta ĩlaa ya mũutĩ.* **She is as beautiful as the flower of a *mũutĩ* tree.**
The axiom reflects Kamba appreciation of flowers and specific plants. Since the Islamic period this maxim has been used during negotiation of a dowry. The Kamba appreciated the fragrance of *mũutĩ*, a low bush species that produces radiant yellow flowers, and which played many roles: precolonial Kamba surgeons undertook brain surgery, sealed the skull, and treated the wound with *mũutĩ*; the flowers of the plant were the epitome of beauty in Ũkamba – during a dowry negotiation parents praised their daughter likening them to this glorious flower, regardless of reality.

77. *Avaĩĩ kĩtathe vayũaa ndathe.* **Where there is a *kĩtathe* (*Albizia anthelmintica*) tree there will be *ndathe* seedlings.**
Kĩtathe (known to botanists as *Albizia anthelmintica*) is a hardwood shade tree used for high-quality firewood and many other purposes. When the tree dies, new saplings emerge from tough seeds (*ndathe*) hardy enough to survive. This proverb emerged during the Monsoon exchange era, when the Kamba occupied ecological niches where the tree grows. It usually conveys a message that bad traits recur in a family and must be suppressed early.

78. *Ĩlaa ya ngwatyo yaĩlaa mũthenya ũmwe.* **A borrowed flower is beautiful only for a day.**
Flowers had medicinal, nutritional, magical, and aesthetic uses. Newborns were named after flowers. People borrowed and gave flower presents to lovers.[1] Beyond this context, the proverb alludes to debt as a malevolent force that interrupts and diminishes both beauty and personal relationships by a pecuniary obligation. It has a darker meaning than 'friendship and money are like oil and water: they never mix'. It implies an opposition between calculation and ideals with calculation likely to win out. Better to work, sacrifice, and save in order

---

[1] Lindblom, *Akamba*, 331; Mailu, *Kĩkyambonie*, 24, 71.

to obtain – in a way that does not interrupt the ethical web of interpersonal relations.

79. *Kamanyĩa kũlĩsa mĩtĩ ĩla mĩnene tũla tũnini kaimanyaa kũlĩsa.* **A boy accustomed to climb big trees cannot climb small trees.**
Climbing trees was part of boys' training to be beekeepers as adults. Big trees in the context of this proverb, however, symbolize women while small trees symbolize girls. If a boy acquires the habit of having sex with adult women, says the proverb, he will find it hard to date girls. Emerging after the Second World War, this axiom means that habits are addictive. If one practises bad habits, it is very hard to expunge them.

80. *Kĩlaa kyumaa nzĩ na mĩw'a ya kyo.* ***Acacia mellera* germinates with its thorns.**
This proverb originated from the Islamic period when the Kamba settled in areas dominated by *Acacia mellera* – a thorny bush used for fencing, edible sap, firewood, and apicultural purposes. This appeared in literature and multiple songs, from which we understand it means that character traits develop early. Each person is born with their own qualities, which can either be encouraged or suppressed.

81. *Kaumaa nthĩ na ũtwii wako.* **A snake is born with its venom.**
In the context of a conversation from which the proverb was drawn in 1985, the meaning is that talents are inborn, comparable to a young snake born with venom already in its system. The maxim emerged during the Vascon era when different types of poison became common in Ũkamba hunting and military realms.

82. *Ĩtũlika ya mũtĩ yoveyawa na ũngĩ.* **A bone broken by a tree is bandaged with another tree.**
Kamba children were fond of climbing trees, which often led to falls resulting in broken bones. The broken limbs were bound with sticks and freshly harvested strings of specific plants. The proverb means certain problems are solved with resources similar to the problem.

83. *Kakuthu kaneyũmba kaiaa wĩvitho ũmĩwa.* **An established bush lacks no cover for someone defecating.**
This axiom emerged between the 1910s and 1940s period of severe environmental degradation in Ũkambanĩ. The region lost so much vegetation cover that homes were exposed and nothing could be hidden. In response some adopted the colonial culture of digging pit latrines. Others encouraged natural bushes to grow near homes in order to hide behind them to relieve themselves, hence the proverb. In its broader application, the proverb means a new leader or institution attracts people.

84. *Ndũkavũthĩĩsye kakuthu kwaa matũ.* **Never underestimate a bush that lacks leaves.**
Bushes without leaves serve many purposes and harbour creatures both profitable and dangerous. The ancient axiom advised close inspection rather than dismissal of an object.

85. *Kĩkoe kĩ mboka.* **Commelina Africana is stew.**
This is a revealing proverb about botany, agriculture, and ecology in Ũkambanĩ, a region that has been known for famines since the nineteenth century. Yet the region has not exploited all its available wild food plants to the fullest. In the past, underdeveloped edibles like *kĩkoe* (*Commelina Africana*) fed humanity during famines. In the twentieth century, there was a contraction of agro-diversity as farming focused attention on mass production.[2] The maxim means a substitute is as good as the object itself.

86. *Ndũkaakĩĩe kĩtheka kũthunga.*[3] **Do not be frightened by the density of the forest.**
Dangerous things lurk in thick forests. The proverb means looks can be deceitful and what appears impossible might be easy.

87. *Mũndũ wa syamata ona akesĩla yalatanĩ syiilea ũmũkwata.* **A man of sticky weeds will always get these weeds even if he passes through bare ground.**
This emerged after the First World War. It means that a person who is accustomed to cohabiting with a lover will always drift towards those habits even if he moves away.

88. *Vayĩ katheka na kaũkuutw'a.* **There is no difference between a little bush and a thicket.**
During the Monsoon era, Ũkambanĩ was characterized by thick forests, but the rapid increase of wild animals and livestock during the Islamic period depleted vegetation, leaving patches of thickets in the middle of grassland. These patches were similar to thick and extensive forests, potentially harbouring the same species. Emerging during the Islamic era the maxim means do not underrate the resources of meek people.

89. *Kĩtheka kĩ matũ.*[4] **The forest has ears.**
This ancient adage appeared in multiple publications. It warns that secrets must be guarded. Second, often what is said in private soon

---

[2] National Research Council, *Lost Crops of Africa*. Vol. 2 (1996–2008).
[3] Kimilu, *Mũkamba*, 117; Mailu, *Kĩkyambonie*, 68; Mutisya, *Proverbs*, 14.
[4] Lindblom, *Riddles*, 30; Kimilu, *Mũkamba*, 116; Mutisya, *Proverbs*, 16; Mwau, *Dictionary*, 650; Mbiti, *Weteelete*, 87.

becomes public knowledge. Sensitive matters must be handled with extreme care. Gossip can be harmful when it spills out.

90. *Kĩtheka kĩthungu nĩ kĩsaa ũtwĩka ĩei.* **A dense forest eventually becomes fallow.**
During the nineteenth century, slash-and-burn farming techniques turned many dense forests into farms and others became wastelands. The end result became symbolic of life itself. Dating from that century, the proverb means that anything plentiful wanes. Wealth, beauty, or strength can decline just as a dense fertile forestland can be reduced to barren land.

91. *Kĩtheka nĩkyo kĩyĩsĩ.*[5] **The forest knows itself.**
Before 1900 there were dense forests across Ũkambanĩ, hence the proverb. This maxim means that just as the deep forest is unknown, certain secrets are personal.

92. *Mbaĩ sya kĩtheka nĩ ilĩ, mũmũ na mwiyũ.*[6] **The clans of the forest are two, the dry and the green.**
The proverb depicts Kamba recognition that society's future depends on females, indicating that the proverb was coined during periods of low population during the Monsoon era. Dry trees symbolize men, who cannot give birth; green trees females, who symbolize fertility.

93. *Sere ndwĩ serasya.* **A clattering sound does not produce itself.**
This means everything has a cause. It is used in part to confront someone who has blundered and then acted innocent when accused of the fact. The results of his blunder are self-evident. The specific dialect used here is from Northern Mwingĩ, an area settled during the Islamic era.

94. *Wĩĩthya mang'ula o kũla twesĩle.*[7] **You are pasturing over stumps where we trod.**
First published by Kimilu in 1962 this axiom concerns levels of knowledge. Whatever a young person experiences is not new to the old and experienced. This is a proverb circulating mainly among women and usually addressed to disobedient girls who are obsessed with romance and carelessly run around with boys.

---

[5] Kimilu, *Mũkamba*, 116.
[6] Lindblom, *Riddles*, 32.
[7] Kituku, *Sukulu*, 47.

95. *Eka ũtumba nthĩ ũvĩvye.* **Stop hiding in a spot burnt bare.**
This proverb reprimands someone lying about an open secret. To warn girls using this proverb, women told them off, *Wĩkungĩla ũvĩvyenĩ ona ũithaũka na tũmwana kũũ nokwo sũsũ wesĩle,* 'You are creeping in the burnt field even when you romanticize with boys on the same path grandma passed through.' Stop lying.

96. *Vau ũkũĩthya mang'ũthĩ nĩvo naĩthasya vuvĩ mwanake.* **Young man, where you graze on scraps is where I grazed on fresh green grass.**
Emerging from the nineteenth century, this is another way of saying, 'it is too late for you; so, stop your deception, I know your tricks already'. Tailor-made for young men, this proverb warns a liar that his deceptions have been exposed.

97. *Ũkonzawa wĩmwiyũ woma ndũkonzekaa.* **It is bent when green, when dried it does not bend.**
This has appeared since the 1910s in poems, songs, and published works expressing the need for early instruction in children. It warns parents that children ought to be corrected early otherwise correction will be ineffective later.[8]

98. *Kyũmati kĩiminawa nĩ kweka.* **Abdominal pangs are not reduced by breathing in.**
This ancient proverb refers to the belief that pain is treated with bitter medicine only. In symbolic terms, it means certain tasks require extraordinary resources and effort to accomplish.

99. *Kavĩndĩ mbĩtũke.* **Little bone pass over me.**
This axiom was said by elders advising someone in a very tense, but still sober moment over serious matters. The listener and those around him maintained complete silence just as the statement implies. In order to win, the listener had to avoid challenging those in power and to use tact to outwit them. The little bone was assumed to be in his throat and to swallow it he had to use those magic words 'little bone pass over me'.

100. *Mũtĩ wa wendo ndũkuawa na ngalĩ.* **The tree of love is never transported in a vehicle.**
Culled from twentieth-century popular songs, this alludes to the Kamba practices where young men travelled to distant places seeking 'love medicine' to win the love of girls. Emerging after the First World

---

[8] Lindblom, *Riddles*; Kimilu, *Mũkamba*, 119; Farnsworth, *Grammar*, 5; Mutisya, *Proverbs*, 2; Thomas Ngotho, *Ngewa Nyanya na Moelyo* (Nairobi: East African Literature Bureau, 1962), 50; Mbiti, *Weteelete*, 91; Mwau, *Dictionary*, 670.

War when automobiles came to Kenya, the axiom was a protest against modernity. While boarding a vehicle to reach one's goal was much quicker, practitioners warned that one must walk on foot to fetch it and return. This means there are things that are not compatible and, if one wants to succeed, one has to be meticulous.

101. *Mũtĩ wĩ mũyo ndũsyaa mwoomboko.* **A sweet tree does not bear much fruit.**
This ancient maxim originated with foragers who observed that plants unfit for consumption produced more fruit than edible ones. The AIM found it across Machakos during the first half of the twentieth century. The Kimilu recorded it in 1962. It implies that good things are rare.[9]

102. *Mũtĩ ndũlĩsĩlawa mbongenĩ.* **A tree is not climbed from its branches.**
The Kamba climbed trees upwards from the base of the trunk, unlike other East African cultures that deployed ropes. This ancient axiom encourages diligence in approaching life's challenges: plan ahead and follow the course to the end.[10]

103. *Mũtĩ ngasũa nĩwonaa ũyambĩĩa kweeka.* **A tree on which I will swing I will see when it begins to bend.**
Kamba children loved swinging as a pastime. They targeted branches that dropped low to form an artificial swing. Children then were on the lookout for such branches. This ancient maxim means the prospects of something can be seen ahead of time.

104. *Mũtĩ ũla ũsyaa nonginya ũsyae na nĩwo wĩkasw'e mbĩla.* **The fruit-bearing tree must multiply and is the one to hit with sticks.**
The tree was considered a mother, providing milk to her human children, but getting the 'milk' was not easy. Those who understood this relationship climbed the tree to harvest the fruit. However, those who could not climb hauled strong sticks for boys to beat the branches to shake off the fruit. This maxim means the provider is always bothered by dependants.

105. *Mũtĩ ũte mbonge ndwĩ munyĩ.* **A tree without branches gives no shade.**
The Kamba located their houses next to shady trees with enough branches and leaves to supply shade. The tree was often given human attributes and names encoding local histories of migration, settlement, and more. The tree symbolized the family as the trunk, children

---

[9] Farnsworth, *Grammar*, 114; Kimilu, *Mũkamba*, 117; Mutisya, *Proverbs*, 42.
[10] Mutisya, *Proverbs*, 71.

as branches, and family harmony as the shade cast by the tree. The proverb was coined in antiquity to show that a person without a family is useless.

106. *Mũtĩ ũvalũkĩlaa ũla wĩvakuvĩ.* **A tree falls on the person near it.**
This ancient proverb has multiple interpretations. It could mean that one gains by being present. It could also mean that one should take responsibility for an unexpected event, dependent on its proximity. For its popular use in these two forms it has appeared in several publications.[11]

107. *Mũtĩ wovosya ndwendekaa mwiingĩ.* **A curative herb is not needed in vast quantities.**
The maxim has featured in election campaign songs and missionary seminars throughout the twentieth century. In a seminar for Christian couples, a counsellor used this proverb to mean that a few well-chosen words are most effective in family discussions.[12]

108. *Mũtĩ wa mũito waa ĩla ũmanthwa.* **A curative herb becomes rare when most needed.**
This alludes to manners of healing and environmental changes during the precolonial era. The Kamba set their settlements in close proximity to curative plants, but both people and livestock decimated such plants. Consequently, when someone was injured or became sick, it took time to find these plants. The ancient proverb means distress occurs when resources have diminished;[13] people do not know the value of things until they become rare.

109. *Mũtĩ wa Ngai ndwĩw'aa nthĩ ũmea kĩĩmani, kwĩ mang'alata kana mbenzi.* **The tree of God does not hear the ground, it grows on mountain tops whether barren or terraced.**
The Kamba use such expressions as 'does not hear', meaning it is tough. The 'Tree of God' refers to natural vegetation spontaneously springing up. It symbolizes strong leaders. Like a natural tree, a leader can rise from anywhere without human input. The natural tree needing neither fertilizer nor watering can grow anywhere. In its original context the maxim concerns the politics of Ũkambanĩ regionalism.

---

[11] Mutisya, *Proverbs*, 58; Mwau, *Dictionary*, 6.
[12] Jones Kaleli, 'Theoretical Foundations of African and Western Worldviews and their Relationship to Christian Theologizing' (PhD dissertation, World Mission, 1985), 518; Mutisya, *Proverbs*, 42.
[13] Kimilu, *Mũkamba*, 117; Mutisya, *Proverbs*, 43.

34   Part II: The Natural World

110. *Mũtĩ wa mwako ndwĩ vala ũtaumaa.* **A building branch can come from anywhere.**
Just as timber can come from anywhere, a leader can come from any part of the country or region. The axiom emerged in the late eighteenth century when construction material became rare and people had to travel far to get the best wood.

111. *Mũndũ atemaa ngĩĩtĩ ũndũ wĩania mwako.* **A man cuts the withies proportionally to his construction project.**
Emerging during the Islamic era when the Kamba transitioned from Tanzanian building styles to something unique to Ũkambanĩ as a result of local conditions, this axiom means, one should cut only the building material needed. Its symbolic meaning is that people should use whatever they accumulate and undertake what they can complete.

112. *Mũtĩ ndũyotaa muunyĩ.*[14] **A tree does not enjoy its own shade.**
This ancient maxim is about the relationship between producers and consumers. Producers usually do not consume what they produce but pass the products to consumers. The tree symbolizes the producer, while the shade is the product.

113. *Mũtĩ mũnini ndũthũũnawa.*[15] **A thin tree is not gnawed.**
This ancient maxim implies there are different resource levels. Certain levels are not fit for certain tasks. A junior officer in an institution, for example, cannot perform the duties of his superiors.

114. *Mũtĩ mũmũ ndũthũũnaa.* **A dry tree does not form a scar.**
The word *kũthũũna* has been mistranslated in the literature. Otherwise, it means healing among plants. When tree bark is taken out, the tree fights back by developing another bark slowly until the cut is completely covered, a process called *kũthũũna*, 'healing'. For non-plants *kũthũũna* means to munch, crunch, or lick bones.[16] The proverb means a dry or dead tree never recovers. In other words, resources are needed for a community to live together. This proverb encourages poor family members to persevere through want and distress, caused by fate rather than failure of the family head to provide.

115. *Mũtĩ wĩ kĩtheka ndwĩ mwene.* **A tree in the bush has no owner.**
Until the 1900s, uncultivated land was open to public exploitation. The word *mũtĩ* is, however, symbolic of a girl. She was open to all young men who would like to seek a relationship. The adage emerged centuries

---
[14] Mwau, *Dictionary*, 660.
[15] Mwau, *Dictionary*, 660.
[16] Kimilu, *Mũkamba*, 117; Mutisya, *Proverbs*, 2.

after the Kamba settled and began to exploit the vegetation of Ũkamba, clearly before the Vascon era. Different variants have appeared in publications since 1912.[17] The proverb means that unmarried girls are open to any suitor, not the preserve of any man. Likewise, there are things in this world that are up for grabs as long as one uses a socially sanctioned path to grab.

116. *Mũtĩ mũnene ũtemawa kĩthũmũsyo.* **A big tree is cut between rests.**
Until the 1900s, the Kamba used axes of locally smelted iron ore. The axes were not as sharp and strong as modern-day axes. Thus, cutting large trees required muscle strength and strategy. A Mwingĩ politician used this proverb to suggest that to beat a seasoned political opponent required strategy, resources, and persistence.

117. *Kinyaa kĩthanze kĩvoo.*[18] **May you always step on calm grass.**
This was a blessing by elders to grandchildren or people of the same age to always wallow in fortune. It appears to have emerged when the Kamba expanded into the plains of Machakos and Kitui, which were covered with tough grass and hard on one's feet. The phrase warns one not to step onto rough terrain and to avoid dangerous situations.

118. *Kĩseũ kĩitonywa nĩ mũkungo.* **The wilderness is not traversed through crawling.**
During the Vascon-era hunting and trading expeditions, Kamba passed through open wilderness or grassland plains, preferred for their safety for their clear views and abundance of game. Such terrains were long, hot, and waterless so travellers were encouraged to persevere to reach shady and well-watered places. They could not crawl but must walk fast. Success is a result of hard work.

119. *Walea syaaki wauta sya aiti.* **You declined the builders', you grabbed those of thatchers.**
This proverb refers to house construction where some build a house while others thatch it with grass. The terms *syaaki* (builders) and *sya aiti* (thatchers) both allude to *nyeki* (grass). Builders and thatchers were distinct professionals. Meals were served separately to the two groups and, thus, the proverb could mean one had crossed the line.

---

[17] Kimilu, *Mũkamba*, 117; Mbiti, *Weteelete*, 166.
[18] Mailu, *Kĩkyambonie*, 22.

120. *Aũme maindaa muu muunĩ na syeew'a maiya.* **Men bury black plums under the ash and eat them when ripe.**
Vitex payo trees played an important role in the environmental history of Ũkamba.[19] Figuratively, this ancient expression has various interpretations. Men bury black plums to ripen; men deposit their semen in women and later enjoy fatherhood; when girls grow up and get married, men enjoy feasting and dowry.

121. *Ĩla ĩtulasya kĩmuu tiyo yosanasya.* **The warthog that knocks the *Vitex payos* tree is not the one that collects the dropping fruits.**
This refers to the warthog that hits a tree to force the fruits to drop. The warthog is fond of resting under the *kĩmuu* tree and consuming black plums – the mother warthog collapses on impact while others feast on the dropped fruits. It means one's effort does not necessarily benefit oneself or one's family. Outsiders reap the benefits. The tree the Kamba call *kĩmuu* is an evergreen tree producing light-green fruits (called black plums) that become black when ripe.

122. *Ngũ isyaa muu.* **Firewood gives birth to ashes.**
This simply means firewood, though hard, burns to ashes. By extension anything under pressure reduces its value just as firewood become worthless ash. Some misinterpreted this as meaning firewood gives birth to black plums since they are buried in ashes in order to ripen.

123. *Mũkũyũ wavalũka ũtiaa mũuumo.* **When a fig tree falls, it leaves the *Ficus thonningii* tree.**
The *Ficus (Moraceae)* (*Mũũmbũ*) and *Ficus thonningii* (*mũuumo*) trees were sacred in Ũkamba. Proverbs relating to these trees date to the Islamic period when circumcision rites came to be centred around the two trees. The *mũuumo* took over the ecological niche, when the sycamore (*Mũũmbũ*) tree died.[20] This can mean a great patriarch leaves a successor with similar traits.

124. *Mũuumo mũnini ũsyaa mũyo mũthonoku.* **A small *Ficus thonningii* tree bears the sweetest fruits.**
Besides mere ritual value, *Ficus thonningii* trees were a source of food. Observing that shorter plants had sweeter fruits, the ancient Kamba coined this maxim meaning not to judge a book by its cover.

---

[19] Lindblom, *Akamba*, 56.
[20] Lindblom, *Akamba*, 56–7.

125. *Vandũ vaĩ mũamba vayaa mũumo.*[21] **Where once stood a baobab there lacks no fig tree.**
During their migration through Taitaland, Kamba ancestors called Evau 'nephews of the Nyamwezi' subsisted on baobab fruits (ng'amba) during a severe and prolonged drought. Subsequently, the migrating group attained a new name, Akamba, 'People of the Baobab'. They observed that when the baobab fell a fig tree soon appeared on the spot, hence this ancient proverb. It means where there was a champion another must be born.

126. *Mwaamba wĩ ng'amba ũkimawa mbĩla maita elĩ.* **A baobab with fruit is hit with sticks twice.**
The baobab is intimately linked to Kamba history. The baobab symbolizes a progressive person. Thus, the proverb means that a prominent person attracts needy people requiring his leadership, guidance, and assistance.

127. *Vayĩ kothumũla kate ngalalũ.* **There is no tamarind fruit that is not sour.**
Tamarind is indigenous to tropical Africa from west to east, and most tamarind-related proverbs date from antiquity.[22] Tamarind juice was used to flavour food while 'the fruit of this tree being very acidic was used to polish the copper and brass ornaments worn by Kamba'.[23] Young men defending their relations with older women used the proverb, implying that even though their partners were older, the romance was not old.

128. *Nthũmũla ĩmwe yĩndua.* **A single tamarind can make gruel.**
Katongu of Kaui River basin sang a song with this axiom in the 1980s. The axiom had historical precedents stretching back to antiquity. Tamarinds were known for their strong sour taste that could make a gruel taste sour. In the context of the song, the proverb means strong leadership can transform a region into a progressive one.

129. *Kũũ twĩ weũnĩ.* **Here we are in the wilderness.**
This proverb depicts the transient nature of migration to towns. In the savannah, people cannot hide, nor can they hide in treeless urban terrains. Urban life is like travelling through a wilderness where one yearns to get home.

---

[21] Mutisya, *Proverbs*, 30.
[22] National Research Council, *Lost Crops*, 3.
[23] KNA: DC/KTI/7/4 Kitui District Report 1909.

130. *Weũ waya nzei.* **The wilderness ate nothing.**
Farnsworth recorded without translation this hard-to-comprehend proverb in 1952.[24] The word *weũ* variously means wilderness, or new or light skin. It may, therefore, translate as 'The beauty eats nothing.' Some informants said that the statement actually may be rendered as *Weũ waĩaa ndei*, 'Even vultures get lost in wilderness.' A man may see a possibility that may take time and distract him from focus and he loses his fortune. Another interpretation is that the hunter said the wilderness had no game.

131. *Weũ ũte ngũ ndũtũawa.*[25] **A plain without firewood is not settled.**
This proverb provides a proxy for historical studies of early Kamba patterns of settlement as well as studies of wood and water resources within a gendered platform. During the Vascon era, with diminishing vegetation cover, most natural watercourses near settlements dried up, forcing the Kamba to walk long distances to fetch water and collect firewood. These two vital activities became onerous chores for females by the dawn of the eighteenth century. This proverb, which emerged in that century, means people are attracted by a leader's resources.

132. *Ũka na ũthyũ mũongo nĩ wa ngũ.* **Come face-forward, the back is for firewood.**
Emerging during the Vascon era, this proverb alludes to collecting firewood in the bush, a regular chore for girls and women. Once collected, the women bound the logs with leather straps and carried the logs on their backs. The axiom is extremely symbolic with diverse interpretations and contains sexual overtones. Among youth, it means romantic cuddling is enjoyable when done face to face as opposed to having coitus from the back. In conflicts this is a way of warning an opponent: slow down lest you tread on sensitive toes.

133. *Vayĩ ũkũ ũtatũmĩka.*[26] **There is no log that cannot be used.**
The Kamba collected only certain woods, as better sources of firewood than those emitting too much smoke. Thus, any log in the pile could be used. Among the multiple meanings of the proverb is that any member of the society or family is useful. Alternatively, all the resources one has can be used even for unexpected purposes.

---

[24] Farnsworth, *Grammar*, 73.
[25] Kimilu, *Mũkamba*, 119; Mutisya, *Proverbs*, 47.
[26] Mbiti, *Ngaeka*, 98.

134. *Kya ngũ kĩtĩawa nĩ kya kĩw'ũ.* **An appointment for collecting firewood is postponed on account of fetching water.**
Emerging during the Vascon era, this proverb refers to water and firewood collecting. These were women's chores and they had to plan trips every week to get these basic items, distant from the villages. Examining these issues can reveal to historians something about Kamba social and cultural readjustments that occurred in response to depletion fuel, water, and food around mountain ranges shortly before Da Gama arrived.

135. *Kathuma kate mbavathi kayĩkalasya mũtumĩa thome.* **A skin without split woods does not hold an elder by the hearth.**
This ancient proverb alludes to old men resting by their hearth. Without logs to fuel the fire, the hearth is dysfunctional. Logs symbolize women or wives. The absence of women – particularly a wife – was equivalent to a cold hearth. Thus, the maxim means without a warm wife, a man cannot sit comfortably by his hearth.

136. *Ũ wĩ kĩvetanĩ ndũthekaa ũla wĩ iko.* **One in the woodpile does not laugh at one in the fire.**
This adage comes in various forms with the bottom line meaning that one should not delight in other people's miseries as tomorrow you may be the one suffering. For cooking purposes, the Kamba collected firewood and piled them at the edge of the compound; those on the woodpile were pulled into the fire. By analogy, privileged people should not mock those in distress.

137. *Ndũkauniĩe kĩthĩnthĩmwa ngũ.* **Do not pile more logs on a weakling.**
By 1900, women were walking far distances to collect firewood. Dry firewood was required, so collecting firewood (*kuna ngũ*) followed periodical patterns. This chore required energy and weak women could carry only a few logs. In one story, someone did the opposite. Instead of giving a weak woman (*kĩthĩnthĩmwa*) fewer logs, she piled more on until the weakling collapsed under the weight. This derisive axiom means do not fool around in important matters.

138. *Ĩlũkũ Ĩ iko yĩilea ũtoa.* **A log in the fire never fails to smoke.**
While specific species burn with little or no smoke, most logs smoke badly and were equated with bad human character. All members of the family or community are valuable; if they misbehave they are like a smoking but still useful log – and are kept as part of the family or community regardless of their behaviour. The proverb emerged when social conflict intersected with the practice of warming up at the hearth.

139. *Vayĩ ũtumo ũtaĩ matatwa.*[27] **There is no ridge settlement without trials.**
This ancient saying was used by someone seeking forgiveness and reconciliation with a spouse, a friend, a relative, or a neighbour. It was an expression of the reality of life in Kamba communities and families. That is, individuals within families and communities were in constant tension, which should be viewed and handled in constructive ways.

140. *Ũtumo wĩ ngũ ndwĩ nyama.* **An upland with firewood has no meat.**[28]
During the Monsoon era the Kamba preferred raised lands and hills for site of their settlements. However, they realized that no site had all the resources needed, hence the axiom. It means no one and no place is ever self-contained. Trade is essential for communal survival.

141. *Ng'oko ĩng'okwa nĩ ene.* **Around the corner is known by the owners.**
This ancient axiom alludes to Ũkamba landscape and how the ancient Kamba lived in hilly terrain where villages were concealed by dense forests. It also means that, if you see a distant land, there must be people living there. Go find out who lives there. The axiom, however, points to secrets, unknown places, and, by extension, to the future. In that sense, secrets are known by the parties involved.

142. *Vayĩ ũtang'okya ũngĩ ũtumo.*[29] **No one can fail to take across a ridge.**
Ridges (long narrow hilltops or mountain ranges usually near a watershed) were important landscapes that defined ancient Kamba settlements. They marked the boundaries of settlement. Since the ridges were miles apart, the intervening ravines were dangerous. If a person visited a ridge, he/she had to be escorted by another over the ridge into the safety of familiar terrain. This fills this maxim with deeply figurative meanings. One interpretation is that anything can serve immediate needs and purposes.

143. *Kũkwĩ ngi kũyĩ nyama na kũla kwĩ nyama kũyĩ ngi.*[84] **Where there is meat there are no flies, and where there are flies there is no meat.**
This proverb, varied in different forms, refers to Kamba preference for meat and mealiepap. It denotes a realization that no one and no place can have all the resources needed to sustain life. Complementarity and

---

[27] Mailu, *Kĩkyambonie*, 28.
[28] Mutisya, *Proverbs*, 43.
[29] Kimilu, *Mũkamba*, 119; Mbiti, *Weteelete*, 30.

exchange are vital elements of existence, a reality of life among the Kamba since the Monsoon era of the emergence of this proverb.

144. *Mũkwa mũkũũ nĩw'o ũlũmasya ngũ.* **An old leather strap ties firewood firmly.**
It was largely women's duty to collect firewood, tie it with leather straps, and carry it home. While this proverb cautions listeners not to judge a book by its cover, it is symbolically a contestation against ageing – as the older one gets the better he or she becomes at many things.

145. *Sisya ũkuĩla ĩkundonĩ.* **Be careful not to carry on the knot.**
Women used leather straps and woven ropes to tie loads onto their backs. Broken ropes were joined together, leaving an uncomfortable knot. Women used only the smooth part of the rope passed over their heads to avoid injury while laden. This is a warning to be watchful of deception and self-inflicted wounds.

4

Wild Game

146. *Andū aa nīmaua mūūngū wasama ng'ombe.* **These people have cooked the quills to the taste of beef.**
The ancient Kamba engaged with porcupines and cattle for complex social and economic purposes. Their reluctance to slaughter their cattle led them to prefer game meat over beef. Porcupine quills were not eaten despite the literal meaning of the proverb. It was a sarcastic criticism of a miser when visitors arrive.[1] It means that these people have exaggerated the matter at hand, alluding to some extreme exaggerations of the miser.

147. *Kīrūngū kīsyaa kīngī, kīsera kyūsyaa kīsera.* **A porcupine gives birth to a porcupine.**
Of the various types of porcupine in Kitui the biggest and most common is the *kīrūngū*, or *nzee*. A smaller and rarer type is the *kīsera*. They do not crossbreed, as the proverb makes clear. In politics this ancient maxim means a leader always gives rise to a leader. Other proverbs, to the contrary, say a guinea fowl bears a francolin and a porcupine a hedgehog, meaning great leaders do not always bring forth great leaders.[2]

148. *Kīrūngū kīyīsaa mūūnda wa mūtheo.* **A porcupine does not raid neighbouring farms.**
This ancient axiom says one should not spoil their own neighbourhood. Local thieves should steal far from their villages, for example. It emerged towards the end of the first millennium.

149. *Nzee ndīsaa maanga ūtūinī.* **A porcupine does not eat cassava in its village.**[3]
While the previous entry dates to the Monsoon era, this proverb emerged during the Vascon era with the arrival of cassava from the New World. Cassava became a symbol of virginity, beauty, and romance. While

---

[1] Lindblom, *Akamba*; Gerhard Lindblom, *Notes on Kamba Grammar* (Uppsala: APA, 1926).
[2] David Korosos, *Tugen Proverbs* (Nairobi: Phoenix Publishers, 1997), 12.
[3] Mutisya, *Proverbs*, 17; Mwau, *Dictionary*, 667.

cassava symbolizes village girls, porcupine stands for a boy, who had to leave the local village girls to date another further away. Do not commit crimes within your community.

150. *Nzee ndīsaa mīingo īlī.* **A porcupine does not eat from both sides of the river.**
Since porcupines cannot wade rivers they browse on one side, concentrating on only that side. One variation speaks of greed and excessive accumulation as a metaphor for romance among youth in polygamous households. Among youth, it warned against too many sexual partners in multiple villages. Stick to one in one area. For greed among large households it was a warning that one cannot use both his own and his children's resources.

151. *Nzee īnyungaa mūtitū ūla yīeye.* **A porcupine smells like the bushland where it lodged.**
There are several variations of this old adage, all reflecting the fact that the Kamba living side by side with nature could tell if an animal was new to the area by the way it smelled. The proverb means that certain traits betray the inner character of a person. What people revere, they resemble, for either ruin or restoration.[4]

152. *Nzee nīyūmīsyaa myūngū yūmea.* **A Porcupine patiently bears the pain as its quills develop.**
The quills of the porcupine are sharp and injurious to people who stumble on the creature. The Kamba assume jokingly that if the quills harm externally, how much more internally? Porcupines must endure a lot of internal pain until all those quills grow. This ancient proverb means that people should be patient and endure the burden of their spouses, families, and communities.

153. *Nzee īkīkūa īsyaa kīthangaitī.* **An ageing porcupine bears a hedgehog.**
Hedgehogs and porcupines are only superficially alike while porcupines are rodents bigger than hedgehogs. For that matter, porcupines are more respected than hedgehogs. This deeply figurative statement means no one is a champion for life since even those who were once invincible do weaken as energy and reason decline with age.

154. *Vala yavūnīa nīvo ītiaa mūūngū.* **A porcupine leaves a barb, where it is satisfied.**
The porcupine habitually drops quills after browsing and the Kamba believed that it does so to say thank you to the area. Therefore, this proverb means people forget important things once satisfied.

[4] Mutisya, *Proverbs*, 35; Mwau, *Dictionary*, 672.

155. *Yũngũ yĩmwe yĩyonawa nĩ nzee.* **A porcupine never sees one bottlegourd.**
Porcupines are fond of bottlegourds and frequent farms that have many, rarely going after a single bottlegourd. A single thing, however important, does not attract attention.

156. *Mbola yũwaa nzou.* **Slow moves kill an elephant.**
Elephants were the most profitable animals of Kamba commerce between the 1300s and 1900s. Hunters killed elephants by stalking and shooting poisoned arrows at close range. The proverb means no matter how difficult a task is, strategic planning is key to success.

157. *Mũkua nima nĩyake onethĩwa nĩ nzou.* **Whoever picks a large load owns it.**
This emerged in the early 1700s when hunters in distant lands had to carry loads of ivory to the coast. Sometimes there were so many of them they buried some in the sand and carried the rest to the market. Since everyone was heavily loaded, there was no chance of relief. If one bore a huge tusk, when he got weary he was told this proverb.

158. *Mũndũ eanasya nyama owaa nzou.* **One has sufficient meat when he kills an elephant.**
As Krapf witnessed, elephant meat could last several families for nearly a month. Trading and hunting parties also enjoyed elephant meat. This axiom means that one is settled when he accumulates wealth.

159. *Mũndũ nũyumasya nzounĩ na mũkuĩle.* **A person can remove himself from the share of an elephant by the way he carries it.**
This maxim alludes to long-distance trade in ivory with the observation that a hunter excluded himself from the profit of the tusk by his own mishandling of it. The heavy object was required to be ferried many miles to the coast without bruises and cracks. By extension it means a person can isolate himself from the family, community, or social club by the way he treats his fellows.

160. *Mũsyĩmi ũtaatha nzou ndaatha nduu.* **A hunter who cannot shoot an elephant cannot shoot a squirrel.**
This maxim dates to the Monsoon era. From its modern political contexts, a leader who cannot win at the opportune time cannot initiate development.

161. *Mũsyĩmi wa nzou e vata na mĩwongo.* **The elephant hunter loves ivory.**
Between the 1300s and 1800s the Kamba were the principal elephant hunters in East Africa, selling their tusks and hair at the coast.

Elephants without good tusks were spared as only ivory had value. This maxim means people act for specific purposes.

162. *Ndĩkyamanaa kelĩ.* **It does not pose twice.**
If the hunter missed an elephant when its massive body was in clear view he was unlikely to hit it the second time. Metaphorically the elephant is luck or fortune. This proverb, therefore, calls on one not to waste opportunities.

163. *Nzou ndyũlawa nĩ kwoo.* **An elephant does not forget its home.**
Most paths and roads in Ũkambanĩ were originally elephant paths. The Kamba say that no matter how many decades and centuries pass, later generations of elephants will walk the paths that their ancestors trod. This proverb emerged during the first millennium and means among other things that there are things that naturally recur.

164. *Nzou yakyamana nĩvenawa ngũngi.* **When an elephant stands across the path, don't let it catch your scent.**
This proverb originated with hunters in the seventeenth century. The Kamba claim that the elephant has very poor sight but a strong sense of smell to detect human presence. To avoid being trampled on hunters approached the animal from the leeward side. This is to say, give way to superiors or the strong in order to avoid tragedy.

165. *Ndũsinda nzou kũmĩa.* **You cannot beat an elephant in bowel evacuation.**
This emerged during the Monsoon era among hunters comparing human and elephant excretion. It means one should not compete with those who are more experienced and resourceful.

166. *Ndũkeke ũndũ ĩsyaa ya nzou.* **Do not take as long as an elephant's pregnancy to do something.**
This catchphrase emerged among hunters who observed the extraordinary gestation period of elephants. This means do not hesitate, hurry up and finish your job.

167. *Thii wa ngovi wĩ mwoo ta metho ana mũtwe ũmwe.* **An elephant's placenta is as scarce as four eyes on one head.**
Kamba hunters claim that elephants take great care and seek ultimate privacy in mating and birth, a claim with scientific merit. The elephant's placenta is rare because like Kamba women the female elephant buries the placenta. This proverb emerged in antiquity and is used as an expression of rarity.

168. *Nzĩa yatũkaswa nĩ nzou.* **An elephant makes a path.**
A strong person pioneers tough things for other people. Elephants opened up most of the paths and roads across Ũkamba. The Kamba used these paths to drive their livestock from pastures to water points, clearing the paths further.

169. *Nzou ndĩmanyaa kana ve syĩndũ sya mwĩĩ wayo syĩ vata.* **An elephant does not know there are spots on its body that are valuable.**
The rich often do not understand their potential or their resourcefulness. This emerged during the Vascon era and encouraged people to pay attention to their capabilities and use them for themselves.

170. *Nzou ndĩemawa nĩ mĩwongo yayo.*[5] **Tusks do not overwhelm an elephant.**
In this proverb *mĩwongo* is not 'trunk' as translated in existing literature.[6] This proverb originated with hunters who killed elephants and transported the heavy tusks from the interior to the coast. On the way the carriers were told this maxim to encourage them to soldier on with their burden. Outside this context, listeners were told to keep up with their responsibilities.

171. *Nzou yoasya vala ĩvalũkĩte.* **An elephant rots where it falls.**
In precolonial times some elephants died of old age rather than wounds. If not discovered in time and butchered the carcass decayed, making the spot rotten. The deeper meaning is that an influential person or facility affects the surrounding area first. Nowadays, for instance, locating a factory in rural areas will uplift the site. Locals will gain employment, markets for their goods, and infrastructure with that factory.

172. *Nzou yũate mbĩa nditalawa ngũmbaũ.* **An elephant that kills a rat is never considered a hero.**
Emerging from the Vascon era, this proverb warns people not to boast of little things. It calls on people to take on tasks that match their strength.

173. *Vai nzou ĩtakalwa mee nĩ kĩthiia.* **There is no elephant whose scrotum cannot be scratched by hooked thorns.**
Small things can harm the most powerful. The thorny tree alluded to has sturdy hooked thorns and would be painful on the scrotum of any animal.

---

[5] Kituku, *Sukulu*, 62; Mutisya, *Proverbs*, 50; Mwau, *Dictionary*, 667.
[6] Mwau, *Dictionary*, 530.

174. *Kavalũkũ keiwe nĩ nzou ũũ nĩ ũsĩ mũliku ndũkaainge ta nzou.* **The hare was warned by the elephant that this is a deep river so do not wade like an elephant.**
This is one of the proverbs that do not follow the common rule of proverbs in pith and metaphorical forms. It derives from a story of the two animals: an elephant found the hare stranded on the riverbank, worried how to cross the deep river. Out of generosity it decided to help the hare cross, saying this axiom. Once on the other side the hare, showing no gratitude, started mocking and insulting the elephant. The proverb means do not bite the finger that feeds you.

175. *Kavũkũ kaemea kyenga.* **The hare wins by dodging.**
The hare is a tricky and slippery animal that runs helter-skelter to evade predators. It is thus considered a wise animal. This proverb means a wise man knows how to respond to tough questions and arguments in a way that avoids conflict.

176. *Mbũkũ ya ũliliinĩ ĩsyĩmawa nĩ mũndũ mũĩ.* **A hare in its hideout is hunted only by a wise man.**
Just as a wise hunter will know where the hare is hiding, a clever person can tell the secrets of a wise man based on how he talks.

177. *Mbũkũ yesĩla kĩtonyinĩ ndĩleaa ũtia wia.*[7] **When a hare passes through a hole in the fence it always leaves behind some fur.**
A hare is a small slippery animal with soft skin and fur such that if it passes through the fence it must leave some fur therein. From antiquity, this has been taken in two different axiomatic ways: First, a wise man passing through has to leave behind something valid. For instance, when political leaders visit rural areas they contribute to development. In another interpretation, the maxim warns that if you take a risk severe suffering is a possible outcome.

178. *Aumie ĩkĩmboo avota ĩkĩngo.* **He fled from the buffalo forest into the leopard jungle.**
Created by hunters in antiquity this axiom describes a transition from a bad situation to the worst condition as a result of arrogance. There are multiple variations and interpretations.[8]

---

[7] Mwau, *Dictionary*, 656.
[8] Christine Ammer, *The American Heritage Dictionary of Idioms* (New York: Houghton Mifflin Harcourt Publishing Company, 2003).

179. *Mboo ila syĩ Kathaana nosyo ila syĩ Kyanzavĩ.* **The buffalos in Kathaana Hill are the same as in Kyanzavĩ Mountain.**
This emerged as Kamba hunters expanded from Mboonĩ to the two mountains and later settled to cultivate pigeon peas. The maxim means: do not think the grass is greener outside your neighbourhood. Innovate and turn your surroundings into your dreamland. Another interpretation from residents of the plains between Kathaana and Kyanzavĩ was that, in old days, herders disparaged each other's fiancées. One would respond with this proverb, often adding some emphasis.

180. *Mboo ndĩkwatawa kĩtimba.* **A buffalo is not patted on its buttocks.**
Folktales said the buffalo resisted being milked like a cow or herded like bulls. Anyone touching its tail or butt suffered from the animal's fury and risked death. Coined at the early stages of domestication of the animals it suggests there are risks one should approach very carefully.

181. *Mboo ndwĩki yendaa yoka.* **A buffalo bull moves alone.**
This is a warning against arrogance and stubbornness. In the wild, strong bulls browse alone while weaker buffaloes graze in herds for security. When a pride of lions strikes, the bull meets a death he could have avoided had he been in a herd.

182. *Mboo nĩlĩsĩlawa mũtĩ.* **Perch in a tree to avoid a buffalo.**
The buffalo was one of the fiercest bovines in Ũkamba. When it charged, people had to run and climb trees for safety. The disappearance of buffalo from human settlement by 1900 led to minimal use of proverbs relating to it.

183. *Walea ũkany'o ũkakanw'a nĩ mboo.* **If you reject admonition, the buffalo will correct you.**
This proverb originated with a veteran who trained novices to maintain silence when hunting fierce animals. Some proverbs were coined within certain classes and trades before reaching widespread circulation. Whoever does not listen to his parents is bound to land in trouble.

184. *Watina cha mboo ndwĩki.* **You poked the bull buffalo's buttocks!**
Large buffalo bulls are fierce and often gore people to death. This proverb was used if a person crossed the path of wizards or powerful men. This meant that one had made a serious mistake.

185. *Kĩtheka kĩyĩemaa mbusya.* **A forest is not too much for a rhinoceros.**
The rhino lives in the forest for shelter and forage. While humans might regard the forest as gloomy and frightening, the rhino prefers it.

Another interpretation is that not all the dangers in the forest bother the rhino, for this large animal is king there.

186. *Mũtĩ weemaa mbusya tyo ntheeũ.* **The tree defeats the rhino, and even more the colobus monkey.**
Whenever rhinos charged, hunters raced up the tallest tree. The animal circled around the tree goring the tree, but finding it futile soon disappeared. Colobus monkeys swing on the branches, bending them – so observers assumed the monkeys could destroy the tree. Hunters then responded with this maxim dismissing this assumption. The ancient proverb assumes different capabilities, but a task that the father cannot do, the son is unlikely to handle.

187. *Mũsingi mũtae ndakĩaa mbusya na ndatulasye ngũka.* **A well-trained initiate does not fear the rhino or hit the bank in fear.**
The proverb alludes to the last stage of Kamba initiations called *nzaĩko nene*. Every Kamba must participate to be a true and properly educated member of the community.[9] This was connected with transition from childhood into adulthood, social relations, and the assumption of responsibilities. Students (*asingi*) spent two months in the home of the circumciser to learn things pertaining to the body, rites of passage, and subjects such as sex, love, pregnancy, childbirth, and death. It was claimed a rhinoceros will come and carry the *asingi* away for further instructions if they failed their examinations, as a trick to test and harden the initiates.[10] Initiates who had listened carefully to instruction were not afraid, and never ran in fear of the rhino. The actual meaning, therefore, is people are not afraid of something they know.

188. *Mũsyĩmi ndasyĩmaa kĩthekanĩ kĩte kĩndũ.* **A hunter does not hunt in a forest without game.**
This proverb has been varied and extended to contexts other than hunting. It can mean that one cannot in economic terms invest where one does not expect good returns; politicians cannot spend time and resources campaigning where they cannot win; and people cannot marry into a family where they know marriages do not last.

189. *Mũsyĩmi ndatiaa tũva.* **A hunter does not leave behind his file.**
Tũva, the metallic file for sharpening blades, arriving with early twentieth-century 'white hunters' became indispensable to Kamba hunters after the First World War. Emerging during the 1920s, this axiom means never leave behind a useful tool, as you may need it.

---

[9] Lindblom, *Akamba*, 56–77.
[10] Lindblom, *Akamba*, 45–51.

190. *Mũthũsa na kĩvĩsĩ ndaa mũlanza ĩtako.* **The hunter who hunts with a boy gets a dart in his butt.**
Mũthũsa was a descriptive term for a raider of livestock or long-distance hunter, while *mũlanza* was a wooden dart for shooting birds. Reputedly, a hunter accompanied by a boy might be injured with this crude weapon. As the hunter aimed at the game, the inexperienced boy behind him also aimed at the game and could accidentally shoot the hunter on the buttocks. The proverb called for separation of age sets. Boys do not keep secrets and can easily reveal embarrassing things. *Mũlanza* in the buttocks symbolized embarrassment.

191. *Mũsyĩmi ũte mũtae ndasyĩmaa mbusya.*[11] **A poorly trained hunter does not hunt rhinoceros.**
The rhino is so dangerous that a hunter needs training. Trainers persuaded hunters to suppress fear, tiptoe behind the rhino, and pull out hair from its tail. If they could do so, they had proven themselves. If the rhino charged, one was to stand still until the animal was close and then jump out of its path, letting the animal harmlessly rush past.

192. *Kathila kasyaa kangĩ.* **A little duiker sires another little duiker.**
A descriptive adage for people whose children ape their bad traits, similar to others using the dik-dik as a symbol of wisdom. It means a child born by intelligent parents will be bright, reflecting parentage, schooling, and general environment.

193. *Mũndũ wĩ mateng'e ndasyĩmaa nzia.*[12] **A bowlegged man does not hunt duickers.**
Bowlegged conditions are known to be caused by rickets – a malnutrition-related disease mostly experienced in childhood. Given that hunters would encircle dik-diks and duikers, who would try to break through the circle and would subsequently be shot, the Kamba joked that if such a person went hunting the duiker would run through his legs, as bowlegs left a gap. However, the proverb means one with a weakness related to a particular task should not undertake the risk of dealing with that task.

194. *Kavii ke Yatta nĩka kĩla mũsyĩmi.* **There is a dik-dik in Yatta for every hunter.**
Precolonial Kamba had individual rights to exploit resources not claimed by others. In that era, everyone had a right to use uncleared

---
[11] Esther Muiu, *Cross-Cultural Religious Interaction of Kamba Community: The Culture and the Missionary Struggle* (Saarbrücken: Lambert Academic Publishing, 2012), 99.
[12] Kĩeti, *Barking*, 109; Mutisya, *Proverbs*, 46.

land between villages.[13] Although the proverb points to communal property, figuratively it refers to unmarried girls. Any suitor could find an unmarried girl. It was likely coined soon after the Kamba began to expand from Mboonĩ Hills towards Yatta during the Vascon era.

195.   *Kũu nĩ nthĩ ĩngĩ kaula lũma.* **'That is another world', as the aardvark said.**
The story is told that once upon a time the lion and the aardvark met. The lion saw the aardvark's long strong claws and said, 'Wow! You really have fabulous claws. Are your teeth the same too?' The aardvark replied shrewdly and tersely, 'That is another world!' The lion, thinking the aardvark was a much stronger animal, backed off. The aardvark's response was interpreted in the mind of the lion as meaning, 'Yes. The teeth are even more fabulous. Do not joke with me.' But the toothless aardvark could have meant the opposite, a different matter.

196.   *Lũma ndwĩ maayo ta ngunyũ.* **The Aardvark has no teeth like claws.**
The aardvark has the strongest and longest claws among all Ũkamba animals. The claws are capable of digging deep holes in the hardest ground. Yet, the animal is toothless. The ancient axiom means that every strong person has weaknesses.

197.   *Lũma ũĩaa nthingii nzaa.* **Aardvarks feed on black ants because of starvation.**
Aardvarks are ant-eating and burrowing nocturnal animals known by various names. The ancient maxim means necessity is the mother of invention.

198.   *Syavinya naekee lũma.* **I left the muscular ones to be dealt with by the aardvark.**
The aardvark is known for its strength in digging deep into hard ground with strong and long claws. This ancient proverb means that the speaker resists any forceful moves of the listener. It persuades listeners to avoid conflict.

199.   *Wĩa wa lũma nĩ kwĩnza maima naw'o wa mbiti nĩ ũkoma nzĩnĩ wa amaima.* **The work of an aardvark is to burrow holes and that of the hyena is to live in the holes.**
This maxim talks about the distinction between freeloaders and providers. The ancient maxim encourages people to work, cooperate, and improve their communities. In one song, a husband who builds a family is likened to the aardvark, while 'hangers-on' infesting prosperous families were depicted as hyenas.

[13] Lindblom, *Akamba*, 164.

200. *Mũthoi wa ngũũe ũaithasya mũatĩĩi.* **The craving for pork soup gets the hunter killed.**
This condemns greed, which entices people to great risks. A greedy person brings injury to himself.[14] In the hunting of wild pigs, hunters undertook risks that ordinary people considered reckless and unnecessary. They chased the animals into holes and followed them into the holes, which were abodes of other dangerous creatures such as pythons, leopards, hyena, and so on. These creatures often killed the hunters as they crawled into the holes.

201. *Mũsyĩmi wa ngũũe ti ũndũmwe na wa ngwae, nĩ mũndũ wa ĩtambya.* **The hunter of pigs is swifter than the hunter of francolins.**
The Kamba hunted birds and hogs, but each used different techniques. While the hunter of francolins could prowl and shoot them easily, that of pigs could not. Pigs sense humans and are fast, requiring the hunter to be as swift. Thus, one task requires different efforts to accomplish. The proverb emerged in the era of subsistence hunting during the first millennium.

202. *Ngũũe yĩkangaa na a ma yo.*[101] **The pig fries itself with its own fat.**
This proverb emerged during the twentieth century when frying became common among the Kamba. The literal meaning is that certain animals have so much fat that when cooking them additional oil is not needed. A self-reliant person deals with his own situation effectively. It might also mean that selfish motives often backfire and cause damage to the person involved.

203. *Mwaathi wĩ nguma ndathaa nthĩ.* **An expert shooter does not miss the target.**
This maxim has been interpreted differently and used in different political and social contexts. In the past, trainees in hunting were often tested for their precision in shooting using thin targets like a piece of grass. Seasoned Kamba politicians used this maxim to indicate that they cannot lose to their opponents.

204. *Kũla kumaa mbĩkya nokw'o kumaa mboveli.* **From where sharp shooters hail, tumblers also hail.**
This alludes to eighteenth- and nineteenth-century duelling practices. Clans rose against each other amid much bloodshed, looting, and forced resettlement along clan lines. These were not serious wars but mere feuds that stopped once a man was shot, wounded, or died. The clan that wounded an opponent withdrew, cheering in victory. It implies

---

[14] Mutisya, *Proverbs*, 66.

that if there is a sharpshooter in a region, there is also a tumbler in the same region. First collected by Lindblom in 1912 this proverb has since appeared in other publications and oral accounts.[15]

205. *Mbovi ndĩsĩ nthwai.*[16] **Those who lay in wait do not know those who drive the game.**

Kamba hunting activities often involved a team of two groups: one group called *nthwai* spread out and drove game towards an ambushing group called *ovi* (single: *mbovi*) who laid ambush at a considerable distance from the starting point of the *nthwai*. The ambushing hunter, referred to as *mwovi* or *mbovi*, shot the animals as they came running towards him. The ancient proverb warns against boasting before people of equal resources who play complimentary roles.

206. *Mwovela weka ndathĩkaa.* **A lone-tumbler is never shot.**

In precolonial days Kamba conducted arrow fights between clans. They ceased at the end of the nineteenth century, but how far back they date is hard to tell. Contests favoured both good tactics and evasion. The proverb means one has competed to prove himself but not to boast. In today's court cases, for example, one person confidently lays out his case only to be shocked at the questions and answers session.

207. *Nthee ilĩ iemwa nĩ mwatũ.*[17] **A beehive cannot defeat two honey badgers.**

The Kamba hang beehives on tall trees with a peg and tie them. However, a honey badger usually pushes through the underbelly of the hive, knocking it off the peg to fall to the ground. Once the hive splits apart the badger helps itself to the honey. Some hives are heavy, properly secured with ropes and so on. It takes more than one badger to dislodge such a hive. This proverb stresses the importance of unity and cooperation in tackling heavy matters.

208. *Kũla ilĩkĩlaa nokw'o imilĩlaa mbya.* **Where they are mauled is the same place they twist horns.**

A giraffe is born in a jungle full of predators, yet it matures, ages, and dies, and still hyenas never lick its bleached bones. This means one can survive even in situations where opportunities are rare and competition stiff. This is an important maxim for young people who are facing joblessness in urban and county terrains of Kenya and elsewhere.

---

[15] Lindblom, *Riddles*; Kimilu, *Mũkamba*, 116.
[16] Farnsworth, *Grammar*, 112.
[17] Mutisya, *Proverbs*, 31.

209. *Ndwĩa nĩ nyamũ nene ĩndĩ yevũthisye nĩ kũmĩa mbiivii ta mbũi.* **A giraffe is a big animal but is disgraced by dropping round goat-like excretion.**
This means that both big and small things have their respective function in human life. Do not underestimate small things.

210. *Ĩvai ĩyũaĩaa kũmbĩaa.* **Poison does not kill because of quantity but quality.**
The proverb originated with hunters in the thirteenth century who pioneered the use of poison. They soon noticed the quality of the poison was more important than its quantity. The value of anything is more important than the quantity of it.

211. *Yamesya maa yĩsawa nĩ aka.* **Women eat it when it develops spots.**
Maa has two different meanings depending on pronunciation. The first is 'intestines', which women appreciate. The second, correct, translation here is spots. An animal with colourful spots like the cheetah is fierce and strong but during old age becomes so weak even women can trap and eat it. This implies that when a champion weakens, anyone can rule over them.[18] Men ate the fat humps of young bulls; when it grew old and tasteless, it was given to women. Persons who are liked and hugged by everyone can be abandoned when they are old. One should tread carefully when his fame is at the peak, lest he regrets it when it is gone.

212. *Makalanzanga nĩ matanĩaa maima.* **Rodents enjoy their holes.**
These animals rush into anthills for shelter and food whenever they see humans.[19] The Kamba interpret this as a joy for these animals just as people feel safe and happy when they are at home. It originated with Monsoon-era hunters.

213. *Makathanga no makaanaa.*[20] **Even rodents scratch each other.**
Rodents are sociable animals living in families and large groups. However, they often fight and even drive some members out of the group. Likewise, there is no group of people that does not experience conflict. The proverb means that we should find solutions rather than simply discussing problems.

214. *Nyamũ ndĩyĩw'aa muuke.* **A beast does not smell its own stench.**
Emerging in the tenth and eleventh centuries, this is a commentary on self-examination, self-criticism, and the folly of boastfulness. Animals

---

[18] Kimilu, *Mũkamba*, 119; Mwau, *Dictionary*, 672; Watuma, *Syĩthĩo*, 58.
[19] Mwau, *Dictionary*, 654.
[20] Mwau, *Dictionary*, 654.

can smell the scent of other animals, but not their own. It points out that a person may not understand the dark side of their actions. We should listen to warnings of other people.

215. *Nyamũ ĩte ngũngi ĩkungĩawa nĩ kĩvĩsĩ.* **A boy stalks a scentless animal.**
Wild animals depend on scent to detect danger. Hunters need stalking skills to get close enough to shoot animals. They have to be in the right direction of the wind so the animal cannot scent them. Less keen-scented animals are vulnerable and can be stalked by less skilful hunters, who are equated with boys. Scent in this proverb symbolizes the ability to discern and avoid deception. Thus, the ancient proverb means that a person without discernible instinct is vulnerable to deception.

216. *Nyamũ ya kũnwa nĩ ngũngĩ ndũmyathaa vala welele.* **When an animal gets your scent, you will not hit it where you were aiming.**
This proverb tells the listener, 'If you hear something act immediately, at the opportune time.' Coming from ancient hunting contexts, this means if one's opponents get wind of his plans it will be difficult to defeat them.

217. *Nyamũ ya nyama ndĩtheaa nyama.* **A carnivore does not select meat.**
This axiom emerged during the Monsoon era as a reflection of the greed and immorality of the speaker. It means that any economically rewarding action is justifiable even if harmful. It also means that any sexual activity is justifiable so long as it quenches one's desires.

218. *Nyamũ ya ũta ndĩtiawaa ĩte nzame.* **A bow-shot animal is never left untasted.**
Hunting was not an easy task, so one could not shoot game and fail to taste its meat. This ancient proverb indicates that people do not labour in vain, but in pursuit of benefits. They engage in challenging tasks hoping for some reward.

219. *Nyamũ yĩ mee ndĩkũnawa kavola.* **A beast with a scrotum is not beaten lightly.**
This talks about handling fierce beasts and, by extension, enemies or risky matters. Kill them before they kill you. The proverb means that hefty matters have to be resolved immediately, lest they become more serious.

56 Part II: The Natural World

220. *Nyamũ yĩ mee ĩkusaa yĩendete.* **A beast with a scrotum dies on the move.**
One interpretation is that, like a bold and powerful male animal, one should be strong and of good cheer no matter the challenges. This is a hunting proverb dating to antiquity.

221. *Nyamũ yĩ nũme ndĩkĩlaa mwaki.* **A male animal does not jump over fire.**
In this fifteenth-century maxim, fire symbolizes danger, while the animal stands for a family head. Thus, the statement means a person with family and friends should never engage in risky adventures that could backfire and put everyone at risk.

222. *Nyamũ mbathe ndĩkalaa ũyinĩ.* **A fierce animal does not live in open grassland.**
The fiercest animals usually live in forests rather than grasslands. Another interpretation is that a fierce animal can be a threat to mass wildlife found in the grassland, which immediately flee.

223. *Nyamũ yĩ ngũlũ ĩmĩaa ĩũngeme.* **A proud animal defecates standing up.**
A proud animal signifies an arrogant person, while defecation symbolizes the blunders an arrogant person might make. The hasty nature of a blunder is referred to in the proverb by 'defecate standing up'.

224. *Ũkamyona ĩkwitheetha wasya nyamũ ĩĩ ndyaũmbwa.*[21] **If you see an animal energetically moving about, you will say it is immortal.**
A young animal displays its strength by its movements until it grows older, gets sick, or injured. Coined by hunters in antiquity, this proverb warns young people that human strength is temporary.

225. *Wakomana na nyamũ sya mavũngũ isembete manya ila syĩ ithu syĩ ĩtina.* **If you meet a stampede of hoofed animals, get to know that those with paws are behind it.**
There is a cause to everything. Look for the motivator behind an action.

226. *Wenda ũmanya nyamũ nthũkũ kiita ĩswii yayo.*[22] **If you want a fierce animal, touch its young.**
The most violent encounter with animals is when humans threaten their offspring. The axiom drawn from hunting from antiquity is a warning to those who tend to be mean to children. Parents and guard-

---
[21] Kimilu, *Mũkamba*, 115; Mbiti, *Ngaeka*, 97.
[22] Kituku, *Sukulu*, 85.

ians will fight to protect their children. It may also mean that one will encounter the fury of those whose core interests are interfered with.

227. *Woona kasamũ kasembete kĩla kakĩĩte nĩ kĩnene kwĩko.* **Whenever you see a small animal running, what is chasing it is bigger.**
Small animals usually run when they see big predators, while a person can only complain, raise the alarm, or solicit help with a task that he or she cannot handle alone. This proverb emerged with hunting in ancient times.

228. *Mũthaimi wa naĩ athekaw'a nĩ kĩao.* **A bad hunter is derided at the game-sharing lodge.**
The word *kĩao* in the context of this proverb means the place or act of sharing game meat after hunting and the place where the reckless hunter sleeps that night. Hunters thus warned the hunting party members of the gravity of failure at the end of the day. The hunting party punished a careless hunter when the meat was shared by giving him a smaller and less desirable share. The ancient proverb persuades people to take seriously their obligations. In schooling, students who do not maintain consistency in their studies regret at exam period and more so during graduation ceremonies. Their peers who maintained consistent grades take home the much-envied trophies.

229. *Sya kũmwe nĩsyo syĩnzanĩaa maima.* **Animals of the same neighbourhood dig holes for each other.**
Tracing from antiquity this proverb has been used during modern times to promote favouritism, nepotism, and corruption in competition for finite resources, particularly in urban areas. People from the same region helped their people to get official services.[23]

---

[23] Kimilu, *Mũkamba*, 118; Mwau, *Dictionary*, 667.

5
Wild Birds

230. *Eka ũlenga ta nzingi ũkũlengala ĩthĩĩ.* **Stop hovering about like a vulture over a carcass.**
An old proverb coined by hunters, this encodes memories of vultures that are now rare. The vulture and carcass symbolize dependency on free and unreliable sources. The proverb calls the listener to do something valuable and refrain from indecisiveness.

231. *Ĩsũni yĩkwĩtũũa yonekaa kwacha.* **A bird with diarrhoea is seen at dawn.**
Circulating in northern and central Kitui, this ancient proverb means bad traits cannot be concealed. It shows the supremacy of the day and sunlight, where all things become clear.

232. *Ĩsũni yĩ mũnuka mũasa ĩyĩĩsawa.* **A bird with a long beak is not eaten.**
Among long-beaked birds in Ũkambanĩ only hornbills were eaten. The beak was the determining factor whether a bird was good for consumption or not. Symbolically, long beaks can mean talkative people cannot be trusted with confidential matters.

233. *Ĩsũni ya kĩvĩsĩ yĩoeaa mokonĩ.* **A boy's bird rots in his hands.**
Birds were sometimes retrieved from nests when they were young, fed to maturity, and then eaten. Such a bird was valuable, so if it died it was a big loss. Likewise, if one is not careful, time and resources can be wasted, leading to financial ruin in today's conditions.

234. *Ĩsũni yaũlekya nĩyoneaa nzevenĩ.* **I spot in the sky a bird about to lay eggs.**
Ancient hunters could tell birds that were about to lay eggs by the way the birds flew. This proverb means that some things are easily predictable through observation.

235. *Ĩsũni yilũ yĩ maa me mũyo.* **A black bird has delicious intestines.**
This was drawn from a riddle that poses a question to be answered and the answer is the pot. The pot is black from the outside but its contents

always gratify. It points to the value of those things or individuals who are unattractive. Unattractive people may be more romantic and morally sound than attractive ones.

236. *Ĩkoto ĩvũthasya na mũũlũkĩle wayo.* **The hornbill disgraces itself by the way it flies.**
The yellow-billed hornbill, Kamba believe, has a disgraceful flight style not matching its beautiful appearance. The ancient proverb castigates people who have no restraint despite their age and social status.

237. *Kĩtaũmwa kya ĩkoto kĩnengawe ivĩsĩ.* **The gizzard of the hornbill is given to boys.**
Boyhood or teenage years are loathsome stages of Mũkamba life, equated with immaturity and stupidity. While care was given to teenage boys, all kinds of trash was thrown at them literally or figuratively. They received the worst meat, such as the gizzard of the hornbill, the least respected part. This was considered mockery. The maxim emerged during the first millennium when hunting wild animals and birds formed a vital part of economic livelihood.

238. *Mũlaki e ndũũ na kasyũngere.* **The honey seeker is friendly to the honeyguide bird.**
Emerging from hunting and gathering contexts, this axiom points to the role that the honeyguide bird played in the history of Kamba hunting and honey harvesting in the wild. *Kasyũngere* refers to a white and crested bird with a long tail, which guided hunters to a fortune or drew them away from danger. If it flew and came back that was a signal for dangerous animals or enemies. To enhance their honey search, the honey seekers (*alaki*) searched for this bird by calling it or whistling in a special way to draw the bird to them. The proverb means that one should respect those who are generous to him/her.

239. *Mũlaki ndogaa ngere.* **The honey seeker does not kill the honeyguide bird.**
This emerged from hunting and honey-seeking contexts in which ancient Kamba formed a symbiotic relationship with the honeyguide, also referred to as the green-backed
honeybird (*Prodotiscus zambesiae*). The bird led them away from dangerous animals and enemies and most importantly led hunters to big game and honey seekers to bee colonies.[1] The axiom means people do not bite the hand that feeds them.

---

[1] Claire Spottiswoode, Keith Begg, and Colleen Begg, 'Reciprocal Signaling in Honeyguide- Human Mutualism', *Science*, 353(6297) (22 July 2016): 387–9.

240 *Kasĩlĩlĩ kosyaĩa ke vata na mauuwĩ.* **The red bird laying eggs loves wasps.**
The *Kasĩlĩlĩ* nests near wasp nests for security of her brood and chicks against predators, including humans, which the wasps will attack. Coined when the Kamba settled in the drier environment of Ũkamba it means that women love strong men.

241. *Kĩndilĩ kĩkalasya kĩla kĩngĩ kyakwatw'a.* **The red-footed partridge keeps a trapped partner company.**
This old proverb has multiple variations and interpretations.[2] According to Lindblom, it means a long wait is well repaid if there is substantial reward in the end. Farnsworth presented a more debatable interpretation, 'A partridge detains another to cause it to be caught. Misery likes company.' Yet, Kĩeti and Coughlin say the proverb cautions listeners to avoid tricky people who will not help in the hour of need. My interpretation is that friends and relatives should keep each other company when they are going through difficult situations.

242. *Ndala ya kĩvĩsĩ tũmĩmanyaa na tũsĩla.* **A boy's nest is known by its feathers.**
This ancient proverb means that a boy cannot wait for the bird to hatch and give him more birds to eat. He secretly captures the bird and eats it as well as its eggs. The little feathers the boy plucked one by one and threw on the path betray his actions. The tricks of a bad character are known through one's little foolish actions and errors committed in secrecy.

243. *Ndituaa vandũ vamwe ta nzũũ.* **I do not stay in one place like the swallows.**
Certain species of swallow flock in communities and constantly hissing what Kamba interpret as *Tuthii! Tuthii*, 'let us go, let us go'. The perched birds hiss but never fly off. Someone who repeatedly claims he will go someplace is taken to be as foolish as these swallows. The axiom persuades the audience to be resolute. It emerged in the age of hunting when Kamba moved into the niches of such birds.

244. *'Nye, Kanyw'amalaa no ngũnyw'a malaa ĩndĩ mũtwe wĩna nziii.'* **'I, the sunbird, am enjoying the nectar, but I have a doubtful mind.'**
Sunbirds are African and Asian songbirds resembling hummingbirds in that they are small, colourful, very active and attractive, and feed primarily on nectar. The emergence of rubber slingshots in 1900s colonial Kenya began to endanger this tiny bird. The axiom emerged

---

[2] Lindblom, *Riddles*, 31; Farnsworth, *Grammar*, 57; Kimilu, *Mũkamba*, 116; Kĩeti, *Barking*, 110.

as a reflection of such ecological changes, but also as an expression of unpleasant changes that came with colonialism and modernity.

245. *Ũsĩa wa ndei ndwosawa ĩtheo wa mũsyĩ.* **The feather of a secretary bird is never found in the backyard.**
The secretary bird is a large bird found in African grasslands. It was the totem of the Amũtei clan, indicating the Kamba interaction with it since the emergence of Amũtei during the first millennium. The proverb emerged between 1000 and 1200, when the Kamba adopted bows and arrows and sought the high-quality feathers of the secretary bird for their arrows and for trade across East Africa. The bird lived far from human settlements so that only a few people could find its feathers in distant places. The proverb implies that valuable things are not found within easy reach. Many want to have a good and productive life, but do not work hard enough to acquire what is needed.

246. *Ũsĩnĩ mũnene ndwaa ngunĩ.* **A big river lacks no ibis.**
This is a long-legged wading bird with a long bill. It was widely distributed in rivers and waterpans, inspiring this proverb during the Islamic era. It means that in any community there is bound to be a champion.

247. *Kĩw'ũ nĩ kya ngunĩ, mang'aa mekaa kweela ngũlimũ.* **Water is for the ibis; the other birds just wet their ankles.**
The ibis was the aquatic king of the watercourses of Ũkamba. Other birds were not as good swimmers as the ibis. Emerging from the Islamic era, this proverb means there are things that some people cannot do due to a lack of power and resources.

248. *Ndala ya ĩvũĩ ndyonaw'a maeo.* **A dove's nest is not smiled upon.**
Doves conceal their nests deep in tree branches and hide chicks or eggs if they detect human intrusion. This ancient axiom means that smiling at the nest thinking that one will harvest chicks from it is self-deceiving. The dove's overnight move will dash one's dreams in the morning. This axiom was told to cohabiters – not to be excessively romantic lest the relationship collapsed.

249. *Ndunduli nĩ nyamũ nthũku ĩkaw'a kĩlĩo ngalĩko wa mũsyĩ.* **The owl is a bad creature; people hurl potshards at it outside the homestead.**
The owl was the messenger of illness, death, and doom. If the owl was heard several nights in succession near a homestead, death was expected to follow. The Kamba will never touch the owl, dead or alive, except for the purpose of rituals. Whenever it perched on a tree near a home, a potshard was hurled at it to kill or drive it away. The ancient proverb means that there are bad characters who should be kept at a distance.

250. *Ndundulu yatilwa ngingo ītwīkaa o ngūkū.* **When the owl is beheaded it becomes just chicken.**
This contradicts other proverbs and appears to have arisen much later as consumption taboos weakened. It means that anything of poor quality can become a resource. Moreover, unprivileged people (owls) can change overnight (decapitated) and become privileged (chicken).

251. *Kasīīlīlī eetīwe Kasīīlīlī nī kūsīīlīla akīsīīlīlīkīla kīsīīlīlonī.*[3] **Kasīīlīlī was so-called because of her piercing voice at the calling place.**
Kasīīlīlī is a common Kamba name that represents Kamba names in general, like *Jane Doe* in English. Such names have a specific history. The proverb also warns that certain habits are harmful and lead to self-harm if one is not careful. In the poem, Mbiti gives the reasons why certain people were given their current names.

252. *Kambee noko kaula kīndalī.* **The first word stands as the grasshopper buzzard said.**
This kind of statement conceals a lot of information while hinting at its origins from oral narratives, riddles, and historical events. This bird has impressed the Kamba from antiquity to the extent that the bird is reputed to have been present during creation. God sent it and the chameleon to deliver a message to the first humans about life and death. While the sluggish chameleon was sent first to tell people that they will die and then be resurrected, the swift bird overtook the chameleon and quickly delivered the message that people will die eternally. Upon the chameleon's dispute that the bird's message was wrong, the bird maintained that the first word is the most valid, hence the ancient proverb.

253. *Ve kavola kathūku ta kala ka kīmbu kīivītīlwa nī ītoloka.* **There is a slow pace I cannot stand like that of a chameleon overtaken by grasshopper buzzard.**
Coming from the same context as the previous entry, this ancient proverb points to the cost of procrastination and is associated with the Kamba myth of origins. According to the Kamba myth of creation, after creation God resolved to endow humans with immortality. He chose the reliable chameleon to tell people that they will die but come back to life shortly after. Assuming this was just another message he was accustomed to deliver, the chameleon took the matter lightly, stopping occasionally to catch flies. When the chameleon reached humans, it began to speak slowly: '*Nīiiwe ... Nīiiwe ...*' meaning 'I was told ... I was told ...' Before he completed his sentence the swift flying and swift speaking *ītoloka* bird also sent by God with a different message arrived and said,

---

[3] Mbiti, *Ngaeka*, 62.

nĩiwe andũ makusae na mololomelelye ta mie ya syongoa, 'I was told you all shall die and disappear into deep infinity like the roots of aloe.' The chameleon countered that, *Eka niiwe andũ makusae na maũsyũka*, 'I was told people will die and resurrect.' The *ĩtoloka* said, *Aka mbee noko*, 'The first word stands.' Death has maintained a firm dominion over humanity since then.[4]

254. *Ngwete ĩmwe ngwete yaana mwikithi nũthi kaula kĩndalĩ.* **One in my hand is equivalent to one hundred, let the multitudes go, as the grasshopper buzzard says.**
This axiom emerged during a period of frequent locust invasions between 1909 and 1931. Swarms of locusts destroyed crops and natural vegetation, with severe consequences for human and animal populations. The swarms that flew for hours from east to west attracted birds of prey, which could only eat a few. The Kamba imagined the birds saying, 'I have enough, let the swarm fly on.' This means the speaker is satisfied with what is at hand with no need to accumulate more.

255. *Mwiiyi wa mũka alĩkaa nĩ nzoka ũtukũ enũkĩte na maaũ.* **A snake bites a man who spies on his wife at night while walking home.**
This emerged in the early twentieth century with changing attitudes to warn men against supervising the sexual behaviour of their wives. It reveals sexual jealousy between husbands and wives during the colonial era. Men of this era did not like sharing their wives with other men, yet there were risks involved in worrying about infidelity.

256. *Nganga ĩ mũũnda thaano.*[5] **Guinea fowl has a garden during the dry season.**
During the dry season the Kamba farms were largely barren yet vulturine guinea fowl kept wandering about the bare farms as if they were harvesting. Indeed, they found bountiful seeds fallen during harvesting. They had the entire farm to themselves. By interpretation, the ancient proverb means that an enterprising person will thrive even in bad times.

257. *Nganga ĩsyaa mbaa.*[6] **The vulturine guinea fowl bears a francolin.**
While the francolin is a less respected bird, the guinea fowl is the queen of beauty. The proverb means a good person can have worthless offspring. A priest seen as the epitome of morality and decency can bear

---

[4] Lindblom, *Akamba*, 253; James Mũĩmi, *Nĩnendete Kĩthyomo Kitũ* (Nairobi: East Africa Publishing House, 1981), 33–4.
[5] Muiu, *Cross-Cultural*, 90.
[6] Mwau, *Dictionary*, 135.

immoral children. Likewise, offspring of worthless individuals can turn out to be quite upstanding. Osborne used this maxim to demonstrate that 'merit warranted respect not birth'.[7]

258. *Nĩ nganga ĩalyũlĩte mwasyo.* **This is a vulturine guinea fowl that changed its voice.**
This proverb warns that in commercial transactions the item for sale must be authentic and of suitable quality. It also condemns deception in transactions, warning of dire consequences once the deception is revealed.[8]

259. *Makanga me nda mayusasya mũsũkũi.* **Vulturine guinea fowls inside the stomach do not make a ruckus.**
According to tradition, this emerged during the famines of the early nineteenth century to cajole people, particularly children, to eat whatever was available. The appearance of food will not harm the stomach. This hints that under normal circumstances, the Kamba cooked and served food with an appealing appearance. But appearance was not a consideration during lean days.

260. *Kĩthũi nĩ kya mwene ũlembwa.* **The bird's breast belongs to the owner of the trapping gum.**
This proverb tracing back to the Monsoon era alludes to the practice of trapping birds with a gum-like sap called *ũlembwa*. The gum was spread on spots where birds congregated. It trapped many birds. Since the trapping required rare skills in preparing the gum, people rewarded the expert with the breast meat, the only worthwhile part of small birds. Therefore, whoever contributes most receives a correspondingly higher reward than others.[9]

261. *Kyelelo kya ĩkenge nĩ kũkwatya.*[10] **The aim of a snare is to lure and trap.**
As early as the first millennium birds and rodents threatened farms during the sowing, ripening, and harvesting seasons, and even ransacked grain stores. The Kamba responded by developing a dome-shaped trap called *ĩkenge*, a patchwork of twigs and strings. Emerging from that period this alludes to the fact that some snares were of poor

---

[7] Myles Osborne, *Ethnicity and Empire in Kenya: Loyalty and Martial Race Among Kamba, C.1800 to the Present* (Cambridge: Cambridge University Press, 2014), 34; Gerhard Lindblom, *Kamba Folklore*, Vol. 3 (Uppsala: Appelbergs Boktryckeri Aktiebolag, 1934), 29.
[8] Mũĩmi, *Ngewa*, 30–1.
[9] Mutisya, *Proverbs*, 73.
[10] Mwau, *Dictionary*, 649.

quality. The builders used this proverb to say that if the trap works it is good enough. The end justifies the means.[11]

262. *Vala kalekelye vonekaa nĩ kĩvĩsĩ.* **A boy knows where a bird lays eggs.**
Finding a nest with eggs was considered a fortune to the finder. However, such a find does not help the boy who will misuse the opportunity. The boy symbolizes an irresponsible and underserving person, who squanders a valuable opportunity.

263. *Katumbĩlĩle tikoneki, nĩko kayonanasya kokĩla.* **It is rarely visible when it conceals itself, it reveals itself when it takes to flight.**
A bird or a small animal hidden in bushes is rarely seen if it maintains its position, but reveals itself by bolting. This proverb was spoken during beer drinking in bars. The speaker meant that one who pays in big bills reveals himself to drunkards and beggars in the bar and becomes a target for pleas to buy them beer.

264. *Wangangaa ĩkengeni ndwaatong'anga ũmwalyo.* **You only wander about inside the trap; you have never pecked on the trigger stick.**
This maxim from the 1300s was incorporated into songs in the 1980s, where the singer chided his opponent for not approaching him head-on.

265. *Ĩvyũvya ya nganga nĩ mũthwa.* **The guinea fowl recuperates with a meal of white ants.**
A sick guinea fowl will scratch to eat ants and get well. This ancient proverb means people have to do what it takes for them to survive or gain profit. In a sense, it encourages hard work to make ends meet. For a sick guinea fowl to survive it has to get out and scratch the ground for food. The widespread use and popularity of this axiom is that it is varied using other species: *Ĩvyũvya ya ĩlaĩ nĩ syaamba*, 'The convalescence food of a monkey is the baobab fruit.' This means the solution to a problem must employ the same resources from which the problem emerged.

266. *Makaanĩ kũti nganga ngũũ.*[12] **In the scratching for sown grain, there is no old vulturine guinea fowl.**
Lindblom translated *makaanĩ* or *makaa* as fields that have been hoed and sown in readiness for the rains. Here, young and old fowls scratch the ground the same way. Lindblom correctly interpreted it as: in preparing gardens for the rainy season no one is exempted from his share of work,

---

[11] Henry He, *Dictionary of the Political Thought of the People's Republic of China* (London: Routledge, 2016), 287.
[12] Lindblom, *Riddles*, 32.

66   *Part II: The Natural World*

regardless of age or status. The proverb also refers to equality within a group that does not have one chief.

267. *Nganga nĩkaa na mwithe.* **The guinea fowl often scratches out seeds with its tail.**
Guinea fowls never use their tails to scratch for food, but this proverb suggests they do. While there is no truth that the tail is ever used for productive purposes, the axiom suggests that there can be. It means that if one alternative fails, try another.

268. *Nganga nĩ mawĩa.*[13] **The value of a guinea fowl is its feathers.**
The Kamba domesticated guinea fowls for feathers, meat, and protective magic. The maxim coined by trappers during the Islamic period implies that the guinea fowl was worth its feathers, without which it was of no value to the trapper. The bird was trapped to harvest its feathers for decoration and feathering arrows. The maxim means an object is worth its value; the kind of premium that humans attach to it.

269. *Nganga nĩvĩĩye kĩthiita.*[14] **The guinea fowl's tail is cooked.**
Farnsworth translated this as 'the guinea fowl is done to the tail', which is Kamba slang for the food is ready and, by generalization, anything is done and ready. The proverb originated with trappers of birds who exploited guinea fowls for their feathers and meat from the 1400s on.

270. *Nganga yatũla ĩtaa ndĩvithaa maa.* **When the vulturine guinea fowl perches on a platform it cannot hide its spots.**
When private matters go public they cannot be hidden any more. It can also mean that as a young girl's beauty matures it cannot remain hidden. People will comment and admire her as the vulturine guinea fowl symbolizes ultimate beauty.

271. *Mũtei wa mũkwa wavĩtya nganga ũtonyaa mwene nzongo.* **If the snare misses the guinea fowl, it pricks the trapper's eye.**
A *mũkwa* was a stringed trap for birds with a trigger string that flashed so fast that setting it endangered the trapper. The Monsoon-era proverb warns against careless decisions and actions that backfire and harm the initiator.

---

[13] Mwau, *Dictionary*, 664.
[14] Farnsworth, *Grammar*, 52; Kimilu, *Mũkamba*, 117.

272. *Eka kwananga maangi na nganga nyamũ syĩ nzĩa.*[15] **Stop wasting arrows on guinea fowls when big game is on the way.**
This warning against using resources in worthless ventures dates from the Islamic period when the Kamba adopted bows. For example, today, this maxim is often told to a person educating his nephews while his own children are young and will need similar efforts.

273. *Ndũkonũve ngoso na kĩvũĩyo.* **Do not forbid a sparrow-weaver a patch on the grain- threshing site.**
The sparrow-weaver is not vermin. It feeds on otherwise useless husks left after grains are thrashed and winnowed. Farmers should not burn such husks as this is a significant food source for wild birds and other creatures. Farmers were admonished after winnowing to allow birds to descend and search for stray grains. This ancient axiom calls for kindness towards people who might make use of things that are not useful to us.[16]

274. *Ngoso ya kyengonĩ ndivivaswa.* **The camp sparrow-weaver is never roasted.**
There were wild birds that lived with people, accompanied them on their migration or journeys, and served in different capacities while they reaped benefits from humans. One of them was called *ngoso*, which made its nest near homesteads, serving the rooster's role as time keeper and warning chickens of approaching predators. These birds were not killed or molested in any way. They were sacred and their nesting trees were never harmed. This axiom means that someone who has experience and has been involved in public affairs is never left out of councils and decision making.

275. *Ndituaa ĩũlũ ndi kĩvalala.* **I do not hover about in the sky, I am not a kite.**
This alludes to the flight of beautiful large kites with black-yellowish feathers and hooked beaks, which until the 1970s hovered in Ũkambanĩ skies spying for carrion. The proverb derives from a story of two wrestlers locked in a bout around the 1940s. After many hours of manoeuvres, one realized it was time to give in and thus told its wife, 'Get the calabashes, gourds and so on out of the way, I do not hover about the sky like a kite.' This was to be done so that he would not fall on these utensils. Fortunately, these words weakened his opponent and he brought him down. Someone in frustration uses this proverb after constant discussion over issues: I have given up. I will do it myself.

---

[15] Mwau, *Dictionary*, 646.
[16] Mutisya, *Proverbs*, 23.

276. *Masũni makũũ mambaa ta andũ.* **The birds of this area speak like humans.**
The word *makũũ* is pronounced with a descending voice to mean 'those of here'. Otherwise, the word means 'old ones'. The proverb is a call to recognize fraudsters and their deceptive tactics.[17]

277. *Masũni mai ũvakũsi.* **Birds do not discriminate.**
When birds attack crops they attack all farms equally without discriminating between farms of poor or rich, friends or adversaries. The variety of birds also focus solely on feeding, rarely showing animosity towards each other. The concept of *ũvakũsi* (discrimination) is recent and thus the maxim dates from the Second World War when the Kamba began to speak of the evils of colonialism with its racial discrimination. This gave way to ethnic, class, religious, and gender discrimination. The proverb advises against discrimination and calls upon people to learn from birds.

278. *Wĩvũa itakũũlũka.* **You are beating birds that do not fly.**
Oral traditions speak of times and places where the Kamba encountered flightless birds. Persistent exploitation led to their disappearance either through extinction or migration. The ancient maxim means that one had profited without much effort. It is also used when one takes advantage of ignorant people.

279. *Kwaa ngũngũũ kũyĩ kimba.* **There is no carcass at the crow's home.**
The pied crow appears in this proverb celebrating cowardice. While cowardice was publicly condemned, the Kamba acknowledged some merits to it. This proverb advises people to avoid trouble whenever others act aggressively. There are no carcasses at the home of the pied crow because it avoids conflict. A second interpretation is that since crows are scavenger birds, corpses cannot last long.[18]

280. *Kaũ wa ĩtoli nĩ ũtanu wa ngũngũũ.*[19] **A fight among grasshoppers is the joy of the raven.**
The ancient proverb means division within a group is the pleasure of its enemy. Whenever two grasshoppers fight, the raven takes advantage of their conflict to swoop down on both. Internal strife distracts people from their common interest to not be overtaken by enemies.

---

[17] Mũĩmi, *Kĩthyomo*, 39–43.
[18] Kimilu, *Mũkamba*, 118; Mailu, *Kĩkyambonie*, 55; Mwau, *Dictionary*, 665.
[19] Mwau, *Dictionary*, 649.

281. *Ngũngũũ ndĩsa ũtuma ndũũ na mũũngũu.* **A crow cannot be a friend of the mongoose.**
This ancient maxim alludes to scavengers that feed on corpses. The two are stiff competitors that can never be friends. The axiom means that equals with minimal resources cannot be friends.

282. *Ngũngũũ yonaa vaasa tyo vaa ve kimba.* **The crow sees far beyond the carcass.**
Crows were introduced around 1890 to control urban rubbish and since then their numbers have exploded, thanks to the growing population's garbage providing the main source of food for the birds. The proverb thus emerged in the early twentieth century. Flying above buildings and trees, the crow could see not just one carcass but many in distant places. This means a leader or any foresightful person can discern things that ordinary people cannot.

283. *Kasũni kala kokĩlaa tene niko kakwataa kiinyũ.* **The early bird catches the worm.**
This is a common adage across world cultures. As an English catchphrase, it was first recorded in 1678. The axiom has been used in all cultures to encourage punctuality and prompt action. There is no indication the Kamba borrowed this maxim from the English.[20]

284. *Kasoni wavĩwe akĩlasya ona mwaki omanya kyathĩ nĩkyavika.* **A little bird whose nest burnt fears smoke.**
This ancient proverb points to the value of suspicion and fear. There are many other proverbs that indicate that fear and suspicions are often valuable. If a person is injured as a result of certain actions he or she is always careful not to repeat the same mistakes.

285. *Ona ke kaunyũsye no kolũkaa.* **Even when the feathers are plucked, it still flies.**
This ancient proverb warns against easy assumptions. When the Kamba captured wild birds they first plucked the feathers, assuming the bird was then helpless. Some, however, had wings that
could still propel them to considerable distances to escape. Thus, be careful as the end can be the beginning.

---

[20] Mwau, *Dictionary*, 667; John Ray, *A Collection of English Proverbs* (Cambridge: John Hayes, 1678).

286. *Kasũni kaikitalasya na ũseki ũmwe.*[21] **A bird does not make a nest with one piece of grass.**
This proverb shows that the task of making a nest is an accumulation of each piece of grass one at a time, just as one cannot do one small task and then stop. Continue until the task is completed. This originated in ancient times with people who were not only observing birds making nests but also the similarity to roof thatching.

287. *Kasũni katanamba kũũlũka kambaa ũtumbĩlĩla.* **A bird lies low before it flies.**
Surely, birds go down low to gather momentum before they fly fast. The ancient moral lesson of this among the Kamba was that the first steps in doing something major are very important.

288. *Kavaa kasũni kamwe ke kwokonĩ kũte twĩlĩ twĩ kĩthekanĩ.*[22] **Better a bird in the hand than two in the bush.**
A little in the hand is more valuable than tons of anticipation. This calls for contentment with little so as to appreciate plenty when it occurs. Kimilu published it in 1962 and appears to have lifted the English catchphrase into Kĩkamba.

289. *Mũtĩ ũla mũnene nĩwo wavĩyawa nĩ nyonyi.* **Birds aim to perch in the tallest tree.**
People look up to the most resourceful person for leadership. This axiom seems to date from the 1600s when leadership became vital in waging wars or defending the Kamba as a group. Sages observed that birds perched on only the tallest trees on the farm in order to enjoy the best view of the ripening crop. If catastrophe struck, the Kamba ran for advice to the oldest person, the wealthiest person, a diviner, or a war leader.

290. *Vai kĩtoli kyaasindana na ndandaalika.* **There is no grasshopper/ grasshopper nymph that has ever competed with the grasshopper buzzard.**
Whichever of the existing and conflicting meanings of the word *kĩtoli* and *ndandaalĩka* one takes, hunters have used this proverb since antiquity to suggest that prey cannot compete with predators. Similarly, weaklings cannot compete with the mighty.

---

[21] Kimilu, *Mũkamba*, 115; Mutisya, *Proverbs*, 70.
[22] Kimilu, *Mũkamba*, 115; Mutisya, *Proverbs*, 46.

6

Predators and Vermin

291. *Ĩkũya ĩngĩ nĩyo ĩ maumĩ.* **The one eating another is the one that roars.**
Precolonial Ũkamba was teeming with wild animals. Bygone generations witnessed predators prowling, capturing, mauling, and devouring their prey, leading to this ancient proverb. It points to power relations between the giver and the receiver, the ruler and the subject, and so on.

292. *Ĩvĩndĩ yaemie mbiti ngitĩ ekanaa nayo ata.* **A bone that defeated the hyena the dog cannot crunch.**
The hyena's strong teeth can clear an entire carcass and crack bones. The axiom admonished people to take up tasks that were within their means. It specifically admonished bachelors not to marry divorcees, lest they end up divorced.

293. *Kala kevwia kenũkĩaa inya.* **The coward returns to the mother.**
This has multiple variations, all advising listeners to avoid confrontation even when they are offended and sure to prevail. Thus, cowardice can be seen as admirably prudent in conflict management.

294. *Kasamũ kanini kaĩĩa kangĩ o nzaa.* **A little creature eats another simply because of hunger.**
Several variations explain why a hungry creature consumes almost anything. They all imply that lack of alternatives force people into peculiar actions.[1]

295. *Kanywa ũumaa mbiti ĩ mũingo wa ũsĩ.* **The mouth insults the hyena only when it is across the river.**
One may talk fiercely about something at a distance or in the future, but when the hour of reckoning arrives, the person becomes dumb. Stop speculations.

---

[1] Mutisya, *Proverbs*, 49; Mwau, *Dictionary*, 649.

296. *Sya vaasa syĩthesyaa mavĩndĩ.* **Those from distant places do not clean bones.**
This ancient proverb addresses transient things that one should not worry about. This comes from a political song in 1974. The singer praising her favourite parliamentary candidate used this proverb to imply that the opponent was a passing cloud.[2] The hyena in the song was the opponent who was from another corner of the constituency and the singer meant that this distant competitor was unlikely to get local votes – the analogy of licking the bones clean.

297. *Kana ka mbiti katũlile nyinya mũtĩ.*[3] **The hyena's cub blamed its mother.**
This ancient axiom was drawn from a folktale. The hyena's offspring killed a leopard cub upon incitation of the mother. The leopard retaliated by killing both the mother hyena and her cub, with the latter blaming the mother for the punishment. This means, if parents encourage evil their children will blame them for not correcting them.

298. *Kyonze kya mbiti kĩminũkĩlaswa nĩ ĩngĩ.* **Another hyena finishes the hyena's weakling prey.**
This proverb refers to an injured animal that having escaped a hyena attack is easily overwhelmed by another hyena. Hyenas ate their fill and left the remains, which were devoured by other hyenas coming upon the carcass. These hungry latecomers cleared everything. The deeper meaning is that if one is weakened by one problem, a smaller challenge will then overwhelm the person. The many proverbs about hyenas reflect close proximity of this animal to Kamba settlements and its place in Kamba lore.[4]

299. *Kĩsaa kya mbiti kĩvoyaa ĩmwenĩ.*[5] **The sore foot of a hyena heals in the dew.**
Even when wounded, the hyena still goes out to hunt in a wet environment. Such observations inspired human zeal to work hard against unfavourable circumstances. The ancient proverb encourages people to ignore challenges and forge ahead to achieve their goals.

300. *Mbiti yĩ kĩsaa ndyendaa mũsolonĩ na iingĩ.* **A wounded hyena does not hunt with other hyenas.**
This contradicts the above entry about the same injured hyena. While the previous entry is more common commentary on hard work even

---

[2] Mutisya, *Proverbs*, 10.
[3] Vincent Kituku and Felisa Tyler, *Multicultural Folktales for All Ages* (self-published, 1998), 8.
[4] Kimilu, *Mũkamba*; Mwau, *Dictionary*, 650.
[5] Kimilu, *Mũkamba*, 116; Mutisya, *Proverbs*, 62.

under bad conditions, this entry is about self-care, precaution, and strategic calculation. If you know you are not up to a given task do not try it, lest you will be embarrassed.

301. *Kũtukĩwa mũno tikw'o kũlĩka nĩ mbiti.* **Too much delay in the dark is not to be eaten by the hyena.**
The actual meaning goes beyond the context of darkness and predatory hyenas. Darkness here embodies evil and failure. The maxim is used in part to imply that failure in a business does not mean the end of an enterprise.

302. *Kũndũ ũkaaya nyama ndũkaawetee mbiti.* **Never mention to the hyena the place you will eat meat.**
Do not tell the hyena where the meat is, lest it finds it before you do. This advises people against exposing plans to the competition. Meat symbolizes opportunity while the hyena symbolizes competitors who may be faster and more resourceful. In the context of joblessness, a jobseeker is advised upon hearing of a job opportunity to not tell others. Secure your own chance first.

303. *Mũkua mbiti ndatalaa maũmangwa.* **One who carries hyenas does not count the bites.**
The hyena is an ambitious listener who faces many challenges. Through this ancient proverb the speaker encourages the ambitious listener to realize that there is no gain without pain. If you benefit from a task do not count the cost.

304. *Mwĩao wa mũonza wa mbiti wasyaa weethĩa ndũkatie.* **The seventh law of the hyena is if you find it do not leave it.**
This emerged after the introduction of written laws in the twentieth century. It advises taking advantage of every opportunity. It can also serve as an axiomatic condemnation of excessive greed.

305. *Vayĩ nyamũ ndoonu ta mbiti.* **There is no animal as mean as the hyena.**
The hyena is depicted as greedy and mean. It was used in this proverb to criticize misers during leans days in the nineteenth century when some resisted sharing food with others.

306. *Ũko wa mbiti nĩ ũmwe.* **The lineage of the hyena is one.**
This ancient adage has multiple variations in published literature and oral circulation. Hyenas in Kamba lore walk as if they are limping, symbolic of a shortcoming. This applies to a group who exhibit negative traits. *Ũko* therefore stands for a family with odd behaviour.[6]

[6] Kĩeti, *Barking*, 114.

307. *Mbiti ĩkwenda kũya syana syayo yaasya syinyunga mbũi.* **A hyena that decides to eat her own cubs argues that they smell like goats.**
Tanzania's former president Julius Nyerere popularized this proverb in the 1960s and 1970s as he expressed disgust at the prevalence of capitalistic attitudes in former prime minister Jomo Kenyatta's Kenya. He considered capitalist greed as essentially cannibalistic, the central claim of this proverb. A common symbol of rapaciousness, the hyena here acts cruelly without even the restraint of the family bond. The point is to limit rapacious behaviour, insisting one's community should never be harmed by one's actions. A person who does not heed this advice is the worst kind of animal.

308. *Mbiti nĩsamawa ĩkekalaa ĩnzame.* **A hyena is tasted so that its taste is known, and remains known.**
The hyena was tabooed such that touching it was unimaginable let alone consuming its meat. The proverb was drawn from a story of starving hunters. After many days without luck, a hunting expedition ran out of water and food and began to starve. After unintentionally killing a hyena the leader told his men, 'Listen carefully, smear it with whitewash so that it looks white like a cow; then roast it until it is black; and then taste it so that its taste will be known.' Before long they were all feasting on the hyena. The ancient proverb suggests that one should try something to know its value.

309. *Mbiti yĩanaa mũlũkũ.* **A hyena increases its gullet.**
Kamba believe the gut is the hyena's most developed organ as it can swallow anything. Even a young hyena is capable of swallowing anything that the mother hyena can. This ancient proverb means people develop strategies for achieving that which they long for in life.

310. *Mbiti yĩ mwana ndĩsaa ĩkamina.* **The hyena with a cub does not consume all the food.**
Despite its rapacious traits, the hyena is a deeply caring animal. When it finds food it always leaves some for its cubs, even when starving. During famines since the nineteenth century, families prioritized children in rationing food. The 'family' – one's community – was off-limits to greedy conduct. The contrast between rapacious behaviour in commerce and reciprocal behaviour within one's 'family' suggests the two worlds ought to be opposed: being selfless in the commercial world, or selfish in the family world, makes one (respectively) either foolish or depraved.[7]

---

[7] Mbiti, *Akamba*.

311. *Mbiti yĩ ũsoa ndĩvithaa.* **A hyena with a stripe does not hide.**
One with conspicuously unique traits must tread with care. Leaders, for example, cannot make blunders without facing public outcry.[8] This axiom predates 1900, when striped hyena virtually disappeared.

312. *Mbiti ĩla ĩtina yonaa ila syĩmbee iithua.* **The hyena at the rear notices the limping of its vanguard comrades.**
It is easy to pick on the weaknesses of others but rarely see one's own. The ancient proverb stresses that self-criticism and re-examination are rewarding.[9]

313. *Mbiti ngeni ndĩthũnaa ĩvĩndĩ.* **An alien hyena does not lick bones.**[10]
A hyena that is a stranger to the pack never gnaws at bones. The ancient proverb calls for restraint particularly for those new to a given area or subject. Let those familiar with the subject talk first and learn first.

314. *No nzunzumangaa ta ĩ mbiti.* **I murmur and hum like that hyena.**
This originated from the story of Hyena and the Calf. The hyena went to visit his in-laws and saw a tethered calf sick with cold. The hyena sat close to the calf and began to hum softly. People asked, 'Are you a singer?' The hyena replied, *Ndinaa ĩndĩ no Nzunzumangaa*, 'I am not quite a singer but I do murmur and hum.' Then people asked 'Can you sing for us?' 'Yes, if you let me run the calf around the house as I sing.' The hyena began chasing the calf muttering repeatedly, *Kĩng'oloto kilya. Kĩng'oloto kilya*, 'Calm down cold. Calm down cold.' Finally, it ran off with the calf. The ancient proverb means, I may not be an expert but I can do the job.

315. *Mbiti ndyenzawa kĩng'ee.* **The hyena never shaves beards.**
This ancient proverb is a figurative rebuke of a wicked person who never contributes to the community in spite of drawing so much benefit from the same community. It also means nothing comes close to the hyena's cheek without being bitten.

316. *Waasa wa mũndũ nĩ mbiti ĩtũĩtye ĩngĩ.* **A paternal cousin is a hyena accompanying another.**
This means cousins can fornicate with each other's wives. In the old days, cousins shared spouses and inherited each other's wives if one of them died. Consequently, this ancient proverb indicates that one cousin anticipated when his older cousin would die and make his wife avail-

---
[8] Mutisya, *Proverbs*, 17.
[9] Mutisya, *Proverbs*, 18.
[10] Kimilu, *Mũkamba*, 118.

able. Thus, the paternal cousin (Wa-Asa, my father's son) was equated with a predatory hyena.

317. *Ona mbiti sioo anyanyae.* **Even hyenas have friends.**
Although the hyena is considered the ugliest and the vilest animal, it has friends. This has been true of human relationships since antiquity. All individuals are capable of making friends, partnerships, and companionships.

318. *Mbiti yambaa ũu yĩ mũingo wa ũsĩ.* **The hyena whimpers differently while across the river.**
When far beyond a river the hyena sounds frightening and courageous, but it calms down and sounds cowardly when near settlements. This is an ancient axiomatic condemnation of boasting. People who boast say many empty words, but coil their tails when encountering the actual task.

319. *Mbiti noyo mũnyambũ.* **The hyena is the lion.**
The hyena is a lesser predator than the lion, symbolizing different levels of challenges. The ancient proverb means even though a challenge be insignificant, it still requires attention lest it develop into a bigger problem.

320. *Kakaaya kangĩ kambaa kũkatĩsya.* **A little animal that would eat another little animal scares it first.**
This ancient maxim is about lovers, predators, prey, and their respective strategies. Today, it applies to where political candidates give tips to musicians and campaigners for their support.

321. *Kakĩlw'a vinya kamelanĩlaw'a na mavwia.* **When it is overwhelmed, it is swallowed with feathers.**
This ancient axiom alludes to predators such as pythons that swallow their smaller animal prey feathers, fur, and all. This means when one's deception is discovered he or she is destroyed.

322. *Kasamũ ke kĩthu kayĩ ai maingĩ.* **A little pawed beast does not have a lot of predators.**
Animals with paws have fewer predators. The ancient proverb coined by hunters means ugly and mean girls have fewer suitors.

323. *Katasemba kaitheaa nyamũ yĩ mbwaa.* **One that cannot run does not provoke an animal with claws.**
Sluggish creatures avoid predators. Similarly, this ancient proverb advises listeners to be less aggressive towards strong people. Nations with weak military and economic structures should not be aggressive against stronger neighbours.

324. *Kĩteng'ũ kyateete ngo ĩndĩ kyakwatya mbiti nĩ kwenda nyama.*
A lair was set for a leopard, but trapped the hyena because of its greed for meat.
This proverb is an axiomatic condemnation of greed from the early twentieth century when European-type traps called *kĩteng'ũ* reached Ũkamba. Before the First World War, the Kamba set such traps to eradicate leopards, but the bait attracted hyenas most of the time, hence this proverb. It means greed leads to destruction and death.

325. *Kwaĩka ngo ti thĩna, thĩna nĩ ũkũmĩkwata yaĩkwe nũũ?* **To circumcise a leopard is not difficult, the challenge is who will hold it down.**
This ancient axiom implies that there are tasks that require courageous people to accomplish them. It is similar to the question raised by an old mouse, 'Who will bell the cat?' It is easy to propose a brilliant idea, but it is not so easy to implement it. Most people are good at making a plausible suggestion but they do not like to take responsibility.

326. *Mwaka wa ngo ndũvoyanawa maiyĩ.* **In a year of leopard attacks, people don't borrow and lend doors.**
This proverb alludes to the Vascon era when the Kamba lived in huts with doors called *maiiyĩ*, made of interwoven soft wood. The doors were fastened with ropes to the hut's entrance during the night. Neighbours borrowed and lent these doors quite often to one another, but the borrowing ceased whenever there were outbreaks of leopards in the villages. The proverb means that one in need cannot help another with similar needs.

327. *Mwiino wa ngo wemelaa uthekeni.* **The leopard's faeces are hardest to come out at the narrowest end.**
In precolonial times Kamba hunters took great interest in observing animal behaviour. Leopards easily pushed out the bulk of the faeces but had difficulties clearing the narrow part. This ancient proverb means the beginning of an endeavour is easy but carrying it through is the challenge. This encourages those labouring to persevere.

328. *Ndikĩaa malũa ma ngo.* **I am not scared of leopard skins.**
This ancient proverb alludes to customs of shapeshifting in which 'Some people skilled in black magic had power to change themselves into wild animals and in this form are able to carry out their ghastly intentions with impunity.'[11] Leopard-men wore leopard skins when attacking opponents in order to lead victims to believe the assault was a leopard attack. Those knowing the trick coined this proverb, for they will face the leopard-men without fear.

---

[11] Lindblom, *Akamba*, 282.

78   Part II: The Natural World

329. *Ndŭkathĩĩye ngo ngingo.* **Do not reveal the neck to the leopard.**
This ancient adage originated from a fable that leopards' tactics of breaking the necks of their prey originated from human rumour. It means warn people to be cautious of what they say. In the business world entrepreneurs should not reveal their trade to competitors and opponents.

330. *Ndĩkŭaa na maa mayo.* **It does not age out with its spots.**
This proverb originated with hunters before the Vascon era. The Kamba observed that young leopards had beautiful spots that darkened as the animal aged. The ancient axiom means nothing is permanent. Senility catches up with all people.

331. *Ũndũ kaswii ka ngo kesĩ tiw'o ka nthia kesĩ.*[12] **What the leopard cub knows is not what the fawn knows.**
Emanating from among hunters during the Islamic era, the maxim means the speaker knows much more than the listener does. The leopard cub symbolizes the speaker who might be young, weak, or poor, but can beat the listener on all respects. The listener is the fawn.

332. *Nditelemaw'a nĩ mũnyambũ waũsola.* **I am not scared of a carved lion.**
The emergence of this proverb is linked to the history of the Kamba woodcarving industry, which went commercial in 1918. By the end of the Second World War, carvings of lions were displayed on the pavement by hotels and exported to the Western word.[13] While a lion can be scary, a carving of a lion is not. Values and strength lie only in the real object, not in a picture.

333. *Kana ka ngo katithasya inyake, naka mũnyambũ kaitithya simba.*[14] **A leopard cub resembles its mother; that of a lion resembles a lion.**
The proverb features in many circumcision songs. Caution is also advised that the word *ngo* means both 'leopard' and the plural form of *ũko*, 'ethnic groups'.[15] The actual meaning of the proverb is that character traits persevere within a lineage.

334. *Ĩswii ya mũnyambũ no mũnyambũ.* **A lion cub is also a lion.**
The ancient adage has multiple interpretations in oral circulation and in literature.[16] Two outstanding interpretations include such views as

[12] Mwau, *Dictionary*, 669.
[13] Joy Adamson, *The Peoples of Kenya* (London: Collin & Harville Press, 1967), 237.
[14] Kimilu, *Mũkamba*, 13; Mutisya, *Proverbs*, 30.
[15] Mbiti, *Ngaeka*, 60.
[16] Mwau, *Dictionary*, 647.

do not underrate people who are knowledgeable about certain things. The second common interpretation is that resemblance is notable and, given proper training, someone can perform the duties of experts.

335. *Ndũkavũthye mũnyambũ muĩe ũũwĩta ĩkinũ.* **Do not mistake a lion that has been rained on for a cheetah.**
This appeared in multiple songs defensively claiming the speaker is capable of handling things better than the derisive audience. Cheetah and monkey were varied depending on which one is locally abundant. Both animals are cowardly compared to the lion and all are used symbolically. Lions symbolize power, wisdom, and ability, while the cheetahs and the monkeys represent cowardice and powerlessness.

336. *Vayĩ mũnyambũ ũtavunya ngũka.*[17] **There is no lion that cannot scratch the riverbank.**
The wiliest lion sometimes misses its prey and lands on the riverbank. Anyone therefore can make mistakes. The adage is an excuse or warning that anyone can fail. Since lions are now rare, the content of the proverb may change.

337. *Mũnyambũ mũkũũ ũkusaa nĩ nzaa.* **An old lion dies from starvation.**
This was an admonition to respect the old, those who had expended their energy building the younger generation and who deserve respect and care by family and community.

338. *Mũnyambũ mũsamba ndũsyaa mbĩwa kana kũrũ.* **A male lion does not sire a fox.**
Drawn from political campaign songs this alludes to things that remain constant. A lion bears a lion cub, not a fox. The animals here are analogies for political leadership. The proverb means a good leader cannot frustrate. He will always deliver something useful.

339. *Mũnyambũ ũiyaa nyeki kũa nyama.* **A lion feeds on grass when it lacks meat.**
This axiom stresses the importance of accepting substitutes when the desired thing is unavailable. The Kamba believe that when the lion is extremely hungry it licks soft grass to quench its hunger. This is not fantasy. Lions are omnivores that may eat grass if they have an upset stomach. Hunters in antiquity created this proverb to justify why they accepted something of lesser value.

---

[17] Farnsworth, *Grammar*, 8; Kimilu, *Mũkamba*, 119; Mwau, *Dictionary*, 670; Mbiti, *Weteelete*, 166.

340. *Mũnyambũ wavĩtya ndwĩa ũvunyaa ndaka.* **When a lion misses the giraffe, it grabs mud.**
Doom can be the result of failure of one's plan. More importantly a substitute is always better. Kitui hunters created this proverb before the Vascon era. They meant to say that if you miss what you wanted, better to make do with what is available rather than nothing.

341. *Ĩteawa na kĩ yĩĩsaa.* **It is baited with what it eats.**
This old maxim refers to bait and baiting. The Kamba trapped animals by baiting with what these creatures liked as food. To sweet-talk someone to honour your request you have to address their interests.[18]

342. *Nding'ĩ ndĩteawa nĩ andũ mate ndũũ.* **Unfriendly people do not set a weighted trap.**
From the Islamic period on, the Kamba trapped animals using a trap with a weight, a trigger, and a sharp blade fixed to the weight. If the trigger went off accidentally, the trapper was crushed dead. Trappers who did not like each other could use this as a stratagem to eliminate opponents and pretend death was accidental. Do not play with your enemy.

343. *ĩtea syene.*[19] **You are setting a trap while the game looks on.**
The proverb derives from the practice of trapping birds and vermin. The trap was set when the animals and birds were absent and everything was camouflaged and the human scent eliminated using herbs. The most common meaning for the proverb is 'You are lying.'

344. *Mũtei wa ndiing'e atea naĩ ndavaumaa.* **If the setter of a snare sets it carelessly he does not come out.**
The ancient snare, the *ndilinge* or *ndiing'e*, was a trap for killing big game, made of a heavy log in which is inserted a knife. It was tied to a strap and suspended from a tree with the aid of a trigger on the ground. Whenever an animal stepped on the trigger spring the weight fell, piercing the animal and causing instant death. This was a dangerous trap to set and often killed the trapper.[20] The proverb warns against carelessness in risky matters.

---

[18] Mutisya, *Proverbs*, 34; Mwau, *Proverbs*, 647.
[19] Watuma, *Syĩthĩo*, 67.
[20] AIM, *A Kĩkamba–English Dictionary* (Nairobi: C.M.S. Bookshop, 1939), 139; Farnsworth, *Grammar*, 46.

345. Ũndũ kĩkame kyambaa kĩtakwete tiwo kyambaa kyakwata.[21] **The way a kĩkame calls before it grasps is not the same after it gets its prey.**
Two versions of this proverb exist amidst confusion. Whereas Kimilu presented it as above, Mutisya gave: *Ũndũ kĩkame kyambaa kĩte kĩkwatye tiwo kyambaa kyakwatw'a*, 'The bush baby makes a different cry when it is trapped.' The axiom means that people change their behaviour when circumstances become unfavourable.

346. Kĩtulya nĩkyo kĩthũku. The forehead is bad.
Mũĩmi elaborated this with the story of the mongoose and the squirrel. The squirrel met the mongoose and asked, 'Why is your muzzle so licked up like you lick fire? What happened to the mongoose so that their muzzles look cracked and red like loquats?' The mongoose replied, 'Tithyĩ kwenda, Kĩtulya nĩkyo kĩthũku, 'It is not our wish, knocking boulders hurts.'[22] It means character traits are hard to overcome.

347. Kĩtutya nĩkyo kyai. Imitation is the worst.
There are several proverbs that castigate resemblance and leave the reader with the impression the Kamba loathed bad resemblance and only encouraged resemblance of useful character traits. This maxim persuades people to steer their life away from their social background if their parents were not successful, and warns against bad company, which can ruin good traits.

348. Kĩnyoe kyaisye mwĩthe nĩ kwĩ yelela.[23] **The rock-hyrax lost its tail because of measuring the tail itself.**
There is a popular folktale behind this adage, which appears in the literature.[24] It explains why the rock-hyrax has no tail, which symbolizes diverse human deficiencies. The grandmother of the rock-hyrax was giving all animals tails, but her grandson assumed he did not have to be punctual. He idled about and came later when only a nibble-like tail remained. The grandmother had no other choice. The ancient maxim warns against procrastination and assumption.

349. Vandũ ve kĩsũlĩ vayiaa ĩkoto. Where there is the common dwarf-mongoose there are hornbills.
There is a symbiotic relationship between the common dwarf-mongoose and hornbills. The mongoose scratches out white ants and the hornbill eats some. As they fight over the ants, the Kamba assume

---

[21] Kimilu, *Mũkamba*, 118.
[22] Mũĩmi, *Ngewa*, 9.
[23] Kimilu, *Mũkamba*, 116; Mutisya, *Proverbs*, 31.
[24] Mwau, *Kĩkamba*; Kituku, *Folktales*; Kĩeti, *Barking*.

that the hornbills and mongoose are mating. The proverb implies that symbiotic relationships are important. However, since this is a weird symbiosis, the proverb may also mean that where a rogue appears other crooks will follow.

350. *Ĩlanga ya ĩvũlũ yumanaa noĩ maswii.* **The scar of the mongoose arises only from the hatchlings.**
Emerging from the Monsoon era, this proverb means certain accidents are avoidable. The mongoose rarely attacks humans, but it bites those who come too close, attempting to seize hatchlings.

351. *Mĩũngũu mĩsamba ndĩthwaanĩaa.* **Male mongooses do not hunt together.**
The mongoose eats chickens and chicken eggs, presenting serious challenges to the poultry industry. As they search for food they do so for themselves, not for other competitors. This means rivals do not help one another.[25]

352. *Mbaa kũtambaasya moaa ĩvũlũ na mbu.* **The lazybones kill the mongoose with screams.**
The mongoose threatened the poultry industry and were hunted out of settled areas by teams of hunters. The mongoose could not be eradicated simply by making noise. Therefore, the proverb rebukes too much talk with blatant inaction.

353. *Mbu ya kĩvũĩ ĩtĩkawa nĩ ũla wĩ maswii.* **The one with chicks responds to the alarm of a wild cat.**
This emerged when the Kamba began to raise chickens during the first millennium. Multiple predators threatened chickens. Whenever wild cats called, those who had chickens took up arms and rushed to hunt them. Those without chickens did not take such actions, hence the proverb. It means it is not your concern: like a farmer without chicks, just ignore it.[26]

354. *Ikĩanĩaa mbosela kũasava.* **They fear each other because of the length of their fangs.**
This is a way of saying respect among peers is advised or give way to something or someone stronger than you.

---

[25] Mutisya, *Proverbs*, 21.
[26] Mutisya, *Proverbs*, 60.

355. *Kŭvathĩkania kĩthu na ĩthayo kŭiyĩvinya.* **It is not hard to distinguish a paw from a hoof.**
Said by a politician aspiring to win a parliamentary contest, but whose prospects dwindled. With this ancient statement he meant that to foresee danger or victory is not difficult.

356. *Mbiti ya ĩvĩsĩ ĩkuanĩasya mbũi na ũkĩĩtĩ.* **A young hyena carries a goat with a building branch.**
Emerging during the first millennium, this talks about a novice who is potentially a liability to the community. For security the Kamba kept their animals in the same house where they slept. A
young hyena pulled out part of the wall along with a goat, leading to injury. This tells the listener to be tactical in doing things to avoid blunder and embarrassment.

357. *Mbiti ĩvũnĩaa kũnosya kĩthu.* **Hyena gains by tiring its paw.**
This is common in the Ngomeni region and is used as a call to hard work: no pain no gain. It encourages innovativeness, searching for solutions and self-reliance. It dates from the entry into Kitui during the Islamic era.

358. *Ũsyao wa mbiti ndũkomaa ũtathũũnĩte ĩvĩndĩ.* **The lineage of the hyena does not sleep without licking a bone.**
This proverb states the obvious truth that the hyena feeds on meat and crunches bones daily. One interpretation (among others) is that someone who has over time developed odd habits will always adhere to those habits.

359. *Ndũkandĩke mbiti mbusalĩ nũndũ ĩthimaa nyama na mbosela.* **Do not employ a hyena in your butchery for it weights meat with canines.**
This emerged during the colonial era when butcheries opened across Ũkamba. Butchers hired assistants who sometimes ate the meat instead of selling it, thus ruining the business. The proverb warns against trusting a thief with treasure.

360. *Kayenee ke mũathi.* **An animal that can see the hunter is hard to shoot.**
Although there is nothing in the phrase to link it with any specific animal this adage refers to squirrels, which had the potential to destroy a village and drive it into famine. While hunters preferred to shoot the squirrel when erect on its hind legs, if it saw the hunter it was difficult. This maxim advised hunters to be tactical and prowl behind the animal. This means it is not easy

to deceive, cheat, or manipulate someone who is aware of your tricks. Also, you will never win a contest of any kind if you reveal too much about yourself.[27]

361. *Keyenee nokesaa kwītūīa.* **Even the watchful one gets diarrhoea.**
This is the opposite of the above maxim and originated from the same period, but it has different meanings. The speaker warned that if you are mean to others it is in vain. You would eventually suffer like others. Want and distress shall afflict you just as you afflicted them. One may boast about his ability to do something but becomes dumb when the hour of reckoning arrives.
Those who make it are few.

362. *Kūmanya katulu nīkūthi kūla kakaa maima.* **If you want to know, a squirrel goes to where it unearths seed holes.**
Tracing back to antiquity, this has nothing to do with squirrels. It means that to end disputes one must put the facts on the table.

363. *Mbīa īkīawa wathe nīūkui wa kīsakwa.*[28] **The mouse is exhausted by the carrying of a maize cob.**
Wathe means exhaustion, fatigue, sickness, or weakness in Machakos, whereas in Kitui it means hostility, cruelty, or anger. For exhaustion or fatigue, the Kitui dialect prefers *tua* or *mīnoo*. This proverb emerged during the Vascon era following the introduction of maize from the United States and an increase of rats that ravaged the corn. This can also mean mice get tired of carrying their food, but are rewarded at the end. The proverb means that people have different resources and what might be the lightest task to one person is an obstacle to another.[29]

364. *Kwī Ngai na kwī ngai.* **There are God and scratchers.**
This dates to the beginning of farming during the Monsoon era when the Kamba not only confronted vermin, generically called *ngai* (exhumers, scratchers), but also appealed to God, whom they call *Ngai*, to drive the vermin (*ngai*) away. *Akamba nī mathembaa Ngai alūngya ngai na ngie myundanī*, 'The Kamba worshipped God to drive vermin and locusts from their farms.' However, the proverb was a derisive statement to Christian converts who preached water and drank wine.

---

[27] Mutisya, *Proverbs*, 9.
[28] Mwau, *Dictionary*, 655.
[29] Mwau, *Dictionary*, 655.

365. *Ngai syĩkaa vathei ikaa vala vavande.* **Vermin do not dig out unplanted fields.**
The word *ngai*, depending on pronunciation, means either God or vermin. Vermin can only exhume sown seeds. This is an ancient rebuke directed to those crying foul when they contributed to the problem they are complaining about.

366. *Ngũa ya arũsi no ĩsaa kũia ngai.* **A wedding dress eventually acts as a scarecrow.**
After the First World War a new practice arose of scaring birds from farms, using human-like scarecrows. As the colonial culture transformed nature, birds and rodents increased and invaded farms. Since killing birds was now prohibited, the Kamba responded by creating scarecrows. But with few Christians, no girls were given in marriage through Christian weddings, referred to as *arũsi*, until the 1950s. Most likely the maxim dates between the 1950s and 1970s. It condemns materialism. All material things are perishable, just as all garments – no matter how nice-looking – eventually become rags, good for throwing on the fence as scarecrows.

367. *Mwiso wa suti nĩ kwiia ngai.* **The end of a suit is as a rodent's scarecrow.**
This proverb emerged after the Second World War when suits became increasingly common in Ũkamba. When a suit was worn out farmers used it to scare vermin. The torn suit was put on a wooden post that resembled a person in order to frighten birds and rodents threatening crops and animals.[30] The moral lesson is that everything ends. Wealth and energy diminish and even life can expire.

368. *Mũvandi ndakĩaa ngai.*[31] **A sower does not fear vermin.**
Across Ũkamba seeds were sown during the dry season close to the first rain but were often unearthed and eaten by multitudes of vermin, generally called *ngai*. Vermin were scared away by scarecrows or trapped and killed for food.

369. *Katulu katumbwa nĩ ĩlea kaasya nthĩ nĩyathela.* **When a squirrel is crushed by a rock-trap it says the earth has ended.**
Squirrels dug up and ate planted seedlings, threatened ripening crops, and even invaded grain stores. The Kamba not only expressed this threat in songs, poetry, and proverbs, but tackled the challenge with rock boulders to trap the rodents, hence this proverb.

---

[30] Mwau, *Dictionary*, 670.
[31] Mwau, *Dictionary*, 661.

370. *Malea nī mavyūka.* **The rock-traps have triggered!**
This was a cheerful way of saying things have worsened. It dates from the Islamic period when the Kamba responded to the challenges of squirrels to farming. They set up a rock boulder with a trigger string and sticks as a sure means of killing the squirrels. For the Kamba, as for the squirrels, it means 'it is over'.

371. *Mūsyīmi ūtaatha nduu ndaatha kīlong'a.* **A hunter who cannot shoot a squirrel cannot shoot an antelope.**
Several proverbs emerged about squirrel hunting, all commenting that to perfect one's hunting skills, the small, difficult-to-hit squirrel was the best practice target. If one could hit squirrels one was ready for bigger game. To be a champion, start low with ordinary things.

372. *Twaa nduu na ūtumo ūla īkwete yavītya mūthūmbī yambate mūtī.* **Chase the squirrel along the edge, if it misses the hole it will climb a tree.**
While squirrels had food in the wild, they preferred the softer and more convenient farm crops. The voracious squirrels could easily bankrupt a village. Farmers trapped and killed them with lairs but these only snared one or two squirrels at a time. Bow hunting was the most effective method. To kill this swift-running and slippery little animal required training and strategy. The best shot was aimed at those jumping onto a tree.

373. *Wona īikaa na mwīthe īneekaa sua ūngī īkavūna.*[32] **If you see it digging up sown seeds with its tail, it has successfully done the same in the past.**
This alludes to something unusual: vermin scratching out sworn seeds using their tail, an impossibility. Emerging from the Islamic period, the axiom means even those people who do things oddly might know what they are doing, so leave them alone.

374. *Ĩvyūvya ya īlaī nī syaamba.* **The convalescence food of a monkey is the baobab fruit.**
This means the solution to a problem must employ the same resources from which the problem emerged. It has longstanding historical precedents back to the first millennium.

375. *Kīseū kī makongo nīwo mūthya wa malaī.* **A savannah with ball thorns is the end of the monkey.**
This early second-millennium maxim means that if a wilderness is infested with ball thorns then pricking a monkey's feet slows it down,

---
[32] Kimilu, *Mūkamba*, 119; Kīeti, *Barking*, 112.

with no trees to offer refuge from predators. Monkeys here symbolize mischievous people whose tricks are restrained when they encounter those equally clever and tricky.

376. *Ndũa yĩ malaĩ ndĩthukawa syaamba.* **A village with monkeys never harvests baobab fruits.**
The monkey epitomizes destruction. Where the Kamba settled near baobab trees as insurance against food scarcity, they attracted monkeys that raided their farms and ate up the baobabs. While humans waited for the fruits to ripen, monkeys would gobble them down still tender green. In the same way, this axiom implies that political demagogues do not allow budding leaders an opportunity to mature as leaders.

377. *Ndũkawete kĩtinya makũlĩnĩ.* **Do not mention the swollen red bottom among the monkeys.**
Hunters and farmers do not expose certain truths everywhere or without careful thought. This maxim emerged when troops of monkeys and baboons first threatened Kamba crops and edible fruit.

378. *Ndiyĩaa nyamũ kũlũngya ta nzũi, ngungĩĩyaa ta ngo.* **I do not eat an animal by chasing it like a wolf, I prowl like a leopard.**
Mũtũlu village elders frequently used this as they debated issues. They meant that strategy is preferable to rushing to achieve objectives. The axiom emerged among hunters in antiquity who observed that the leopard and the wolf had two different hunting strategies. The leopard prowled and pounced on the neck of the prey while wolves worked in teams that chased the prey until it was tired of running. Wolves expended time and energy while leopards minimized resources.

379. *Ndũkakĩĩe ngũlĩ kũthungya wia.*[33] **Do not fear a monkey because of its thick fur.**
This encourages people not to give up on a task even if it appears difficult. Monkeys have fur that make them appear like lions. Yet, unlike lions, mere shouting can scare monkeys away.

380. *Ngũlĩ ya nzamba yamina vata na ĩla nga ndyũmĩsyaa ĩminzaa ũminza.* **A male monkey finished with a female does not hesitate to throw her off.**
The Kamba believe that after mating the male monkey simply pushes away the female. Tracing back to antiquity, the axiom rebukes people who are not grateful for what others have done for them and are compared to such monkeys.

---

[33] Mwau, *Dictionary*, 664.

381. *Ngũlĩĩthekaa iingĩĩtesĩ kyayo kĩthekawa nĩ ingĩ.* **A monkey laughs at others without knowing its own bottom amuses other monkeys.**
A warning against scoffing at other people in trouble because one may fall into the same problem and be jeered at in the same way. The sore bottom of the monkey is a source of derision among the Kamba, who believe when monkeys yap they are laughing at other monkeys' buttocks.

382. *Syalĩsa ĩĩma syĩvithanaa ngarũ.* **When they climb the hills, they do not hide their nudity.**
The word *ngarũ* (in Mwingi dialect) is a euphemism for nudity. When monkeys climb mountains they expose their buttocks to those behind. The ancient proverb means that there are situations where people should not keep secrets. Climbing mountains symbolizes handling difficulties like terminal illness, or accidents where one person needs to rescue another person even if custom demands social distance. Children should never see the private parts of their parents, but if the parent is in danger or during terminal illness, such customary decorum becomes baseless.

383. *Kĩkangũ kya ngũlĩ kĩtutasya kya nyinya.* **The monkey's sore bottom resembles that of its mother.**
Aside from resembling their mothers, young monkeys also develop or imitate her behaviour. This ancient adage focuses on negative aspects, meaning that if bad manners appear in children, their upbringing was inadequate.

384. *Ĩla yĩliawa nĩyo ĩ kĩtinya.* **The suspicious monkey is the one with a sore butt.**
Emerging from the Monsoon era this refers to the frequent behaviour of monkeys where they constantly look at their scarred buttocks. The Kamba interpret that behaviour as the monkey's sensitivity to wounds and scars. The same way, a guilty person is often nervous, betraying himself to the public. The maxim, therefore, means a culprit cannot hide his guilt when subjected to grilling.

385. *Ĩlaĩ ĩlekasya kĩla ĩkwete yakwata kĩngĩ.* **A monkey drops what is at hand only when it gets a better one.**
The word *ngũli* is often used in place of *Ĩlaĩ*, but the latter has a rhyming effect here. The proverb means better something than nothing. Even if an item is not completely satisfying now, bear with it until something better comes along.

386. *Kyathũ kye nani kĩtunĩvĩtwe nĩũkilitw'a*. **Excess scooting reddens a monkey's butt.**
A monkey's bottom looks like sores and wounds, which the Kamba explain in various ways. This maxim may have multiple interpretations and meanings. It can mean that a good thing deteriorates in quality through persistent misuse, just as monkeys rub their bottoms against rocks, trees, and hard ground instead of sitting like humans. Dating to the Kamba encounter with monkeys in the first millennium, this maxim warns against acts that lead to self-injury.

387. *Mũthenya wa ngũli waũkw'a mĩtĩ yonthe yĩthĩawa yĩ mĩtendeu*. **The day of the monkey's death all branches are slippery.**
It is an exaggeration to claim there are trees too slippery for monkeys. Similar to a Swahili saying, this means that fate is unpreventable. When it strikes, it carries on its ugly eventuality to the end. Emerging in antiquity, this is a statement of despair and fatalism.

388. *Kĩswaili kya ĩlaĩ kĩtheleaa ũyinĩ*.[34] **The treachery of the monkey ends in the savanna.**
This appeared in a song that criticized boastful politicians by suggesting that their fate will be sealed at the election box. The monkey may be slippery in the forest where it can hide in trees, but when it gets in the open savanna grasslands it cannot do tricks but must run. Notice that here the term *Kiswaili* is deceit. The Kamba use a euphemism for lies. Someone who does not want to admit that he lied says *Nĩkie kũmwĩkĩsya Kiswahili*, 'I just threw some Swahili at him.' Kamba precolonial traders found treachery quite common along the coast and began to consider Swahili the language of deceit.

389. *Mĩtĩ mĩtendeu yaminie malaĩ Kyũlũ*. **Slippery trees vanquished monkeys in Kyũlũ.**
This proverb illustrates environmental changes since the colonial era, particularly new species of trees in the Kyũlũ hills during the early colonial era. Monkeys were not used to these trees and the Kamba observed the monkeys falling off branches more often. The proverb is more of a commentary on human life than monkeys. It cautions against obsession with sexual pleasure.

390. *Mũeewa nĩ ĩkũlĩ atithasya ĩkũlĩ*. **One nurtured by a monkey resembles a monkey.**
The Kamba believed a person who associated with monkeys would start aping their manners, climbing trees, and yapping like monkeys.

---

[34] Mwau, *Dictionary*, 650.

This was said when people saw bad traits in a teenager who had been under the care of a bad character.

391. *Ndŭkakĩe ĩkŭlĩ ŭyĩta simba.* **Do not fear a monkey thinking it is a lion.**
This axiom encourages people to bear their burdens with fortitude. The task before them is not as challenging as they may assume. The use of the Swahili word *simba* for lion indicates a twentieth-century creation after Kiswahili became more widespread.

392. *Ngŭlĩ ngŭŭ ĩthĩaa yovelie syano mbiingĩ.* **An old monkey has evaded many arrows.**
This is an expression of strength and pride in one's accomplishments. It can also mean a long and healthy life involves avoiding dangerous places and risky habits.

393. *Ngulĩ ngŭŭ ĩkaa iima yĩkaĩle ĩĩngĩ.* **An old monkey digs out one hole while sitting in another.**
This came from a political speech in which the speaker meant that some mean politicians seek opportunity while blocking younger aspirants. It has historical precedents going back to the Monsoon era of increasing farming among the Kamba.

394. *Ngŭlĩ ngŭŭ ĩtwaa oĩngĩ ngŭŭ.* **An old monkey marries another old one.**
This axiom, which emerged during the twentieth century, talks about unmarried people, admonishing them to stay within their social status and age bracket: an old man should marry an old woman. But, of course, that is not always the case.

395. *Ngŭlĩ no ngŭlĩ ona wamĩvaka ĩga.* **A monkey remains a monkey even if you paint it with whitewashing soda.**
Such monkey-related expressions mean character is often incurable. Vincent Kituku and Mũĩmi illustrate the proverb in a story in which a man domesticated a monkey. Whenever he went out the monkey ransacked the grain store. Thinking that it was another wild monkey that was eating his grains, he set a trap. When he left, the monkey was trapped as it tried to steal again. When the man came back to find his domesticated monkey on the trap he said, *Ngŭlĩ no ngŭlĩ ona ŭkamĩkĩa kĩtonyeo,* 'A monkey is a monkey even if you dress it up.'[35]

---

[35] Mũĩmi, *Ngewa*, 10.

396. *Nĩnakwatĩwa ngũlĩ nĩ ngakaa.* **Premna oligotricha shrubs kept the monkeys at bay for me.**
This proverb alludes to ancient understanding of the natural environment in which the blue and black berries of *Premna oligotricha* shrubs were favourite food for farmers. Whenever these were ripe, monkeys vied for them, sparing the farm crops so that farmers did not have to watch over their farms. Farmers who knew this game set their farms next to blueberry plants and never depleted them. The plants, which also have beautiful flowers, thickened and made excellent fences around the farm. Their impenetrability kept other vermin out and provided the farmer with a ready source of firewood and kindling. Several other proverbs signify the expression 'I am lucky.'

397. *Vandũ ngaathi nditavasyaa ngũlĩ ndĩkangĩlye mũooko.* **If I go somewhere I do not tell the monkey lest it get there before me.**
Monkeys were usually punctual and often raided farms before farmers were ready for them. This maxim means a competitor claims he will beat the speaker by getting to the point first. It emerged during the Islamic era of expanding farming.

398. *Kwenda kwa nzeng'a tikwo kwa mwene mũũnda.* **The intentions of the colobus monkey are not the intentions of the farmer.**
This animal is destructive to farm produce, to the farmer's annoyance. It means that at work the interests of employees and employer often conflict.

399. *Mũtĩ ũnaema ngũlĩ nzeng'a ndĩũlĩsa.* **A tree that a baboon cannot climb a colobus monkey cannot climb.**
Although baboons and colobus monkeys climb rocks and trees alike, bigger monkeys were considered more prolific climbers than smaller ones. This warns young people not to marry divorcees. What defeated the first suitor (baboon), you (colobus monkey) cannot overcome. Until 1900 separation and divorces were rare, therefore this proverb emerged during the twentieth century when social changes brought broken marriages, and young unmarried men were cautioned against marrying divorcees.

400. *Nzeng'a yũvenwa mwana ĩkĩaw'a ũngũ.* **To kidnap the young of the colobus monkey one must give it a bottlegourd.**
While the Kamba did capture monkey babies by exchanging bottlegourds with the mother, this axiom was more about marriage. It was said during dowry negotiations by the uncle of the bride to the uncle of the bridegroom: the listener should give the speaker something.

401. *Thuva wa nzeng'a ndwatĩawa.* **The footprints of a colobus monkey are never tracked.**
Among herders it was essential to know the shapes and sizes of the hooves of livestock. When they strayed, the herder tracked them down using those skills. However, such skills were useless with colobus monkeys since the trail ended at a tree. This ancient axiom means that a liar's words are unworthy of following. Futile projects are not worth trying.

7
Insects in Kamba History

402. *Eka kũaa mawa mwene e kĩtĩnĩ.*[1] **Stop crushing honeycombs while the owner is up the tree.**
This old proverb has deep cultural and historical meaning for honey harvesting. In Kamba apicultural norms no one tasted honey before the person up the tree came down safely. Therefore, the proverb tells us to stop making decisions over other people's affairs.

403. *Kĩthwĩĩ kya nzũkĩ vayĩ mũndũ ũtombũa.* **Anyone can disperse a bee colony.**
While bees are fierce, attacking any creature approaching their colonies, the colony itself is easy to disperse. Boys used rocks and sticks to disperse bee colonies, hence this ancient proverb. It means that with tact and strategy anyone can overcome a formidable task.

404. *Kyaumĩla mũthenya kĩvithawa maliũ.* **If it juts in daylight, it is not hidden from birds.**
The objects jutting in broad daylight are the millet ears or flying ants coming out of the anthill and visible to birds.[2] The axiom, which dates from the Vascon era, means that secrets that are too open are hard to conceal.

405. *Kũweta ndĩngĩ ti kũkatha yalata kũma.* **Mentioning *ndĩngĩ* is not praising the hardness of the bare ground.**
This axiom emerged from the 1940s as land was degraded, and bare areas emerged upon which a burrowing insect called *ndĩngĩ* made their homes. This axiom means exaggeration does not make something real.

406. *Mũgii wa kĩvĩsĩ ndũkosaa ĩkundo.* **The honey-rope of a boy is always knotty.**
The honey-rope (*mũgii* in Mwingi dialect) was a special rope used once or twice a year during honey harvesting. It needed to be stored and cared for, something a boy would often not do. When honey-harvesting

---

[1] Mailu, *Kĩkyambonie*, 24.
[2] Mutisya, *Proverbs*, 17.

time came such boys had to repair it with knots, but the rope had to be without knots to function properly.

407. *Mwanīki e vata na nzūkī.* **A beekeeper loves bees.**
Beekeepers anticipate attracting bees and thus getting honey. But the bees also like the protection they get from the beehive. The beekeeper forms a symbiosis with the bees. Tracing from antiquity this proverb means people do things that benefit them.

408. *Mwatū ūla wī nzūkī syī kaū nīwo wīthwaa na ūkī.* **The beehive with fierce bees is the one with honey.**
Kamba beekeeping experts claim bees have different temperaments, some being polite and docile, others fierce and aggressive. The most aggressive swarm of bees have honey because they have something to defend. Signs of valuable opportunities are always challenging.

409. *Mwatū wamesya watūku wīthīa wakūa.* **When a beehive develops cracks it signifies old age.**
This ancient proverb means that nothing is valuable forever. Depreciation is part of the manufacturing world.

410. *Mwatū wa nthī ūtwesawa mūthenya.* **A ground beehive is harvested during the day.**
Some farmers suspended beehives up in tree branches high off the ground. Honey harvesting from the hive was done at night by men. However, if a hive was low enough to reach, it was tempting to grab some honeycombs during daytime. The term *Mwatū wa nthī* (ground-based hive) symbolizes an easy woman whom men can easily convince to have sex during the day. Sexual intercourse was limited to nighttime.

411. *Ndūkakimanīsye nzūkī na mawa.* **Do not pound or crush bees with honeycombs.**
Kamba beekeepers harvest honey twice a year. The proverb talks about processing the honey. Combs are put in a container, bees and maggots carefully picked out, and the clean combs pressed into liquid honey, while the leftovers are spared for other products. The proverb calls people to distinguish between good and evil, or what is valuable and what is not.

412. *Ndūtindania na nzūkī wakosa ngoyo.* **One cannot associate with a bee yet lack honey.**
This is about the contagious nature of companionship as much as it is about symbiotic relationships. The idea is expressed in other terms elsewhere, generally meaning there are some associations beneficial to members.

413. *Nzũkĩ ĩla manthi ndĩvĩvaw'a nthwau.*[3] **The worker bee's wings are not burnt.**
To harvest honey from a beehive the Kamba use a smoking torch to force the bees to evacuate the combs so that the combs can be extracted. In the process some bees get burnt. Harvesters have to be extremely careful to distinguish various types of bees in the colony. Injury to the worker bees is to be avoided. The deeper meaning is the most important person in a family or community ought to be cared for.

414. *Vau nzũkĩ nĩ syatwa mai.* **The bees have harvested excrement there.**
The quality of honey depends on the flowers that the bees use to make honey. According to Thorp, the best honey is made from creepers, fragrant tree flowers, and bulrush millet.[4] Bees occasionally produce a poisonous honey from a species of rubber tree and a thorn bush. If bees suck human faeces, although they rarely do, the result would be more tragic. The proverb is a satirical way of saying the plans have collapsed.

415. *Nzũkĩ ya ĩvia yũnũvaa mũlaki.* **A bee colony in a rock frustrates the honey seeker.**
Expert honey seekers were skilled in tracking bees to their hives. This ancient proverb was said when the tracker realized that the bee colony was in an inaccessible rock crevice. Thus, the proverb talks about futile endeavours where one craves for something impossible to achieve.

416. *Nzũkĩ yũmbaa kĩthwĩĩ nĩkana yusũsya mwatũ.* **Bees make a colony to fill up a beehive.**
This proverb means unity is important in overcoming a challenge. For instance, individual votes are important for a party to win any election. The proverb may date back to precolonial times, when the Kamba started making beehives to attract bees.

417. *Ũthea mana ta ĩwa.* **You will seem clean falsely like a honeycomb.**
This ancient proverb was used by women disparaging each other. It alludes to the situation where a honeycomb may appear enticing but has no honey, implying the woman being criticized has nothing real to offer.

---

[3] Mwau, *Dictionary*, 667.
[4] John Thorp, 'African Bee Keepers: Notes on Methods and Customs Relating to the Bee- Culture of the Akamba Tribe in Kenya Colony', JEAUNHS 17(1943): 255–73.

418. *Vandũ nalĩkĩle nĩ nzũkĩ ndivakomela.* **I cannot camp again at the spot where bees attacked me.**
This originated with a Vascon-era trade expedition to the coast. It refers specifically to the area between southern Ũkamba and the Taru Desert, where travellers were often attacked by wild animals as they slept. Leopards, lions, and other now rare animals attacked travellers at night. Those returning from such travels through the area created the proverb. The terrain was also a black spot for the British imperial builders of the Kenya–Uganda Railway. Trade routes to the coast, mainland Tanzania, and Mount Kilimanjaro passed through this area. It means once bitten twice shy.

419. *Ya mũlaki ndĩsawa nũngĩ.* **A bee colony predestined for the honey seeker is never consumed by another honey seeker.**
The Kamba apiculture was in full swing by the beginning of the Islamic era. As demand for honey increased and persistent exploitation decimated nearby natural bee colonies, honey-seeking expeditions became fully organized economic activities, with specialized men called *alaki* or singular *mũlaki*. The seekers travelled long distances combing trees and rocks for bee colonies. In due course, the Kamba came to believe that each bee colony was predestined for a specific honey seeker (*mũlaki*) as implied. The honey seeking depended on chance, and one stumbled on the bee colony predestined for him. The maxim means that one's luck cannot be stolen.

420. *Aĩwa nĩ mũthwa ũte nzwa.* **Flightless ants consumed him.**
Termites and ants played significant roles in Kamba history. This proverb means that someone perished without a cause and in vain. The Kamba believed that ants gnawed corpses, turning them into useful humus for plants to feed the living. It was preferable for a corpse to be gnawed by ants that can usefully reproduce.

421. *Kĩthũmbĩ kĩyĩyũmbaa kĩte mũthwa.* **An anthill does not form itself without ants.**
The red tall anthills littered across the plains of Ũkamba are products of the united, cooperative, and systematic work of the white ants. This proverb originated around the first millennium and means any major and visible achievement is a result of hard work.

422. *Ndyĩsũvaa kĩthumbĩ kĩte nzwa.* **I do not plead with an anthill that has no ants.**
This is an ancient Kitui women's maxim said in protest against men who were uncooperative in certain desired proposals. *Kĩthumbĩ kĩte nzwa* means an anthill that has no ants, pointing to the precolonial multipurpose importance of anthills and ants themselves. The state-

ment was used in altercations when the speaker finds that the opponent will not yield to compromise. An anthill without ants symbolizes that fruitless argument.

423. *Nditikũ na nziingii syiyĩ mũngamĩi ĩndĩ syĩ wĩa mũseo.* **The army ants have no chair, but they do a great job.**
These tiny insects work without supervision the whole day and accumulate considerable amounts of food for future use. During the infamous famine, *Yũa ya nditikũ* (famine of the army ants) of 1868, the Kamba of Kitui survived by digging the grain reserves of these little workers. According to oral accounts, a single colony yielded about a ton of grain. Diggers secured both grain and ants for cooking. From this symbiotic relationship the Kamba let them roam around their compounds and discouraged killing them.

424. *Nguku nĩyaiye mũvakũi.* **Red ants lacked a castrator.**
Aggressive red ants, called *nguku* or *nzule*, prevented hunters from entering forests where they lurked. If hunters could theoretically castrate them to make them docile, the forest would then be exploitable, but no one can castrate ants. Tracing back to the Monsoon era this axiom means that certain issues cannot be tackled even if minor.

425. *Nguthu ya mũthwa yĩ ngwatanĩo ĩvalũkasya nzou nima nthĩ.* **A cooperative group of ants brings down a whole elephant.**
This ancient proverb stresses the value of teamwork and unity of purpose. If ants pile on an elephant, the behemoth will eventually come down. The maxim means coordinated efforts can easily wear down a challenging task.

426. *Nĩ wasĩwa nĩ mũthwa.* **The ants made the beehive for you.**
In the early days of Kamba settlement of Ũkamba, ants hollowed large trunks in the process of feeding. Next came bees who made their homes in there. The Mũkamba who coined this proverb made a fortune, but also learned the principle of hollowing trees into beehives from the master white ant. The axiom means that one got something easily.

427. *Ĩkũtũ ĩnyamaasya mwene.*[5] **A bug in the ear torments the victim.**
The black ant called *nzũngũ* often entered people's ears when they lay on the ground. Before the bug could be taken out it stung inside the ear. The proverb, first collected by Lindblom in 1911, emerged during the Monsoon era and is similar to: 'It is the shoe wearer who knows where it

---

[5] Lindblom, *Riddles*, 35; Jeddy Kaleli, 'Towards an Effective Christian Cross-Cultural Youth Training Model: A Youth Ministry International Case Study' (DM Thesis, Liberty Baptist Theological Seminary, 2004), 66.

pinches.' The intensity of the pain or passion is felt individually. One must go through a problem to understand its intensity.

428. *Ĩkomba yĩiekaa ũnyeea ona yĩ ĩkw'ũ.* **The hairy caterpillar does not stop itching when it is dead.**
There are several variations of this ancient maxim. They also suggest: do not be surprised by bad traits in a family for they start early and persist over time with severe consequences.[6]

429. *Ĩkomba ĩsyaanĩaw'a na ũnyeeo.* **The hairy caterpillar is born with its itchiness.**
The profusion of caterpillars after the rainy season caught the attention of the Kamba. Many could be noticed perched on food plants or wandering around looking for a place to pupate. They could cause mild to severe stings and rashes.

430. *Mũkoma kweene ekalaa eyũmbanĩtie ta yaamũ.* **One who sleeps in other people's homes is always alert like the hairy caterpillar.**
The hairy caterpillar is always ready to pierce intruders with its itchy spikes. Someone who habitually lodges in other peoples' homes, for good or bad reasons, is always ready for contingencies such as eviction. Coined in ancient times it warned people to be self-reliant.

431. *Nĩkalaa nĩyumbanĩtye ta maamũ.*[7] **I am always prepared, like rash-causing caterpillars.**
Maamũ are fuzzy caterpillar species associated with castor seed trees. If they encounter human flesh they cause irritation and boils. If livestock eat the caterpillar with leaves they can die within hours. The itchy caterpillar is therefore seen as always ready to defend itself. Humans are cajoled through this ancient axiom to be prepared for contingencies.

432. *Kĩng'auwĩ kĩyũmaa kelĩ.* **A scorpion does not sting twice.**
All the known stingers can only sting once. This was extracted from a preacher's story at a funeral. According to the story, a man went to harvest honey with his two sons. The youngest feared bee stings. As they approached the beehive, a rogue bee came speedily down and stung the older son. His brother knew he was next and fled. His father ran after him and convinced him that his elder brother had taken the sting away. The bee was now harmless. The preacher concluded thus: likewise, Christ, the elder brother of humanity, has taken away the sting of death. The bereaved should live in hope. The proverb, however, predates that story narrated in 1985. It has been in circulation from antiquity.

[6] Mutisya, *Proverbs*, 26.
[7] Kimilu, *Mũkamba*, 118.

433. *Kĩtoli kĩng'endaw'a nĩ mwiino.* **The grasshopper becomes obstinate yet its body is full of excrement.**
The proverb covers itself in the word *kĩtoli*, which is both a noun and verb meaning the grasshopper, and 'to poke'. It admonishes people to take no pride in things of little value. Beyond that it has other deeper meanings that trace back to its precolonial context: boys used this proverb against girls who were mean and proud. This was a mocking or teasing axiom, which held up to ridicule a girl who was conceited or proud.

434. *Ngũlamee ikomanĩaa malaanĩ iitwa.* **Pincer wasps meet among flowers while harvesting nectar.**
Ngũlamee (scrotum pincers) is a rare species of black wasp that feeds on flowers. The word *malaanĩ* both means in flowers and in hooked thorn bushes. The proverb dating from the 1300s preserves memories of this nearly extinct species of insect. It means common interests bring people together.

435. *Mũkoma kwene ndamanyaa kĩtanda kĩla kĩ ngũngũni.* **One who lodges in other people's homes does not notice the bedbug-infested bed.**
The word *kĩtanda* (Swahili for bed) indicates the emergence of this proverb after the Second World War when modern beds became widespread. It warns of the danger facing an irresponsible and ignorant person as a lodger who does not know his host's secrets.

436. *Ngulu ĩaniaa ĩeinĩ.*[8] **The weevil develops in the abandoned farm.**
This bug is so dependent on farm produce that no one would expect it to survive without food crops. This ignores the reality that, before it infested crops, it originated from the wild.

437. *Ĩithaanũka yasyaa ndĩũmwa nĩ ngala.*[9] **When it is swift, it says fleas cannot sting it.**
This proverb has been presented in various ways, which indicates its widespread use since the advent of fleas during the nineteenth century. In spite of use of the word *ngala* (flea) this proverb should never be taken as a variation of the next entry, which is older. Even though they have the same meaning they use the word differently. Both caution against underestimating danger.

---

[8] Mwau, *Dictionary*, 665.
[9] Mailu, *Kĩkyambonie*, 59.

438. *Ĩtũlĩla yaasya ndivya ni ngala.* **When it springs, it boasts it cannot be burnt by sparks.**
This axiom uses the term *ngala* as 'spark' and existed before the arrival of fleas in East Africa. It admonished young people who were strong in their youth and felt invincible, meaning that they could also be vulnerable. Figuratively, they might stumble and fall into the fire (injury) as they jump over its flames (danger).[10]

439. *Vandũ va mwaki vaitĩaa ngala.*[11] **A fireplace lacks no sparks.**
This ancient maxim is veiled by the word *ngala*, which means both 'spark' and 'flea'. Both fly off, both are found in a fireplace. Since the flea came with the colonial empire during the late nineteenth century and is implied in the proverb, this proverb emerged during the first half of the twentieth century.

440. *Ũko wa mbaa ngala nĩw'o ũmwe.*[12] **The lineage of fleas is the same.**
Literally, the proverb means that although there might be different species of fleas, they are basically the same and cause similar harm. By application, a person from a bad lineage is not expected to be any better than his forebears and tends to perpetuate bad habits within the family.

441. *Ngala nĩuthĩna Mũnyambũ ũndũ Mũnyambũ ũtathĩnia ngala.* **A flea can trouble a lion more than the lion can harm a flea.**
The flea is so tiny that the mighty lion cannot catch it yet it inflicts considerable torment to the lion. The only alternative for the king of the jungle is to roll on the ground to get the fleas off. Its final recourse is to flee from the fleas.

442. *Kavaa ndaa syaku ĩlĩ wĩsĩ kũte sya mũndũ ũngĩ.* **Better two lice of your own that you know than someone else's.**
The itchy history of the Kamba and lice began with their acquisition of clothes from the coast during the Monsoon era. Where one wore clothes for days without being washed, or at the same time not bathing, body and hair lice infestation followed. Like bedbugs, lice symbolized intimacy. Often spouses were referred to as lice or bedbugs. In this proverb 'lice' signifies two wives, or people close to the speaker. The statement means that despite inherent conflict at home, it is easier to handle that which is familiar.

---

[10] Blanche Watuma, *Mũkamba na Syĩthĩo Syake* (Nairobi: Sengani Publishers, 2011), 51.
[11] Farnsworth, *Grammar*, 44.
[12] Ngotho, *Ngewa*, 22; Kimilu, *Mũkamba*, 118; Mutisya, *Proverbs*, 28.

443. *Mwanaa Nyenze, mwanaa Ndaa na mwanaa Ngũngũni no mũndũ na mwenduethe.* **The sons of roaches, lice, and bedbugs are nephews.**
Historically, the cockroach, the louse, and the bedbug originated and spread across Ũkamba with the Vascon exchange. They are all bloodsuckers and a nuisance. This axiom probably arose in the seventeenth century when these three suckers became a common phenomenon within Kamba settlements.

444. *Muaĩwa ũsũe ndaĩvawa ũsũe.* **One whose grandmother is murdered is not paid a grandmother.**
This ancient axiom alludes to blood-money customs. As Penwill illustrates in *Kamba Customary Law* (1951), murder of a woman was paid at seven cows and other miscellaneous fees. The proverb implies that compensation is of less value to the lost object.

445. *Mũtinda na ũsũe ndaa ndaa.* **A constant companion of his grandmother lacks no lice.**
During the nineteenth and twentieth centuries, lice-infested grandmothers would be seen plucking the creatures from clothes and cracking them between their teeth. The actual meaning of the proverb has nothing to do with lice and grandmothers. A positive interpretation is that an apprentice always benefits from a master. Negatively it means intimacy is contagious. If a good person and a bad person associate for a while, they can pull each other either way from their respective behaviours.

446. *Mũya ndaa esaa kũya wakũlũme.* **He who eats lice eventually eats a bedbug.**
This expression is used as a threat in a contest. One might say this to inform the opponent that he is stronger than the opponent's scarecrow threats. It points to the fact that the aggressor has habitually challenged other people (lice), but will soon meet his match (the speaker) who compares himself with a bedbug. The proverb means that you have been trying easy tasks but have never confronted the arduous ones. Although the Kamba killed lice by crushing them between the nails or teeth, no one dared bite the bedbug. Since bedbugs originated from the coast through commerce it must have emerged during the Monsoon Exchange era. While lice have a long history in Africa, bedbugs are byproducts of commercial interchange.

447. *Kyaa kĩmwe kĩyũwaa ndaa.* **One finger alone cannot kill a louse.**
This adage dates from the Monsoon era. One way to eradicate lice was to pick them up one by one and crush them between fingers. It took two fingers to accomplish the crush. Thus, the proverb means unity is strength. It reinforces the belief in interdependence and condemns

individualism. While individual worth is emphasized, individual rights that alienate a person from the community are discouraged.[13]

448. *Ndaa yĩ mũũmano ĩmanyĩkaa ngalĩko ĩla yĩĩ nĩ mwene.* **One wearing lice-infested clothes knows which side the biting louse is.**
This talks about personal issues including one's family members. Only the household head knows all their character traits.

449. *Wosiwe na mata ta ndaa.* **You were picked up with saliva like a louse.**
Using saliva on the index finger, the Kamba picked lice from clothes, hair, and body. This statement castigates the listeners for having let themselves be exploited and seen as easy. Like other proverbs dealing with lice, this emerged in the early years of the Kamba ethnogenesis and has been in circulation for many centuries.

450. *Kwaa mwĩkathĩĩi kũikomekaa nĩ ngũngũni na ngala.* **A smug man's house is hard to sleep in because of bedbugs and fleas.**[14]
This Vascon-era adage is varied, using bedbugs, fleas, and green peas as an axiomatic condemnation of bragging. Taken together, where green peas are used the proverb reflects the significance of green peas as a staple food, but where thorn bushes are used the proverb signifies the rarity of thorny bushes for making fences. Self-praise is usually a cover-up for shortcomings.

451. *Kĩla mũndũ nĩwe wĩsĩ kaũ wa ngũngũni sya kwake.* **Everyone knows the war of his own bedbugs.**
This Vascon-era axiom means only individuals involved in a given matter know the pain and pleasure experienced. Another interpretation is a man knows the character of his wife and the wife alone knows the temperament of her husband.

452. *Ĩki yĩtomo ĩtumbawa nĩ mwiino ũwambee.* **The first excrement kills a greedy fly.**
Whenever people went out for a nature's call in the bush, flies descended upon the faeces as the person evacuated, many flies being killed in the process by the falling lumps of faeces they intended to feed on. This ancient axiom warns against taking the lead before carefully assessing

---

[13] Farnsworth, *Grammar*, 84; Kimilu, *Mũkamba*, 116; Watuma, *Syĩthĩo*, 67; Kaleli, 'Theoretical Foundations', 233; Kaleli, 'Christian Cross-Cultural', 64; Kituku, *Folktales*, 78; Mutisya, *Proverbs*, 31; Mwau, *Dictionary*, 653; Mbiti, *Ngaeka*, 90; Muiu, *Cross-Cultural*, 91; Charllotte Leslau and Wolf Leslau, *African Proverbs* (New York: Peter Pauper Press, 1962), 34.
[14] Lindblom, *Riddles*, 31; Kimilu, *Mũkamba*, 116; Kĩeti, *Barking*, 103; Mutisya, *Proverbs*, 32.

the situation. Be patient and strike at the right moment. Otherwise, greed will drive you to recklessness and ruin.[15]

453. *Kaki katumanu kaatĩaa kimba mbũanĩ.* **A foolish fly follows a corpse to the grave.**
Flies that hover about corpses to be crushed in the grave are foolish. Therefore, this axiom warns of dangerous cravings. By extension, obsession with certain things can draw people to dangerous situations and places. This appears to be a recent coinage because, before the colonial era, corpses were buried almost immediately after death so that flies were avoided. Other variants mean that people who do not listen to warnings run into tragedies that were avoidable.[16]

454. *Keka ngi yĩ ũtumanu yĩthĩwa ĩtwesaa ũkĩ ta nzũkĩ.* **If the housefly was not foolish it would be harvesting honey like a bee.**
This ancient axiom compares two different insects – the housefly, which feeds on excrement, and the bee, which delights in flowers and honey. The two insects and their living habits are symbolic of varied human behaviour, one beneficial to all and the other repulsive. Therefore, the bee is considered a wise insect, honourable, and king among insects. These proverbs date from antiquity.

455. *Ũtumanu wa ngi nĩwo ũtumaa ĩthaũka na mai vandũ va malaa ta nzũkĩ.* **The foolishness of the housefly makes it play with excrement instead of flowers like the bee.**
The two insects in such comparisons represent people who behave in certain ways and how the outcome of their actions are equally different. The housefly feeds on faeces that is repulsive while the bee feeds on sweet honey that is treasured. The Kamba interpreted the course of the two insects' temperaments to have resulted from their respective levels of intelligence.

456. *Kũtaanĩsya na ngi nĩ kwiia kyondo kĩla kĩ nyama nthĩ.* **The best way to get rid of flies is to put down the basket containing meat.**
Woven baskets were carriers of meat attracting pesky flies. Once a person dropped the basket, the flies ceased to follow him. To deal with an obstacle effectively, identify the root cause.[17] Avoid certain individuals or places and the problems associated with them will no longer bother you.

---

[15] Mutisya, *Proverbs*, 67; Mwau, *Dictionary*.
[16] Mutisya wa Ngai, 'Kyuo kya Ngoso, number 21', https://www.youtube.com/watch?v=msEF7lcYafk. Accessed 23 May 2021.
[17] Mutisya, *Proverbs*, 61.

457. *Mũthoi ũtanyw'a ndũkavule ngi.* **Do not pluck out flies from a soup that you cannot drink.**
This means if you have no use of something, leave it to the weak. Treat nature with kindness and those below your authority with respect. The maxim emerged during the Vascon era, according to oral traditions.

458. *Ũnoa mana ta mũĩthikisya ngi.* **You will labour in vain like a housefly's midwife.**
Coming from folktales this ancient proverb condemns greed and pursuit of worthless causes.[18] It rebukes conflicts that not only profit no one, but give adversaries opportunity to attack both conflicting parties.

459. *Vayĩ ngi ngũũ mainĩ.* **There is no old fly in the stools.**[19]
Before the age of latrines, houseflies fell passionately on excrement. Likewise, every person is active where good things are involved. The proverb is used to rationalize uncouth behaviour. It means that even though a person might be unfit for the occasion, he/she can do it.

460. *Vai itho ĩtona ngi ngwũ.* **No eye cannot see a dead fly.**
This old maxim is a statement of hostility towards detractors who talk negatively about bereaved families. Those who mock the bereaved will eventually face death in their own families.

461. *Ũkeew'ĩa mwĩĩnĩ ta ĩtangua.* **You will feel it on the body like a tick.**
In this maxim *ĩtangua* is a sluggish tick stinging people and animals alike. The victim did not notice until the bitten spot itched and swelled as the tick sucked more blood. This is what the Kamba call 'feeling it in the body'.

462. *Nyamũ yĩ ngũlũ ĩkũawa mbili nĩ Ngai.* **God plucks ticks from a proud beast.**
The Kamba usually plucked ticks from calves but left the violent ones alone and said this proverb. The oxpeckers and other tickbirds, which took care of the ticks from such calves, were assumed to be God-sent. Thus, one who cannot be admonished either perishes, or survives through thick and thin.

463. *Mathanyũka ma kĩmbalutya mathelelaa mwakinĩ.* **The swift flight of the moth ends in fire.**
In Ũkamba, the brown moth with fragile dust-like wings is attracted by light at night and will drop into and perish in the fire. Coined during

---

[18] Mũĩmi, *Ngewa*, 18.
[19] Mutisya, *Proverbs*, 43.

the Monsoon era, this axiom warned listeners to think faster than they acted. Just as the moth is a good-looking insect, good people often are ruined by bad habits that can be avoided.

464. *Mbili ndiumaa ng'ombenĩ.* **The tick does not leave the cow.**
This maxim goes back to antiquity. It talks about adamant and stubborn behaviour that leads to self-destruction, exactly the same way that the tick sticks on the skin of cows until the moment the animal is roasted for food, when the tick is destroyed in fire.

465. *Mbili ĩvindũkĩaa kyambĩonĩ.* **The tick comes to its senses at the places where hides are pegged down to dry.**
This maxim appeared when modern hide-drying houses became common features in Ũkambanĩ after the First World War. It warns people to abandon bad habits before it is too late.

466. *Waema kwĩwa ũkewia kyambĩonĩ ta mbili.* **If you don't hear you will hear at the tannery like a tick.**
This axiom emerged after the First World War, when the British colonial administration opened tanneries across Kenya. The Kamba, for obvious reasons, were among the earliest labourers in the process of drying hides and skin. They observed that ticks remained on the skin long after the animal was slaughtered, only dropping off as the skin was tanned. This is an axiomatic way to emphasize the importance of listening to an elder's counsel lest you ruin your life.

467. *Ndũti nĩtũmaa nzũngũ.* **The red ant often sends the black ant.**
Ndũti (red ant) and *nzũngũ* (black ant) are two tiny biting ants that abound in Kamba compounds. While red ants feed on both vegetable and meat debris, the black ant feeds on grains. Both store their food underground. Since they are different species, no communication is expected between them. However, the black ant can accidentally carry food to the tinier red ant. This is interpreted as service to the smaller insect. The axiom was coined in ancient times about situations where, under stressful circumstances, a son could ask the father for help. It means the lesser authority can order around the greater authority.

468. *Nzũngũ ĩ mũsyĩ ĩsaa mũndũũme.* **A black ant at home eats a man.**
Within the ancient Mũkamba compound there were multiple insects crawling around as they fed on food debris. The stinging black ants (*nzũngũ*) frequented sandy outdoor grounds where family members spend most of their time. They were pesky to people. The symbolic meaning of the proverb is that all the family affairs are the responsibility of the head of the household.

469. *Ĩũma ĩkĩvuva ta nyenze.*[20] **It bites and blows like a cockroach.**
Nyenze, a large cockroach, reached Ũkambanĩ following imperial commerce during the nineteenth century. Ũkambanĩ, being on the imperial path, was infested by them, feeding on food dropped in the houses and biting people when they were sleeping. The roaches were said to be clever enough to blow cool air on the bite so that the person did not wake up and disturb their search for food. This proverb dates to the late nineteenth century, when roaches became widespread in Ũkambanĩ.

470. *Wenda ndaa imanthe itaninĩ.* **If you want lice, look for them in the aprons.**
This proverb alludes to archaic Kamba womenswear that disappeared after the Second World War. Until then the Kamba women wore a short thick apron called *kitani* (plural *itani*) from the Monsoon era to the early colonial era. This apron, described by European travellers, was a patched textile, usually neatly beaded, and often smeared with red ochre and scented with herbs. If not properly cleaned it became the abode of lice, which had spread through trade from the coast. This axiom emerged during the Monsoon era, and broadly means certain things have their proper place – if something odd happens people suspect odd characters within the village.

471. *Ĩng'ata ya kwĩtambĩĩlya ĩyĩ mbũni.* **A bug forced to perch has no satisfaction.**
The Kamba believed that it was an indication of a plentiful harvest if the beetle *syũngũthĩ* perched on someone. However, if one forced the bug to perch, there was nothing. In other words, anything done without cause is worthless.

472. *Kwaa syũngũthĩ kũyũaa ũsũũ mwaandu.* **There is always stale porridge at the house of syũngũthĩ.**
Syũngũthĩ is a female name derived from a sluggish insect, which was a pest in precolonial Kamba houses. It fed on food bits and often died in porridge containers, turning the porridge stale. However, it was taboo to kill the insect, for it was believed to bring good luck to people. The maxim means that braggarts do not accomplish the goals they profess. They are always embarrassed in public.

---

[20] Kimilu, *Mũkamba*, 115.

8
Amphibians and Reptiles

473. *Ekanĩsya kĩmbu na mũsũũ.* **Leave the chameleon with the pigeon pea plant.**
The evergreen pea plant is home to insects that attract chameleons. Harvesters usually never bother chameleons. The axiom was said about someone in an inappropriate romantic relationship who will not heed admonitions to end it. Counsellors said this in despair: leave it to fate. The proverb dates to the introduction of the pea plant in Ũkambanĩ.

474. *Kĩmbu kĩemaa kwĩkalaata nĩ kũlea kũingwa.* **The chameleon fails to run because it is never driven.**
Emerging during the Vascon era this proverb and its variations speaks about those who are slow and in need of prodding. People need mentors, custodians, and peers to cheer them up.

475. *Ũko wa kĩmbu ndũaa mĩngũkũ.* **The chameleon lineage lacks no scales.**
The back of a chameleon is scaly and all chameleons conform to that appearance. This is to say that family character traits are inherited and circulate within the family. This statement has a negative connotation of bad traits: a thief will most likely bear a thief.

476. *Ĩtaa yĩĩyaa nguu nzaa.* **A python eats a tortoise due to starvation.**
This is a good instance of nineteenth-century ecological events in Ũkamba. A series of severe droughts during the first half-century depressed the population of herbivores. Predators depressed the remainder so severely that some species could find no prey – causing pythons, for instance, to invade villages in search of domestic animals. Failing to find prey in the villages they turned to anything they could find and began to attack tortoises, whose shells were not only hard to swallow but also impossible to digest. The proverb, which emerged in the 1850s and 1860s, therefore talks about doing the unthinkable for survival.

477. *Mwathĩnzĩlwa mwongonĩ ta nzana.* **They flayed your back like a monitor lizard.**
This alludes to the practice of skinning monitor lizards from the back. The skin of these reptiles was valuable for covering dance-drums. The proverb means you are decisively defeated.

478. *Mũthĩnzi wa nzana e moo, nũndũ ndĩthĩnzawa ta na nyamũ iingĩ.* **The skinner of the monitor lizard is rare, because it is not skinned like other creatures.**
The history and practice of skinning the monitor lizard is encoded in multiple proverbs. These emerged in antiquity when Kamba dances began using drums requiring tough skin covering that only this reptile could provide. The proverb means there are certain things requiring rare expertise. This reptile is skinned from the back, unlike other animals whose skin is flayed off by cutting the throat and working down the belly. The Kamba skin this reptile this way to save the hard part of its skin.

479. *Nzyĩma ĩtesene ĩteelemawa nĩ mwĩlũ.* **The black lizard scares a hunting party that does not know each other.**
Hunting was one of the most professional undertakings of precolonial Kamba. Each member was well informed what, when, and where to act. A group without planning can be distracted by little things.

480. *Muutĩa wa ĩvia ũmanyĩkaa nĩ ĩtelembũ.*[1] **The lizard knows the rock's warmth.**
The lizard referred to is a specific species of reptile fond of lying flat on a rock almost immobile, waiting for prey or just resting. The Kamba thought it was lying there for the rock's warmth. By analogy, husbands lie on their wives in the same manner. It is only the husbands who knew why they loved their wives even if others disapproved the union.

481. *Katuto nakonea nzoka ndikotea sua ĩngĩ.* **I cannot bask again on the ground in the clearing where I saw a snake.**
From antiquity, this maxim has been used to warn that one cannot play with known dangers. One should avoid known dangerous places or risky endeavours.[2]

482. *Ndata ndaasa ndĩũwaa nzoka.* **A long stick does not kill a snake.**
This ancient axiom alludes to the practice of killing snakes by beating them dead with sticks. A long sting will have less force, as the axiom indicates. It points out that some options are not viable at all.

---

[1] Kimilu, *Mũkamba*, 117; Mutisya, *Proverbs*, 59; Mwau, *Dictionary*, 661.
[2] Kĩeti, *Barking*, 109; Muiu, *Cross-Cultural*, 90.

483. *Nzoka ĩsyaa o nzoka.* **A snake gives birth to a snake.**
The 'snake' is symbolic of evil character. Literally, the proverb describes the bad traits of a snake, and similarly, in the deeper meaning, the meaning of 'snake' transcends the reptile to likening its behaviour to humans. There is also the relation of the snake and its offspring '*Kaswii*', which denotes generational traits. Therefore, the proverb relates to bad character traits that run in human families from generation to generation.[3]

484. *Mũndũ akũnaa nzoka na kĩla ũkwete.* **One hits a snake with what is at hand.**
One accomplishes a duty using the resources available. This means a person responds to new situations or experiences by seeking to integrate them into the pre-existing mental structure.[4]

485. *Kĩmbuva kyũmĩaa ũthewa.*[5] **The puff adder bites because of provocation.**
The puff adder does not attack unless it is provoked. The lesson is that people must refrain from provocation. Enmity and conflict are byproducts of provocative behaviour.

486. *Syĩmbuva iitwĩlanaa mata.*[6] **Puff adders do not spit on each other.**
Strong parties respect each other. Snakes spit on prey to drive them away or kill them through their poison. But the poison of a puff adder is harmless to another and it would be futile to spit on other puff adders. Like sides repel or respect each other. A corrupt judge cannot be expected to deliberate over a case involving a corrupt police officer.

487. *Ndũkageeye nzoka ũkũnĩ.* **Do not nurture a young snake to maturity in the wood.**
This proverb from antiquity circulates as a warning against enriching enemies who will bring one down. In spite of Mwingi rendition, the axiom has been known throughout Ũkamba.

---

[3] Mary Mulatya, 'Comprehension of Kikamba Proverbs: A Study of Standard Eight Pupils of the Kawethei Primary School, Kangundo District, Machakos County', MA dissertation, University of Nairobi, 2013).
[4] Kaleli, 'Theoretical Foundations', 23, 273–4; Mutisya, *Proverbs*, 50.
[5] Mwau, *Dictionary*, 650.
[6] Mwau, *Dictionary*, 667.

488. *Mata mathũku no ma nzoka.* **The only bad saliva is that of a snake.**
Saliva had multiple functions both bad and good. Others were blessed by spitting on them in a special way like mist. During child labour, saliva was part of the liquid offered to the spirit to let the baby come out. However, the saliva of a snake, also ejected as a mist, was lethal. This symbolized human saliva when it was spat on the ground for cursing. These practices and proverbs have existed since the beginnings of Kamba society in the first millennium.

489. *Nzoka ĩkomaa mũthya wa iko.* **A snake sleeps at the edge of the fire.**
This is a short way of telling someone they are committing folly. This is a common proverb with many variations across Kamba dialects. The proverb is a commentary on 'lethal ignorance'.

490. *Yĩima ĩthũku nĩ ya nzoka.* **A bad hole is the one with snakes.**
In rural Ũkamba there are many holes in the ground, some with bird nests or bee hornets that were exploited for food. Other holes had only poisonous snakes. Whenever one saw a snake going into the hole they ceased pursuing birds and honey and repeated this statement, meaning they are not foolish and will not proceed.

491. *Yaũmwa nĩ nzoka yoona ĩkole yĩ kalaa yĩ tũĩye.* **Once bitten is afraid of snake scales.**
There are varieties of snakes, many of them shedding their scales in fences near homes. Snakes attack chickens at night. A fowl that was attacked but survived a snake bite became afraid of scales. This is another way of saying 'once bitten twice shy'.

492. *Wanake mwiingĩ wekalilye nguu thing'ai.* **Excess beauty made the tortoise look like *thing'ai*.**
This was drawn from a fable explaining how the tortoise was originally beautiful and how it became hard shelled as a result of mischievous behaviour. The word *thing'ai* connotes the
creature's crouched shape seen as unsightly punishment. The moral lesson of the proverb is a caution to be moderate in life.

493. *Ũsĩ ũkuaa nguu na ing'ang'i ndũkaayele maaũ.* **Never try your legs, a river sweeps away turtles and crocodiles.**
This is an ancient warning against entering a risky matter that can harm even champions. Turtles and crocodiles are avid swimmers as they live in water. If a river can sweep them away, how much more a human being. Trying the legs is attempting what has defeated those who are stronger than the listener.

494. *Ndŭkatwetetee ngewa ya nguu na kavalŭkŭ.* **Do not bring to us fables of the tortoise and the hare.**
This is another way of telling the listener: tell the version of your story straight. Keep your deceptions out of this conversation. This dates from antiquity when the Kamba encountered these animals.

495. *Kyathĩ kya nguu nĩ mathookonĩ.*[7] **The appointment of a tortoise is in the cowpea vines.**
During the rainy season in Ũkambanĩ, the tortoise appears frequently among the cowpea vines. Since tortoises love to eat the soft green leaves of cowpea vines, its habits are predictable. People hunting the reptile for sale or for its valuable liver usually searched for it in the vines. By analogy, people can expose liars and thieves by tracking their habits and places they frequent.

496. *Ĩsemba ya ngitĩ tiyo ya nguu.* **The race of a dog is not that of the tortoise.**
This appeared in a song that meant people have different resources and capabilities. The dog is fast and a hunter. The tortoise is a slow creature that eats leaves. The two cannot compare.
Human relationships are like that in many cases.

497. *Saa wĩvo wa kũuwa nguu ĩsame ndĩla.* **There is enough time to cook a tortoise until it tastes like a castrated he-goat.**
This is said when the listener complains of too much pressure to carry out an arduous task. The Kamba often consumed tortoises, believing that its meat had healing powers. Its liver was believed to cure beriberi or night blindness. This Kamba myth is not outlandish or lacking in cultural context.

498. *Woona nguu yeethika yĩthĩaa yĩitunga sheria.* **If you see the turtle ducking, it is making laws.**
This is a call not to underestimate someone or something. It alludes to colonial legal changes, where laws became written and codified and given a name, sheria. The tortoise is reputed to live more than 350 years, making it the symbol of wisdom and justice.

499. *Ndũvatĩlĩlea nguu suluali ĩte matako.* **Do not struggle to put trousers on a turtle for it has no buttocks.**
This proverb emerged from the 1920s when shorts and trousers, both called *sualuali*, arrived and spread across Ũkamba. The challenges of wearing these garments became a source of much derision. Many proverbs were carved out of this encounter because one had to have the

[7] Mwau, *Dictionary*, 653.

right shape of buttocks to wear shorts, hence the proverb. People whose bottom could not hold the new garment because they were shapeless or too lean were categorized as unshapely tortoises. The proverb warns that it is unprofitable to try the impossible.

500. *Ũmanyaa nĩ nguu nĩkwona yethika.* **You know it is a turtle when it dives.**
The turtle lives in Ũkambanĩ waterways, often hibernating in the mud when the water recedes. This species keeps its snake-like head slightly above water. It is distinguished from snakes by its striking behaviour of diving and coming up again, an act referred to in this proverb as *yethika*. The truth is known when it is revealed.

501. *Mũthi wa tene nĩwosaa nguu nthĩ.* **An early riser picks up a tortoise on the ground.**
This emerged in the 1930s after establishment of the National Museums of Kenya. Subsequently, the museum began to solicit reptiles from across the country. Between 1935 and 1955, the tortoise, which was previously so plentiful, became rare due to collection and transfer to the museum. The axiom emerged as people desperately sought for tortoises to sell.

502. *Ndambũka ya tene ndĩvata.*[8] **The early morning journey is not always fruitful.**
Contrary to the previous entry, this adage means better walk in daylight than at night. Tracing back to the Monsoon era of great travels, the proverb persuades people to wait until daylight to leave the safety of their homes.

503. *Mũtei wa makũyũ nĩwe wĩsĩ ngalĩko ĩla mũkũnga wĩĩ.* **A fisherman knows which side has the shark.**
Before the colonial era the Kamba did not consume fish, viewing fish as akin to snakes.[9] This axiom, therefore, emerged after the First World War where dams were constructed and stocked with fish. The caretakers of the dams were trained in fishing and fish consumption. The proverb means entrepreneurs know the risk involved in their investment.

504. *Mũtei wa makũyũ ndateaa weũnĩ.* **A fisherman does not fish in the wilderness.**
Fish is obtained in watercourses not in the wilderness. The listener, therefore, should not engage in futile endeavour. Proverbs about fishing

---

[8] Mwau, *Dictionary*, 663.
[9] Lindblom, *Akamba*, 141.

emerged in the 1930s when the Kamba began to engage in fishing in artificial dams.

505. *Ũkanga ndwĩvawa na kĩsungi.* **The sea is not scooped up and emptied with a strainer.**
This is a recent coinage with deep figurative meaning. The strainer or sieve came to Kenya through the imperial culture of tea and coffee drinking from the early twentieth century. Since the strainer has holes that cannot hold water, to drain a sea using a strainer is a futile endeavour. It means that an opponent cannot be beaten with weak blows.

506. *Ũkanga wĩ makũyũ ũmanyĩkaa nĩ atei.* **A sea full of fish is known to fishermen.**
While Ũkamba stands some three hundred miles from the sea, the Kamba have engaged with the Indian Ocean for millennia. Some settled and formed diasporic communities along the Indian Ocean, from Mozambique in the south to Somalia in the north. Others accessed the sea during trade missions. They never fished in it but they knew about fish, producing proverbs since the days of contact with the sea to the age of imperialism.

507. *Ĩla ĩmelasya ĩngĩ nĩyo nene.* **The one that swallows another is the biggest.**
In the dry lands of Ũkamba, snakes swallow smaller reptiles while scavenger birds swallow smaller creatures. Merchants dominate small businesses while in politics predominant politicians dominate regional and national politics, often with negative consequences.

508. *Ndũkew'a kyoa thano.* **Frogs do not croak during the dry season.**
This is an old expression of the order of things. People do certain things when circumstances allow. The moral lesson is that one should do things at the right time and place.

509. *Ũtanu wa kyoa nĩ ĩla kwĩ mbua.* **The joy of a frog is when it rains.**
This is a simple way of saying people are happy when they have resources to support their livelihood. The maxim can also be in jest when suggesting lazy people (frogs) are happy when there is free food.

510. *Ũthelaa kyoa ũyona kokyũwaa kaĩ wakĩta kũkĩnenga livuti ya kũthi mbee.* **You keep the frog thinking you are killing it but in fact you are lifting it forward.**
This is a recent coinage given the English word 'lift', meaning to give one a ride in a vehicle. The slow-moving frog when kicked is 'lifted' to

a desired distance. One may unknowingly assist his enemies to prosper so the rich should be considerate to the poor. Harsh actions against poor neighbours and employees may inspire them to innovate and overtake the rich.

511. *Ndŭkaaumange kĭng'ang'i ŭtaingĭte Athi.* **Never mock the crocodile before you cross the Athi River.**
There are many stories about the Athi River and its role in the history of Ũkambanĩ. By the time the Kamba arrived the river was full of crocodiles and hippopotamuses such that crossing it was quite a challenge. Several fords were almost impassable because of the danger crocodiles posed. It was out of that context that the proverb emerged during the Monsoon era. It means that one should desist from speculation.

512. *Ve kwaa mana ta mũsyĩ wathĩte mbiti.*[10] **Perishing without a cause is like an arrow that shot a hyena.**
This was an axiomatic description of a man who died without children. The most miserable thing that can befall a Mũkamba is sudden death without leaving behind posterity.[11] The analogy is that when the Kamba shot a hyena, it was taboo to retrieve the arrow. The proverb cautioned
against endeavours that could result in irreparable damage. There were two levels of loss whenever one shot these creatures, the animal itself and the expensive arrow.

513. *Ndia ĩmwe ndĩtumbĩawa nguũ kelĩ.* **A single pond never snares a hippo twice.**
Riverine Kamba frequently hunted hippopotamus in the major rivers. These animals were exploited for their nutritious meat and commercially valuable body parts during severe drought and famines. The Kamba soon realized that once a hippo was killed in a given pool, the rest migrated to other parts of the river and never returned to that pool.

514. *Ve ndia yaũtiva andũ na yaũtiva nguũ.* **There is a pond for people to swim and another for hippos.**
Emerging from Kamba encounters with hippopotamus along the Athi and Tana during the first millennium, the proverb alludes to different levels of political power. It calls on the audience to take up their appropriate political positions.

---

[10] Kaleli, 'Theoretical Foundations', 261; Jeddy Kaleli, 'Towards an Effective Christian Cross- Cultural Youth Training Model: A Youth Ministry International Case Study' (DM thesis, Liberty Baptist Theological Seminary, 2004), 63–6.
[11] Mbiti, *Akamba*, 31–2.

515. *Nguũ ndĩsaa ũtũinĩ.* **A hippo does not browse in the neighbourhood.**
Young people were admonished not to engage in sexual activities within the village lest they suffer shame of an unplanned pregnancy. There was a contradiction to this admonition, which is discussed in other entries. This is a call to look for opportunities away from home.

Part III

Kamba at Home

9

Farm, Hearth, and Home

516. *Atũi nĩmo mavoanisya mwaki.* **Neighbours extinguish fire for one another.**
Those close to you are the first to come to your aid when catastrophe strikes. Fire in this case symbolizes tragedy, calamity, catastrophe, and the like, whereas neighbour symbolizes anyone close to the subject. It encourages cooperative action to achieve communal goals. While this is about cooperative coexistence, the next entry is about conflict within a settlement.

517. *Ĩima ĩliku iyĩnzawa thome.* **A shaft is not dug in a hearth.**
Emerging between the twelfth and fifteenth centuries this axiom means a risky undertaking is not done within one's community. Certain activities like metalwork and hunting big game were done far away from villages. Metaphorically it cautioned against making enemies in the neighbourhood.

518. *Kĩlĩko kyaĩkĩawa thome na nzaĩko yĩ woo.*[1] **The mind is circumcised at the hearth and circumcision is painful.**
It is at the hearth that ideas were discussed and lessons learned from antiquity. The shaping of minds at the hearth was equated with circumcision based on the idea that debate removes people's preconceived notions about the world.

519. *Kũmina ngalali nĩ kũthi kwa kamwana thome.* **To settle a dispute is to go to the boy's hearth.**
Settle matters with your adversaries by confronting them on their home turf.[2] This ancient proverb emphasizes the need to confront a dispute with evidence and resolve it instantaneously.

---

[1] Mailu, *Kĩkyambonie*, 59.
[2] Kimilu, *Mũkamba*, 116; Mutisya, *Proverbs*, 12; Mwau, *Dictionary*, 652.

520. *Mũtumĩa ekalaa thome nũndũ wĩũka.* **A man stays at the hearth ready for all upshots.**
The hearth was both the reception office and seat of the family patriarch. He stationed himself there to receive visitors and to resist intruders or fierce animals. That is why the hearth was rarely enclosed, in order to enhance visibility of all things foreign and domestic.

521. *Mũtumĩa ndalũngaw'a thome.* **An elder is never chased from the hearth.**
The hearth was always open to elders. They were never asked to leave, because an elder had wisdom and experience to offer.

522. *Mwana ũte ĩthe ataĩwaa mathome.* **A fatherless son is nurtured at hearths.**
Boys learned almost everything about life from their fathers. However, those who were fatherless got their lessons at the hearths of village men. This maxim was said to encourage young men to listen carefully when older men were talking, and to learn from them.

523. *Ngenda nzele yĩ thome ndũma mũsee.* **If I wanted a calabash bowl in a hearth, I would send an elder.**
If a young man wanted to date and marry a girl he did not go directly to her parents but sent his uncle to the father of the girl to discuss it at the father's hearth. The matter was taken from there to the mother – and negotiations moved on from there.

524. *Thome wĩ ngũĩ waaĩyaa ĩkoma ya mũtumĩa.*[3] **An old man's snuff container disappears in the hearth full of jokes.**
It is futile to hang around places where people perpetually make jokes when necessity of seriousness and respect are required. The maxim means to stay focused whenever serious matters are being handled.

525. *Thome nũthelaa ngewa na ũkatiĩwa mbaka.* **Stories often end leaving only the cat at the hearth.**
This emerged from about the 1920s. Cats frequented the hearth, often spending the night there for warmth. At the hearth men spent hours telling stories and chatting. When such stories ended, the men dispersed leaving only the cats, thus everything ends.

526. *Thome wa ĩtulya wĩ kavaa kwĩ wa nduu.* **The hearth of a lizard is better than that of a squirrel.**
This proverb appeared in a political song in which the singer meant that his favourite candidate was better than the opponent. The singer

---
[3] Kĩtukũ, *Folktales*, 46; Muiu, *Cross-Cultural*, 90.

compared the two animals, condemning the squirrel as shrewd, cunning, careless, unclean, and unreliable. Voters were challenged to prefer the abode of the lizard (*ĩtulya*), which is clean, firm, and reliable.

527. *Thome wa ngũi umaa wĩnĩmya ũnĩ.* **The hearth of a singer makes cooperative teamwork.**
Precolonial Kamba had professional musicians whose role in society was not just to entertain the public but also to educate people and bring them together, socializing and making deals.

528. *Thome wĩ ivĩsĩ ndũsilĩalwa ĩkoani, ũtumĩa wĩ vinya na ti wa ngũĩ.* **Litigation is never deliberated at a hearth with boys, leadership is not a joke.**
Elders and their respective hearths were the anchor of Kamba lifestyles. The opposite was true of boys, playful and uncommitted to serious transactions. In the case of arbitration, young boys were asked to leave. This practice, and thus the proverb, emerged during the twelfth century.

529. *Thome wa ngũmbaũ wĩsaa kũangwa nĩ mũlote.* **The hearth of the mighty is eventually tumbled by a weakling.**
This alludes to championship, heroes, and heroines, using them to show that human strength is transient and limited, something that is also true of economic and political power. It implies that a weakling takes advantage of the strong when the latter weakens. It may also warn the strong that they should not underestimate the ability of those who appear weak.

530. *Thome wa aũme ndwĩ nzamba.*[4] **There are no heroes among men or at the hearth of men.**
Thome can mean a locality or compound while *nzamba* in this context can mean a hero or a mighty man. One cannot claim supremacy among men; he will be brought down eventually.

531. *Thome wĩ mũtumĩa ndũnyaa.*[5] **A hearth with an old man does not dry up.**
The word *ndũnyaa* means 'does not dry up' or 'does not degenerate into indiscipline'. Elders were reservoirs of wisdom and experience and provided solutions to daily challenges. The male elder was the anchor of the Kamba community. His base was the hearth where the fire and whetstone symbolized his personality.

---

[4] Mwau, *Dictionary*, 668.
[5] David Mwandia, *Kũsoma Kwa Kelĩ* (London: Macmillan, 1958), 37.

532. *Thome ūte nzili ūvūawa nĩ Mūkavi ūmwe.*[6] **One Kwavi warrior beats a hearth without a decision maker.**
This adage emerged during the Vascon period with the arrival of Kwavi Maasai in the plains adjacent to Ūkamba. From the 1600s, the Kwavi challenge prompted social and political reorganization among the Kamba. Each settlement had a commanding warrior entitled *nzili* or *mūsili*, 'decision-maker', who, in the event of an attack, mobilized fighters and advised them accordingly on how to defend their settlement or flee along the safest route to refuge. Small bands of Kwavi easily routed any settlement without such a decision maker.

533. *Ūmaala thome ūtaawe.*[7] **Get out of the hearth to be admonished.**
Emerging during the Islamic period, this axiom indicates people who stayed indoors never learned their lessons. One had to get out of his family and village to learn life lessons.

534. *Woona ūkwĩtheemea thome e kwake.* **If you see a man clearing his throat at the hearth he is at home.**
The hearth was a special place in the minds of people who lived in a family, a space providing self-satisfaction, pride, and courage, where the owner could do as he wished. Clearing one's throat was a symbolic gesture of authority and one would rarely do so at another's hearth.

535. *Woona thome wa ngeke wikoma kiinyū manya ngeke mbene nĩngwū.* **If you see the *ngeke's* hearth full of caterpillars, the *ngeke* is dead.**
A *ngeke* is a foul-smelling bird that never ceases to feast on caterpillars until full. If any caterpillars appear anywhere near its nest, assume this creature is dead. By interpretation this means surpluses are an indicator that the consumers have had enough to eat.[8]

536. *Woona thome wa nzatū wĩmūtheu manya ĩ nzatū ĩnyomba.* **Whenever you see the python's hearth clean, it is inside the hole.**
This ancient proverb means stability is easy to discern. If you find a man sitting at his hearth, his wife is present. Behind a successful man there is a woman and a family.

---

[6] Kimilu, *Mūkamba*, 118.
[7] Kimilu, *Mūkamba*, 118.
[8] Mutisya, *Proverbs*, 48; Mwau, *Dictionary*, 188.

537. *Thome wa mbĩwa ndũkosa mbuvwa.* **The hearth of the fox lacks no *mbuvwa* fruit.**
The fox sometimes feeds on fruits of the *kĩvuvwa* tree. The hard-to-digest nuts pass through the gut with faeces and litter the fox's den, sometimes germinating into new plants. These reveal the fox's presence just as each profession is revealed by its tools. Scholars will always have a collection of books; farmers will have hoes and machetes.

538. *Thome wa mbĩwa ũtũvaa ngitĩ.* **Dogs enjoy the hearth of a fox.**
Kamba traditions say that dogs do not attack foxes. The dog and fox in the wild supposedly play but do not attack. Whenever chased from a home compound by a dog, after some distance the fox goes down and wags its tail so the dog will refrain from attacking. This folk observation is not substantiated. The maxim implies that only friends can visit each other.

539. *Kelele sya mwango itivataa ene nyũmba kwaka mũsyĩ.* **A squeaking door does not hinder the house occupants from building their home.**
Building one's house signifies procreation, which cannot be hindered by a squeaking door. In other words, opposition to one's plan cannot deter success. This proverb emerged after the First
World War when modern doors called *mwaango* became common. The precolonial word was *yĩiyĩ* or *iiri*, so this proverb was not coined at the time these terms were in use.

540. *Kũtwaanĩa ndia nĩ kwongela ndia mũsyĩ.* **To wed a fool is to add fools to the family.**
This ancient axiom represents the ironies of Kamba attitudes towards fools and simpletons, individuals of poor mental faculties. If a son was incapable of initiating a marriage on his own, the father stepped in and secured a wife for his son and paid a dowry. Ironically, people feared that the simpleton would have mentally weak children, thus raising a family of fools. However, the term 'fool' here refers to an immoral and arrogant person. The axiom warns against trusting a worthless person with vital community resources.

541. *Mũsila aithi nde mũsyĩ.* **Whoever arbitrates on his way out has no house.**
This ancient proverb is about family management, targeting patriarchs and matriarchs. It was the head of the family who set rules and maintained order in a family. The maxim advised family heads not to arbitrate in a hurry.

542. *Mũsyĩ ũmanyĩkaa nĩ mwene.* **The family head knows his household.**
Circulating from antiquity, this axiom advised families to resolve their own problems. If an outsider wanted to know anything about a given family, he should ask the patriarch.

543. *Mũsyĩ wa ũkya nĩ wa ũkya ona ũkesa ũthua mũndũ mekalaa me atwĩke.* **A poor household remains poor; even if one person becomes rich they all remain tattered.**
Of twentieth-century coinage this proverb alludes to the well-known fact that clothes are indisputable identifiers of one's wealth, learning, character, and religion. A poor beginning to a social unit creates a vicious cycle of poverty and psychology such that improvements make no difference.

544. *Mũsyĩ mũnene wombokaa mwene akw'a.* **A large household disintegrates after the death of its patriarch.**
Tracing back to the Islamic era, this is a true observation that large households tended to disintegrate when a patriarch or matriarch died. It describes an alternation of chaos and order like the solar system centred on the sun. If the sun is removed, chaos befalls the solar system.

545. *Mũsyĩ mũnene ndũkosaa makothe.* **A big household does not lack mischief.**
Some family members behave in ways unacceptable to family norms. The message is that other family members ought to bear with it considering that all families have similar challenges.

546. *Mũsyĩ wĩ ngũmbaũ ndũkosa ĩngĩ.* **A household with a hero lacks no other hero.**
Intense conflict over livestock emerged during the Vascon era when the Kwavi emerged as a challenge in East Africa between 1680 and 1880. These military contests defined heroism. Once a family produced a hero, another one emerged later in the same family. Traits can be nurtured and inherited. This maxim with multiple variations means that legacies are hard to erase. Family traits persist within the family.

547. *Mũsyĩ nĩ kakuthu kathĩnĩaa mwene.* **A household is a bush where the family head is afflicted.**
This ancient maxim points to the fact that families are riddled with conflicts and the household head should wade through the quagmire of this conflict with patience and foresight. The maxim tells the listener: your obsession should be the only thing that should bother you. Pursue your passion with vigour and confidence.

548. *Kũũ nĩ kĩthambĩonĩ ũnyaĩyo nĩ mũsyĩ.* **We will dry ourselves at home, this is just a bathing place.**
This proverb depicting Kamba attitudes in the context of rural–urban migration was coined during the independence period when towns with readily available water and bathrooms were seen as a temporary residence to figuratively clean oneself up and retire to Ũkambanĩ.
Rural immigrants saw their movement to cities as a temporary relocation with the sole purpose of fetching wealth and returning to rural homes.

549. *Mũsyĩ wĩ indo ndũkosa kĩteng'ũ.* **A household with livestock lacks not a trap/branding iron bar.**
A patriarch always set a modern trap for predators. The proverb refers to a European type of trap introduced after the First World War. This means that the proverb emerged around the 1920s. It means certain things compliment those making life function properly.

550. *Mũsyĩ wĩ ndia ndwĩtawa kĩthoi.* **A household with a fool wastes no soup.**
This is an axiomatic condemnation of immaturity and impatience. It means every individual is useful in some ways to the community. Another interpretation is that nothing can be saved where there are greedy people.

551. *Mũsyĩ ndũkumbatĩlaw'a ndũkakĩlye ũnyiila.* **The family is never squeezed lest it oozes.**
Arising during the first millennium when the Kamba desired large families, this advised heads of families to handle family members softly.

552. *Mũsyĩ nĩ mũndũ mũka.* **A household is a wife.**
The phrase *mũndũ mũka* in this context means a wife not a woman. This has been around as long as the Kamba community. It encourages marriage and maintenance of a family.

553. *Mũsyĩ nĩ mũtĩ iveti syoteaa muunyĩ.* **A home is a tree where women enjoy the shade.**
Particularly in the postcolonial era men found themselves preoccupied in their endeavour to provide for their families as enterprising men found themselves slapped with infidelity, gossip, misuse of resources that they had accumulated, and even threatened divorces. At the end of such tensions the victims and their counsellors used this proverb to rationalize their frustration.

554. *Mũsyĩ mũseo ndwaa tuthunguta aeni.* **A notably good household lacks no benefit.**
This ancient axiom can mean a good household attracts guests by various means, encouraging families to be decent, generous, and hard-working.

555. *Mũsyĩ wa kĩvĩsĩ ndũvuvawa mwaki.* **A boy's home is never lit by fire.**
Two things are incompatible: 'the boy', representing immaturity, and 'fire', symbolizing the anchor of life. The first thing that an elder did when he got to the hearth was to light the fire. His wife did the same in the kitchen. These were not mere acts of production but symbolized continuity of life. Boys never cared about fire. Additionally, fire may refer to a wife and sex. A man who neglected his wife sexually was considered foolish and without fire.

556. *Mũtumĩa ũkakola mũsyĩ akomaa na mĩkalya.* **A man who will abandon his family sleeps with his firestone sandals on.**
This is a recent coinage tracing back to the period the Firestone Company expanded into East Africa. The Kamba wore rough sandals made from used tyres, originally Firestone products. One can never imagine these rough sandals on the bed – wearing them would mean the wearer is about to leave. There is even deeper symbolism: *mũsyĩ* is used in this context for wife. A man cannot sleep with his wife with such rough sandals on.

557. *Sya mũsyĩ ti somo.* **Family secrets are not for reckless revealing.**
This is an ancient axiomatic condemning the betrayal of passionately guarded family secrets.[9] It warns the listener that family affairs should never be discussed in public.

558. *Kelele wa kĩtimba ndwomboaa kyoo.* **The noise of the buttocks cannot demolish the toilet.**
Latrines and toilets as colonial innovations appeared in Ũkamba during the twentieth century. Before 1900, the Kamba used the bush, sandy soils, and anthills as depositories of excrement and urine. Near each home there were sections of the surrounding forest designated for adults, children, and visitors respectively. Toilets or latrines called *syoo* (singular *kyoo*) became widespread in Ũkamba in the 1970s, but are still resisted as a bad omen in rural areas since latrines were dug up to six feet deep, the same as graves. The proverb alludes to the fact that the latrines were prone to collapse, but the collapse was by no mean the result of farts.

---

[9] Leslau, *Proverbs*, 34.

559. *Ndũtinda kyoonĩ weteele yumaa yĩngĩ.* **One cannot overstay in the toilet waiting to pee again.**
This emerged among urbanized youth after independence. It calls for systematic disposal of duties and responsibilities at their proper time.

560. *Ũteli wĩvakuvĩ na kyoo ndũkaũlike wĩ mbanga.* **Do not dine in a restaurant located near a toilet, danger lurks therein.**
This has deep symbolic meanings. The hotel represents a woman while toilet embodies odd characters. A woman who would date loose men might be vulnerable to venereal disease and the phrase 'do not enter' is another way of saying do not have sex with her lest you contract venereal diseases. The maxim hints about the poor hygienic nature of public toilets before the dramatic changes that followed the 2002 general elections.

561. *Maanzonĩ kwĩ mĩaawa.* **One does not defecate in deserted places.**
This ancient axiom indicates abandoned places are not to be polluted for they may be of value in the future. Polluting a deserted place was symbolic of insulting one's roots.

562. *Maanzonĩ no kũsyokawa.* **Deserted places are often returned to.**
This axiom rationalized reconciliation with a separated or divorced partner. The allegoric epithet involved is that *maanzo* (deserted home sites) do not always lose value or meaning to those who once lived there. A settlement was deserted when the land became infertile and unproductive, unhealthy, or neighbours became unfriendly. If circumstances improved, people often came back.

563. *Mũsyoka maanzonĩ ndaĩawaa nĩkyaosa.* **Whoever returns to the old deserted home compound lacks nothing to pick.**
This proverb alludes to the once peripatetic lives of the Kamba. With plenty of land at their disposal, the Kamba lived and farmed in one place for decades before relocating to a new site of settlement. Not all objects were removed from the old to the new location, so if someone returned to the deserted compound they might find useful objects.

564. *Ũnou nĩ maanzonĩ.*[10] **Fertility is in deserted settlement sites.**
Deserted settlements have all sorts of litter that turns into humus and fertility. Crops do very well in these places just as there is benefit in things apparently of little value.

---

[10] Mailu, *Kĩkyambonie*, 59.

565. *Maanzonĩ nokw'o mũndanĩ.* **Deserted fields are also farmland.**
This early nineteenth-century axiom was said with regard to men who abandoned their first wife to cohabit with another, only to return permanently to the first wife. Original things are more valuable than new and shiny ones.

566. *Vandũ vaĩĩ yanzo vayũaa muu.* **The site of an abandoned homestead lacks no trace of ash.**
Ash is one of the most reliable identifiers of old settlement sites in Ũkambanĩ and offers an important clue to archaeologists. While other identifiers may disappear, ash, which leaches deep into the ground, endures longer. Yet the proverb has nothing to do with ash and means that certain traits circulate within a family for a long time. For instance, a rich household will always have rich people in the family.

567. *Nyũmba yĩyusya yambĩĩa kusya muumbĩ.* **A house bound to leak starts leaking fog.**
The proverb, which emerged during the Vascon era, means signs of destruction are known in advance. Fog has so little water, such that if a house leaks during fog it is a sign that it needs repair. Fog or mist represent the slightest opportunity to reveal the weaknesses of a given character who is the subject of the proverb. Therefore, someone who will become a social misfit begins by stealing eggs from his parents, and so on.

568. *Nyũmba yĩyusya yambĩĩa kango.* **A house leaks from the pinnacle.**
The word *kango* (leopard spot – pinnacle) hints that the proverb dates from the time leopards (*ngo*) frequently attacked sleeping families and their animals through the roof. Until the 1880s, the Kamba lived in small conical grass-thatched huts having no *kango* (pinnacle).[11] In the 1890s, they began to build taller round huts called *mũsonge* with a distinct *kango*. An outbreak of leopards during that decade misled some to assume that the *mũsonge* structure was adopted in response to the predators. That was not the case and is certainly not our focus here. In short, emerging around the early 1900s, this axiom means bad things start from the top brass of leadership.

569. *Nyũmba nzeo ti mũomo vota nthĩnĩ.* **A good house is not the door, get in.**
This axiom dates from the seventeenth century when the Kamba adopted what they call *nyũmba*. It is about people rather than dwell-

---

[11] Richard Gehman, 'The African Inland Mission: Aspects of its Early History', *Africa Journal of Evangelical Theology*, 23(2) (2004): 115–44.

ings: a good spouse (house) is not to be judged by physical appearance (door).

570. *Nyũmba ĩkũtoa yonekaa nĩ ala me nza.* **Those outside see a smoking house.**
This is said when elders are handling family disputes. It means they saw the mistakes of one partner in the marriage. Outsiders often observe family weaknesses quite early. The emergence of *nyũmba* occurred during the Vascon era and this proverb emerged around the 1800s, as evident in linguistic and ethnographic data.[12]

571. *Ona nyũmba yũvya mwene nĩwotaa.* **Even when a house is burning, the owner warms himself.**
This seventeenth-century axiom means that in every calamity there is a consoling factor. If one's house is on fire, one gets some warmth.[13] By extension this means there are positive things for people to see even in the worst circumstances.

572. *Mũlika mbake ndaamanyaa kana kwaka kwĩvinya.*[14] **One who enters houses already built does not know the pain of construction.**
This is condemnation of dependency, laziness, and freeloading. It encourages men to build their own houses and to provide for their families. The word *mbake* provides clear clues that the maxim emerged between the seventeenth and twentieth centuries.

573. *Muma nyomba akũnaa mũtaania.* **One who comes out of the house beats a mediator.**
The Kamba often fought during drinking brawls in the open part of the compound, giving an impression of an organized occurrence. Some responsible persons would intervene and separate the fighters. If someone came out of the house having no knowledge of the combatants they might accidentally beat the mediator. The proverb thus means information or intelligence is vital in conflict resolution. This axiom emerged after the Kamba settled and built modern round huts called *nyomba* (or *nyũmba*), not the old structures called *ikuri*. I surmise this occurred during the Vascon era and the proverb emerged during that period.

---

[12] Hildegarde Hinde, *Vocabularies of Kamba and Kikuyu Languages of East Africa* (Cambridge: Cambridge University Press, 1904), 32–3; Wilfred Whiteley and M.G. Muli, *Practical Introduction to Kamba* (London: Oxford University Press, 1962), 25.
[13] Mutisya, *Proverbs*, 56.
[14] Mwau, *Dictionary*, 657.

574. *Mūtumīa ndekalaa nyūmba indo ikīsyaa.* **An elder does not stay in the house when livestock is multiplying.**
Dating from the Monsoon era this proverb has multiple interpretations, foremost that a man does not rest when he can do something productive. He has to go out and pasture the animals. The second interpretation is: he has to find another wife since he can afford a dowry.

575. *Vundi wa nyūmba nde nyūmba.*[15] **The house builder has no house of his own.**
This proverb emerged after the Second World War, when a class of builders of modern houses emerged. They built coastal or European-style houses but rarely for themselves. The word *vundi* is borrowed from Swahili, *fundi*, instead of the old Kamba word *mwaki* for builder.

576. *Mūvīīa wa andū aīngī ūkomaa ūtemūvinge.* **The public gate sleeps unclosed.**
This old proverb talks about responsibility. It originated from polygamous families where co-wives had to take turns in shutting the gate at night and opening it in the morning. If these duties were not regulated the gate was often left unclosed. The proverb is therefore a call for regulation of responsibilities.[16]

577. *Kīla kītūngaa mūtumīa iko nī mbevo.* **It is the cold that draws an old man back to the fireplace.**
One of its many variants helps clarify this old adage: *Kīla kītūngaa mūtumīa ndīthya nda kīsī*, 'An old man doesn't know what makes him resume herding.' Traditionally, herding was the job of young sons and grandsons. If an old man herded, there was a reason. This is not about herding livestock, however, but marrying a young wife and raising children at an advanced age. 'Drawing an old man back to fire or to herd' may be interpreted as old men marrying young women to bear children, which can be for many reasons.

578. *Mwaanga kwoo ndomasya.*[17] **A trampler on his homeland does not harden it.**
A family member who tramples on farm crops will not make them dry up. This proverb calls for the need to tolerate the harm and mistakes made by family members.

---

[15] Mwau, *Dictionary*, 670.
[16] Lindblom, *Akamba*, 80; Kimilu, *Mūkamba*, 117; Mutisya, *Proverbs*, 60.
[17] Mutisya, *Proverbs*, 31.

579. *Kĩthima kĩ mbee kĩtyĩ kwataw'a.*[18] **A well ahead is never trusted.**
Something in the future or ahead of you along the path is not predictably useful. Emerging from the Vascon era, when digging of wells began, this axiom tells the listener to trust what is at hand.

580. *Kwataa mbee nguvĩ.* **Seize a short yard.**
This was a common axiom among farmers during the twentieth century when hoes appeared in Ũkamba farms. Kamba families cultivated in teams where each person marked up a square area that they would clear within a specified time. That marked area in front of the cultivator was called *mbee* (front cultivation yard). The axiom was to advise children to take a small area for their share. This axiom has been applied in almost all aspects of life.

581. *Mũĩmi eyonaa na kalombe kala kake onethĩla nikakwĩtũũa.* **A farmer is proud of his cow even if it has diarrhoea.**
A person appreciated whatever achievement he had, no matter how. The Kamba used to bring bulls to watering holes to fight. In such circumstances every person boasted of the ability of his bull, reflecting the owner's pride even if the animal was sick and weak.

582. *Mwĩĩmi wĩ nzaa nde nzaa.*[19] **A farmer with hands does not starve.**
A hardworking farmer does not suffer food shortages. This proverb emerged after independence to encourage agriculture. Two words spelt the same but with different pronunciations and meanings increase the difficulty of understanding it. *Nzaa*, depending on pronunciation, can mean hands or hunger. The prefix *nde* adds yet more complexity, typical of Kamba proverbs: *nde nzaa* can mean has no hands, does not starve, or does not dig.

583. *Mũndũ ũtanamesya ndaekaa kũvanda.* **The sower does not cease sowing until the seeds germinate.**
This emerged from farming in the Islamic era. Sown seeds were often threatened by animals or too much or too little moisture. Farmers had to struggle until their seeds germinated and the crop flourished. This proverb is about persistence and fortitude to endure challenges in pursuit of profit.

584. *Vala ĩvalũkaa tivo ĩmeaa.* **Where it falls is not where it grows.**
Where the seed is cast may not be where it will germinate and grow. Natural forces and animals may move it to a new location just as people

[18] Kimilu, *Mũkamba*, 116.
[19] Mbiti, *Ngaeka*.

may land in unpleasant places, situations, or relationships. As times change, their fortune is bound to change as well.

585. *Kalila ndonya ndiketīa mwethya.* **A little weed patch that I can manage, I do not call a cooperative group.**
Kalila can mean either 'a little milk', or, as in this context, 'a little weed'. Weeding, harvesting, threshing, and winnowing were labour-intensive operations with little available labour. Farmers could call one another to help in groups called *mwethya* but only as a last resort. The hidden meaning is that certain things need personal initiative before appealing for assistance.

586. *Ĩkũna nĩ ya mwene mũũnda.* **It is the farmer's turn to beat.**
This axiom was said during droughts when crops had withered and people, seeing no point of keeping animals off the farms, let them roam and eat the withering crops. If a farmer objects, the community holds him responsible for keeping animals off his farm. It denotes drought and crop failure and emerged during the nineteenth century.

587. *Mũũnda ngaĩma nditavasya ndia ndĩkese ũmbandia makongo.* **I do not tell a simpleton about a farm I will cultivate lest he plant ball thorns beforehand.**
Makongo refers to ball thorns, which creep into abandoned farms. Between 1893 and 1933, following the introduction of sisal, the word came to refer to sisal seedlings, which were even thornier. Either may fit this proverb, which emerged during the twentieth century when ball thorns spread from the north and sisal from the south.

588. *Mũũnda nĩwoona thaano.* **I notice a farm during the dry season.**
Kamba farmers surveyed fertility and layout and prepared their farms long before the rains. The hidden meaning is that certain signs can tell the future of an investment. It is imprudent to plunge into a venture with limited knowledge.

589. *Mũũnda wĩanawa nĩ kwengeewa ũtee.*[20] **A farm is developed by extending the edges.**
Clearing forests for cultivation was not easy, particularly in an age when axes were the only tools. So the Kamba adopted the strategies of extending their farms gradually from the edges outwards. It is gradual accumulation that makes one rich.

---

[20] Kimilu, *Mũkamba*, 117; Mutisya, *Proverbs*, 69.

590. *Mũũnda mũnene ũvisaa na ũtee.* **A large farm burns from the edges.**
This figurative statement alludes to the fact that large farms were not easy to sow, weed, or harvest. The owner started these processes from the farm's edges inward. Obstacles can be handled bit by bit until done to perfection.

591. *Nĩmia ĩngĩ yumanaa na mwene mũũnda.* **Help me cultivate again comes from the farm owner.**
Until the Vascon era, Kamba farms were small compared to later years. During the Vascon era newly enlarged farms called for larger labour demands. Farmers responded by asking fellow farmers to help or by organized village self-help groups, or *myethya*, the basis of the nationwide *harambee* movement. It was an individual farmer who called a friend, relative, or neighbour to come and help with cultivation. This maxim stresses that the cause of action rests with the decision maker.

592. *Kĩla mũndũ na mũũnda ũla wake.* **Everyone with their own farm.**
This axiom has two interpretations worth considering here. First, it is a call for respect of other people's space, said in part to tell immoral individuals to keep off, stick to their own families, and stop flirting with married women (the farm). Second, it was said in the context of disagreement that people ought to take care of their own business (the farm).

593. *Mbanda nĩ thano.* **Sowing is best before the rains.**
Farming is crucial to the Kamba. Success depends on what, where, and when seeds are sown. Seeds sown before the rain stand a better chance of germinating early, maturing early, and being able to resist shortages of moisture should the rain be low. The proverb emphasizes the importance of punctuality and quick action to achieve something vital.

594. *Mũĩmi wĩ nzaa aĩmaa mbuanĩ.* **A farmer with 'hands' cultivates during the rainy season.**
Comprehension can be tricky because the word *nzaa*, depending on pronunciation, can mean dig, hands, or hunger. This proverb is about hands and thus means a hardworking farmer cultivates during the rainy season. One who needs something vital accumulates resources to purchase ahead of time.

595. *Kamŭlo kaumbĩke kaumbŭawa nĩ ŭla wakaumbĩkie.* **A concealed digging stick is unearthed by whoever concealed it.**
The most popular precolonial digging tool was the *mŭo*, carved out of hardwood, later with a metallic blade inserted into the wood.[21] After work, it was buried somewhere in the farm known only to the owner. Emerging during the Islamic era this means that only those who were initially involved in secret affairs can reveal such secrets.

596. *Wiio nĩ kwiĩĩya.*[22] **A fence is to fence out.**
This probably emerged during the first half of the twentieth century when fencing became necessary to keep stray animals from crops. This also tells the listener, if you resolve to do something, do it right away.

597. *Mŭũnda wa mũtũi mũkilo ndwĩ mavavaĩ.* **The neighbour's farm across the border has no pawpaws.**
This emerged from the Vascon era when cultivation of pawpaws became common. The first historical mention of it was in 1513. Subsequently, the plant reached East Africa through the agency of the Portuguese. In the middle of the eighteenth century, it expanded from Zanzibar to the mainland by way of the Tanga-Pangani-Kilimanjaro route.[23] During the colonial period pawpaws became the measure of progress among farmers, but the plant bred envy among neighbours. This maxim emerged as a condemnation of such envy. It encouraged listeners to improve their situation instead of engaging in jealousy.

598. *Mũndũ wĩngĩmya nĩmwonaa thaano.* **Someone who will help me cultivate I see during the dry season.**
Farmers prepared their farms for sowing during the dry season. Failure to do so was risking starvation. Those who did not sow their farms during the dry season had to work for other farmers in exchange for food.

599. *Ndileaa myethya no moko ndaĩ.* **I do not decline cooperative work, only that I do not have hands.**
This is said when one is reluctantly accepting an invitation to do something of low value. However, it denotes a Kamba way of undertaking hard chores through cooperative engagement of neighbours, called *mwethya* (plural: *myethya*). This model was adopted after independence as *harambee*, an important contributor to Kenya's development.

---

[21] Sultan Somjee, *Material Culture of Kenya* (Nairobi: East Africa Educational Publishers, 1993), 28.
[22] Kimilu, *Mũkamba*, 119.
[23] W. Conradie, 'Origin of the Papaya: Carica Papaya; Caricaceae', *Quandong* 19(1)(1993).

600. *Mbee ĩmwene ndĩnzĩlawa mũo.*[24] **Do not peg a digging stick in a man's yard.**
This proverb speaks to the custom of woman-to-woman marriage practices called *ĩweto* by which a barren woman took a young woman to bear children on her behalf. The children took the name of the barren woman as their surname although they address her as grandmother. The young woman was free to mate with any man of her choice. To avoid conflict and embarrassment, before the First World War, when a man visited the *ĩweto*, he would peg down a digging stick at the gate before entering. The stick told passersbys that there was a man in the house. The proverb suggests something like: too late, your place has been taken. By implication one is not to compete with someone superior. It means one has made their attempt too late.

601. *Vau vomũ nĩvo ve mũo.*[25] **The hard part is the seeder.**
By 1900 the Kamba were using wooden implements for cultivation. These were carved out of hardwood among which was a species called *Mũvĩngo*, which has a hard-black pith. The axiom alludes to the carving of that 'hard-black pith', a rather arduous thing to do. By application this precolonial axiom means major achievements result from toils and risky investment.

602. *Mbeũ nĩ lĩu ĩndĩ tĩ yĩ mũthanganĩ.* **Grain is food, but not when in the dirt.**
This was a common saying of Kitundumo wa Mulike, a female rainmaker near the Maai Mountains (Mwingĩ, Kitui) from the 1950s to the 1980s. Musician Musyoka WaMaiyu popularized this during the 2007 national elections, when he called for peace rather than a chaotic demand for power.

603. *Mũvandi ndaiaa mũo mbeũ ĩtenamba ũmea.* **The planter does not store the sowing stick before the seeds germinate.**
This dates from the first millennium when wooden sowing sticks were developed. *Mũvandi* was a long stick, carved from particular woods and sharpened at one end. It was kept in a special place after planting season but kept close when planting. If the seeds were dug out by animals or rotted, the farmer had to replant. After germination, the stick was still used to fill any remaining gaps. Only after this process was the stick stored away. This implies that one must carry through any project undertaken rather than start a new one while it is incomplete.

---

[24] Kimilu, *Mũkamba*, 116; Mwau, *Dictionary*, 654.
[25] Kimilu, *Mũkamba*, 119.

604. *Mŭvandi wa mbeũ tiwe ũmĩkethaa.* **The sower of seeds is not its reaper.**
What people produce is often used by non-producers. Tracing from the Monsoon era, this axiom stresses the fact that some initiatives benefit others more than the initiators.

605. *Mŭvandi wa mbeũ ndakĩaa ngai.* **The sower of seeds is not afraid of vermin and rot.**
Farmers had to defy the threat of poor rains causing seeds to rot, while vermin also dug out the seeds. This maxim encourages people to keep on investing in different fields with courage. It emerged during the Islamic era when farming intensified.

606. *Kyanda kĩvĩsaa kyombĩĩya.* **A valley burns when it thickens.**
Mutisya (2002) translated this proverb as 'A sugarcane plantation catches fire only when it becomes fully developed. Misfortunes usually strike when things are at their best. The bigger they are the harder they fall.' However, the word *kyanda* refers more generally to a depression, normally along a river, whether farmed or not. Second, it refers to a farm, a plantation of any crop. Additionally, the proverb can be interpreted as 'unity is strength', implying that warmth and profit come with cooperation.[26] Originating from precolonial farmers cultivating sugarcane in river valleys, it probably emerged during the first millennium of the Christian era.

607. *Kyanda nĩkyo kĩyĩmaa.* **A valley cultivates itself.**
Farms located in river valleys and other depressions were long cultivated because their fertility renewed annually through silt brought from upstream during the rains. This proverb dates to the Islamic era.

608. *Mwaĩma ũĩme.* **You weeded on a weeded farm.**
This proverb emerged after the Kamba transitioned to farming where farmers cleared weeds around germinated seeds. It is foolhardy for anyone to later start weeding where weeds had already been removed. This maxim's actual meaning is that an opponent's deceptive designs will not work any more. Some readers can mistakenly read this as 'You people cultivated the tongue!' for the two words are tonal and subject to pronunciation.

609. *Makwata nde mũũnda, aĩmĩaa atũi.* **The land-grabber has no farm, he cultivates for neighbours.**
This adage has appeared in multiple publications in varied forms.[27] It emerged during the colonial period, particularly after individualized

---

[26] Kimilu, *Mũkamba*, 116; Mutisya, *Proverbs*, 54.
[27] Kĩeti, *Barking*, 114; Kituku, *Folktales*, 44; Mutisya, *Proverbs*, 65; Mwau,

land ownership, as a condemnation of land grabbing. Hunger for land drove individuals to seize land wherever they could find it. The proverb refers to people who started one project and before it was over switched to a new project. The axiom points to the concept of double-dealing: the land grabber has no farm. Applied to young people, when one has many secret lovers and the lovers learn they are dating the same person, they all quit, leaving the deceiver alone. Therefore, by lacking a partner, they have no 'farm', that is, a partner to call their own. Someone who handles too many things at the same time has nothing to show.

610. *Mũũnda now'o mwene mũsyĩ.* **The farm is the family.**
The Kamba are chiefly agricultural with the farm as the anchor of family life since the Monsoon era. During the Vascon era, they enlarged farming with new crops coming through the Vascon exchange. The colonial regime encouraged farming after 1900. A song was aired carrying this proverb from the late 1960s to encourage farming in post-independence Kenya.

611. *Ndũkakomeeye manda kũnoa.* **Do not fall on valleys because of their fertility.**
Once the Kamba had exhausted the resources of the hills and springs they began to locate their farms on fertile depressions along river basins. New farmers were warned to examine such terrain first instead of being lured by mere looks.

612. *Vaiĩ mũũnda ũtamesya ĩia.*[28] **There is no farm that does not turn weedy.**
Someone seeking forgiveness and reconciliation says this. The speaker acknowledges their mistakes but calls attention to the fact that error is part of life. The maxim arose during the Islamic era when farming intensified in Ũkamba.

613. *Walea ũvũna wĩ mũũndanĩ ndũvũna mũtikũlyo.* **If you cannot be satisfied in the garden, you cannot be satisfied at the end of the harvest.**
During the rainy season people consumed considerable amounts of green millet raw. As the millet matured, the green became rare and people craving it were advised to eat their fill at the right period. The message is that people must act and secure their positions or resources at the appropriate time.

Dictionary, 654; Watuma, *Syĩthĩo*, 54.
[28] Mailu, *Kĩkyambonie*, 28; Mutisya, *Proverbs*, 23.

614. *tesĩ ĩngĩ ĩmĩnyungĩaa kĩtimba.* **A dog that does not know another dog sniffs at its bottom.**
When dogs meet for the first time they will sniff at each other's bottoms. The proverb is said as a warning not to underestimate another person. Sniffing at someone's buttocks is a mockery, denoting the sniffer is in a position of authority. However, the sniffing stops when the alien dog fights back.

615. *Ĩvĩndĩ ĩthũũnĩtwe nĩ ngitĩ ũyosaa ũvaumye kyaũ?* **What will you get from a bone licked by a dog if you pick it up?**
This precolonial catchphrase has multiple interpretations and can apply in many life situations. Just as a bone licked by a dog has no meat on it, there is little value in discarded things. Look for alternatives elsewhere.[29]

616. *Kakitĩ kalĩsĩlaa kaangĩ ĩthaũ.* **A dog mounts another out of playfulness.**
Dogs have played the role of assistant hunters, security guards, and keepers of herds or flocks on behalf of their masters. They were rarely seen as pets.

617. *Kũnũva ngitĩ ti kũmisya silanga; nĩ ĩthambĩaa ĩkaumĩla mũingo.* **To get rid of a dog do not throw it into the reservoir, it may swim to the other embankment.**
This was coined from the 1940s when dam construction became common and the canine population became excessive. Dogs began to go astray to towns where many were killed by shooting or poisoning. By Kamba custom, such slaughter was immoral. In the villages, dogs were left to die naturally. Attempts to throw them into newly built dam reservoirs to drown did not work, hence this proverb. Its true meaning is that to impoverish an enemy is not to leave him or her to starvation as that will not be their ultimate end – eliminate them.

618. *Mũndũ aikũmĩwa nĩ ngitĩ aũngamaa meyane ata?* **If a dog is barking at someone, will he will stop for a conversation with the dog?**
Since antiquity the Kamba kept dogs for security to bark at those approaching the homestead. Here, the dog exemplifies a person in a mocking sense. It means if someone (whom you do not respect) says bad things to you (barks), what business do you have with him? It also implies the barker is of no consequence to the speaker.

---

[29] Mutisya, *Proverbs*, 47.

619. *Kĩvĩsĩ kyosaa ngitĩ kĩte mũũnda.*[30] **A boy picks up a pet dog before he gets a farm.**
Adopting a dog signified that one had resources to defend and feed the dog and other people. Picking up a puppy before one had a farm from which to raise food to feed the animal was foolish. The boy here symbolizes anyone incautious in their actions. Picking up a puppy symbolizes attachment to something major and serious without the resources to execute and sustain the attachment.

620. *Mũsyĩ wĩ mwĩĩtu ndũeawa ngitĩ.* **A household that has a girl never keeps a dog.**
Since Kamba youth would undertake their romantic affairs at night when parents were asleep and barking dogs were a danger, girls sometimes killed the dogs to pave the way for these trysts.

621. *Mũndũ akwata ngitĩ ĩnyũũ ndĩlea ũmũũma.* **If one touches the dog's nose, it is bound to bite him.**
This ancient proverb appears in popular music. One should not go about poking into trouble lest dire consequences follow.

622. *Ndivatwa ũvĩta nĩ ngitĩ ĩkĩkũma na ndĩnoma.*[31] **A barking dog that has not bitten yet cannot stop me from passing through.**
This proverb was said by someone aware of some slander behind his back without affect. It alludes to barking dogs hindering passage. Some would bite and others just bark at passersby. Opponents were likened to barking dogs making mere noise, which the speaker simply ignores.

623. *Ndikwata ngitĩ takwa ndikatwĩke mbĩwa kaula Sange.* **As Sange said, I cannot capture a dog like myself lest I turn into a fox.**
James Mũĩmi used this proverb as a conclusion to a short story about the dog and the fox. The story goes: the fox entered the home of a man named Mũindũ and stole a goat. Mũindũ called his dog Sange, telling it to kill the fox and rescue the goat. When the fox saw Sange running after him he barked 'Mbwa! Mbwa!' like a dog. Sange thought, 'So when the fox kills a goat it turns into a dog!' Turning back, he said, 'I cannot capture a dog like myself lest I turn into a fox.' The proverb, emerging from the Monsoon era, means a thief cannot catch another thief.

---

[30] Mwau, *Dictionary*, 651.
[31] Lindblom, *Riddles*, 34; Patrick Ibekwe, *Wit and Wisdom of Africa: Proverbs from Africa & the Caribbean* (Trenton: Africa World Press, 1998), 188.

624. *Ndŭkookĭlye ĭkitĭ muu ŭteŭkomeea.* **Do not arouse the dog from the ashes that you will not lie on.**
Do not deny people things that you have no use for. Like other entries relating to the dog, the axiom dates from the earliest times. Traditions stress that the dog, like the chicken, was attracted to human settlement by fire and human protection. The most common interpretation is let a lying dog sleep. Let stubborn and ignorant people continue in their ignorance. Dating from antiquity, this axiom alludes to the habit of dogs sleeping on the warm ashes outside the house.

625. *Ndŭkose kakitĭ kate kalĭkye metho.* **Do not adopt a puppy before its eyes are formed.**
This ancient adage encodes the Kamba cultural practice of doing things at the right time, but not too early. Upon birth, puppies' eyes take several weeks to develop, reaching full vision around the eighth week, while the ears take up to eighteen weeks to fully develop. The Kamba emphasized that it was inappropriate to remove puppies from their mother during the period of development. All projects should be executed at the right time, but not prematurely.

626. *Vayĭ ngitĭ ĭte mŭnyanyae.* **No dog is without a friend.**
This axiom originally used the hyena, but as they retreated from close proximity to settlements they were replaced with the dog. Dogs in the old days were fewer and indispensable to hunting and security, and thus always had a 'friend'. Always, people are alike or share interests.

627. *Ndŭkakathe ngitĭ nzaa kŭtanatuka.* **Do not exaggerate a dog's hunger before dusk.**
Despite suggestions in oral interviews that this proverb traces back to antiquity, the majority of informants convinced me the maxim emerged during the difficult years of famines during the nineteenth century. A dog is a hunting animal that is not entirely dependent on humans for survival. Starving dogs went out and hunted for food. Hard-working people are in this case compared to such a dog.

628. *Ngitĭ ĭkŭmaa vala yosetwe, na yalekelw'a nzaa ĭikŭma kwa mŭtŭi.* **A dog barks where it is adopted, but if starved, it barks at the neighbour's home.**
This can be applied to the brain drain in Kenya, which invests in education only to see most graduates end up seeking employment and further education abroad due to lack of opportunity at home. Arguably Kenya's best professionals live outside the country's boundaries, 'barking' in the West and more recently the East and the Middle East.

629. *Ũyosa ngitĩ wambaa kwosa inyia.* **When you are picking up a puppy, you pick the mother.**
The mother of puppies had to be appeased in order to bless the adaptor. In order to select a puppy, the mother had to be made comfortable. Some mother dogs could track their puppies to the homes where they were taken. This was not taken lightly – it meant recognition that animals had feelings like humans and such feelings were not to be abused or ignored.

630. *Ve mĩsyĩ ũtamyosa ngitĩ.* **There are homesteads where you cannot pick up a puppy.**
The Kamba obtained puppies and kittens from neighbours and distant villages, preferring puppies from those families they knew best. It was believed that a dog from a degenerate owner would share similar traits. This means some households were so degenerate that one would not contemplate getting a bride from it or giving a girl in marriage to it.

631. *Mwĩkootele wa ngitĩ nowo mweendele wayo.*[32] **The stretching of a dog is also its manner of taking off.**
There are many interpretations and applications of this proverb. Some say habits are next to nature. If one decides to ignore you he does not have to say it but simply turns to other things. As a trained Mũkamba, you have to understand tiny signs, which indicate change. You have to adjust accordingly.

632. *Ngitĩ ĩkũnunanuna ndyendaa kwona ĩngĩ ĩkinunanuna.* **A sniffing dog does not like another sniffing dog.**
There is a sexual element in the first level of its meaning: a male dog looking for a female one does not like to see another male dog. Likewise, young men pursuing young girls do not like competitors and vice versa for girls. The metaphorical meaning depicts the nature of competition. Monopoly of any kind is preferred at all levels of society.

633. *Kurũ onayatinda ũlĩsa ĩngĩ ndĩsyaĩthya mbĩwa ĩsyaithya o kurũ.* **Even if dogs mate repeatedly, they will never bear a fox, but will bear a dog.**
Persistent endeavour in the wrong place and wrong way will not yield the desired outcome. In the song from which this maxim was drawn, an incompetent leader will always remain incompetent and will never bring development to his electorate.

---

[32] Mwau, *Dictionary*, 657.

634. *Ngitĩ ndyũngi ĩnũkĩsyaa mwene mũlanza.* **A stray dog takes an arrow home to its owner.**
If a stray dog became a nuisance to a particular home it was shot with a wooden arrow, not only to chase it away but as a symbolic gesture that the owner should restrain his animals. The axiom warned against uncouth behaviour. Married men or women involved in adultery, for example, suffered severe embarrassment and corporal punishment by the community when their mischief was discovered. The proverb was therefore a specific critique of men who flirted with other people's wives, or wives who committed adultery. *Mũlanza* symbolized punishment, while the offender was equated to a stray dog.

635. *Ngitĩ ya ĩtomo yũmaa mwene.* **A greedy dog bites its master.**
The Kamba attributed dog bites, particularly when trying to feed the animal, as a result of sickness or a lack of gratitude. This proverb, however, is about misers, people who are greedy and gluttonous. A wife who does not show generosity to guests, for example, is a burden (the bite) to her husband.

636. *Ngitĩ ĩkũmĩaa ngo ndĩkũmĩaa nduu.* **A dog barks after a leopard not after a squirrel.**
This proverb means that in any competition people criticize the strongest not the weakest competitors. In politics, criticism is directed at the strong candidate (a leopard) not at the weak (a squirrel).

637. *Ngitĩ ĩkuete nyama mũsyĩ yĩthaa ĩvũnie.* **When a dog brings meat home, it is full.**
Dogs among the Kamba were used as pets, security guards, and hunting dogs. The dogs often killed small animals and dragged them home. Most dogs, however, fed themselves first before delivering the remains to humans. This axiom points to selfish characters who benefit from but give little to their communities.

638. *Ngitĩ ya mũng'ethya yambĩĩa na mwene.* **A rabies-infected dog bites the owner first.**
During the colonial period there were at least three major outbreaks of rabies among dogs. The first case of rabies in Kenyan dogs was recorded in 1912 on the outskirts of Nairobi. Subsequently, rabies spread to Machakos. The proverb, therefore, emerged between the 1910s and 1950s. As a new disease, the Kamba blamed the dog for lack of gratitude, for the attack usually came when the owner was feeding it.[33] This

---

[33] Philip Kitala, et al., 'Community-Based Active Surveillance for Rabies in Machakos District, Kenya', *Prev Vet Med.* 44(1–2) (2000): 73–85; Austine O'Bitek, et al., 'A Hundred Years of Rabies in Kenya and the Strategy for Eliminating Dog-Mediated Rabies by 2030', AAS Open Research 2019, 1(15 Feb 2019): 23.

is an axiomatic condemnation of situations where some people mock their beneficiaries.

639. *Ngitĩ ya mũnene onayo no mũnene.* **The dog of the boss is also a boss.**
This is said in reference to the children of the privileged, who are accustomed to getting exactly what they want from adoring adults. This was coined in colonial days when new leaders were called *Anene*, originally meaning chiefs, but were broadened to other high-status positions. Peter Mutua told how his teachers could not correct children of a senior priest in Nairobi lest the teachers face his wife's fury – the couple eventually were forced to pull their children out of the school.[34]

640. *Kũnĩa ngitĩ vala yaumaĩya ĩthanze.* **Beat the dog where it peed on the stubble.**
Ĩthanze is a species of grass that grows mainly in loam soils, denoting the origin of this proverb from such areas where the Kamba trained their dogs not to pee on stubble. With the disappearance of the *Ĩthanze* the proverb was modified to *Ngitĩ ĩkũnĩawa o vala yamĩĩa*, 'A dog is beaten where it excreted.' In training, the Kamba disciplined their dogs by beating them whenever they peed or pooped in the wrong place.

641. *Kũna ngitĩ wone mwene.* **Beat the dog to see its owner.**
In Kamba society it was an abomination to beat someone's pet. Beating a dog kept for defence and hunting often led to furious confrontations. The Kamba were very much attached to their animals and treated them very well. Thrashing a dog obviously occasioned severe hostility, even a life-and-death struggle.

642. *Mũsemba weka eany'a kũũ kĩlinga.* **One who runs alone has long legs like a loop.**
Another version is *Mũsemba weka ndakwatĩka*, 'No one can catch a lone runner.' This talks about a braggart who praises himself about his capability before he is shown the task.

643. *Ve nzĩa mbiingĩ sya kũwaa ngitĩ.* **There are many ways of killing a dog.**
This adage might have colonial origins. The English have had this proverb in documented form since the 1600s.[35] Since it is universal to many cultures, there is no evidence that the Kamba borrowed this

---

[34] Peter Mutua, 'Bringing Up Children in the Family Business: Engaging the African Village', http://biasharasme.sasahivi.com/blogs/coffeeblog/item/16-bringing-up-children-in-the-family- business-engaging-the-african-village.html. Accessed 10 June 2019.
[35] John Ray, *A Collection of English Proverbs* (Cambridge: John Hayes, 1678).

adage from the colonial culture. The proverb means that there are many ways of solving a given problem.

644. *Ngitĩ mbose ndyosaa ĩngĩ.* **An adopted dog does not adopt another.**[36]
The majority of dogs were not bred at home but adopted as puppies elsewhere in a process called *kwosa* (hence the adverb *mbose*) because one did not pay for the puppies. The new dog obviously had no ability to care for another dog. This means dependants cannot help dependants.

645. *Ngitĩ ngũũ ndĩkũmaa mana.* **An old dog does not bark in vain.**
Appearing in songs and literature, this is one of the maxims that revere old age. While young dogs bark consistently, an old dog barks only when it scents a stranger or a prowling animal. The phrase 'old dog' refers to an experienced leader who does not say things for the sake of making a speech.

646. *Ngitĩ ngũũ ndĩkwataa mĩao myeũ.* **An old dog does not obey new laws.**
At one level this means train and admonish the young early since older people do not learn as easily. This appears to have diffused into Kamba from English: 'One cannot teach an old dog new tricks.' It means that people will not abandon ingrained habits.

647. *Ngitĩ ĩsaa thii ĩtunge kyũũmati kya mwana.* **A dog eats the placenta to reduce post-labour pains.**
A dog eating the placenta of its young is scientifically called placentophagy but there is no consensus on why dogs do it. Kamba nannies coined this proverb to justify their habit of nibbling on baby food claiming that dogs' practice placentophagy to rebuild their strength. The maxim is therefore an excuse for unusual behaviour. Experts in canine behaviour argue that placentophagy encourages milk production and speeds up birth. The mother needs to eat some of the placenta for its high vitamin and hormone levels, which induce milk supply. These hormones help the uterus to contract, speeding up the birth of the remaining puppies. Others argue that dogs eat the placenta to clean the den and hide the scent from predators.[37]

---

[36] Mutisya, *Proverbs*, 40.
[37] Ann Seranne, *The Joy of Breeding Your Own Show Dog* (Hoboken: Wiley Publishing, 1980), 137; Myra Harris, *Advanced Canine Reproduction and Puppy Care* (Wenachee: Dogwise Publishing), 53; Martin Coffman, *Sports Medicine for Hunting Dogs* (Belgrade, Montana: Wilderness Adventures Press, 2011), 30.

648. *Wĩĩthasya ngitĩ ĩtina ĩkesaũkũũma ngele.* **You feed a dog and it later bites your leg.**
Dogs are often used in Kamba lore to express a lack of gratitude among humans. Owners care for their dogs with passion but the animals eventually attack their owners. It is extremely disconcerting among the Kamba when a dog nips at its owner. Here the dog symbolizes an ungrateful person whose attitude and actions are considered as biting its benefactor.

649. *Kyongo kya mbaka kĩemeaa mũtũnginĩ.* **The head of a cat remains in the water can.**
This is a recent expression, for *mũtũngi* is a Swahili word for a water container introduced around the 1950s. The metallic container was replaced by plastic containers from the 1970s. The statement is slightly contradictory given that the mouths of these containers were too small for a grown cat's head.

650. *Mbaka ĩtakwata mbĩa ti mbaka.*[38] **A cat that cannot catch a rat is useless.**
Before 1870 there were no cats in Ũkamba. However, by 1910 the Kamba had numerous cats obtained from Europeans and Swahili traders. The introduction of the cat was a solution to a problem that came with European interlopers – the inadvertent introduction of mice just when the transformation of the local environment increased the number of snakes. The cat was quickly adopted as mice and snakes increased during the 1880s and 1890s. This proverb can be another way of saying that an idea that is not implemented is worthless, or a person who cannot deliver is of little account.

651. *Maũndũ nĩ ma Ngai asũvĩaa mbaka nzangili.* **Things belong to God who provides for the wild cat.**
This creates hope that even in the face of impossibility something good can happen. The Kamba could have obtained the practice of taming cats from the coast where the animal is called *paka* (corrupted to *mbaka*). However, some Kamba call the animal *kaka*, perhaps giving rise to Swahili *paka*.

652. *Mbaka ĩmanyaa nĩkwakya nĩũlika mamwenĩ.* **A cat knows it is daylight when it steps on the dew.**
Nighttime in Ũkamba is sometimes dry and hot but there is still dew at dawn. People knew that dawn was approaching as they walked at night when they began to feel it on their feet.

---

[38] Mwau, *Dictionary*, 654.

653. *Nzĩa syaũthĩnza mbaka nĩ nyingĩ.* **There are many ways of skinning a cat.**
Although the Sokoke cat originated in Giriama land where Kamba hamlets have existed since the first millennium, cats reached Ũkamba through imperial commerce between the 1880s and 1910s. This witty twist of the older maxim, 'There are many ways of killing a dog', probably emerged during the second half of the twentieth century.[39] It means there are many solutions to a given problem.

654. *Ona mbaka ngũũ nĩnyusaa iia.*[40] **Even an old cat drinks milk.**
The philosophical meaning of this twentieth-century coinage is that no one, regardless of his or her age or status, is averse to pleasure. The deeper meaning is that even old people can fall in love, enjoy sex, and even procreate.

655. *Ona mbaka sya mũsyĩ no ing'ei.* **Even domestic cats are thieves.**
This proverb comes from a story where people thought only wild cats stole eggs but found that domesticated cats also stole eggs.[41] Coined in the twentieth century, it means anyone can be a culprit.

656. *Wĩa wa ngitĩ nĩ ũkũma mũsyĩ, naw'o wa mbaka nĩ ũkwata mbĩa.* **The work of a dog is barking at home, that of a cat catching mice.**
This appeared in a song of Kiwmele wa Mutava of Mutulu village in the 1970s. The proverb means different people have different functions in society and all the functions are equally important.

657. *Mbaka ĩla yĩĩsaa mbĩa yĩ na ĩvu ndĩsoanĩaa ũnĩ ĩkaya kyaũ.* **A cat that eats a pregnant rat does not consider what it will eat tomorrow.**
This is a postcolonial coinage and has since become an adage for a moral and ethical issue, developed in the minds of households with cats. In free-range situations, the rats are meals for the cats, but humans noticed that cats kills rats of all ages and conditions. They do not bother to store or spare some rats for tomorrow.

658. *Mbaka yoaie mwana na ũnyenya yũmwĩtaa O Mũng'wau.* **The cat killed its child while caterwauling 'meow'.**
Emerging from the early 1900s when cats reached Ũkamba, this proverb came from a story where a cat ate her kitten while licking it and purring. The proverb warns that love for children must be moderated lest it become toxic and even fatal.

---

[39] Nancy Robbins, *Domestic Cats: Their History, Breeds and Other Facts* (Morrisville: Lulu Press, 2013).
[40] Mutisya, *Proverbs*, 43.
[41] Mũĩmi, *Ngewa*, 23.

659. *Mũtwaano wa mbaka ũthelaa ngitĩ syakũma.* **The wedding of cats ends when the dogs bark.**
Kamba cats and dogs are not good friends. Even if pets in the same home, they keep out of the way of each other. While the dog stays outside the house, the cat roams both the compound and inside the house. Sometimes the dogs' barking scares the cats. The statement symbolically means that the mischief of juniors ends when seniors appear on the scene.

660. *Mbaka ngũũ nĩ ĩsĩ lelo.* **An old cat is tactical.**
This was a common saying of a man named Muthengi of Maai Mountain range in Kitui, talking about the importance of tactics and experience. Old people might be physically weak but they know how things work.

661. *Mbaka na mbĩa ĩĩsania ĩsaaninĩ yĩmwe.* **A cat and a mouse do not share a bowl.**
This is a recent coinage given that the cat, the mouse, and the bowl are all recent additions in Ũkamba. The Kamba started using modern plates early, but they only became widespread after World War Two. The cat kills the rat on first encounter, so opposite sides repel.

662. *Nĩsĩ ũĩ ũmwe na nũmbĩanĩtye. Maũĩ maingĩ nĩ ma mana.* **I know only one wise thing and it is enough for me. Too many wits are void.**
This came from the story *Mbaka na Mbalũkũ* by James Muimi.[42] The cat and the hare were arguing about wisdom when the cat said with finality the above axiom. Shortly after saying it, a predator ambushed them. The cat jumped up a tree to take refuge. The hare ran here and there, but to no avail. It was captured and devoured. This proverb emerged between the 1910s and 1940s, when cats became widespread. It means that too much argument without action is useless.

663. *Kĩtindo kya mbaka na mbĩa kyaĩ ngalawanĩ vevoka.* **The companionship of the rat and the cat was on the ship only.**
This proverb alludes to the cats carried on ships to control Asian black rats, which threatened the ships' grain cargo and supplies. While the cat was carried on board by human choice, the rat sneaked into the ships and reached East Africa during the seventh and eighth centuries. Sailing ships later spread the domestic cat and the rat throughout the world so that the rat and the cat were unlikely companions in travel to East Africa. Nonetheless, neither animal reached Ũkamba until the colonial era, the probable time of the emergence of the proverb. The proverb is said by disagreeable parties who cannot get along. The

---

[42] James Muimi, *Ngewa Sya Syana* (Nairobi: Mowa Publishers, 1981), 21.

speaker means that what united them in the past is gone and they have no common ground any more.

664. *Mũkua mbaka ndatalaa mavalo.* **One carrying a cat does not count the scratches on his body.**
To adopt a cat the Kamba carried them in their arms but the animal would scratch the person carrying it. To avoid injury, they began to carry them in sizeable bottlegourds with holes to let the cat breathe. The maxim, which emerged in the colonial period, means that one who engages in a risky but rewarding business should ignore the cost.

665. *Mũvakũi wa mbaka ndaa wia nguanĩ.* **The castrator of cats lacks no fur on the clothes.**
This is a recent coinage for castration of cats and dogs was not common in Ũkamba. The practice probably emerged in the 1950s for reasons associated with colonial views of animals at the time. The proverb actually means that association or companionship is contagious. The careers and individuals we associate with no doubt shape our character.

666. *Andũ me ndũũ mayũũthaa nguũtũ.* **Friends do not gamble among themselves with white shells.**
Friends should not make fishy deals or withhold secrets from each other. The word *nguũtũ* is the historical marker in this proverb encoding the history of precolonial Kamba long-distance trade, circumcision customs, and gender affairs. *Nguũtũ* were white shells imported from the coast and used as currency before 1800. Between 1896 and 1920, their use changed dramatically when the rupee and the shilling replaced *nguũtũ* as new colonial currency.[43] Among men, shells became dice for gambling, symbolically pointing to the loss of one's wife to the winner. As this form of gambling was replaced with the colonial version called *karata* or *kalata*, the term *kalata* replaced *nguũtũ*. The proverb, however, deploys *karata* as a vehicle emphasizing the critical importance of friendship and familial relationships – one should never play games in these types of relationships.

667. *Nzĩa ĩkooa ĩkwataa ĩmwe mũthenya.* **A path that is overgrown gets dew by midday.**
This ancient axiom talks about signs of a teenager drifting into bad behaviour and ruin. The path symbolizes a youth, while dew represents habits that are visible and point to immoral tendency.

---

[43] AIM, *Kĩkamba–English*, 150.

668. *Nzĩa ĩkaĩya mwana ĩmeasya ĩmwe mũthenya.* **A path where a child will be lost develops dew in broad daylight.**
Rising from antiquity with the preceding entry, this axiom has a slightly different meaning. It points to bad trends of a youth that will lead him into immorality. His habits are noticed as they develop slowly.

669. *Nzĩa ya avĩti yĩ ũtee.* **The path of passersby is on the side.**
This adage was drawn from Kamba home settings. Kamba dwellings had two ways of entering, one going into the compound and another around the fence. The path outside was cut for the public so that one who had no appointment in the home compound just passed by. It is applied to warn those less involved in certain matters not to interfere but mind their business.

670. *Wĩkũlya kwaa ũsuu nĩkĩ, ũendete ũendo na mwenyu?* **Why are you asking the way to your grandmother while absconding with your mother?**
This proverb emerged during the Islamic period. Sometimes women absconded from their matrimonial homes with their children, who out of curiosity asked the mother as they walked, 'Which way leads to my grandmother's home?' The mother would respond, 'I know the way. That is where I came from in the first place.' The proverb, therefore, admonishes one not to ask about obvious things.

671. *Wĩsĩ nĩwĩsĩ mũndũ wa ũndũ nde kĩndũ kĩasa ĩndĩ wa ndia ndesa ũkwatya.* **A knowledgeable person knows that a friend's thingy is never too long, but a fool does not comprehend it.**
This ancient maxim alludes to obsession that drives some people to perfection and others to excessive habits. It concerns persons who, more than unique physical endowments, are good at romance due to their style of love making.

10

Crops and Other Plants

672. *Nĩ kya mwee kĩĩsawa na ũtee.*[1] **It is made of millet and is eaten along the sides.**
Traditionally, the Kamba consumed their food in ways differing from modern styles. Hot mealiepap prepared from millet flour was spread over a calabash bowl and then eaten from the edges, which cooled faster. It was eaten with bare hands (subject to scorching) or wooden spoons. In human relations, a hot-tempered person was equated with this hot mealiepap and should be spoken to cautiously.

673. *Maisha nota kĩteke kya wĩmbĩ maĩsawa na ndee.* **Life is like millet mealiepap, it is eaten from the edges.**
Millet was a staple before the eighteenth century. Mealiepap made from millet was eaten hot and very slowly from the edges. The maxim advises the listener to slow down and proceed with caution. While this proverb may have precolonial precedents, its use of the Swahili word *maisha* indicates its emergence in the twentieth century.

674. *Mũnuka wakĩle mwee ndũvuvaa ũngĩ.* **A mouthful of millet does not blow millet.**
Ripening millet ears were cut and pressed in large calabash bowls to separate seeds from husks. The husks were then blown with the mouth (a process called *kũvuva*), leaving clean seeds. The mouth had to be clear in order to blow. Dating to the Vascon era, the maxim advised the listeners to focus on a task they can complete rather than leaving many things unfinished.

675. *Mwee ũũlũkaw'a kenda wewa ũthi na ũkũngi.* **Millet is winnowed to let the husks go with the wind.**
This proverb emerged from the Vascon era with the cultivation and processing of millet. The millet seeds were procured through winnowing using large calabash basins with the aid of wind to take out husks. It means effort is needed to achieve desired goals.

---

[1] Watuma, *Syĩthĩo*, 57.

676. *Mwĩĩtu wa mwee ndakusaa na ĩvu.* **A daughter of millet does not die pregnant.**
Where other crops wither and die, drought-resistant millet thrives, hence this proverb. The proverb emerged during the 1930s, when increase in droughts coincided with a surge in teenage pregnancies and deaths at birth. Proverbs relating to premarital pregnancies doubtlessly increased during the interwar period.

677. *Ndũketange mwee ngũkũnĩ.*[2] **Do not sprinkle millet before the chicken.**
Kamba chickens were raised on millet and other grains and stray chickens often damaged unguarded grain stores. Emerging in the mid-twentieth century, the proverb warned against situations of intimacy that could lead to seduction.

678. *Nzeesya ĩsaa mwee na kĩelelo.*[3] **Pearl millet munias eat millet strategically.**
Millet became a staple grain during the Islamic period. It was a favourite of weaverbirds, especially the pearl millet munias, which consumed standing millet crops without spilling grains, carefully picking one grain at a time until the millet husk was exhausted. Its name *nzeesya* even derives from the word *kũ-thesya*, to clean or exhaust. The axiom admonishes one to approach a challenge with precaution and strategically.

679. *Ti mwee woonthe ũkimawa mũnyinginyi, mũnyinginyi nĩ kũthea.* **Not all millet makes *mũnyinginyi*, it has to be selected.**
Dating from the Islamic era, this proverb points to the necessity of selectivity. The Kamba gathered millet grains selecting the biggest and healthiest seeds for a cuisine called *mũnyinginyi*. Those selected were soaked in water and eaten raw. The proverb means not all women are married, some remain unmarried.

680. *Vayĩ kĩndũ kĩthũku ta kũtavĩka mũvya mavũĩnĩ.* **There is nothing as bad as vomiting sorghum in front of doves.**
Doves feed primarily on sorghum whenever they invade ripening crops. If one consumed sorghum and vomited it before the doves, these birds descended on it fast, human nausea notwithstanding. Emerging from the twentieth century this axiom warned against behaviour that was conducive to seduction and infidelity.

---

[2] Mwau, *Dictionary*, 664.
[3] Farnsworth, *Grammar*, 131.

681. *Vayĩ mwando mũvĩte nĩ sua.* **There is no green millet flour that missed the sun.**
This refers to pearl millet, the staple crop until maize replaced it during the twentieth century.[4] Millet was domesticated in West Africa and spread to East Africa thousands of years ago.[5] However, it did not become popular in Ũkamba until the Vascon era, precisely the time of the emergence of this proverb. The proverb encourages young people that there is always hope for opportunities.

682. *Ĩiyũ ya kĩw'ũ yendaa ona kĩw'ũ.* **A banana planted on the waterfront drowns in floods.**
Bananas reached East Africa from Southeast Asia about the beginning of the Christian era. By the Islamic era, bananas were established inland as far as Kilimanjaro. The Kamba favoured cultivating them along river basins and depressions. Floods, however, swept them away, hence the adage.[6] It means that what you get often disappears.

683. *Ĩiyũ yumaw'a kĩĩ nĩ kũsyaa.* **A banana plant acquires consumers by bearing.**
The banana plant bears multiple bunches of fruits weighing it down to attract many species of insects, birds, reptiles, and herbivores. This proverb implies that an adult woman would attract men, even rapists, by exposing her body or flirting. Another interpretation is that a mother is worn out physically by childbirth.

684. *Aũme ti ivĩsĩ maindaa ndũla mũthiti na syeew'a maiya.* **Men are not boys; they bury loquats in the anus and eat them when they ripen.**
Before explaining this proverb, a brief mention of loquats is needed. Contrary to previous mistranslations, the fruit tree locally known as *ndũla, ndunda,* or *lũkati* should not be translated as almonds, but loquat.[7] Loquat, an ornamental fruit plant native to China and Japan, flowers in shade. Loquats reached Ũkamba through the Monsoon Exchange era and became popular trees in the highlands. During the colonial period, British planters imported more loquats from England, South Africa, and their native Far East.[8] Using obscene epithets and the lure of loquats as speech devices, Kamba women coined the above proverb to warn teenage girls to avoid unplanned pregnancies.

[4] Maundu, *Traditional Food*, 125.
[5] James McCann, *Stirring the Pot: A History of African Cuisine* (Athens: Ohio University Press, 2009); National Research Council, *Lost Crops*, Vol. 1.
[6] Kĩtukũ, *Folktales*, 91–3.
[7] Mwau, *Dictionary*.
[8] Edward Buck, *Annual Colonial Reports Number 519 East Africa Protectorate Report for 1905–1906* (London: Wyman and Sons, 1907), 74.

685. *Mũtinda na kĩvĩsĩ ndaleaa kwindwa ndũla mũthiti.*[9] **Associates of boys will definitely have loquats pushed up their anus.**
Women admonishing girls to be wary of immature boys to avoid mischief and embarrassment usually said this. The unripe loquat (*ndũla*) is symbolic of an immature boy's penis, whereas the anus signifies embarrassment for the girl.

686. *Kanywa mũtheke ũĩsaa ndũla na aka ma weũ.*[10] **A thin mouth eats loquats with the damsels of the wild.**
There are multiple symbolisms in the proverb – a thin mouth, loquats, and the lasses of the wild – necessary for comprehension of its allegoric meaning. A thin mouth represents sweet words while loquats symbolize sweeter results, and the company of women of the wild, the most delightful romance. In other words, sweet rewards are the results of sweet investments. This advises salespeople they have to sweet-talk their customers.

687. *Kũya ndũla nĩ kũatĩanĩsya.*[11] **The pleasure of eating loquats is swallowing them in quick succession.**
Loquats, the sweetest fruits in Ũkamba, are so tasty it is difficult to stop with just one, hence this proverb. It is worthless to have something good that is not sustainable. The first taste does not make one fully appreciate the fruit's sweetness. Try it again to understand its value. The political speaker from whom the axiom was heard meant, re-elect the incumbent to test him again.

688. *Kĩkondu akengie kĩtũla masyaie nzĩanĩ kĩtũla alike athela.*[12] **The eggplant Solanum deceived the loquat; as they both bear fruit on the wayside the loquat was vanquished.**
Another illustration that loquats are an emblem of a victim of deception. The loquats are favourites of humans and animals. The proverb cautions against deceit and aping others without forethought. It provides a forum for dialogue between alien imperialists and local subjects. Solanum is an indigenous inedible plant, while loquat is an alien delicacy. The two plants are in dialogue just as the Kamba entered into dialogue with imperialists.

---

[9] Mwau, *Dictionary*, 660.
[10] Mwau, *Dictionary*, 648.
[11] Mwau, *Dictionary*, 652.
[12] Kituku, *Sukulu*, 17.

154 Part III: Kamba at Home

689. *Mbalũkũ yaemwa nĩ kũvikĩla nzavivũ yaisye ti mbĩũ.* **When the hare failed to reach the grapes, it said they are not yet ripe.**
Emerging in the 1930s when grapes reached Ũkamba, this axiom is close to the European fable of the sour grapes. It points to lame excuses that people give for their failures and missteps.

690. *Ndũkaainde ndũla na syana syiikaindũwe syĩ mbĩthĩ.* **Do not bury loquats near children lest they be unburied raw.**
This talks about immaturity, impatience, and relations between adults and youth. Children symbolize immature intellect and impatience; loquats symbolize pleasure; the act of burying loquats represents intercourse, while exhuming unripe loquats signifies embarrassment. Plans made with a fool will be exposed before maturation, just as children will not wait patiently for buried loquats to ripen. Coming from the Vascon era this warned against having affairs with immature persons.

691. *Kĩtũngũũ nĩ mũkaangĩle.* **The onion is the style of frying.**
Onions from central Asia reached Ũkamba through imperial commerce during the nineteenth and twentieth centuries. However, frying began in earnest after the First World War, with tremendous changes in the character of Kamba cuisine.[13] The proverb means success is predicated upon one's strategies.

692. *Mũndũ nowe wĩtũngaa nguu akaya mathooko soko.* **One turns himself into a tortoise to feed on greens in the market.**
Dating to the 1920s this is a form of protest against public misconduct within the marketplace. A person without dignity is like a wild beast fed on grass, or worse, as a tortoise fed on cowpea leaves. The Kamba consider eating raw leaves as the lowest ebb of humanity.

693. *Vaita wa sukuma ũminawa nĩ wa nyunyi.* **The value of kales is surpassed by that of green leaves.**
A recent maxim, as collard greens were only recently introduced from Eastern Europe. The proverb speaks to replacing indigenous species with foreign ones. Collard greens' advent substantially reduced consumption of traditional greens. Such plant transfers came with cultural baggage: colonial planters advocated new plants as superior to traditional ones. The idea was to create a market for imperial products and prove to the colonial subjects that imperial products were supreme. When collard greens were not available people fell back on traditional greens. In that sense the proverb warns against disregarding original objects in pursuit of novelties.

[13] Stanley Alpern, 'The European Introduction of Crops into West Africa in Precolonial Times', *History in Africa* 19(1992): 13–43.

694. *Ndũlũ ĩteteaa na kũlũla.*[14] **Chilli pepper defends itself with its pungency.**
The migration of the chilli to East Africa began in 1492, when Christopher Columbus shipped to Europe the spicy plant from the Caribbean. The Portuguese introduced chilli peppers into East Africa in the early 1500s. However, chillies spread so slowly inland that by the 1930s they were still rare in Ũkamba. Thus, this maxim must have emerged during the early twentieth century when cultivation and consumption of chilli peppers became widespread in Ũkamba. The proverb means people defend themselves with the best weapon they have.

695. *Ĩnyanya yĩla ĩtune nĩyo yĩthĩawa na kĩinyũ.* **The reddest tomato has the worm.**
Although tomatoes had reached East Africa by the early Vascon era, they were not common in Ũkambanĩ until the colonial period. The proverb appears to have been coined during the colonial period. In the 1980s and 1990s it was applied to sexual behaviour and HIV/AIDS, a disease that was figuratively referred to as 'the little worm'. The reddest tomato symbolizes the most beautiful girl, whose beauty attracts male attention so her chance of contracting HIV is higher.

696. *Maluu menzawa nthĩ.* **Irish potatoes are dug from the ground.**
This emerged soon after British farmers introduced Irish potatoes (called *maluu* in Kĩkamba) in the 1880s.[15] Nearly all of Ũkamba potatoes are consumed locally and are considered a high quality and prestigious food. The proverb emerged during the 1920s and 1930s, for only after the First World War did African farmers grow potatoes for home consumption. It means certain objects have their specific sources, which one must understand first before benefiting from the object.

697. *Ndũkaatate kũvũthya ĩnanasi nũndũ nĩ ĩtũaa lakini yĩembe nĩya ĩvinda.* **Do not mock the pineapple for it lasts longer than the ephemeral mango.**
This emerged during the twentieth century when pineapples reached Ũkamba. To the Kamba both pineapples and mangoes taste similar, but the mango is preferred except that it keeps for less time than the pineapple. The maxim is about comparison of quality and strength.

---

[14] Mwau, *Dictionary*, 664.
[15] B. Laufer, 'The American Plant Migration, Part One: The Potato', *Anthropology Series. Field Museum of Natural History*, Vol. 28, No. 1, Publication 418 (Chicago, 1938); J.H.G. Waithaka, 'Potato Cultivation in Kenya', paper presented at the First Regional Workshop on Potato Seed Production and Marketing, Nairobi. International Potato Centre, October 1976.

698. *Ndūkatate kūya yīembe ndasuite.* **Do not try to eat the mango before I peel it.**
This proverb dates from the mangoes' introduction in mountainous regions during the Vascon era. The fruits are eaten often by peeling the green or yellow skin to consume the tender, juicy flesh. Speakers mean they are experts in the subject under discussion and the audience should not jump to conclusions.

699. *Ndūkaye maembe na mūnyū o ūtonya kweteela makaetheta na aūke makew'a.* **Do not consume mangoes with salt while you can patiently wait for them to ripen.**
The mango as a foreign tree, romanticized in lore, symbolizes a young girl ripening into maturity. As a euphemism for sex, the mango is extremely appetizing and attractive to boys. Unwise boys do not wait for mangos to ripen, and get an undesirable result.

700. *Kūīsya kīsūanīo ndūkakūīsye īkonge.* **Transfer the thoughts, do not transfer the sisal.**
This proverb emerged in the 1930s when land ownership became a major concern in the Ūkamba highlands. As land fragmentation took root and overcrowding began, sisal demarcated farm boundaries. The sisal demarcation symbolized social divisions, hatred, and enmity, not wealth and progress. For dire want of land, neighbours often transferred the sisal a few meters over the designated boundary line. The proverb admonished neighbours to change their thoughts instead of involving themselves in such activities.

701. *Ngwatanīo nzeo nī ya makonge.* **The only good companionship is that of sisal.**
Having emerged during the First World War, the maxim reflected the success that the sisal industry realized between 1914 and 1944 across East Africa where Kamba labour was crucial to commercial success. However, the maxim implies social tension. While sisal in a plantation will never fight, humans cannot live without conflict.

702. *Mūtumīa mūonge ndamanyaa īkonge īsongye.* **A bribed elder never identifies sisal that has been uprooted.**
This proverb emerged in the 1930s when sisal (a major tropical fibre plant from the Americas) were introduced as farm border markers in Ūkambanī. Subsequently, it came to symbolize social division, enmity, and conflict over land ownership.

703. *Mwĩw'a wa ĩkonge ũtonyatonyaa nyamũ syonthe.* **The sisal spike pierces all animals.**
Sisal arrived in Kenya from the New World during the twentieth century as an imperial cash crop. Its thorns, however, became problematic to humans and animals. This proverb emerged in the 1930s using sisal as a symbol of a bad character who bothers the community.

704. *Tumanwe ta mũthemba wa ĩvia na ngongoma nĩ mavandie ĩkonge.* **Let us part our ways like the tick and the rock, they have planted a sisal.**
By 1914, sisal was firmly established as a cash crop, and by 1944 Kenya had become one of the world's largest producers of sisal. Emerging from the 1930s, this proverb is an axiomatic expression that the differences between two disagreeable people were as wide as that of the tick and the rock. 'Planting' symbolized physical and moral division between farmers, since sisal plants marked the boundaries between farms.

705. *Ĩlimba yĩ mboso.* **Dark loam soil has beans.**
This proverb emerged out of comparison of a short black girl and a tall fair-skinned one. Furthermore, in olden days *malimba* were left as grazing lands. With the introduction of beans from Latin America during the colonial era, these landscapes became coveted farmlands. Something considered of less value may have the most valuable.

706. *Vata wa ĩtimũ nĩ ngaati.* **The purpose of a lemon is sour taste.**
This proverb emerged during the late nineteenth century when Catholic missionaries introduced lemons (from India) into Kenya. Subsequently, the acidic variety was consumed solely for its sourness, as the proverb indicates. The broader point is that something is used only for its value and nothing else.

707. *Mũendi wa kyalo ndaumbĩkaa ĩkwasĩ.* **A traveller does not bury a sweet potato.**
This is a warning not to leave behind unfinished business. You cannot be sure when you will return to it. Sweet potatoes (*ĩkwasĩ*) reached the East African coast via the Portuguese during the sixteenth century. From the coast, Kamba traders carried the plant to the mainland, where it acquired multiple cultural meanings and uses. Potatoes were buried under hot ashes and vigilant watch kept lest they burn. After some hours, they were fully baked and taken out for consumption, something impossible for a traveller, who might return shortly, later, or never.

708. *Ĩkwasĩ yĩmwe yiitũsya ndũũ munyĩnĩ.* **A single sweet potato cannot keep friendship under shades.**
This reveals Kamba perceptions of sweet potato as a source and builder of friendships, families, and communities. Such was not always the case with other alien plants. During the day, the Kamba spent time with friends and relatives under shade as protection from the scorching sun. Snacks, commonly potatoes, were shared and slowly eaten as people talked. These customs emerged in the 1500s after the arrival of potatoes. In a social context, the proverb means that limiting friendship to a single thing that defines it is impossible as friendship demands many different inputs. In politics, it points out the importance of democracy and inclusiveness. Free choice is better than intimidation.

709. *Sisya ũkũanĩswa ũkwasĩ na walĩku wa nthĩ.* **Be careful lest your sweet potato vine be shortchanged by a crack on the ground.**
This axiomatic warning against deception emerged from the Vascon era after sweet potatoes became popular. Sown under loose soil the plant often makes a crack in the ground as its bulging tubers spread outwards. Some people tricked others by showing them cracks in the ground in exchange for potato vines. Here the potato represents the farmer's most valuable possession.

710. *Ũtumo wa ndoanĩlyo ũmeasya ũkwasĩ.* **A neighbourly hillside settlement produces a sweet potato vine.**
Once introduced into Ũkamba the sweet potato emerged as a symbol of village unity, cooperation, and peaceful coexistence. How? Someone brought a single vine from the coast and planted it. As it produced daughter vines, he cut some and gave them to neighbours to plant. Close ties of friendship developed out of that valuable gift. Others waited for those first planters to give them vines for their own farms. In this way, the village developed from a single sweet potato vine, which became a symbol of unity and prosperity. Coined in Machakos, this proverb warns against mischief and boastfulness and shows that it is good to live with others in a community.

711. *Eka kũathimũa ũtananywa mbakĩ.* **Stop sneezing before you inhale snuff.**
In 1560, Portuguese merchants shipped tobacco from the New World to East Africa.[16] Its products, especially snuff, makes consumers sneeze, symbolizing multiple things in Kamba lore. The speaker in the proverb was derisively telling the listener that there were greater challenges ahead, so quit complaining and wait for the main challenge.

---

[16] Judith Mackay and Michael Eriksen, *The Tobacco Atlas* (WHO, 2002), 18.

712. *Kĩthangai kĩtwaite myei ata?* **How does the turf grass spread its roots?**
This proverb depicts the struggle with invasive plants introduced in the region by imperial commerce before the Second World War. It originated from a question that a white overseer asked a shrewd Mũkamba in Machakos. The white man was supervising a gang uprooting the invasive turf grass in order to eradicate it. During his rounds with a whip he saw a man sitting idle, usually an act of defiance and laziness punishable by whips on the buttocks. He asked why he was idle. The Mũkamba replied, *Eka ngunde mbakĩ nĩmanye ũndũ kĩthangai kĩtwaĩte myei*, 'Let me take my snuff in order to know the direction of the couch grass roots.' The white man's anger subsided. He told him, 'Okay! Tell me when you are done.' Later he asked the Mũkamba, *Kĩthangai kĩtwaĩte myei ata*? 'How does the turf grass spread its roots?' These statements spread widely and became proverbs. The question is used as a happy way of asking peers, 'Howdy'?

713. *Kĩthangai kyendaa ũkũwa nesa na kĩivaunzwa.* **Couch grass must be removed carefully and shaken.**
A Machakos politician used this maxim to imply his opponent was so invasive to local politics that his ideas needed to be uprooted and suppressed. Originating from sub-Saharan Africa and the islands of the western Indian Ocean, couch grass is common in the Ũkamba highlands.[17] It is invasive in parts of Ũkamba.[18]

714. *Mũĩmi mũĩ ndathatĩaa kĩthangai kĩmeete levunĩ na nĩwĩsĩ kyũkitawa na lelo.* **A wise farmer does not rage against couch grass growing on the furrows, he knows it is fought strategically.**
Since the late 1930s, when couch grass was introduced in Ũkamba as an aid to soil conservation and land reconditioning, the weed has become a symbol of challenge, arduous tasks, and an unlikeable character. This axiom means a wise person does not complain, but understands his challenges and devises strategies to handle them.

715. *Kĩndũ kĩseo kĩkũaa no kumbatũ.* **The only good thing that lasts is tobacco.**
This proverb emerged from Kamba struggle against ageing, which reduced one's strength, value, and attraction. Snuff was widely consumed in Ũkamba from the seventeenth century on by inhaling or lumping it in the mouth and was said to improve with time. It was used

---

[17] Holm et al., *The World's Worst Weeds: Distribution and Biology* (Honolulu: University Press of Hawaii, 1977).
[18] Elizabeth Lyons and Scott Miller (eds), *Invasive Species in Eastern Africa: Proceedings of a Workshop held at ICIPE*, 5–6 July 1999.

on that account as a preservative and medicine. Other products may deteriorate with time, but tobacco leaves processed into snuff improve with age.[19] Through persistent interaction with tobacco, the snuff came to symbolize human genitals, romance, novelty, and sex.

716. *Kumbatũ mũkũũ wĩ mbakĩ mbĩu.*[20] **Old tobacco makes good snuff.**
Kumbatũ referred to unprocessed tobacco leaves. The longer the leaves stayed in storage, the better the snuff produced. By analogy, old people have good words and good advice.

717. *Mauta makũũ maithiaa mbakĩ.* **Old oil does not process snuff.**
Butter from cow's milk was used for seasoning mealiepap, processing tobacco, and as perfume in circumcision ceremonies. In each case, freshly produced butter was preferred. The adage alludes to Kamba attempts to respect generational differences in tackling similar tasks. A more common interpretation is that old enmity is irrelevant. Reconciliation is the solution for disagreements that took place years previously.

718. *Ndia ndĩkolaa mbakĩ.*[21] **A fool never has enough snuff.**
Traditionally, *mbakĩ* symbolically refers to a man. This then means a foolish woman is never satisfied with sex. However, it can apply the other way around. Among male interviewees, the word *mbaki* means woman, thus the proverb means foolish men are addicted to sex. The lesson of the maxim then is there must be limits even to good things.

719. *Mũtong'i nĩ kwĩkwatĩsya.* **The owner better light the pipe.**
This proverb emerged during the Vascon era, when supplanting cannabis and Datura, as principal sources of narcotics, newly introduced tobacco from the New World, was smoked in dry pipes and rolls called *mũtong'i*. The word *mũtong'i* symbolizes children in this proverb. Symbolically a man who had not lit a pipe of his own (sired his own children) had no joy, that is, his name will be forgotten after death with no children to carry on his legacy.[22]

---

[19] Kimilu, *Mũkamba*, 116; Mutisya, *Proverbs*, 43; Mwau, *Dictionary*, 650.
[20] Mailu, *Kĩkyambonie*, 59.
[21] Mutisya, *Proverbs*, 44; Mwau, *Dictionary*, 663.
[22] Lindblom, *Akamba*, 35, 85; Douglas Penwill, *Kamba Customary Law: Notes Taken in the Machakos District of Kenya Colony* (London: Macmillan, 1951), 70; Chris Duvall, *Cannabis* (London: Reaktion Books, 2015), passim; *Kenya Gazette*, 15 October 1913: 882, and 4 March 1914: 203.

Crops and Other Plants 161

720. *Aleani mayĩkĩanaa mbakĩ.*[23] **Disagreeable people do not share snuff.**
Snuff symbolized friendship, and friends usually exchanged gifts of snuff whereas foes would not. Failure to share snuff and liquor was a sign of enmity, it was also dangerous to share such things with enemies: they could contain poison. Tobacco reached East Africa around the sixteenth century and the proverb dates no earlier than that period.

721. *Mbakĩ ĩla mbĩu ĩkunyawa ũkwĩw'a ĩsu ndĩkundĩka.* **When the ripest tobacco is sniffed, you hear people say 'that is unbearable'.**
This proverb, using tobacco as the basis of quality, implies that a good leader does not have to beat about the bush. The leader's first action is effective and bears results. Wa Maiyu framed it differently but the proverb has been around since the introduction of tobacco in Kenya.

722. *Mbakĩ ya mũeni nĩyo ĩthĩawa ĩmbĩu.* **A visitor's snuff is the best.**
The proverb literally means 'A guest has ripe tobacco' or 'The snuff of a guest is most ripe' and has been in circulation since the eighteenth century. Variants have been published.[24] Several institutions used this proverb as a justification for reshuffling staff to new regions, interpreting it as schools getting new teachers would appreciate them for their new ideas of teaching or administration. Sex or genitals were often called jokingly *tobacco*, thus new partners would provide more excitement than old ones. It was applied broadly to mean the contributions of outsiders to a community are most welcome as they bring new resources.

723. *Mbakĩ ya neneva ĩtilawa matuny'o nĩkenda ĩthanthaĩe nthĩ.* **When a tobacco plant grows tall, it is trimmed so that it develops near the ground.**
This reflects a unique Kamba practice for the cultivation of tobacco. Tobacco was grown in deserted cowsheds, chicken runs, and goat pens, which were no longer useful but were still sufficiently fertile for the crop. The Kamba preferred the short tobacco plant, pruning it to develop multiple leaves at the base. The meaning has to do with investment, profit, and reinvestment.

724. *Mbakĩ ya nzili ĩnywĩĩwaa mũsama.* **The snuff is consumed for its taste.**
This is drawn from a song in which the singer, separated from his wife, meant he needed his wife who was irreplaceable; he could not be content with another woman. The tobacco type that the Kamba call *nzili* is of

---
[23] Mwau, *Dictionary*, 660.
[24] Mwau, *Dictionary*, 660.

inferior taste and quality according to Kamba tastes. This proverb indicates that *nzili* is taken in the absence of snuff and only because its taste is close to that of the snuff. In the context from which the maxim originated, another woman will suffice, but will not be comparable to the speaker's wife.

725. *Mbakĩ nĩ kwĩsengesya mwene.* **Snuff is worth keeping for oneself.**
This emerged in the 1700s when the manufacture and sale of snuff became widespread. While men smoked tobacco, women preferred snuff taken through the nose or lumped into the mouth. As snuff became a market commodity, the Kamba preferred to taste it to determine which one fitted individual tastes.

726. *Mbakĩ yamboya ndiminaa munyalo.* **Borrowed snuff does not quench.**
When the Kamba ran out of snuff they borrowed from neighbours, which developed into a pastime, becoming an act of socialization. However, those involved were reminded that self-sufficiency was preferable. The maxim encouraged property accumulation and ownership.

727. *Sembaa ngũnywa mbakĩ.* **Take off while I take my snuff.**
This is a threatening or a teasing phrase to someone else using tobacco as a source of power. Tobacco is a stimulant, a source of energy and mental clarity, as several proverbs attest. This proverb traces back to the eighteenth century when the Kamba began to make snuff, which was inhaled through the nose. It can mean 'prepare for battle or flee from me'.

728. *Ĩtina ĩseo nĩ ya kĩwa.* **A good base is that of a sugarcane.**
Sugarcane reached the coast from India via Arab traders during the Monsoon era. Kamba and other traders carried it inland before 1500.[25] In 1910, the British brought more sugarcane to Kitui and Kibwezi. Thus, proverbs related to sugarcane emerged as early as the Monsoon era to as recently as the 1910s. The current proverb hides the sexual connotation – *ĩtina* – which translates as 'behind', 'base or bottom', or 'poke' – all euphemisms for sex. The proverb means just as the base of the sugarcane is the sweetest, sex is pleasurable.

---

[25] Lindblom, *Akamba*, 506; Gregory Maddox, *Sub-Saharan Africa: An Environmental History* (Santa Barbara: ABC-CLIO, 2006); A. McMartin, 'Sugarcane in Central and East Africa: Some Observations on Its History and Present Positions', *Proceedings of the South African Sugar Technologies' Association* (April 1961):104.

729. *Kĩwa kyakũa kĩtũngaa mũyo ĩtina.* **When a sugarcane plant ages it relegates its sweetness to the bottom of the plant.**
Sugarcane was cultivated and consumed in Ũkamba from the Monsoon era to the colonial period. The cane is sweetest at the bottom of the stem, symbolizing the maturity and experience that comes with age.

730. *Kĩwa kĩĩla mũyo vakũũ.* **The sugarcane is sweeter at the oldest part.**
Nineteenth-century European explorers found sugarcane flourishing on Kamba farms. Sugarcane is indeed sweeter at the bottom with the sweetness fading towards the top. The proverb treasures the quality of older things.

731. *Kĩwa kĩtheke kĩtyĩ mĩnoo wĩsaa kĩte kyasũvye ĩndĩ kĩnene wĩsaa ĩvinda yĩasa.* **A thin sugarcane is effortless; you eat without chopping it but a big one you eat for a long time.**
Thin sugarcane here symbolizes attractive objects, persons, or lifestyles ultimately worthless. There are less attractive but sustainable choices worth pursuing. Similarly, select individuals can provide long-lasting friendship.

732. *Kĩwa kyanangawa nĩ waasa wa ngolwa.* **The excess length of the unpalatable long top end spoils sugarcane.**
Sugarcane is sweet and enjoyable but the top part, considered the life source, is less tasty. The same is true of life, with setbacks at all stages. This proverb calls for patience and understanding of such circumstances.

733. *Mũyo wa kĩwa wĩwĩkaa nĩ ũla ũkĩĩte.* **Someone who has tasted it knows the sweetness of sugarcane.**
This proverb emerged shortly after the introduction of sugarcane in Ũkamba. It generally means that no one can appreciate another's pleasure or pain.

734. *Kĩnze kĩ ndawa ta maanga.* **Music is vital like cassava.**
Although the cassava from the Amazon basin had spread inland as far as Uganda by the early nineteenth century, it did not become popular in Ũkamba until the 1920s.[26] From the 1930s, however, its cultivation gave the Kamba new fuel for axioms such as this one, with sexual overtones. This axiom from the second half of the twentieth century stresses the

---

[26] John Jameson (ed.), *Agriculture in Uganda* (Oxford: Oxford University Press, 1970); N. Simmonds (ed.), *Evolution of Crop Plants* (London: Longmann, 1976), 81–4; W.O. Jones, *Manioc in Africa* (Stanford: Stanford University Press, 1959); J.W. Purseglove, *Tropical Crops: Dicotyledons* (London: Longman, 1968).

importance of music and entertainment. The words *ndawa* (medicine) and *maanga* (cassava) are key historical markers in this proverb.

735. *Mũndũ ũtew'aa maanga me ũũ ew'aa matavĩka.* **One who does not sense the taste of bitter cassava senses vomit.**
To some this Vascon-era axiom refers to a community regarding endurance and patience as vital virtues. The Kamba raised their children to endure hardship in response to continual drought and famine. Another interpretation is that an arrogant person does not realize an approaching danger, only waking when catastrophe strikes.

736. *Mũyi wa maanga ndew'aa me ũũ.* **The consumer does not sense the bitterness of cassava.**
Several Kamba traditional stories credit characters who manifest perseverance and endurance, qualities that Kamba parents inculcate in their children.

737. *Yaanga nĩ mwĩnzĩle.* **Cassava is how you dig it out.**
This proverb means romance requires a lot of tricks and styles. It also applies to almost any other aspect of life requiring tact, diplomacy, and strategy. Clearly it emerged after several decades of experimenting with cassava cultivation in the early twentieth century.

738. *Yaanga ĩla ĩkũũ yĩthĩawa na mũyo mwiingĩ.* **Old cassava is the sweetest.**
This is a woman's proverb using cassava as a way to express sexual messages. It is a contestation against ageing. It suggests the older one grows, the more sexual she becomes and the more experience she brings.

739. *Yaanga yĩ mwene yĩingwa mũyo.* **Cassava with an owner is not sweet; go dig your own.**
Cassava symbolizes romantic relationships. This axiom tells a girl that a boy with another girlfriend is worthless, find your own boyfriend, and do not take other girl's.

740. *Kanywa ũla waĩsaa nthooko nowo wĩsaa nyama sya ngũkũ.*[27] **The mouth eating cowpeas is the same that eats chicken.**
This is a colonial-era coinage when consumption of cowpeas began to be taken as a sign of poverty, while chicken consumption represented the opposite. This inspirational proverb encourages the poor to believe that their situation will change for the better if they persist and persevere.

[27] Mwau, *Dictionary*, 648.

Crops and Other Plants 165

741. *Nzookonĩ vatyaa mbĩtĩa.*[28] **In cowpeas there lack no odd seeds.**
This old maxim means that there are always odd characters in all societies. The proverb dates back to the original cultivation of cowpeas in the first millennium. In a handful of cowpeas there were several odd seeds. The same with people, bear with their uncouth manners.

742. *Mbĩtĩa ndyũwaa andũnĩ.* **Oddities are never absent among humans.**
In every group of people there will always be an odd character, just as every handful of cowpeas contains bad seeds. This encourages communities to endure deviant behaviour and live with odd characters.

743. *Mbeũ mbĩthĩ ndĩtheleaa vamwe.* **Green seeds do not perish in one spot.**
People always find a way to escape danger. In the event of catastrophes in precolonial times entire families and settlements were wiped out. Survivors, however, rebuilt their populations and thrived.

744. *Wangangaa mathookonĩ na matakĩthĩnĩ ndwanganga mavembenĩ na mavumbũnĩ.*[29] **You have toured cowpeas and green-grams stands, but you have never been to corn and *Lablab purpureus* fields.**
This compares the novelty and appeal of introduced plants to scorn for old things. The speaker tells the listener, 'You are going too far. If you try me, you will see fury and fire.' Wandering about in cowpea and green-gram fields is a pleasure, but *mbũmbũ* and cornfields are itchy and uncomfortable to movement.

745. *Kĩtheete kĩsamaa nzũũ nziũ.* **A predestined tragedy tastes like green pigeon peas.**[30]
This concerns pigeon peas, a perennial legume that reached East Africa from India through the Monsoon Exchange as an important food crop. The word *kĩtheete* has previously confounded translation and interpretation. The proverb was coined in Machakos where the word can mean aggression (*kũ-thea*), or predestined misfortune. The common meaning therefore is that the beginning of a project can be easy and promising but the results shocking. Grandmothers said this to admonish girls about the pleasure of sex resulting in an unwanted pregnancy. More broadly, something that will breed misfortune entices the victim. Tragedy is hard to forestall. *Kĩtheete* refers to *kĩtai* – tragedy. In this context, the proverb is used in conflicts warning aggressors of the benefit of backing off. There is danger at the end of aggression.

[28] Mutisya, *Proverbs*, 23; Mbiti, *Weteelete*, 165.
[29] Kimilu, *Mũkamba*, 119.
[30] Watuma, *Syĩthĩo*, 53.

746. *Kĩng'oo kya ndũti kĩwĩkaa nĩ mũsũũ.* **The snore of a red ant is known by the pigeon peas.**
Ants build colonies on pigeon-pea plants and the Kamba maintained that the little ants snored. Sages argued that since one would find red ants sleeping on the pigeon-pea plant at night, only the plant could hear how much the ants snored. This is not literal but a symbolic way of saying those in love understand the reason for their love.

747. *Kwaa mwĩkathĩĩi kũyũwaa nzũũ nziũ.* **The braggart's home lacks no green pigeon peas.**
Families with pigeon peas were not only respected but were considered wealthy and progressive. It was not abnormal therefore for some people to boast how many pigeon peas they possessed.
Emerging at the same time as other proverbs related to this plant, it is a warning not to trust what others claim.

748. *Malaa onthe ti ma kanywa.* **Not all flowers end in the mouth.**
This emerged after the Kamba acquired pigeon peas. The pea plant produces flowers of different colours and fragrances before the seedpod develops. Bugs and blight attacked flowers and seedpods, ruining them before they produced edible peas. Hence, not every pea flower is destined for consumption, just as whatever the prospects of success, the end may be a failure.

749. *Malondu maaminie nzũũ mayĩwa maing'elela ũlũ.*[31] **The sheep finished the pigeon-pea plant since it was assumed they could not look up.**
This means the culprit may not always be obvious. That is, the Kamba blamed jumpy goats, not docile sheep, for mischief.

750. *Mĩsũũ ĩkũnanaa ĩla yĩanene.* **Green-pea plants of the same height beat each other.**
This can be taken as an admonition for peers to stick to their own age, status, and so on. People should respect those who are older and limit their exploits to their own age group. The same applies that elders should respect the young.

751. *Mũsũũ ũtũlawa nĩ kũsyaa mũno.* **A pigeon-pea plant is broken by overproduction.**
This maxim emerged from 1800 to 1900, for it talks about the burden of parenting too many children. In the remote past the Kamba bore on average five children per woman. It was noted that the more chil-

---

[31] Mwau, *Dictionary*, 654.

dren, the weaker she became physically and less capable of feeding the family.

752. *Nzũũ syaema ũsyaa syaisye sua yĩĩ ĩvyũ mũno.* **When pigeon peas fail to bear, they blame the hot sun.**
Extremely hot sun stymied pigeon-pea crop yields, hence this proverb about lame excuses. It was coined shortly after cultivation of pigeon peas became widespread across Ũkamba.

753. *Nzũũ syekalanga mũno syeeyetelilye kĩvooi.*[32] **Pigeon peas' procrastination brought them the blight.**
Pigeon peas were a delicacy across Ũkamba and widely cultivated. They sprout after the first rain, but do not mature until after the second. Within the intervening period, their pods often incurred blight. This proverb warns against procrastination as failure to perform at the right time usually leads to misfortune.

754. *Kĩumo kĩtambaa ta ũlenge mbuanĩ.* **A curse creeps like squash during rainy season.**
The squash, native to North America, reached Ũkamba during the Vascon era. It grew by spreading tentacles from the centre. The growing of this plant intersected with the social milieu including curses, which was believed to spread within a lineage like squash tendrils. The axiom warns of blunders that could become established and afflict other community members.

755. *Malenge maũtusya mbuanĩ maotaa na thano matakaw'ona.* **Squash harvested during the rainy season dreams of a dry season that will never come.**
This proverb means wherever one is and whatever he is doing, tomorrow will be different than today and dreams cannot be relied on. The squash's dream fails because it will be eaten before the hot season begins. It is important to point out that the right translation of *malenge* (singular, *ĩlenge*) is squash, not pumpkin as commonly translated. While pumpkins are mainly round, bigger, and yellow, squash have long oval shapes and range from green to a dotted mix of green and white.

756. *Mongũ ma ũvoya maikamasya mboka.* **Borrowed bottlegourds do not thicken the stew.**
Yũngũ, calabash or bottlegourd, reveals the historical connection between Africa and the rest of the world.[33] Careful selection of seeds

---
[32] Kimilu, *Mũkamba*, 118; Kĩeti, *Barking*, 105.
[33] Gayle Fritz (ed.), *Transoceanic Drift and the Domestication of African Bottle Gourds in the Americas* (St Louis: Washington University in St Louis, 2013), passim.

produced types suitable for canteens, dippers, ladles, and storage containers. The maxim warns against dependency. Cultivate your own food crops to enjoy life.

757. *Vai ndũũ ndauĩa mongũ.* **There is no friend I cannot cook bottle-gourds for.**
Fresh green bottlegourds are tender and tasty – hence by analogy friendships should be as tender as bottlegourds. The ancient maxim means the speaker can make friends with anyone or can overcome any obstacle.

758. *Yũngũ ĩvyũ ĩmanyĩkaa nĩ mũyi.* **A hot bottlegourd is known by the consumer.**
A bottlegourd is grown for its fruit, harvested young either to be consumed, or, when mature, dried and used as utensils. Seeds of dry bottlegourds were fried and eaten for their nutritional value. When fresh it was cooked and consumed warm. The axiom suggests the bottle-gourd is so hot it could scald the mouth of the unwary. One meaning is that only that person knows the conditions they are in. It rose in the age of farming.

11

Domesticated Animals

759. *Chaemie ala me mbya no aa me mĩthũkũ?* **It defeated the horned, how much more the hornless?**
This proverb originated in parts of Ũkamba and the Kamba diaspora where th letter /c/ is used in place of /k/ and /s/. As bullfighting emerged as a common pastime during the Vascon period, herdsmen believed that horned bulls were stronger than the hornless. The bigger, longer, and sharper the horns the better the bulls fought. If a horned bull beat other horned bulls, it was expected that the hornless would stand no chance against it. By extension, the poor cannot challenge wealthy people, and so on.

760. *Eka kũmbovea kasaũ suanĩ.* **Stop tying my calf in the scorching sun.**
This is another way of saying stop delaying my plans. Calves were tethered under shade while their mothers went to pasture. Family members who did not like each other tethered their opponents' calves in the sun so that they might suffer or even die.

761. *Ĩla ĩtindiĩte ndĩvataa ĩla yũngye kũya.* **The animal resting does not prevent one standing from browsing.**
Kamba goats and sheep usually came to rest under shade trees around noon. The herdsmen observed that some animals continued grazing, paying little attention to those resting. In the past it dealt with freedom to make individual choices. Go ahead with your plans despite what others are doing.

762. *Ĩla ĩkomete ĩtalawa ta ĩla ĩkũya.* **The resting animal is counted just as the browsing one.**
As the herdsman counted his animals, both browsing and resting beasts were counted the same way. The proverb calls for fair sharing of resources even if a member of a given community, family, or group was absent. It was an abomination to eat all the food, for example, without sparing some for absent siblings.[1]

---

[1] AIM, *Kĩkamba–English*, 54.

763. Ĩketũũwa yambĩyaa na ũkolotya. Before diarrhoea, it farts and blows frequently.
This refers to cattle frequently constipated or with diarrhoea. The latter was preceded by loud releases of gas. Do not ignore small things: they can build to major things. Particular cattle will show signs of oncoming diarrhoea. The alert leads to treating the problem early.

764. Ĩkombalasya mbya nĩ kũengeya ngongo. It twists horns to avoid crevasses.
As bulls grow older their horns twist from age. Likewise, people who live a long life do so because of avoiding things dangerous to their health, following the right lifestyles, observing good health practices, and avoiding life-threating situations. It also depends on luck. This proverb appears to have emerged during the twentieth century when gullies became common features of Ũkamba, something abundantly clear in environmental studies from across Africa.[2] The proverb provides a source material for environmental historians to gauge the age of gullies in Ũkambanĩ.

765. Ĩkũnoa ndĩ mũĩthĩlye. An animal destined to be fat has no special breeding.
The Kamba have always respected fat as part of their diet, and animals were usually fattened before slaughtering for feasts. The proverb arises from the observable fact that some animals take more work to fatten and others requir less. For humans, it means poor or hard backgrounds do not matter for one bound to succeed.

766. Ĩtalĩsa ĩsoma ndĩlĩsa moi. A bull that cannot mount old lean cows cannot mount youthful cows.
This justifies odd sexual behaviour. While it implies that a young man who cannot date an older woman cannot date a girl, its actual meaning is that anything can serve a given purpose.

767. Ĩla yĩna wĩnyeelo nĩyo ĩtwaa kĩtingũnĩ. The itchy one takes itself to the stump.
The Kamba kept livestock separated by a fence close to the home compound. In that animal space, there were many tree stumps. Itch-ridden animals used these stumps to scratch themselves. The proverb means that people in need of something must express their needs

---

[2] Jeremiah Kitunda, 'Culture and Social Erosion in Ũkambanĩ: The Disintegration of African Culture and Environment, 1889–1989', MA thesis (Miami University, 1998); Melissa Leach and James Fairhead, *Misreading the African Landscape* (Cambridge: Cambridge University Press), Passim.

clearly. Whoever is in need submits to the giver. This proverb is applied mostly during negotiations for bride price.

768. *Ĩla ĩkwenda mwana nĩyo yũkĩlasya mwĩthe.* **The one that needs a baby raises its tail.**
This proverb alludes to a cow in heat raising its tail to entice the bull. For humans it talks about submission or power relations between a giver and a receiver. The receiver stands on the lower end of the relationship and has to be acquiescent. This is used during dowry negotiations in which bridegrooms are the recipients in the relationship. He must sweet-talk would-be in laws and offer a fair price.

769. *Mũndũ ũte ng'ombe akinyaa kyaa kwa mũtũi endete kwa mũthoni.* **A man without cattle steps in dung at the neighbour's shed on his way to in-laws.**
This alludes to suitors who, wanting to marry a girl from a distant village, would try to impress the girl and her parents by not showering and visiting with cow dung reaching up to his knees. This would give the impression that the suitor had many cattle. A poor suitor tricked girls and parents by going to the cowshed of a neighbour to soil his feet and legs. The origin of this
custom (and the proverb) dates to the Vascon era. The proverb reflects the high premium that cattle acquired among the Kamba during the Vascon era. It means that there are multiple means to an end – so, be smart.

770. *Mũndũ ũte ng'ombe ndaendaa ũmbanonĩ wakũseũvya mũnanda.* **A man without cattle does not go to meetings for constructing cattle dips.**
This emerged from the late 1950s. The colonial regime required all cattle be inoculated against ticks and other disease and initiated dip construction projects. These were shallow and narrow concrete pools with acaride mixed in water to kill ticks. Only herders participated in the construction of cattle dips.[3]

771. *Mũlũngyo wa mũtwe ũsyaĩthasya moi.* **Mental intercourse sires [a] heifer.**
This has two interpretations. From the eighteenth century to the twentieth century, the heifer (*moi*) was seen as a good investment since it multiplied. The bull was worth five goats, while the heifer fetched ten goats in exchange. From the late twentieth century, bulls found their utility as working animals and sources of meat for butcheries and meat

[3] Richard Waller, '"Clean" and "Dirty": Cattle Disease and Control Policy in Colonial Kenya, 1900–40', *The Journal of African History* 45(1)(2004), 45–80.

factories that developed in various parts of Kenya, fetching higher prices. This proverb was a warning that one's aspirations and plans could backfire; his heifer might turn out to be a male.

772. *Mŭvakŭi wa ndewa e ĩvu ĩnene na asunĩte ota mŭvuvi wa mbwevwe.* **The castrator of bulls has a big belly and is as filthy as the flute blower.**
This is a hidden way to say the weaknesses you see in others are the same unacknowledged ones in you. In olden days castrated bulls were treasured for tender meat. The castrator was not paid but was given the scrotum to eat, which made him fat. He was dirty because of running over cow dung in the struggle with the bulls. On the other hand, a piper who entertained people played the instrument while seated on dusty ground, making him dirty.

773. *Mwene aingaa syakela.* **The owner crosses when the livestock crosses the path.**
Kamba herders did not lead their livestock but drove them from behind to ensure safety. They only crossed a path after all the animals had crossed. Coined during the Monsoon era this points to the head of the family who was responsible for the security and survival of his family. He slept last to ensure safety of his family members.

774. *Ndĩtŭlĩka kŭŭ ĩkaĩwa nĩ mŭthuĩle.* **It cannot break a leg and avoid limping.**
The hidden meaning is if one loses something valuable in a transaction, he gains treasure in return for it. It is said in regard to someone who has just given his daughter in marriage. The loss of the daughter is equated with a broken leg on the part of the parents, but in return they get bridewealth. It is noteworthy that the word *mŭthuĩle* means both limping and getting rich, and thus conceals the truth of the axiom from the novice.

775. *Noĩsyawa ĩtina na ĩkavĩlanya mbya.* **It can be born last but still twist its horns.**
This has many variations within the literature and oral circulation.[4] A bull can be born last but still grow to be bigger than its siblings, and with greater twisted horns. In life, a late start is not necessarily disadvantageous.

---

[4] Kituku, *Folktales*, 73; Mutisya, *Proverbs*, 5.

776. *Nĩwamĩkwatĩle mbyanĩ.*[5] **He seized it by the horns.**
This phrase has multiple interpretations. First, it means deal with difficult situations with determination and bravery. Second, it means: he is victorious for he tackled the problem directly. The phrase can also mean if speakers handled the hard part, listeners should finish the easy part.

777. *Wavingũaa mĩvĩĩya ĩlĩ esaa kwova na kĩtheko.*[6] **One who used to open two shed gates eventually tethers.**
From the 1650s to 1950s, all Kamba economic activities had the ultimate goal of acquiring livestock. Those who had just a few animals tethered them at home with ropes. As their number increased, they were put in a shed with one gate. If too many they were divided into multiple sheds or one large shed with multiple gates. This was the greatest display of wealth. Often the trend took a reverse direction. The proverb warns that a rich person should never be arrogant, and should handle his wealth carefully, knowing that fortunes change. Such changes and hence this proverb appeared between the 1880s and 1910s, years of the devastating rinderpest epidemic and famines. In 1891when rinderpest passed through Ũkamba those who owned five hundred head of cattle, for instance, had only five to ten left.[7] The ancient proverb gained currency during this period.

778. *Yemaa isyĩmbya tio isyĩmĩlungu.* **It withstands the horned, how much more the hornless ones.**
This is about power relations among animals and henceforth among humans. Kamba herders observed that horned bulls did better than the hornless in fighting others off. If they dominated the horned animals, it was assumed that they will have an easy time fighting the hornless. A person who has prevailed against greater odds should have an easy time with smaller challenges.

779. *Ndewa ngũũ yũkitaa na lelo.* **An old castrated bull fights with tactics.**
When oxen were castrated they became weaker than other bulls. To adjust to challenges they used stratagems rather than muscle, and always did well in a fight. Similarly, in a competitive world one can remain on top if he/she employs tactical skills.

---

[5] Kĩeti, *Barking*, 115.
[6] Kĩeti, *Barking*, 105.
[7] Lindblom, *Akamba*, 478.

780. *Nzaũ ngũũ ĩisolo na yũkitaa na syelelo.*[8] **An old bull has tricks and fights with stratagems.**
This ancient adage emphasizes the importance of strategy over strength. Using the symbolism of the sexuality of an old bull, the adage means experienced people approach difficult tasks with caution and so prevail. The older one grows so does his/her experience.

781. *Nzaũ yanasya yakomana na ĩla ĩngĩ.*[9] **A bull bellows when it meets another.**
From the Islamic period the Kamba raised large numbers of livestock with numerous bulls. The herdsmen loved to see them bellow and fight other bulls. This means people adapt different attitudes when they meet challenges, just as bulls bellow to challenge other bulls.

782. *Nzaũ ndyanasya ta ng'ombe nga, ĩkivaa ũkiva.* **A bull does not low like a cow, it bellows.**
This adage dates to the Islamic era when bulls came to symbolize power. It calls on leaders to assert their authority. Make firm decisions and show the way forward.

783. *Nĩnĩsĩ nesa ngelekanio ya Kĩkamba, ng'ombe ĩkuma ndĩthya yanĩsyaa kasaũ.* **I know well the Kamba example of a cow returning from the pasture lowing for the calf.**
This is a variation of the above, which should be kept separate. The two have a different structure and are used in different contexts.

784. *Ndanyuka mbola ĩsaa o kũmelya.*[10] **One that chews slowly eventually swallows.**
It is advisable to do things cautiously and at one's own pace, step by step, and eventually you will finish. Some use this maxim to advise young men that courting women should be done slowly.

785. *Yakũa ĩkũaa wia ndĩkũaa ĩtema.* **When it grows older, its fur ages not the liver.**
This means the liver of an old animal is still valuable. Symbolically, this means a woman can be sexually active even in old age, and young men can enjoy the same quality of sex offered by younger women.

---

[8] Kituku, *Folktales*, 28.
[9] Kimilu, *Mũkamba*, 118; Mutisya, *Proverbs*, 19.
[10] Lindblom, *Riddles*, 34; Farnsworth, *Grammar*, 4; Kimilu, *Mũkamba*, 117; Mailu, *Kkyambonie*, 14/71; Mũĩmi, *Kĩthyomo*, 21; Kĩeti, *Barking*, 112; Kituku, *Folktales*, 55; Mutisya, *Proverbs*, 4; Mwau, *Dictionary*, 663; Mbiti, *Ngaeka*, 90; Muiu, *Cross-Cultural*, 91.

786. *Sya kwaasa syĩĩaa mbũno.* **Animals from afar feed for satisfaction.**
Where water and pastures diminished near settled areas, herders drove animals over long distances to pasture and drink. Such animals browsed in haste, almost as if they were stocking fodder in their stomachs for the lean days. This maxim emerged during the Vascon era, when depletion of nearby pastures and water resources intensified as the Kamba accumulated more livestock. It admonishes the listener to take just enough for the day and not to worry about tomorrow.

787. *Syeeliwa mũĩthi syĩthĩawa syĩ mbau.*[11] **When they suspect the herder they are lost.**
Depending on pronunciation, *mbau* can mean 'ribs' or 'lost things' but here 'lost' is the right meaning. The proverb means people who do not trust their leaders are like flocks without a shepherd, left to stray in the wilderness.

788. *Syetĩka ũsĩnĩ syĩnũkaa na kasaũ.* **When they birth at the watering point they bring back a calf.**
This proverb reveals the history and manners of Kamba's animal husbandry before 1900. Animals were taken out to grazing areas and then driven considerable distance to watering points. This proverb can mean that a herd descending on a watering point could return with a stray calf. The deeper meaning is that animals mate at the watering point and thus take home a breed the herder never intended. Interaction with other cultures produce new influences. In-depth interviews revealed that this proverb emerged from a period called *Ĩvinda ya ũvoo* – the era of peace, a period of *peaceful trade* where traders were men of peace (*andũ ma ũvoo*) because as Kamba traders approached borders of other ethnic groups they held out grass. The other side did the same and laid down their weapons. The proverb exemplifies the fact that Kamba interaction with the coast, southern Ethiopia, and other parts of East Africa produced considerable cultural changes within Ũkamba.

789. *Nyamũ yĩ nondo yunawa nĩ nda.* **A beast with breasts benefits from the womb.**
Emerging in ancient precolonial times this appears to have encouraged childbearing. Mothers endure privation and aggravation raising their children, but once teenagers they become men of valour and women of repute, leading to marriage and grandchildren. Thus it means the mother who had rough times is rewarded by the womb.

---

[11] Kimilu, *Mũkamba*, 118.

790. *Mũĩthi wa naĩ ndakosaa kũya nyama syĩ mũthanga.* **A bad herder never failed to eat soiled meat.**
The herdsman's duty was to protect his livestock from predators. If he failed they were often killed by predators. The recovered animal was then cleaned to be eaten but the meat was usually
dirty. This is what the proverb means by 'he never fails to eat soiled meat'. This ancient proverb today advises employees to do their jobs properly lest they be fired.

791. *Mũĩthi wa ngũũe ndakĩaa mako.* **The herder of pigs does not fear filth.**
This originated from Machakos after colonial planters introduced hogs in 1904 and 1905. A serious outbreak of African swine fever in 1907 wiped out 90 per cent of the pig population. The industry revived in 1909. It is likely the maxim emerged shortly after 1964, when African farmers began to raise pigs.

792. *Mũĩthi wa indo ndekalaa nthĩ ateũsemba semba.*[12] **The cow herdsman cannot sit down without also having to run.**
If a herdsman sits down in the shade for a moment to rest, he definitely has to run to catch up with the herd. The axiom is a warning not to let things get out of control: do not get behind in your work. The axiom emerged in the Islamic period when the keeping of livestock intensified.

793. *Mũĩthi atĩĩya thuva nake mũsyĩmi atĩĩyaa ũlaso.* **A shepherd tracks hoofprints, while the hunter follows blood trail.**
If animals strayed, herders were able to track their own animals for long distances by recognizing individual hoofprints called *thuva*. Similarly, hunters followed blood trails to track wounded game. Emerging during the Vascon era and now common in political songs, this proverb means that politicians go where the votes are.

794. *Syaa ngomya vaasa.*[13] **They lodged me far away.**
Stray animals may wander so far the herder must sleep for the night on their trail. Nothing in the statement is literal but rather coded erotic language. Marriages took people far from their homes.

795. *Syũaa vala syĩĩ.* **Where they exist, they stray.**
Although the word *syũaa* refers to *indo* (livestock), which often strayed, it can also refer to other possessions. The ancient proverb means that unless one has livestock, one cannot lose them. It is a way of persuading people to accept the reality of loss.

---

[12] Kaleli, 'Christian Cross-Cultural', 63–6.
[13] Kimilu, *Mũkamba*, 118.

796. *Mũlungu nũlungũkaa katune akakamwa nũngĩ.* **God asserts His majesty so that someone else milks the red cow.**
This means things may change in favour of those previously disadvantaged. *Katune* (little red) is a common name for a milk cow because of its reddish colour. One interviewee said that the proverb was told to a daughter-in-law whose gift of a milk cow was being revoked and given to another daughter-in-law. This proverb then serves to study colours and shapes of cattle in ancient times.

797. *Nzele mbũĩ iingĩanĩsyaa ng'ombe nasyakwatana ĩkwathukanga itiwe ikwalĩkania.* **A wise chap instigates bulls to fight, and then steps away leaving them to butt each other.**
This was sung by Kiwmele wa Mutava during a *mũkanda* dance in the 1970s. The proverb points to people who cause strife between two friends and leaves them to sort out their disagreement. However, the proverb may stretch back to the age when the Kamba not only raised bulls but started bullfighting.

798. *Vandũ vaĩĩ ng'ombe yĩũkilũ vayũwaa ũkilũ ũngĩ.* **Where there was a milky-coloured cow there is always another milky-coloured cow.**
The Kamba owned cattle in many colours, from which most names derived. This proverb implies that the milky-coloured cows were a strong breed. Even if the colour disappears in the herd it later reappeared. Dating from antiquity the proverb means family traits endure.

799. *Woona ĩteanĩsya kasaũ nĩyongisye.* **If it does not low for the calf, it has been fed already.**
When a cow returns from pasture it lows for its calf. If it does not it signifies that it has nursed the calf. This was coined in the first millennium: no complaints means one is satisfied.

800. *Woona yeana yĩ mũvakũi.* **When it grows, it has a castrator.**
This is a bull that becomes hard to subdue for castration. A champion is symbolized in this statement, but foremost the axiom points out that certain things must not be left until they get out of hand. Even children get to a point where they cannot easily take orders from parents.

801. *Woona ĩkũtĩsya manya veo mũthenya wĩkya ĩkime.* **If you see it threatening there is a day it will gore.**
Lindblom reported that fierce cattle trying to butt were made harmless by the following process, undoubtedly of a magic character. First, a night-jar's feathers and skeleton were burnt and the ashes put in water to be given to the animal to drink. Alternatively, the eggs of this bird

were thrown at the animal that is to be cured of its bad habit. This magical process of making animals tractable is called *kŭvovya*.[14]

802. *Mŭingi wa ĩsoma ndanoaa.* **The driver of a weak animal does not tire.**
This concerns patience for slow learners and difficult members of family or community. Pragmatism and patience are needed in dealing with challenging but potentially beneficial matters. One may choose the unsuitable in the absence of the preferable.

803. *Mŭndŭ ŭtaya ĩsoma ti mŭiyi wa nyama.* **A man who cannot eat lean beef is not a meat consumer.**
This proverb speaks of meat consumption during the Monsoon era. The Kamba consumed considerable amounts of both wild and domesticated meat. Most Kamba believed consuming fat meat nourished them more than lean. However, this ancient proverb employs meat as a symbol of romantic behaviour, implying that someone who never dates ugly women is not a suitor, a sentiment advocating a balanced life. The axiom also cautions strong and wealthy people to be considerate towards the meek and the weak.

804. *Mbee wa ng'ombe vaiĩ nyeki mbothu.*[15] **Before cattle, there is no excessive grass.**
This emerged during the Islamic period. Many parts of Ũkamba were treeless grasslands according to traditions. Introduction of livestock diminished grass and brought about
regeneration of trees and bushes. The maxim is saying that anything frequently used will be exhausted soon, just as persistent grazing depletes grass.

805. *Vayĩ nyama ĩsamaa tengĩ ng'ombenĩ.* **No meat parts taste like others in a cow.**
This appeared in a political song claiming that politicians are different and proposing different strategies. It has precolonial precedents dating to the first millennium. The Kamba distinguished and gave symbols to different meat parts. Some were not eaten, others preferred, and all tasted different. As the singer said, there are hooves, gullet, and another called 'do not chop me that dead part'.

---

[14] Lindblom, *Akamba*, 496.
[15] Mailu, *Kĩkyambonie*, 14, 71.

806. *Mwenda mũka nĩ kũvatha ng'ombe.* **A man who desires a wife must produce cattle.**
To marry, an exchange of cattle was required. The term *kũvatha ng'ombe* (select cattle) refers to going into a cattle shed to select cattle for dowry. One had to do so to get a wife. Tracing from the Monsoon era, this maxim means life is about give and take.

807. *Ngi ĩmwe nĩyo yowasya nyama.* **Only one fly spoils the whole meat.**
This adage appeared in several publications and in oral accounts. It points out that a bad person can damage the reputation of a large group.[16] It takes a single person or a single simple action to spoil big plans, in the same way a single fly induces bacteria into a carcass that soon starts rotting.

808. *Syakũmwe syĩtulanasya syĩkaa kũthauka.* **Animals of the same shed do not gore each other, they only play.**
This is about a mixed basket of conflict, reconciliation, and forgiveness in a community. Animals caged together tend to make friends and fight less. This means villagers should not fight but cooperate.

809. *Sya mũtavo syendaa nongĩ.* **Raided livestock often depart with a counter-raid.**
This proverb encodes a tripartite structure of cattle rustling among the Kamba, Kwavi, and Galla in southeastern Kenya from the 1600s to the1900s. One of the three could rustle cattle but, before they could rest, raiders from another community would drive the animals away. Octogenarian eyewitnesses of such episodes clearly collaborated this story.

810. *Syaawa na mĩomo ya nyũmba.* **Livestock is shared according to the house doors.**
When an elder passed away his livestock was shared among his wives (house doors). Each wife was given an equal share of the livestock to distribute to her sons.

811. *Mĩomo ya nyũmba ndĩmelanasya na ndyotanĩaa mwaki.* **The doors of households do not swallow each other and do not warm themselves together.**
In polygamous marriages, two households cannot use each other's resources, except through mutual exchange. With multiple wives, each wife had to have her own house and kitchen as no woman shared a

---

[16] Farnsworth, *Grammar*, 26; Kimilu, *Mũkamba*, 17, 117; Kituku, *Folktales*, 20; Mwau, *Dictionary*, 665; Mutisya, *Proverbs*, 35.

cooking stove with another. Each wife had her own animals and farm. They were living in the same compound but leading different lives. Such proverbs ensure separation of responsibilities and division of family obligations and resources.

812. *Syalisya inyusaa muuluũ.* **Those coming last drink muddied water.**
Kamba free-range livestock were driven to a watering point such as a particular part of a river (*isyuko*) or a water pan. The animals simply walked into the water to drink. In the process, they urinated, excreted, and stirred up mud so that soon the water was almost a broth. For the cattle arriving last the drinking water was already turned muddy by earlier arrivals. The proverb warns that if people take a backseat to life they will live on leftovers or worse.[17]

813. *Syanyiiva syũanĩa mũkũũ mũnini otiwa omanzĩwa.* **When the animals are few, they pay dowry for the eldest son.**
In the old days it was the parents' responsibility to pay their sons' dowries. Whenever parents had less livestock than needed to pay dowry for more than one son at once, priority was given to the older of the two. This proverb emphasizes the significance of prioritization.[18]

814. *Tisya atavi nĩ sya atavĩwa, nĩsyumaa ũkavi ĩkethĩa ene.* **They are not for rustlers, but for beneficiaries of rustling; they often come from Kwavi only to find new owners.**
The term *atavĩwa* can mean both beneficiaries of booty or victims who have been raided. These proverbs emerged between 1600 and 1800, a period of engagement with Kwavi and Galla cattle rustlers. The word 'they' refers to livestock. The message is that livestock rustlers do so to enrich their families more than themselves.

815. *Kavaa ĩsoma yaku kũte kĩtũũ kya mũka waku.* **Better your weakling cow than your wife's herds.**
This is a mother-to-son proverb, with the mother advising her son that his property is better than his wife's opulence. If they divorced the woman took her wealth with her, leaving the man in poverty. Western attitudes have silenced such gender power relationships. It is generally assumed that Kamba women had no economic or political power. Yet Kamba women had more economic and political power than their husbands as prophetesses, healers, wizards, and leaders. Interestingly,

---

[17] Farnsworth, *Grammar*, 106; Kimilu, 118; Kituku, *Folktales*, 2; Mutisya, *Proverbs*, 3; Mwau, *Dictionary*, 667; Mbiti, *Weteelete*, 91.
[18] Lindblom, *Akamba*, 78.

they did not carry their husbands' names, yet such men were respected and proud of their wives' success.

816. *Kavaa kũvundĩsya ng'ombe kũĩma, kũte kũvundĩsya mũndũ mwĩkalĩle.* **Better to train oxen how to plow than to teach a man how to behave.**
This dates to the introduction of the plow in Kenya and the decline of morality in Ũkambanĩ in the 1910s and 1920s. During these early years of the plow the Kamba practised plowing on settler farms, but plowing only became widespread after the Second World War.[19]

817. *Vala syokitĩa nyeki nĩyo yũmĩaa.* **Where bulls fight, the grass suffers most.**
This is an adage found in many African languages, to persuade parents and leaders to minimize conflict. Children (grass) under a parent's (bulls) care or community members under the suzerainty of the leaders are the ones that suffer. Similar to a Zulu proverb (When elephants fight only the grass suffers) that only appeared in the eighteenth century, this axiom goes back beyond the 1600s.

818. *Vala ya kwoko yakinya nĩvo ya kũũ ĩkinyaa.*[20] **Where the front leg steps so does the hind leg.**
When a cow is walking the hind hooves step where the front hooves stepped. The proverb warns to avoid establishing a bad precedent. If the first-born performs well in life his younger siblings follow the same trend. Parents and leaders should also provide good examples for the young to follow. This axiom has multiple variations.[21]

819. *Mũkamba nĩ indo, ngisũ syĩvata na ameũkunda ĩthumo.*[22] **Cattle are valuable for those who love milk.**
By most accounts, this proverb emerged during the Vascon era when obsession with livestock intensified. As Charles Dundas remarked, the greatest pride and joy was a man's cattle, and nothing could equal them in his estimation.[23] Consumption of dairy and beef products was believed to be behind longevity for most precolonial Kamba. Cattle were almost sacred.

---

[19] John English, Mary Tiffen, and Michael Mortimore, *Land Resource Management in Machakos District, Kenya, 1930–1990* (Washington: World Bank, 1994), 48.
[20] Kimilu, *Mũkamba*, 118; Mbiti, *Weteelete*, 96.
[21] Kituku, 62, 119; Mutisya, *Proverbs*, 29.
[22] Kimilu, *Mũkamba*, 22.
[23] Charles Dundas, 'History of Kitui', *Journal of the Royal Anthropological Institute of Great Britain and Ireland* 43 (1913): 480–549.

820. *Ya mũka ndyoneka nĩ mbiti.* **A cow for dowry is never seen by hyena.**
Herdsmen said this when livestock spent a night in the wilderness and wandered home in the morning without being attacked by hyenas. The proverb shows that the ultimate goal of raising livestock was to exchange it for a bride – it denotes a sense of predestination, and determination to survive.

821. *Yanĩsyaa vala yovewe kasaũ.* **It moos where its calf is tethered.**
The Kamba would separate calves from their mothers during the night and reunite them after milking. The calves were often tethered on trees during the daytime. The cow will then moo, facing where its calf was tethered. This maxim was said during bride price negotiations referencing favours that in-laws had to do for the parents of the girl.

822. *Yatulw'a ĩtulasya ĩngĩ.* **When an animal is butted, it knocks another.**
This proverb emerged during the Vascon era during negotiations for bride price. If the groom's father does not have the resources, he can charge the price needed on to families where his daughters are married. During debt disputes among traders a trader with an overdue debt passed it on to those for whom he had advanced credit.

823. *Ya ũkw'a nĩ ya ũkw'a onekakima wuti.*[24] **The one fated to die will surely die.**
The Kamba observed that sometimes a predator will prowl as close as possible without the prey showing signs of alertness. Hunters could crawl close to game without difficulty. In its deeper context, it means some people are so devoid of foresight that they cannot detect when plans are not working and are doomed to fail.

824. *Yenda mũno nĩnyenyaa ĩkatila mũkaũtĩ.*[25] **If it loves too much it licks to the point of cutting the umbilical cord.**
Emerging from antiquity the proverb in all its varied forms calls for balance between parental love and children's discipline, desire, and responsibility.

825. *Yambo ĩmwe ĩitumwa ũa ũtoma.*[26] **One peg cannot stop a hide from drying up.**
Wet skins (after slaughtering) were spread on the ground and pegged down at many spots to keep the skin stretched out. The pegs were

---

[24] Mwau, *Dictionary*, 672.
[25] Kimilu, *Mũkamba*, 119; Kĩeti, *Barking*, 110; Kituku, *Folktales*, 79.
[26] Kimilu, *Mũkamba*, 119; Mutisya, *Proverbs*, 25.

called *syambo*. By interpretation a single blunder cannot put on hold an entire project.

826. *Walea ũvũnĩa nyama ĩthĩĩ syavika mũsyĩ syĩvũnika.* **If you do not eat enough meat at the slaughter you will not be satisfied at home.** This talks of exploiting opportunities at hand to secure one's future. When hunters trapped or killed a large animal, meat was indiscriminately eaten on the spot. Once it was shared and taken home there was no more.

827. *Mũndũ aitawa nĩ nyama ĩla yĩ nzelenĩ.* **One is choked by the meat in the calabash bowl.**
The proverb dates back to the Monsoon era of herding and farming gourds. Greedy people choked trying to chew fast enough to grab more from the plate.[27] The axiom advises that one should tackle the matter at hand before rushing to something else.

828. *Nyamũ ngaathĩnza ndimyonasya kavyũ.* **I do not show the knife to an animal that I will slaughter.**
This proverb means that the speaker does not rush into matters he knows will be dealt with successfully. It may also mean that the speaker will not tell his secrets to an opponent whom he plans to overwhelm in competition. However, in the most common interpretation, the symbolic meaning is that the speaker does not reveal his emotions since he knows he has already won the girl's friendship.

829. *Nyamũ nzyau ndĩkosaa manina.* **An animal that has given birth lacks no mucus.**
This ancient axiom alludes to the mucus that female cows excrete after birth. It means there is always chain effects in every action we take. There are demerits that come with benefits. Some people interpret this as meaning that one must be bold in certain circumstances.

830. *Nyamũ ĩte mwĩthe ĩlũngaw'a ngi nĩ Ngai.* **God whips flies off a tailless animal.**
The Kamba believed that the crucial purpose of a tail in animals was to whisk off flies and other bugs. While some animals had long tails, others were tailless. However, flies rarely bothered the latter. The Kamba rationalize the absence as an act of God.

---

[27] Mutisya, *Proverbs*, 66.

831. *Ve kũvuva yakane na ve kũvuva ĩvoe.*[28] **There is blowing out and kindling.**
This was popularized by Mutisya wa Ngai in the early 2000s to talk about hypocrisy and deception. While it mentions two forms of blowing on fire, one to kindle it and the other to blow it out, it figuratively refers to sexual relations between men and women. A woman may think her lover is keen on marriage while the man is only interested in sexual satisfaction. Beyond this, Mutisya explained, some people may promise to help you, but in reality fail to help.

832. *Yenda maa ĩthongaa iko.*[29] **When it desires spots, it throws itself into the fire.**
Kĩeti and Coughlin (1990) interpreted this to mean if one heeds wise advice all well and good, but if one does not he/she is doomed to perish. There are more ways of applying it. It implies that ill-fated people always get themselves into trouble. Spots symbolize beauty and tragedy at the same time.

833. *Yenda mũno yĩũlũkaa yĩkathi ũvuĩla mĩw'anĩ.* **When it craves too much, it flies and perches on thorns.**
This refers specifically to a kite, which craving for the chicken flies so fast that it tragically lands on thorn trees. Dating from the Monsoon era, the proverb calls for a balance between desire and ethical responsibility.

834. *Yakũa ndĩkũaa ĩtema.* **When it ages, the liver does not age its own liver.**
This refers to a bovine to be eaten no matter its age, for the liver will always be nutritious. However, the hidden meaning is erotic. Initially it suggests that sexuality does not cease or decline with age among women. While speakers agree that *yakũa* refers to the cow, this applies to any animal with a liver.

835. *Ve ndeto ithonokete ng'ombe.*[30] **There are words that go beyond cattle.**
Originating in the tenth and eleventh centuries with cattle herding among the Kamba this proverb explores the relationship between materialism and morality. Cattle were exchanged for a bride, but one had to balance his words before in-laws. If one was not kind and noble to a bride's parents the engagement was terminated because cattle were not meant as payment but as a token of sealing a covenant of friendship between two families.

---

[28] Mutisya wa Ngai, 'Kyuo kya Ngoso, number 16'.
[29] Kĩeti, *Barking*, 107; Mutisya, *Proverbs*, 66.
[30] Mailu, *Kĩkyambonie*, 58.

Domesticated Animals 185

836. *Ũtumo wĩ ivĩsĩ weeiwe ndwĩsaa ũkũĩa mũtumĩa wa kwĩvakwa, akũaa ithukĩ asũnzũmele.* **A settlement with boys never matures a trustworthy elder, he pulls out stumps squatting.**
This is said of individuals who regardless of age still act immaturely. It is the worst insult that can be said about a man among the Akamba. The word 'elder' refers to both sexes.[31]

837. *Vaiĩ yanasya ũtumo ũmwe myaka yonthe.*[32] **None bellows on one ridge forever.**
Kamba villages before 1900 were demarcated by ridges, each with a chief bull replaced by younger ones over time. The proverb therefore means that no one remains famous forever. New heroes and heroines are constantly born and rise to replace old ones.[33]

838. *Vaiĩ ĩtewa ndĩnenũka.*[34] **There is none that cannot be said 'it has not returned home'.**
Every homestead had a dominant bull as a symbol of family strength and economic stability. From the Monsoon era, whenever such a bull died the household head pondered and recited the above proverb. It could also be said in burial ceremonies for village champions equated with bulls.

839. *Mumanĩsya ndĩthya na mũthoni ndaasyaa kĩmboloa.* **One who alternates herding duties with in-laws does not give barren cows for dowry.**
If one lets the father-in-law tend the livestock it gives the father-in-law an opportunity to assess the son-in-law's wealth and demand the best of the herd as dowry. This proverb reveals the underlying deception involved in paying dowry. The best animals were not given to in-laws. The maxim tracing back to the Vascon era indicates that someone who knows you well cannot be deceived.

840. *Ndũkakũlye kũsyaiwe kĩ wangĩĩye kyengonĩ.* **Do not ask what was born since you are approaching the ranchlands.**
This was coined in the 1700s when the Kamba developed the system of taking cattle to ranches for breeding. Upon hearing of the birth of a calf, family members travelled to the ranch to see the newborn. People joked do not ask whether the calf is male or female, we will know once we get there.

---

[31] Mwau, *Dictionary*, 660.
[32] Mailu, *Kĩkyambonie*, 16, 59, 71.
[33] Kĩeti, *Barking*, 112; Kituku, *Folktales*, 24; Mwau, *Dictionary*, 670.
[34] Mwau, *Dictionary*, 670; Watuma, *Syĩthĩo*, 58.

841. *Ndŭkavĭvye kyengo ŭthama.* **Do not burn the camp on your exit.**
Based on oral accounts and documented estimates this emerged during the Vascon era, when increased livestock numbers and decline of pasture nearby necessitated grazing away from settled areas. Ranching camps were set on the most suitable spot for the herdsmen to live. It was a taboo to burn, urinate, or defecate on the ground when taking off as its ground was now sacred by being trampled on by cattle as they multiplied and fattened. Usually as herdsmen broke camp they offered tobacco, milk, and water to that ground and prayed to spirits there to give the humans and their animals a safe journey.

842. *Nzaa ndĭsĭ mbŭi ya ŭko.*[35] **Hunger does not know the lineage of the goat.**
Hunger does not allow one to choose which type of goat to eat or sell. In a flock, some animals were designated for specific purposes. Such animals were not to be slaughtered or sold but hunger often pushed people to break those laws to survive. When a famine strikes goats are sold to procure food, regardless of significance.

843. *Ĭlondu yevulĭlye kavyŭ iko.* **The sheep revealed the knife in the kitchen.**
A family wanted to slaughter a ram for dinner but had misplaced the knife, concealed under the ash in the kitchen, but the sheep scratching the ash revealed the knife and thus surrendered its life. The proverb means foolishness leads to self-injury so think and act with caution. Sheep were among the earliest animals that the Kamba domesticated.[36]

844. *Ĭlondu yŭaa mbisŭ na mŭlungu.* **A sheep breaks the pots with its hornless head.**
This ancient proverb appearing in varied forms in oral accounts and literature means that everyone has a potential to do the unexpected.[37] Just as the hornless ewe more often than the horned goat breaks clay pots, individuals who may appear unequal to the task may be perfectly capable. Goats often invaded houses to lick pots, but because the mouth of pots are usually narrow, their horns would not allow them to get out; so, they would shake the pot hard, eventually breaking it. Whenever the Kamba saw broken pots they would blame the goats, little suspecting the sheep could do it.

---

[35] Mwau, *Dictionary*, 667.
[36] Kĭeti, *Barking*, 109; Mwau, *Dictionary*, 647.
[37] Kimilu, *Mŭkamba*; Mutisya, *Proverbs*, 14; Mwau, *Dictionary*, 647; Kĭeti, *Barking*, 112.

845. *Ĩtulasya mbisũ yĩnamĩte.* **It knocks pots when its face is downcast.**
This ancient axiom tells the listener: never underestimate the meek. Shep are considered meek and less aggressive than goats, but they have higher potential to damage things than people suspect.

846. *Inyaa ndũũme nde mbya.* **The mother of a ram has no horns.**
This adage trace back to the Monsoon era during which period the Kamba bred hornless female sheep with thinner tails than the fatty ones of her male offspring with attractive horns. This means heroes can come from humble backgrounds.

847. *Malondu kwĩ mbua mathekawa nĩ mbũi.* **Goats jeer at the sheep during the rains.**
Kamba observed sheep and goats' different behaviour and concluded that one was cleverer than the other. During the rain, sheep with their wool soak up wetness while rainwater runs down the goats' skin.

848. *Mbee no mũlungu ta mboya ya ĩ ndũũme.*[38] **The future is in the hands of God like the prayer of a ram.**
This involves a story of spiritual competition between the cock and the ram. A farmer who kept all kinds of animals invited a friend for dinner. They had a good time. After the dinner, and as the guest was ready to leave, the host made a promise: 'Next time you come', he said, 'we will have this ram for your banquet.' Many days passed and at last the visitor came. Since the cock and the sheep were kept in the same enclosure, the ram was always urinating on the cock. In response, the cock crowed repeatedly, saying, 'When will the dawn come, so that this ram will be slaughtered?' Every time the cock hurled these insults, the ram responded, 'The future is in the hands of God.' At daybreak, the guest made a plea, 'My friend, why should we waste such a fine ram on a feast? I suggest you slaughter the cock.' The host agreed and the cock faced the knife in place of the ram. The moral lesson of the proverb, from the early 1900s, is that people should not delight in the demise of others. The future is unknown to all of us.

849. *Mũingi wa ĩlũnga ndanawa na wia.* **The driver of sheep lacks no wool.**
A driver of sheep gets a bit of its wool, which translates as people whom we interact with give a bit of their character to us. If you associate with enterprising people you will become an entrepreneur. Similarly, if you stay with odd characters you will get a bit odder.

---

[38] Mũĩmi, *Kĩthyomo*, 33.

850. *Mũĩthi wa malũnga anyungaa otamo.* **A shepherd of sheep stinks like them.**
The shepherd indeed smells like his sheep. Therefore, if one keeps bad company they will contract bad habits.

851. *Mũĩthi wa mbũi ndowaa waia kĩtimba.* **A shepherd does not lack wool on his hips.**
This says a good shepherd is one who had sexual intercourse with sheep and is said in tense moments to mean the most fitting is the most daring.

852. *Mũndũ ũte mbũi anengawe mĩkamo.* **One who has no goats is fed on udder.**
The Kamba had a structured custom of meat consumption. Some sections of an animal were for different age sets, men, women, the rich and elders, some for dogs, birds of prey, wild animals, and spirits. Disliked people were often given what the owner would not consume such as the udder. This ancient axiom reflects the extremes that poverty can push someone to, since the udder is a piece of meat for no worthy person.

853. *Katena kathi ndĩthya kakũnawa ta mbũi ngima.* **When a kid goes to pasture it is beaten like a mature goat.**
Shepherds carried a whip to urge goats along or to keep them from straying. Kids were not beaten, but if they joined the flock they were treated like other goats. This maxim means if one indulges in serious matters they should expect the repercussions that come with their decisions.

854. *Ate mũthee ndetawa kĩveti.* **Before she is cleansed she is not called a wife.**
This ancient proverb alludes to Kamba marriage customs, specifically the prerequisite *kuthea mwiitu*, to clear a girl. The process has been described in the next entry. The maxim is spoken at certain critical junctures and plainly means a woman is not one's wife if this preliminary custom is not fulfilled. The couple may have as many children as they want, acquire as much property as
they can, but until this seemingly minor rite, *ntheo*, is cleared, the woman is not the wife. He cannot even bury her if she dies.

855. *Kĩka kĩivingĩaa kĩngĩ.* **The female does not lock in another female.**
Once a man married he was duty bound to pay in-laws seven goats. Of the seven one must be male, which is killed to close in or lock out the remaining six. This process was the *Kũthea mwĩĩtu,* the six goats the

ntheo. This was a crucial part of paying bride price and must be done before the traditional marriage certificate was completed.

856. *Kũũ tũkwongesya ngenge nokw'o mũkwongesya makũmũ?* **Are you nursing weaned babies, where we are nursing infants?**
This old proverb means that things should conform to their correct order and proper place, time, and status. Kamba women preferred to nurse different age sets of babies separately in feeding infants and weaned babies. However, the maxim really was a challenge to someone ignoring protocol: follow established procedures and the general order of things. The axiom appears to have emerged during the Monsoon era after settlement and creation of a social order in Ũkamba.

857. *Mũsyĩ ũ te tũtena ndwĩ mbũi.* **A home without kids has no goats.**
This derisive statement means that in families where there are no children, men have either stopped procreation or are simply impotent. This is mockery, sarcasm, and a reflection on the centrality of procreation in Kamba world milieu.

858. *Ndiyĩaa mbũi kũnoa.* **I do not eat a goat because it is fat.**
As early as the first millennium, the Kamba were raising goats for economic and social purposes. The Kamba ate only the fattest in the flock leaving the lean to fatten. This maxim states the opposite: a lean goat is as good as a fat one. Sometimes an object can serve a given desire regardless of its quality.

859. *Ũkaema ona mbũi nziũ mũthenya ona ũtukũ ndũmyona.* **If you cannot see a black goat during the day, you cannot see it at night.**
This deeply figurative statement is open to manifold interpretations. If one cannot accomplish simple things at the opportune time, they cannot achieve anything in difficult times.

860. *Ndũkavundĩsye mbũi kwĩna ndanzi.* **Do not teach a goat how to dance.**
This is a more recent proverb, appearing in popular songs and posters in the 1970s. It means there are people who are unteachable. Do not waste time, energy, and resources in ventures that cannot bear beneficial returns. The word *ndanzi* is a Kamba corruption of the English 'dance'. This new form of music featured new rhymes and movements. Participants had to learn how to do it. Since some people never managed to dance properly, trainers coined this maxim in frustration.

861. *Thoosya mbũi ĩ mbaika.*[39] **Sell a goat while it is a doeling.**
Younger animals were preferred in trade because they would bear more offspring than older animals, an attitude dating to the eighteenth century and hence the proverb.

862. *Mbũi nga ĩkũlĩsa nthenge ĩlĩsĩlaa ndee.* **A she-goat mounts a buck on the sides.**
Female goats do not normally mount he-goats. When they do, the Kamba say, they mount on the sides or awkwardly. This maxim appeared in a song performed by women political singers, meaning a person who will ruin community affairs begins to commit small political blunders.

863. *Mbũi ngeni ĩkũvawa matũ nĩ ila ngũũ kĩtũũnĩ.* **A new goat is fucked in the ears by the older ones in the pen.**
By interpretation this axiom dating from the first millennium means a sojourner is exploited in foreign lands and newcomers are harassed by experienced veterans.

864. *Mbũi ya mana ndĩsiawa wia.* **One does not inspect the fur of a gift goat.**
This axiom is similar to, 'Do not look a gift horse in the mouth.'[40] The receiver of a gift ought to receive it as a symbol of gratitude, not as a thing to be used or deployed in the usual way.
Goats sometimes lost their wool due to skin disorders. These made poor gifts, though it was not acceptable for the recipient to complain about it. This points again to the underlying economics of the gift: its meaning as a gift is tied closely to the size of the sacrifice made in giving it away. Whenever the maxim is uttered, it implies that the gift is of low quality but a very welcome tentative solution to the problems of the recipient.

865. *Mbũi yĩ mwana ndĩsawa ũ mwana nĩwe ũthĩnzawa.* **A goat with a kid is not eaten, the kid is eaten.**[41]
This proverb provides moral and ethical guidance in dealing with domesticated and wild animals. Female game and their young ones were not to be shot and killed. At home, adult livestock were not killed or sold, selling their offspring being more desirable. It made economic sense to leave female animals alone to nurse their babies and their young in order to increase the wealth of the community. It can also apply to children helping parents. As they grow and help the parents with domestic chores, satisfied parents repeat this statement.[42]

[39] Kimilu, *Mũkamba*, 118.
[40] Henry Hart, *Seven Hundred Chinese Proverbs* (Stanford: Stanford University Press, 1937), xxv.
[41] Kimilu, *Mũkamba*, 18, 116; Kituku, *Folktales*, 49.
[42] Kimilu, *Mũkamba*, 18, 116; Kituku, *Folktales*, 49.

866. *Mbũi yũwaa mbisũ vala yovawa.*[43] **A goat breaks pots where it is tethered.**
This proverb encodes cultural practices rarely found in historical texts. Precolonial Kamba tethered some special goats (for ritual purposes) under their beds. The goats often invaded areas of the house where pots were kept, often breaking them, as they searched for food rich in iron and salts. This custom dates from the Monsoon era, as does the proverb. It means an influential person affects the area he hails from. It may also mean damages occur at the epicentre of activity.

867. *Kavyũ ka mũeni kaithĩnzaa mbũi.*[44] **A guest's knife does not skin a goat.**
This proverb refers to the belief that if one slaughtered a goat with a visitor's knife, a precedent would be established where anyone will bring a knife to one's home and slaughter all the goats in that household. This emerged during the Vascon era when goats became central to Kamba customs and were frequently slaughtered for meat.

868. *Mbũi ĩĩsawa na kyaa kyamwene.* **A goat is eaten with the owner's index finger.**
This ancient maxim was applied during bride price negotiations when the groom's side had a disagreeable opinion. Whenever one killed a goat for guests, it was he who directed which part should be served to each person. This means leave final decisions to those directly responsible.[45]

869. *Mbũi ndĩtumwaa ũsyaa mavatha nĩ kwekewa ĩtuuva.* **Letting a goat have *Ĩtuuva* (*Grewia similis*) bush does not cause it to bear twins.**
If a goat gave birth to twins, the whole family celebrated. Yet a goat does not bear twins because of eating vines. Good results are often a matter of strategy, luck, and fate.[46]

870. *Vala mbũi ivatawa nĩvo syendaa, syĩvata na kwĩthongo nzũinĩ.*[47] **Goats go where you block them; they love to plunge themselves into the wolves.**
This axiom uses goats to show the lethal result of failure to heed advice. It also points out that it is futile to advise an arrogant person. After harvest deadly caterpillars infested the remaining crops. If the goats got away from the herder and consumed leaves with caterpillars most died within hours.

[43] Kimilu, *Mũkamba*, 116; Mwau, *Dictionary*, 656.
[44] Kimilu, *Mũkamba*, 115.
[45] Mutisya, *Proverbs*, 60.
[46] Kĩeti, *Barking*, 106; Mutisya, *Proverbs*, 55.
[47] Mbiti, *Ngaeka*, 98.

192   *Part III: Kamba at Home*

871. *Ĩkũvuna ĩtindiaa ota ĩkũsyaa.* **When it is miscarrying, it rests like it is giving birth.**
Livestock often miscarried. Herders observed that the pregnant animal lay on the ground the same way as one with a live birth. Originating in antiquity this proverb warns that one's plans can also abort. It may also mean offenders defend themselves as if innocent. In short, give your own version of the story.

872. *Ĩnĩũthaumya ndyumasya mũkũũta.* **An animal that chews does not produce thirst.**
The term *mũkũũta* refers to a species of tree whose bark is boiled with meat to treat diarrhoea. This is often eaten by livestock, which retain it as cuds, *mũkũũta*. However, in the context of the proverb, *mũkũũta* is thirst or dehydration. The proverb therefore means, a little bite is better than starvation.[48]

873. *Mbũi nzeke ĩ ũa.*[49] **A lean goat has a skin.**
A thin goat produces leather skin too. Everything has some value. Size or appearance has little implication on quality and ability.

874. *Mbũi ya mwana ĩsũvĩawa nĩ mũsyai.* **The parent takes care of the child's goat.**
Children received gifts at birth and in different stages of growth such as initiation, which parents could save for the child or use up. Parents used the proverb to justify the use of children's savings.

875. *Mbũi ya ũkĩ ndĩmanzaa ĩngĩ.*[50] **A goat of beer does not look for another.**
This warns drunkards who sell their goats for liquor: once they gave away their goat, it was gone for good while they will sober up. This is a call to be realistic in economic transactions.

876. *Mbũi ndĩsyaa mavatha nĩkũkindwa nĩ nthenge ilĩ.* **A goat does not bear twins because of being mounted by two bucks.**
This axiom dissuades sacrificing discipline on the altar of parental love. Children do not benefit from excess affection without discipline.

877. *Kengaa mbũi marũnga nĩmoĩvie.* **Flatter goats; the sheep have become wise.**
This originated in Mwingĩ (given the use of the word *marũnga*) during the Vascon era. The sheep was the most docile animal, which the

---
[48] Farnsworth, *Grammar*, 50; Kimilu, *Mũkamba*, 115.
[49] Mailu, *Kĩkyambonie*, 59; Mutisya, *Proverbs*, 47; Mwau, *Dictionary*, 655.
[50] Kimilu, *Mũkamba*, 27, 116.

Kamba interpreted as stupidity and thus an animal easy to deceive. At the same time the goat is seen as even more foolish and less intelligent. The proverb means it is easier to deceive goats than sheep. It implies the speaker is wiser; the listener would better take his/her deception elsewhere.

878. *Mbũi ĩkasa ĩngĩ ndyũla.* **A goat that can be bartered for another is easily identifiable.**
The phrase *Mbũi ĩkasa ĩngĩ* refers to a goat that can be given in exchange for another one to be slaughtered and eaten. As in any exchange, not all goats are worth exchanging. The metaphorical meaning is that a person of note, value, and ability is easily identified.

879. *Katena kakavya konekaa tene.* **A kid that will be burnt is noticed early.**
Unlike older goats, kids jumped around fire with some stepping into hot charcoal concealed under ashes and got burnt. This Vascon-era proverb was said about a young person undertaking risky adventures that will explode and harm the youth.

880. *Mbũi kĩng'ei nĩyo yĩkĩawa mbwii ngingo.* **A thievish goat is made bellwether.**
The Kamba put little bells around the necks of their animals from the Monsoon era. The goat that was straying most or ransacking kitchens and farm crops, hence called thievish, was targeted as the bellwether. Dating from the Monsoon era, this proverb means someone with peculiar behaviour is always put in the public spotlight.

881. *Mbũi ndĩvatawa mũtĩ ĩkwenda.* **A goat is not denied a shrub it wants.**
Goats were adamant to eat certain plants and guided humans to discover edible plants such as coffee. The shepherds initially denied goats access to the plant, thinking they were harmful.
Eventually the shepherd gave in to the goats only to discover what a remarkable find it was.

882. *Mbũi ngũũ ndĩtivĩaa mana.*[51] **An old goat does not snort in vain.**
In flocks, older goats could scent or spot a prowling predator and snort, warning other animals to run for cover. Likewise, elders do not give warnings in vain.

---

[51] Farnsworth, *Grammar*, 24; Kimilu, *Mũkamba*, 116; Mutisya, *Proverbs*, 19.

883. *Mbũi nzaũ yonekeaa kĩĩmanĩ.* **A white goat is spotted from the hill.**
The proverb points out that people should guard their public reputation through proper conduct. Leaders cannot do trivial things, for example, lest people notice and think less of them.

884. *Mbũi nzaũ yaĩĩaa muumbĩnĩ.* **A white goat disappears in the mist.**
A good person can go astray as people watch helplessly. A white goat points to visibility of something good, like a child that is spoiled as people watch. This points to the fact that a stubborn person who refuses admonition may be drifting to his downfall.[52] It may also mean a good person may get spoiled while people are protesting in vain against their declining morals.[53]

885. *Kĩla mbũi ĩ mwanĩlye wayo.* **Every goat has its own specific bleat.**
Character traits differ. This diversity of persons within a community is of benefit to the community and should be given a chance to shape the character of the community.

886. *Nzenge ya kũtũ ĩlungĩlĩlyaa kwaasa.* **The he-goat of the ear mounts from afar.**
A traveller could easily tell where there was a homestead by the sound of the billy goat at night whose call was heard from afar. Its call lessened after mating. The role of the he-goat became symbolic of things to come. The phrase 'Calling from afar' signifies unforeseeable things. This ancient proverb means hearsay is unreliable. Secondly, one may hear something dangerous and flee. From the context within which this proverb was extracted the speakers meant that they heard would-be in laws had an ill reputation.

887. *Nthenge ya kĩvũvũ ndĩlũngasya mbaika.* **A hasty buck does not mount a doeling.**
This has several interpretations. A doeling that has never mated needs to be 'prepared' emotionally. The billy goat that would not prepare the inexperienced doeling will never mount her. Likewise, a man who cannot take time to arouse a woman's sexual feeling will not have any success with others. The actual meaning of the proverb is that patience and tact are vital to success.

[52] Kĩeti, *Barking*, 114; Kĩtukũ, *Folktales*, 15; Mwau, *Dictionary*, 655.
[53] Peter Mutua, 'Bringing Up Children in the Family Business: Engaging the African Village', http://biasharasme.sasahivi.com/blogs/coffeeblog/item/16-bringing-up-children-in-the-family- business-engaging-the-african-village.html. Accessed 19 June 2019.

888. *Kathenge kailīsa inya kambaa kumaīīa metho.* **A buckling urinates on its eyes before it mounts its mother.**
This is about arrogance, figuratively meaning someone who wants to commit evil ignores many warnings. He is blind to them.

889. *Mathenge matesene manyungīanaa isithe.*[54] **Big billy goats that do not know each other sniff each other's tails.**
This indicates that one who is unaware of the strength of a task or a person may make serious mistakes. It is better to be cautious beforehand.

890. *Yaelw'a mūkuva ītwīkaa ndīla.*[55] **When a needle is applied it becomes a neuter.**
Dating from the Islamic era, this axiom means a castrated he-goat remains castrated: what is done cannot be undone. Indeed, there are certain things that are stable.

891. *Mathīna ma nzenge mathelea ikonī.* **The troubles of a buck end in fire.**
This line is literal but symbolic. The buck symbolizes a sexy man who treasures romance, while fire represents tragedy and death. The speaker means someone obsessed with romance ends in tragedy and death. Control yourself and live a moderate and balanced life.

892. *Mbūi yūgaawa mwene aangī nī ai manyama.* **A goat is killed for the owner, the public eats meat.**
This deeply figurative statement rose about the 1700s when the slaughtering of goats as gifts to a guest emerged. Since the guest could not eat the whole goat by themselves certain parts of it were served while the rest went to the public. There are symbolic meanings in the sentence but the most common is that one person may be responsible for every matter in a family, or community.

893. *Mūthīnzi wa mbūi ndaa ngeeti.*[56] **Those who slaughter goats lack no pieces of meat lodged between his teeth.**
Kamba readers rarely know the word *ngeeti*, tiny pieces of meat remaining stuck between the teeth, removed with toothpicks. This proverb dates from the eighteenth century, an age of mass slaughter of goats for family and public celebrations. Specialized butchers slaughtered goats for individual families or large communal gatherings and perhaps tasted their work before others. It was uncommon for them to

---

[54] Kimilu, *Mūkamba*, 116; Mutisya, *Proverbs*, 38.
[55] Lindblom, *Riddles*, 29; Kimilu, *Mūkamba*, 119; Mutisya, *Proverbs*, 61.
[56] Mwau, *Dictionary*, 660.

leave the celebration without consuming meat. The sentence means that there are always signs showing the trail of a person.

894. *Mūthumo ūū wĩ mauta.* **There is fat in this bone marrow.**
A poor young man begging to be allowed to marry his sweetheart uttered this statement to her parents. He meant that he was young, strong, and capable of raising bride price if given a chance. The future is an investment itself. This proverb illustrates that poverty is not natural but structural. In the eighteenth century, while some grew wealthy, others were impoverished.
Lacking cattle to pay their bride price, they promised that given the opportunity they could eventually pay for their marriage. This can be seen as a loaned wife who can be withdrawn if the young man defaulted.

895. *Mūthumo wa mbūi ndwĩkaw'a ītheka ūtemwalye.* **A goat's bone marrow is never thrown away before it is broken.**
Among precolonial Kamba, goat bone marrow was an invaluable source of protein. Consequently, during mealtimes every bone was carefully crushed and inspected to see whether it held any of the life-enriching red or white marrow. This maxim means valuable objects are never discarded.

896. *Ona syaūlūka no mbūi.* **Even when they fly off they are still goats.**
This maxim originated from two men, Kita and Kyeni (son and father) in the 1920s. They competed to see who was more powerful in magic. The son struck first. He saw his father's farm filled with fine corn and declared (*kwathĩĩsya*), 'Why don't porcupines come and taste the maize?' Suddenly a large number of porcupines came and devoured the maize. When the father saw the porcupines destroying his farm he commented 'What are they doing? Why don't they stop and run back into the forest?' Suddenly all the porcupines left. Then the father saw the goats of his son browsing on leaves and he declared, 'Why don't they reach to the top of the trees and eat like monkeys?' Suddenly the goats were all on top of the trees. The son, surprised to see the unusual scene, declared, *Ona syaūlūka no mbūi*, 'Even if they fly they remain goats.'

897. *Mbūi ītindiaa na ūko wayo.* **A goat rests with its kind.**
People of the same ancestry settle in one location for many reasons. Another interpretation is that one should stay with those who share the same ideas with him/her.[57]

---

[57] Mutisya, *Proverbs*, 36.

Domesticated Animals

898. *Wĩkama nzenge mayiani meiko.* **You are milking a billy goat while black tea is boiling.**
The origin of this proverb is linked to the history of tea production, consumption, and commercialization after 1924. Although tea is not grown in Ũkambanĩ, its consumption became widespread from the late 1920s. In Ũkambanĩ, tea is mixed mainly with goat milk and sugar to produce a drink called *Chai*. The Kamba set the water boiling and go out to milk the goats. He-goats do not produce milk but their scrotum appears to some as udders, hence the ticklish axiom. It means you are trying the impossible.

899. *Syaawa syĩmbĩthĩ syauw'a syĩyĩ mũthoi.* **Meat is shared while uncooked, when cooked it has no broth.**
This alludes to sharing meat of a fallen animal. Only uncooked meat was shared. The ancient proverb means premature actions yield unsatisfactory results.

900. *Woona kaivingĩanĩw'a na iingĩ nĩkeanĩĩye mũnzyũ wa mũĩthi.* **If you see it driven with others it is fit for the shepherd's whip.**
This dates from the first millennium when the Kamba began to raise larger flocks and herds. Kids and calves were left home while mature animals were driven long distances to pastures and water points. They were driven with a rod – *mũnzyũ*. It was immoral to whip young animals, but when they matured, they were driven with a whip like their mothers. If one volunteers to do something challenging for adults, it is assumed he or she is mature enough to bear the responsibility.

901. *Ngethi ndĩ kĩsomba na ndĩvũnĩasya.* **Greetings have no granary and do not cause constipation.**
Young people who salute one another excessively coined this around the nineteenth century. Greetings and salutations were part of daily life in East Africa. This axiom means that people are never tired of salutation. Do it more often.

902. *Ngethi ya mbũi nĩ mbya, nayo ya ngitĩ nĩ maayo na mbosela.* **The salute of goats is by horns, that of dogs is canines.**
The salutation of goats by horns symbolizes peaceful encounters. When goats meet other strange goats, they engage in what appears as mock fighting for a few seconds only. When dogs meet strange dogs, they gnash their sharp teeth while sniffing each other's bottoms. The Kamba have since the age of domestication interpreted this behaviour as offensive, provocative, and aggressive. The most common interpretation is that most people are not grateful and despise peace. Be ready for them and respond to their evil actions with resolve.

903. *Ĩtumbĩ nĩ ya mwei na kĩlungu.* **An egg is only for a month and a fraction.**
This observes that freshly laid eggs last about a month before rotting or hatching. It can mean pride is short-lived and haughtiness does not last long.[58]

904. *Ĩtumbĩ yĩ mokonĩ ma kĩvĩsĩ ndĩtĩaa ũkw'a.* **An egg in the hands of a boy is bound to break.**
This ancient axiom alludes to the habit of boys gathering wild bird eggs to mishandle and spoil them. Sages then said a young inexperienced person was like such a boy and could not handle friendships or partnerships and could not be trusted with anything valuable.

905. *Matumbĩ maitheũkaw'a onthe ve maũvwĩkĩa.* **Eggs are not boiled altogether, some are for brooding.**
The Kamba did not use chicken eggs as food until after the First World War. Therefore, this emerged in the 1920s. It means that there must be savings so do not use all the resources at once.

906. *Matumbĩ maitalawa tũswii matemalĩku.* **Eggs are not counted as chicks before they are hatched.**
Since the brood does not all hatch into chicks, this proverb advises farmers that they should wait for the chicks to hatch and mature before they can think of their profit. This advises against speculation, which is so common in economic investments. The maxim dates to antiquity.

907. *Mai nĩ ma ngũkũ, makitĩ mekaa kwĩtolongania.* **Excretion is for the hen, dogs only mess themselves up.**
This axiom points to the importance of specialization. While dogs often consume faeces, chicken always clear it. This is an emphatic statement for people to understand their limitations compared to the speaker who claims superiority. By most oral accounts this axiom emerged among the urbanized generation of the 1950s.

908. *Mũgei wa ngũkũ e vata na matumbĩ.* **The keeper of chickens loves eggs.**
This proverb came from Mwingi dialect after the First World War. This maxim means one who raises chicken loves to eat eggs. The actual meaning is someone who does something knows the profit of it. However, this one proverb demonstrates that the way a proverb is presented depends on the dialect of the speaker.

---

[58] Kĩeti, *Barking*, 105.

909. *Mŭthoosya wa matumbĩ methĩ ndaetae ndŭŭthĩ ndŭnyŭ.* **A seller of raw eggs does not cause commotion at the marketplace.**
During the great famines of the 1890s, the Kamba trekked to Nairobi, government stations, and missionary stations to sell chickens and eggs. Subsequently, eggs became the commonest items in the market and hence the emergence of this proverb. Simply stated, since eggs are fragile, any commotion in a crowded marketplace might destroy the trader's eggs. The most vulnerable people should not cause trouble, lest they will suffer first.

910. *Ĩla kĩlŭĩ kyakosie kaswii kyavĩtie na kavuvu.* **When the kite missed the chicks, it survived on bats.**
This was drawn from a folktale. It is tailor-made to educate the audience that even when you miss a desired target do not give up, there is another option even if of lesser value.

911. *Ĩtaatemwa nĩ lŭĩ ti mbŭĩ.* **One that has never been attacked by a kite is not wise.**
This proverb originated with poultry keeping during the Monsoon era. The Kamba kept chickens for aesthetic purposes, food, and trade. Kites threatened poultry. The proverb emphasizes that experience breeds wisdom, caution, and precaution in conduct later in life. We learn through mistakes. It means if someone missed something that they wanted through ignorance, with that experience they will have a better chance next time.

912. *Kaswii ka ngŭkŭ kaimanyiaw'a kŭthelya.*[59] **A chick is never trained to scratch the ground.**
Nature teaches people methods of survival. A child born in poverty is never trained to search for basic resources. He is led by his instincts.

913. *Kaswii kakatwĩka nzamba konekaa o kaalĩkw'a.* **A chick that will become a cock is spotted after hatching.**
This means good quality comes from another quality source. Otherwise, success has its own signs, which can be detected.

914. *Kyuumo kya ngŭkŭ kĩkwataa ndiŭ.* **The hen's curse never harms the hawk.**
There were multitudes of eagles that preyed on chicken and swooped upon homesteads carrying away young chicks. At such moments, the mother hen was believed to be cursing the eagle when she clucked incessantly, but observably that did not kill the eagle. Ignore detractors and forge ahead with your plans despite criticism.

---

[59] Mulatya, 'Comprehension of Kĩkamba', 29.

915. *Mũthia wa ngũkũ nĩ suvu.* **The end of chicken is soup.**
Kamba kept chicken for consumption and thus the lifespan of a chicken ended in the kitchen. There is an end to everything and a reason why we do things in this and that manner.

916. *Ngũkũ ya kwosa soko yĩĩsaa kũũlũka na maswii mayo ĩkasyoka kũ yaumie.* **The hen collected from the market eventually flies its chicks back to its original home.**
The Kamba started buying chickens from the market during the colonial period. Because fowls are accustomed to their human adopters, whenever they were traded they tried to escape and return to their original owners. The moral is that one should be cautious in choosing a future wife, husband, or business partner. Beware of tricksters and the deceptive tactics.

917. *Ngũkũ ĩkũea ndĩ mawia maseo.* **A hen raising chicks has no good feathers.**
This is about self-sacrifice for a goal. Parents spend most of their resources, time, and energy raising children and making self-sacrifices for the sake of children.

918. *Ngũkũ ĩvwĩkie ndyendaa nzamba.* **A brooding hen does not need a rooster.**
Most living things, except perhaps humans, mate for procreation not recreation. Hens need roosters for procreation only. This means you should not do something without a reason. There is a time for every season.

919. *Ngũkũ iyũkita iisũvĩanaa metho.*[60] **When cockerels are fighting they make no special effort to avoid inflicting eye injuries on each other.**
Chickens often fight and poke each other's eyes with no concern about injury. The proverb means that there is no courteous rule in confrontations.

920. *Ngũkũ ĩkũlekya ndĩthĩnzawaa.* **A hen laying eggs is not slaughtered.**
This is a statement that there is more profit in letting such hens brood and thus bring more chickens to the owner. The proverb means the source of profit is worth caring for.

---

[60] Mutisya, *Proverbs*, 23.

921. *Ngũkũ ya kĩvĩsĩ ndyalĩkasya.* **A boy's hen does not hatch.**
Tracing from the origins of poultry farming this proverb warns against excitement, anxiety, and lack of caution in all life's undertakings. When a boy is gifted a hen by his grandmother and it begins to brood, the boy keeps on picking it up to show other boys, 'Here is my hen given to me by grandmother!' At the end the eggs, which require consistent warmth from the mother hen, go bad.

922. *Ndivokaa na nyama sya ngĩĩ nene ngũkũ.* **I don't dine on warthog meat when I have chicken.**
This appeared in a political song that compared a favourite candidate as a chicken and the opponent as a warthog. While chicken is an expensive delicacy, warthog meat tastes gamey and is eaten for lack of alternative. In the proverb, dining symbolizes electing candidates. So, why elect a weak and vile one when there is a better, organized, and seasoned candidate in the running.

923. *Ngũũe na ngũkũ syĩvulanaa.* **Pigs and chickens do not mix.**
This maxim emerged during the 1950s when Kamba farmers took a more aggressive role in pig farming. They did not put pigs and chickens in the same pen. The maxim means healthy people should not be mixed with the sick, neither should thriving institutions merge with declining ones.[61]

924. *Mathae ma nzamba mayalĩkasya ĩngĩ.* **Cock eggs do not hatch into a cock.**
This ancient proverb has multiple interpretations. Farmers across the globe believe roosters lay gooey eggs with no shell. A deeper meaning may be people of good character do not always produce similar offspring.

925. *Mũĩthi wa mwela ndaumanĩaa nzamba ya mũtũi.* **One who keeps hens does not curse the village rooster.**
This ancient proverb symbolically alludes to ways of raising children. Young hens symbolize girls while the rooster stands for boys. A household with no rooster borrowed one from neighbours to mate with the hens. Although sexual contact was mutely discouraged within a village the proverb also persuades families with girls not to despise the village boys. It means individual villagers have something that by itself cannot benefit the holder. Trade an item with fellow villagers in exchange for what you do not have.

---

[61] Anthony Bottrall, 'The Marketing of Fruit and Vegetables in Kenya. Case Study No. 4, Machakos District of Eastern Province', unpublished report, 1969.

926. *Mũsyĩ wĩ nzamba ndũlekasya matumbĩ ma ũkũngi.* **A household that has a cockerel does not lay unfertilized eggs.**
The Kamba believed unfertilized eggs were inseminated by wind. As the proverb says, a household with a rooster will have all eggs fertilized. This ancient maxim means that a rich family will resolve all matters requiring payment.

927. *Nzamba ya mũika ndĩseleawa too yasasya tene.* **A young rooster does not oversleep, it crows early.**
Young roosters crow early. Similarly, Kamba youth are sharp, traditions say, in doing things. They should be given the opportunity and responsibility of public development.

928. *Nzamba yakaa kĩsenzemwe vandũ ve mwela.* **A cock makes its rest place next to the hen's dust bath.**
Hens create a dust-bath area by scratching out a bowl-shaped depression in the dirt. It then settles in, fluffs its feathers, and scratches up loose dirt, sand, or litter through fluffed feathers. This dirt bath also serves other purposes. The dust bath is an important part of keeping chickens healthy and clean. Roosters wait for the hens to bathe first, rarely making their own dust baths. They use those the hens make. The proverb means that one invests where there is profit. A farmer does not plant in sandy, rocky, or barren soil that will yield nothing.

929. *Nzamba yaũtũla ndĩtũlaa mwela mũongo.* **The mounting cockerel does not mount on the back of the chick.**
A knowledgeable person knows the target and gets results. This is a quiet way of boasting that the speaker does not do things in vain. This is a men's proverb coined shortly after the raising of chickens became widespread.

930. *Nzamba yĩkaa ũkinya ndĩkinyawa.* **The cockerel mounts it is never mounted.**
A men's ancient axiom as an assertion of authority. A man gives orders and directives in his home. Women and children do not rule over him.

931. *Vai nzamba ya mwela ũmwe.*[62] **There is no cockerel for one hen.**
The Kamba kept the best cockerel, the largest and healthiest for that matter, among hens. They observed that the cock had no favourites. The cock mounted them equally. The hen in this case symbolizes the woman. Thus, the proverb was used as protest against monogamy as well as an excuse for involvement in extra-marital affairs. It implies that a man is worth multiple women. Beyond sexuality, this coloni-

---
[62] Mwau, *Dictionary*, 670.

al-era coinage may mean that there are always alternatives to something; there are diverse options to every life situation.

932. *Vayĩ mboswa ya mũnuka yosea ĩngĩ.* **No beaked creature pecks for another.**
This alludes to the ways in which birds feed using their beaks. Observably, each picks grain for itself only. This proverb talks about individualism. There are things that one has to do for himself or herself. From oral sources, it appears to have emerged during the Vascon era even though poultry and farming predate the Vascon era, when both economic activities intensified and individualism increased.

933. *Ndũa ĩsyaĩye ndiũ ndeeyawa ngũkũ.* **Chicks are not raised in a village where hawks nest.**
Appearing in recent political speeches, this Monsoon-era proverb alludes to the existence of political machinations. The speaker was castigating another politician who was undermining the progressive work of local political leaders.

934. *Ona nyũmba yusũĩye ata ngũkũ ndĩkosaa kakona kaũlekelya na ũvwĩkĩa.* **Even in the hardest situation you have an opportunity.**[63]
It means that matters whose time has come, naturally find a way to an end. This is about hope and determination. One should never give excuses for failure as solutions exist.

935. *Vai ngũkũ ĩtoasya.* **There is no hen that does not incur rotten eggs.**
This has multiple variants but by its use of chicken eggs it distinguishes itself, and its context and meaning appear distinct. Among its multifaceted meanings is that anyone can make errors and all people are potential victims of tragedy.

936. *Ũtheele wa ngũkũ ndũaa kaswii.* **The kick of a hen does not kill the chick.**
Hens scratching for food often kick their chicks but to no harm. By extension, correcting a child cannot cause injury. This proverb has been in circulation from antiquity and has been renewed through songs.

937. *Kũthosya mbata ngũkũ itathelete nĩ wĩa wĩvinya.* **Selling geese before chickens are finished is hard work.**
This exposes Kamba preference for chicken over geese. The latter are rarely kept and their eggs and meat are considered of lower value than chicken. Things of higher value are given priority.

---

[63] Mutisya wa Ngai, 'Kyuo kya Ngoso number 14'.

938. Ĩkyaĩe mang'oi kyosyokea matandĩko. Whatever ate the donkeys, may it return to consume the saddles.
This is a statement of despair and protest. Someone who is willing to take any option of a given task says this in despair. However, the proverb must have evolved after 1900, when donkeys were introduced from Meru and Isiolo. Evidently, in the 1840s Kamba caravans that Johannes Krapf followed from the coast to the inland had no beasts of burden.[64]

939. Ĩndĩ yathi ata na ti ĩng'oi? How did it go and not a donkey?
This proverb emerged around the late 1930s after the introduction of donkeys. It emerged out of the behaviour of the donkey straying away without notice. The question is asked as an expression of wonder when some plans have backfired or if someone changed plans without informing partners. However, the original key word from antiquity was monkey (ĩlaĩ/ĩkũlĩ), which like the donkey could disappear in an instant.

940. Ĩng'oi yĩsaa ndaĩanĩ ya ng'ombe. The donkey feeds on the honour of the cow.
The Kamba consider the donkey to be less intelligent than the cow. It is widely believed that once cows rest after drinking water, donkeys also rest. If one group of cattle rises up to go, even if the donkeys do not belong to that group they follow those cattle, to the annoyance of the herdsmen. This proverb emerged shortly after the Second World War. It is in part a mockery statement that certain people benefit because of their parentage rather than merit.

941. Ĩng'oi ĩtwaa ĩng'oi na yatata mũno itwaa nzaĩ. A donkey marries a donkey, and if it tries hard it marries a zebra.
This delves into a field of study easily dismissed as a fairy tale. Although zebras and donkeys rarely crossbreed, in some places such as Lamu donkeys historically crossbred with wild zebras, giving birth to striped-legged offspring called zonkeys. In 1859, Charles Darwin wrote about zonkeys in the *Origin of Species*. The maxim, which emerged around the time of the Second World War, means that many people take a long time to marry, but still get a partner of their class among latecomers like themselves.

---

[64] Hellmut Epstein, *The Origin of the Domestic Animals of Africa 2* (New York: African Publishing Corporation, 1971).

942. *Kŭtata ĩsyŭko nĩ kŭinga ŭkwete ĩng'oi.* **To try a watering point is to cross it holding a donkey.**
This proverb, from the postwar period when donkeys became common in Ũkamba, means that companionship with a foolish man is costly and dangerous.

943. *Mŭĩthi wa mang'oi ndakĩaa nzeele.* **A shepherd of donkeys does not fear kicks.**
This was coined after the Second World War when donkeys became common. These animals often kicked their owners. People who owned the animals knew that they had to put up with or avoid the kicks. The proverb actually means one should bear responsibility for loss or risk in any transaction.

944. *Ndingaa mang'oi maka kĩtheyonĩ.* **I do not drive jennies down the hill.**
This has a hidden vulgar meaning. Usually said by men, the jennies refer to women while downhill represents a compromising circumstance. It can also mean walking behind women. The speaker cautions that closeness between men and women can lead to unnecessary promiscuity.

945. *Ndwaaona ndanzi ya mang'oi.* **You have never seen the dance of donkeys.**
This axiom emerged shortly after the introduction of donkeys in Ũkambanĩ in the 1930s. The term 'dance' symbolizes two things – donkey mating styles and donkey fights with kicks and bites. In both cases, the speaker warns the listener not to cross a red line.

946. *Thooa wa ĩng'oi ŭmanyĩkaa yĩ nthĩ.* **A donkey's price is known when it is down.**
This proverb emerged after the introduction of donkeys in the 1930s. Animals were purchased from pastoralists for carrying burdens. During transactions, the best-tamed donkey usually lay down and the seller would boast about its tameness and bargain for a higher price. The proverb suggests that in trade, goods are only valuable if they can be viewed.

947. *Nthĩnĩ wa mũatĩnĩo ngamlĩa ila syũ mbee nsĩyo iseleasya andũ ĩndĩ ila sy ĩtina nsĩyo itandĩkawa mũno.* **In a caravan the camels in front cause delay, but rear guards are whipped most.**
This is a recent coinage with political implications. The Kamba have never owned camels except a few individuals who were in contact with camel-keeping Cushitic speakers. The maxim means that in politics, leaders are to blame but citizens suffer most.

12

Men and Masculinity

948. *Aũme mai kiima na maivandaa vathei.* **Men are not mean and do not sow in vain.**
Grandmothers admonishing girls about the risk of sex said this sarcastically. Men will not say no if girls make moves toward them, and they will be quick to impregnate the girls. This is an ancient aphorism about male–female relationships, but it became common in the early 1900s when procreation was no longer a preoccupation and premarital pregnancies began to rise.

949. *Aũme maiananaa ve ala me ngome.* **Men are never equal, some have cockrings.**
This ancient maxim alludes to one of the rarest subjects in public discourse – intimate details about genitals. Women coined this axiom to describe different penis sizes. Some are too long requiring a ring to size down the organ. A cockring was thus worn at the base of the penis in order to shorten the section of it entering the vagina. By extension people have different resources and capabilities and can never be the same.

950. *Aũme maithambanasya mũongo.* **Men do not wash each other's back.**
This is an ancient erotic and deeply symbolic proverb. It is said in a light moment to stress that there are certain things that people should do for themselves and never rely on others.

951. *Aũme ti aa Monika.* **Men are not Monicas.**
Monika (Monica) is a cover for women, so the proverb means men are not women. This maxim was coined in the postcolonial era. *Monika* is not a traditional name, but one arriving with European imperial culture.[1] This is normally said by men in appreciation of their achievements against the odds.

---

[1] Patricia Lorcin, *Historicizing Colonial Nostalgia: European Women's Narratives of Algeria and Kenya, 1900–Present* (New York: Palgrave Macmillan, 2011).

Men and Masculinity

952. *Aũme ndĩa kĩnyũũto.*[2] **Men, get your hoop rolling.**
This ancient proverb refers to hoop rolling or hoop trundling, a children's game that has been well documented. Kamba boys made wooden hoops and rolled them as they ran to deliver
messages. In free translation it says 'Men get your hoop rolling.' It calls on men to work unceasingly.

953. *Aũme nĩmo matusaa kĩtheka kĩthungu ĩei.* **Men are the ones who turn a thick forest into fallow.**
This is varied in many ways that point to a process of exploitation and depletion of fertile land. In other words, it is men who turn a thick forest into a fallow one. Men cleared forests for farms and left exhausted fields fallow where livestock grazed and small creatures invaded. It was normally grandmothers who used this old proverb (although grandfathers often used it with astounding effect on their granddaughters) admonishing girls to be careful in their romantic adventures. Figuratively, a man fertilized a woman turning her into a mother (a fertile farmland), gradually exhausted like fallowed land. In this context *ĩei* symbolizes infertility, uselessness, unattractiveness, and condemnation. The proverb points to girls who became pregnant before marriage and the male suitor abandoned her as fallow.

954. *Mbendwa ĩkusaa ĩte mũka.* **The most loved man dies without a wife.**
The word *mbendwa* refers to a loose person quick to win women for sex but not committed to a relationship. Such a person ends up having no wife. Women were also victims of the same tendency and ended miserably, although their case was better than that of loose men. By most oral accounts, this emerged during the late Vascon era between 1700 and 1800.

955. *Mbendwa yĩnũkasya mũyo ta nzenge.* **A womanizer takes home pleasure like a he-goat.**
This refers to the practice of billy goats being often borrowed among neighbours to mount she-goats, after which the billy goat is returned to the owner. When asked what have you brought with you from previous visits, Kamba say, the billy replies 'pleasure'. This axiom is varied, all implying a man who flirts with women in his neighbourhood gains nothing but his immorality. Although the best breed was loaned, it returned with nothing to show for it.

---

[2] Watuma, *Syĩthĩo*, 67.

956. *Mbendwa ndĩsĩ ĩngĩ.* **A debauched man does not recognize another.**
This axiom condemns habits of flirting with married women. It targets specifically men of perverse character. It means that one dissolute person does not know another. He thinks he is the only one who can carry out his mischief.

957. *Mũndũ akw'a ate mũka akimawa na muu kĩtimba.* **If a man dies without a wife he is hit with ash on the bottom.**
There was no excuse for a man not to marry, as much as it was an abomination for a man not to engage in sex. If a man died without a wife, he was not granted the same burial rights accorded normal people. He was buried naked, turned upside down and interred lying on the stomach, and smacked with white ash on the buttocks. The burial was conducted as an indication that he died
as worthless as ash. Other single men who died past the age of marriage were wrapped in gunny bags and their bodies thrown into a gully to be devoured by hyenas. The ancient proverb warns people that they should have possessions and raise a family.

958. *Mwendwa nĩ aka ndendawa nĩ aũme.* **Men do not like one who is liked by women.**
This proverb alludes to competition and envy among equals who desire to outshine their compatriots. It was also used by chief Mukwekwe in the 1910s and 1920s. It reflects the sentiments of that time: men did not appreciate womanizers and were reluctant to elect such men as leaders.

959. *Syaamba kala, ngethe nzeo ndũkosa.* **When they tinkle you cannot miss a good girl.**
A recent proverb created by popular *benga* musicians it means where money is involved, good things are also gained. It points to the fact that money has become critical for almost everything in life. Men need money to get a good girl. The phrase *syaamba kala*, 'when they clatter', is onomatopoeia for the sound of silver coins, which has become symbolic of many things.

960. *Syĩna aũme itiĩasya angĩ.*[3] **Things in the hands of men do not make other men cry.**
Men do not envy what other men have. This is about the search for wealth, and given its rendition, emerged during the Vascon era of economic expansion. The maxim sought to reduce envy and encourage people to work towards building their wealth and legacy.

---

[3] Mwau, *Dictionary*, 668.

961. *Mŭndŭŭme ekw'ŭŭwa nĩ kĩŭmati.* **A man is subdued by stomach cramps.**
In the context of masculinity, men have been unpredictable since antiquity. However, while wayward men boasted of their invincibility, stomach cramps subdued them. In a way people can swindle others, but they are no match for nature. Do not trust every person you come across.[4]

962. *Mŭndŭŭme atwaswaa no kĩw'ŭ endete kŭla kwĩ mŭka.* **A man drowns while reaching out to his wife.**
An ancient proverb emphasizing the centrality of a wife. Its common interpretation is that nothing will stand between a man and his wife. During rainy season, people were warned not to wade into flooded rivers because in a few hours the water will subside making it safe to cross. Nevertheless, the passion for their wives forced some men to try, and thus they drowned. The ancient proverb means some actions are not worth the risk.

963. *Mŭndŭŭme ŭte kĩveti avyŭvĩswaa lĩu nĩ sua.* **The sun warms food for unmarried men.**
This ancient maxim alludes to the critical role that a wife played as a source of warmth and comfort for men. That role is represented here as warming food to eat. It implies that if a man had no wife he would pick up his bowl of food and place it in the sun to warm, whereas a married man's wife would warm the food, season it, and serve it to him. Symbolically this means that a man who is not married suffers.

964. *Mŭndŭŭme nĩ musyĩ.* **A man is a family.**
This ancient proverb points to the centrality of the wife, family, and marriage. It is clear from ethnographic data that every man, dead or impotent, was required to marry. Even people who died before marriage were secured a wife then given to a surrogate husband who sired children on behalf of the dead. The woman and her children took the surname of the dead man.

965. *Mŭndŭŭme avitha ŭkya wake ŭkuthŭawa nĩ mŭka.* **When a man conceals his poverty, his wife exposes it.**
If you are not providing for the family, the wife will struggle to provide. If she appears stressed, unhealthy, or poorly dressed, people will take that as a reflection of a man's poverty. This may be mundanely through the appearance of her skin and grooming or through destructive gossip.

---

[4] Mutisya, *Proverbs*, 36.

966. *Mŭndŭŭme nŭthŭĩwe nĩkŭthekw'a na syĩndŭ sya mŭndŭŭme iyĩsawa mana.* **A man despises ridicule, and a man's things are not eaten in vain.**
Open to multiple interpretations, this has sexual connotations. The ridicule usually comes from women who also prey on the toil of a man, at a time when the man endeavours not to labour in vain without some return.

967. *Kanywa wa mŭtumĩa ndŭtŭngawa mana.* **The mouth of an elder is not returned empty.**
'Mouth of an elder' symbolizes an elderly messenger referring to ancient situations where an old man would send another to a son-in-law for a cow. If the son-in-law had no cow to give, he was taught this proverb, meaning a substitute was imperative. This proverb traces back to the Vascon era when marriage institutions became explicit, and livestock central to marriage customs.

968. *Mŭtumĩa ailye nthĩ onaa vaasa kwĩ kĩvĩsĩ kĩŭngye.* **An old man sitting sees farther than a boy standing.**
This is a common adage claiming age was the gateway to experience and ultimate learning. Elders were possessors of vision and focus. The sight alluded to is not that of the eyes but vision and thought about the near and far future. Younger people may not have that capability.

969. *Mŭtumĩa ndakŭaa masŭnzŭmele.* **An elder does not age while squatting.**
This proverb is said in reference to individuals exhibiting immature conduct regardless of their advanced age. Even though they may look mature, their maturity stagnated at adolescence. It is the worst insult that can be said about one's character, and the phrase 'old men' can refer to either sex.

970. *Mŭtumĩa ndavŭĩawa ngŭĩ.* **An elder is never derided.**
This is one of the multiple proverbs calling for respect of elders.[5] To insult an elder was unfathomable at least before 1900. This proverb concerns honour and respect to elders. The Kamba have symbolic names for toes and fingers. The little finger, *kala kamwela*, 'splinter finger', is rarely used to point at objects. Using it to point at an elder was the worst form of disrespect. Elders were revered and respected as leaders.

971. *Mŭtumĩa nĩ kavĩsĩ keanaa.* **A man is a growing boy.**
While men loathe to be compared with boys, there was clear recognition among elders that there was always room to learn new things. This

[5] Mwau, *Dictionary*, 660.

ancient proverb views learning as a continuous process until either senility or death.

972. *Mũtumĩa etawa mũtumĩa nũtumĩa.* **An elder is called a senior because of his maturity.**
An elder is recognized as such because of how he behaves in public. The services a man above fifty years old offers to the younger generation and society in general was a prerequisite to entering the class of elders. Such proverbs emerged with the crystallization of Kamba society in the late first millennium.

973. *Mũtumĩa nĩwe wĩtusaa kĩvĩsĩ.* **A man makes himself a boy.**
A person was expected to grow, mature, and distinguish himself from youth by the way he conducted himself. His morals were expected to be distinctly different from those of young people. If an old man behaved like a boy, for example by dating a young girl openly, it was considered acting as teenage boys act. How a man spoke in public also measured his maturity into 'elder' class. To revert to teenage behaviour in words and deeds was considered the worst thing that could happen to a man. As part of social control, this maxim emerged in antiquity.

974. *Mũtumĩa ndaumanawa na nthoka.* **An elder is never done with visitations.**
This ancient axiom alludes to the business of marriage, which was the prerogative of old men and their wives. An old man with children spent most of his life giving away his daughters for marriage and negotiating for his son's marriage. He was also involved in the marriage of his grandchildren and the children of his brothers, cousins, and neighbours.

975. *Ũtumĩa ti mbuĩ na kũkũa ti kũkũa ithukĩ.* **Elderliness is not grey hair, as old age is not pulling out stumps.**
Elders said this when they saw an old person behaving immaturely. This is one of the proverbs that proves that proverbs did not just target the young. Targeting elders, peers usually said this to convince an erring elder of the importance of maintaining the highest level of maturity and morality.

976. *Mũndũ aekaa kũmbwa akw'a.* **One ceases to be created only when he dies.**
A deeply symbolic ancient maxim noting that growth can stop at some point with age, but circumstances lead to weight gain or loss. These changes are marked in the phrase 'creation', but it is more about changes in knowledge than body mass. The older a person becomes, the more experience they gain.

977. *Mũtumĩa mũĩ ndaasya ndyĩkwa.* **A wise man never says 'I cannot stand that behaviour.'**[6]
Patience is a prime character of an elder and a parent. Since families and communities are prone to conflict, parents and elders were duty bound to bear with misbehaviour. They never say 'I cannot condone this or that behaviour.' Misbehaviour happens and the way forward is to correct the error.

978. *Ngũlũmbũ ya mũtumĩa nĩ ĩkuti.*[7] **The tiny skin inside a snuffbox comes to the rescue of an old man when the snuff runs out.**
This emerged during the eighteenth century, when snuff consumption became common and the Kamba developed a cache of items to accompany the habit. A decorated snuffbox included a tiny piece of leather placed inside to keep the snuff fresh and loose. Whenever the snuff ran out, the old man relied on sniffing this skin to quench his desire for snuff. This axiom means that small things matter and they are often indispensable.

979. *Mũndũ mũĩ athimaa syuo ta vetha.* **A wise man measures words like money.**
This axiom provides insight into the history of currency in East Africa. Long before the Monsoon Exchange across the Indian Ocean, East African communities were exchanging livestock, ironware, foodstuffs, and other products through barter. In place of the cumbersome salt bars normally used as payment, Arab traders introduced money as an alternative in the form of foreign coins, including everything from Indian rupees to Austrian silver thalers reflecting the multinational nature of precolonial maritime trade. Between 1888 and 1890, the British imperial administration of Kenya and Uganda issued the Mombasa Coins in a mixture of rupees, annas, and pice minted in India.

980. *Mũndũ mũĩ ndamĩaa kyengonĩ.* **A wise man does not defecate at the ranching camp.**
The moral of this ancient axiom is do not abuse your privileges. If people help you, return their actions with a gesture of gratitude. This emerged in the early eighteenth century when declining pastures forced livestock keepers to establish seasonal ranches in distant places with water. When rain fell and grass bloomed near the villages, ranchers returned with their herds. They were warned, however, not to urinate, defecate, or do any other indecent act on the place as they left. Instead, they offered tobacco, beer, cold water, or milk to the ground to appease the local spirits, thanking them for caring for people and livestock.

---

[6] Kimilu, *Mũkamba*, 86.
[7] Mwau, *Dictionary*, 665.

981. *Mũndũ ũkwenda ũndũ e syalavo mbingĩ.*[8] **One who desires something has many tactics.**
This ancient axiom is open to interpretation. Among other things it means a person desiring to get something employs all kind of tactics to get it.

982. *Mũndũ mwonzu e wake mũnou.*[9] **A weakling has a relative who is fat.**
This ancient proverb warns against underestimating others based on body size, appearance, or resourcefulness. Such people may have hidden strength. It also warns against mistreating the weak for they have sympathizers, defenders, and relatives. If you do not like them leave them alone and mind your business.

983. *Mũndũ ndamanzĩka akĩtaa ũsyawa.* **A human being cannot be acquired, he is born.**
This ancient adage emphasizes the value of people who are important to their families and communities. People are not commodities to be acquired with money, but have to be born and nurtured to maturity by families and communities. This calls for love and appreciation of relatives and neighbours, particularly when we do not appreciate their value.

984. *Mũndũ ndaleaa wĩto, aleaa kĩla ũkwĩtĩwa.* **A person does not decline a call, he declines what he is called for.**
This common adage circulating since antiquity calls on people to be open-minded when asked to give help. Some pretend to call for help when they are actually inviting you to a banquet. The maxim calls on the listener to answer the call, investigate its intent, and then decide to accept or not.

985. *Mũndũ no ũla ũmwe.* **People are the same.**
This axiom emerged during the Islamic era as the Kamba intermingled with non-Kamba immigrants claiming common blood interconnections. Those involved claimed they were kindred despite their language differences. Kamba clans have historical ties with almost all their neighbouring ethnic groups in Kenya and Tanzania. This alludes to the manner in which the Kamba greeted people whom they met for the first time. After formal interpersonal salutations they enquired about clan, homeland, and so on. At the end they discovered bonds and concluded with this proverb. It was used during the colonial era to forge affinity with Europeans and Asians aiming at unity rather than enmity.

[8] Mwau, *Dictionary*, 658.
[9] Kimilu, *Mũkamba*, 117.

986. *Mũndũ wa kĩsalĩ aĩsaa syĩ mbĩthĩ.* **A hasty person eats them raw.**
This ancient proverb condemns habits of haste and lack of strategy. An impatient person does not wait for food to cook and ends up eating it raw. Similarly, haste is not good for other aspects of life, resulting in immature action and inadequate outcomes.

987. *Mũndũ ũmũmanyaa na andũ make.* **You know a man by his family.**
This old saying means the character and resourcefulness of a person is reflected in the manner by which he conducts his family affairs. The way the family dresses, socializes, and dines reflects the character of the patriarch.

988. *Mũndũ ndavandaa mũtĩ ũtaĩsaa.* **A man does not plant a tree he does not eat.**
Farmers planted mostly consumable plants but also shade trees, medicinal plants, and fodder. This proverb has been used to argue against accusations of immoral behaviour, but for the most part it means people do not produce what they do not consume.

989. *Mũndũ ndekaa ũndũ wake ekaa ũthũmũa na akasyokea.* **A man does not stop his habits, he only rests before he resumes.**
This common maxim dating to antiquity appears in many songs. It means habits die hard. A thief may appear to cease stealing but will later repeat.

990. *Mũndũ mũseo nĩwe wĩthikaa e thayũ.* **A good man buries himself while he is alive.**
The Kamba care how their remains will be handled after they have died. In order to ensure a good burial ceremony, one endeavoured to live well with neighbours and relatives through helping them when death struck in their family and by donating items to the community. Good deeds were an investment for one's own burial, for people will pay them back by making sure that when such a good person died, his body would be handled carefully and many praises said about him. Before 1900 old men performed all burial matters.[10]

991. *Mũthiki wa andũ ndathikawa.* **One who buries people is never buried.**
This old adage reveals some ironies in the Kamba world. People who did good to others were not properly rewarded. There were men who specialized in burial customs. When such people died there were no

---

[10] Lindblom, *Akamba*, 116–17.

specialists to bury them, hence the proverb. Being good is not good enough.

992. *Woona kĩwandu kyongela nthanga manya kĩũmati kĩo vakuvĩ.* **If you see your pregnant wife changing a button, get to know that labour pain is close.**
This appears to have emerged in the twentieth century when specially made maternity dresses with buttons became available. These dresses had overlapping pieces that were adjusted according to the way the buttons were laid out. Lacking a word for buttons, the Kamba called them *nthanga* from an earlier word. When the buttons reached a particular point, the observant husband knew the 'labour date' was close. One should know the signs of time.

993. *Mũndũ ũtoĩtye kĩndũ ndonaa kĩngĩ.* **A person who has not forgone something cannot gain something else.**
Tracing from antiquity this proverb is similar to 'no gain without pain'. In order to make profit, one must invest or sow the seed in order to reap much more than what he/she put in.

994. *Mũndũ wĩkũasa ndetawa na kĩwe.* **Someone at a distance is not summoned with a whisper.**
This ancient proverb means distant people cannot help one, but only those nearby. It thus emphasizes the importance of good neighbourliness and family unity. It is also applied in many other contexts.

995. *Mũndũ ũkũsembania na kyuu kyake akusaa na thĩna.* **A shadow chaser chases and dies miserably.**
This statement is deeply figurative and not easy to comprehend. The phrase *ũkũsembania na kyuu* (chasing shadows) means pursuing futile goals. One should be realistic and pursue goals that can be executed, not building castles in the air.

996. *Mũndũ ũte kyake ndona kyene.* **One who does not have his own cannot see that of others.**
This figurative statement emerged during the Vascon era of commercial exchange. A trader exchanged something for what he wanted. He could not get it if he did not have items of trade. The maxim expanded and applied to many other contexts. It means that, to survive in a community, one needs property to acquire property. This is a figurative condemnation of poverty as a result of laziness. A lazy man who cannot create wealth was not treated well by society.

997. *Mũndũ wĩ kĩndũ nĩ kyake.* **One with something owns it.**
Tracing from antiquity this axiom emphasizes self-reliance. People can use their property as they please, and others should not give orders about what to do. It is better to be self-reliant than to depend on other people for basic necessities.

998. *Ũte kyake nde ngoo.* **One who does not have something of his own has no heart.**
Whoever has nothing has no temper and never gets upset. The maxim suggests hard work and accumulation of wealth rather than begging. It admonishes people who ask others for favours to accept what is offered back.

999. *Mũndũ ndathelaa athelaa avwĩkwa mũthanga.* **A person is never exhausted; he is finished when he is buried.**
Appearing in a popular song, this axiom means that fortune and opportunities will always appear in life. The possibility of richness should not be ruled out until one dies. It can also mean that if the listener is a beneficiary, it is imprudent to exhaust the resources of his/her benefactor, for tomorrow is another day. The resources will still be available.

1000. *Mũndũ ũla wĩsĩ andũ angĩ nĩ mũsomu ĩndĩ ũla wĩyĩsĩ we mwene nĩ mũĩ.* **One who knows other people is learned, but who knows himself is wise.**
While this might have emerged from the 1950s when formal education became fashionable and the measure of a man's worth, it appears to have been borrowed from Chinese wisdom. This is identical to the Lao Tzu catchphrase 'He who knows others is wise. He who knows himself is enlightened.' Sages always remind audiences that wit is about knowledge of the people around them rather than pursuit of learning.

1001. *Mwethya nĩ ndũngo.* **Self-help work is exchange.**
The most common interpretation is if a neighbour or relative organizes a group to help someone with weeding or building a house, the recipient of these services has to pay back by organizing a similar workforce to help that neighbour next time. This cooperative spirit dates from the late seventeenth century as per most oral accounts. Original settlements in Machakos and later Kitui did not require as much cooperative work as they did later under strained labour resources and increased work demands.

1002. *Mũkindĩwa kĩveti aasya kĩyĩsĩ mũndũ ũngĩ.* **One whose wife cheats says she knows no man.**
This emerged during the twentieth-century transformation of attitudes towards sex and marriage. Previously, the Kamba had less

concern about what is known today as infidelity, trusting male relatives and clan members to take care of their wives during their absence, including their sexual needs. As society changed during the course of the century, nuclear families scrupulously restricted sexual contact to the Western ideal of one man, one wife. This restriction was not easy to enforce since men had to go to work in urban areas, hundreds of miles away from home for several months, returning home only briefly. These circumstances forced couples to rely on 'faithfulness' to one another, on biblical teachings against adultery and on occasional visits of wives to their husbands in towns. Under these conditions, spouses often had extramarital sex. Men who trusted their wives barely suspected such things, hence the proverb, which is applied in other aspects of life.

1003. *Mūndū nī vaasya valūa yī nzīnī.* **A man is an envelope, the letter is inside.**
This emerged from the 1930s when letter writing began to emerge. In the West letters were sealed in envelopes so their contents remained secret until opened and read. The maxim therefore means the secret held by a person lies within him. Only when he reveals it does the public learn his inner content and character.

1004. *Nthimo ya Mūkamba itivalūkaa vathei.* **The proverb of a Mūkamba is not in vain.**
If a hunter shot an animal he would predict the animal was pregnant. When the hunters caught up with the fallen animal they exclaimed this proverb, if the animal was indeed female and pregnant. Such a person's proverbial words were true, not just empty words. Proverbs are significant in revealing the truth.

1005. *Yamūka ndīsaa katūti na ndyoneka nī mbiti.* **A cow that will pay dowry never eats the deadly ant and is never seen by the hyena.**
This ancient maxim reveals the challenge of animal husbandry. In farms where cattle were allowed to browse after harvest there were small poisonous ants that killed bovines within hours of their consumption. In the surrounding forest there were numerous hyenas that also preyed on cattle. The Kamba were never passive to these problems but the problems persisted. The maxim means that something that will profit never fails.

1006. *Mūndū ūmwe ndovaa na kūthwaa.* **One man does not simultaneously lie in wait and scare the game to ambush.**[11]
This came from the context of hunting small game for meat with two teams. The duty of one was *kwova* (to lie in wait to shoot the game) and

---

[11] Farnsworth, *Grammar*, 63.

the duty of the other *kũthwaa* (to drive the game towards those lying in wait for the game). It means one person cannot do both at the same time. By the 1940s when Farnsworth collected the proverb in central Machakos, hunting had severely declined in the region, leaving proverbs to carry the memories of ancient hunting. The maxim means there are things that a person cannot do simultaneously. Alternatively, there must be division of labour.

1007. *Mũndũ akolaw'a too nĩ Kĩthuma kya ng'ombe yake.*[12] **A person cannot sleep soundly with his neighbour's blanket.**
This adage emerged from the early seventeenth century according to oral traditions. It means one can only sleep soundly on a cowhide from his own cow. The hide symbolized a wife; hence the proverb means a man's life was only complete with a wife whom he paid for with cattle. Beyond wives and hides, it means that whatever people own is best for them; other people's property will never give satisfaction. The maxim encourages independence and hard work.

1008. *Mũndũ ndaemaa ũmanyana na ng'ombe yake ona yĩ nzeele.* **One does not fail to know his cow even if it kicks.**
This ancient proverb alludes to the fact that milk cows were treasured among the Kamba. However, some were kickers. Women trained them to be docile by giving them salt licks and hay or by tying their hind leg. Nevertheless, men used the maxim to justify their ability to cope with their wives.

1009. *Kyonze kĩthĩnzaa ng'ombe kwa mbaa naũme.*[13] **A weakling slaughters a cow at the uncle's home.**
This deeply figurative statement arose in Kitui when cattle became the economic mainstay of what is now Kitui County. With multiple interpretations and applications, it reveals the significance of maternal uncles in precolonial Kamba. The uncle who is called *mama*, a word pronounced slightly differently to distinguish mother and uncle, had a soft spot for his sister's children.

1010. *Ũnene wa ng'ombe nĩ mana, kĩng'ee kyanengiwe mbũi.* **The big size of the cow is nothing; the beard was given to the goat.**
Within Kamba lore bovines are characterized as foolish, and the cow is probably the most idiotic according to Kimilu. The indication of wisdom is the beard but since bulls have none they are considered less intelligent than he-goats, which have a long 'goatee'. Dating from the seventeenth century this proverb has multiple meanings, the most obvious

---

[12] Farnsworth, *Grammar*, 130; Kimilu, *Mũkamba*, 117; Kĩtukũ, *Folktales*, 4.
[13] Kimilu, *Mũkamba*, 116; Mwau, *Dictionary*, 653.

being that a rich, highly educated, or well-built person may not make a good leader but someone less resourceful and meeker might.

1011. *Mwambi wa kīthuma akusasya ngalīko yake.* **One draws the skin towards himself.**
This is a common saying from ancient times when the Kamba used cowhides as blankets. Whenever more than two people slept on one bed and had to use a single hide, those on the edge of the bed pulled the hide to cover themselves. The proverb means that one favours his own side. Variants (see below) have developed different meanings.

1012. *Mūndū ūkomelete katī ndakusasya īvula.* **One sleeping in the middle does not pull the blanket.**
This emerged after the First World War when blankets became widespread, quickly replacing skins and hides as favoured beddings. Because blankets were scarce, sets of siblings slept under one blanket. Those in the middle had no need to pull the blanket but those on the edges pulled to cover themselves. There are other meanings beyond these literal interpretations.

1013. *Mūndū wa mūndū nī mūnene.* **One's relative or friend is important.**
Friendship is extremely valuable and appears in many proverbs. This one calls for care in friendship and filial relationships as they are fundamental to one's material wealth and good life. It was used from antiquity to appreciate help from others, or to caution that one should not handle friends and relatives lightly.

1014. *Kamūlilo ka wīa nī mbau sya mwene na kayīingwa kīthambusyo ta mūatine.* **A little work tool is the owner's ribs and it does not have holes like the kigelia fruit.**
This proverb with multiple interpretations emerged from the Vascon era. The phrase *kamūlilo ka wīa*, 'a little work tool', refers to the wife, while *mbau sya mwene*, 'ribs of the owner', symbolizes intimacy and closeness, since the wife ought to be kept as close as one's ribs. In this context the proverb is a romantic expression of a man's love, feeling, and concern for his wife.

1015. *Kathūngī ke twīndū tūseo kakuawa na ndanī.* **A basket of valuables is carried on the bosom.**
This refers to romantic intimacy between man and wife. A man means this as an expression of his feelings and concern for his wife and intimacy with her. She is given the best care, kept in the most favourite position, figuratively and literally. The axiom emerged during the

Vascon era, with similar proverbs that indicate rising aesthetics and romance in Ũkamba.

1016. *Kĩtete kya ndia kĩthũsaa na ũla mũĩ.* **The wise one uses the gourd of a foolish man.**
During the Vascon era hunters and raiders carried food supplies in bottlegourds. As expeditions lengthened to months and supplies ran low, the wise survived on the supplies of the foolish by tricking them into sharing, then disappeared after supplies were finished, resulting in starvation and even death. It was applied in many other areas of human life.

1017. *Mũndũ ũte kĩtete ndasilĩaa kyene.* **He who does not have a calabash does not arbitrate over other people's calabashes.**
This proverb derived from hunting and long-distance travels, during which the Kamba carried their food supply in bottlegourds. When the expedition paused to rest, they would decide whose gourd to use first. Someone without a gourd remained silent. The deeper meaning is that a man without a daughter cannot negotiate dowry for a girl. Only married men with daughters could speak on such occasions.

1018. *Mũndũ ũte yĩuna ndauna ũngĩ.*[14] **One who cannot help himself cannot help another.**
Someone who cannot sufficiently work to create wealth cannot enrich other people. There are many variants, some of which reveal the meaning of the proverb said during courtship as a young man sought the hand of an old man's daughter. The elders looked at his performance in farming, herding, hunting, or any other means of bringing fortune to himself, to conclude that if he had done none of these well he could not support a family. However, this is just one source of the origin and application of the proverb. Since such applications are so varied and changeable it is not worth a detailed discussion. Kituku's context is, however, vital for excavating the history of proverbs. By tracing the custom of bridewealth to the sixteenth century, we surmise that the proverb originated during the early years of the Vascon era.

1019. *Mũndũ ũtesĩ ũngĩ amwĩtaa kaa.*[15] **A man who does not know another habitually calls him that little one.**
One who does not know the capability of others always underestimates them. It is a warning never to underrate your opponent. This is varied in multiple ways to imply a double attitude towards the mother. She was the ultimate refuge, but, at the same time, to be associated with her

---

[14] Kituku, *Folktales*, 3.
[15] Lindblom, *Riddles*, 33; Mwau, *Dictionary*, 658.

was the worst insult. A man was not addressed as the son of his mother. Girls also protested being addressed as the daughter of her mother. Children preferred to be associated with the father's prowess.

1020. *Mũndũ ekĩawa ĩvu nĩ mũnyanyae.*[16] **One is impregnated by her friend.**
This was said when the girl asserted that the father of her pregnancy was not her friend. If rape was not involved those listening to the case assumed that there was some level of acquaintance involved between a boy and a girl. By interpretation, people get into trouble trying to accommodate colleagues. Another interpretation is that it is one's friends who will help him/her.[17] Moreover, whatever problem you get yourself into, it is likely that people close to you put you there.

1021. *Mũndũ ekĩwa wathe nĩ kĩndũ ũvikya.*[18] **One is weakened by something they can carry.**
If something is too heavy obviously someone will not carry it. However, a seemingly light object wears the carrier out. People are affected by things that they do repeatedly. For instance, one can consume alcohol responsibly or to their own ruin.

1022. *Mũndũ elũkaa kĩla ũĩte.* **One belches what he has eaten.**
People add other appendices to this axiom, which make the proverb more effective in the conversation but affect the historical period of emergence. It means what is in one's mind is what he/she speaks out.

1023. *Mũndũ mũĩ e atai aingĩ maseo.* **An intelligent person has many good advisers.**
Originating from antiquity this talks about sources of learning and knowledge. One is considered wise if he often listens to many wise people and learns from them. The axiom informs the audience that they should listen to different people to grow in wisdom.

1024. *Mũndũ mũĩ ndewaa ambatĩe.*[19] **A wise man is never told to go higher up.**
The proverb may be widely applied, including an interpretation that it has a sexual connotation in which it means a mature male youth is not told what to do in an intimate relationship with his girlfriend. The origin of this proverb is unknown, but by all accounts it emerged in antiquity.

---

[16] Kimilu, *Mũkamba*, 117; Mbiti, *Ngaeka*, 28; Mutisya, *Proverbs*, 37.
[17] Mutisya, *Proverbs*, 37.
[18] Kituku, *Folktales*, 66.
[19] Mwau, *Dictionary*, 658.

1025. *Mũndũ mũima ndaleaa ũndũ ta kana.* **An adult does not object like a child.**
The Kamba try to avoid disputes as far as possible, avoiding the word 'no' even to an unreasonable request. An adult always answers such requests with canny answers that leave him unscathed in the future.

1026. *Mũndũ mũwau ndaumĩaw'a ndĩthya.* **A sick person is not given the duty of herding.**
Dating from the Vascon era, this proverb means a person committed to a valuable cause is not charged with an extra task. Pass the task on to someone else.

1027. *Mũndũ ũmwe ndetawa mbaa ngania.*[20] **A single man is not referred to as a clan.**
This is an old adage with multiple variations emphasizing the importance of marriage, family, clan, and life in a community of people.[21] Numerical strength for a clan was vital, and it was the duty of individuals to build it through procreation and serving in multiple functions. Historically, the Kamba arrived in Ũkamba as a group of twenty-five families during the first millennium. By the beginning of the Islamic period, they were already a distinct cultural group, with a structured clan system. Each clan occupied its own mountain across present-day Machakos and Makũenĩ.
The proverb urges individuals to multiply.

1028. *Mũndũ ndayenzaa na ndayonaa ĩkoti.*[22] **A person does not shave and see his nape.**
It was taboo for someone to cut his own hair, as others doing it strengthened friendships. The nape before the age of mirrors was impossible to see, and people depended on others to shave it. The proverb emphasizes the near-sacred importance of interdependence in a community.

1029. *Mũndũ mwaanu ndakũngĩwaa yembe.* **A lazy person has never sharpened a hoe.**
This emerged with the introduction of hoes for cotton cultivation in Kitui after 1932, revolutionizing Kitui agriculture. Weeding in Kitui was by digging sticks and a short-handled iron hoe called the Machakos hoe.[23] The maxim implies the new hoe cultivation was for courageous and strong people. A lazy person was not worth giving a hoe.

---

[20] Kimilu, *Mũkamba*, 117; Kituku, *Folktales*, 83.
[21] Mutisya, *Proverbs*, 31.
[22] Mutisya, *Proverbs*, 31.
[23] Colin Maher, 'Land Utilization as a National Problem with Special Reference to Kenya Colony', *East African Agricultural Journal* 2(2) (1936), 72.

1030. *Mũndũ ndameneaa mũka kũmya itani.* **A man does not despise his wife for having hard, rough underwear.**
This axiom emerged during the Vascon era when this type of apron (*itani*) became common among women. It disappeared after the Second World War. The bulky underwear were elaborately oiled, softened, and perfumed to impress husbands. If this were not the case, elders admonished the husband to bear with the wife for there were other more significant matters in life than soft underwear. The actual meaning is sexual: a man should not disown his wife because of her inability to exude sexuality.

1031. *Mũndũ ndatũaa ũsũnga na kĩtuo kĩmwe.* **A person does not dance with one shoulder.**
The most popular dance was *kũsũnga*, predominantly done by shaking both shoulders. The shoulder figuratively points to wives in a polygamous context, meaning a polygamous man does not sleep with one wife all the time. By extension, it may be applied to mean that one must change tactics rather than doing things repeatedly.

1032. *Mũndũ ũmanza undũ ũkwenda ũkoa akwata ũla ũtekwenda.* **If one searches for a desirable thing and fails, he takes an undesirable option.**
This has been associated with an unknown elder in the remote past. The unknown ancestor used it to mean an alternative can suffice when one has no choice. According to interviewees, this proverb emerged around the late eighteenth century with elders only vaguely known today, though their settlement is well known.

1033. *Mũndũ wĩ thayũ ndakwataa mũthanga.* **Dust doesn't stick on a living person.**
Public administrators created this maxim after independence to persuade public crowds to sit on bare ground (for want of seats) as they listened to official speeches. The maxim means dust that gets on the skin will not remain there permanently. It will be washed off.

1034. *Mũndũ wĩ thayũ ndaleaa ũsukwa.* **A living person is frequently slandered.**
Certainly, people talk about others all the time. The ancient axiom encourages people to endure when they are slandered rather than fight the gossipers.

1035. *Mũkaakaania ndew'aa ũkaanio.* **A disputatious person does not heed warnings.**
This ancient maxim is about listening and considering advice and suggestions. Such affairs demand less argument and more listening.

People who like arguments do not listen to warnings and perish at the end. There are still other interpretations to this proverb.

1036. *Mũndũ ũkũtwa ndaleaa ũsũna kavyũ.* **A person harvesting honey never fails to lick the knife.**
This proverb emerged during the precolonial era of apiculture. The Kamba hung their beehives on tree branches away from vermin and thieves. Keepers harvested the honey with an assortment of tools and vessels, including a knife with which they cut the combs very carefully to extract them. While eating honey during harvesting itself was discouraged, as the sweet fresh honey dripped from the knife the harvester often licked the knife. The proverb is thus an excuse for small oddities like pilferage in business stocks.

1037. *Mũndũ wĩ nthongo ndaũkitĩaa kĩthangathĩnĩ.* **A one-eyed person never fights on sandy ground.**
Fighting as a game as well as a conflict was common among precolonial youth. Most of this fighting was conducted on soft sandy ground to avoid injury. Since sand often entered into the eyes, those with bad eyes avoided sandy places for such fights. Once the single eye was blocked by sand, the victim would be overwhelmed quickly. This emerged in the Islamic period when the Kamba occupied riverbanks, and valleys with sand. It means one should avoid certain risky adventures and places. It is advisable not to expose one's underbelly.[24]

1038. *Ũtanakw'a ndoasya nthongo.* **One who is not dead has not escaped blindness.**
This is a common ancient adage with deep symbolic meanings. The term blindness or one-eyed is not literal but symbolizes accident, death, and misfortune as well as good luck and
wealth. The speaker first warns listeners not to boast of achievements because their fortunes may change. At the same time the proverb may encourage listeners to work hard, have hope, and trust that fortune will change for the better.

1039. *Mũndũ wa mũndũ e ũtukũ na ũngĩ.* **A friend has a night and another.**
This ancient axiom emphasizes the importance of friendship. A friend will spend a long time with a friend without alarm. This is open to many interpretations and applications. It means that a good companion is rare.

---

[24] Mutisya, *Proverbs*, 46.

1040. *Mũndũ ombawa ũtukũ.* **A person is created at night.**
This old proverb emphasizes the importance of dinner and good sleep, for that is when the body adjusts to many conditions. It may also point to intercourse, which was restricted by law to nighttime or liable to punishment, often with banishment from the village if done in daylight. The man not the woman was the one who was punished that way, according to most interviewees.

1041. *Mũsyawa wa mũndũ nde mũiwe.* **Twins have no co-wife.**
This symbolic and complicated axiom with historical antecedents appears in a song by musician Ben Mbatha in which he meant that no one is born with another. People are born with different temperaments, talents, and outlooks on life. No musician performs like any other. Mbatha appears to have coined this axiom but it could have historical precedents tracing back to the emergence of organized music.

1042. *Mũndũ ũte mũka ndakwatawa ũtumĩa.* **A man without a calabash is not called into eldership.**
This proverb uses *kĩtete* as an allegory for girl, wife, or family. Except for very old oral testimonies, historians cannot date it from its content. But those familiar with the history of Kamba farming and the cultivation of gourds and calabashes estimate its emergence to the pre-Vascon era. Another lead is to be found in its hidden meaning. The proverb means that a man who has no daughter or family can never officiate in social and political matters reserved for elders.

1043. *Mũndũ ũte mũka athanaa mĩkaawanĩ.* **One without a wife gives orders in coffee shops.**
This is a postcolonial coinage when coffee shops emerged from the late 1920s and subsequently transitioned into tea and coffee shops as well as eating places or restaurants. Married men ordered their wives to serve drinks and food, but an unmarried one ordered no one except in restaurants. The maxim was meant to encourage young men to marry and build wealth.

1044. *Ũte ngũkũ ndaumanaa na ĩya ya ngũkũ.* **A person who does not have chicken does not chase away the mongoose.**
In a large family there were chickens that belonged to different members. However, only those family members who had chickens suggested that the family could have one chicken for dinner. The ancient maxim means that the ultimate decisions over use of resources lie with the owner. The buck stops here!

1045. *Mũndũ ũte ngũkũ ndaendaa ũmbanonĩ wa mĩkololo.* **A man without cattle does not go to a gathering of dip or dam builders.**
Emerging from the Monsoon era, this proverb admonishes listeners to avoid matters not involving them. It is also an excuse by someone suggesting that since he is not an expert in the field under discussion it will be unfitting for him to get involved. This is said in reference to who should participate in bridewealth negotiations. Only married men with daughters can do so. The origin of bridewealth provides clues to the origin of this proverb. During migration to Ũkamba and early settlement, the custom of bridewealth was non-existent, hence the proverb emerged during the seventeenth century when the Kamba acquired more livestock to exchange for brides.

1046. *Mũndũ mũĩ nde kĩveti.* **A clever man has no wife.**
Emerging from the Vascon era this common phrase has multiple interpretations and applications. First it admonished young men how to handle married life. Wives make mistakes but not every mistake should cause tensions. The man should ignore some errors, mistakes, and weaknesses of his family members.

1047. *Mũndũ e kĩndũ atũaa e kĩndũ.* **One who has something remains with something.**
Someone is attractive to creditors if he has property. This maxim emerged during the age of long-distance trade during the Islamic period. The Kamba borrowed and loaned among themselves. Those with property were more likely to get credit than those with nothing.

1048. *Ũuĩte na ũngĩ ũuĩte maithenganaa.* **Two brewers do not beg each other for the brew.**
The maxim implies two things: self-sufficiency and similarity. Since each brewer is self-contented there is no need to beg. Second, since they have the same resources they do not need the other's resources.

1049. *Mũndũ akaw'a oondũ ũtwĩte mĩtĩ.* **A man is assisted in building by the way he harvested building material.**
Whenever a Mũkamba was ready to build, he went to the forest and cut building materials. Then he called neighbours to assist in erecting the house. Those helping contended with the available material whatever their quality. This means people should abide by the rules and resources of the person on the receiving end. Leave to their peril those who cannot make firm decisions on their own affairs.

1050. *Mũtai ũte mũtae ndataa mũtaawa.* **An untrained adviser cannot admonish advisees.**
This ancient axiom has a simple interpretation: to advise others one first needs to learn from knowledgeable people. Traditionally, whenever novices needed knowledge in a given area they consulted specialists.

1051. *Vaati nzeo yũkaa yĩvakĩte wailo.* **Good luck comes smeared with black oil.**
This provides insights into the history of urban pollution in Ũkamba. Automotive oil and grease, poorly disposed of after use, appeared around 1921. Urban areas became greasy from the 1930s on. This means good things are often disguised, just like the blackened oil-covered grass and land.

1052. *Mũndũ akuawa o mbola.*[25] **A person is carried gently.**
Drawn from the romantic realm, this axiom means an opponent is defeated gradually. Cajoling a girl to be one's friend was referred to as 'to carry', because young men carried their sweethearts and the groom gently carried off his bride to his home. In the same manner, the proverb suggests that, in politics, a candidate running against a stronger contender must employ carefully couched strategies and remain consistent in efforts to erode the power of the opponent.

---

[25] Mwau, *Dictionary*, 657.

13

Women and Motherhood

1053. *Aka mayĩsĩ ngũ ta mathendũ.* **Women do not distinguish dry bark from logs.**
This is a women's maxim in which is meant that a woman can marry any man without considering his worth at sex. As a critique of that free choice, the proverb compares two men as equivalent to bark and logs. The bark (a worthless man) blazes brightly but tires quickly – its warmth (romance and material support) is short-lived. On the other hand, the log burns longer, and its warmth is satisfying and sustaining. The effort to secure a log matches the effort of securing a long-lasting marital relationship. This maxim emerged in periods with intense competition for suitors in the seventeenth and eighteenth centuries.

1054. *Aka me kĩtũlĩ ve ũndũ mawetaa.* **Curvy women have something to say.**
This maxim, popular since the 1970s, has featured in many cultural dances. According to oral accounts it means curvy women lure men into temptation.

1055. *Aka me ũko ta indo.* **Women have types like livestock.**
Elders said this to young men advising them to seek carefully for their brides. The maxim has multiple variants, all meaning not every woman is suitable as a wife. It is applied in other ways such as in business partnerships or any long-term commitment to a joint undertaking.

1056. *Aka nĩ mamĩthemba ta mathamba.* **Women are of different kinds like iron sheets.**
Corrugated iron sheets were initially called *mathamba*. Since the Second World War that name has faded, which means that the proverb emerged sometime between the late nineteenth century and the outbreak of the Second World War, the period when such a term was used. As such, this maxim warned young men to be meticulous in choosing life partners. It also calls for keen scrutiny of whatever field of work one wants to venture into.

1057. *Aka nĩ ndia ndiku na ndũlika nzĩnĩ wa mĩkuthũa.* **Women are deep ponds that a man cannot swim through successfully.**
This was used among womanizers who ironically persuaded listeners to refrain from being womanizers. A man cannot exhaust the energy of women if he chooses to be promiscuous. Although with longstanding precedents, it emerged during the twentieth century.

1058. *Aka maasya mũndũũme akw'a ũsu nĩ ũvonge ngasava ũngĩ.* **When a man dies, women say, 'that is a branch, I will cut another one'.**
This ancient proverb alludes to gender issues. A widow gets another man while maintaining her residence, whereas a widower living with a new partner must move outside his home. The bereaved female chose whom to stay with among male relatives of her deceased husband.
Sometimes a widow defied these procedures and found a lover of her own outside the household. The free choice of a new sexual partner was equated to cutting a new log in the forest.

1059. *Aka nĩ othu na iveti nĩ mbũthũ.* **Women are many and wives are few.**
This is said in many variants to warn young men that not all women are fit for longstanding relationships; it has multiple interpretations and applications. Although quite old it appears to have emerged from a particular period of Kamba history. Before 1700, the Kamba were not particular about whom to marry. Procreation was more important than beauty and romantic sentiments. This suggests that the proverb emerged between the 1700s and early 1900s. Mailu recorded it in 1972, which could reflect the changing politics of gender in the last 70 to 100 years.

1060. *Iveti syĩ ĩkũmi kya mũndũ no kĩmwe.* **Out of ten co-wives, one's wife is only one.**
Polygamy is normal among the Kamba and a fair number of men had multiple wives, but love and tender care towards the husband came from one wife only. This maxim means not everyone excels.

1061. *Kava mwolyo wa lĩu kwĩ mwolyo wa mũũme.* **Better queuing for food relief than queuing for a husband.**
Kamba women who experienced the stigma of queuing for relief food (*mwolyo*) imported that experience into polygamous marriages and coined this proverb around the late 1920s. In polygamous marriage, a man usually slept with one woman at a time and never at the same time, keeping co-wives waiting their turn in their own houses. The proverb means there are things that are not comparable.

1062. *Mūkamba mūka ndatwesaa mwatū.* **A Kamba woman does not harvest honey.**
Women used this axiom as an excuse to be excluded from hard tasks. It was taboo for a woman to extract honey from a beehive, due to the risks involved. The proverb talks about division of labour along gender lines.

1063. *Mūūme ti suti atī nakola ngatūnga ndukanī nīsakūe mbola.* **A husband is not a suit that if I am dissatisfied I can return to the shop and select another one slowly.**
This together with the previous entry demonstrate the manner in which the new economy centred on fixed shops in Ūkambanī operated from the First World War onwards.

1064. *Mūndūmūka wī ngoo akūīaa kwoo.* **A bad-tempered woman grows old at her maiden home.**
This ancient axiom unveils certain secrets of choosing marriage partners among the young. For men, a woman who was bad-tempered had to be avoided at all costs. This is one of the proverbs discouraging bad temper. *Ngoo* means both temper and heart.

1065. *Kīla mūndū mūka mūmbe nesa e īlavata īthūkū thayūnī wake.* **Every beautiful woman has a dark spot in her life.**
The Kamba were not historically selective in partners, a reality tied to the availability of women to marry. Since the sexes were fairly equal in number until the 1700s, proverbs like this emerged when the Kamba became selective during the Vascon era, signalling political, economic, and demographic stability. The Kamba began enquiring carefully about the character and behaviour of the would-be wife and her family. If she was found to be quarrelsome, prone to wizardry, theft, or chronic diseases, the young man diplomatically abandoned the quest.

1066. *Vayī wītīawa mūisīsya ūtesī mūndūūme.* **No virgin calls a midwife.**
One meaning of this axiom is pregnancy comes through coitus and conception. There is an explanation for all occurrences. One cannot make excuses for mistakes.

1067. *Kīmbithī kya aka kīsīīwe no aka aangī.* **Other women know women's secrets.**
Those in partnerships know the secrets of their association. Still, the ancient proverb has deep cultural and historical meaning. With regard to sexuality, motherhood, pregnancy, and other matters, women and men learned things during initiation that they were never to reveal across gender lines.

1068. *Kya mũndũ mũka kĩkwataw'a kyakoma.* **That of a woman is trusted when it sleeps overnight.**
This proverb can be pronounced, interpreted, and applied in diverse ways because it holds suspense. It raises the question: 'What is it that can be trusted or touched when she is
asleep?' By most oral accounts it is *kyuo* (word), implying a woman changes her mind frequently and the man can only patiently take her word. If she does not change, it was assumed that she honoured her words.

1069. *Kũtwaa mũndũ mũka mũkũũ no ta kũthoowa ĩkaseti kũituka.* **You may be late to do certain things.**[1]
Of recent coinage, this proverb expresses the domineering view of marriage as solely for procreation rather than a mere general life partnership. An old bride cannot bear children. This axiom tells the listener to do things in the right time and the right way.

1070. *Kwĩ aka makũtwawa na angĩ mauta Kĩthuma.* **There are some women destined for marriage and others a bed full of ointment.**
This emerged in the postcolonial era and reflects social changes in attitudes towards women, marriage, beauty, and morality. It reflects resistance against foreign perfumes and other products. Appearing in popular music this means there are women worth marrying and others who have merely applied perfumes and cosmetics who do not seek a long-lasting relationship. The Kamba society, both men and women, had unspoken opposition to the modern idea of beauty. Women who dressed elaborately or applied cosmetic perfumes were associated with 'immoral sex' or prostitution. The axiom was used not by elders this time but in public discourse, to warn young men to carefully seek whom to marry.

1071. *Mũndũ mũka akũnaa wĩa mwiingĩ kwongya mwana na ĩthe.* **A woman does a lot of work, suckling the baby and the father.**
This appeared in a song in Machakos during a female politician's campaign. It means while a lactating woman nurses the baby, her husband watches closely and waits for his turn for love. Here these two different duties cannot be handled at the same time as the woman has to jump between them, not an easy task psychologically. A woman candidate, in her opinion, was preferable since she was likely to manage public affairs better.

---

[1] Mutisya wa Ngai, 'Kyuo kya Ngoso number 44'.

1072. *Inyaa ngũmbaũ olotawa na ngundi ndoloteka na kyaa.* **The mother of a champion is pointed at with a fist not a finger.**
The mother of champions is highly respected. Pointing at someone with a finger implies they are insignificant, while persons of stature are indicated using the entire hand, implying the big nature of such mothers who are respected and revered.

1073. *Mũndũ wĩ nguma no nyinya mũndũ mũka ũta mwenda.* **The only hero is one's mother, a woman one cannot marry.**
This is a deeply symbolic statement and hard to understand for most. It means one's mother is the only woman to bring someone into life, but that offspring cannot sleep with their mother.

1074. *Mũndũ mũka ũlalasya itho ĩmwe nĩ mũng'endu sũvĩa ũkũnwa.* **A woman who winks one eye is proud, take care lest you be struck.**
There are hidden meanings in this statement. It points to the need for care and precaution when dealing with attractive matters that may lead someone into intractable problems. This postcolonial coinage uses female moral decay as a commentary on other aspects of life.

1075. *Mũndũ mũka wa ũtwaawa kũasa kwoo nde mũsamo.* **A woman married far from home is not attractive in her homeland.**
This ancient statement represents contradiction, but one historically explained. In the very early days when the Kamba population was small, marriages occurred between adjacent clan villages.
By 1900, however, it was preferred for women and men to marry in distant villages. This statement means that a girl who is married far from her village was not attractive to her male agemates, for diverse reasons. One meaning is that unwanted items can be thrown away in natural sites that find use for them. Second, if a trade product is not in demand in the local market, it can find markets elsewhere.

1076. *Mũndũ mũka nzeleke e kanywa ke lũkwata.* **A cunning woman has an enticing mouth.**
This postcolonial coinage may probe a historical study of Kamba mirth and laughter, innovative subjects that historians rarely dare look at. Although Kamba women laughed easily (*kũtheka na ũkula*), the kind of laughter that came with the emergence of prostitution during the colonial period was different. After the First World War the manner of smiles and laughter became yardsticks of female morality. The way a woman laughed, including physical gestures and tone, differentiated her from normal behaviour. People said she laughed like a prostitute. In political speeches this axiom meant that misleading leaders had enticing words and if the electorate voted for them they would get nothing in return.

1077. *Mũndũ mũka mũito asũngĩlaa ũtee.* **A pregnant woman dances on the side.**
This has sexual connotations. Indeed, in a crowded dance, a pregnant woman will most likely avoid the crowd, but that is not the actual meaning. It means a pregnant woman cannot have sex normally on her back. This is a warning that a person who is weak or disadvantaged must employ strategies suitable for the task.

1078. *Mũndũ mũka mũseo ti kĩtimba.* **A beautiful woman is not the shape of her hips.**
This view of beauty was nonexistent before 1900, which means the proverb certainly emerged during the twentieth century. Beauty came to be viewed from the shape of the body, particularly the hips. This proverb emerged as a protest against the trend to view beauty according to modern tastes.

1079. *Mũndũ mũka nĩ waandũ onthe.* **A woman is for all people.**
This ancient axiom has multiple variations and interpretations: first, all people belong to the woman and she (mother and symbol of hope) should treat them all fairly and equally. Second, a woman is free to take any man she wants to mate with, having no predestined husband. This dovetails into the concept of the nuclear family and patriarchy, challenging the historical notions of women's constricted sexuality. Third, a woman belongs to anyone who wants to take her hand in marriage or for sex. In this context, the maxim advises men against fighting over women as no one has authority over her, her choice being the paramount factor.

1080. *Wasamya kĩvĩsĩ nĩũkwanangĩa wiiyo.* **If you give a boy a taste he will destroy your fence.**
This ancient axiom admonished girls not to date immature and irresponsible boys who might bring embarrassment. Kamba dating involved boys going to the home of the girl at night and getting into the compound through cracks in the fence. If a boy became intimate with a girl, such cracks in the fence developed into paths.

1081. *Ũvyũ wa mwana ũmanyĩkaa nĩ mũsyai.* **The parent knows labour pain.**
This ancient adage does not have a Swahili origin as some suggest, it is merely similar. The parent is used instead of the mother because the context points not to labour pain but the pain of upbringing a child, particularly if the child is in danger or dies. Only the person involved knows the details of the episode.

1082. *Wavitha ūthei ndūsyaa.* **If you hide your nakedness, you cannot procreate.**
This proverb points to the need for individuals to promote procreation. It calls on both male and female to be open to sex and let their partners have their way. This contradicts the overall performance of sex, which was almost ritualized and done mostly at night or in complete secrecy during the day. In a literal sense, the proverb means that the end justifies the means. If you want something, go for it no matter the cost.

1083. *Kwiiya mūndū mūka nota kwiiya ūkethe.* **To spy on a woman for infidelity is like guarding an already harvested grain field.**
This emerged among farmers during the colonial period. When a field was harvested, it was called *ūkethe* and birds descended on it to eat spilled grain. Farmers ignored them, just as it is futile to watch over one's wife. Women ridiculed the practice of *kwiiya mūndū mūka* – guarding a wife against committing adultery – as futile. The Kamba appear formerly to have had relaxed attitudes towards sex and marital infidelity, even sharing spouses. However, as polygamy declined during the colonial era, men kept keen eyes on their wives to ensure they did not cheat, but observers noted that vigilance over women was futile as they always outwitted the watchers.

1084. *Wenda ūmantha mūndū mūka mūseo īlya yiiko na wīī.* **If you want a good wife, try her in the kitchen and the bed.**
Emerging in the 1900s this maxim prompts a discussion on urban-based work, bedrooms, and kitchens from 1900 to 2000. A good wife was considered one good in bed and in the kitchen. A woman who prepared well-cooked food was ideal. But this good cooking involved new recipes, challenging women's ability to master them and innovate, since cooking now required new utensils that the women did not have. It was the new tastes of the colonial era that gave rise to discourse over recreational sex and kitchen politics.

1085. *Mūndū mūka wī kītimba atwaawa kyathela.* **A woman with a big behind is married when it is finished.**
Emerging during the twentieth century, this axiom speaks of morals, beauty, romance, and reality in life. Girls used to brag before men and would not give in to men's pleas for marriage, but as a girl's beauty waned with age she became less attractive. She ended up marrying someone she previously scorned as worthless. It condemns bragging.

1086. *Mūndū mūka ūte kītimba nota mwanasiasa ūte mbesa.* **A woman without hips is like a politician without money.**
This is a recent coinage depicting the nature of post-independence politics in Kenya. It compares wealth and women. To the creator of this

proverb the beauty of a woman is largely in her hips and, without hips, a woman is less attractive. Likewise, a broke politician will attract no voters. This reveals the nature of Kenyan politics and sexuality. It indicates that, while money drives politics and the election of leaders, beauty among women is not to be found so much in the content of their character but in the shape of their bodies and physical appearance.

1087. *Ĩsu nĩ nguano ya ũtilĩlwa.* **That is a borrowed wooing ploy.**
This is a racy proverb collected from Ĩkanga in southern Kitui county, referring to the Kamba practice of sweet-talking girls into sexual intercourse. If a young man wanted to sleep with a particular girl, he had to pick his words carefully in order to convince the girl that he was a valuable suitor. It is elaborated with a story of a boy who relied on his grandmother's words to cajole girls. One day he asked his grandmother, 'There is this girl who does not talk to me. Whenever I salute her she gets upset. What shall I do grandma?' The grandmother said, 'That is easy my grandson. If you find her in a gloomy mood you do this and that' (the actual directives are withheld here). The boy was excited and left his grandma's house full of confidence. When he approached the girl, this time she came smiling and begging for a hug. The boy was stupefied and ran very fast back to his grandmother. *Nayo sũsũ kauka kathekete kekanawa nako ata?* 'Grandmother, what if she comes smiling?' The grandmother, shocked by his behaviour, simply exclaimed, 'You must be a foolish grandson.'

1088. *Kamwanda kavukĩaw'a aka ona aũme makaingaa masembete.* **A vale where women are defiled, even men cross running.**
Emerging during the Vascon era, this maxim reflects gender equality in risks and abilities. It is close to 'What is good for the goose is good for the gander.' Increased population and relative insecurity during that period led to cases of rape. Beyond that context, it means there are things that are universally feared across gender lines.

1089. *Mũsũnga na mũthoni ekasya mũsũng'ũ angĩĩsye kĩĩrĩnĩ ndakaume mũthoni.* **Whoever dances with in-laws hugs the spectators lest he insults the in-laws.**
Dances were called 'group music', where all participants revelled and sometimes spectators joined in with anyone willing. The rules were that one could not dance with relatives. Above all, no one was permitted to dance with in-laws. If that happened due to excitement, the dancer had to hug spectators in order to avoid accusations of having insulted the in-laws. Dances were for the most part simulations of sex and, if a man danced facing and hugging a member of his wife's family, it was taken symbolically as having sex. The ancient axiom warns caution in handling delicate matters.

1090. *Mūthokania ūtukū esaa ūthokya mūthoni.* **Whoever invites guests at night eventually invites in-laws.**
Lindblom related a story that illustrates this proverb. A certain man habitually jumped onto any bed available whenever he was tipsy. One day he accidentally slept on the bed of his mother-in- law, to the disgust of all villagers. Not only was he embarrassed, he was also severely punished according to custom. Far from immorality, this ancient axiom cautions against carelessness of any kind.

1091. *Vata wa nthenga nīkūmilwa.* **The object of beer drinking is intoxication.**[2]
The current form of this ancient maxim is *Kyelelo kya mūlevi nī ūmilwa*, 'The aim of a drunkard is to get tipsy.' The variant employs the Swahili loanword *mūlevi*, indicating a twentieth-century origin. Beer was popular in Ūkambanī and diasporic Kamba in Tanzania.[3] This adage serves as a simple explanation of alcohol's purpose: to relax the mind and achieve intoxication. However, some used it to justify consumption of low-quality liquor.

1092. *Ūkī wa ūthoni ūthelaa na ūthoni.* **Wedding beer ends with the wedding.**
In-laws were respected even more than political authority. The proverb, which emerged during the twelfth century when marriage customs became clear, alludes to how the Kamba exchanged daughters in marriage. Negotiations for weddings between in-laws involved consumption of specially made beer. The men from both sides drank and talked to the end in friendly terms.
The ancient axiom means serious associations last long in harmony.

1093. *Ūthoni ndūtunyawa.* **In-law-relationships are not trampled on.**
By the Islamic period, the Kamba had firmly settled around Mboonī and created elaborate social networks, in part based on intermarriage. Since that time, this proverb has remained a central philosophy guiding relationships among in-laws. It means that in-laws need space and freedom and should not be given any of one's burdens.

1094. *Ūthoni ndūvūthaw'a.* **The inlawship is never derided.**
The Kamba took great care of marital relationships. To do so they minimized contact and visits with in-laws, probably the most highly respected of all social relations. Any small mistake was counted as disrespect for in-laws and was automatically fined a goat.

---

[2] Mwau, *Dictionary*, 670.
[3] Lindblom, *Riddles*, 17.

1095. Ūthoni ndwasaw'a kīwa ndūkasimbe athoni. Dowry is never paid in sugarcane lest you mock the in-laws.
Dating to the Monsoon Exchange era when sugarcane reached East Africa, this proverb reflects the period of its integration into cultural practices. It was often associated with sexuality. Squeezing the sweet juice out of the sugarcane replicated kissing on the mouth, which is a taboo act in the presence of in-laws according to Kamba customs. The Kamba maintained one must send gifts of honey rather than sugarcane to in-laws. The brew drunk even now during dowry negotiations and formal socializations with in-laws must be made from honey.

1096. Ūthoni wa kīvīsī ūthonekelaa mbua. The inlawship of a boy results from the rain.
This is a rebuke of persons of uncouth manners. Marital relationships were the most revered associations, where every care was taken to ensure mutual respect and no offence. A boy could not reach to such levels of respect.

1097. Kūsyaa ti kūmīa, kwīvinya taūkusya nyololo.[4] Childbirth is not comparable to defecating, it is as difficult as pulling chains.
Women use this saying with varying motives and objectives such as to advise younger women who have never been pregnant, or to challenge men who will never experience childbirth. It could also warn that to attempt an arduous task for the first time is challenging. A young man who had not yet begun paying bride-price was warned that dowry was not as easy as he imagined. Mutisya took another interpretation: no mother will disown her child no matter what, since labour pains establish permanent bonds far different from excretion, which people soon forget.[5]

1098. Sya mūndū mūka italawa syaingīīwa. Livestock herded by a woman are counted when they get home.
Women were rarely entrusted with herding, for security and moral reasons. Moreover, this ancient axiom is not about livestock in women's care. The symbolic meaning is that a girl is worth so many animals and gifts as a dowry. But these dowries are not counted as the father's property until they are brought to his home.

1099. Mūndū mūka mūī ndenzeawa mwana.[6] A wise woman does not let others shave her child.
Precolonial Kamba women rarely trusted other people with the safety of their children. Other women who were envious poisoned other

---
[4] Kimilu, *Mūkamba*, 1.
[5] Lindblom, *Riddles*, 31; Mutisya, *Proverbs*, 36; Mwau, *Dictionary*, 652.
[6] Mwau, *Dictionary*, 658.

women's children if they had a chance to bath, cuddle, or cut their hair. Wise women avoided such contacts.

1100. *Mũndũ mũka wĩ ngoo akũĩaa kwoo.* **A bad-tempered girl ages at her maiden home.**
Dating back to the Islamic period when Kamba social fabric took the current form, this maxim alludes to a girl's ability to secure a suitor. Young men were least attracted to introverts and girls who did not talk nicely. Thus, bad-tempered girls ended up as spinsters if they did not marry old men. The proverb with multiple interpretations foremost cautions against temper and ignoring other people.

1101. *Mũthewa nĩ kwaa eyovaa mũthiita waelye.*[7] **One bound to perish adorns beautiful ornaments.**
This alludes to the types of dress and dressing styles used in Ũkambanĩ before 1900. These had a flowing tail, which Krapf described in the 1840s and 1850s. The tail is a symbolic way of saying she is deceitful in every move she makes to cover her tracks and has secret plans to run away. Fearing pressure from family members to stay in the marriage without a permanent solution to her complaint, a woman designed her departure in a disguised manner. Secret absconding was seen at that time as a sound way out of a deteriorating marriage. As Kieti says, by disguise one avoids being recognized from afar.

1102. *Mũndũ mũka ndoanĩsw'aa ta ũta.* **A wife is not discussed like a bow.**
This proverb laces sexuality and martial masculinity. It compares a wife to a bow, both of which are very personal. No one was ever comfortable with someone else's bow. Likewise, men usually preferred their wives to other women. In this context, men may think other men's wives were not beautiful enough, not sexy enough, and so forth. In response to such criticism, the husband responded: one chooses the bow he can draw.

1103. *Ũta wa mwene wĩtawa ngoma nĩ andũ.* **People ridicule the owner's bow.**
Just as the bow fits its owner with no second opinion needed, so with a woman one wants to marry. It is the sole decision of the suitor, not the public, to scrutinize the bride. There are many auxiliary statements to this proverb. The buck stops here at the desk of the man alone, not even with his relatives. This proverb predates the Vascon era and set the stage in antiquity on how and who one should marry.

---

[7] Kĩeti, *Barking*, 114.

1104. *Mũndũ mũka ndasungawa, nĩwe wĩsungaa.* **A woman is never guarded, she guards herself.**
This speaks about morality and infidelity issues in married women. It is not the business of the husband to guard the wife against having extra-marital affairs. If the woman wishes to commit adultery nothing will stop her. Do not strive after wind.

1105. *Kyathĩ ngathi nditavasyaa ndia.* **I do not tell a fool my appointment.**
There are several variants but they address different contexts and may have different meanings. This emerged in the context of competition for girls. Young men preferred to approach girls privately, in the absence of other young men. During the twentieth century, this concept was extended to job seeking in urban areas. Jobseekers kept their interview appointment secret lest other applicants spoil the interview and be hired instead.

1106. *Kĩveti kyũĩ kĩnthaa yũa na kĩveti kĩtaku.* **A wise woman digs famine with a foolish woman.**
Since the nineteenth century surviving a famine has been referred to as 'digging out the famine'. The phrase derived from a famine called *Yũa ya ngaatu*. During that famine, which occurred during the 1860s, the Kamba survived by digging wild bulbs for food. The axiom talks about exploitation among the poor. Women were the most affected by famine because they were responsible for young children and any incapacitated individuals in the family. Some took advantage of other women. She would seek her company to distant places to find food and let her carry the food most of the way. However, the proverb is a symbolic pointer to other aspects of social life.

1107. *Kĩveti kĩtoonu kĩĩsawa kyasyaa.*[8] **A mean woman is eaten after childbirth.**
Whenever neighbourhood women noticed that one of them was not generous, they waited until she was in labour and as they took care of her at her weakest moment they helped themselves aggressively in her kitchen and pantry. A feast was held at home for the newborn and people revelled. This ancient maxim advocates getting the better of misers when they appeal for help.

---

[8] Muiu, *Cross-Cultural*, 91.

1108. *Kĩveti kyakũlw'a wĩ mũmwaũ kyasyaa 'Mũtwii mwĩvwa kwa Atangwa.'* **When a woman is asked about her lineage, she says 'Mũtwii clan and niece of Atangwa clan.'**
This proverb appeared during the Islamic era. It is notable that Kamba clans emerged out of some twenty-five families that migrated from central Tanzania during the first millennium. Clans were clearly defined by the end of the Islamic era, hence the axiom dates from that period.

1109. *Kĩveti kyaũsyaa ndia kyonekelaa mwĩvĩkĩlenĩ wa mata.* **A pregnant woman who will bear a simpleton is noticed by the way she spits.**
Simpletons are known to have limited control of their saliva. So, Kamba believe that if a pregnant woman spits consistently she is likely to deliver a simpleton. Emerging from antiquity this axiom means signs of time are detectable.

1110. *Kĩveti kĩkalaa na ndia.* **Only a foolish man lasts with a wife.**
This axiom emerged around the late nineteenth century. It implies that marriage, partnerships, and friendships are not easy. To maintain them requires patience and wisdom to forgive mistakes and ignore offensive behaviours.

1111. *Kĩveti kyũkaa kũveta na kĩkawa nĩ ndia.* **A woman puts aside what a fool does.**
This alludes to the responsibilities of married women. The first, to keep objects orderly and away from where people sit for meals. Symbolically she keeps family secrets out of public view. Due to tensions with the husband, it is only a patient woman (what is called foolish) who can bear this burden.

1112. *Ĩvu ya kĩveti yĩinenevaa mana kĩte kĩito.*[9] **A woman's abdomen does not protrude if she is not pregnant.**
Precolonial Kamba women were usually healthy and active with little trace of belly fat. The belly protruded only during pregnancy. Thus, this axiom means a woman's belly swelling is an indicator of pregnancy. Hence, there is a cause behind every incidence.

1113. *Mũndũ ndavũthasya mũthoni kĩveti kyake kĩtanamba kũkũa.* **One does not mock his in-law before his wife gets old.**
This proverb warns against getting a second wife while the first is still young, an act considered insulting to in-laws. In democratic societies leaders are not replaced unless they prove themselves incompetent.

---

[9] Lindblom, *Riddles*, 33.

1114. *Kũmantha kĩveti kwĩ vinya.* **The search for a wife is tedious.**
The Kamba see 'a search for a wife' – looking for a fitting partner and convincing the bride to leave her home to stay with a foreigner she calls husband – as a hard endeavour. This maxim emerged during the Vascon era, driven by balances in sex ratios and the rise of selectivity in choosing partners for marriage.

1115. *Mũsyĩ wakawa nĩ kĩveti ndia.* **A foolish woman builds a family.**
Foolishness is associated with harmony since it implies patience to endure challenges within a family or community. Those who endure keep their marriages and families together. Those who do not suffer family dissolution.

1116. *Mwaĩkwa ndaneenaa na kĩveti kyene.*[10] **An initiate does not speak to a married woman.**
The purpose of circumcision was to educate young men about secret society, customs and traditions, roles in conjugal affairs, history, society, and ideas on manhood. Circumcision ceremonies were performed during the summer between August and September and lasted between six and ten days.[11] Through this proverb the initiates were warned against speaking to female relatives. This was because the community upheld the morals of society and initiates were to honour women.

1117. *Ngũngũ ĩĩaa nda ĩla ya yo.*[12] **The barren eats for her stomach.**
The term *ĩĩaa* is key to comprehension of this proverb. It can mean cries, worries, or 'eats for'. The latter is the actual usage in the context of this proverb. The barren has no child to feed and thus eats just for her satisfaction. Women with young children eat less and let the children eat first. This proverb emerged among starving communities during the nineteenth century when ecological cataclysm brought about new levels of infertility, poverty, and starvation.

1118. *Ngũngũ ndĩkũaa.* **A barren woman never ages.**
While in backstage discourse the truth and causes of infertility were clearly known and sympathized with, in public discourse infertility was scorned and condemned in both sexes. This ancient proverb means that without the burden of childbirth the woman's body remains intact

---

[10] Naomi Musembi, 'Evolutionary Changes in Thematic Lyrics in Songs with Reference to Kamba Circumcision Songs in Kenya' (Thika: Mount Kenya University), 299.
[11] Paul Kavyũ, *Traditional Music Instruments of Kenya* (Nairobi: Kenya Literature Bureau, 1980).
[12] Mwau, *Dictionary*, 665.

and never weakens in her sexual performance. Related to that is the assumption that she remains sexually more viable than women who have been worn out by childbirth. Another interpretation is that she never ceases to have sex, with the hope that she will conceive. It means, until your dreams materialize keep on dreaming.

1119. *Mŭkŭngŭi wa ngŭngŭ aminawa nĩ ngŭngŭ.* **A man who tries to impregnate barren women is broken down by barren women.**
This proverb alludes to infertility. Some men thought they could impregnate barren women. If a man succeeded impregnating one he kept on sleeping with barren women until he became a habitual partner of barren women. Such a man never marries and leads an absurd life. The moral lesson is do not engage in futile endeavours.

1120. *Mŭmanzi wa mŭka ndamanzaa ngŭngŭ nŭndŭ ngŭngŭ ndĩsyaa ĩngŭŭ.* **A searcher of a wife does not search for a barren for the barren does not bear at old age.**
Extracted from a song its meaning is clear as far as marriage is concerned. Nevertheless, the message of the proverb is not about childlessness but about other life aspects. That is, one cannot invest valuable resources in a venture that will not bear returns. One cannot try impossibilities. The proverb traces back to antiquity even though barenness has fluctuated throughout history depending on diet, public health, and status of medical treatment.

1121. *Ngŭngŭ ĩsyaawa yĩ ngŭngŭ.* **A barren woman is born barren.**
The ancient proverb talks about inherited problems and precedents. It reflects societal condemnation of barenness and childlessness. The common view was barenness was inborn and one grew up with it. However, the proverb has nothing to do with barenness. On the contrary, it talks about things and situations that are hard to change.

1122. *Ngŭngŭ na mŭoi me ndŭŭ.* **A barren woman and a witch are friends.**
The truth of this proverb may be misleading or contradictory to the Kamba perception of barenness and childlessness. In reality, witches kill children while barren women crave children. This is referring to characters who do not like progress in the community.

1123. *Ngŭngŭ ndĩtei na mwana.*[13] **A barren woman has no mercy for a child.**
This proverb is crucially important given that it is assumed that proverbs supposedly express condensed folk truth. This statement

---

[13] Mwau, *Dictionary*, 665.

exists with a known fact that barren women and impotent men were extremely kind and loving to children. Other proverbs exist that show that childless people engaged in adoption and had large numbers of children that they passionately cared for. The maxim features in songs of all kinds, but the musicians who sang the songs admitted that it does not have a grain of truth in it.

1124. *Kĩthing'ĩĩsyo kĩ mũka.*[14] **Persistence lands one on a bride.**
A bus line spread this maxim in the 1980s. It means even though a girl may say no to a lad's marriage proposal, if he persists she will eventually give in. However, its real application has less to do with love affairs and marriage and more with the importance of persistence in all endeavours.

1125. *Wenda kũmanya mũkau akekala ata akũa, sisya inya wake.* **If you want to know the shape of your wife in her old age, look at your mother-in-law.**
It is believed that character traits are passed from mother to daughter. From the Second World War, when this axiom emerged, young men were advised that if the mother-in-law is mean to her husband, it can happen to you after marriage. This appears to have been lifted from, 'Like mother, like daughter.'

1126. *Kĩveti kĩseo ti wanake nũndũ vai kĩndũ kyanake kĩte ĩlanga.* **A good wife is not just beauty because nothing beautiful is without blemish.**
This is about selecting a wife. Since this practice is somewhat recent, the maxim emerged during the colonial and postcolonial periods. The Kamba appear to have summarily declared beauty to be a matter of common sense. The determinant of a good wife is not beauty alone but also the person's inner content.

1127. *Kĩveti kĩ syana kĩkũlaa mbisũ.* **A woman with children does not scratch the pot.**
This unveils the relationship between Kamba mothers and children, particularly in lean days. It is part of the joy of motherhood. It is a coinage of the period between 1800 and 2000. During the famines of the 1800s and 1900s, every bit of food was secured and eaten. Pots and bowls were licked clean of any food. During the nineteenth and twentieth centuries, poor families cooked food in earthen pots; the food was scooped out of the pot and served to family members. If there was not enough the cook, normally the mother, let the family eat while she contented herself with the burnt remains, which she carefully removed

[14] Mwau, *Dictionary*, 651.

with a snail shell. However, if she had little children she abstained from such actions and let the children scratch the pot. The application of this proverb goes beyond the kitchen and means a leader is not fit to deal with trivial matters and should leave certain things to juniors and so forth. There are other interpretations and applications.

1128. *Wenda kĩveti kĩkavaa manthĩla weũnĩ.* **If you want a good wife search in the wilderness.**
This is an axiomatic mockery that means there is no woman who is perfect. One will never find a perfect woman with no defects to marry. If one stubbornly insisted on getting such a wife he was directed to the wilderness to find a spouse – but there are no people in the wilderness. This maxim emerged during the age of imperialism.

1129. *Kaveti kakaenda wendo konekaa tene.*[15] **A wife who will abscond her matrimonial home is noticed quite early.**
The Kamba practised marital customs that appear unique and contrary to Western cultures. When a married woman was dissatisfied with marriage she ran off secretly to her parents. This act was called *kũthi wendo* and there are several proverbs that relate to this practice. Coined during the eighteenth century the proverb tends to carry the same message about young couples. They are more concerned about women who were careless about their marriages. The proverb, however, is about predictability of different aspects of life.

1130. *Mũmanthi wa mũka ndatalaa ĩthasya.* **One seeking for a wife does not count broken relationships.**
This is a twentieth-century coinage, when separations and divorce intensified. It refers to separation among the young and calls on young men seeking a permanent relationship to persevere and persist until they find their match.

1131. *Mũmanthi wa mũsyĩ nde syĩngokoa mbũmũ.* **The founder of a family has no hard elbows.**
This proverb tracing back to the Vascon era admonished household heads to be polite and gentle to their wives, children, and other dependants. It derives from people often using their elbows to nudge others. It calls upon patriarchs to develop soft elbows. The maxim can be applied in other contexts.

---

[15] Mwau, *Dictionary*, 648.

1132. *Mŭmanthi wa mwana ndakĩaa nzakame.* **One who needs a child never fears blood.**
This refers to people who are desperate to conceive. Sometimes conception is difficult, and this elicited such proverbs. Spouses would have sexual intercourse even during menstruation; this means one will achieve one's desires at all costs. The proverb also means one in need does not keep secrets.

1133. *Ngungi ya iveti ndĩ kĩtanda.* **One who flirts with women does not have a bed.**
Different versions of this proverb have appeared in many songs since its creation after the Second World War. Beds became common during that period. The axiom means an immoral person has no home and is rootless.

1134. *Mŭtŭania alikaa kwake na ĩteta, na kwene aneena na kĩwe.* **A cohabiter enters his home with noise but whispers in other persons' homes.**
The cohabiter was a man who lived with a widow to the extent of neglecting his own wife and family. As a result of tensions with his wife, the cohabiter is always quarrelsome. However, he has no voice at the widow's house. This is a deeply symbolic statement meaning a thief makes a lot of protests. If someone protests loudly against an accusation, the listeners assume that he has done something wrong.

1135. *Katheka wakinyie mai ndŭlwa nĩko.* **You cannot forget a thicket where you stepped on excrement.**
Human excrement was deposited in bushes but immediately buried to prevent people from stepping on it, and thus magically harm the person stepping on it.[16] Burying excrement was of ritual significance as much as it was hygienically valuable. People will not want to pass through a place where they previously stepped on faeces. This ancient axiom applies to broad life aspects with a brooding meaning, once bitten twice shy. In the Old Testament, God tells the Israelites the same thing as the Kamba elders said about handling excrement.

1136. *Kyŭŭtŭ kĩnyungaa kyŭvakŭŭwa.*[17] **The curded excrement smells when it is being collected.**
The word *kyŭŭtŭ* in the context of this proverb means faeces in a semi-dry condition. The ancient proverb means that trouble will not get in your way if you avoid it.

---

[16] Adamson, *Peoples*, 238.
[17] Mwau, *Dictionary*, 653.

1137. *Watola mai na kyaa kĩmwe, kwata na kĩtaa kyonthe.*[18] **If you touch faeces with one finger, immerse the entire hand.**
This ancient maxim talks about commitment and resolve to deal with problems head-on. If you are involved in a particular matter be fully committed and pursue the matter to the end. You cannot be lukewarm.

1138. *Mũtiwa ĩtina avulawa mai nĩ kĩng'onde.* **The rearguard has his faeces plucked by a beetle.**
Hesitation breeds embarrassment. Young boys who ran in single file sang this; the last one in the run was infuriated and ran faster. Adults turned these children's words into highly symbolic statements. It has multiple variants that are used differently by different age sets.

1139. *Mũtuma ndũũ na kĩngolondo kĩsaa ũmũthokea nyũmba kĩvingilitĩtye ngũmbwa ya mai.*[19] **If one befriends a beetle, it eventually brings him excrement.**
The beetle is attractive and some people collect them for aesthetic value. But whenever beetles escape they roll dung into a ball to roll into humans' quarters. This is a warning against intimacy with bad characters or with underage people.

1140. *Mũndũ atuma ndũũ na kĩngolinda kĩsaa ũmweete mai.*[20] **If one befriends a dung beetle, it eventually brings him excrement.**
Many dung beetles, or 'rollers', roll dung and human faeces into round balls, used as food for their brooding chambers. They then roll the ball around, sometimes into people's compounds. This warns the listener that if you associate with evildoers, you will be implicated in evil deeds. While flies consume faeces but pollute food and water, dung beetles, in contrast, clear faeces out of the proximity of human settlement (although it is not an attractive sight).

1141. *Mũthia wa kĩngolondo nĩ ũkũtanĩ.* **The end of the dung beetle is at the wall.**
The term *ũkũtanĩ* (against the wall) came into common use after the Second World War when walled buildings became common. Previously the Kamba had mud walls but rarely used the term *ũkuta*. They observed that though the beetle could roll its ball of dung endlessly it was stymied and stopped when it hit a wall. Thus, the proverb means there is always an end to any form of mischief. Imperial architecture was a major blow to beetles.

---

[18] Kimilu, *Mũkamba*, 119; Mutisya, *Proverbs*, 61.
[19] Kimilu, *Mũkamba*, 117.
[20] Kimilu, *Mũkamba*, 117; Mutisya, *Proverbs*, 34.

1142. *Mai ma mũeni nĩmo manyungaa.* **The visitor's faeces stinks the most.**
A guest always takes the blame if something unusual happens during his visit. If a neighbourhood has never experienced theft, for instance, the villagers will blame the newcomer, although the visitor may be innocent.

1143. *Mai ma mũviki mayonekaa.* **The excretion of a bride is never seen.**
A bride took every care to hide her weaknesses, to the extent of pretending that she never goes out for nature's call. The first week of marriage she ensured that no one saw her go out to answer nature's call, so that her faeces or urine was never seen by anyone. Nevertheless, the ancient proverb means that the secret of someone in the spotlight is clear.

1144. *Ndiwa nĩyĩsĩ vala mũũme wĩĩ ndamũkenga.* **A widow knows that her husband cannot cheat where he is.**
This means that among women only a widow is absolutely sure that her husband cannot cheat during his absence because he is dead. Only a dead man does not cheat on his wife. This is a postcolonial coinage pointing out that there are certain things that are fixed.

1145. *Ngingo ndĩkĩlaa mũtwe.*[21] **The neck will never be above the head.**
Although mostly used to compare the husband as the head and the wife as the neck, this gendering of the term is a misinterpretation, as in olden days this was about respect in society. It signified layers of power relations and rarely male–female power relations. As society changed in the twentieth century women began to use it to imply that the ultimate decision lies with the husband as the head of the family. It is that twentieth-century gendered statement that gave rise to the current meaning: a woman is subservient to a man.

1146. *Mũiani ndathelawa nĩ nzika.*[22] **One who watches over his wife never stops worrying.**
Anthropologists have argued that the nuclear family and the patriarchy are as old as society itself and with family and patriarchy came the male demand for fidelity. This anthropological truism does not appear to hold in Kamba history. The Kamba practised liberal sex with not only equality among men and women, but also few sexual restrictions in wedlock. Men shared their wives with clansmen and friends

---

[21] Mwau, *Dictionary*, 665.
[22] Mwau, *Dictionary*, 656.

such that men did not have to guard the sexuality of their wives in the manner that appears today. Things changed around 1800. Men increasingly began to guard who was seeking sexual intimacies with their wives and girlfriends. This maxim emerged sometime during the late nineteenth century, coinciding with changed attitudes towards sex and women.

1147. *Mũndũ mũito ndamanyaa woo wa kũũmwa akwananasya na kwemelwa nĩ mai.* **A pregnant woman equates labour pains with constipation.**
This is a woman's proverb aimed at women who do not understand childbirth and labour pains. Dating from antiquity, this statement talks about inexperience in certain hard tasks. It cautions young people to refrain from underestimating life matters that they have never dealt with. Once they try, they can be frustrated and defeated. In this saying, constipation is compared with labour pains, which are not similar in any way.

1148. *Mwenda ũkomo nĩwe ũyalanĩliaa.* **One who wants to go to bed prepares one for himself.**
The speaker of this proverb means that one in need of a wife is responsible for finding one. There is no point starving for marital love and romance when the opportunity is there to get married. The word 'bed' symbolizes the wife who traditionally prepared the bed and made it comfortable and perfumed. It was against customary norms for a man to prepare the bed for this was a woman's responsibility. There are many other proverbs that allude to these bedroom matters.

1149. *Ndeto sya kaveti kakũũ ililikanawa kakw'a.* **The words of a little old woman are remembered after her death.**
Although this axiom emerged during the Islamic era, it became popular through the career of a twentieth-century devoted matriarch and protector of Kamba culture, named Mũsailĩ Mũvanya from Nziũ in Makũenĩ. Growing up at a time when the Christian missionaries and imperial culture were systematically destroying Kamba culture, Mũsailĩ lamented the death of African pride. She dissuaded the Kamba from taking Western names after conversion since westerners were not taking Kamba names. Indeed, 90 per cent of the Kamba have foreign names and only a handful of Asians and Europeans have taken up Kamba names. As the proverb implies, there were many women before Mũsailĩ who prophesied, but the Kamba recognized their prophecies and advocacy only after the women died. Today female prophets are more remembered and revered than when they lived.

1150. *Ũla wĩyoneaa aũme ndesa kũkwata mwana.* **A woman who is fussy about men never procreates.**
Arising from ancient times this points to the importance of procreation. Conception was highly esteemed in precolonial societies. Mature women who needed to procreate did not have to be married to do so. If one was selective, conception became problematic. The maxim means that one should take the opportunity to get what he/she wants right away. This proverb appeared in the twentieth century when pressures of modernity and social change caught up with Kamba society.

1151. *Vatyĩ mũtĩ wĩlĩsaa kana kĩnaa kĩnyusaa.*[23] **There is no tree that climbs itself, or porridge that drinks itself.**
This is a deeply symbolic statement with sexual connotations – that a woman needs a man and a man needs a woman in order to be sexually satisfied. However, its application goes beyond sexuality and points to the importance of the commonwealth of a given society to the individual. All complement each other in one way or another. The maxim was coined in antiquity in forested terrain where climbing trees was the norm, unlike for people who lived on plains and in treeless terrain.

---

[23] Mbiti, *Ngaeka*, 98.

14

Children and Adulthood

1152. *Ĩthaa ya kĩvĩsĩ yaĩaa nzaanĩ kyũkwatangania.* **The ornament of a boy is damaged in his hands as he mishandles it.**
Ĩthaa was a brass ornament imported at high cost from the coast and worn around the neck during the Monsoon era. To damage or mishandle such an ornament was unthinkable. The proverb admonishes that one should be careful with opportunities, lest they slip away.

1153. *Kavaa kũtindania na atumĩa ivĩsĩ syĩ mũĩsyo.* **Better a day in the company of elders, boys are problematic.**
Grandfathers admonishing their granddaughters said this. Boys were openly encouraged to date girls since society scorned chastity. Mature boys had to ensure chastity was not found within their village lest they be embarrassed and fined a black bull. Girls on their part were not to be seen as morally loose nor completely aloof from sexuality. This female reaction made boys act more aggressively, the problematic nature that the ancient proverb alludes to. Older men who married young girls were less aggressive.

1154. *Kavĩsĩ ka mbaĩ kainyivaa.* **A clan boy is never little or belittled.**
This ancient axiom alludes to the Kamba political structure based on *mbaĩ* – the clan system.[1] The clan was the ultimate authority where male members were highly respected irrespective of age. In the absence of an adult male the female guardian usually probed the oldest boy to handle family matters.

1155. *Kĩvĩsĩ kĩ mbesa kĩtũmaaa ĩthe sikala.* **A monied boy sends his father to fetch a cigarette.**
This talks about the evil and transformative power of money (as the basis of wealth and power) during the twentieth century. Although the history of cigarettes in Kenya traces back to 1907, when the first shop opened in Mombasa, the Kamba restricted its consumption to

---

[1] KNA: DC/MKS/4/10 Machakos District Political Record Book 1930–1938; Kivuto Ndeti, *Elements of Akamba Life* (Nairobi: East African Publishing House, 1972); Mwau, *Dictionary*, 673.

adults until independence. During the late twentieth century, access to money through employment and business enterprise gave youth a chance to smoke and also to challenge traditional authority. Sending a father to buy cigarettes is seen as an insult and a sign of moral decay.[2] The proverb calls for balance between wealth and morality, traditional authority and economic power.

1156. *Kĩvĩsĩ kĩsovaa kyakũa.* **A boy becomes handsome when he grows older.**
The Kamba loathed the behaviour of teenagers and longed for the time that children would outgrow their teenage behaviour. Growing older does not imply physical ageing but maturity and improvement of behaviour. The adage dates from antiquity and applies in different social settings.

1157. *Kĩvĩsĩ kĩng'endawa nĩ ũsũe aĩkĩta mũemewa.*[3] **A boy brags of his grandmother calling him 'my husband'.**
Grandmothers proudly referred to grandsons named after their grandfathers as 'husband'. Outside this context of joking relationships, the names had implications that the grandson could have coitus with the grandmother. Among other things this ancient maxim means that too much praise can turn a good character into a social misfit.

1158. *Kĩvĩsĩ no kĩvĩsĩ kyũwaa ngũngũni na kiinyungĩa.* **A boy is a boy, he crushes a bedbug and takes a whiff of it.**
The Kamba loathed immaturity, which is expressed in the actions of a boy and a bedbug. The stench of bedbugs symbolized bad manners. Bedbugs reached East Africa's interior during the Monsoon era, hence the proverb. They could be killed by hand between the index finger and thumb. However, Kamba boys always sniffed at the dead bedbug. The proverb warned that enemies can go to extremes.

1159. *Ndũkatavye kĩvĩsĩ nthimo ndũkakyaangĩthye nyamũ.* **Do not tell a boy a proverb lest a beast gore him.**
This is an ancient proverb alluding to proper use of proverbs. Individuals taking proverbs as pieces of folk entertainment might use them uncritically. This warns that people who do not understand proverbs should be addressed in plain language.

---

[2] Peter Odhiambo, *The Truth about Tobacco and the Economy in Kenya and What Kenya Must Do about Tobacco and the Health of Kenyans* (Nairobi: National Tobacco-Free Initiative Committee, 2006).
[3] Mwau, *Dictionary*, 651.

1160. *Ĩthaũ ya kĩtandanĩ yumaa kana.* **A game in the bed results in a baby.**
This emerged after the Second World War when modern beds, called *kĩtanda*, a new loan from Swahili, became fashionable, and the Kamba became concerned about 'unplanned pregnancy'. It cautions against risky ventures of any kind.

1161. *Kana kationeka nĩ mũndũ ataumĩtye ng'ombe athoowa ninya.* **A man cannot have children without cattle.**
Without payment of cattle, biological parentage was meaningless in Kamba society. As Colin Maher learned from Kitui, 'If a woman runs away from her husband and lives with a lover, the latter is supposed to refund to her husband the amount of the marriage price. If he does not do this any children which are born will be the property of the legal husband who will not fail to remove them as soon as they have finished suckling since ... the children are considered to be great assets to Kamba, biological parentage notwithstanding.'[4] This maxim means there is no gain without pain.

1162. *Kana ke kaa masavu ma vakuvi.* **A child makes simple calculations.**
This twentieth-century coinage by elites alludes to one of the most popular educational courses, mathematics. The word mathematics came to symbolize strategies. While adults have well-thought-out calculations, children do not. However, 'child' is not literal but figurative of an imprudent person who does not think before acting.

1163. *Kana kesĩ akoo.* **A child knows only the sibling.**
This talks about favouritism, as in blood is thicker than water. In a group of children, siblings care for their own first. It is an old lesson that people should take care of themselves first before reaching out to help others.

1164. *Kana kaka kekalaa kakũnĩte ngũa.* **A girl keeps her dress smacked down.**
As noted elsewhere, the Kamba adopted manufactured clothes during the Monsoon era, but wore them as beaded aprons until the Second World War. Until then the practice of smacking the dress down between the thighs to minimize exposure was non-existent. Thus, this proverb emerged around the 1940s and 1950s, when European dresses were adopted and overcrowding in Ũkambanĩ brought men closer to their female relatives. 'Smacking the dress' was a women's innovation to cope with such male closeness and to reduce seduction. Although

---
[4] KNA: DC/KTI/5/1/1 Soil Erosion and Utilization, 1937: 40–5.

the axiom admonished girls about 'proper seating' position, it is also a call to relegate private matters to backstage discourse. Certain family matters should never be thrown into public discourse. This is an endangered proverb given that the custom of 'smacking the dress' is disappearing rapidly as new clothing styles are adopted.

1165. *Kana kaka kaitukĩawa nza.* **A girl never stays outside till dark.**
For their security and morality girls were expected to be home before dusk. This ancient maxim means to play safe in all conditions if you know your strength and weakness. Stay out of trouble.

1166. *Katatavw'a katavĩaw'a mai me ngele ndũnyũ.* **The stubborn girl is taught only when faeces trickles down her legs in the marketplace.**
There are several variations of this proverb, all referring to arrogant girls who will not listen to their parents, for which reason they eventually suffer self-inflicted embarrassment in public. This dates to the early 1900s, when marketplaces emerged. In this proverb, arrogance is punished by embarrassment in public, with the marketplace as the public space where it was most humiliating.

1167. *Kelĩtu katavũa ngũĩ na tũmwana kesaa kũkwata mũsee mũseo.* **A girl who cannot play with boys gets a good old husband.**
An incorrect interpretation is that a girl should not have sex so that she will find a good husband. On the contrary, the Kamba did not encourage abstinence. While moderation in sexuality was an important virtue, girls who were less willing to date boys were eventually married to polygamous old men. The moral lesson in this ancient proverb is that practice and experience are indispensable in life.

1168. *Kelĩtu kambĩĩa ũkwatwa nĩ nthoni kethĩaa kambĩĩa kwĩmanya.* **When a girl becomes shy it is a sign that she is conscious of herself.**
Girls exhibited shyness at puberty, a sign of their awareness of their biological changes. This ancient axiom points to maturity of both humans and projects.

1169. *Mwĩĩtu ũtathong'oa kĩthana ndauĩa mũtumĩa na avetanganawa na mĩthũmbĩ nĩ kĩkw'ũ.* **A girl who cannot harvest curded sap does not cook for an old man and is saved from ruin by death.**[5]
This ancient axiom means a morally unsettled girl never makes a good marriage partner and squanders her life in immoral ways until death.

---

[5] D.L. Patel, *Ĩvuku ya Ngewa na Mbano: Kĩkamba* (Nairobi: D.L. Patel Press, 1956).

Its wording has considerable concealment. The phrase *ũtathong'oa kĩthana*, 'extract curded sap', refers not to tree sap called *kĩthana*, but to initial human lactation. Thus, the full meaning is that a sexually immature girl cannot marry an old man.

1170. *Mwĩĩtu nĩ nyama syĩ mathangũnĩ, syatũngwa mathangũnĩ niaawa ĩngĩ.* **A girl is like meat on leaves; they are redivided once returned to the leaves.**
The ancient maxim emerged from the context of sharing meat in the hunt. When hunters killed an animal, they laid it on green leaves for skinning and cutting into portions. Such meat on the leaves was public property subject for sharing among the hunters. Nevertheless, it actually means a new bride cannot continue to reside in her parents' house after the wedding. If she does, she will be remarried to someone else. Its application can be broadly applied. If you buy some goods, it is prudent to take them away with you rather than leave them in the shop as the seller might resell them.

1171. *Kana kĩng'ei konekeawa ngoinĩ kaitw'a matũ kayikia ngoinĩ.* **A baby bound to be a thief is noticed in the baby sling as he grabs leaves and puts them in the sling.**
This ancient adage means that bad things can be detected early. So, look for the signs and forestall future damages and loss. Certain traits are early warnings of bad character and should be addressed promptly.

1172. *Ka kwaa kambaa kwaa matũ.* **A child bound to perish turns deaf first.**
This maxim emerged in antiquity and points to the risk of stubbornness, arrogance, ignorance, and failure to heed good advice. The child here symbolizes an arrogant person who cannot be advised. Kamba children were instructed from infancy to listen to their parents, older siblings, grandparents, and elders. If a child appeared arrogant, people said the child was becoming deaf, growing horns, developing a hard head, or lost. Deafness symbolizes arrogance and stubbornness.

1173. *Kana kavenwa kavyũ kanengawe kamũtĩ.* **Whenever a knife is taken away from the child, a stick is given in its place.**
This ancient adage derives from dowry negotiations. It means when one's daughter is taken away for marriage her parents should receive livestock in exchange. A substitute suffices for the real thing.[6]

---

[6] Leslau, *Proverbs*, 34.

1174. *Mwana atithasya ūla ūmūsyaete.* **A child resembles the parent.**
This talks about resemblance including both good and evil traits. The word *mwana* in this context means son. It was desirable that a son aped the father since fathers trained their sons to be out in the field as herders, hunters, traders, and warriors. A son was encouraged to follow the character traits of his father in these skills.

1175. *Mwana wa kĩtai atusaa ngoi na kĩni.*[7] **The jinxed baby cuts the baby sling with his gums.**
Women made leather baby slings called *ngoi* from animal skins from as early as the Islamic period. The proverb indicates that there were accidents in which babies fell off and died from injury. It was an axiomatic rationalization of such accidents, blaming predestination and thus escape from punishment.

1176. *Mwana ūte ĩtūmwa ndawaa ngũmbũ.*[8] **A child who will not mature to adulthood never develops mumps.**
This talks about precolonial child mortality and health. Mumps were common during the wet season. Herbalists treated them using varieties of plant medicine.[9] However, the proverb means that an unprofitable affair has no defect. It remains deceptive.

1177. *Mwana ūtemūsuke ndeanaa.* **A child who is not slandered does not grow.**
This was not a justification for slander, but a way of coming to terms with slander as part of social discourse and an intractable human vice. It traces back to antiquity, when neighbours talked about neighbours in their absence.

1178. *Mwana wĩ wia ūtũasya ūkya mūsyĩ.* **A cowardly son keeps his family poor.**[10]
Once a son grew up in a poor family, he changed the family fortunes by going out and undertaking risky ways to gain wealth. Such ways included hunting fierce animals and selling their skins, teeth, fur, claws, and so on. Others went on cattle-raiding expeditions and honey-collecting expeditions in remote and dangerous places. Cowardly sons never dared take such risks. Emerging from the Islamic period this axiom means cowards do not hunt.

---

[7] Mwau, *Dictionary*, 662.
[8] Mwau, *Dictionary*, 661.
[9] Wycliffe Wanzala, et al., 'A Survey of the Applications and Use of Ethnomedicinal Plants and Plant Products for Healthcare from the Ūkambanī Region in Eastern Kenya', June 2016.
[10] Mwau, *Dictionary*, 662.

1179. *Mwana mũtumanu oloota ĩthe na kala ka mwela.* **A foolish son points at his father with the index finger.**
This ancient proverb alludes to the relationship between sons and fathers. Pointing at someone with the little finger symbolized great mockery. For a son to point at his father in that manner represented both the highest gesture of disrespect and a sense of foolishness on the part of the son.

1180. *Ndũkethĩelanĩle kĩatũ na au.* **Do not compare your shoes with those of your father.**
Emerging shortly after the First World War when the Kamba adopted modern footwear called *syaatũ* (singular *kĩatũ* from Swahili *kiatu*), this refers to power relations between fathers and sons. The son has to obey and respect the father. Difficult tasks were the responsibility of the father and the son could not handle them. By extension the axiom alludes to national political and economic power, where proper respect for authority is advised.

1181. *Mwana ndia ndamenawa kwoo.* **A deformed child is not despised in his community.**
A family and community should always care for their offspring regardless of their health. Emerging from antiquity, this axiom points to the fact that disabled children were cared for by their communities.

1182. *Mwana ũtakauna athekaa na mwei wa mbee.* **A child who will not help laughs within the first month of birth.**
It is a good thing for a baby to smile and giggle but not too early. Emerging in antiquity this axiom warned the audience not to be overjoyed when they see the first results of their investment. Things can change quite quickly.

1183. *Mwana ũtanakw'a ndavĩtũkĩtye nzũmĩ.* **A child who is not dead has not escaped crooked teeth.**
With multiple variant versions, this ancient axiom alludes to one body feature that distinguished the Kamba from their neighbours – the teeth and what they did with their teeth. Al-Masudi described the Kamba filing teeth in the late 800s.[11] Historically, no other group along the coast filed teeth but the Kamba. Teeth had to be clean, straight, and healthy. Overlapped teeth among children was considered a misfortune. Specialists had a way of correcting those teeth.

---

[11] Al-Masudi, *In The East African Coast: Selected Documents from the First Century to the Early Nineteenth Century*, ed. Stewart Parker Freeman-Grenville (Oxford: Oxford University Press, 1975).

1184. *Mwana ũneana ndavithawa nzama.* **Secrets are not hidden from a grown-up child.**
This is an ancient saying that is subject to multiple interpretations and applications. First, the Kamba assumed that children never knew the secrets of adults and that adults could speak about certain things in coded language in the presence of children. However, when they grew up, such coded language was no longer secret to them. Adults were, therefore, cautioned to be careful what to say in the presence of their young adults. Another interpretation was that young adults were ready to take community responsibilities and it was time for them to be involved in decision making.

1185. *Mwana ũkatwawa nĩ kĩw'ũ athaũkaa kĩthangathĩnĩ thano.* **A child who will drown plays with sand during the dry season.**
This ancient proverb originated in areas of seasonal rivers where sand-bathing was common. During the dry season, rivers become dry and sandy, after the rains they are flooded beyond capacity. So, someone who plays with sand during the dry season will have no idea that the same sand will be under water a few months later. This translates into issues of underestimating danger. Do not underestimate your enemy.

1186. *Mwana ndowaawa nĩ kũkũnwa.*[12] **A child is not killed by beating.**
This ancient axiom is related to the correction of children. One of the things adults took as their responsibility was discipline of all children in the village. Spare the rod, spoil the child.

1187. *Mwana mũseo ndaa waũmũthambya.* **A good child lacks no one to bathe him.**
A beautiful baby is admirable and attractive to all people. Such traits entice people to take care of that baby. This ancient proverb emerged in the context of raising children. However, its actual meaning is that good traits are a resource; physical decency, humility, moral decency, and the act of generosity lure people to a good person. The person is equally rewarded in diverse ways.

1188. *Mwana mũsyae ndakimaa mbiti kwoo.* **A child does not hit hyena in his own community.**
A relative is valuable no matter what. This argues for the need of forgiveness. People will not disown a relative even when he becomes deviant. The ancient adage also means that even if a child is lame, he/she cannot be left to die. The community is morally responsible for that child.

---

[12] Kimilu, *Mũkamba*, 86.

1189. *Mwana mūsyae ndaa ngoi.* **A baby lacks no baby sling.**
Emerging from antiquity, this proverb means that there is providence for every soul. As long as one is born, there will be material resources for the person, in just the same way a baby is provided with a baby sling by the family or community, regardless of the level of the family wealth.

1190. *Mwana mūkūū nīwe umaa ngwa.* **The eldest son curses thunder.**
This ancient proverb alludes to the practice of cursing thunder in the hope that the curse will drive it away. However, it was only the eldest son in the family or the grandmother who could do so. The cursing was done at night in pitch darkness. It means that in a large family it is the eldest son who takes over when a patriarch dies.

1191. *Mwana mūkūū no ta īthe.*[13] **The eldest son is like his father.**
The eldest son was the deputy to his father. The maxim has more to do with responsibility than with sexuality, as some tend to interpret it. It means as the father aged, he gave most family secrets and estate to his eldest son as the caretaker or custodian.

1192. *Mwana nī inya kwa mūkaa īthe nī woteo wa mwaki.* **A child is worth its mother, the house of its stepmother is just a hearth.**
This proverb refers to certain situations where some children were brought up by their stepmothers. When the care was not sufficient, people referred to her care as a mere hearth where the child just warmed her/himself.[14]

1193. *Mwana nī wa Ngai, inya nī yaya.* **A child belongs to God, the mother is a nanny.**
This proverb alludes to relationships between mother and child. It appears to have a colonial or even Swahili etymology because the word '*yaya*' is a borrowed concept from the coast. The Kamba used relatives as nannies for babies and rarely employed nannies. The proverb therefore emerged during the twentieth century. The deeper meaning is that God is the giver of life and the mother's care is limited. The mother can nurse and train the child in good manners but in the course of life that child can die or become an irresponsible person. It is believed that the mother's job ends in breast feeding, weaning, and warning the child of the beauties and the beasts of life on earth. God's duties assume the rest of the child's personality development.

---

[13] Lindblom, *Riddles*, 72–84, 164; Kituku, *Sukulu*, 59.
[14] Farnsworth, *Grammar*, 105.

Children and Adulthood 259

1194. *Mwana ti wa mūsyai ūmwe.* **The child is not of a single parent.**
From ancient times when this maxim emerged, raising children and bequeathing them the right manners was the responsibility of all adults. Although this is interpreted narrowly to refer to disciplinary responsibility, the meaning was broader than that and included feeding and general care.

1195. *Mwana wīna īthe ndavanaa mīatine.* **A son with his father does not brand kigelia strainers.**
This alludes to brewing beer. Most very old men knew the skills of making beer for their personal use. For that purpose, they acquired all the apparatus for beer brewing, including the processed fruit of the kigelia Africana tree. These were special assets harvested from the forest, dried, treated, and then branded with a hot metal rod and stored for use. They were passed on to sons as part of their inheritance. This proverb is significant in that no other oral tradition captures the history of how all this transpired. If a son wanted his own kigelia Africana for fermentation he had to take it to his father for branding. He could use his own marks only when his father had passed on.[15]

1196. *Mwana ndeleawa ngoi ate mūsyae.* **A baby sling is not designed before the baby is born.**
This ancient axiom rose out of experience with infant mortality, sterility, miscarriage, and infirmity. A baby sling was cut out of animal skin, soon after the baby was strong enough to be carried in it. However, the Kamba believed that if the sling was designed before the baby was born the mother would miscarry. As Kīeti and Coughlin argue, the proverb illustrates a summary of experience. It admonishes people to desist from abrupt decisions to carry out ventures that may backfire and put one at risk.[16]

1197. *Mwana nīwakawa na ndwakawa sua ūmwe.* **A son is constructed but not in a day.**
This appears in a political song in which context the axiom meant a leader is built over time. A leader gains experience and reputation through persistent practice of leadership and engagement with the public.

1198. *Mwea mwana naī esaa kwona ayiewa nī atūi nesa.* **One who rears a child badly eventually finds the child well nurtured by neighbours.**
Dating from the Vascon era, this proverb has two interpretations. A child who is abused by parents is nurtured well by neighbours to the

---
[15] Lindblom, *Akamba*, 518.
[16] Kīeti, *Barking*, 102–3.

embarrassment of the parents. The second figurative and sarcastic interpretation is that when parents bring up a child in an immoral manner, the child is disciplined or even killed by the public for his immoral behaviour.

1199. *Ndenye nĩ ya mwana.* **Curdling is for a baby.**
This is rarely used but when employed it is effective in warning youth about the dangers of sex. It derived from a children's game called *ndenye* in which one child sat on another and the one on the floor bounced the one on top, as both sung repeatedly *ndenye ndenye ya mwana*. Although the children did not know it, the game was symbolic of sexual intercourse among adults. This game was forbidden among teenagers.

1200. *Kana ka thavu kaĩvĩtaa.* **A vile child cannot survive.**
This points to Kamba beliefs about childbirth and parents' moral standing. These circumstances are well documented. *Thavu* (not to be confused with *thaavu*, gold) means sin, uncleanness, or illness caused by infringing tribal customs. A child born before this uncleanness was dispelled through purification was feared to die shortly after birth.

1201. *Kana nĩ yũmba yĩũ.*[17] **A child is wet clay.**
Adults can mold clay into any shape, and likewise, in many ways, a child's behaviour. Youthfulness is valuable and this is seen in the way people mourn for different ages of deceased persons.

1202. *Kĩĩyo mũsyai ũĩĩ mwana, mwana ndamũĩĩya.* **The intense grief the parent can feel for a child, a child cannot feel in the same measure.**
This means parents are merciful and their attachment to their children is deeper than that of children to their parents. Children distance themselves from parents as they grow up, but parents seem not to. Children often move away from parents to establish their own homes and families, but parents stick to their children until they are adults.

1203. *Ngalĩko ya mwana nĩ ũitonĩ, nayo ya ĩthe nĩ mwakinĩ.* **The baby's side is by the wall and the father's is on the fireside.**
For a couple having a baby, the sleeping arrangement was that the baby was put near the wall, the mother in the middle of the bed, and the father near the fire as an assurance of complete security of the baby and mother. The fire in this context symbolizes all forms of danger and the father is the protector. This ancient axiom means people must know their obligations and respect division of labour.

---

[17] Kituku, *Sukulu*, 22.

1204. *Vayĩ mwana woosawa nthĩ.* **There is no child that was collected from the ground.**
This ancient axiom was drawn from a song sung in eastern Ngomeni in the early 1970s by old men in the type of dance called *mũsĩvo*. It points to the fact that it takes procreation for a child to be born. It means that anything has a cause and a beginning.

1205. *Tata nĩ ũtatania.* **Fatherhood is a show of it.**
This is a common axiom that establishes a relationship between sons and fathers. It was coined by sons protesting against their fathers' excesses and harshness. In other words, if one wants to be called father, he has to act like a father.

1206. *Vayĩ mwana na ĩlũmwa nĩ mbiti.* **There is no child for the hyena's bite.**
No child should be rocked while another is offered to hyenas to bite. This proverb means that people should not exhibit favouritism when dealing with their children. It is worth noting that *ndanĩ* (in front) implies special treatment such as attending to the baby after it soils itself or even breastfeeding it.[18]

1207. *Vayĩ mwana wa ndanĩ na wa mũongonĩ.*[19] **There is no baby of the bosom and of the backside.**
This ancient proverb was born out of a situation where a woman was charged with babysitting the baby of her daughter and that of her son simultaneously. The woman carried the daughter's baby on the bosom and the son's baby on the back, yet to the Kamba the back was a vulnerable position for a child who was exposed to sun, rain, and injury. A child on the bosom was completely secure and protected.[20] In this context, *ndanĩ* (in the bosom) implies special treatment. This proverb notes that parents and the general public should not employ favouritism in handling children and by extension public affairs. This calls on the listener to be fair between two people.

1208. *Vayĩ ĩsyĩtwa yĩtaea mwana.* **There is no name that cannot raise a child.**
The Kamba had a flexible naming system and naming children was important. In most cases, the first two boys and the first two girls were named after the grandparents on both sides of the family. The first boy was named after the paternal grandfather and the second after the maternal grandfather. If these died, then the naming system switched

---
[18] Kĩeti, *Barking*, 106.
[19] Kĩeti, *Barking*, 106.
[20] Kĩeti, *Barking*, 106.

to ugly things, obscenity, and the natural world, while some names were noble and pleasant. Parents of a person with a natural-word-derived name had health issues at the time that child was born. For example, children named after crocodiles, hyenas, or monkeys were so named so that they would survive child mortality. Parents rationalized their decisions using this first-millennium maxim.[21] Names had unique stories behind them. They revealed a wealth of information about the bearer's birth circumstances and family lineage, and can be tips into the past of Ũkamba.

1209. *Ũimwĩvaasya ndasuvasya.* **She didn't fart when you were dating her.**
This ancient axiom refers to courtship leading to marriage and its joys and risks. When a girl was courting she put out the best of her character – even pretending she does not hunger, thirst, or attend to nature's call. Soon after marriage things unravel quickly. Therefore, this warns of people who want to exploit you by pretending to be other than they are.

1210. *Mũsyĩ wĩ kamwana ndwĩyaĩyawa nĩ mũndũ mũka.* **A woman does not lead a household with a boy.**
This alludes to mid-to-late colonial-era power relations when political decisions became concentrated in the hands of male members of family and clan. It was assumed by the end of the Second World War that men were born to rule and boys could overrule even their mothers' decisions. Families who negotiated these turns of events had mothers acting as regents to their sons, particularly in matters of dowry and sale of family properties. This is where the invention of tradition thesis could make sense – by the end of colonial rule and until the publication of ethnohistorical studies on egalitarianism among the Kamba, such trends were considered very old and even ordained by God.

1211. *Mwei wĩ ĩtunĩ na kĩa mwana kĩ nthĩ.*[22] **The moon is in the sky and the predator of the child is on earth.**
This ancient axiom was used by a girl refusing to marry a passionate suitor in favour of another of her choice. While a suitor pushed and cajoled the girl's parents, another young man was already flirting with her right then and was not far from the point of such negotiations. The axiom was pronounced to let the cat out of the bag and thus bring the negotiations to an end for the passionate suitor.

---

[21] Mutisya, *Proverbs*, 47.
[22] Lindblom, *Riddles*, 32.

1212. *Mbanga ya mwana ĩvalukĩlaa mũsyai.* **The child's tragedy falls on the parent.**
This axiom rose from ancient behaviour of some children falling into trouble, causing them to be fined. If they could not pay the fine, the parents were obliged to pay it. Sages coined this axiom in which they meant that if a child made blunders like stealing, the responsibility fell on the parent to compensate the offended party.

1213. *Kakũnza ngundi kakũnawa ta ĩthe.* **When a boy clenches a fist, he is beaten like his father.**
In twentieth-century drinking brawls, women uttered this statement meaning that if a youth asked for liquor he was ready to drink like his father. Besides other meanings and interpretations, the maxim indicates that if a boy wants to prove himself he will be treated as an adult.

1214. *Kĩĩma kĩlĩswa nĩ mwĩĩtu kĩlĩswa nĩ ũta.* **A mountain that can be climbed by a girl cannot be climbed by a bow.**
Traditionally, a daughter was extremely valuable to her father. It implies that the services a daughter assumes in a household cannot be handled by anyone else in the family. She is an indispensable resource to her parents and family. In-laws are more valuable than the material things exchanged in the form of dowry.

1215. *Mwanake akũaa ayasya akaina.* **A lad ages while saying I will dance in the future.**
There were several songs and dances that were part of rites of passage. They all involved acrobatic performances that were challenging to some young men. The axiom condemns procrastination and calls listeners to act promptly.

1216. *Ng'ondu ĩ mwana.*[23] **A purifying medium has a child.**
In other words, herbs are a cure to infertility. The cure for infertility involved administration of the products of *mũthea wa nzĩ*, a plant of rare occurrence from which the concoction called *ng'ondu* was made. One way of treatment was washing the patient for some days with a decoction of this plant. Some of it was also rubbed on the patient's head. When next she menstruates, she has coitus with her husband and can then have children.[24] This was a protest proverb from the early twentieth century, challenging the aggressive criticisms of traditional medicine.

---

[23] Kimilu, *Mũkamba*, 54.
[24] Lindblom, *Akamba*, 270–1.

1217. *Woongolo ũmwe ndũtw'a mwana ĩkũmũ.*[25] **One lullaby cannot make a baby a weaned child.**
Lullabies were thought to be essential to child development, but it was observed they did not make babies grow faster. Success comes with more than casual involvement.

1218. *Kala kamanyie kũsũna kayũlawa.*[26] **A finger accustomed to licking never forgets.**
This is a common maxim with multiple variations and manifold interpretations. The most common interpretation is that habits and addictions are bad. Avoid the temptation of engagement in bad behaviour that could become habitual.

1219. *Mwĩĩtu ũvĩtĩtye na ĩthe ndathelawa nĩ nzoni.*[27] **A girl who has slept with her father is always shy.**
This proverb warns against actions leading to permanent and damaging embarrassment. Its origin is unknown but appears to have emerged in the early twentieth century. Before the 1900s distance between father and daughter was strict. Social context of that period excluded the possibility of incest. The dramatic change since involves the shrinking social distance between fathers and daughters in the context of 'modernity'.

1220. *Mwĩĩtu anakavaw'a nĩ kwovwa mavuo.*[28] **A girl is beautified with ornaments.**
The father was responsible for beautification of his daughter. He bought elaborate assortments of ornaments and a supply of aromatic herbs to apply on the ornaments, generically called *mavuo*. Without such ornaments a girl was considered unattractive. The Monsoon-era maxim has multiple interpretations. The most common is that to make something attractive something external ought to be applied to the object to make it unique.

1221. *Mwĩĩtu mwanake ndatethya.* **A beautiful girl does not help.**
This is another adage that carries some contradiction within it. The Kamba public generally appreciated beautiful females and objects. However, most proverbs about beauty condemn its deceptive aspects. In another version, beauty is depicted as weak and unproductive. These attitudes, particularly of beautiful girls being of less use, emerged in the context of societal change under pressures from modernity.

---

[25] Kimilu, *Mũkamba*, 119; Mutisya, *Proverbs*, 72.
[26] Kimilu, *Mũkamba*, 115.
[27] Mwau, *Dictionary*, 662.
[28] Mwau, *Dictionary*, 661.

1222. *Mwĩĩtu mwanake nĩ ndũla yĩ mũinyũ.* **A light-skinned girl is a worm-infested loquat.**
This means a light-skinned beauty does not always go together with morals, gentility, and decency. This interesting sociological observation emerged out of circumstances of the late colonial era, increasing during the early era of independence as modernity began to take a toll on traditional senses of romance, sexuality, and marital partnership. It emerged out of the circumstances where beautiful girls rarely maintained their marriage. Two songs related to this topic of comparing dark- and light-skinned girls have appeared in previous publications by this author.[29] As William Shakespeare once said, 'All that glitters is not gold.'[30] This is an aphorism stating that not everything that seems true turns out to be so. This can be applied to just about any experience in life. Watch out, lest you will be deceived.

1223. *Mwĩĩtu wĩ kĩsaa ndendaa myethyanĩ.*[31] **A girl with a sore toe does not go to group-work congregations.**
This admonishes against taking unnecessary risk. Sore toes often occurred during the rainy season. One suffering from such had to take good care and avoid dew, which was a risk if one went cultivating on the farm.

1224. *Mwĩĩtu wa kwĩita ndaĩyawa.*[32] **A girl who commits suicide is not mourned over.**
Lindblom informs us that suicide was rare in Ũkamba, but girls sometimes hanged themselves. The ancient axiom means that one should not expect sympathy for self-inflicted injury. People will be reluctant to rescue a careless person.

1225. *Mwĩĩtu mũseo ndakataa ngalĩ.*[33] **A beautiful girl does not pay bus fare.**
This emerged during the late twentieth century when travel by buses became common. To travel one had to buy a ticket (*kũkata ngali*) – to cut a ticket. This was an exaggeration or a teasing statement that the conductor will waive the fare on account of the beauty of the passenger. Its actual meaning is hard work is readily rewarded. On account of her beauty someone will be automatically moved to carry her across the flooded river.

---

[29] Jeremiah Kĩtũnda, 'Love is a Dunghill and I am the Cock that Gets on it to Crow', in *Hemingway and Africa*, ed. Miriam Mandel (New York: Camden House, 2011).
[30] William Shakespeare, *Merchant of Venice*, Act II Scene 7.
[31] Kĩeti, *Barking*, 109.
[32] Farnsworth, *Grammar*, 22; Kimilu, *Mũkamba*, 117; Mutisya, *Proverbs*, 26; Mwau, *Dictionary*, 670.
[33] Mwau, *Dictionary*, 662.

1226. *Mwĩĩu ndathelelawa.* **A girl is never finished.**
Anthropologist Lee Cronk exposed the fascinating story of a preference for daughters over sons among the Yaaku (or Mukogodo) people of Kenya. It is noteworthy that tendencies of liking girls over boys or vice versa was not unique to the Yaaku. The patrilineal Kamba had their own perceptions of boys and girls. The daughter was special, as evidenced in multiple proverbs that expressed that receptivity. That did not necessarily translate to preference over any sex of the child among the Kamba. This proverb was about dowry. To some extent it was an expression of greed on the part of in-laws but also a revelation of the meaning of dowry in general terms. That is, dowry was not a price but a token, a symbol of a friendly bond between in-laws, which never ends even after the death of the girl given in marriage.

1227. *Eĩtu ala aseyo matithelaa.*[34] **Beautiful girls are inexhaustible.**
Grandmothers admonishing grandsons about sexuality said this. This proverb has broader implications about anything good one may be anxious to get. Such things, this proverb says, remain available.

1228. *Eĩtu no ta mbaĩki, italĩkaa syaathi ũlũma vala syatwawa nĩ kĩseve.* **Girls are like castor beans, they spring and land wherever the wind takes them.**
The castor bean plant, indigenous to Africa, occurs across the continent and the Indian Ocean islands. Precolonial Kamba cultivated the plant for multiple uses. The ancient axiom talks of the dispersal of the seeds of this plant, which scatter from the pod through a process called ballistic dispersal. The wind propels the seeds far away from the mother plant. This is comparable to how girls in a given family disperse as they are married in different parts of Ũkamba and beyond.

1229. *Mũthei wa eĩtu mwisyo nĩwe wĩsaa kũthewa na moomwĩkya ngemi.* **Whoever selects girls will eventually be the last one to be selected as they jeer at him.**
This is one of the ancient proverbs that discouraged selectivity in marriage and romance. This axiom admonished young unmarried men against excessive selectivity in courtship and marriage. This emerged at a time when women outnumbered men, and society unconsciously needed to balance marriages to ensure all girls were married.

1230. *Wakoma na eĩtu ĩkala tamo.* **If you sleep with girls be like them.**
This was illustrated with a story in which a young man secretly went to visit a girl at night. Around midnight a honey badger struck the chicken

---

[34] Mbiti, *Weteelete*, 43.

run with considerable commotion. Instinctively he jumped out of bed to save the chicken but came face to face with the girl's father on the same mission. In full moonlight they stared at each other. The old man knew what had happened and said this proverb before he retired to his bed.

1231. *Niwe waisye nũkundwe ndũkaaleana.* **You said 'let them drink, I will never divorce'.**
This alludes to precolonial Kamba covenants. It specifically points to girls' ability to marry men of their choice regardless of parents' decisions. It is a mistake, as stated in some publications, to suppose that, among the Kamba, women are usually given in marriages without any regard being paid to their own inclinations. The majority of marriages were founded on mutual attachment. The suitor sought the girl's consent before he approached her father to negotiate the marriage.[35] During formal negotiations, the girl usually took a small portion of the liquor that the suitor's representatives brought. The girl sipped the liquor and gave it to her paternal uncle, saying *Ũkĩ ũũ nũkundwe ndikaleana*, 'drink this beer, I will never break the marriage'. That was another way of saying she had agreed the marriage could proceed. The girl's uncle then passed the beer to his brother, the father of the girl, and then served the rest of the guests in the negotiation.

1232. *Kĩveti kĩkathi wendo kyambĩaa na ũkoma kĩkĩĩte mĩkalya.* **A wife who will abscond sleeps with firestone sandals on.**
This is a recent coinage and a witty twist of earlier forms. The type of sandals called *mĩkalya* began to be worn in Ũkamba during the 1930s. They were carved from used car tyres. Replacing skin footwear, these were preferred for their tenacity and durability. They were suitable for rough country use in farming, hunting, herding, and travel in bushland. They are not the type of shoes one would wear for fashion and good looks. One therefore is not expected to go to bed wearing these types of shoes. The axiom, which emerged during the 1930s, means that signs of trouble appear early and in conspicuous ways.

1233. *Mũndũ wĩ ngũlũ alumangĩawa ndũnyũ katĩ nĩ iveti na mathũngĩ.* **A proud man is knocked about with baskets by women.**
This is a postcolonial coinage dating from about 1900. It comments on social conduct in public and across gender lines. While pride was misconduct, the worst insult a man could suffer was to be assaulted by a group of women using baskets. If such an assault occurred in the marketplace, the insult was grievous. The proverb condemned boastfulness and lack of self-restraint in public places.

---

[35] Lindblom, *Riddles*, 72.

1234. *Mũndũ mũka ndatiaa leso.* **A woman never leaves behind her leso.**
This axiom emerged in the 1950s as a female way to force other women to wear *leso* as a headgear, baby carrier, or a wrap around their hips.[36] From the 1960s, *leso* became a carrier of proverbs as cultural, gender, and political messages of politicians seeking to mobilize voters during elections. They printed proverbs on each *leso* in the same way Americans use T-shirts. The garments were worn exclusively by women, making the proverb even stronger because a woman leaving her *leso* behind symbolized abandoning her political messages. Winning support of women, the majority, and, arguably, the more politically committed of the populace, was the most effective path to election victory. That way the axiom assumes considerable complexity in meanings and interpretations. The axiom meant that a politician cannot leave women out of his political calculations and survive an election, just the same way a woman without *leso* would not pass her moral test.

---

[36] Charles New, *Life, Wanderings and Labours in Eastern Africa*; Charles Hobley, *Ethnology of Akamba and Other East African Tribes* (London: Frank Cass, 1910); Lindblom, *Akamba*.

Part IV

Kamba Society

15

Place Names and Ethnic Names

1235. *Aũi ma ndakĩthĩ mambaa ũsama matanathi Ngunĩ.* **Produce merchants consult before they head out to Ngunĩ.**
This axiom emerged in the late twentieth century in Mwingĩ sub-county. It alludes to trade in green grams introduced from India and grown across Kitui. Ngunĩ town emerged as one of the major trading towns for that crop. From the mid-1960s, traders from Mwingĩ began to descend weekly on market fairs to buy green grams from Ngunĩ, creating a nightmare for sellers. The buyers gathered ahead of time and set prices to their advantage. This axiom emphasizes dialogue and agreement before embarking on a major project.

1236. *Ĩsoma yĩmwe yĩituma ila ingĩ itathi Mavoko.* **One weakling cannot prevent others from going to Mavoko.**
This emerged in the 1940s when Mavoko town was developed as a livestock trading centre and the seat of the Athi River Kenya Meat Commission station.[1] Thousands of cattle poured into the
town from Ũkamba, Maasailand, Taita-Taveta, and Tanzania, mostly on foot. Weaklings that could not endure the trek were rested while the rest marched on to Mavoko. The proverb usually suggests that one coward cannot halt the launch of a military expedition. There are two interpretations: the crowd does not think much about outliers; and small doubts should not hold back an important undertaking.

1237. *Wĩtiwa weng'ee mbasi Kariakoo.* **You will be left gazing at buses at Kariokor.**
There is a section of Nairobi city called Kariakoo (carrier corps) and buses are the key historical markers here. Whereas Kariakoo was established in 1914 as a station for a Carrier Corp unit of King's African Rifles (KAR), bus services in Kenya began in 1934. Subsequently, many Kamba flocked to Kariakoo to watch these new vehicles, creating a sense of idleness leading to loss of precious work time. The proverb sought to dissuade such laxity, warning if a person is not careful he or she will miss opportunities.

[1] Mutisya, *Proverbs*, 62.

1238. *Kumawa nīkūsyokawa.* **A point of departure is also returned to.**
This ancient adage encodes the history of Kamba migration, warning listeners not to sever ties with their roots for they may return there in the future. In fact, Kamba groups have returned south to ancestral lands. Closer to home, however, the proverb addresses contemporary relationships. It warns that if you are leaving a place for good, you should not pollute the point of departure in case you may return.

1239. *Kwīthonga aīīwe Mwala.*[2] **Kwīthonga was consumed in Mwala.**
This is embedded in a story of a bird in the company of quelea birds that was killed along with them even though it was not eating farm crops. The moral lesson is look before you leap and stay away from bad company. Do not be greedy when invited for a feast, it may be a lethal trap. This is also used in a crowd to signal to fellow speakers that there is danger and they need to get away.

1240. *Mwana ūte ūno aīsaa syatweewe Mwala.*[3] **An obedient child eats things harvested in Mwala.**
This proverb emerged after beekeeping intensified in Mwala during the Monsoon era. It means that wealth generated in a given place often benefits distant people. It means that an obedient child is rewarded. He also becomes favoured and gets free things from Mwala.

1241. *Kīkamba kya metho na ngove ndūkīsī.* **You do not know the Kīkamba of eyes and eyelashes.**
This proverb emerged out of conversation in Kīkamba between the Kamba and two colonial officers nicknamed *Kīlaka* (patch-rag) and *Katune* (Little Red One) who served in Machakos District in the 1940s and 1950s. They had learned the language, but the Kamba could communicate in public through sign language that was difficult for *Kīlaka* and *Katune* to decipher. The officers complained that they understood Kīkamba but not sign language. The proverb means that one may know things superficially but communal secrets remain unknown.

1242. *Malī ya Akamba ti ndaany'e.*[4] **Kamba wealth is not divisive.**
This points out that the Kamba help each other in their villages. They lived in a social egalitarian communal life where the welfare of an individual was the responsibility of everyone in the community, as much

---

[2] Thomas Ngotho, *Ngewa Nyanya na Moelyo* (Nairobi: East African Literature Bureau, 1962), 4–5; Muiu, *Cross-Cultural*, 104.
[3] Mwau, *Dictionary*, 662.
[4] Kimilu, *Mūkamba*, 114.

as the individual was responsible for the defence, wealth, and health of the community.

1243. *Mũkamba athaa nyamũ yakyamana.*[5] **A Mũkamba shoots an animal when it poses well.**
The hunter did not shoot at an animal until he was sure the arrow would hit the target. The ancient proverb has many variations but it is usually about doing things at the opportune time.

1244. *Mũkamba ainĩaa nzaũ ĩla yake onethwa nĩkwĩtũũa.*[6] **Mũkamba cheers his bull even if it has diarrhoea.**
Treasuring bullfighting Kamba herders cheered their bulls in early fights until the bull learned fighting tactics. The animals appeared to be encouraged to fight harder whenever they heard cheers. One interpretation is that people are most concerned with their own affairs, as is fair in a contested situation. This idiom emerged out of singing contests in the 1950s, pitting men from different villages who were cheered by their clansmen.

1245. *Mũkamba mũĩ ndatusaa mũtĩ ũkwenyenya ndata.* **A wise *Mũkamba* never cuts a tree that has no walking sticks.**
The first armed clash between the Kamba and the British centred around the colonial officials' insensitivity to the sacredness of trees. An imperial officer ordered an age-old tree chopped for raising the Union Jack without permission of Kamba leaders. In subsequent exchanges this maxim emerged, meaning a wise Mũkamba does not cut a tree whose canopy covers the light of stars and has no branches worth a walking stick.

1246. *Mũkamba mũĩ aathaa nyũnyi ĩla yĩ nyama.* **A wise Mũkamba shoots a meaty bird.**
Having emerged first among hunters, this maxim has environmental overtones to prevent environmental mismanagement. The proverb stressed that people should kill birds that they need for food only.

1247. *Mũkamba mũĩ nũla wĩĩthukĩĩasya vala ũangĩte.* **A wise Mũkamba is one who looks before he leaps.**
This is an emphasis on precaution. Emerging from the Islamic era, this proverb persuaded people to think ahead and take precautions where necessary.

---

[5] Mwau, *Dictionary*, 656.
[6] Mwau, *Dictionary*, 656.

1248. *Mūkamba mūĩ nūla omboasya asalūkĩtye.* **A wise Mūkamba dozes with open eyes.**
This is an axiomatic condemnation of idleness, around since antiquity. Certainly, one can doze with eyes open. Accordingly, this proverb discourages excess sleeping and idleness.

1249. *Mūkamba nandū na mūsyĩ wakawa na kavyū katuvu.* **The Mūkamba is worth his people, and families are built with a blunt knife.**
This ancient proverb emphasizes the centrality of the family: a man is worth his family and only patience (a blunt knife) builds a family. Since a family is a collection of members, to keep them together the patriarch was advised to be slow to anger, and to be patient and forgiving.

1250. *Mūkamba avika matanĩsyonĩ ma nzĩa akwataa nzĩa aitia matanĩsyo.* **When a Mūkamba reaches the crossroads, he takes the road and leaves the crossroads.**
This is about conflict resolution. Precolonial Kamba lived in a world of path-webs that knotted together villages and distant places. Walking on a long, wide path one often came to a point where the path forked. The one that the traveller had to follow to his desired destination was called 'the path' and the other 'the fork'. Taking 'the path' and leaving 'the fork' symbolized leaving a place of disagreement and quarrel. The axiom means leave quarrelsome people to continue with their quarrels.

1251. *Mūkamba ndanyaĩĩa vala wathambĩa.* **A Mūkamba does not dry off where he bathed.**
During hot seasons, when people bathed, they walked dripping wet so the water kept them cool for some time. The proverb means a certain step may be the beginning of a given project, but the end is different.

1252. *Mūkamba ateūya akwataa wĩa waūneena.*[7] **When a Mūkamba is not eating he takes to talking.**
This proverb reflects the historical practice of the Kamba using various forms of folklore or gossip whenever they had no serious matter to discuss. The maxim emerged in antiquity when narration of folktales was a common pastime.

1253. *Mūkamba akĩana ndew'aa akūa nĩw'o wambĩĩa kwĩwa.* **A man does not hear when growing up; he begins to hear when he gets older.**
This is inverted truth. At advanced age people lose hearing ability, but the statement suggests old age is the high-noon of hearing. The term

---

[7] Kimilu, *Mūkamba*, 42.

'hearing' symbolizes an ability to learn. This ancient proverb warns people to be careful with their lives and listen more to others.

1254. *Mũkamba atalaa mavatw'a ndatalaa manewe.* **A Mũkamba counts denials not gifts.**
Exchange of gifts was a common social aspect of Kamba society. Some people will not take no for an answer. This maxim condemns lack of gratitude if someone gets upset when a neighbour or relative says no to their requests.

1255. *Mũkamba atusaa nzama ĩla yĩvo yaemwa.* **The Kamba form a council when the existing one fails.**
This was drawn from the ancient Kamba customary judicial system, which was comprised of a council of old and prominent men. The system has been well documented since 1910. The statement reflects the truth that such councils of elders could remain as judges as long as they were able to handle the cases brought to them.[8]

1256. *Mũkamba mũlau ndanyaĩawa.* **A generous Mũkamba never wants.**
Tracing from antiquity, this proverb encouraged people to share material things and cherish generosity in society. Generosity begets generosity.

1257. *Mũkamba nde muuke nĩ metho wĩĩ.* **A Mũkamba does not have smell sense but eyes.**
The Kamba emphasize sight over scent and hearing. To ascertain the truth, it was better to see it than to rely on hearsay. This ancient proverb stresses the significance of eye-witnessing.

1258. *Mũkamba ti mũthingu kyake nĩ nguano.* **A Mũkamba is not generous, he only cajoles.**
This ancient axiom speaks of Kamba stratagems, deception, and truth. When people want something, they will entice with niceties. *Nguano* translates as seduction, coaxing, or enticing of any kind. It is used when men persuade a girl to marry or sleep with them.

---

[8] Dundas, 'History of Kitui'; Anthony Thomas, 'Oaths, Ordeals, and the Kenyan Courts', *Human Organization* 33(1) (Spring 1974), 59–70; Sarah Kinyanjui, 'Restorative Justice in Traditional Pre-colonial "Criminal Justice Systems" in Kenya', *Tribal Law Journal* (2010), 10.

1259. *Mũkamba ti ndia onaa ĩsembete na asya nĩ ngito ũkamĩthĩa na katheo.* **The Mũkamba is not foolish; seeing it running, if he says it is pregnant you will find it with a foetus.**
Kamba hunters were experts in observing animal behaviour and health. Pregnant females were not to be shot. Disputes occurred in observing female game. If the leader thought one was pregnant, but other hunters killed it, this ancient axiom was pronounced if a foetus was found. It advises listeners to be cautious.

1260. *Akamba matilanaa kasũni.* **The Kamba share a little bird.**
The proverb originated with hunters where teamwork and cooperation were vital for survival. If hunters were starving and one killed the tiniest bird, it was roasted and its meat shared among all for just a bite. Herders who killed birds also shared the meat no matter how small the bird was. This teaches the significance of sharing and reflects not just hunting but also Kamba socialism and cooperation in all difficulties.

1261. *Akamba maasyaa ona walea kũthi kĩĩmani, kĩĩma kĩkooka vala ũĩ.* **The Kamba say that if you do not go to the mountain, the mountain will come to you.**
This proverb has a Koranic etymology for Prophet Mohammed said something similar: 'If the mountain will not come to Muhammad, then Muhammad must go to the mountain.'[9] The proverb means if you do not come to me I will still search for you; I need you; I will vanquish you. Another interpretation is that if things are not going your way you should adjust to the way they are.

1262. *Akamba maithũwe nĩ kũtheka.* **Kamba do not loath laughter.**
This was said to encourage entertainment. From antiquity, the Kamba women in particular had a peculiar way of laughing. '*Mathekaa namaũkula*', said Mũlewa wa Mũvinga, an octogenarian matriarch. However, the axiom is another way of saying people appreciate gifts and amusements.

1263. *Mũkamba athũkĩaa kwenda ũsamĩthwa.* **A Mũkamba is spoiled by desire to taste.**
With the opening of weekly market fairs across Ũkamba in the early 1900s, new edibles flooded the markets. First sellers enticed customers by asking them to taste Swahili-Asian cuisine whose taste enticed passersby to buy. With time it became customary for customers to demand a little taste. The maxim reflects a growing tendency among the Kamba for trying different things, even in politics.

---

[9] Francis Bacon, *Essays of Francis Bacon* (New York: Cosimo, 2007), chapter 12.

1264. *Mũkamba mũima ndeawa ambatĩanga.* **An adult is never told to get up a bit.**
This is an old, erotic axiom said in jubilant, derisive, or stern moments to emphasize the importance of learning certain life matters. A mature person was never instructed on what to do during coitus. The objective and application have nothing to do with obscenity. The speaker meant that he was up to the occasion.

1265. *Mũkamba aanangiwe nĩ kyong'oi.* **A Mũkamba was destroyed by deceit.**
This is an axiom from the Vascon era of immense deceptions in commercial exchanges. It emerged as a condemnation of deception in economic and social transactions. It calls upon listeners to be honest in all spheres of life.

1266. *Akya Mũkavi ovala waia ngĩĩtĩ.* **Help the Maasai build where he sets the building material.**
This proverb originated from the Kamba–Kwavi inter-ethnic border region on the southwestern edge of Ũkambanĩ during the Vascon era. The two raided each other for livestock, but also laid down weapons and cooperated in building their societies. Along the border, they settled next to each other. In the Kamba view, Kwavi nomads did not take much care to select the right spot for putting up a dwelling. Thus, the Kamba began to say 'respect the choice of your neighbour even if he does not make the right one'.

1267. *Mũkavi eĩtavĩwa ndew'aa iamba.*[10] **A Masai whose livestock is to be rustled does not hear the anklets.**
This proverb emerged in the 1600s when Kwavi encroached on Ũkamba, attracted by pastures and waterpans. During the seventeenth century they raided the scattered eastern Kitui Kamba settlements. The Kamba responded by organizing their own raiding expeditions with warriors wearing anklets called *iamba*. Whenever the Kwavi heard those anklets they fled, took cover, or prepared for battle. Someone doomed to die would not hear these warning sounds. The proverb points to the risk of arrogance, stubbornness, and ignorance of warnings and counsel.[11]

---

[10] Kimilu, *Mũkamba*, 116; Mutisya, *Proverbs*, 53; Mwau, *Dictionary*, 657; AIM, *Kĩkamba–English*, 155.
[11] Charles Ambler, *Kenyan Communities in the Age of Imperialism* (New Haven: Yale Press, 1988).

278 *Part IV: Kamba Society*

1268. *Ũkavi mwoneku ndwĩ nzevũ.* **The Kwavi rustling party spotted already has no magic medicine.**
In their contest with the rising power of the Kwavi during the Vascon era, the Kamba deployed magic medicine called *nzevũ* believed to be capable of driving away enemies or making one invisible. Missionary Johannes Krapf related how in 1849 the Kamba put *mũtheea* in the campfires to become invisible to their Galla and Kwavi enemies.[12] These tactics were abandoned for more realistic defensive actions whenever the rustlers struck, hence the proverb.

1269. *Mũkavi ndoaa ũngĩ.* **A Kwavi does not kill another Kwavi.**
This emerged between 1600 and 1900 in the context of Kwavi–Kamba cattle counter-raids. It is another way to say that, even though Kwavi warriors were fierce and merciless, they never killed comrades. An enemy does not kill one of its own. Second, people cannot send a thief to catch another thief.

1270. *Ũkavi ndwingwa mwene.*[13] **No one can claim ownership of Kwaviland.**
This has multiple interpretations. Unlike the Kamba, the neighbouring Maasai had limited individual ownership. They grazed over the communal land as they pleased. At least this was the impression outsiders got without asking the Kwavi themselves. At another level, this was a way of saying any Kamba warrior was free to raid the Kwavi livestock but at his own risk.

1271. *Ũvaa wa Masai nĩwoneaa ũyĩnĩ.* **I notice the bald of a Maasai in the wilderness.**
This is a postcolonial coinage given the word Maasai, which was rarely used before 1900. Kwavi was used for all Maa-speakers. The proverb is an expression of one's ability to detect malice.

1272. *Masai yaemwa ni ndĩthya yasya mĩkalya yĩĩngito.* **When a Maasai cannot keep up with herding he claims the firestone shoes are heavy.**
This emerged after the Second World War, when the footwear called *mĩkalya* emerged in Ũkambanĩ. *Mĩkalya* originated with the establishment of the American Firestone Tyre and Rubber Company in Kenya in the 1930s to supply pneumatic tyres. The Kamba and the Maasai began

---

[12] Johannes Krapf, *Travels, Researches, and Missionary Labours, During an Eighteen Years' Residence in Eastern Africa. Together with Journeys to Jagga, Usambara, Ũkamba ni, Shoa* (London: Trübner and Co., 1860).
[13] Mwau, *Dictionary*, 668.

to use discarded tyres for making *mīkalya* footwear in the 1940s. The axiom means people always make lame excuses for their failures.

1273. *Nīsyumaa Ũkavi na īkethia ene.*[14] **They often come from Kwaviland only to be owned by others.**
This proverb reveals complex cattle-rustling activities involving the Maasai, the Kamba, and the Galla during the Vascon era. This is depicted in a Mijikenda myth that says that the Galla, Kamba, and Kwavi were originally siblings. Galla was the eldest of them. Galla raided another community's cattle. When his brothers Mũkamba and Mũkwavi asked for a share of the booty brother Galla refused. Mũkwavi raided Galla and in turn was robbed by his brother Mũkamba. Thus, there arose an endless enmity among the three brothers. This myth depicts a scenario where the Kamba raided the Kwavi cattle, but as soon as they reached Ũkamba the Galla warriors struck and robbed their booty. The proverb calls for caution lest one labours in vain.[15]

1274. *Ũkavi nīwatũla mbenge.* **The Kwavi have broken the barrier.**
The Kwavi encroachment starting in the 1600s forced the construction of strong wooden palisades (*mbenge*) to keep raiders out. If the enemy broke through the barriers, that catastrophe was expressed through shouting this statement, which means things have worsened.

1275. *Ũkavi watũla mbenge walikaa musyĩ.* **When the Kwavi broke the barrier, they entered the home.**
In its context this Vascon-era axiom means, if famine and drought struck they decimated the family's livestock. It is thus a coinage of the times when the Kwavi raided Kamba cattle more frequently during the eighteenth century. Chronic droughts and famines followed during the nineteenth century. Likening the famine to Kwavi raids, the Kamba coined this maxim.

1276. *Kĩswaili kya ngomakomi kĩtheleaa kĩvavaĩnĩ.* **The trickery of the woodpecker ends at the papaya tree.**
The papaya or pawpaw from the tropical Americas did not reach Ũkamba until the 1890s when British planters brought it from India. Therefore, the proverb emerged during the twentieth century. The woodpecker is regarded as sacred by some and evil by others. The pawpaw presented unique challenges to the native woodpecker that makes its home in woody trees by pecking out debris. Pawpaws defy this activity since it is usually watery and fibre-ridden.

---

[14] Kituku, *Folktales*, 70.
[15] Krapf, *Travels*.

1277. *Natuvie athiani nzuku syĩ Ũsũĩnĩ.* **I tipped the army chaplains before the copper arrived from the coast.**
This proverb has two versions – one coined and used by women and another by men for men, but both allude to trade, copper, smiths, and Giriama middlemen in the precolonial commerce between Ũkamba and the coast. The Kamba referred to the Giriama and coastal people as *Asũĩ* and the coast, *Ũsũĩnĩ*. The proverb emerged out of the context of Monsoon-era trade, hunting expeditions, trade in copper, and processing the copper into finished products in Ũkambanĩ. To ensure success on an elephant hunt, for example, a hunter who wished to succeed in the hunt consulted with the leader of the hunt (*mũthiani*). To gain in the hunt he paid the *mũthiani* in the form of *nthuku* (also spelled *nzuku*), coils of copper wire bound closely about arms and legs as signs of social status.[16] During the hunting expedition the *mũthiani* then asked the hunter for clearly marked arrows. When the elephant was felled, the *mũthiani* had to investigate it first. He implanted the arrow of 'the briber' and when the party later found the arrow, the briber was given an appropriate share of the ivory and meat. Thus, prudent planning, specifically payments to gatekeepers or intermediaries, is affirmed as conduct according with known and established rules and customs surrounding exchange. Consulting and compensating key players obtained access to goods, and planning with this in mind ensured honourable success, bringing with it a combination of the coveted esteem and wealth.[17] On the home front women had their version of this proverb, *Natuvie mwalĩli nzuku syĩ Ũsũĩnĩ*, 'I paid the smith before the copper coils arrived from the coast.' The long-distance trade in copper from the coast stimulated the emergence of copper artisans called *mwalĩli*, who transformed the imported wire into varieties of ornaments for women and girls. Stacks of these archaic relics are found, along with extensive notes in the galleries of the National Museums of Kenya and the Kenya National Archives in Nairobi. A wise patriarch paid in advance and as soon as the copper arrived his relatives' ornaments were prioritized, hence the proverb. Someone who had planned ahead cited this proverb. The term *mwalĩli* was largely feminine. It came from the root verb *alĩla* (set up a grinding stone) hence *kwalĩla ĩvia yaũthia* (to set up a grinding stone) and later *kwalĩla kĩanda kyaũtua syũmaa* (to set up the anvil in order to

---

[16] AIM, *Kĩkamba–English*, 155; Mwau, *Kĩkamba*.
[17] Edward Steinhart, 'Elephant Hunting in 19th Century Kenya: Kenya Society and Transformation', *The International Journal of African Historical Studies* 33(2) (2000): 335–49; Kennell Jackson, 'Ngotho (The Ivory Amulet: An Emblem of Upper-Tiers Status Among the 19th Century Akamba of Kenya, ca. 1830–1880', *Kenya Historical Review*, 5(1) (1977): 34–69; Kennell Jackson, 'The Family Identity and Famine among the Nineteenth Century Akamba of Kenya: Social Response to Environmental Stress', *Journal of Family History* 1 (1976): 192–216.

forge metallic implements). The smiths used the feminine principle of the setting of grinding stones to set up of their anvils for metalwork.

1278. *Nzou ĩkinyĩtwe nĩ Mũsũĩ ndĩthoeka.* **An elephant stepped on by a Giriama cannot be purchased.**
This alludes to the ancient ivory trade between Ũkamba and the coast in which the Giriama, called *Asũĩ* (singular *Mũsũĩ*), were middlemen in the trade, making bargaining for better exchange harder for Kamba traders. Consequently, the Kamba found ways to trade directly with the island-based coastal merchants. The proverb means the speaker knows the subject under discussion better than those who just joined the conversation. It can also mean that in a dispute the playing field is uneven if one party makes secret decisions ahead of the meeting. This 'insider information,' speaks both to the importance of knowledge as a possession, and to the fact that it only conveys advantage if only one side knows. It therefore touches on the central motif of withholding in proverbs: a warning not to fall behind in one's due diligence.

1279. *Ĩthyoma ĩmwe ĩitĩwaa mwana mwĩkũyũ.*[18] **A single stammer does not make a child a Kĩkũyũ.**
The Kĩkũyũ stammer Kamba words. According to Kamba oral traditions, the Kĩkũyũ ethnic group originated as a branch of the Kamba. As one section of the Kamba moved further north of Ũkamba highland towards Mũrang'a, they intermingled with other non-Kamba groups and began to speak differently. Gradually losing their Kĩkamba tongue, their language sounded to the Kamba as a baby learning to speak. When Kamba children stammer, they are said to be speaking Kĩkũyũ. This ancient maxim means 'man errs' and it is not a mistake to make a mistake, it is only a mistake to repeat it. This is another way of saying 'I am deeply sorry' to a respectable person when a serious error occurs.

1280. *Kĩkũyũ kĩsila mbakĩ ĩ kũtũ.* **There is a case in Kĩkũyũ when tobacco is in the ear.**
This emerged during the eighteenth and nineteenth centuries when snuff became popular. Between 1700 and 1900 snuff was used to get confessions out of suspects. Among the Kĩkũyũ, snuff was inserted into the ear of the suspect. The Kamba found this method gruesome and warned listeners that if they do not change they will face the Kĩkũyũ version of justice.

---

[18] Kimiu, *Mũkamba*, 15; Watuma, *Syĩthĩo*, 67; Kituku, *Folktales*, 14.

1281. *Kĩkũyũ kyaĩaa mũndũ eeyĩelela.*[19] **One vanishes into Kĩkũyũland by choice.**
Many Kamba settled in Kĩkũyũland against the wishes of their communities of origin. This proverb means association with certain unfit characters or habits eventually corrupts. Another interpretation is that one can be tripped up by the familiar. Since the Kamba were among the earliest ancestors of the Kĩkũyũ, this proverb dates to the times when the Kĩkũyũ and the Kamba separated into distinct linguistic and ethnic groups during the Vascon era.[20]

1282. *Kũthyoma kũitumaa mũndũ mwĩkũyũ.*[21] **Speaking the language of the Kĩkũyũ does not make you one of them.**
This is a variant version of proverb 1280 in this book, but with a twist in meaning and interpretation. The Kamba consider Kĩkũyũ dialect as a corruption of Kĩkamba and claim that the Kĩkũyũ branched off from the Kamba and began to stammer their way away from Kĩkamba as they moved from Mboonĩ towards Mũrang'a. The proverb means that a single error cannot make someone a bastard.

1283. *Mwĩkũyũ aemwa nĩ nzaĩ aasyaa nza yĩ maima.* **A Kĩkũyũ who cannot dance says the compound is pot-holed.**
Nzaĩ was a form of a dance using small anklets attracting mixed borderline Kamba and Kĩkũyũ revellers. Tracing from the Vascon period the axiom points to lame excuses that people give when they cannot succeed.[22]

1284. *Mwĩkũyũ mwavika ũsĩnĩ akwĩyaa nĩkya ngũlimũ.* **When you get to a flooded river, a Kĩkũyũ tells you the water is just ankle high.**
This derived from a Kĩkũyũ axiom, 'The river is just ankle high. Everyone wades by himself.' In the early nineteenth century, a group of Kĩkũyũ warriors who raided the Maasai were routed and fled into a flooded river. With the enemy on their heels, the Kĩkũyũ men had no time to help each other cross the river, as was their custom. Their leader shouted the proverb, which means that under duress individuals care about their own safety first.

---

[19] Kimilu, *Mũkamba*, 115.
[20] Godfrey Muriuki, *A History of the Kikuyu* (Nairobi: Oxford University Press, 1975); Bethwell Ogot (ed.), *Kenya Before 1900* (Nairobi: East Africa Publishing House, 1976).
[21] Mwau, *Dictionary*, 652.
[22] Leslau, *Proverbs*, 33–6.

1285. *Kĩkũyũ kĩsawa mwanake.*[23] **In Kĩkũyũland it is the youth who come in handy.**
This is said in reference to the youths sent to seek food in the Mount Kenya region. It means difficult tasks are assigned those who can do them.[24] It is also used by older people who want to exploit youth, so young people should be wary.

1286. *Ekũyũ masyaa 'Mũkamba aisye nũtonya kũeka syĩndũ syoonthe eka kĩveti na ũkĩ.'* **The Kĩkũyũ say 'Mũkamba said he can give up everything but not wife and wine.'**
This is a type of proverb that not only quotes the wisdom of neighbouring linguistic groups but also uses those ethnic groups as a Wellerism. The proverb emerged during the eighteenth century.

1287. *Ekũyũ makwatwa masyaa, 'Ndukũ ndale itiasavaa.'* **The Kĩkũyũ when arrested say days that are counted do not last long.**
This originated from the 1950s mass incarceration of the Kamba and Kĩkũyũ Mau Mau rebels against colonial rule. The Kamba version of the story says that their Kĩkũyũ inmates played down the length of their imprisonment, saying the days cannot prolong themselves. We will be out soon, they consoled themselves. This axiom was meant to encourage those imprisoned to look forward to their day of release.[25]

1288. *Mũũkwa wa Mũmbee ũkwatasya wa vuka.*[26] **The trap of a Mbere man snares when it grows old.**
The precolonial Kamba and neighbouring Mbere people of the upper Tana River basin trapped animals until the dawn of the 1900s. While the Kamba set traps to snare animals immediately, the Mbere set and left the traps in the forest. After several months, human scent disappeared and animals sensing no presence of humans walked freely into the trap. The Kamba respected Mbere trapping skills through this proverb, which not only teaches patience and focus, but also reveals inter-ethnic cooperation in trapping during the Vascon period.[27]

1289. *Ĩkĩthi ne ĩkĩtaa tyomũkwĩw'a?*[28] **Whenever 'it' is going and advising, don't you hear?**
The origin of this axiom is associated with the eighteenth-century prophetess Syokĩmau. The prophetess who served the Kamba and Kwavi

---

[23] Mwau, *Dictionary*, 649.
[24] Mutisya, *Proverbs*, 45; Mwau, *Dictionary*, 649.
[25] Myles Osborne, 'Kamba and Mau Mau', *International Journal of African Historical Studies* 43(1) (2011), 63–87.
[26] Kimilu, *Mũkamba*, 116.
[27] Krapf, *Travels*.
[28] Kimilu, *Mũkamba*, 115.

people spoke the following words: *Ĩkĩthi nthĩ na ĩ kĩtaa tyomũkwĩwa ũndũ ngwasya?'* These words were shortened to the above proverb. Syokĩmau played tricks on the Kwavi to benefit Kamba raiders. She would hide Kamba warriors in the attic of her large house. When the Kwavi came to her for treatment, she would enquire about their opponents' herds. As they answered, she would repeat this proverb, with so many layers of hidden meanings, translations, and interpretations. The Kwavi present at the divination thought she was speaking to the spirits above. When the Kwavi left, the hidden Kamba warriors would come down, get their charms and instructions, and raid the Kwavi, taking care to leave unscathed those who had visited her. This proverb therefore reveals the complexity of precolonial Kamba– Kwavi relationships. Sometimes the Kwavi used translators and sometimes they knew Kĩkamba sufficiently to communicate with the Kamba.

1290. *Mbĩse nasyo ngũtavye ila niyĩĩe Atwa.* **Bring it on, I will tell you those I have preserved for the Atwa.**
This refers to the Kitui Kamba relationship with the Galla, whom they called Atwa since the Vascon era. The Kitui Kamba competed with the Galla for livestock raiding, waterpans, and pasture. From that context, this axiom was used as an expression of confidence in meeting a challenge against opponents.

1291. *Mũndũ aganaa na Mũthaisũ nĩ kũa mũndũ wake.* **A person carries out burial rites with a Mũthaisũ for lack of kindred.**
This proverb alludes to an ancient burial custom in Kitui where the lots of a patriarch had to be ritually 'divided up'. Once the body was disposed of, a cleansing ceremony (which Mwingi-Kitui dialect called *kũgaa*; Machakos, *kũaa*) followed. A Mũthaisũ was usually called to sleep with the senior wife as an act of 'dividing up the family'. The bereaved women actually preferred to have such ritual sex with a member of their husband's family. Nevertheless, for lack of a next of kin they put up with a Mũthaisũ. The proverb talks about exhausting resources and coping by whatever means available.

1292. *Mwĩsilamu ti kĩlemba.*[29] **A Muslim is not a headgear.**
This proverb has a Swahili origin. Mũĩmi illustrated it with a story of a hyena who converted to Islam and was instructed not to eat corpses, something the hyena found difficult. It went back to its old ways of crunching anything that came its way. The maxim means there are things that require discipline and restraint. Test something or someone to determine their quality.

---

[29] Mũĩmi, *Kĩthyomo*, 31.

1293. *Mũsele mũvyũ ndwĩ mũindi mũkũũ.* **Hot rice has no old Indian.**
This originated from colonial multiracial encounters. The British Empire attracted Asian immigrants, generally classified as Indian, who introduced new cuisines involving the consumption of rice served on large flat plates and eaten in mixed age groups while sitting on mats. The maxim originated between the 1920s and 1960s.

1294. *Kĩsũngũ kyesie na ndeke.* **The English language came by air.**
The Kamba have engaged with the English language since the 1820s and with aviation from its inception in East Africa during the First World War. The axiom, however, emerged in the 1970s among students making excuses for not speaking English fluently. They meant it was not their fault they spoke broken English, rather it was because the language was alien to them. This shows how a generation without understanding historical facts can formulate misleading proverbs. It was not the twentieth-century airplane, but the nineteenth-century ships that originally brought English to Kenya.

1295. *Mũsũngũ aneena mũindi ndatũmuaa.* **When the white man speaks, the Indian keeps tight-lipped.**
The proverb was born out of the racialized Kenyan society of the early twentieth century. Whites held ultimate authority, Indians followed, with Africans on the lowest rank. This proverb, however, elaborates seniority in age and status. When the senior decides, juniors must follow.

1296. *Ngitĩ syoonthe syaĩĩ sya Kĩsũngũ.* **All dogs were once upon a time of English breed.**
This proverb emerged from the early 1900s, alluding to the fact that white settlers kept large numbers and varieties of dogs. The English dogs had sufficient food and were healthy compared to the skinny Kamba hunting dogs. This proverb was first a mute response to colonial disdains for African dogs. Second, it meant that anyone can improve and excel; those who are lean can be fat and healthy.[30]

1297. *Sore nĩyo yaminie ikombe kwa Mũsũngũ.* **'Sorry' finished the cup at the European house.**
The origin of this proverb is attributed to G.C. Leith whose Kamba nickname was *Kĩkombe*, 'cup'. He served as District Commissioner of Machakos from 1888 to 1892, hence the proverb emerged shortly after

---

[30] Lindblom, *Akamba*; Brett Shadle, 'Cruelty and Empathy, Animals and Race, in Colonial Kenya', *Journal of Social History* 45(4) (Summer 2012), 1097–1116; Binyamin Blum, 'The Hounds of Empire: Forensic Dog Tracking in Britain and its Colonies, 1888–1953', *Law and History Review* 621 (2017).

that period.[31] His Kamba servants – upon realizing that giving apologies for mistakes calmed the white man's fury – abused this Western custom and supposedly broke all the ceramic cups in Kĩkombe's house, as the maxim suggests. The moral lesson is that an apology must be genuine. This was a protest against Western etiquette. If a Mũkamba wanted to apologize to fellow Kamba, he had to use different terms, not the imperial, 'sorry'.

1298. Kĩswaili kyanangawa nĩ avana. The word 'no' spoils the Swahili language.
This is a twentieth-century creation given that Swahili was not spoken in East Africa inland, Kĩkamba being the language of trade. As it penetrated the interior, fraud in transactions became common. As a result, by the end of the colonial era, Kiswahili was Kamba slang for lies or cheating. Colonial traders used the new language to cheat, relative to the value of their goods.

1299. Kĩtui nĩ kyumawa kĩ mbũmbũ. Despite an abundance of *Lablab purpureus* lentils people still depart Kĩtui.
This adage was used as a justification for migration from fertile central Kitui to drier Mwingĩ and eastern Machakos from the late nineteenth century. *Mbũmbũ* is a variety of lentils (known among botanists as *Lablab purpureus*), which was first successfully cultivated in central Kitui. It was a favourite legume that attracted many to emigrate from less productive locations. The axiom warned rich men to be kind to the poor, for the poor can do without gifts and tips from the rich.

1300. Ũte mwana nĩwe wĩtwaa Kitui kũya mbũa. A childless person takes themselves to Kitui to eat skin meat.
This localized proverb hints at the emergence of beggars and vagrancy in Kitui town between 1898 and 1958.[32] Until the colonial era ended, the Kamba used to send their sons to Kitui to bring back meat and other valuable goods. Those who had no sons to take care of them in their old age travelled to Kitui town to eat miscellaneous pieces of meat left on the skin and spread to dry, locally known as *mbũa*. That is what the sages called *Kwĩtwaa Kitui kũya mbũa*, to go to Kitui to eat skins. The maxim encouraged people to care for themselves under any circumstance.

---

[31] KNA: DC/MKS/4/9 Machakos District Political Record Book 1930–1938.
[32] KNA: DC/KTI/1/1/5 Kitui Annual Reports, 1942–1948; Stanner, 'Kamba Market'; G.C.M. Mutiso, 'Kitui Ecosystem: Integration and Change', in *Ecology and History in East Africa*, ed. Bethwell Ogot (Nairobi: Heinemann, 1979): 126–52: Jackson, 'Ethnohistorical Study'.

1301. *Nakũthianie ta Kalekye na Ũkavi.* **I have spied you out like Kalekye and the Kwavi.**
This proverb, from the Vascon era, is important in Kamba written history. Pioneer historian Kennell Jackson mistakenly identified Kalekye as female. That error has since circulated in written histories. Lately, Myles Osborne in *Ethnicity and Empire* repeated the same error. It is not hard to find female warriors, but at the same time, it was taboo for a woman to wield a bow or even carry one for her husband. It is therefore not possible that Kalekye could have been a woman.[33] Kalekye ee Nzeleele was a male historical figure and has featured in several scholarly publications. He is very well known in oral accounts as a shrewd military leader who lived on Engamba Mountain in the eighteenth century. He single-handedly beat Kwavi invaders many times through unexpected battle tactics. With time, the Kwavi spied on him carefully, broke through his *mbenge*, and overwhelmed his army. The proverb emerged soon after the tragic end of Kalekye's heroism.

1302. *Ũkavikya mbu Malũng'ũyũnĩ?* **Will your wails reach to Malũng'ũyũnĩ?**
The maxim is tied to the above events of the eighteenth century involving Kalekye and Kwavi invaders. The Kwavi who were about to attack asked Kalekye the above question. This proverb therefore encodes the history of scattered Kamba settlements and their struggle with the Kwavi during the Vascon period. In those days, the land between Eengamba mountain and Ngomeni rocks was uninhabited. Malũng'ũyũnĩ was the only other *mbenge* settlement. Interestingly this was not on a mountaintop, but on a plain below Kathũngũ and Twoolotwa rocks. The men of this *mbenge* were the most feared by the Kwavi. Its fighters used to rush to the aid of those who were beating war drums in distant hills as far as Eengamba. The proverb rose soon after the tragic death of Kalekye. It means soliciting for someone to attempt the impossible.

1303. *Katatavw'a oowaiwe nĩ ĩnai.* **Katatavw'a was killed by a tapeworm.**
This female historical figure, *Katatavw'a*, died from tapeworm infection in the early twentieth century because she would not heed any hygienic advice. The proverb is, however, a camouflage for a stubborn person who does not accept admonition. There are multiple variations to this proverb, which points out the fatal consequences of arrogance.

---

[33] Osborne, *Ethnicity*, 31.

1304. *Wĩvaati ta Singũ.* **You are as lucky as Singũ.**
This is associated with a poor man named Singũ who lived in Machakos during the 1890s. The story as recounted by Mũĩmi is that during the devastating famine of the 1890s Singũ could
not secure food for his starving family. In despair he laid down under his grain store from noon to late afternoon hoping to die. While sound asleep a gazelle wounded by hunters fell next to him. He rose up, skinned it and cooked it for his family. That night heavy rain fell, his family sowed the land, and out of the harvest, they never suffered want again. Subsequently, people who achieved something unexpectedly would say the proverb.[34]

1305. *Maũndũ meo kwene aangĩ me kwakwa, kaula Mũnyasya wa Nzivũ.* **Strange affairs occur in homes while others occur in mine, as Mũnyasya wa Nzivũ used to say.**
Mũnyasya wa Nzivũ of Kalanga in Kitui coined this proverb around the 1910s. He was commenting on an incident of incest between a man and his stepmother, an extreme social absurdity. Spreading widely through songs and dances, the proverb has since been applied as self-criticism and complaint.

1306. *Kavola Kamengele.* **Go slow Kamengele.**
While some proverbs emphasize the importance of speed, others urge slow deliberation. Hasty and thoughtless action can be disastrous. This emerged during the late colonial era and was featured in popular music in the 1970s. It was a caution to young girls to slow down in the move towards romance. It also advised that rushing into urban, modern lifestyles was potentially harmful and one needed caution.

1307. *Kaminda aanangiwe nĩ ĩtava ĩnene yatũla kĩko.* **Kaminda was ruined by a big scoop that broke the spoon.**
This alludes to the tragic story of Kaminda wa Kamũtĩ of Kakongo village in Kyuso, a mentally challenged herder. This demonstrates that proverbs are not always about notables. Around 1988, Kaminda was guarding the cattle of a Kyuso merchant at Mboloinĩ waterpan. He had just finished his mealiepap with dik-dik stew when rustlers ambushed him. As he ran with the cooking of the day, he became confused and wandered back to the enemy camp and was killed. Subsequently, people began to play down Kaminda's tragedy using a barrage of axiomatic expressions including this one. The proverb tells the listener to waste no chances. Do something fast.

---

[34] Mũĩmi, *Kĩthyomo*, 7–8.

1308. *Kanonga akwie akwaatha ĩtu na ndoe.* **Kanonga died while shooting the sky with a fart.**
This emerged in the late nineteenth century. Old women usually told young girls this axiom while warning them against bragging of something that they were ignorant of.

1309. *Ve ngathĩĩyo mbiingĩ syatumiswe Kanonga akavũka mũthiti akwaatha ĩtu.* **Too much boasting made Kanonga split his buttocks trying to shoot the sky.**
This also emerged in the late the nineteenth century after an episode where Kanonga tried to shoot clouds to bring rain. Even though this looks foolhardy, Kanonga can be seen as a visionary who believed clouds could be induced to yield rain long before colonial scientists shot clouds in Ũkamba. It is also possible that Kanonga had heard of this science and tried his own method.

1310. *Nzasũ syatumie Kanonga aitũlwa kũũ nĩ ĩng'oi.* **The donkey broke the leg of the proud Kanonga.**
Kanonga gained widespread fame through his extraordinary behaviour. He was constantly doing abnormal things. In the story of his encounter with the donkey during the Second World War he boasted that he could handle an unruly donkey like a goat. He kicked the donkey, angering the animal, which kicked his leg so hard that it broke. People around him asked, 'Kanonga! Are you a donkey to kick a donkey?' Out of that context came this proverb.

1311. *Wĩ ngũlũ ta Kanonga aitwaĩya Ngai nzanzimbaa.* **You are as proud as Kanonga gifting God Zanzibar bananas.**
While other proverbs associated with Kanonga are older, this one emerged during the late colonial period when the new species of bananas, called *nzanzimbaa*, were named after their place of origin, the island of Zanzibar. These are the tiniest species of bananas the author has seen; they are very sweet and revered in Ũkamba. They surfaced through trade in the late 1940s.

1312. *Wĩ ũvũngũ ta Mbuvi ayasya nthenge yĩ mũthũkũ ndĩtheũkaa.* **You have lies like Mbuvi's declaration that a hornless buck never bleats.**
He-goats bleat loudly when in rut. Anyone assuming the head with or without horns determines behaviour in he-goats is wrong. The speaker condemns this lie, arguing that it emerges from pride and ignorance. This statement dates from the story of a man called Mbuvi living in the early 1900s. He spoke so dishonestly that people dismissed all his declarations.

1313. *Matenzawa auniwe nĩ kwĩthika.* **Matenzawa was saved by diving.**
This proverb is based on a story of a poor man named Matenzawa who lived in Kangundo in Machakos. Apart from admonishing people not to despair, it illustrates the tenuous and perseverant life of Matenzawa. There are two versions of his story. He had a long beard and long unkempt hair, and the colonial law required that all bearded men should pay poll tax. However, through the entire colonial era he evaded paying taxes for whenever the tax collectors appeared he ran off and dived into a nearby river. The second version of the story is that when Matenzawa tired of abject poverty and decided to commit suicide by diving to die, he found ivory buried in the muddy bed of the dam. He sold it and became rich. This incidence happened between 1927 and 1957, when dams were built across Machakos.[35] This proverb emerged afterwards. In short, there is no room for despair in life; fortune awaits a man who exerts himself.

1314. *Nondo sya mwĩĩtu ũsu wĩtawa Kokĩ itivalũkaa.*[36] **The breasts of that girl called Kokĩ never sag.**
Emerging from the twentieth century, this axiom warns against excessive drinking. One who loves drinking is like one in a romantic relationship with a girl called Kokĩ (meaning Madam Little Beer) whose attractiveness never fades. The word Kokĩ is a female name given to a baby girl if the mother had just consumed a little honey (ũkĩ) before labour, or a baby born when the father was having a little beer.

1315. *No ĩ kya Ngelanĩ.* **It is that from Ngelanĩ.**
This emerged shortly after 1938 when Kamba of Ngelanĩ region led by Mũindi wa Mbingu marched from Machakos to Nairobi to protest before the colonial governor against the destocking policies. They camped along Racecourse Road for many days and when asked to call off the strike they said *No kyuo kĩ kũũ, tũngai ng'ombe*, 'We maintain our original word, return our cattle.' Other ethnic groups joined the protest, rendering their own version of this proverb. Since then people who know each other and wish to conceal their secrets have used this maxim.

---

[35] Mutisya, *Proverbs*, 56.
[36] Kimilu, *Mũkamba*, 27.

16

Beliefs, Rituals, and Cosmology

1316. *Andũ maemie Ngai me elĩ tyo mũndũ?* **Two people defied God, how much more for a man?**
This ancient axiom means that the quest to control people is futile. There is a long history of human defiance of law since humanity began. The axiom alludes to the biblical story of creation in Genesis where Adam and Eve disobeyed the creator. That original defiance, the maxim suggests, involving two people against a stronger supernatural force, is a lesson that mere mortals cannot easily control people.

1317. *Ĩthaa mũndũ nĩ nzuke ya Ngai.* **One's father is an age-mate of God.**
Around 1970, a musician wove this axiom into a song calling his countrymen to return to the farms, shun idleness and drinking, and respect their fathers. The proverb means a father deserves the utmost respect and reverence from children.

1318. *Kula ya Ngai ndĩ mũlolongo.* **God's vote does not queue.**
This emerged during the second half of the twentieth century, when massive voting by queuing was introduced. People stood in long lines (*mũlolongo*) behind the candidate of their choice. They were counted but did not cast a vote. Appearing in traditional songs, the proverb means that if fate should be on your side, it will be so. One does not have to queue for God's blessings.

1319. *Ngai nde kĩmena na ndaĩsaa ongo.* **God has no hatred and does not take bribes.**
This is a recent coinage given the word *ongo* (bribe), a concept of the postcolonial era. Colonial society was full of hate, conflict, corruption, and bribery. Religion played a key role here as the place of escape. While every administrator and police officer had to be bribed to render services, sages condemned these vices through such idiomatic expressions.

292   *Part IV: Kamba Society*

1320. *Ngai nĩ mũnene kwĩ Mũthũngũ.*[1] **God is greater than the white man.**
This is drawn from colonial culture, racially organized with the white man at the top, Asians in the middle, and Africans at the bottom. European leaders had all the power to the extent that colonial subjects confused divine and human powers. This proverb was crafted to separate the two: human power is limited.

1321. *Ngai nĩ mũĩ kwĩ wenzi.*[2] **God's mind is sharper than a blade.**
The hidden part of the proverb is making the audience confuse sharpness and wit, as the word for both is *ũĩhe* both wit of the mind and the sharpness of a blade. Only the term *wenzi* helps to make the distinction between wit and sharpness.

1322. *Ngai wa kĩng'ei ndakomaa.* **The god of a thief does not sleep.**
This maxim recognizes God as material provider for all. A thief is even given an opportunity to thrive through stealing from others. While not recognizing theft as a virtue, it implies that whichever god a thief worships, that deity answers their prayers.

1323. *Aimũ ma mũthiani maiingĩawa kĩlumĩ.* **A seer's spirits do not need drumming.**
To understand this proverb definitions must be clear and the proverb's historical context understood. Contrary to conventional definitions, the word *mũthiani* means more than a spy or scout.[3] *Mũthiani* was a member of the Kamba elite responsible for major matters such as war, hunting, long-distance trade, and prophecy. *Athiani* were the most revered personalities in precolonial Ũkamba.[4] Unlike specialists whose spirits were induced to act through libation and a drum dance (*kĩlumĩ*), seers did not go through such long processes to cure, hence the saying. The proverb calls for practical, rational thinking and action: if one wants to do something they should do it immediately, like the *mũthiani* who healed without elaborate rituals.

1324. *Aimũ maetae thĩna maithĩnzĩwa.*[5] **The spirits torment when sacrifices are being offered to them.**
Precolonial Kamba believed that spirits were of different types – those for the family and those for healers. The latter were spirits of the

[1] Mũĩmi, *Kĩthyomo*, 33.
[2] Lindblom, *Riddles*, 34; Mwau, *Dictionary*, 664.
[3] AIM, *Kĩkamba–English*, 122, 60.
[4] Lindblom, *Akamba*, 149; Jackson, 'Ngotho'; John Fage and Roland Oliver (eds), *The Cambridge History of Africa* (Cambridge: Cambridge University Press, 1985).
[5] Mwau, *Dictionary*, 645.

departed. All were offered sacrifices at their own times, usually at hillsite shrines. It was said that they inflicted people during such processes. The deeper meaning is that some people often bite the hand that feeds them.

1325. *Aimũ mathĩnasya ũla ũmathembeaa.* **Spirits molest those who make offerings to them.**
This ancient proverb alludes to the Kamba belief that God's abode were spirits of the dead who interceded for living or troubled humans. If they did not offer gifts to the spirits, the spirits would visit them in their sleep and throttle (sleep apnea) them. People who did not sacrifice to spirits did not have such problems. The maxim means change your habits and all will be well for the root cause of the problem is self-inflicted.

1326. *Aimũ nĩ mesĩ kwa etĩkĩli.* **Spirits know the abode of Christians.**
This proverb entered Kamba culture through gradual Christianization of the Kamba from the 1850s to 1950s, meaning people know their own capabilities. A weakling will never dare challenge a strong man.

1327. *Ĩimũ ya mũndũ nĩ mũndũ.* **A person's demon is another person.**
This ancient axiom means a person's needs are known by another person and are catered for by another person. Similarly, another person also initiates one's nightmare. This profound Kamba observation is similar to the French philosopher Jean-Paul Sartre's 'Hell is other people.'[6]

1328. *Mũndũ mũka nĩ ĩimũ na ndaiimawa nzele.* **A woman is a spirit and is never denied a calabash bowl.**
This ancient proverb equated a woman with a spirit, the ultimate authority and value in both dead and living realms. Spirits took care of the living as the woman took care of the community. It is for that reason that men revered women while at the same time controlling them and their feminine power. Spirits were propitiated with calabash bowls of beer, water, milk, or porridge. Women among the Kamba were to be handled the same way.

1329. *Kĩla kĩĩma na aimũ makyo.* **Every mountain and its spirits.**
Hills were believed to be colonized by specific spirits that could be beneficial or harmful to people. This may be interpreted as every person has his own strength, value, and virtue.

---

[6] See the play *No Exit* (written in 1943).

1330. *Kĩĩma ngathi ndyathĩaa maimũ maikese ũthi ũvuva mwaki.* **I do not reveal to spirits a mountain that I will visit, lest they light fire there.**
The phrase 'light fire' symbolizes destroying the plan. Revealing one's plans gives opponents a chance to destroy such plans.[7] This alludes to beliefs that spirits resided in mountains and were fond of fire. The Kamba would not want a mountain with evil spirits, which symbolized opponents. Therefore, do not let your opponent know your plans.

1331. *Thĩimũ yĩkwĩsĩ yĩĩkũĩsaa yĩkaũmina.* **A devil that knows you will never finish you.**
This proverb originated with the Kamba diaspora in coastal Kenya. A person who wants to harm or exploit a friend or employer will not engage in open rampage but quietly pilfer to dip into your resources repeatedly. The axiom emerged during the twentieth century when Swahili axioms found their way into Kamba wit and wisdom.

1332. *Wenda ũya na aimũ wasaa kĩko kĩasa.* **If you want to dine with spirits, you will need to carve a long spoon.**
This was drawn from the woodcarving industry emerging around the Islamic era. The head of each household made necessary wooden articles like spoons. The Kamba fretted about dining with ghosts because these could attack without warning. The message is that if one wants to avoid trouble stay far from aggressive individuals.[8]

1333. *Mũndũ ũte mĩtwe ĩlĩ ti mũndũ.* **A man without two heads is not a man.**
There were certain things that one with only one gender of children could or could not do such as purchasing witchcraft. This is one of the proverbs revealing that, unlike other societies, the Kamba greatly valued both boys and girls. It also helps us debate whether the precolonial Kamba was gendered or not.

1334. *Ũoĩ wa aimũ ndwingwa kĩvingũo.* **Witchcraft of the spirits has no key.**
In Kamba belief there are different kinds of witchcraft with corresponding remedies. One version is called *mbingo* (the closure), which involves a wizard 'closing' a victim's ability to prosper or bear children. The remedy involved a healer 'unclosing' the person to release his or her potential. This was called *kũvingũa*, thus supplying *kĩvingũo* to that type of witchcraft. However, if the spirit condemned one, he or she was doomed.

---

[7] Mutisya, *Proverbs*, 16.
[8] Lindblom, *Akamba*, 545.

Beliefs, Rituals, and Cosmology 295

1335. *Kũndũ nĩ ĩya ya mbũi nditavasya aimũ.*[9] **I do not tell the spirits where I will eat a goat.**
This ancient axiom talks about competition among youth. It stresses the importance of controlling one's excitement for potential success and keeping it secret. It shows the intersection of spirits and goats in Kamba beliefs. The spirits symbolize evil, while the goat stands for something adorable, which is envy of peers. The adorable thing sparks competition between
speaker and peers, cast here as spirits. The goat is the most important object for it reveals that the proverb emerged during the Monsoon era when the Kamba adopted goats as domestic animals.

1336. *Kakw'a kosawa nĩ mwene.* **Whenever it dies it is picked up by the owner.**
This ancient maxim comments on child mortality rates. As an explanation of death, it alludes to the Kamba belief that the creator grants children to couples but can also takes a child's life. This encourages couples to procreate after a baby's death. When a child died, it was the creator who took the child away.

1337. *Kĩkw'ũ kĩkalaa andũnĩ.*[10] **Death dwells among people.**
This means death is part of life and should be accepted. It is meant to console a family suffering a loss. It asks people to accept their fate because humans have no control over life.

1338. *Kĩkw'ũ nĩ kĩng'endu nũndũ kĩyĩsĩ mwĩĩtu mweũ.* **Death is proud, it does not know a beautiful girl.**
Here, *mwĩĩtu mweũ* refers to a light-skinned girl, the epitome of beauty among the Kamba. The axiom means death is beyond human control, striking even the most desired.

1339. *Mũndũ aikw'a nowĩkasya ntheele.* **Even a dying person kicks.**
The dying show signs of life by moving their limbs, often seen as resistance against death and symbolic of endurance, persistence, and hope. The proverb tells the listener, even if you are defeated, you can persist in resisting.

---

[9] Mwau, *Dictionary*, 650.
[10] Mwau, *Dictionary*, 649.

1340. *Mũkamba ndakusaa.*[11] **A Mũkamba does not die without a cause.**
This ancient proverb exemplifies the Kamba's deep belief in witchcraft as the principal cause of death, suffering, and misfortune. Unless a person was a centenarian, their death was attributed to witchcraft and divination was sought to determine the cause.[12] Virtually every tragic incidence was attributed to some malevolent force and supernatural powers.[13] As condemnation of lame excuses the proverb admonishes one who makes a mistake – accept responsibility, apologize, and correct it.

1341. *Ĩsũvĩane na athani ma ũvũngũ.* **Guard against false prophets.**
This proverb was lifted from Matthew 7:15–20. Christian converts incorporated it into Kamba wit and wisdom before the Second World War. It appeared at the end of a published story by James Muimi about girls and ogres.[14]

1342. *Ĩtumo nĩ ya kyamana naĩ.* **The spear has crossed the wrong way.**
This expression of a conspicuous death of a man in a large family emerged in antiquity when the Kamba used spears before they switched to bows and arrows. When a man died in suspect
circumstances, the community asked the deceased's brother to take his place as a leader. The brother responded with this proverb, indicating it was risky to take over without establishing what killed his brother. In the old days the Kamba stretched out a corpse in a special way while a specialist pulled out the dead man's penis (spear) to a forward-facing position. If the penis fell between the legs it was considered bad luck. The family had to seek divination. The maxim became an expression of doubt and a worsening situation.

1343. *Avautani ya Ngai ndĩ matuu.* **God's about turn has no reverberations.**
This means God's plans have no reverberations, like drilling soldiers. Many Kamba served in the colonial military forces. This involved drilling, where the most memorable feat involved ordering recruits with a loud 'About turn!' The recruits turned and stamped their feet,

---

[11] Festus Kavale, 'A Biblical Study of Witchcraft', *African Journal of Evangelical Theology* 12(2) (1993), 117.
[12] Lindblom, *Akamba*, 278.
[13] Richard Gehman, *African Traditional Religion in Biblical Perspective* (Wheaton: Oasis International, 2012); Richard Gehman, 'The African Inland Mission', *Africa Journal of Evangelical Theology* 23(2) (2004): 115–44.
[14] Muĩimi, *Kĩthyomo*, 5.

making quite a remarkable sound. The proverb means that when God makes one's life change no sound is heard.

1344. *Ĩvĩtũkanĩaa kĩthyũwonĩ.* **They separate at the cleromancy.**
This ancient proverb alludes to Kamba divination, but with far-removed meaning and application. When a misfortune struck, it was suspected that the victim had been bewitched. A diviner's counsel was sought. The diviner assembled several pebbles called *mbũũ* (dice), each representing suspected individuals.[15] When the culprit's pebble separated and fell off as the diviner turned them up in a circle, called *Kĩthyũwo* (hence *kĩthyũwonĩ*), the audience pronounced this proverb. Nevertheless, this proverb was used when a contestant distinguished himself/herself from others in a positive way.

1345. *Maũndũ maũkaa andũnĩ.* **Incidences occur among people.**
This is a consolation axiom told to those suffering a loss such as the death of a relative. When losses occurred, elders gathered to console the affected family members with this maxim, meaning that, as long as people exist, bad things will occur, so be strong.

1346. *Mũkalĩĩli wa ĩthembo nde liũ.* **An impatient altar priest has no food.**
In the old days every village had a central shrine with a specialist priest. Their sites today encode the history of the earliest settlements known in oral traditions. As Mutisya puts it, a priest who prepared the shrine quickly did not get food on which he depended.[16] Another interpretation is that one who depends on offerings of shrines will certainly starve after the food runs out. One must work.

1347. *Mũthembi wĩ nthembo yake ndowaa wa ũmwaĩka.* **A person with his own offering does not lack someone to circumcise him.**
The most important part of a Mũkamba's life was circumcision. At each of its three stages, one had to pay the circumcision expert. If one had no payment, the ceremony was put on hold. This maxim appeared during the Islamic era when circumcision ceremonies emerged in Ũkambanĩ.

1348. *Nthembo ya kĩvĩsĩ ĩtethasya avĩti.* **The offering of a boy benefits passersby.**
Emerging shortly after the Second World War, before which young people were not involved in offerings, this axiom means crafty people misuse a fool's valuables. People take advantage of those who do not

---

[15] Lindblom, *Akamba*, 158–60.
[16] Kimilu, *Mũkamba*, 116; Mutisya, *Proverbs*, 6.

protect themselves. This statement suggests that a boy's offering was unconcealed and anyone could pick it up.

1349. *Kĩlumĩ kingĩvawaa mũyo nĩ nthele.* **Ritual dance is embellished by kicks.**
This ancient axiom alludes to organized ritual dances that involved trance among women. The trance was taken to be a sign the rain spirit had descended to communicate its message through the affected women. In reality, the maxim means that conversations are sweeter when seasoned with some axioms.

1350. *Ndũkongele kĩlumĩ nzeele.* **Do not add kicks in the *kĩlumĩ* dance.**
This alludes to ritual dances called *kĩlumĩ*, which were performed by women with two drums accompanying the *ululations* and singing of a leader. One session of the *kilumi* dance could last about half an hour, during which many women went into trance, fell on the ground, and started kicking as if they were dying. Some dancers faked the kicks and hence the proverb, which condemns exaggeration.

1351. *Nzevũ nĩyongelawa mũkungo.*[17] **Magic is often combined with crawling.**
Nzevũ was a commonly used black-magic powder used to protect one against fierce beasts or enemies. A pinch was taken in the hand and blown in the direction of the beast or enemy.[18] The ancient axiom means when these magical tactics failed practical actions were taken such as crawling away from danger.

1352. *Kĩkalo kya nthĩ kyunaa mũndũ mũe.* **Idleness benefits only the healer.**
This emphasizes hard work and castigates idleness. The healer was the only person who earned a living by sitting, not really idle, but waiting for customers.

1353. *Mũe wa ũkunũlw'a ndang'endeaa mũe wa ĩtiima nũndũ mũthya wa ngomakomi nĩ kĩvavaĩnĩ.* **An apprenticed healer does not mock a disabled healer, since the end of a woodpecker is on the pawpaw tree.**
Dating to the Vascon era when the pawpaw reached East Africa, the proverb calls on the audience to respect people's status and stage of development. Second, it means the two types of healers prove themselves when they are confronted with complex ailments. Like the

---

[17] Kimilu, *Mũkamba*, 118.
[18] Lindblom, *Akamba*, 263.

woodpecker, which cannot drill the pawpaw tree, the boastful healer is embarrassed at the hour of reckoning.

1354. *Mũe ũvoasya nde ithitũ mbiingĩ*. **A true healer does not have many charms.**
Healers used charms and chants but the most effective were practical and used fewer charms. The proverb suggests that hitting the nail on the head is better than beating about the bush over important public matters.

1355. *Nasyaiwe mũe no kĩnandũ ndaĩ*. **I was born a healer save for the healer's gourd.**
This ancient proverb refers to healers who used no charms. They simply healed. It is said in a light moment when the speaker means that even though the listeners may underestimate him, he is an expert in the matter at hand.

1356. *Mũndũ mũe ti kĩtiti*. **A diviner is not a divinatory calabash.**
Kĩtiti is a medicine man's small gourd in which divining dice are kept and from which they are shaken. The medicine man uses the dice to draw conclusions. As Mũĩmi illustrated in the story of the bat and the antelope, the actual meaning is strength is not always in body mass. It is close to the axiom 'actions speak louder than words'.[19]

1357. *Mũndũ mũĩ ndaendaa ũwenĩ na inya*. **A wise man does not go to a divination with his mother.**
Divination was central to precolonial Kamba cosmology. Prudence required that a man should never be accompanied by his mother to the diviner. There were male secrets that were not to be known by women. The ancient maxim means that it is not wise to expose kin to risks.

1358. *Mũndũ mũe ndeyaũĩsyaa*.[20] **A diviner does not divine for himself.**
This proverb points to the importance of interdependence, medicinal specialization, and even ignorance about certain medical conditions. Diviners had limited knowledge over matters of cosmology and had to leave certain matters to specialists. Those who could divine about rain, the health of animals and family, or serious expeditions were not specialists in matters of fertility and marital affairs, for example. This ancient proverb persuades the audience to listen to good counsel and value interdependency.

---

[19] Mũĩmi, *Kĩthyomo*, 31–2.
[20] Mwau, *Dictionary*, 657.

1359. *Mũndũ mũe nde nguma kwoo.*[21] **A healer has no fame in his own homeland.**
This proverb means people rarely recognize the credentials of acquaintances. After infiltration of Christianity, it was varied as *Mwathani ndakathawa kwoo,* 'A prophet is not without honour, save in his own country.' Although appearing several times in Christian scripture, the Bible only strengthened the nineteenth-century opinion.

1360. *Kĩumo na ũoi nĩ mũndũ na mwanainya.* **Curses and witchcraft are siblings.**
The Kamba explained economic and social failure of a person in terms of witchcraft from a jealous neighbour and a curse from parents. A person cursed or bewitched behaved the same way. A series of misfortunes followed the person. This maxim called on the listeners to lead good lives in their communities and particularly to care for their families.

1361. *Mũndũ mũe nĩ ĩvose.* **A diviner is arms akimbo.**[22]
Emerging from the Monsoon era, this was an idiomatic condemnation of inaction and idleness. It points to Kamba views about the career of healers. The healer appeared idle and spent time bathing, concerned about hygiene and appearance. Society recognized that everyone could not do this and acquire wealth. One must get dirty, work, and build wealth.

1362. *Kwaa mũoi no kwĩsaa kuma mũtavania.* **From the wizard's house often comes a priest.**
This emerged in the 1940s when evangelism became widespread and evangelists increased in number. The Kangundo area of Machakos was the first to produce renowned evangelists such as the African Brotherhood Church founder Simon Mulandi. This proverb was used first to defend the stereotype associated with young women of Kangundo, who were said to be proud and unable to maintain stable marriages. It means all people cannot be the same. In a large family, for instance, some children can be moral and responsible people while others are not.

1363. *Mũoi wa mũndũ tiwe mũvingũaa.* **One's wizard is not the healer.**
This axiom appeared in the songs of Kareria wa Mulandi of Ngomeni, meaning there is an exit to all challenges. The proverb alludes to witchcraft and healing. According to Kamba beliefs, wizards could bewitch someone to be mute or infertile. Such people would be said to be 'closed' and a healer had to 'open' the voice or womb in order for it to function properly. The wizard cannot do that but the healer can.

---

[21] Kituku, *Sukulu*, 51; Mwau, *Dictionary*, 657.
[22] Mwau, *Dictionary*, 657.

1364. *Ngũkũ ndĩmelya mbembe.* **The chicken will not swallow maize seed.**
Another expression of witchcraft this implies how fast and lethal one's magic could be. The chicken could bewitch a cock between the time it picks up a corn seed and attempts to swallow it. The proverb emerged during the Vascon era when corn became common and witchcraft surged.

1365. *Vau vayĩkw'a mũtĩ.* **A stick cannot be thrown there.**
This statement was used in two ironic senses: when a river flooded, people repeated this axiom, meaning the river is dangerously flooded and cannot be crossed. However, the axiom originated in the realm of magic, where ancient Kamba were said to use magic to cross flooded rivers. If the magician failed in his efforts, he said, 'You cannot throw a stick into the river' – meaning it was too dangerous.

1366. *Ndavĩtya nduu.* **She cannot miss a squirrel.**
During lean days when hunters could not supply meat, women used witchcraft to bring down animals for their communities. Animals killed magically were feared so such women had to say some other words to undo the wizardry so their magic would not harm humans. This profession required expertise and precision. The maxim means the person in question is an expert in the subject under discussion and is qualified for the issue under review.

1367. *Ndithakĩawa mwana nĩ mũoi.* **I do not let a wizard toss my baby in the air.**
This proverb refers to women playfully tossing their babies in the air. It was believed that wizards took advantage of such baby-tossing occasions to bewitch the baby, hence the proverb. Tracing from antiquity, this means the speaker will not let ill-intentioned individuals meddle in their affairs.

17
Wealth and Poverty

1368. *Kasaũ ka thĩna nĩ mwalimũ.* **A poor calf is a teacher.**
An orphaned calf is a symbolic expression of human bereavement. This maxim is a post- independence coinage for the word *mwalimũ*, which appeared in Kĩkamba only after 1900.[1] Since the 1910s, this adage has appeared in seven publications. As Lindblom explained, 'The proverb is said of a poor orphaned youth, who has to fend for himself including finding the means of paying the bride-price and establishing his own family.'[2] An orphaned calf teaches itself how to survive while teaching humans that not all is lost, even in the worst tragedy encouraging self-reliance and hard work.

1369. *Kũthĩna mũno tikwo Kũkw'a.* **Abject poverty is not death.**
This emerged during the nineteenth and twentieth centuries to encourage endurance, since poverty and suffering constitute only one form of trouble and will be over soon. As other proverbs demonstrate, people suffered to the point of despair but, as they readied themselves for death, their fortunes changed.

1370. *Tei nĩ ũkya.* **Mercy is poverty.**
This emerged with the capitalist penetration of the Kamba economy after the Second World War. It represents the emergence of a class that cared less about neighbours. Traders used the proverb to deny credit to those who requested loans but were unlikely to repay them. If they cannot repay, do not pity them.

1371. *Thĩna ũyietawa nĩ kwathĩĩw'a.* **Poverty is not caused by dreaming.**
Some blamed wizardry as the cause of their poverty but this proverb implies that such lame arguments are worthless. Positive thinking and hard work are the path to wealth.

---

[1] Lindblom, *Riddles*, 31; Kimilu, *Mũkamba*, 115; Kĩeti, *Barking*; Kĩtukũ, *Folktales*, 76; Mutisya, *Proverbs*, 49; Mwau, *Dictionary*, 649.
[2] Lindblom, *Riddles*, 31.

1372. *Thĩna ndwonaw'a methoi.* **Poverty is not shown tears.**
This encourages people to keep their heads up during their duress. It encourages poor or needy people to work hard to pull themselves out of despondency.

1373. *Thĩna ndũaa ũkĩtaa kũnyamasya.* **Poverty does not kill, it torments.**
This adage emerged during the devastating famines of the nineteenth century and has appeared in several traditional songs. The moral of the adage is simple: hope. Keep hoping for a better tomorrow.[3]

1374. *Thĩna nĩ mũthũku ũkũindaa vathũku.* **Poverty is bad, it drives you into trouble.**
This came from a popular song that pointed to the extremes one can get into because of want and distress. As Iliffe said in *The African Poor*, there are different 'sources' of poverty. The words of this musician elaborate Iliffe's idea of the overbearing forces of nature and the cruelty of men who take advantage of others.

1375. *Vandũ vate kiinga vayanasya kasalũ ka nzamba ngalĩko wa mũsyĩ.* **A young bull does not bellow in a home without a grain store.**
Food security was a priority to ancient Mũkamba. Surplus food was always exchanged for livestock. If food stocks diminished, bulls were exchanged for food. If famine continued, all livestock were sold. The maxim emerged during the Vascon era when the Kitui Kamba intensified grain cultivation and made storage facilities called *syiinga* (singular: *kiinga*). It emphasizes the significance of a savings account.

1376. *Wavitha yũa ndũvitha kĩkoro.* **If you hide your starvation, you cannot hide your tailbone.**
This adage emerged during the devastating famines of the nineteenth century, which wounded the pride of many previously wealthy families who pretended to be still holding their own. This adage persuaded people to openly talk about their suffering, reach out for help, and thus prevent further catastrophe behind the curtain of baseless pride. When a person experiences starvation and emaciation, the tailbone sticks out and thus betrays the man's meagre diet, so do not pretend while you are languishing. Ask for help right away if trouble strikes. The deeper meaning is that certain things cannot be kept secret as their harm grows bigger.[4]

---

[3] Kĩtukũ, *Folktales*, 34; Ambler, *Communities*.
[4] Mwau, *Dictionary*, 667.

1377. *Kava kũthaũka na malĩ kũte kũthaũka na mwene.*[5] **Better play with one's wealth than the person himself.**
The message of the proverb is a clear and stern warning that wealth can be gained, lost, and regained, but a person cannot. As the Kamba accumulated wealth between 1500 and 1800, this adage emerged. It says that if an opponent abuses his children or wife, he is courting death. It is said in a serious and tense environment where jokes are minimal and the audience understands that no lines should be crossed at that point. Money is fleeting and transient, negotiable, and flexible – even possibly a little comical, whereas personal honour and dignity are none of these things.

1378. *Kũnyamaa ũkathua.* **After hardship comes relief.**
This is a nineteenth-century expression of Kamba philosophy vis-à-vis suffering often repeated to people in serious tribulations to encourage them to persevere. It means there is a reward at the end of hardship. It encourages listeners to endure knowing that the obstacles they face are transient.

1379. *Mũmanthi ndanoaa.*[6] **One who strives for wealth never tires.**
This truism urges industrious people to soldier on even when incurring losses. You can regain wealth. Such statements emerged during the eighteenth century when the Kamba shifted from subsistence farming and hunting to long-distance hunting, trading, livestock rustling, and large-scale animal husbandry. Such activities were tiring, so participants were persuaded to persist for the reward at the end.

1380. *Kavaa ũkya wa malĩ kwĩ ũkya wa wendo.* **Better poverty of wealth than of love.**
In this Vascon-era statement, poverty expresses the pain one endures if he lacks love. It cajoles people to take their romantic relationships seriously. It appeared in songs heard by Lindblom in 1911 and was certainly in circulation going back three hundred years.

1381. *Kavaa kũya ũkya mũnyau.* **Better endure dry poverty.**
This was an expression of protest against colonialism from the First World War. Kamba nationalists used to tell their colonial masters loudly: it is better to endure poverty in peace and honour than to relish affluence in servitude. Even though the colonial regime promised economic development, the Kamba insisted that honour was better than benefits that come with insults.

---

[5] Kĩtukũ, *Folktales*, 35.
[6] Mwau, *Dictionary*, 657.

1382. *Kavaa tũthĩne tweteele kũathimwa.* **Better toil in anticipation of blessings.**
Counting wealth as a divine blessing is the language of Christians rather than traditional Kamba. This axiom was formulated after independence when such language became common. It plainly means better a happy end after suffering than squalor at the end of life.

1383. *Ũndũ ũendeka ndũemaa.* **A popular matter never overwhelms.**
This is similar to 'Where there is a will there is a way.' Proverbs like these reflect the difficult times when they emerged.

1384. *Malĩ na malĩ iyananganaa.* **Property and property do not destroy each other.**
This encodes the history of conflict between farming and stockbreeding. Starving animals sometimes destroyed planted crops. Despite the loss, this was used to suggest livestock and crops are simply the property of one owner.

1385. *Malĩ nĩyonawa ĩndĩ mũndũ ndoneka.* **Wealth can be found but not a person.**
People are more valuable than material possessions. This cajoles someone to marry sooner or to help a relative needing costly medical care. The proverb emerged before migration to Ũkambanĩ and acquired many modernizing variations.

1386. *Kũvoya mũno nĩ kwĩsea.* **Begging is self-embarrassing.**
This catchphrase calls for moderation when asking for help. It points to the value of self-reliance and promotes hard work instead of dependency. However, the maxim *Kũvoya ti kũũya* means 'Begging is not stealing', indicating that the Kamba recognized it was preferable to beg than to steal.

1387. *Ka mwene ketawa kaketĩka.*[7] **The owner responds whenever called.**
This ancient adage means one's property is easier to use than depending on others, which is neither beneficial nor reliable.

1388. *Mbua ndĩsĩ ngya na kĩtonga, yuaa nginya kwa mũoi.* **Rain does not distinguish between poor and rich, raining even on the farms of wizards.**
There is no discrimination in nature: if competitors and enemies had a choice they would stop rain from falling on the farm of their opponents, but nature does not operate that way.

---

[7] Kimilu, *Mũkamba*, 115.

1389. *Mwana wa ngya asasya mwĩĩtu mwanake na kĩswe.* **A poor son pays dowry for a beautiful girl with a rage click.**
Emerging from the nineteenth century, this means the poor youth has no resources to pay dowry for the girl to be his wife. Opportunities pass those who have no resources. Young men from poor families married late, having missed girls they admired because they could not afford dowry at the first encounter. Elders used this axiom when they were not prepared to procure something admirable.

1390. *Mwĩĩtu mwanake esĩlaa kwa ngya thome.* **A beautiful girl passes through the hearth of a poor lad.**[8]
This emerged during the nineteenth century, when poverty became widespread as a result of severe natural and human-induced changes. Dowry in livestock skyrocketed. Still, the first choice of a wife was her beauty. Beautiful girls were usually married to those rich in livestock to pay dowry rather than a handsome but poor boy. This is a figurative condemnation of poverty and a warning that if one has no resources, opportunities will go to the rich.

1391. *Mbũi ya ngya ĩiitaa na awe elĩ.*[9] **A poor man's goat heals with two healers.**
Dealing with deception and with multiple interpretations this proverb implies the listener cannot pay the amount he offers. It comes from a story of a poor man needing divination who promised two diviners the same goat. A cleansing ceremony was officiated by a healer, using a prescribed goat each time.[10]

1392. *Mũndũ ngya e mũnuka mũseo wa kũĩva makwani.* **A poor person has a sweet mouth for paying debts.**
As a negative commentary on the poor, the maxim can be a warning to the lender that the borrower is shrewd and deceptive; a thorough investigation about his credit history is needed. On the positive side, it advises the borrower to be bold and to design their application for loans in words that attract the lender.

1393. *Mũtũa ngya ndanoaa esaa kũnoa yakw'a.*[11] **A pauper's neighbour never fattens until the pauper dies.**
Whoever lives near a pauper never fattens until the pauper dies since he shares his food with the pauper. Among traditional Kamba weight gain

---
[8] Mutisya, *Proverbs*, 42; Mwau, *Dictionary*, 661.
[9] Kimilu, *Mũkamba*, 116; Charlotte Leslau and Wolf Leslau, *African Proverbs* (New York: Peter Pauper Press, 1962), 33–6.
[10] Mutisya, *Proverbs*, 65.
[11] Kimilu, *Mũkamba*, 117.

was revered. The material status of a person and his family was known by physical appearance, fat, proper dress, and hygiene. The proverb was a warning against encouraging poverty among neighbours since rich neighbours were more beneficial than poor ones.

1394. *Ngya ndĩthekaa ĩngĩ.* **A pauper does not laugh at another.**
This has multiple interpretations. One is that the poor had shared interests and therefore held the poor fellow in esteem. The second is a warning against mocking people who were suffering for the same fate that could befall the mockers.

1395. *Ngya ndyosaa, yosa ĩwaa nĩ yang'ea.* **Paupers are never lucky, if they stumble on luck they are said to have stolen it.**
One way out of poverty was to discover something valuable. This proverb deprecates longstanding attitudes between rich and poor during the colonial period. In urban areas where people often lost money, finders who were poor would count it as their divine luck but if they explained their luck most people suspected that they had stolen the money. The same would not be the case if a rich man stumbled upon lost money.

1396. *Nyonyi sya kũũ syĩyĩsĩ ngya na itonga.* **Local birds do not distinguish rich and poor.**
This proverb from a folktale reflects threats of natural forces on agricultural life. The proverb emerged from farmers cultivating crops that were targets of weaverbirds, which did not discriminate between poor or rich farms, hence the proverb.

1397. *Ua ũkwetwe nĩ ngya ndũthekya ĩngĩ.* **A calabash bowl held by a pauper does not thrill another.**
This means the poor cannot help other poor people since people in competition are of little use to one another. One should not put one's hopes in people with meagre resources.[12]

1398. *Sila mũasa nĩ ũkya.*[13] **Prolonged judgement of a case brings poverty.**
This deeply symbolic statement originated with the creation of modern law courts between 1890 and 1960. Natives were allowed to practise African Customary law as the colonial authorities empowered village elders, headmen, and chiefs to settle disputes as before. These traditional dispute institutions gradually evolved into tribunals officially recognized in 1907. Legal cases can last many years, forcing both parties

---

[12] Mutisya, *Proverbs*, 40.
[13] Mwau, *Dictionary*, 667.

to expend resources and time. Some parties are financially ruined by court cases, hence this proverb from the interwar period. It urges that if you conceive an idea, execute it immediately.

1399. *Kava mūthūūna īthei kwī wīkonotete.*[14] **Better a licker of bare bones than a starver.**
This teaches people to appreciate whatever resources they have rather than having nothing. Work with what you have, no matter its quantity or quality, to achieve a better end. The popular proverb has been used as business slogans throughout Ūkamba such as the *Mūthūūna īthei* Bus Transport of Machakos in the 1970s and 1980s. In a sense, these mobile slogans on buses were forerunners of the internet, challenging the view that modernity is an enemy of proverbs.

1400. *Nzaa nzei syīnyenyawa.* **Bare hands are not licked.**
This comes from licking honey. This delicacy was never consumed with a spoon but with bare hands, licked until no sweetness was left. In the nineteenth and twentieth centuries parents said this to children, meaning, 'I do not have what you need my child. Do not complain. If I have something you will have it.'

1401. *Kanini kanyivasya nzaa.* **A little morsel reduces hunger.**
Emerging from the nineteenth-century famine contexts, this adage has appeared in different versions in literature. It encouraged people to tackle challenges systematically, little by little.[15]

1402. *Ndyumaw'a nzaanī na ngetūnga.* **I cannot be rescued from hunger and turn myself back to it.**
This axiom means it is illogical to be rescued from starvation and give the food donation to another starving person. You must take care of yourself first. It emerged during nineteenth-century famines when individuals had to care for themselves first before they were able to feed starving neighbours.

1403. *Nzaa nī mūtūi wa īvu.*[16] **Hunger is the stomach's neighbour.**
No matter how much one eats, hunger always returns. The belly and hunger interact daily. An old proverb concerning only natural phenomena, it has nothing to do with famines or shortages.

---

[14] Mwau, *Dictionary*, 660.
[15] Farnsworth, *Grammar*, 93; Kimilu, *Mūkamba*, 115.
[16] Kimilu, *Mūkamba*, 118.

1404. *Līu mũvye ndwĩnzaa yũa.* **Cooked food does not dig out famine.**
When drought and pests destroyed farm life the Kamba resorted to digging roots, tubers, and grains stored underground by ants – and even the insects – to consume. Named 'digging out famine', the process is still in use. The proverb can be traced to the 1879 famine called *yũa ya nditikũ*, 'the famine of the red ants', when some *nditikũ* ants saved many Kamba families. The ants store grain in large reservoirs underground, which desperate Kamba dug out to survive during famines.

1405. *Mũtĩ wĩ mũyo ndwĩnzaa yũa.* **A delicious tree does not dig out hunger.**
During lean days the Kamba lived on wild plants most of which, while not delicious, satisfied hunger. The proverb's moral is that the value of an object is more important than its stigma.

1406. *Yũa nĩ yumawa ĩndĩ ntheko ndĩthelaa.* **Famine ends but ridicule does not.**
This cautions against meanness and greed during lean days, deriving from Ũkamba's nineteenth-century famines. The Kamba quickly noticed that while it was possible to lessen famine's impact, bad behaviour left permanent scars. The axiom cautioned that people must maintain their morality even during lean days.[17]

1407. *Mũĩthi nĩ wa nzaa mbyũ.*[18] **A shepherd has hot hunger.**
This proverb appears in songs, poems, and oral narratives. Dating from the Monsoon era, it warns people to be wary of fake opportunities.

1408. *Mboswa ndyosaa ĩngĩ.* **An adopted pauper does not adopt another.**
This dates from the early eighteenth century when Kamba families began to adopt impoverished client families. During famines, unlucky Kamba and non-Kamba families were co-opted to richer households.[19] The maxim calls for family members to increase their wealth on their own. They will never be able to help another if they do not build wealth. It is also used as a protest telling those seeking help that the speaker does not have enough. Read thus, it sounds like a defence of selfishness.

---

[17] KNA: Ref 307.72.OLE; Siri Eriksen, et al., 'Vulnerability to Climate Stress – Local and Regional Perspectives', *Proceedings of Two Workshops January 27–28, 2005, World Agroforestry Centre* (Gigiri, Nairobi, 14 February 2005); Kennell Jackson, 'Dimensions', in *Kenya Before 1900*, ed. Bethwell Ogot (Nairobi: East Africa Publishing House, 1976).
[18] Mũĩmi, *Kĩthyomo*, 34–6.
[19] Ambler, *Communities*; Jackson, 'Dimensions'.

1409. *Vwĩa wĩ thĩna.* **Fear is poverty.**
This ancient proverb identifies fear as the chief source of poverty and suffering. Because of fear, as many folktales illustrate, a strong person can be defeated by a weakling through tricks. Fear can lead to great loss.[20]

1410. *Weteelete ndakusaa.* **One who is waiting does not die.**
Suggesting proverbs are valuable tools of scholarship, John Mbiti used this proverb as the title of his book encapsulating his ideas. He used the picture of the famous Nzambani rock to argue that one who waits is like a rock; they abide forever and never give up.[21]

1411. *Muunyĩ wa kĩtĩ wĩwĩkaa nĩ ũla wĩ ĩtina wa kyo.*[22] **The one under it experiences the shade of a tree.**
This indicates that the household head knows his responsibility and the challenges of his family. However, multiple interpretations and applications have arisen. This can mean that pleasure or pain of something is only known by those involved.

1412. *Vayĩ kĩthũi kĩtetĩkĩwa nĩ ĩvyũvya.* **There is no chest that cannot have porridge dropped on it.**
This is an ancient warning against boasting about one's strength because no one is naturally invincible. Illness can subdue the strongest man.[23] The sick were fed on soft food, usually *ĩvyũvya* (warm porridge), usually a lukewarm liquid food. The gruel often spilled on the chest and on necklaces, so it dates from the Vascon era when necklaces made of material from the coast became common.

1413. *Mũthui ndavũnaa too.* **A rich man never gets enough sleep.**
A rich man is always preoccupied with acquiring more wealth and protecting it, which means he does not sleep enough. This ancient axiom encourages listeners to work hard and shun idleness, but also to consider the value of sleep and good health.

1414. *Mũthui nĩwĩsĩ ũtalo wasyo syĩ kĩtũũnĩ.* **The rich man knows their number while they are in the kraal.**
This alludes to men rich in livestock with so many herds and flocks that neighbours said *Indo syake ityĩ ũtalo*, 'his livestock is uncountable'. However, the proverb claims the owner knew the exact number even

---

[20] Mũĩmi, *Kĩthyomo*, 22–3.
[21] Mutisya, *Proverbs*, 72; John Mbiti, *Weteelete Ndakusaa* (Nairobi: Vide-Muwa Publishers, 2012), 30, 214.
[22] Mwau, *Dictionary*, 661.
[23] Mutisya, *Proverbs*, 55.

to when they were in the shed. This ancient proverb also means the person involved knows when he is in control.

1415. *Mũthui mũnene athĩnaw'a nĩ kalĩo ka mbakĩ.* **A rich man lacks a potshard for snuff.**
Tobacco cultivation coincided with growing wealth in the seventeenth century. The maxim suggests individuals first made snuff for themselves using potshards. Wealthy Kamba could afford a whole pot so they kept no potshards. Potshards, however, were indispensable: the making of snuff was never done in pots but in pieces of broken pots. Since the wealthy discarded such pieces, they suffered when the need to make snuff occurred.

1416. *Mũthui ndaumawa.*[24] **A rich man is not insulted.**
This concerns respect accorded different Kamba classes. Rich men were often leaders and were by law not insulted. The proverb implies that people should never insult a rich man because tomorrow they may have to beg for help from him. Wealthy men and women feature prominently in proverbs and other oral arts. Kennel Jackson noted the existence of a class of wealthy persons whose status was distinguished by the wearing of *ngotho* (ivory armlets), which were disappearing by 1900.[25]

1417. *Ũthui nĩ matialyo ma nda.*[26] **Wealth is what remains after the stomach has had its fill.**
Said to encourage hard work, this maxim emerged in the 1900s. It has two interpretations, one quite simple: do not eat everything. Save in the present to enjoy the future. The second is that wealth comes only when someone is satisfied. One cannot be wealthy while lacking the basics.

1418. *Ũthwii nĩ muunyĩ ũthyũkaa.* **Wealth is like shadow, it changes direction with the rotation of the sun.**
This axiom emerged during the Vascon era and compares changing positions of shadows and shade with changes in the position of the sun to an alternation of wealth and poverty. One person may be rich today but poor tomorrow, while the poor become rich. It calls for ethical use of wealth and for hope among those who are materially suffering.

---

[24] Mwau, *Dictionary*, 660.
[25] Jackson, 'Ngotho', 35–69.
[26] Mwau, *Dictionary*, 670.

312   Part IV: Kamba Society

1419.   Ũthwii wendanasya na mwene.[27] **Wealth departs with its owner.**
This is an observed fact that when rich people died their wealth dissipated. People who built wealth knew how to care for it while the heirs tended to neglect it, such that, within a decade after the death of a patriarch, accumulated wealth dissipated.

1420.   Ũthwii wa nda ndũlũkasya kĩvũnzi. Belly wealth does not blow dust.
This maxim traces back to the Vascon era. It encouraged saving and accumulation of visible wealth as opposed to lavish but ephemeral lifestyles. Livestock, a symbol of wealth across Ũkamba, kicked up considerable dust as they moved between home and watering points, which was quite admired. I heard this first from Mutulu village elders who were debating between eating well immediately and raising livestock for future use.

1421.   Kĩthangwana kya mũsyĩ kyambaa ũmina malĩ kĩikoaa mwene. A family ritual clears out wealth before killing the owner.
Large households had rituals that were observed very carefully, for a broken ritual meant devastating misfortune. The head of the household was usually the last to be devastated.[28] This is one of the Kamba's reasonings about loss of resources that historians ought to examine to understand the sources of material improvement and impoverishment among the Kamba.

1422.   Malĩ ndĩetwe nĩ kwĩtwa.[29] **Wealth cannot be beckoned to one's possession.**
This emerged in the 1600s and 1700s when the Kamba accumulated huge amounts of material wealth. There were ways to acquire wealth and several had to be exploited to become wealthy. All involved hard work and careful investment.

1423.   Waĩ nĩ waĩwaa, notaĩ akamesya.[30] **A rich man is often divested and the poor possess.**
Tracing from the Vascon era, this proverb concerns fluctuations of wealth and poverty. People's situations in life may change suddenly or eventually.

---

[27] Farnsworth, *Grammar*, 54.
[28] Lindblom, *Akamba*, 281–2.
[29] Kĩtukũ, *Folktales*, 5.
[30] Kĩeti, *Barking*, 105.

1424. *Waĩĩ mbee nũsyokaa ĩtina.* **A pioneer becomes the rearguard.**
Be careful with your resources. They are exhaustible, so do not boast. This proverb emerged during the nineteenth century when fluctuating fortunes became common.

1425. *Kĩsoso kĩvivaa kĩngĩ.* **A honeycomb does not squeeze another.**
Tracing from the Monsoon era of apiculture, this was my father's catchphrase by which he meant a pauper cannot help another. A person depicted as *kĩsoso* is therefore a rascal who is not useful to the community.

1426. *Mũvoyi nowe wĩ ngingo mbololo.* **The beggar is the only one with a flexible neck.**
This proverb highlights precolonial Kamba beggary as part of an age-old social phenomenon in world cultures. Dating from the Islamic era, this axiom implies that 'beggars can't be choosers'. They must content themselves with what is offered. The recipient, borrower, seller, or beggar is expected to use language or gestures that will entice by deference to customers or potential creditors. The neck refers to how the Kamba begged; employing gestures of deference – a soft voice, a pliant neck, twisting one's lips – to request support and succor. Dating to the Islamic era, the proverb suggests that such deferential gestures are expressions of poverty and powerlessness, qualities viewed in Kamba culture as belonging to victims of their own life choices. Along with condemning begging, the proverb advised beggars to behave deferentially to get one's way.[31]

---

[31] John Iliffe, *The African Poor: A History* (Cambridge: Cambridge University Press, 1979); Donald Worster, *Dust Bowl: The Southern Plains in the 1930s* (Oxford: Oxford University Press, 2004).

18

Cuisine and Consumption

1427. *Ĩlũkũ yĩla yĩsaa nyũnyi noyo yĩsaa mauta.* **The gut that eats greens is the same that eats fat.**
This reveals an appreciation of fat over greens. The proverb was used during lean days to encourage people to consume what was available to survive. While fat people were revered, obesity was associated with mental retardation and leanness a sign of poverty.

1428. *Ĩtomo yaakomya aĩngĩ kĩlute.*[1] **Greed makes many sleep hungry.**
The Kamba discouraged greed with short stories and proverbs. This maxim refers to popular stories such as the greedy dog with a bone crossing a bridge who upon seeing its reflection dropped the bone to attack its own reflection and to get its bone too. As a result, it lost everything.[2] The moral of the proverb is greed breeds loss instead of anticipated gain.

1429. *Ĩtomo nĩ ĩthũku nĩyoaie mbiti.* **Greed is bad; it killed the hyena.**
This ancient adage appears in multiple oral narratives and songs. The axiom condemns greed.[3]

1430. *Kĩtheri kĩĩwa kakũti.* **Kĩtheri is eaten for starvation.**
This is a recent coinage. The food *Kĩtheri*, a mixture of beans and corn, came with colonial culture. It has become the main dish of poor Kenyans since the early twentieth century. This axiom indicates that with new cuisine and tastes *kĩtheri* is eaten for lack of better. The axiom therefore means a substitute is only good for lack of an alternative.

1431. *Kĩtavi nũkwĩtya mũka.* **The Kitavi is demanding a wife.**
Dating from the Vascon era when the Kamba came into contact with the Kwavi pastoralists, this is an axiomatic light way of saying 'I am

---

[1] Mũĩmi, *Kĩthyomo*, 26.
[2] Mũĩmi, *Kĩthyomo*, 26.
[3] Mũĩmi, *Kĩthyomo*, 17–18.

hungry.' It is said in the company of happy family members, friends, and associates who will know the meaning right away.[4]

1432. *Mũndũ ũkosa nyama nĩũvoka na kakũna.* **If one misses meat, he can dine on *kakũna*.**
This emerged in the late 1970s famines when Kamba cooks innovated new recipes, called *kakũna*, an improvised stew comprised of boiled water and flour. Boiled water, salt, and onions was one type; another odd stew was a mixture of salt, onions, flour, and water. These two types of famine stew were dubbed *kakũna*, hence the proverb.

1433. *Mũndũ wa ĩtomo avĩvaw'a nĩ ngima ĩkomie nza.* **An avaricious one is burnt by mealiepap that slept over outside.**
This proverb originated in the Islamic era as a condemnation of greed as much as it speaks to the etiquette of dining. The Kamba were strict on the etiquette of dining. One should be slow to eat in the presence of others, even when facing starvation. It was also good etiquette to eat and drink in moderation. Cold mealiepap that spent the night in the open could not scald anyone. Its deeper meaning though has more to do with general behaviour involving such vices as envy, corruption, and greed that bring down whoever engages in them. Scalding symbolizes the final destruction of uncouth behaviour.

1434. *Mũnoi tiwe mũi.*[5] **The labourer is not the consumer.**
Pregnant with meaning, this proverb can point to deprivation or benevolence. Those who create wealth support those who have little or nothing. Sometimes people may labour hard only to see their property stolen or confiscated.

1435. *Kava kũvũnĩwa kũte kũtinda na nzaa.* **Better constipation than starvation.**
This ancient maxim compares two unpleasant conditions: constipation and starvation, implying the speaker faces a decision between two equally unpleasant courses of action.

1436. *Ndyeew'a ka ũye ngekala.* **I have never heard someone say take, eat, I will starve.**
With respect to starvation during famine in the nineteenth century, individuals ate before giving others a bite. Take care of your welfare first. This proverb was used by a person who meant there was just enough to sustain the speaker.

---

[4] Farnsworth, *Grammar*, 89.
[5] Kĩtukũ, *Folktales*, 61.

1437. *Mũkii wa ũsũũ nĩwĩsĩ vala ve lũng'ũyũ.* **The maker of porridge knows where to get herbal sweetener.**
Before sugarcane arrived from Asia, Kamba women sweetened porridge with an aromatic plant called *lũng'ũyũ*. Any woman who wanted to season her porridge knew where to get these sweeteners. This means people know the profit of what they are doing.

1438. *Mwĩko watũlĩka ũĩ ndũnatũlika.*[6] **When the stirring rod breaks, the skills have not.**
Use of the Swahili word *mwiko* for cooking ladle means this proverb emerged in the twentieth century when this word, along with the Swahili cooking ladle, came into common use. The Kamba were prolific carvers of wooden kitchenware, as this proverb indicates. If a crafted product is broken, the skills are still intact and there is hope to replace the broken ladle. Symbolically this is about hope, fortitude, and endurance. Do not give up – even if one option fails, try another.

1439. *Ndyĩsaa kwa mũndũ.* **I do not dine at anybody's kitchen.**
The speaker asserts their self-reliance and can do without the opponent's help. The Kamba encouraged both socialism and independence. Consuming food at someone's home submitted the partaker to the homeowner's authority. Even though said to date from antiquity, it appears to have been created by scarcity in the nineteenth century.

1440. *Ndyĩsaa wando wĩnawaki ngaya woma.* **I do not eat green millet when it is sour but when it is dry.**
Millet, the staple crop of Kitui, was eaten from the time it showed signs of maturity up to harvest time as a dry and ripe crop. At its green stage the grain crop was cut and put out in the sun to dry a little and then processed. This is called *mwando*, which is sour, implying that people should wait for the millet to mature. This semi-ripe millet – *mwando* – is compared to a maturing girl with the hidden meaning that the speaker does not like sex with immature girls (*wando wĩnawaki*); sex is better when girls mature (*woma* – mature millet). This axiom emerged with the arrival of millet in the seventeenth century. By the late 1700s millet had replaced *wimbi* as the staple grain crop in Ũkamba.

1441. *Kava kũya ngima naũtialya kwĩkwĩw'a nĩyathela.* **Better to eat a mealiepap and spare some than to hear it is finished.**
Mealiepap was a favourite meal. Since it was produced from flour that had been laboriously ground by women, it was unfathomable not to have enough of it. Its supply was lower than demand. The proverb implies preference to sufficient supply of the most favourite objects.

---

[6] Mbiti, *Ngaeka*, 98.

1442. *Wenda ūmanya mūyo wa ngima myakīle īmbyū.* **If you want to appreciate the deliciousness of a mealiepap, swallow it when it is hot.**
This appears to sarcastically warn people to be careful with things their emotions drive them to acquire. This is often used in a sexual context, where the speaker refers to a woman who is sexually ready. If she is unreceptive, the sexual experience for both is different. By most oral accounts this axiom has been around since the introduction of maize during the Vascon era. The word mealiepap is used here for lack of a better translation for what is called *ngima*, a thick cooked mixture of grain flour with water or milk.

1443. *Vai kyai kya kana mūkawanī.* **There is no tea for a baby in a coffee shop.**
This alludes to growing capitalist tendencies and economic immorality. Until 1920, it was honourable for a nursing mother to stop by a coffee shop and ask for water and food to feed her baby free of charge. This generosity disappeared as profit drove the new economic dispensation from the interwar period. The only tea, water, or food available was for sale even for babies.

1444. *Wathiaa mūvinyu esaa kūthia mūkalatyo.* **One who once ground fine eventually grinds coarse flour.**
This proverb emerged during the first millennium as the Kamba cultivated grains and women ground them on grindstone into fine flour. It symbolically points to the weakening of an individual due to age. An old woman will not grind flour as fine as she did when she was youthful. Fortunes change with time and place; do not boast about your present status.

1445. *Wīse nīwīsaa kwīsa wavinyasya akathia mūkaratyo.* **Something happens to those who ground coarse flour.**
This ancient axiom talks about women flour grinders. The maxim emerged in northern Kitui for the rest of Ūkamba does not use the letter /r/. The word *mūkaratyo* is normally rendered as *mūkalatyo*, but without the letter /r/ the maxim loses its northern Kitui flavour. Grinding fine flour to feed her family was the ultimate goal of every woman. However, with a decline in health and age, her capabilities decline and she can grind less fine flour. The proverb cautions that people should not boast of their capabilities because they are not permanent.

1446. *Wīsī nī ūkaa syethe akathia mbeke.* **The knowledgeable at times fails to split a grain.**
This means that someday the expert flour grinder might underperform and grind coarse flour. The axiom, dating from the Vascon era, thus

means, nothing is permanent. Time and fortune change imperceptibly.[7]

1447. *Yelũkaa kĩla ĩgĩte ona ethĩawa nĩ thiĩ wa mwana.* **It belches what it has eaten, even the child's debt.**
Given the word *ĩgĩte*, it is obvious that this axiom originated from the Mwingi North dialect. The key word, however, is *thiĩ*, not *thii* (placenta) as found in traditional practice of *kũkovea mwana thiĩ*, to take the 'debt for a baby'. This was done with a special *nzele ya kũkova* (a borrowing calabash bowl), stored after borrowing so that at the time of repayment the same bowl would be used in order to maintain accurate measurements. Beyond this, the Vascon-era adage means people behave according to their training, and performance depends upon one's resources.

1448. *Lĩu nĩ mai.* **Food is excretion.**
The obvious meaning is quality food makes one full and makes one excrete well. If food eaten did not turn into shit, it became poisonous. Second, cooked food should not be denied others because it will soon rot, while friendship will endure. The proverb appears to have emerged during lean times in areas that suffered food shortages from the mid-nineteenth century. Today it calls the Kamba back to their traditional generosity.

1449. *Lĩu wĩ mũyo ndũkolawa.* **Delicious food is never eaten to fill.**
Predating the colonial era this adage cautions against excessive indulgence in pleasure. Themes of famines and food shortages began around the turn of the nineteenth century for many ecological and demographic reasons. During the nineteenth-century famines unpalatable food helped people survive. Delicious food would not last long because it was eaten up quickly, while unpalatable foods lasted much longer.

1450. *Kũtũlĩka kwa muĩ tikw'o mũthia wa kũua kĩteke.* **The breaking of a stirring wood is not the end of consuming mealiepap.**
This talks about alternatives, substitutes, and fortitude. To make mealiepap of wimbi, millet, and sorghum before the advent of maize, women used a wooden stirring utensil called *muĩ* before Swahili *mwiko* arrived. This device was the anchor of the kitchen, at least for mealiepap. Accidental damage was a major blow. While comparable to a popular Swahili adage, we cannot assume such proverbs derived from the coast. Since Kĩkamba was one of the Bantu languages, intermingling at the coast to form the Swahili language, it is possible that the Swahili wit and wisdom drew their inspiration from Kĩkamba.

---

[7] Kimilu, *Mũkamba*, 119; Mutisya, *Proverbs*, 55.

1451. *Navũna nasya makũmbi nĩmavye.*[8] **I ate to satisfaction and said 'let the grain stores burn'.**
Light-hearted and thankful persons say this, revealing the history of grain storage in Ũkamba. There were at least three major grain storage facilities – *ĩkũmbĩ* (*makũmbĩ*), *kĩsomba* (*isomba*), and *kiinga* (*syiinga*) – where food was stored. The first, from the Vascon era, was the largest of the thatched structures and could include the third as one of its compartments. All were vulnerable to fire and care was taken to avoid such a disaster.

1452. *Mũndũ ũtaatembea aasya inya nĩwe wĩsĩ kũua.* **A person who has not travelled thinks their mother is the best cook.**
This proverb appears among other African cultures in varied forms.[9] This adage of the Vascon era has been used to persuade policymakers to look beyond boundaries instead of focusing only on home-grown solutions. One learns by going out, eating other's food (ideas and practices), and knowing what kind of cooks (technology and practices) are available.

1453. *Mwĩĩ ti kavumbu ndwĩyũmbaa.* **The body is not a mound, it does not create itself.**
This ancient proverb encouraged proper food consumption. Unlike mounds arising across Ũkamba, the body has to be fed through the mouth in order for someone to grow.

1454. *Mwĩĩ ndũmanzawa na taa, ũmanzawa na kĩteke.* **The body is not searched with flashlights, but with mealiepap.**
Since people struggled to be fat, it was jokingly likened with searching for something. The proverb was said to encourage people to eat in order to be healthy. Since torches (flashlights) are postcolonial introductions, this proverb was definitely created after the First World War when such items became common.

1455. *Mũkamba etaa mũyo waingĩva tiiki.* **A Mũkamba calls excessive pleasure a noxious taste.**
This means that too much of anything devalues it. The key word '*tiiki*' translates in different ways, including an obnoxious or repulsive taste. On one simple level, this applies to quantity: the proverb refers to *quality*, and makes a subtler point: there is a threshold for a *decent quality* that, if overdone, overcooked, oversold, or overtold, becomes *worse* than boring and badly wrought, distorted, and ugly. Appetites,

[8] Farnsworth, *Grammar*, 53.
[9] Farnsworth, *Grammar*, 120; Kimilu, *Mũkamba*, 116; Mbiti, *Ngaeka*, 90; Mbiti, *Weteelete*, 1; Joseph Healey and Donald Sybertz, *Towards an African Narrative Theology (Faith and Cultures)* (New York: Orbis, 1997), 337.

if overdone, are not merely wasteful, but degenerate. Moderation is the way of life of the ordinary Mūkamba. A Mūkamba calls excessive sweetness repulsive.[10]

1456. *Mūkaĩ ndesĩ ūvūnie.* **A miser does not know the rich.**
Coined during the nineteenth-century famines, this maxim means that misers cannot distinguish poor from rich. The behaviour and attitudes of misers close off great opportunities.

1457. *Ūkaĩ nĩ mūvithe.* **Meanness is that which is hidden.**
Sages advised that the more people hid their meanness the better. Meanness arose out of a period of scarce resources. Except for one mention of famine during their migration upon the plains of Taita-Taveta, the Kamba oral traditions do not recall food shortages before 1800. This maxim emerged between 1835 and 1895, when the Kamba experienced unprecedented and devastating famines.

1458. *Kakima kailũ kaĩsawa nĩ kwaa mũnyũ.*[11] **A little black mealiepap is eaten because of lack of salt.**
During the Vascon era, the Kamba consumed and traded in locally made and imported salt. There were times when salt ran out, forcing people to make do with a dark and saltless mealiepap. Contrary to Lindblom's interpretation, this proverb reflects narrow choices and alternatives that one faces at a particular time due to distress.[12]

1459. *Ngima mbyũ ĩsawa na ndee.* **Hot mealiepap is eaten from the edges.**
This adage emerged during the eighteenth-century intensification of millet cultivation. Millet was pounded with mortar and pestle before grinding into fine flour from which mealiepap was made. Since the edges of mealiepap cool first, people ate from there downwards until they reached the bottom. Thus, the proverb says approach difficulties cautiously.[13]

1460. *Ngima yumaa mũtuni.* **Mealiepap comes from flour.**
Emerging from the Vascon era, this adage stresses the importance of hard work. *Ngima* made from millet flour, wimbi, sorghum, and later corn flour required tedious grinding by women. Much that is great and fine originates from toil and sweat.[14]

[10] Mutisya, *Proverbs*, 67.
[11] Lindblom, *Riddles*, 30.
[12] Lindblom, *Riddles*, 353.
[13] Kĩeti, *Barking*, 109.
[14] Lindblom, *Riddles*, 36; Farnsworth, *Grammar*, 66; Kimilu, *Mūkamba*, 117; Mutisya, *Proverbs*, 69; Mwau, *Dictionary*, 665.

1461. *Ve ma ngima na ma mboka.* **There is water for mealiepap and for gravy.**
Differences always exist among people and human actions.[15] This was coined after colonialism when the loan word *mboka* was adopted and eating stew and mealiepap became common.

1462. *Kĩla nyũmba kalia.*[16] **Every house should have some milk.**
This originated in the Vascon era of enlargement of the svcale of livestock rearing across Ũkamba. Every household was expected to have at least a cow. A household that did not have one was considered poor and its honour within the community was shaky. Another interpretation is that it calls for fairness and justice in large households and in politics. All members of the household or state must be treated equally and fairly.

1463. *Ũtatia ndethĩa.*[17] **Someone who cannot leave something behind cannot stumble on anything.**
This ancient axiom has multiple interpretations and applications, one as a caution against pursuing unrealistic dreams by abandoning unfruitful endeavours. Another cautions against greed. There is a time to say enough is enough and spare something for tomorrow.

1464. *Mũya weka akusaa weka.* **He who eats alone dies alone.**
Dating to antiquity, as Mbiti explains, 'This proverb highlights the value of sharing both joy (food) and sorrow (death). If there is no fellowship, no sharing of food during one's life, there will be no sharing of grief and bereavement at one's funeral. Happiness conquers grief and fellowship defeats separation by death.' It also speaks about the value of hospitality, which can be made more palatable to avoid the state in which 'a person who eats alone dies alone'.[18]

1465. *Ndũkaĩe ũivoeswa.* **Do not cry while it is cooling down.**
This old proverb concerns feeding children on hot porridge. Adults used to cool the hot stuff by tossing it between two gourds, blowing on it or shaking it around, processes called *kũvosya*. If children were too hungry to wait, they cried. The proverb means if something is under way, be patient.

---

[15] Mutisya, *Proverbs*, 74.
[16] Farnsworth, Grammar, 2.
[17] Kimilu, *Mũkamba*, 118; Kituku, *Folktales*, 50.
[18] Kimilu, *Mũkamba*, 117; Mutisya, *Proverbs*, 39; Mbiti, *Ngaeka*, 97; John Mbiti, 'A Person Who Eats Alone Dies Alone', in *Crises of Life in African Religion and Christianity*, ed. Hao Mwakabana (Geneva: The Lutheran World Federation, 2002), 83.

322   Part IV: Kamba Society

1466.   Kaĩsawa ke kauwe.[19] **It is eaten when cooked.**
The Kamba usually consumed cooked food and ate it while hot. Use something when it is ready for its particular purpose. This is open to interpretation.

1467.   Mũya naĩ aĩsaa syana i syake. Careless feeders consume their own children.
This ancient proverb is not about cannibalism but about an immoral person who may end up committing incest. It can also mean a person who is careless with resources ends up impoverishing his family.

1468.   Kauwa kaĩsawa nĩ ala me thome. When food is cooked, it is eaten at the hearth.
This means people close to a property benefit from it, but those who are distant do not.[20] It emerged during the Islamic era, when the Kamba consolidated their settlements in Ũkamba. Until the end of the Second World War, male members of a family congregated at the hearth in the evenings before bedtime and in the mornings before worktime. Women cooked food in the houses located inside the home compound and served it to the males gathering at the hearth. Those absent around the fire, of course, received no food.

1469.   Mũthoi na kĩthoi nĩ ma inya ũmwe. Stew and soup are kindred.
Figuratively this means too much love destroys, but it can be interpreted as comparing two unequal things.[21] A person likened to bean soup is less important than the person depicted as stew, encoding the preference for meat over a vegetable diet.

1470.   Ũthoninĩ kũyĩtaw'a kĩthoi. One does not ask for soup at the in-laws' house.
Proverbs that are structured this way provoke the question why. This axiom appears in varied forms in oral circulation and literature.[22] It castigates dependency and promotes independence.

1471.   Kũya nesa tikũya mũkaango. To eat well is not just to eat fried food.
This proverb appeared after the First World War, when the practice of frying food penetrated Ũkamba. Prewar cuisines included seasoning with homemade salt, herbs, ghee, or animal fats. Mũkaango (frying food

---

[19] Kimilu, Mũkamba, 115.
[20] Kimilu, Mũkamba, 115; Mutisya, Proverbs, 58.
[21] Mwau, Dictionary, 672; Mbiti, Ngaeka, 81.
[22] Kimilu, Mũkamba, 116.

with onions as the key ingredients), an addition to the Kamba cuisine, stimulated a series of proverbs. Everything has an alternative.

1472. *Kũya nĩ kũthinĩka.* **To eat is to save.**
This proverb dates to when the Kamba lived in grass-thatched houses. Inside the thatches were concealed such paraphernalia as knives, needles, medicines, arrows, and seeds. This concealment was called *kũthinĩka*, akin to saving unused resources for the future. The axiom encourages saving for rainy days.

1473. *Kũya nĩ kũĩva.* **To eat is to pay.**
This emerged following the development of dining in restaurants from the 1920s. Before 1900, neighbours borrowed necessities from each other and repaid in kind. It puts an emphasis on paying promptly bills, debts, and promises.[23]

1474. *Kũya tene ti kũtoona.*[24] **Eating early is not parsimoniousness.**
Eating early is not an indication of avarice since it usually pays to have an early start. This alludes to precolonial practice where wives kept porridge in a gourd for their husbands. Normally, when an old man woke up in the morning, he would sit and be served porridge and then go out to the hearth. This is what 'eating early' means, but the axiom means punctuality is a good thing.

1475. *Lĩu wa thome wathĩswaa avĩti ma nzĩa.* **The food of the hearth is given to passersby.**
The hearth was located outside the home compound where a passerby could stop and chat with those present. If there was food or drink, the passerby was served without question. In part, therefore, this proverb refers to open material, which becomes victim to public exploitation. Keep your things concealed. In public bars today, people make friends by buying beer for strangers who then become permanent friends.

1476. *Lĩu wa mũeni nĩwo wĩmũyo.*[25] **The visitor's food is the most delicious.**
The fact that Kimilu published this maxim in 1962 indicates the possibility of its circulation by 1900 and in bygone centuries. It points not only to the value of new things, the Kamba appreciation of visitors, and strangers, but also warns against the temptation to engage in attractive but dangerous undertakings.

---

[23] Farnsworth, *Grammar*, 129; McCann, *Stirring the Pot*.
[24] Kimilu, *Mũkamba*, 74, 116; Mutisya, *Proverbs*, 4.
[25] Kimilu, *Mũkamba*, 63, 116; Mbiti, *Ngaeka*, 90.

1477. *Lĩu wĩ lung'a ũmanyĩkaa nĩ muui.* **The cook knows delicious food.**
The precolonial Kamba women coined this axiom, at a time when cooking was largely their preserve. The cook certainly knew the quality of the food she prepared. The axiom means certain matters are known only to those involved.

1478. *Ĩkalaa wĩvalĩe nĩ kĩvĩsaa ngwatĩlo.* **Always be prepared that its handle may burn off.**
Oral interviews confirm the object is the handle of the ladle carved from wood or dry bottlegourds. The ladles often caught fire, rendering them useless without the handle. The actual meanings are that one should be cautious and ready to adjust to changes, find a way to evade tragedy, and anticipate bad luck, accident, or catastrophe. The proverb dates back to the first millennium.[26]

1479. *Mũthinzi ndaisaa mavũngũ.* **The skinner does not consume hooves.**
This alludes to the ways Kamba shared meat of a slaughtered animal. Certain parts of the meat were divided among the skinner, hunters, elders, women, and children. While women and elders treasured the head and hooves, these were never given to the skinner. It was an insult to do so. He was given the most meaty and fatty parts. This axiom arising with the hunting conditions of the pre-Vascon Kamba means property owners must enjoy the best part of their possessions.

1480. *Mũtumĩa ndasũnaa nzele.*[27] **An old man does not lick the calabash bowl.**
Elderly Kamba frequently consumed thick gruel and porridge. These two semi-solid foodstuffs left considerable residue in the calabash bowl. The bowl in such a condition was given to children to lick. An adult rarely licked the calabash. The proverb means that certain duties, responsibilities, and opportunities should be left to younger people. It discourages greed and selfishness.

1481. *Mũtumĩa wĩ mwĩĩtu ndakĩlaw'a nzele.*[28] **The calabash bowl never passes over a man with a daughter.**
One who owns property is not denied something. Notables at the hearth communally drank gruel from a single calabash bowl. They sat in a circle passing the bowl one to another. Sometimes worthless persons were not given a portion and the bowl was passed over them. However,

---

[26] Mwau, *Dictionary*, 646; Watuma, *Syĩthĩo*, 51.
[27] Mwau, *Dictionary*, 660.
[28] Mwau, *Dictionary*, 660.

a poor man who had daughters was considered potentially rich and extremely revered, receiving gruel with the notables. This proverb emerged from the 1300s with the rise of bride-price customs.

1482. *Mauta ma kwĩvaka mainoasya.* **Body lotion does not fatten.**
Precolonial Kamba treasured weight gain and deliberately consumed oils of all kinds, and smeared the same oil on their bodies to achieve fatness. Sages cautioned that fat applied on the body did not change the internal body conditions. One cannot conceal evil intent. There are things that will not serve the desired purpose.[29]

1483. *Mauta makũũ masisaa ngima.* **Old oil does not season mealiepap.**
As already explained elsewhere, mealiepap was the main dish since the Monsoon era, seasoned with ghee. If the ghee was kept for too long it was used as perfume instead of food seasoning.[30] Among other things the proverb means old disputes should not impact relationships. Forgive, forget, and work together.

1484. *Mauta maseo maitombolawa maingĩ.* **Good perfume oil is not drawn in large lumps, but small bits.**
This ancient proverb refers to perfume in the form of fat and oils. It emphasizes quality rather than quantity. Precolonial Kamba were fond of ointment for beauty, perfuming, and massage. To make good use of such ointment, small amounts were found to be better.

1485. *Mauta mausũaa ndue nĩkwĩyemeanĩsya.* **Ghee fills a gourd container bit by bit.**
The principal source of precolonial cooking oil was ghee extracted from churned milk. Small fat lumps from the milk were stored in a special gourd called *ndue*. From 1900, a metallic container called *ngeleni* (corruption for gallon) was introduced. Thus, the proverb was slightly altered to *Mauta mausũaa ngeleni nĩkwĩyemeanĩsya*, 'Ghee fills a gallon by gradual accumulation.' This points to the importance of persistence to get something done.

1486. *Ũtumanu ndwĩ ng'ondu.* **Foolishness has no cure.**
With the coming of Western medicine (*ndawa*, after Swahili *dawa*), this proverb changed slightly to *No ũtumanu ũte ndawa*, 'Only foolishness has no cure.' The Kamba had cures for almost every illness but could not cure foolishness.

---

[29] Mutisya, *Proverbs*, 13.
[30] Kimilu, *Mũkamba*, 116; Mailu, *Kĩkyambonie*, 52, 71.

1487. *Mũthengi mũkũũ ndaa malanga.* **An old drunkard lacks no scars.**
This ancient proverb alludes to precolonial Kamba attitudes towards drinkers and drunkards. During the Vascon era there emerged a class of poor drinkers called *athengi* (singular *mũthengi*), literally 'beggars of beer'. These men of few means and lower morals often got in trouble when drunk and were often bruised in fights.

1488. *Mũthengi nde kĩvĩla.* **No seat is reserved for a drunkard.**
Since *athengi* brought nothing to the drinking party, they were not offered a seat (as notables were) and did not ask for one. They sat on the ground waiting in anticipation that they might be allowed a sip. Thus, if one begs from a donor, they must bear with all circumstances including compromising his honour. While the previous entry dates to the Vascon era this proverb, for its use of the word *kĩvĩla*, which refer to modern chairs as opposed to Kamba three-legged stools, indicates its emergence after the First World War introduction of chairs.

1489. *Makunda maiananaw'a.* **Mouthful sips are never the same among drinkers.**
Formerly drinks were communally consumed from the same calabash. People stood or sat in a circle and one person took a sip and passed the bowl one to another. Each drew a sip proportional to their mouth. This method was devised during lean days so that people could share fairly the same amount of scarce food and drink. With time it became a measure to guard against poisoning, particularly at beer-drinking parties. Such circumstances appear to have emerged in the seventeenth and eighteenth centuries, and the proverb dates from that period. It tells people to be contented with what they have while recognizing people have different talents and resources.

1490. *Mũndũ akundaa ĩkunda yake yavika.* **A person sips when his turn comes.**
Traditionally, the Kamba drank liquor or porridge from the same bowl, passed one to another so that one had to wait for his turn. The proverb means one's opportunity is always on the way and cannot be taken away. Patience pays.

1491. *Ndũkasembee ĩkunda, wĩkunda ũkunde makindi.* **Do not rush to sip, you will sip lumps.**
This alludes to the manner in which the Kamba consumed a gruel of mixed sour milk, millet flour, and water. During the Vascon era, the gruel *ndua* was served in large calabash bowls and consumed by a group of men seated in a circle. Since the gruel normally had lumps, it was prudent to sip carefully to avoid them. Greedy men betrayed their poor

dinning etiquette by taking big sips, with lumps, which was to their great embarrassment. The proverb calls for gentility and observance of public values.

1492. *Lũkindi wa makindi avĩsaa nĩ makindi matemavye.* **One who lumps of flour is burnt by the lumps before they are cooked.**
Although akin to the above entry, this ancient adage with its tongue-twisting structure is both different and difficult to translate. One interpretation of it is that Lũkindi is the name of a person, son of Makindi. Because of a craving for food he is scalded by porridge before it is cooked. The second interpretation is that Lũkindi is a descriptive term for a character who gobbles lumps of uncooked porridge and is scalded. This means too much indulgence in unsettled issues leads to negative results. A person who is not cautious ruins himself. That is, a person who has epicure for porridge will end up munching uncooked lumps. The proverb discourages people from having too much desire. Approach issues with patience.

1493. *Ndũkasembee ĩtava yĩ yaku, no ũkwĩsa kũtava.* **Do not rush, when the scooping turn is yours, you will eventually scoop.**
This emerged during the Monsoon era as the Kamba elaborated their social structures and turned to farming. Food and drink were normally consumed communally, served in large calabash bowls with wooden spoons. This communal consumption was established to ensure all members received the same share in both lean and abundant times. The partakers took turns scooping from the bowl. The axiom calls for patience.

1494. *Mũtindania na nyinya asyaa nowe wĩsĩ kũua.*[31] **He who lives with his mother thinks she is the only cook.**
This well-known African adage points to the fact that the mother was chief cook, while other relatives may help. With variations in oral circulation this axiom emerged during the Vascon era. It encouraged travel, experience, and extensive interaction with different peoples in order for one to grow in knowledge.

1495. *Ngeũwo nguvĩ ndĩ mwĩthũi.*[32] **A little beer has no buyers.**
Old men treasured beer from antiquity. *Ngeũwo* referred to beer specially prepared for in-laws, which guests consumed at the home of the in-laws. It lost meaning if it was prepared in a hurry, which not only compromised quality, but also gave prospective partakers no time to prepare. The moral is one should act cautiously over important matters.

---
[31] Kituku, *Folktales*, 29.
[32] Kimilu, *Mũkamba*, 117.

1496. *Ũkĩ nũla ũsesengaa.*[33] **Beer entices and cajoles.**
When the Kamba wanted to get special services or items from someone they did not trust would yield easily, they brewed beer carefully and took it to him. Before he was too tipsy, they began to make their request in a conversation called *kũsesenga*.

1497. *Mũtoewa nĩ syũki nĩwe mũmĩa nzĩanĩ.* **Smoke drifts towards the person who defecates on the road.**
This emerged in antiquity out of the context of warming up around the fire. On chilly mornings children sat around the fire to warm up. Since no one can control wood smoke, whenever smoke drifted in the direction of a particular person the rest said the cause was that the victim had defiled the path. The proverb has multiple interpretations and applications. It was a form of social control among youth, warning them of the dire consequences of relieving themselves on the path.

1498. *Vai mwaki wĩ ũvuvĩo nongĩ.* **There is no fire that is set in the same place as another fire.**
This ancient saying simply states no fire is set on top of another. However, the actual meaning stresses that certain things should be handled separately. Figuratively, fire stands for co-wives and their respective houses. No woman shared fire or house with another. Co-wives were bound to have their own houses in which to cook and warm themselves with their children. The maxim enforces that fact.

1499. *Mwaki ndũvwĩkawa nyeki.*[34] **Grass does not cover fire.**
This ancient proverb has changed with successive cultural changes. The original form used grass until the Monsoon and Vascon ages when clothes replaced grass. During the twentieth century, clothes gave way to blankets and its meaning became more complex. It means the truth cannot be concealed. Second, sensitive matters should never be left unattended lest delay leads to something worse, just as covering fire with grass or clothes will lead to an inferno. Open secrets cannot be concealed forever.

1500. *Kĩka kĩ mwaki kĩthekethawa kĩ kyũmũ.* **A flint is drilled when it is dry.**
The ancient Kamba fire-making implements consisted of two sticks representing male – *wĩĩndĩ* – and female – *kĩka*. Both sticks were supposed to be dry, as the proverb implies. The male drill was twirled around into the female with hands greased with saliva for traction. After twirling for a few seconds fire was produced. This process was

---

[33] Lindblom, *Riddles*, 36.
[34] Farnsworth, *Grammar*, 7; Kimilu, *Mũkamba*, 117; Mutisya, *Proverbs*, 12.

figuratively equated with coitus – and the resulting fire, a baby. The proverb is about sex and sex education. It means that something that will bear good results should be done on time.

1501. *Mwaki wakana mũno nĩũngũasya nyama.* **If the fire flames high it burns meat.**
Preferably, meat is roasted on charcoal rather than flames. Ambitious and boastful people are compared to meat flames whose arrogance brings them to ruin. In other words, do not overdo something, moderation is advised.

1502. *Ve kũthea nthĩ ta mwaki wa ĩnea.* **Some deeds exceed their intentions, like a dung fire that consumes the ground on which it is set.**
An axiomatic rebuke of misconduct, aggression, and greed this maxim derives from the practice of using dung as fuel to repel insects. Once set on fire, it burnt evenly and, as the proverb says, the dung-fuelled fire burnt the soil dark black. No other fuel can burn like dung. The Kamba have taken that phenomenon to symbolize aggressiveness, greed, or immoral conduct.

1503. *Woona vaitoa ve mwaki.* **If you see smoke, there is fire.**
This ancient proverb implies that smoke means there must be fire. It is similar to the English saying, 'Where there is smoke there's fire.'

1504. *Ĩnĩũtoa yoo mwene.*[35] **Even the one that smokes must have its owner.**
This ancient proverb and its variations have been used to advance the view that all individuals have relatives. The phrase 'a smoking log' refers to an odd character, but who is protected from harm because the person has relatives who may seek revenge if the person is harmed.[36] Smokey logs had less value but the person collecting the log attached value to it even if other people did not. It was used to persuade listeners to respect the decisions and property of their neighbours.

1505. *Vayĩ kwota na kwĩingĩthya.* **There is no difference between warming up fully and just a little bit.**
This ancient proverb and its published variations warn against double-dealing. In customary law the person simply observing a theft was considered as guilty as the thief.[37]

---

[35] Mwau, *Dictionary*, 647.
[36] Kimilu, *Mũkamba*, 115.
[37] Mwau, *Dictionary*, 670; Mutisya, *Proverbs*, 61.

1506. *Ũkwĩvĩvya ndayũngũasya.* **One roasting himself doesn't burn himself.**
This ancient axiom was said when someone engaged in risky affairs. It meant self-inflicted injury is not harmful because the person involved can control things.

1507. *Mwaki ndũvuvawa mana.* **Fire is not lit in vain.**[38]
For travellers, the sight of smoke in the wilderness was a sign of people nearby cooking, who could be either friendly or hostile. The adage means there is a reason for everything. However, fire symbolizes conflict and speakers mean to say there is a source for every conflict. If the causes of conflicts are found, then they may be resolved. It is applied differently in a social context.

1508. *Ndikĩaa syũki ngwota mwaki.* **I do not fear smoke as I warm by the fire.**
This is an ancient protest axiom that appears in many songs and variations since Kimilu recorded it from Machakos in 1962.[39] If you want to be competent, be prepared to lose. To gain, one has to be ready to take some risk, for there is no gain without pain.

1509. *Ũsu nĩ mwaki wa kwotea vaasa.* **That is fire to warm from afar.**
Emerging in antiquity, this is an axiomatic way to say 'that is a great thing'. The way it was used during field interviews also signifies that an object is appreciated by all. No one wants to miss it, it is famous. Something popular can be a 'fire to warm from afar'.

1510. *Mũndũ aetawe nĩ mbevo kwota mwaki.* **The cold brings a person to the fireplace.**
With variations in oral circulation and literature, this proverb means the listener may ignore the speaker but later find his assistance indispensable.[40] This emerged during the late Monsoon era as population and migration increased in the context of families struggling to retain members.

1511. *Mũndũ okeaa makaa elekelye ngalĩko syake.* **One draws coals towards his side.**[41]
This adage illustrates the behaviour of men warming themselves at the hearth. As the night advanced the weather cooled, even as the firewood burnt out leaving glowing charcoal. As those around the fire

---

[38] Mwau, *Dictionary*, 662.
[39] Kimilu, *Mũkamba*, 119.
[40] Mutisya, *Proverbs*, 26.
[41] Kimilu, *Mũkamba*, 117; Mutisya, *Proverbs*, 31; Mwau, *Dictionary*, 658.

needed warmth they scratched the charcoal with a stick as if stirring the embers, but really to move it towards their side. Dating from antiquity the saying admonishes people to take care of their own affairs first. It also suggests that people can be selfish, so beware.

1512. *Mata ma kwĩtangĩthya mai nyama.* **Self-choked saliva has no meat.**
This proverb emerged when highly valued meat became relatively rare, creating the idea that one could tell meat was coming if they choked on saliva. Some forced choking on themselves so they would get meat. Such people were warned that only reflex actions bring fortune, not human designs. The proverb suggests that humans cannot manipulate nature to their selfish ends.

1513. *Mũndũ mũĩ atiaa ngathĩ akaathya mongũ.* **A wise man leaves fatty humps to beg for bottlegourds.**
Circulating in Ũkamba since the first millennium, this is a figurative statement alluding to humility and restraint in social affairs. In a society where meat was esteemed, begging for bottlegourds amounted to stooping too low. The fatty hump meat was more valued than bottlegourds. The fact that a wise man would switch options to such a low-valued cuisine suggests that in society humility is a strong virtue.

1514. *Kũvoka na nyama sya ngĩĩ ngũkũ syĩvo nĩ mbanga.* **Consuming warthog meat in the presence of chicken is a travesty.**
This appeared in political songs in Mwingĩ North political campaigns of the 1970s and 1980s. Competing candidates were depicted as worthless warthogs and others as chickens, a local delicacy. It has Monsoon-era precedents and means that one should go for the best alternatives.

1515. *Mũsembea nyama aĩsaa kĩtimba.* **Whoever rushes for meat eventually eats the buttocks.**
Meat was a favoured food and was often consumed cooked, roasted, or even raw. However, people who were known to be glutinous were often slipped bowels or reproductive organs without their knowledge, as punishment. Yet the proverb talks about carelessness in handling sensitive matters, leading to irreparable damage to reputations and objectives. This emerged particularly after the Kamba adopted livestock as a meat supply.

1516. *Nyama ya kwĩtanyukĩa ĩ mũyo.*[42] **The meat one chews for himself is delicious.**
In the past, the Kamba used to chew food for young children. It is not clear whether this also happened with toothless adults. Either way the axiom derives from that context. It emphasizes the importance of independence and hard work. Self-made achievements through personal efforts are more rewarding and satisfying.

1517. *Nyama ya mathunya ndĩ ĩtanyukia.*[43] **Fatty meat is unchewable.**
Collected by Farnsworth in the 1940s from central Machakos, this proverb emerged in antiquity. The Kamba consumed meat frequently from both wild and domestic sources. While fat was appreciated, the Kamba preferred tough meat that they could chew. The Kamba understood and talked about chewing foods as part of the long process of digestion, whereas fat glides down the throat easily, denying the diner an opportunity to chew. This proverb means that good-looking things are not always valuable.

1518. *Nyama ya weemu ndũmĩvikĩla.* **Stubbornness and arrogance are unreachable.**
This ancient axiom discouraged spanking and flogging. Non-violent methods can correct people. Men and women who abused their families were severely flogged in clan meetings. However, as such laceration did not yield positive results, sages used this maxim to suggest that one cannot impart knowledge or instil discipline through the infliction of pain.

1519. *Nyama sya kũkw'a iĩsawa nĩ mwĩyendea.*[44] **Dead animal meat is consumed by choice.**
Meat was revered, but as freshly slaughtered healthy animals were preferred, meat from natural death was never offered to other people. The consumer aware of the potential risk made a choice. The ancient maxim suggests that the choice to enter a risky business is an individual choice.

1520. *Nyama ĩla yĩ vakuvĩ na ngathĩ ndyaa mauta.* **The meat near the hump lacks no fat.**
Fatty meat was valuable and concentrated largely around the hump. Metaphorically this ancient axiom means proximity to wealth, power, and knowledge is beneficial.[45]

---

[42] Kimilu, *Mũkamba*, 118; Mutisya, *Proverbs*, 31.
[43] Farnsworth, *Grammar*, 1117, 129.
[44] Mwau, *Dictionary*, 666.
[45] Mutisya, *Proverbs*, 58.

1521. *Ndūkathekw'e nīkwona syī iko.*[46] **Do not be delighted just because they are cooking.**
Men often shared food while it was still cooking; you may wait patiently, but when the food is cooked they will say everyone is on his own. This ancient maxim implies several things: presumption leads to disillusionment; wait to be invited in order to avoid embarrassment; or plans can backfire, be ready.

---

[46] Kimilu, *Mūkamba*, 117; Mutisya, *Proverbs*, 10.

19

Health, Healing, and the Body

1522. *Itho ĩkatonyeka ĩsalũkĩlyaa kĩlaanĩ.* **An eye bound to be blind blinks in the *Acacia mellera* bush.**
This depicts the nature of Ũkamba landscape, full of thorn bushes that tear clothes and skin if walked through carelessly. In thorny terrain travellers closed their eyes or kept them semi-closed until they passed through such an area. Sometimes thorns got in their eyes and hence this proverb. The ancient proverb warns people to be careful to avoid danger.

1523. *Kĩthimo kya metho kĩthimaa kĩtumbo.* **The eye scales weigh a carcass.**
The Kamba say a weighing scale in the eye weighs dead animal meat, alluding to rarely documented practices in rural villages. When an animal dies from unexpected causes, the meat is chopped without using scales in a process called *kĩtumbo*. The maxim means people cannot rely on eyes to measure things. One may think they see pride in someone and be wrong. This is now the 'eyes' measure' since eyes only see the surface.[1]

1524. *Kimbaa kĩisyaa.*[2] **It swells when it is giving birth.**
This may refer to an expectant mother's body. After childbirth she gains weight and most parts of her body swells. It means changes occur at the hour of reckoning. Pleasure is transient, pain inevitable. Coined by women, the proverb has been in circulation for millennia and has more meanings than are given here.

1525. *Ũkũne ũvwaa ũkũve ndumaa mwĩĩ.* **Laceration is like coitus, it does not get out of the body.**
Both laceration and coitus or rape are incisions into the body and cannot be retrieved. The message is that certain things are better avoided or prevented. The damage they cause if they happen is irreparable. This emerged out of conflict in precolonial times. In other words, tit for tat. This axiom is akin to the next entry.

---

[1] Mulatya, 'Comprehension of Kĩkamba', 59.
[2] Mwau, *Dictionary*, 650.

1526. *Kĩkatĩ wa maaũ kĩyĩ mwathũkĩĩle.* **An object between the legs has no way to evade.**
This axiom alludes to coitus where penetration is assumed to be hard to evade. Certain things perpetuate themselves when they happen and should be avoided.

1527. *Kuusya ona kyaasava no kyaku.* **Pull it; even if it elongates, it is yours.**
The proverb emerged around the 1970s in a fight between a man and his wife. The woman grabbed the husband's penis to demobilize him, leaving the man to resignedly say this axiom. There is a clear sexual meaning in the statement. First, it meant that, if the penis is elongated the woman will eventually have to bear with that length during coitus. It also means that she has crossed the line and will face more serious problems. Clan intervention often followed and both were punished gravely. Subsequently, the statement gained wide popularity and spread across Ũkamba as an axiomatic way of saying 'you are adding injury to a wound'.

1528. *Kyaasava nĩkĩtilawa.* **When it is too long, it is cut.**
This emerged in the same circumstances as the above entry. It was pronounced by the woman involved in the fight with her husband in which she meant, if the penis becomes unusually long, it can be cut. Subsequently, people began to use the axiom beyond its original locality, setting, meaning, and application.

1529. *Metho mavandiwe na mũo ũmwe.* **Eyes were planted with one digging stick.**
Said of those who think they are doing malice secretly although observant people can discover them. It dates from the Islamic period when such tools were adopted.

1530. *Metho maingaa ũsĩ mbee wa mwĩĩ.* **The eyes cross the river before the body.**
Circulating in radio programmes and orally this proverb means eyes can be deceptive. When they see a flooded river, they suggest one can cross it without testing the current's strength. This ancient axiom is a warning not to underestimate tasks or people.

1531. *Mũatha na itho nde mbĩtya.* **One who shoots with the eye never misses.**
Hunting required training, practice, and experience. Emerging from the first millennium, the proverb means that what is imagined is not always practicable.[3]

---

[3] Lindblom, *Riddles*, 32; Kimilu, *Mũkamba*, 119.

336   Part IV: Kamba Society

1532. *Mweeni aiyĩawa mĩiyo ndaiyĩawa metho.*[4] **Only the guest's basket is stored up not the eyes.**
This adage has appeared as variants amidst translation errors in literature. It means although guests' luggage is stored up until their departure, they still notice the host's weaknesses. The adage dates to the beginning of weaving in the Islamic period.

1533. *Kĩvuti kĩ itho kĩwĩkaa nĩ mwene.* **A speck in the eye is felt by the victim.**
This concerns personal problems, the magnitude of which is only known by people involved. They should speak out about their conditions, for none will fathom their suffering otherwise.[5]

1534. *Ngelekanio ti kala ka itho.* **An example is not a little finger stuck into the eye.**
One easy way to provoke a fight among youth was to poke someone's eye. This ancient proverb therefore warned against provocation.

1535. *Vai kĩndũ kĩyĩetae mũndũnĩ eka masombi.* **Nothing brings itself to a man except eye boogers.**
Dating from antiquity, this axiom encourages hard work and self-reliance because nothing comes out of idleness. During sleep, the eyes produce mucus known as rheum that leaves behind eye boogers, which are loathsome to viewers.

1536. *Kũtũ kũla kwĩwaa ngania nũnakwie kwĩwĩkaa nĩ kũngĩ.*[6] **The ear that hears that someone died is heard by another ear.**
This ancient axiom is deeply figurative. Literally it means a person hears someone else has died, but when they die, someone else gets the news. It urges people to be kind to others and grieve with the bereaved, for all meet the same fate.

1537. *Kũtũ kwĩ mbĩtya itho nĩyo tũ.* **The ear can miss it, real sight is reality ascertained.**
This ancient truism has multiple variations, both in oral circulation and literature.[7] It means better to trust an eyewitness than rely on hearsay.

1538. *Kũtũ kũkaa kũyĩw'aa ndawa.* **The ear that is bound to be deaf does not hear medicine.**
This proverb alludes to ear infections that caused deafness in the twentieth century when modern medicine was sought as treatment. Some

[4] Mutisya, *Proverbs*, 13.
[5] Mutisya, *Proverbs*, 59.
[6] Kituku, *Sukulu*, 9.
[7] Mwau, *Dictionary*, 668; Mbiti, *Weteelete*, 10; Watuma, *Syĩthĩo*, 58.

cases could not be helped. Figuratively, the proverb means a doomed person does not recognize useful warnings.

1539. *Ndeaa kũtũ syũke imbĩthĩe.*[8] **I keep ears open, they come find me.**
A figurative condemnation of idle talk, this implies that simply listening to gossip one gains much information. This ancient axiom is said by someone who intends to ignore disagreements.

1540. *Mũsii wa kũtũ nũmwe.* **The ear tunnel is single.**
This axiom means let people speak one at a time. During dinner time it encouraged children to talk less as they ate their food. It emerged from antiquity as the Kamba desired social deliberations to handle life matters.

1541. *Nthaa matũ ĩtũlaa kyano na ũtambĩ.* **The deaf break an arrow with their thigh.**
This ancient adage warned against disobedience. The so-called *mbaa matũ* or *nthaa matũ* ('deaf clan') are people who do not listen to advice, paying attention too late when catastrophe has arrived, symbolized by the fatal breaking of the arrow on their soft thighs. Such folly leads to self-injury and death from poison.[9] When proverbs warn, they are forceful in clarity and depth.

1542. *Kũũ kwaĩ ngove nokwo kwaĩ metho.* **Where the eyelashes were, so were the eyeballs.**
While the eyelashes are clearly visible, eyes lay behind them. The axiom is varied in different ways.[10] The Kamba insisted that sight comes not from the whole eyeball but from the small black part, the pupil. This is another way of saying, 'I know your tricks. You cannot deceive me.'

1543. *Ndanyuka mavia na maeo mene ndamanyaa kana me woo.*[11] **One who chews stones with another's teeth does not know the pain.**
With multiple variants this belongs to a small category of proverbs employing impossible concepts to rebuke odd behaviour.[12] Certainly, one cannot eat rocks or food with someone else's teeth. Dating from the late Monsoon era, it means an adulterous person sees his actions as simply pleasure but the offended have a different view.

---

[8] Kimilu, *Mũkamba*, 116.
[9] Kimilu, *Mũkamba*, 116; Ngotho, *Ngewa*, 34; Mailu, *Kĩkyambonie*, 58; Mutisya, *Proverbs*, 7; Mũĩmi, *Kĩthyomo*, 26–7; Kĩeti, *Barking*, 107; Mwau, *Dictionary*, 654.
[10] Kimilu, *Mũkamba*, 116; Mwau, *Dictionary*, 651.
[11] Kimilu, *Mũkamba*, 117.
[12] Mwau, *Dictionary*, 658.

1544. *Vata wa ĩvu nĩ kũvũna ona yakũthĩĩwa kĩthangathĩ.* **The purpose of the stomach is satisfaction, even if it is filled with sand.**
This is an encouragement to listeners to eat what is available. People cannot eat sand though as some informants insisted warriors were often fed on sand as part of their training. This statement emerged during nineteenth-century famine conditions to persuade children to bear with unpleasant meals. The end justifies the means.

1545. *Ekana na maayo mooka oyu namotia kĩni na nĩkyo kĩkũũ.* **Leave the teeth alone; they just came and will leave the old gums standing.**
This ancient axiom compares the gums and teeth to demonstrate the significance of old things. A baby is born with gums but without teeth. The teeth come later but in old age the teeth fall out, leaving the gums intact. Old things are more valuable and stable than new things.

1546. *Kathekya ĩthe kate maayo.* **The baby smiled at the father before teething.**
This ancient axiom alludes to practices surrounding childbirth, an entirely female affair. When a woman conceived with a man who was not her husband, to hide her infidelity she secured the saliva of her lover and put it in a container to reveal the affair to the midwives. They mixed the saliva with water in a calabash bowl and passed the bowl to the unsuspecting husband as libation to ensure safe childbirth. Once the baby arrived, the midwife burst into laughter saying, *Nĩkathekya ĩthe kate mayo*, 'This baby smiled at the father without teeth – the man has been fooled.'

1547. *Syavĩta mwana syĩtavaswa ĩthe.* **When they bypass the son, they are not told the father.**
This is another female proverb about moral secrets, from the eighteenth century. Women can tell a child secretly of his biological father but the father cannot. The axiom warns that some words are not repeated.

1548. *Kĩndũ kĩmũyo kĩtyona maeo.*[13] **Something sweet will not spare the teeth.**
This truism, although with precolonial precedents, became evident during the modern period. Heavy consumption of sweets and sugary drinks has considerably compromised dental health. Thus, the proverb is a call to listeners to avoid sugary diets and consider their dental health. Figuratively, however, it means good things are not always beneficial.

---

[13] Mwau, *Dictionary*, 650.

1549. *Mũtanuka na maeo meene ndamanthaa syĩ mavia.* **A person chewing with other people's teeth does not know when food is mixed with rocks.**
This ancient proverb suggests multiple developments. One was the techniques used in threshing grains and legumes and the consequences in consumption of food processed that way. The Kamba threshed grains and legumes on a flat patch of hard ground (*kĩvũĩyo*) smeared with cow dung to keep rocks and dust from mixing with food. Husks were spread on the patch, left for about an hour to be scorched by the sun and then beaten with sticks. Sometimes they beat them down to the bare ground, stirring dirt and stones into the grains. If this was not cleaned properly, consumers found rocks in the cooked food. The proverb rebukes dependency, complacency, and idleness. It particularly calls on men to stop depending on their fathers and to establish their own homes and families.

1550. *Ve ĩeo ĩkũka mbemba ikaemea uanĩ.* **A particular tooth may fall out keeping corn intact in the bowl.**
The key historical marker is maize corn, which reached East Africa during the 1500s. The original varieties called *ngasue* required strong molars to chew boiled corn seeds. The proverb means there is always an indispensable item or person in every place and situation.[14]

1551. *Mũsyai nde ngoo ekalaa na ilĩ yakwova na ũthasye.* **A parent does not have a temper, they have two, to tie and untie.**
This ancient adage has appeared in songs and poetry across the twentieth century. Farnsworth recorded it from central Machakos in 1952.[15] It is usually directed to parents and officials, advising them to be flexible as they deal with children and subjects respectively.

1552. *Mwaĩki nde ngoo.*[16] **The circumciser has no temper.**
Circumcision appears to have emerged shortly before the Vascon era. By the 1500s a class of professional circumcisers had emerged. Such a person was calm and even tempered. He or she was also kept entertained and relaxed through the process in order to avoid injury on the initiate. This maxim means that sensitive operations require a calm mind.

---

[14] Mutisya, *Proverbs*, 74; Masao Yoshida, *The Historical Background to Maize Marketing in Kenya and its Implications for Future Marketing Reorganization* (Kampala: Makerere Institute of Social Research, 1966); James McCann, *Maize and Grace* (Cambridge: Harvard University Press, 2007).
[15] Farnsworth, *Grammar*, 77.
[16] Mwau, *Dictionary*, 661.

1553. *Ngoo īsaa kīla īkwenda yalea īkaya mūthanga.*[17] **The heart eats what it desires, once it rejects food it consumes dirt.**
Appetite drives consumption patterns. The ancient proverb has a hidden meaning. While appetite drives consumption, sometimes it drives the body into peril and death.

1554. *Mwīkya na ngoo ndathaa.*[18] **One who shoots with anger never hits the target.**
This warns hunters not to shoot at animals angrily but tactically. They must be sober and focused. Angry people do not accomplish their objectives.

1555. *Mwīkya wa ngoo ni mūmbīwa.* **Whoever gives in quickly is a loser.**
This emerged in the early colonial period in a business context. It admonished creditors to be persistent in pursuing their borrowers.

1556. *Kīla kyaīlaa ngoo nīkīmīthūaa.* **Whatever fits the heart hurts it.**
This is said when separated lovers are counselled to reconcile. It means one disagreement is not unusual. It is okay to reconcile and move on with maturity. Not all that is fitting in the eye of the beholder is acceptable and morally relevant.

1557. *Kūmya ngoo no kīndu.* **Hardening the heart is a good thing.**
This was sung by Katuta wa Mutunga of Mutuendo in the 1940s and 1950s in which he meant being hard and remorseless can be valuable. It can enable one to achieve what appears impossible.

1558. *Īvu īnene ītakīaa mwene thaano.* **A big belly confuses the owner during the dry season.**
This refers to farmers storing as much food as possible during the dry season. Those who would not save are referred to as having a big belly, symbolizing greed, whereas the dry season stands for lean days. A person accustomed to extravagant ways is unable to survive on minimum resources.

1559. *Kyalewa nī īnyūū ti kya īvu.* **What is rejected by the nose is not for the stomach.**
This is a common adage about scent and taste. To eat, the scent must endorse the food for the stomach to be receptive. This may have multiple applications outside body parts; in a family, if the wife says no to some-

---

[17] Kimilu, *Mūkamba*, 118; Mwau, *Dictionary*, 665; Mbiti, *Weteelete*, 143.
[18] Mwau, *Dictionary*, 662; Watuma, *Syīthīo*, 57.

thing, the husband would most likely follow suit and vice versa. The ancient adage has been published in different versions.[19]

1560. *Kala kanyenyawa kelĩ mũyo.* **A little finger is licked twice for its sweetness.**
From after the rise of apiculture this adage is open to multiple interpretations, including romantic ones. Something good is repeated, such as eating delicious food or dating an attractive person.

1561. *Moko ma ndũũ nĩ eli, kwakũnengane na kwosa.*[20] **The hands of friendship are two, one for giving and one for receiving.**
True friends know how to give and receive. The ancient axiom alludes to a longstanding habit of making friendships through exchanges of gifts and even of relatives in marriages.

1562. *Moko maingĩ manenawa yũanĩ.* **Too many hands are loathed during famines.**
This has both figurative and symbolic meanings. People appreciated extra labour during planting and weeding seasons yet loathed the same help coming around their homes during lean days with no food to share.

1563. *Mwimbo walea kũtonywa nĩwĩtonyaa.* **If a boil is not lanced, it bursts itself.**
To appreciate this maxim a brief description is worthwhile: a boil usually begins as red bumps on the skin, which over time fill with pus. Some people prick it to reduce the pressure and pain. Because this process is painful, some leave the boil intact until it ruptures on its own. This ancient proverb points to acts of hiding secrets, which leak and ooze to the embarrassment of those involved.

1564. *Muunyĩ wa kyaa ndwotawa.* **The shade of a finger is not basked under.**
People should accept conditions of scarcity and endeavour to create wealth for family and community. A finger's shade symbolizes 'meagre resources' insufficient for a community. This proverb emerged from the degraded ecological conditions of the early colonial era. Shade trees became rare and, if travellers came to a scrawny tree, they called it a finger's shade.

---

[19] Kituku, *Folktales*, 82; Mwau, *Dictionary*, 653.
[20] Mailu, *Kĩkyambonie*, 52.

1565. *Mŭyovo ŭmwe ndŭyovawa mbyŭ ilĩ.* **One loin is not girdled with two swords.**
This was an admonition to polygamous men not to sleep with their wives in the same bed or even the same house. Each woman must have her own space. Almost every word in this line is symbolic. The word *Mŭyovo ŭmwe* (one loin) stands for a man, while the term *mbyŭ ilĩ* (two swords) represents women. The term *ndŭyovawa* (never girdled with) symbolizes sexual intercourse.[21] The proverb cautioned against greed and excessiveness.

1566. *Moko maikŭnaa na kĩtaa kĩmwe.* **Hands do not beat with one palm.**
One cannot clap with one hand but for good results one uses both hands. In that sense it emphasizes the importance of complimentary coexistence and unity.

1567. *Kwĩthŭwa kumanaa na waasa wa kwoko.* **Scratching depends on the length of the hand.**
This ancient maxim implies that the length of one's hand determines where he/she can scratch his/her body. By extension, it means that achievement depends on one's effort and ability.

1568. *Ndŭkakaĩye kwoko ŭtakomeeye.* **Do not groan over a hand that you are not lying on.**
Alluding to how the Kamba rested in bed with head on arms, this ancient proverb means that if the arm is injured this will produce groans. Someone else cannot make the same complaint for he cannot feel pain in another's arm. The axiom is said in a legal dispute over who committed a crime. Even if one is a relative, the speaker means 'I do not deny the allegation for I was not
there when the offence was committed.'[22] The proverb dates back many centuries.

1569. *Mŭndŭ ŭkumaa asisasya ngŭngi ndaketolongania na maumoo maaŭ.* **A person urinating checks the wind direction to avoid spattering his legs with urine.**
This ancient proverb calls for focus and strategic calculation in any undertaking. A politician used it in a context in which he meant a candidate must look at where other contestants are heading. Also, it means when doing anything, be cautious of risks.

---

[21] Mutisya, *Proverbs*, 64.
[22] Mutisya, *Proverbs*, 37.

1570. *Ndũũka ikwataa ũla wĩ maaũ maũsemba.* **Madness strikes one who has legs to run.**
Precolonial Kamba had few cases of mental illness, one of the common characteristics of which was stripping naked and running off. Its origin is linked to consumption of narcotics from Asia. The proverb means that people should undertake tasks that they can handle.[23]

1571. *Maaũ maamũkaa vala mũtwe ũkomie.* **The legs wake where the head slept.**
The head controls the legs and, therefore, if one goes to bed with a desire to go somewhere he will not sleep well. He will depart for the destination before time. The ancient axiom points to obsession and appears to warn the listener to be careful and slow down on certain things.

1572. *Mũndũ avitha ũndũ avithaa kĩtau na kĩimũtũla kũũ.* **If a person conceals a secret he conceals a wound that will break his leg.**
This ancient saying originated when incurable wounds were considered a stigma. Some people even covered the wound with clothes and kept the status of their health a secret. The alternative was to reveal the wound and get treatment. It means that in a dispute one ought to speak his mind lest there be no solution. It is risky to hide problems, so reach out for help.

1573. *Mũndũ avuĩkaswa mũthanga nũ wake.* **Only kindred cover a person with dust.**
This ancient proverb emerged from burial customs. When a person died and the body readied for burial, the eldest son took a handful of dirt to throw into the grave as a symbolic gesture that the next of kin had sanctioned the burial. The rest of the people then finished the burial process. Another interpretation is that harm can also come from relatives. When a community condemned a criminal to death by stoning, a relative threw a pebble at him/her and then the assembly finished the execution. The ancient proverb implies that people who need community assistance must show the way.

1574. *Ve kĩtau na mũsivo.* **There is a wound and a boil.**
A wound and a boil are not the same, and serious matters should not be compared with others. Sores and wounds were the most common ailments among the relatively healthy Kamba.

---

[23] Mutisya, *Proverbs*, 45.

344 Part IV: Kamba Society

1575. *Kĩnene kĩthũku no kĩtau.*[24] **A big bad thing is only a wound.**
This catchphrase implies that, to the Kamba, small is not better but big evil is undesirable. Rising from antiquity it can apply to almost every aspect of life.

1576. *Wiingĩ mũthũku nĩ wa itau.* **Too much bad stuff is that of a wound.**
By most oral accounts, this proverb dates from antiquity, wounds being the most common malady among the Kamba living in brushy landscapes. It implies that while good things are welcome, people normally resist things that are bad for them.

1577. *Mũyo mwiingĩ nũtũlaa ĩvĩndĩ.* **Too much pleasure breaks bones.**
This maxim originated with honey harvesters during the Monsoon era. It rose out of their realization that sweet things had to be eaten in moderation. As an admonishment for moderation, it also cautions that no condition is permanent. Pleasure gives way to pain.

1578. *Mũtemi wa nguso ndamanyaa kana syĩ woo.* **The expert of cicatrizations does not know that they hurt.**
Kamba women beautified themselves with cicatrizations over their body using the latex of the euphorbia tree, and tattooed their cheeks by rubbing the powdered root of plum mixed with milk into their scratched skin.[25] Cicatrization is an old custom that appears in Arabic records as early as the 800s, indicating the proverb emerged during the first millennium. An expert called *Mũtemi wa nguso* who performed cicatrization did not feel the pain he inflicted on women. In other words, the offender does not know the feelings of the offended.

1579. *Kĩlunzu kĩituvĩaa mwĩĩ.* **A blunt machete is not blunt on the body.**
The proverb emerged shortly after the twentieth-century introduction of the machete. Without frequent sharpening a machete becomes too blunt for wood but can still cut human flesh.
It means, things that may not harm one person may be harmful to another.

1580. *Mwĩĩ ũng'endasya ndia ĩndĩ mũthanga ũũ ũkwona ũvindasya aũme aingĩ.* **The soil on which we stand covers many virile men, for virility is the pride of fools.**
This proverb warns that humility is better than pride. Strength and beauty should be used as resources naturally bequeathed to carry out

---

[24] Kituku, *Folktales*, 77.
[25] Adamson, *Peoples*, 238.

moral duties. Live well with friends, serve humanity, and serve God. Here *mwĩĩ* means strength, masculine prowess, or feminine beauty as a source of power and advantage.

1581. *Ve nzuĩ sya kwenzea nza na ingĩ sya kwenzea nyũmba nzĩnĩ.* **There is hair for shaving outside and others for indoors.**
Among the Kamba hair has specific names depending on where it is. This proverb illustrates how the ancient Kamba dealt with body hair. Lindblom tells us that the Kamba never kept their hair long except when someone was sick for a long time. From the seventeenth to the twentieth century, body hair was shaved with a sharp knife while eyebrows, eyelashes, and beards were plucked one piece at a time with copper pincers. Pubic and armpit hair was trimmed using sharp blades in complete privacy, hence the proverb, which calls for an order of doing things in all spheres of life.

1582. *Kwia ti kũũngũa nzakame nĩ ndune.* **Being black is not being charred.**
This is a protest maxim that emerged in the twentieth century as colonial culture led to light- skinned girls being associated with beauty and thus being more popular. By the end of the Second World War, light-skinned girls were already associated with beauty and were the target of multiple lovers. Popular musicians in the 1970s and 1980s used this maxim in songs.[26] The proverb means that there are certain things that have invisible value and beauty.

1583. *Nthakame nthũkũ ndĩkomaa mwĩĩ.* **Bad blood does not sleep in the body.**
This means an odd character cannot last long in a community of morals. It may also mean bad things cannot be kept secret forever. It has been in circulation since antiquity to encourage openness and sincerity.

1584. *Nthakame nĩ ngito mbee wa kĩw'ũ.* **Blood is thicker than water.**
Even though Kamba speakers do not quote English as the source of this universal axiom, it appears to have been borrowed from classrooms between the 1930s and 1950s. As in English, it recognizes the supremacy of familial relationships and loyalties. It also applies to friends versus strangers, neighbours versus immigrants, and so forth.

---

[26] Jeremiah Kĩtũnda, 'Love is a Dunghill and I am the Cock that Gets on it to Crow', in *Hemingway and Africa*, ed. Miriam Mandel (New York: Camden House, 2011).

1585. *Kũsũnga nĩ kũmya ĩtheka.* **To dance is to restrain laughter.**
This alludes to the use of drums for dancing as both a rite of passage and part of schooling among precolonial Kamba since the Vascon era. The *ngoma* served three main purposes, each determined by the beat. The *mũkanda* dance was an important rite of passage and entertainment. One would not be allowed to marry before participating in dancing. One dance, the *Kũsũnga*, has performers shake and swing their shoulders to the tune of drums and whistles. This amused spectators, causing them to smile, laugh, and chant. Since laughter is contagious, the performers would often laugh, causing a distraction leading to poor performance. The proverb means that, to overcome a challenge, one has to persevere. Whatever the obstacle may be, persistent and concentrated efforts will wear it down.

1586. *Kwĩtiing'a nĩ kũseo.* **Self-restraint is good.**
The ancient proverb encourages self-control. It means someone who is self-restrained gains more from people than a beggar.

1587. *Ĩteng'e ya kanywa ĩlũngawa na kanywa ũngĩ.* **The bowleg of the mouth is straightened by another bowleg.**
This ancient proverb means that many blunders are verbal. They need to be corrected through rebuke, and counselling.

1588. *Ndũkandũe vala ĩnyũũ ĩtũĩĩye kanywa.* **Do not dwell where the nose dwells next to the mouth.**
As one of a series of ancient proverbs dealing with body parts next to each other, they all mean do not be constantly provocative. These are angry words hurled at opponents. They also represent protest against cruel behaviour.

1589. *Mũyo ndũtũaa kanywa.* **Deliciousness does not stay in the mouth forever.**
This ancient adage has appeared in varied versions in literature since the 1910s.[27] The Kamba observed that lusciousness did not last long in the mouth after one had eaten sweet or delicious meals. This proverb is a warning that good things cannot last. Hard work and caution are advised.

1590. *Kanywa kaasya nathi kyoonĩ na kaimĩaa.* **The mouth says 'I have gone to the toilet', but it does not defecate.**
This is a warning against conceited behaviour, especially when one derides a disadvantaged person. It emerged during the twentieth century when toilets became common.

---

[27] Mwau, *Dictionary*, 662; Ibekwe, *Wit*, 198; Lindblom, *Riddles*, 32.

1591. *Kanywa ndwĩ ũndũ ũtaweta, ũw'o na ndeto mbiingĩ. Ũwetaa wathi kũmĩa na wavika ũivindya ki.* **The mouth can say anything, both truth and verbosity. It says, 'I am going to the toilet', but keeps mum when it gets there.**
People can say things that they cannot accomplish. Indeed, when nature calls, people excuse themselves saying, 'I need to go to the restroom', but in the act of relieving their bowels, their mouth remains shut. This ancient axiom is a stern warning against talking without forethought.

1592. *Kanywa kaumaa ngwa katavika ĩtunĩ.* **The mouth curses thunder while it cannot reach the sky.**
This ancient axiom means that in competition one has to understand his resources against a stronger person. Braggarts backpaddle when they are confronted with reality.

1593. *Kanywa nĩ mũthũku, ũĩsaa mbeũ mũũnda waanywa kĩw'ũ.* **The mouth is evil. It eats sowing seeds leaving the farm to drink water.**
This derives from the context of farmland poverty where famished families with meagre food supplies consumed everything, even the seed crop. It emerged during the nineteenth century when droughts created severe food shortages, creating exactly such situations. When rains fell, farms flooded with water but no seeds for planting were available. To deter this practice some people mixed grains with sand and ashes so that no one would dare cook them.

1594. *Kanywa mwatũe ndwaĩĩwaa nĩ kyaũya.* **An open mouth cannot fail to find a morsel or does not lack something to eat.**
This originated in famine-stricken areas to mean that food will be available some way or another. Kamba lore provides a yardstick of the impact of famines from 1800 to 2000, each bearing a metaphorical name suggesting its horrific dimensions. During *Yũa ya Nzana* (the Monitor Lizard Famine) the Kamba were reduced to consuming the scaly monitor lizard in the 1880s.

1595. *Kanywa ũmwe ndũmanyaa kana lĩu nĩ mũvye.* **One mouth cannot determine whether the food is well cooked.**
In precolonial days, the Kamba used to work in teams to build houses and stores, digging wells, clearing forests for farms, weeding, and so on. These cooperative activities are the symbolic meaning of 'cooked food'. If people cannot succeed by themselves, they need help from relatives and community members. Such cooperative activities emerged during the Vascon era. This proverb, and one to follow, emerged therefore with the practices of self-help groups called *myethya* during that period.

1596. *Kanywa wene ndwĩsaa muuma.* **Another person's mouth does not swear an oath.**
This originated around the thirteenth century with the rise of oathing customs called *kũya muuma* as a means of settling cases. The disputing parties in a given case were given an object to bite. If one lied, death supposedly followed and could even wipe out the offender's lineage.[28] The proverb became common during the Mau Mau uprising in the 1950s, when taking oaths became widespread in Kenya. It calls upon people to be self-reliant, independent, and to desist from using resources not their own.

1597. *Mũnuka mũĩ ũtonyangaa mwene.*[29] **A sharp mouth pierces its owner.**
This is a warning to people to say few words in public lest they incur embarrassment later. There are chances that one can make blunders if they say too much.

1598. *Mũnuka nĩ mũthũku, mũnuka tiwo kanywa.* **The muzzle is evil; the muzzle is not the mouth.**
This axiom has circulated in social media and school drama across East Africa, educating the public about the evils of gossip. It employs two body parts that are often not clear even to Kamba speakers – the mouth where food is processed (*kanywa*) and the opening of the mouth or muzzle (*mũnuka*) encompassing the lips and the voice. The muzzle is taken negatively, particularly where idle talk is involved. The axiom warns that gossip from one's lips is destructive.

1599. *Mũnuka nĩ wa kũneena nawo kanywa nĩ wa kũya.* **The muzzle is for speaking and the mouth is for eating.**
The mouth and muzzle are figurative reflections of how the Kamba understood the functions of these body parts. The Kamba have a name for the mouth for eating, and a word for the mouth for talking, slander, and conspiracy. The latter is considered the evil aspect of this body part. This ancient axiom is a warning to shun gossip and any form of idle talk.

1600. *Kana kaĩtomo kavĩvaw'a mũnuka na kĩsinga ke kanini.* **A greedy child is burned with a glowing torch while still young.**
This is not literal but means that children who show signs of deviant behaviour have to be corrected, nurtured, and trained to be gentle and generous while they are young. Gluttonous traits were considered a

---

[28] Lindblom, *Akamba*, 165.
[29] Mailu, *Kĩkyambonie*, 55.

vice. This ancient maxim implies that, if a child is left alone with such traits, they will extend into other aspects of life.

1601. *Wa kanywa watulĩka ndusyuliawa mwaitha, wovawa na ũngi.* **When the bow of the mouth is broken, it is not repaired with herbal fibre but with another mouth.**
This ancient maxim rose from a conflict context. It means verbal mockery is repaired with verbal apology and forgiveness.

1602. *Mũnuka nũkengaa mwene.*[30] **The mouth lies to its owner.**
With a number of published variations, this adage is similar to the biblical verse Galatians 6:3, 'If anyone thinks they are something when they are not, they deceive themselves.' It warns to beware that plans can backfire; so be cautious.[31]

1603. *Mũnuka ũla ũĩsaa mbeũ now'o wĩsaa ũkũlya twĩvanda kĩ?* **The mouth that eats the seeds is the same that asks, 'What shall we plant?'**
Seasonal harvests are barely enough to sustain farm families until the next harvest in Ũkambanĩ. About a month or two before the planting season, food is so short that some families eat grains that are meant as seeds for planting, leaving them asking what are we going to plant now?

1604. *Mũnuka ũla ũĩsaa nyama now'o wĩsaa ũya nyũnyi.* **The mouth that eats meat also eats greens.**
In Kamba culture consuming meat is deemed better than eating greens. One may enjoy meaty cuisine but, when poverty hits, greens will do. There is no recognition of greens as healthy food, only that greens are inferior to meat. This maxim warns the listener that resources change imperceptibly. It emerged in the nineteenth century to give hope to people who were surviving on a poor diet – the future will be better.

1605. *Kyuo kĩ mũtwe kiyaa mũũnda.* **An idea in the mind does not guard a farm against weaverbirds.**
To keep birds away from ripening crops one had to shout at them. If one remained quiet and kept thinking of what words to shout the birds would destroy the crops. Circulated from antiquity, this maxim encourages people to speak out. If you have thoughts about something, some ideas of how to improve the life of the family or the community, share them.

---

[30] Mailu, *Kĩkyambonie*, 16.
[31] Mailu, *Kĩkyambonie*, 24.

1606. *Ĩsanduku ya mũtwe ĩte ĩvingũe nĩ mwene ndũmanyaa kĩla kĩnzĩnĩ.* **The content of a mental box is hard to tell unless the owner opens it.**
As Kamba men moved to towns in the 1900s, they adopted the culture of putting their personal effects in wooden or metallic boxes. These were locked with a padlock, such that no one had access unless the owner opened it to show what was inside. The maxim advised listeners: if you want to know what people are thinking, you have to ask them.

1607. *Nzama ya mũtwe ndĩ mũae.*[32] **A mental counsel does not have division.**
The proverb means that someone who decides to avoid a problem of soot by shifting the kitchen, but does that only in his mind, gains nothing. Mutisya interpreted this proverb to mean an 'unpublicized change of mind invites no controversy'.

1608. *Nzama yĩ mũtwe ĩmanyĩkaa nĩ mwene.* **A conspiracy is known only by the conspirer.**
This ancient axiom warned the listener to beware of conspiracy at all levels, including close friends. If a person planned to cause harm to the listener, there was no way of knowing but to read body signs. Another interpretation is that people can keep their secrets for no one will know unless they reveal what they are thinking. Whenever one has a headache only he or she knows its severity.

1609. *Mũtwe ũĩsaa ũngĩ na uĩawa lĩu nĩ ũĩme.* **The head consumes another, and the tongue prepares its food.**
This ancient proverb with multiple interpretations has three phases: one where the tongue gets food ready for swallowing, then tongue and jaw move it around so it can be chewed, and finally to swallow. The Kamba equate this process as cooking with the tongue. A literal interpretation is that the Kamba loved to eat the head, which was prepared differently than other meat and involved some thought. It means people use their minds to deceive others, often speaking their designs loudly, and even gossiping about them.

1610. *Mũtwe mũmũ ndwatũaa ũkuta.* **A hard head does not crack the wall.**
'Hard head' refers to arrogance. No matter how stubborn one may be, life's challenges will always need strategy to overcome them. The Swahili term *ũkuta* refers to the walls of modern buildings that became common in Ũkamba during the twentieth century. This proverb encouraged people to think and act.

---

[32] Kimilu, *Mũkamba*, 118; Mutisya, *Proverbs*, 17.

1611. *Nzele ya mũtwe ĩsũnawa nĩ mwene.*[33] **The owner licks his mental calabash.**
Licking calabash bowls and honey barrels are the same process and appear to have originated from the same period in antiquity. The calabash bowl was used for drinking thick porridge. Once the porridge was finished, the Kamba cleaned the residue with their index finger and licked the finger – a process called *kũsũna*. This process was a delight to many people: friends and relatives invited each other to the licking. However, this would not happen if one thought only of an imaginary future calabash bowl or honey barrel. One must be practical. Dreams are not strategy.

1612. *Wona kene kũnĩĩlya ngingo, wona kaku syokeelya ngingo.* **Stretch out your neck when you see other people's morsel, shrink your neck whenever you get your own.**
This axiom, tracing back to antiquity, can be interpreted as a call to aggressively search for wealth. It can also serve as a sarcastic rebuke of greed. Sticking out the neck is symbolic of admiring other people's things, while shrinking the neck signifies protecting one's property and keeping secrets.

1613. *Nzũngi nesa ĩmilaa no wayo.* **A good dancer twists with his own.**
This refers to ornaments that enhance the beauty of dancers. Good dancers used their own ornaments, not borrowed ones. This ancient maxim means self-reliance is most desirable.

1614. *Nzũngi yĩ ngũlũ ĩtwaa kĩlaalai.* **A proud dancer marries a whore.**
This axiom emerged during the colonial era when prostitution first emerged and the category of women labelled *ilaalai* (singular *kĩlaalai*) – a Christian term denoting an adulteress – increased. The term came to cover prostitution and uncontrolled sexual behaviour. The maxim discouraged selectivity of women in marriage as well as mistreatment of women during courtship. Men too fastidious or simply nasty were rejected by all women of honour, so such men attracted only the worst of their kind.

1615. *Nzũngi ĩte wia ĩsũngaa yelekele nondo.* **A courageous dancer dances towards the breasts.**
Kamba drumming music and dance, emerging about the Islamic era, was performed at night by girls and boys under flaming torches. Boys formed a line facing girls and danced to the rhythms of the drums,

---

[33] Kimilu, *Mũkamba*, 77, 118; Mutisya, *Proverbs*, 60.

songs, and whistles. The lead singer frequently ordered one side to charge against the other, dancing and shaking their shoulders to the song. Bolder boys danced all the way into the chest of the girl directly opposite him, demonstrating he was not timid. The symbolic meaning of the proverb is, if you like something, go for it.

1616. *Nzũngi ya vaasa ĩsũngaa ĩsyaitye sua.* **A dancer from afar dances facing the sun.**
Literally, this ancient proverb refers to a girl who should leave a dance to get home before sunset if she comes from far away. The deeper meaning is, if you want to enter a given venture, measure yourself against your circumstances. Do you have time and space to do it safely and conveniently?[34] The sun in this context measures time while 'dance' symbolizes sex. A girl involved in romance should balance her pleasure with time to return home before sunset. Outside that context, the axiom is about caution, strategy, and tact in stiff competition or risky business.

1617. *Ĩĩ nĩ ndaĩ ya katondoli tondolia vala wĩkitya.* **This is a touch riddle, touch where you may reach.**
Originally a children's chant while swimming in waterpans, but recently politicians have turned it into an expression of political games and secrecy. Adults use it in both light and tense moments, meaning the matter at hand involves guesswork and personal interpretation. This emerged during the Islamic era as the Kamba moved to areas with waterpans.

1618. *Mwĩkathĩĩi nde ĩlũũ.* **The braggart has no defects.**
This adage has several variations published since 1958, but all mean that one should never praise himself because he will never see his own weaknesses.[35] Better to let others judge you and point to your weaknesses.

1619. *Nzũki ndĩmbula.* **I can tell an evil person if I see one.**
Popularized through *mbenga* music in the 1970s, this ancient maxim means that people with bad intentions may conceal their wickedness, but the public will still detect and expose it.

1620. *Nzũki yosanaa na ĩngĩ syiiw'ana ta nguthi na kĩng'auwĩ.* **An ugly fellow picks another ugly one and they match like a scorpion and crab.**

---

[34] Lindblom, *Akamba*, 343; Mutisya, *Proverbs*, 9; Mbiti, *Weteelete*, 28.
[35] Mutisya, *Proverbs*, 18; Mwandia, *Kusoma*, 14; Kimilu, *Mũkamba*, 117; Watuma, *Syĩthĩo*, 57; Mwau, *Dictionary*, 663.

With historical precedent, this saying emerged from a song of Kimanzi wa Mbiti of Nzemeli within the Kabati area of Kitui in the 1940s. It means a bad character is matched with equals.

1621. *Yumaw'a katĩ nĩ kwongwa.* **Consistent sucking drains milk from the breast.**
While women created this proverb in antiquity, it was popularly used in military expeditions to encourage persistence and perseverance. It encourages labour with hope. Women rarely use it.[36]

1622. *Yũmbwa ĩiyũmbũawa.* **In-born traits are not undone.**
The Kamba believed that behaviour was in-born and unchangeable. This ancient axiom does not recognize the value of training and education to turn a vile character into a morally upright champion. By ignoring the essence of reform, it reveals the nature of proverbs: they do not always represent the truth. They are products of experience and observation of a few subjected to scrutiny in later generations.

---

[36] Mutisya, *Proverbs*, 39; Mwau, *Dictionary*, 646.

20

Trade, Markets, and Industries

1623. *Ĩleve ĩtheiĩ kĩlonzo kiingĩ.*[1] **An empty tin has a lot of noise.**
Some attribute this adage to the first Speaker of the Kenya National Assembly, Fred Mbiti Mati, in 1962 during a campaign against a voluble opponent. The Speaker took two tins, one filled with water and one empty. Beating both before the gazing electorate he demonstrated that an empty tin is louder. The Speaker, being of the first generation of Kamba elites, might have borrowed this maxim from literature because there is an older English phrase, 'Empty vessels make the most noise', meaning that people with the least talent and knowledge usually speak loudest.

1624. *Kwandĩkwa ti kũsyawa.*[2] **To be employed is not to be born.**
This axiom alludes to the new version of paid employment. Between 1895 and 1945, the Kamba enlisted in large numbers as soldiers, porters, clerks, and other servants of the British Empire. Paid employment soon became highly esteemed to the extent that the wise had to remind people that employment was not a substitute for blood relationships.

1625. *Malĩ ya Mũsa ndĩminwa nĩ Ali.* **Ali never exhausts the wealth of Moses.**
This proverb emerged during the colonial period as coastal Muslim traders increased in Ũkamba. They often employed Islamized Kamba as business caretakers who engaged in pilferage. But pilferage did not bankrupt their employers, hence the proverb. By implication all relationships are mutually exploitative; and when a web of understanding and cohabitation has formed an *organic* web, it becomes its own criterion. The players will never ruin one another any more than a hand would ruin a foot.

---

[1] Kimilu, *Mũkamba*, 115; Mwau, *Dictionary*, 647; Mbiti, *Ngaeka*, 90–1.
[2] Kimilu, *Mũkamba*, 116.

1626. *Mūkui wa tūvanzania nīwīsī vata wa tw'o.* **The carrier of sacks knows their value.**
In the 1980s synthetic nylon sacks, *mbasania*, replaced sacks (*ngunia*) made of sisal fibre. *Mbasania* are very important since no food moves from one place to another except in these sacks. The moral is that people should respect other people's decisions even when they sound disagreeable.

1627. *Mwaki ndambaa kīthuma.* **A builder does not stretch out the bedding skin.**
This maxim is deeply figurative and tricky to comprehend. The word *mwaki* means fire or builder depending on pronunciation, while the word *kīthuma* (bedding skin) is euphemistic for stomach, firmness, or resolute and inflexible in principles. The proverb is subject to several interpretations: one is that a household patriarch does not have harsh rules. He has flexible principles and cares for family members. The second interpretation is that he does not crave for food; he lets the dependants eat first, they are his priority. This maxim emerged during the nineteenth century when feeding large families became challenging.

1628. *Mbuvaa soo mwene aimba ngŭmbŭ.*[3] **I blow the megaphone when the owner develops mumps.**
The megaphone was an imperial introduction, but traditional trumpets from animal horns have been in existence for millennia. These 'natural trumpets', used solely for entertainment, did not have the finger holes, keys, slides, or valves found in Western megaphones and by which the pitch of an instrument might be altered. This means the speaker is calculating and acts when people are exhausted.

1629. *Soo wa mwīnzīo ndwambaa.* **An underground-based megaphone cannot be loud.**[4]
This emerged between 1920 and 1950. It means that certain resources have to be invested in their right place in order to be beneficial. Kamba megaphones adopted through Christian missions were used mainly for evangelism. It may also tell readers you cannot hide your talents, use them for your benefit and the benefit of others. In its religious context, it was used to persuade converts to testify about Christ; to proclaim their new faith.

---

[3] Mailu, *Kīkyambonie*, 15, 71.
[4] Kimilu, *Mūkamba*, 118.

1630. *Ndũkaavute simũ ya mũisikya ũtanaminĩte masyaa.* **Do not erase the midwife's phone number before you cease to bear children.**
This maxim serves as proof that proverbs are not relics of the past, but are constantly created. It also provides a proxy for scrutinizing the mobile phone's journey in Kenya, and its subsequent revolutionary impact on public life.[5] This axiom emerged in the early 2000s with the advent of cellular phones, where people stored the phone numbers of their contacts. Young women coined and spread this axiom through social media. In rural areas, midwives play crucial roles and expectant women kept phone numbers of the nearest midwives. After birth, they were warned to keep the contact. This axiom is a rephrasing of the previous entry, again illustrating how younger generations twist proverbs to fit their generational material conditions. Do not mock those who helped you into success.

1631. *Simũ wa Mũkamba nĩ mbu.*[6] **The telephone of Mũkamba is wailing.**
This emerged between the 1920s and 1990s, when telephones became common. Before that, information was largely word of mouth. It means if you need help make some noise.

1632. *Kwĩ silanga na maia ĩndĩ mwiso wasyo no ũkanga.* **There are dams and lakes, but the ocean is largest.**
This emerged during the twentieth century, given the term *silanga* (dam reservoir), artificial water catchments constructed from the 1920s. There are no major lakes in Ũkamba, but Kenya's two major rivers pass through Ũkambanĩ.

1633. *Mwĩnzi wa silanga tiwe mũnywi wa kĩw'ũ kyawo.* **The digger of a dam does not drink water from the dam.**
This is an expression of some truth that builders of dams often do not drink water from it. They are paid and move on with their activities elsewhere. Most endeavours benefit other people, just as parents accumulate wealth not for themselves but for posterity.

1634. *Nzũngĩ yautwa mũtu ĩtwĩkaa yondo.* **A basket full of flour becomes an old basket when the flour is pinched.**
This is a figurative statement referring to stages of development of a girl. It means that once a girl is exposed to sex, she ceases to be a virgin and engages in sex throughout her life in the same way a basket is used

---

[5] Jeremiah Kitunda, Jerry Fox, Joel Gazier, and Emily Smith, 'The Effect of Child Labor in Africa on the Cell Phone Industry', *International Journal of Information Systems and Change Management* 6(2) (December 2012): 147–59.
[6] Kimilu, *Mũkamba*, 58; Mbiti, *Weteelete*, 90.

consistently. The maxim is also a commentary on girls who had an unplanned pregnancy. Their personal worth was damaged like an old basket, few men admired them. The proverb condemns exploitation of other people. It also warned the listener to be vigilant in romantic relationships.

1635. *Kĩkavũ nĩnauta mũtu nĩkĩtaa kyondo.* **A big basket whose flour content has been pinched becomes a small basket.**
This axiom compares modern Swahili and traditional baskets, depicting the modern basket as better. It implies things depreciate in value over time. A new Kamba basket is attractive, but as it ages it transitions to a mere junk receptacle. The maxim has sexual meanings: once a girl conceives she can only marry an old man.

1636. *Mũndũ mũima ndekalaa ate ndĩnĩ.* **An adult does not live without debt.**
In the 1930s a white man named Paul was in charge of limestone mining in eastern Kitui. He owned an old lorry that frequently broke down, but he never paid the cost of repairs whenever he took it to the mechanic. Upon his return to the camp he would call out his African assistant (*Mnyampara*) in broken Swahili: '*Nyampara! Hii gari kwisha tengenezwa mzuri. Lakini pesa bando Lipa. Mtu mkubwa kama mimi ukosa deni namgani?*' This translates to, 'Overseer! This lorry has been repaired so well but I have not paid yet. How will a big man like myself live without debt?' The Kamba turned these words into their own catchphrase, meaning in capitalist societies debts are part of life. It also means 'Man errs, forgive me for my blunder.'

1637. *Nduka ĩsu ũlea noyo wĩthooa ngua.* **The shop you rejected is the same that you will buy clothes from.**
This emerged after the First World War when textile shops emerged in trade centres across Ũkamba. It points to the vital role that the shop came to play in the psyche of the Kamba during the twentieth century. The Kamba were no longer making their clothes or sending expeditions to the coast for bales of clothes. Shops were the place to go to now. The axiom admonishes the listener to be careful in disputes. Do not sever links with those whom you may need in the near future. Do not be too selective and dismissive.

1638. *Ngũkũ ĩmĩaa nyũmba nũndũ ndĩvikĩla konzi.* **The hen drops inside the house because it cannot reach the latch.**
This axiom emerged during the twentieth century since *konzi* (door bolts) was derived from Swahili and colonial culture. It circulated in Kĩkamba radio programmes from the 1980s and talks about things that people resort to because of lack of alternatives. Hidden in it is the story

of diminishing job opportunities in the 1970s and justification of odd measures that youth resorted to as means of survival.

1639. *Thimaa wĩanu wa ndũnyũ na nduka ti ndũũka.* **Measure the development of a town by shops not the population of its lunatics.**
This appears in the poems of Mutisya Mbatha, but has historical precedents stretching to the early 1900s.[7] It reflects how urbanization progressed in Ũkambanĩ during the 1900s and how locals measured economic progress. Towns were considered developed not just by the number of businesses but also by the population of lunatics attracted by food scraps in dumpsters. In short, their growth went hand in hand with invasions by people with mental illness. It is a polite way of telling someone to not be silly.

1640. *Ndũnyũ ĩkĩawa vinya nĩ ala matũnyaa vo.* **Shoppers energize a market.**
There is a link between the wealth of a people and the development of a marketplace. Rich people build strong towns with sufficient revenue to pay for social amenities. The proverb emerged between 1915 and 1955.

1641. *Ndũnyũ nĩ tene, kata mbanga nĩ kĩtoo na mũkwatangano.* **The market is early in the morning; at noon it is commotion and touching.**
This depicts a typical Kamba marketplace. As Stanner observed, 'In the dust and chatter of the *ndũnyũ*, where often 1000 people come together to buy, sell, gossip, and flirt, the pulse of these influences (of the markets) beats strongly.'[8] The *soko* (borrowed from Swahili) refers to the marketplace, while *ndũnyũ* denotes exchange – buying and selling. The proverb reveals the way this exchange was conducted. The exchange began at about ten o'clock in the morning. By noon, the place was noisy, buzzing with people and filled with sales items. At that time competition of all sorts gave an image of confusion emerging from the din of people and animals.

1642. *Ndũnyũ ya isũlĩ ĩtũnyawa nĩ makoto.* **Hornbills enjoy the marketplace of the common dwarf mongoose.**
The symbiotic relationship between hornbills and common dwarf mongooses is unclear to most Kamba. While some believe that the mongoose mates with hornbills the truth is that common dwarf mongooses scratch here and there on the ground seeking food. In the process they raise all kinds of bugs that hornbills eat, hence the moral – symbiosis is beneficial.

---

[7] Mutisya wa Ngai, Mumbunĩ (Machakos), personal communication, 26 October 2019.
[8] Stanner, 'Kamba Market', 63.

1643. *Nthũngĩ ya ũkua isyo ndũnyũ yokotheawa nthanga mĩongo mingĩ yambwe.* **Scores of threads are twined to stabilize the shopping basket.**
The common carriers of merchandise in Ũkamba were woven baskets (*nthũngĩ*) of different sizes and colours. Their strength derived from strong strings, twisted to make them even firmer. As a result, the more strings the better for carrying valuables. This proverb – coined during the early years of the colonial era when trading centres (*ndũnyũ*) opened across Ũkamba – admonishes that to achieve something permanent and good one had to invest heavily. Weaving proverbs also encode examples of how women organized and encouraged weaving work among the younger generations of women.

1644. *Vai soko ĩte mũũki.* **There is no market without a mad person.**
Apparently nearly all towns in Ũkamba have at least one person who is mentally ill, a phenomenon of the colonial era. The rise of urban space in Kenya during the colonial period corresponded with deteriorating public health and sanitary conditions. After the First World War, newly created trade centres began to hold weekly market fairs (in Swahili, *soko*) with merchandise from near and far. Mentally ill people and stray dogs became welcome members of these marketplaces. The establishment of Mathari Asylum in Nairobi for mentally ill Africans reflects the magnitude of mental illness before the 1920s. As official and societal negligence of this aspect of health continued, the population of mentally ill persons increased to the extent that every town in Kenya had at least one mentally ill person roaming the streets, ignored by the state and society. Madness became a measure of the growth of a town, confusing its development with hygienic deterioration. This proverb has two connotations: first, a market is madness, has madness wandering freely in it; and second, a lack of proper care and attention to boundaries allows madness to spread, implying a need for controls and regulation of markets. At a symbolic level this proverb from the early twentieth century means there are causes for everything in life.

1645. *Vai soko ndatwaĩa ndĩa.* **There is no market I cannot hoop roll.**
This is an expression of defiance against colonialism and social restrictions of the early twentieth century. The marketplace was out of bounds to African children so fond of hoop roll. Therefore, if the speaker overcame such restrictions, it means he was invincible. The market was a vehicle to communicate something about romance and immoral conduct. It means that no one would stop the speaker from doing what he wants even if society and state consider it illegal.[9]

---

[9] O.F. Raum, 'The Rolling Target (Hoop-and-Pole) Game in Africa', *African Studies* 12(3) (1953): 104; Cullen Gouldsbury, *The Great Plateau of Northern Rhodesia* (E. Arnold, 1911), 273.

1646. *Vai nduka ndaĩĩsya kĩsululu.* **There is no shop I cannot lean a bicycle against.**
Said to mean anything can satisfy, this axiom is an instance where the market is depicted in the context of moral decay in colonial Ũkamba. The act of leaning a bicycle, which had no stand, is a symbolic euphemism for sex. Rough men and womanizers used this to express their nature, that nothing would stop them from getting any female they desired. The bicycle introduced in Ũkamba shortly after shops were established symbolized moral behaviour. Leaning it means having sex with someone. The shop is a symbol of any female – girl or woman. The speaker means he can sleep with any woman regardless of age and social relation.

1647. *Wĩmwoo ta vombo wa kamii.* **You are as rare as a wheelbarrow pressure pump.**
This dates to the period after the First World War when wheelbarrows were introduced in Kenya. The wheelbarrow had one pressurized rubber wheel to last for many years. Unlike bicycles and automobile tyres, there were no pressure pumps sold in Ũkamba for pumping up the tyre on this particular device. The maxim is a simple expression of rarity.

1648. *Wĩwi ndwĩ ndũnyũ, wĩnaw'o vau ũũngy'e.* **Obedience is not in the market, you have it where you stand.**
Elders from the 1920s said this to the young. It depicts the marketplace as the ultimate centre of authority and a place where all-important things could be retrieved or accessed. One of the things that could not be obtained from the marketplace was obedience, however, a virtue highly valued in Kamba society. The maxim meant that one did not have to be potty-trained in obedience.

1649. *Kĩtambaa kĩkekala kĩmanyĩkaa na kĩtatw'a na ũito wakyo.* **A durable garment is known by its thickness and weight.**
This proverb means that someone who can perform a given task is known right away by his first action. A potential bride is known early. The word *kĩtambaa* is a Swahili-loaned word, which indicates that the proverb emerged during the 1900s when Swahili trade in clothes expanded to inland markets.

1650. *Kũla syumaa nĩsyĩvwĩkawa.* **Where 'clothes come from', there they are worn too.**
This refers to importation of clothes from distant lands during the Monsoon era. People do not produce what they do not consume: those who manufacture clothes themselves wear them. Figuratively, it means people need the same resources that they avail to others. It stresses the significance of reciprocity. Moreover, it assumes, and proclaims, a close,

experiential symbiosis between manufacture and use, between local labour and local taste. It also, more subtly, suggests that trade ought to be a channel by which needs and surpluses are balanced.[10]

1651. *Kavuti kekumbaa ta mwene.* **An overcoat curves in the shape of the wearer.**
This emerged after the Second World War when Africans began to wear Western-style suits and overcoats. Before the war, it was illegal for natives to dress like Europeans. Afterwards missionaries began to give used coats to African clergymen and other associates. Observers noted that the coats conformed to one's body shape, hence the proverb. The actual meaning is that there are certain rules that cannot be changed. Even if you cover them with a coat, it will reveal them.

1652. *Ve kũsya yaana ũvũthanĩtye na ĩkũmi.* **You may lose a hundred while chasing after ten.**
This emerged from the 1960s when Kenya minted banknotes of ten and one hundred shillings. In some business transactions, and through the ploys of conmen, some people lost one hundred shillings in the hope that, if they invested it in the black market, it would yield an extra ten shillings, making the total in the pocket one hundred and ten. When that did not happen, the moral lesson was that it is not worth quarreling over minor things as they may cost dearly.

1653. *Kambũni ya tũmisi yaminwa nĩ kambũni ya mbaĩka.* **The biker-pants company finished off the petticoat company.**
From about the Second World War Kamba women adopted European dresses worn with petticoats called *tũmisi* (plural). Up to the 1980s, petticoats were fashionable, but in the 1990s, as new undergarments called bikers (so-called because it was adopted from the tied short pants that cyclists used) appeared. Unlike the petticoat that was worn for beauty, the biker was for protecting thighs from friction. It quickly eroded the petticoat industry. The proverb emerged in the late 1990s and spread through music, radio, and the rural–urban population movement. The maxim means that a new commodity replaces the old and gives birth to new forms of wit and wisdom. In other words, people have to change with the times.

1654. *Vau nĩ vathei vove na ĩthangũ.* **That is a vanity wrapped in paper.**
This emerged from the Second World War as shopkeepers began to use old newspapers as wraps for sales that they gave to customers. The wrap gave the impression that the inside content was valuable.

---

[10] Mutisya, *Proverbs*, 41.

The maxim implies that a wrap can be given to someone with nothing inside. Things that have less value were equated with 'nothing in the wrap', to be distinguished from the Western concept of 'That's a wrap!' so common in the film industry, meaning that it is completed.

1655. *Kala ndūtūaa kīthembenī.* **A sloshing sound does not last in a barrel.**
Here *kala*, 'splattering sound', represents good things. Honey kept in barrels was one such good thing, but it lasted only a short while. This observation was extended to human possessions and situations. The proverb thus means good things are not permanent.

1656. *Kīthembe kīminawa nī ūseki ūmwe.*[11] **A honey barrel is drained by a piece of grass.**
The Kamba often drew honey out of honey barrels using a piece of green grass, and then licked the honey from the grass. This insignificant dipping eventually drained the honey out of the barrel. The ancient proverb means that a challenging task can be done bit by bit or, viewed negatively, many small mistakes lead to a tragic end.

1657. *Kīthembe kīu kiū nīkyo kī ūkī.* **The black keg is the one with honey.**
Persistent use darkened the wooden honey keg dressed with skins. The longer a keg was used, the darker it became and the better the quality of honey it contained. The proverb means that, despite the unappealing physical appearance, its quality still abides. So, do not underestimate the value of older, weaker-looking things.

1658. *Kīthembe nīkyo kīkuaa.* **The honey barrel carries itself.**[12]
This ancient proverb concerns self-reliance, independence, and resourcefulness. Because a keg carried valuable honey, the owner could hire someone to carry it and pay him in honey. Likewise, rich people are independent and rely on their own resources.

1659. *Ngelekanio ti kīthembe.*[13] **An example is not a honey barrel.**
The honey barrel was a delicate and important vessel requiring careful handling. The Kamba held that, if one wanted to demonstrate how something fell from the sky, the honey barrel was not a good example. This is an ancient axiomatic warning against mishandling delicate matters.

---

[11] Kimilu, *Mūkamba*, 116; Mutisya, *Proverbs*, 70.
[12] Kimilu, *Mūkamba*, 116.
[13] Kimilu, *Mūkamba*, 117.

1660. *Mboloi ya kĩtai ndĩkavũkaa kĩtavikĩte.* **A hooked stick of tragedy does not break until tragedy arrives.**
While the hooked stick for hauling fencing thorn bushes often broke, frustrating the farmer, metaphorically, a hooked stick hauling misfortune never breaks before catastrophe arrives. The proverb points out that harmful habits are hard to stop. The stubbornness of the individual is equated with *mboloi* while the accident is likened to the thorn bush. Stubbornness leads to calamity.

1661. *Mboloi ĩkusĩtye mbanga ndĩkavũkaa.* **A hooked stick hauling misfortune does not break.**
As stated in the previous entry, another common use of the hooked stick was to snag thorny bushes and drag them for use in fencing and blocking the gates at night. Under such weight, the hook often broke. Five proverbs relate to this device and they all allude to tragedies. Each variant is unique, reflecting the central role that *mboloi* played in Kamba villages. As testimony to the popularity of this adage, many variants circulate orally, of which at least two have appeared in literature.[14]

1662. *Mboloi ya mbanga ndyanĩkaa myatũ.* **A hooked stick of tragedy does not dangle beehives.**
From the Monsoon era, the Kamba developed two ways of hanging beehives on trees. One was to set the beehive between branches on a stable bend in the branch, enhanced with a strong peg driven through the beehive and securely into the branch itself. The second way was using a hooked or forked branch called *mboloi* or *ngolya*, which was tied to a branch on one end while the beehive dangled on the other. The hooked branch was used for many other purposes, sometimes ending in tragedy, like killing a snake or whacking an opponent. Such *mboloi* was not fit for dangling beehives. In the Kamba lore, *mboloi* represents a means to an end while the beehive symbolizes valuable things. Literally, it would be suicidal to hang beehives with hooked sticks that had been involved in accidents. Rising from the Monsoon Exchange era, the proverb means that careless people cannot handle weighty public matters.

1663. *Mwanĩki wa myatũ ambaa kwĩyanĩka.* **The beehive hanger hangs himself first.**
Someone setting beehives in trees first finds a stable place on the tree where he can sit. This implies that if one wants to do something, he must have a proper foundation.

---

[14] Mutisya, *Proverbs*, 53, Mbiti, *Ngaeka*, 99.

1664. *Mwatũ wa kĩvĩsĩ ndũkwatasya.* **The beehive of a boy never traps bees.**
This is an axiomatic condemnation of anxious and tactless actions. During the Monsoon era, the Kamba carved beehives and hung them in tall trees to attract bees. The process was carefully done with a fairly natural environment maintained for the bees. Boys, naturally inexperienced at this, grew impatient and drove the bees away by constantly checking and disturbing the beehive.

1665. *Mwatũ wa mbengei ndũlika ndũti.*[15] **Red ants cannot enter the beehive of an expert carver.**
Contrary to its plain meaning, this axiom censures boastfulness and cockiness. Hollowed tree-trunk hives had lids on both sides with tiny holes so expertly carved that only bees could enter or exit. If not done right, snakes and rodents could also enter. Certain tiny ants, smaller than bees, often invaded, driving out the bees. While experts could prevent snakes and rodents from entering with well-fashioned lids it was impossible to prevent such tiny ants from entering. This is a sarcastic rebuke against boasting about something that one cannot do.

1666. *Mwatũ wemaa kĩtheka tyo mũndũ.* **The forest defeats the beehive and less will a man persevere there.**
This is a popular old adage that is often posed in question form, *Kĩtheka kyemaa mwatũ no mũndũ?* 'If the forest defeats the beehive, how much more for a person?'[16] It means that even though a beehive is destined to stay in the forest forever it can collapse and be retrieved from the forest and taken home. While a beehive remains in the forest where it was placed, people return home no matter how long they stay in foreign lands. This was said when a family member who had been away returned permanently. It was coined during periods of migration towards the coast, Kilimanjaro and mainland Tanzania, Mount Kenya, and the Tana and Athi River Basins of Kenya.

1667. *Myatũ myathe na mbengeo syayo.* **Fierce beehives and their lids.**
This is an old exclamation said when two disagreeable parties disengaged. It alludes to beekeeping where, if the beehive had fierce bees, the harvester replaced the lid and fled. If women were fed up with marriage, they left everything behind and invoked this maxim as explanation. Thus, if you find something unbearable, leave it immediately.

---

[15] Kimilu, *Mũkamba*, 117.
[16] Mwau, *Dictionary*, 650.

1668. *Ndingũ ya myatũ yaina ũlĩsa ndĩkũlasya mwene.* **The honey badger does not ask permission of the beehive owner when it climbs to the hive.**
This ancient maxim alludes to honey badgers as the main vermin in apiculture. The honey badger climbed to the site of the beehive, got under the hive, lifted it off the pegs securing it, and let it fall to the ground. As the hive split and bees scattered the honey badger climbed down and enjoyed the honey. This act symbolizes men who misuse other people's resources or flirt with their wives.

1669. *Ndumbĩ nzeo ndĩkosaa mwatũ.* **A good flat surface on a tree lacks no beehive.**
This proverb represents a compliment, rewarding good behaviour and action. In Kamba apiculture, beehives were hung on trees with good bases between branches. The proverb means something like, a good shop cannot lack customers. Good things are attractive.

1670. *Ndia nĩ ndũyũ, yasaa mwatũ na ndĩsaa ũkĩ.* **A fool is like *ndũyũ*, it carves a beehive, yet it cannot eat honey.**
This axiom alludes to the tools used for carving beehives. Sir John Thorp described and illustrated one of them as *thia*, a long handle with an iron blade fitted to one end by means of a leather ring (*ndũyũ*).[17] This leather ring, he explains, was formerly of rhinoceros hide, but by the 1900s it was made of palm-tree nuts called *ndũyũ* or *ngũyũ*. These were traded across the region for such purposes. Once fitted with such nuts, the tool, used for scraping out the barrel, was called *ndũyũ*. While the tool made all the beehives in Ũkamba, it was never rewarded with sweet honey from those beehives, just as a foolish man makes a good thing and fails to use it. The proverb has multiple interpretations, first as a warning against foolishness. The second is a condemnation against the malice of denying others resources of no use to themselves.

1671. *Ũkew'a mwatũ ũvengewa wasya nũkwanangwa.* **If you hear a beehive being prepared, you would assume it is being destroyed.**
With multiple published and unpublished variations, this proverb means that inexperienced people cannot distinguish between altercation and constructive dialogue.[18] To resolve matters, since antiquity the Kamba discussed them and often their heated discussion sounded like altercation so that passersby mistook discussions for quarrels and fights. In the context of this proverb, '*mwatũ*' symbolizes family or any

---

[17] John Thorp, 'African Bee Keepers: Notes on Methods and Customs Relating to the Bee- Culture of the Akamba Tribe in Kenya Colony', *JEAUNHS* 17(1943): 255–73.
[18] Kimilu, *Mũkamba*; Mutisya, *Proverbs*.

social unit, while 'destruction' symbolizes construction of the unit through serious dialogue. In democratic systems, for instance, parliamentary debates involve such heated debates that people from undemocratic systems may think that it will soon degenerate into physical conflict. Within Ũkamba, when passersby hear a dispute in a household or in a development planning committee, they may assume that the group is tearing things apart.

1672. *Akimi elĩ maileaa kũtinania myũthĩ.* **Two pounders never fail to rub their pestles.**
Men carved the mortar, which subsequently became an exclusive property of women for blending, processing, and grinding food. As two women (*akimi*) pounded grain in a mortar using two pestles, taking turns raising the pestles up and down, they hit each other's pestle, hence the proverb. The proverb circulated first among women. It points to inevitable conflict when people are put in a crowded space or compete for finite resources.[19]

1673. *Ĩtuvi ya mwasi wa ndĩĩ nĩ mũkimwa.* **The reward for a mortar maker is pounded grains.**
The carver was not paid but rewarded with food pounded with his mortar, an act with symbolic meanings. His blessings on the mortar ensured decades-long use, producing healthy food. This axiom means that good deeds are rewarded accordingly.

1674. *Kĩvindu kĩmanyanaa ona ndĩĩ.* **Only the mortar endures darkness.**
The Kamba kept their mortars standing overnight outside the home compound, which often scared passersbys who mistook the upright object in the dark as a person guarding the home. By interpretation, only the foolish man would stand in the dark as a mortar does.

1675. *Vate mũthĩ na ndĩĩ ndũkima mbemba.* **Without a mortar and pestle, one cannot pound corn.**
The historical marker here is corn (maize), which came with the Portuguese during the sixteenth century. During the 1500s, Kamba traders secured corn from coastal traders and spread it across East Africa.[20] The proverb is an expression of reciprocity and interdependence in social interaction. As much as neighbours need each other to build a village, a man needs a wife to build a family. The mortar and pestle symbolize male and female reproductive organs, with corn signifying the outcome of sex, a child.

---

[19] Mwau, *Dictionary*, 645.
[20] McCann, *Maize and Grace*.

1676. *Mwasi wa mũkanda nĩ mũsyĩmi wa nzana.* **The carver of musical drums is a hunter of the monitor lizard.**
As evident from oral accounts, written records, and museum collections in Kenya, Kamba musical drums were covered with skins of monitor lizards. The drum called *mũkanda* was made of a hollowed log and covered on both sides with monitor lizard skin. The carver's first step was to hunt for monitor lizards. Once found he finished the drum and returned to the bush, killed the reptile, and skinned it. The proverb alludes to complementarity and interdependence.[21]

1677. *Mwasi wa ivĩla ekalĩlaa kating'ĩ.* **The maker of seats sits on a stump.**
This ancient adage points to the ironies of Kamba industries. Experts in carving stools rarely carved good ones for themselves and their families. They carved for their social networks. Carving of household furniture began with the settlement in Ũkamba during the first millennium and continued to grow in sophistication until the nineteenth century when documentation about them appeared for the first time.

1678. *Ndũkasuke kĩthembe wĩkaĩle mwatũ.* **Do not slander the honey keg whilst sitting on the beehive.**
This axiom condemns ingratitude. The honey keg and beehive were interrelated vessels that the Kamba carved for apicultural purposes. Both were often sat on. While the beehive attracted bees, the Kamba used the keg for storage of honey. If someone while sitting on a beehive said the keg was bad, the message was that when the time comes to harvest honey you will need that keg.

1679. *Ndũkasuke muasĩ wĩkaĩle kĩvĩla.* **Do not gossip about the *muasĩ* (*Lannea schweinfurthii*) tree while sitting on a stool.**
The Kamba carved furniture predominantly from a tree called *muasĩ* (botanically called *Lannea schweinfurthii*), which was reverently given human attributes. The proverb appears to have emerged when the species became rare near villages. According to documented sources, depletion of natural resources began around the 1600s, causing Kamba to migrate from the Mboonĩ hills in different directions. This means the axiom emerged around the seventeenth century. There are many variations of this proverb. The moral message is that it is imprudent to gossip about someone in the presence of his relatives.[22] The deeper meaning is that one cannot slander in-laws and still expect to enjoy his or her marital relationship.

[21] George Senoga-Zake, *Folk Music in Kenya* (Nairobi: Uzima Press, 1981).
[22] Mutisya, *Proverbs*, 16.

1680. *Yasaa navinya ndyambaa.* **A strongly wielded adze makes no sound.**
Woodcarving with an adze was bound to be noisy, but with enough force the adze would make no sound.[23] The proverb is a deeply figurative statement: if one changes the rules of the game, the result will be unpleasant. Sometimes to avoid conflict, particularly during the colonial era, the Kamba protested against authority by quietly refusing to obey orders.

1681. *Mũtĩ ũte ngumbo ndwĩ ngomo.* **A branch without kinks has no adze handle.**
Ngomo refers to the handle of an adze and the adze itself, as well as the combination of the two. Woodcarving using adzes began in the 1300s, hence the emergence of the proverb. The axiom means that quality products often come from unattractive source materials.[24]

1682. *Ngomo ndĩyasũvasya.* **An adze does not carve itself.**[25]
To gain knowledge one should be educated by those who are learned in the subject. The proverb emerged during the Monsoon era with Kamba woodcarvings of furniture, tools, and other common products. Travelogues and ethnographic studies confirm that woodcarving was an established industry in Ũkamba during the Vascon era. The proverb alludes to the principal tool of woodcarving, which was normally made with an older one.

1683. *Ndũkavũthye mũtumĩa ngomo ĩla ngũũ nĩyo yasaa ĩla nzaũ.* **Do not mock an elder, the old adze shapes the new ones.**[26]
This ancient maxim alludes to the central role played by elders as patrons and matrons of the younger generations. Elders and experts used this proverb as self-defence against someone underrating them. Said in light moments or tense, it implies the speaker is more experienced in the matter at hand.

---

[23] Sultan Somjee, *Material Culture of Kenya* (Nairobi: East Africa Educational Publishers, 1993); Eugene Burt, *An Annotated Bibliography of the Visual Arts of East Africa* (Bloomington: Indian University Press, 1980); Andrew Tracey, 'Kamba Carvers', *African Music Society Journal* 2(3) (1960): 55–8.
[24] Kimilu, *Mũkamba*, 117; Mutisya, *Proverbs*, 45; Mwau, *Dictionary*, 660; Somjee, *Material Culture*.
[25] Somjee, *Material Culture*.
[26] Mwau, *Dictionary*, 646; Stephen Lammers and Allen Verhey (eds), *On Moral Medicine* (New York: Wm. B. Eerdmans Publishing Company, 1998), 926.

1684. *Ĩtava ĩnene ĩtũlĩaa mwene kĩko na yĩthanzasya kanyw'a.*[27] **A large scoop breaks one's spoon and enlarges the mouth.**
This statement combines two proverbs similar in meaning but different in structure. As they dined in groups from the same bowl, precolonial Kamba used wooden spoons. Some greedy partakers tried to take large scoops that broke the spoon, leaving them embarrassed. Hence the proverb, which means either 'a large scoop breaks the spoon but widens the mouth' or 'a large scoop breaks the spoon, yet it does not widen the mouth'. This means the person starves; so, never tackle a job bigger than you can manage.

1685. *Ĩlũkũ yũtoa nĩvĩvasya mbisũ.* **A smoking log also cooks a pot.**
The Kamba selected firewood carefully, but even their preferred woods emitted smoke. Used in the context of family feuds it meant that even straying family members are still useful and cannot be shunned. Other members have to tolerate their behaviour.

1686. *Kĩinga kĩminawa nĩ kasele.*[28] **A calabash bowl drains a silo.**
This is the opposite of *Kĩinga kyusũawa nĩ kasele*, 'a small calabash bowl fills a granary'. To store grains after threshing, the Kamba made large cylindrical containers out of twigs and tough grass. These containers, *kiinga* in singular, kept the grain safe from the elements and from vermin for a long period. They were filled and drained one bowl at a time. The proverb compares the power of the small bowl to fill or empty a large container. Thus, persistent work brings success.

1687. *Kakwĩthanda kayĩwoo.* **Self-thud is not painful.**
This axiom was first told to children when they threw objects into the sky that would then land on their own heads with a thud. The child was told to endure the pain that he inflicted on himself and to be more careful. Soon this extended to adults with the same message.

1688. *Andũ elĩ maithianĩaa ĩvianĩ ĩmwe.* **Two people do not simultaneously grind using the same grindstone.**
The proverb originated with women, the chief operators of these tools, meaning it is important to take turns. Unlike the mortar, the carving of a grindstone from rocks and its use was an exclusive innovation of women. The origin of this practice is as old as Kamba society but an archaeological analysis of relics of Kamba grindstone may reveal when

---

[27] Lindblom, *Riddles*, 29; Mwandia, *Kũsoma*, 47; Mailu, *Kĩkyambonie*, 61; Mutisya, *Proverbs*, 66; Mwau, *Dictionary*, 646.
[28] Kimilu, *Mũkamba*, 115; Mutisya, *Proverbs*, 70; Watuma, *Syĩthĩo*, 67.

the practice began. Oral traditions date the proverb to antiquity, as the grindstone itself.[29]

1689. *Ĩvia ĩtumbĩaa kũlĩta.*[30] **Stone crushes because of weight.**
This proverb refers specifically to a grindstone. The proverb emerged during the first millennium when women established stone-based food-processing systems in Ũkamba. Grindstones litter forests, deserted precolonial home sites, and burial sites across Ũkamba needing urgent archaeological study. The meaning of this axiom is far removed from stones. It implies that resources matter and one's ability to accomplish anything is dependent on resources.

1690. *Ĩvia ĩthiaa na ĩngĩ.* **A grindstone grinds with a stone.**
The grindstone was the anchor of life in every home since antiquity but by itself it could not accomplish its function. A grindstone required a grinder to process food, and other necessities. This proverb was said to emphasize the importance of complementary roles between husbands and wives. Thus, it means for anything good to endure, complementary resources are essential.

1691. *Ĩvia yĩmwe ĩtyũaa tũsũni twĩlĩ.* **One stone does not kill two birds.**
Stones were extensively used as hunting weapons for small game and birds. The ancient Kamba realized that, practically, one could kill two birds with one stone. The maxim was a condemnation of double-dealing.[31] It means achievements are incremental and one should work step by step.

1692. *Kavila kala kavũthũ nĩko kakimaa kasũni nayo yĩla ĩnene nĩyo yĩtuĩkaa mũomo.* **The small stone shoots the bird, the big stone anchors the door.**
An important axiom meaning that while leaders handle great affairs of family and society, subordinates handle minor matters. In the past the Kamba hunted birds with stones, thrown by hand with precision.

1693. *Komangaa ĩvia no ũkomanga nthio.* **Sharpen both the grinder and the grindstone.**
This ancient proverb appears in many songs implying blame should never go to one party in any dispute.[32] Consequently, be fair in settling controversial issues. The maxim can also be used to cajole college

---

[29] Mwau, *Dictionary*, 645.
[30] Mwau, *Dictionary*, 648.
[31] Mwau, *Dictionary*, 648.
[32] Mutisya, *Proverbs*, 20.

students to critical evaluation of primary sources and to interrogate documentary evidence.

1694. *Kũtata ĩvia nĩkũthia nayo.*[33] **To try a grindstone is to grind with it.**
When a woman needed a new grindstone, she called a group of women to accompany her to a site where loose rocks abounded and carved a suitable size and shape. Then she set up her new grindstone on the ground and tried to grind sand. Thus, obviously, try something out first. Symbolically, the grindstone is a woman. If a man wants to marry a particular girl, it would be beneficial to court her for some time and sleep with her before they marry.

1695. *Vamwe vatũawa nĩ ĩvia.*[34] **Only the rock abides in one place.**
In this ancient proverb the word rock is a euphemism for a fool. It means the rock never moves, but people should. Disagreeable parties should change their attitudes, forgive, and forget their disputes.

1696. *Mũsyĩ wĩ mũtumĩa ndũwaa ĩnoo.* **A homestead with an elder lacks no whetstone.**
A man was associated with certain indispensable tools symbolizing different aspects of life, one being the whetstone for sharpening blades symbolizing advice, counselling, and training of the young. Where there is an elder, there is no lack of counselling and training. Future archaeological studies of remains of such whetstones might yield more information regarding Ũkambanĩ during the first millennium when this proverb emerged.

1697. *Mũsyĩ wĩ ĩnoo ndũtuvasya ĩthoka.* **A home with whetstones never blunts axes.**
The whetstone symbolizes an old man as the anchor of the family, whereas the axe symbolizes male members of the family schooled and admonished by the elder. The proverb describes the virtues of a whetstone – it renews the axe blade, extending its usefulness. It depicts the important role played by elders in family, community, and society.

1698. *Nthio kwatũka tikwo mwisyo wa ĩkie.* **The splintering of the grinder is not the end of mealiepap.**
The grinder was indispensable in the use of the grindstone. If the grinder splintered for any reason the family faced starvation. Yet the proverb is also a statement of hope. There are many alternatives, so do not give up.

---

[33] Kimilu, *Mũkamba*, 64, 116.
[34] Kimilu, *Mũkamba*, 119.

1699. *Ndũkasyũlie ũlii ĩvianĩ.* **Do not strip fibre out of a rock.**
This warns against attempting the impossible. It emerged during the Monsoon era with the use of vegetable cordage for multiple purposes. The Kamba extracted fibre from trees and shrubs as early as the birth of Christ. In the 800s, Arab-Muslim geographers and historians portrayed the Kamba along the coast as practitioners of such skills. This implies that they had been using fibre back to the Monsoon era.

1700. *Mũkwatanĩsya mbisũ ilĩ ĩmwe nĩyũngũaa.* **One who cooks with two pots burns one.**
There are several published variants of this adage, from 1911 to 2011.[35] These have been used since antiquity to caution against double-dealing, greed, and other excesses. Older women used it to explain to younger women the necessity of doing one chore at a time. In a deeper sense in polygamous households, a man can only handle one woman at a time.

1701. *Mbisũ ĩla yuaa mavĩndĩ ma nzou yũaawa nĩ mavũi ma ngũngũ.*[36] **Chicken lungs eventually break the pot that cooks elephant bones.**
Dating from the seventeenth century, this proverb refers to power relations at different levels of society. A weakling can bring down the strongest. Elephant bones symbolize the pinnacle of power while the soft chicken lungs represent the lowest ebb of power. No matter how strong or privileged, the strong can be outwitted and defeated.

1702. *Mbisũ ngũũ ĩtyaa wũmea.*[37] **An old pot never lacks crust.**
This proverb dates from the invention of pottery during the first millennium. Coined by women who did the cooking it is deeply figurative with many interpretations and applications. The longer the pot cooked, one interpretation says, the darker it became and the more it retained bits of food scraps, called *wũmea*. This means an old pot is beneficial. The second interpretation, based on a translation of the word *wũmea*, reinterprets the proverb as saying 'An old pot lacks no injury.' This means an older person is weak, having endured so many challenges.

1703. *Mbisũ ya ũmanzi ndimbaa ũvũyũ ũketĩka.* **A pot of wealth creation does not boil to overflowing.**
Dating to the Monsoon era when pottery emerged as an industry among Kamba women, this proverb means, among other things, that wealth is built slowly rather than rapidly. As the women cooked, whatever it was – usually a mixture of water and food – always made foam on top. Once

---

[35] Lindblom, *Akamba*; Farnsworth, *Grammar*, 133; Kimilu, *Mũkamba*, 119; Mutisya, *Proverbs*, 64; Mwau, *Dictionary*, 670.
[36] Mwau, *Dictionary*, 655.
[37] Mwau, *Dictionary*, 655.

the foam subsided, it was assumed that the cooking was over and the food was ready for consumption. The proverb suggests that is not the case with building wealth.

1704. *Mbisũ yavya ĩsamawa na kĩvũli.* **When a pot is done, it is tasted with a ladle.**
According to oral traditions collected in the 1890s, the Kamba initially cooked in shells. After a medicine woman discovered the art of making pottery during the first millennium, pots were made for cooking. Once the food was cooked, the Kamba used a ladle to check its condition. This points to the significance of a complementary role in community life. The pot and the ladle are complementary, and so also should humans have a complementary role.

1705. *Mũmbi wa mbisũ auaa na ilĩo.* **The potter cooks with broken potshards.**
This is analogous to 'A cobbler's child has no shoes.' While potters made elegant pots for sale, they rarely possessed good ones of their own. It advises people with skills to tend to their families while helping others. It also warns against mocking potters for the crudeness of their vessels – the potter is not stupid.

1706. *Kĩtete kĩ ĩtina nĩkyo kĩtwĩkanasya.* **A bottlegourd with a base supports itself.**[38]
This proverb originated from a farming context during the Monsoon era. Bottlegourds, which were the prime liquid vessels in precolonial Ũkamba, had either flat or cylindrical bases. The two shapes symbolized stability and instability of all kinds. Extoling self-reliance, the proverb figuratively means that resourceful people do not need to beg for support. They can thrive on their own. The proverb was used during dowry negotiations, pointing to the bridegroom's ability to entertain the in-laws and pay the required dowry.

1707. *Kĩkuu kĩtumawa na ũluuti.*[39] **A gourd is stitched up with needle string.**
Whenever bottlegourds broke they were expertly and beautifully sewn with two sticks and two strings, the combination of which was called *ũluuti* – the pusher. Wax and fibre were lined up along the crack to make it waterproof. The proverb emphasizes the merits of joint action and cooperation in the workplace, within the family, community, and state using the right tools and approaches.

---

[38] Lindblom, *Riddles*, 31; Kimilu, *Mũkamba*, 115; Kituku, *Folktales*, 67.
[39] Lindblom, *Riddles*, 31; Mutisya, *Proverbs*, 70.

1708. *Ua ūla ūūtwekya nīw'o ūthaawa.* **The calabash that winnows is sealed first.**
When gourd vessels broke or cracked they were expertly sewn together again, a process called *kūthaa*, to sew. The proverb calls for prioritization. The most urgent and important matter is the one that deserves more attention.

1709. *Kīkuu kīūaīwa kwaa yia.* **A bottlegourd is not broken for lack of milk.**
Bottlegourds were commonly used as reservoirs for milk storage. It would be unimaginable if one broke such a container because it did not have milk. One cannot blame the gourd for lack of milk. The person ought to put milk into the gourd and consume it sparingly. In that sense, the axiom is about blame and how to treat accidents.

1710. *Kīkuu kīmwe kiigaatasya kalūvū na kalia saa ūmwe.* **A single gourd does not ferment milk and beer at the same time.**
This emerged in the early twentieth century when beer called *kalūvū* began to be made from sugar. However, the bottlegourd used for brewing beer was never used for fermenting milk. This talks about separation of duties for different family members.

1711. *Kīkuu kīseo nīkyatūawa nzele.* **A good gourd is split into a calabash.**
This truism reflects the Kamba fascination with gourds. Calabash bowls were made from attractive gourds. This means a well-behaved child is rewarded accordingly or an industrious worker is rewarded with promotion and monetary benefits.

1712. *Kusu wī kīkuunī ndūtūaa.* **Sloshing in a bottlegourd does not last long.**
This implies that liquids inside the gourd made a sloshing sound described as *kusu*. Since the Monsoon era, variations of this adage have been used to mean that nothing is permanent. A colleague told me of a story that involved migration with the family livestock. On the trail, they put the cow's milk in a leather container and tied it to the ox's tether. As the ox lumbered along, the milk in the leather turned to butter, something that doesn't slosh.

1713. *Sava ndwīsavasya.* **A clattering does not make itself.**
This was twisted from the previous entry to mean that people have to act in order to better their lives. Nothing makes itself for people to enjoy, they have to create their own sources of joy. There is a reason for everything. Dramatic changes have to be made occasionally to perpetuate communal life.

1714. *Vata wa kĩkuu no kũkaatya.* **A gourd's purpose is to ferment.**
In order to make liquids sour, the Kamba put the liquids in bottlegourds that were selected for that specific purpose. This proverb means that, as long as the goal is achieved, the end justifies the means. It justifies use of substitutes that satisfy immediate needs. Otherwise, quality does not matter so long as the object serves its purpose.

1715. *Kaula katune katunĩvaw'a nĩ ũnengelanĩlwe.* **A red calabash bowl is made red by changing hands.**
Emerging from the Vascon era, this adage appears in at least five earlier publications.[40] Watuma explained the context succinctly. Women used to exchange gifts of oiled food in beautiful, small calabash bowls, which were returned with another serving of oiled food. Consequently, the calabash became red because of the oil. Red symbolized beauty, friendship, and romance.
The moral lesson was friendship is predicated upon the exchange of gifts.

1716. *Kyakw'a mwĩta kĩtisyokaa mwĩta.*[41] **If it breaks full, it does not return full.**
What is done cannot be restored. This is said when someone suffers an irrecoverable loss. The proverb emerged from the practice of collecting water in bottlegourds, which broke quite often leading to loss of precious water. The practice of fetching water in gourds emerged from the 1100s when cultivation of such gourds increased, and hence the creation of this proverb.

1717. *Kĩsengũla kĩyeendaa nesa kelĩ.* **A broken piece of a gourd does not go straight twice.**
Broken gourds littering home compounds had various purposes. Children often played with them by throwing them at some desired target. While one might luckily hurl one straight at the target, it was hard to repeat success. This axiom calls on people to be careful with opportunities that can slip away.

1718. *Aathĩa ũanĩ.*[42] **He shot at the bowstring.**
Dating back to the Monsoon era, this proverb has multiple meanings. One cannot shoot at the bowstring because that is where the base of the arrow launches. Whenever a good hunter aimed at an animal, he knew he would hit the target before he released the arrow. Symbolically the terse statement is about a third person with a connotation of simul-

---

[40] Lindblom, *Riddles*, 34; Watuma, *Syĩthĩo*, 52; Mwau, *Dictionary*, 648.
[41] Lindblom, *Riddles*, 34.
[42] Kimilu, *Mũkamba*, 115.

taneous negation and affirmation. In negation, the person in question tried in vain an arduous task and failed. In affirmation, it can mean someone got something easily without much effort.

1719. *Atumĩa matumaa ndoo nduãnĩ ĩkĩnyunga.*[43] **Elders repair a stinking sheath in the village.**
This is an old saying regarding the crucial role elders played in maintaining harmony within their villages. *Ndoo* was a hide-sheath for a sword. Exposed to water, the hide-sheath inevitably began to stink. Seen as a bad omen, experienced elders opened, cleaned, and resealed it symbolizing the sealing of the bad omen. Adult men remain calm and bear with many unpleasant things. The proverb stresses the importance of a neighbour who is useful at critical moments and should be respected.

1720. *Ĩkoota ĩnene nĩya mwene kwĩkya.* **A long draw of the bowstring belongs to the shooter.**
Archery involves various skills and tricks. Some draw and release their arrows quickly while others aim and concentrate on drawing to ensure targeted game is hit squarely. The maxim means a risky action belongs to whoever decides to take that particular action. It cautions against greed. Do whatever you are doing but the buck stops with you. In short, the proverb means a man is worth his ambition.[44]

1721. *Walea kwĩkya na vanda wĩ mũnini ndũlea kwĩkya wakũa.* **If you do not use the slingshot in your youth, you will do so in your old age.**
The word *vanda* (slingshot), made in part from rubber, is the peculiar historical marker in this proverb. The rise of the rubber industry in the world between the 1890s and 1920s inspired many innovations around the globe including Ũkamba. The slingshot, in part made from discarded tyre tubes, was one of the most spectacular examples of such innovations. This powerful new weapon appeared in Ũkamba in the 1920s as a direct borrowing, or with slight modifications, from European slingshots. Subsequently, as the slingshot became fashionable among Kamba youth, several proverbs, including the current one, emerged out of its use during the interwar period.[45]

---

[43] Kimilu, *Mũkamba*, 115.
[44] Robert Hardy, *Longbow* (London: Bois d'Arc Press, 1992), 24–7.
[45] John Munro, 'British Rubber Companies in East Africa Before the First World War', *Journal of African History* 24 (1983), 368–79.

1722. *Kakwĩtema kayĩ woo.* **A self-inflicted cut is not painful.**[46]
This means it is futile to complain of loss resulting from one's irresponsible action. It emerged out of the context of the Kamba making knives and swords from iron. The knife was sharpened for various purposes. The sharp blade would cause injury if the user was careless. Those nearby used this adage to inform the victim that they were responsible for the injury and should endure it.

1723. *Ndwoona ke kakũe ndoonĩ.* **You have never seen it drawn from the sheath.**
During the first millennium, the sword and sheath, bow and arrows were popular weapons. Evidently, the Kamba were using such weapons along the coast and Kilimanjaro during the Islamic era. During heated arguments the speaker used this maxim to warn the opponents that he/she was crossing the line and dire consequences would follow soon after.

1724. *Mwaĩki ndatiaa wenzi.*[47] **The circumciser does not leave behind a blade.**
Circumcision experts possessed and always carried the sharpest blade among precolonial Kamba whenever they travelled. The symbolic meaning of the proverb is that the principal object of production should be kept close.

1725. *Vai ũta ũtaatha onaethwa nĩ wa mũvou.* **Any bow can shoot, even one made of *mũvou* tree.**
While unsuitable for archery, even a bow of the soft wood *mũvou* (a medicinal plant) will shoot. Emerging during the Islamic era, this maxim is an expression of principles that remain constant. A bow – no matter the quality and no matter the output – is a bow. The proverb symbolically refers to male abilities: men irrespective of age were able to engage in sex. It was also applied in defence of someone who is disparaged as inconsequential. The defender implied that he had his own strengths and achievements.

1726. *Ũta nĩ mũvaũ.* **The bow is the *mũvaũ* tree.**
During the Islamic period the Kamba were certainly using bows made from *mũtuuva* (*Grewia similis*) shrubs and later from *mũvaũ* trees, as evident in colonial literature. The best bow was that made from *mũvaũ* and, by extrapolation, the quality of an object is determined by what it is made of. A person is worth the material he/she is made of.[48]

---

[46] Mutisya, *Proverbs*, 26.
[47] Mwau, *Dictionary*, 661.
[48] John Hunter, *Hunter: With Introductory Note by Captain Archie T.A. Ritchie*

1727. *Ũta ũte nthuke na maangi ndũendaa nzyĩma.* **A bow that does not match the arrows does not hunt.**
This was an axiomatic call for respect of age grades, classes, and gendered associations. A person involved with an older woman was rebuked to pick his own age mate for romance. Another interpretation is that some tasks need more effort than smaller tasks.

1728. *Ũta ndwĩ nthuke na maangi.* **The bow is not of the same age as the arrows.**[49]
Women coined this adage to rebuke young men who wanted to date older women. There are two interpretations, the first historical: the bow was adopted for rituals before it became a weapon and arrows added to it. Second, and practically, once the hunter made a bow, he kept it until death while arrows were replenished periodically, so when the son inherited the bow some arrows were thirty to sixty years younger than the bow.

1729. *Ũta ũla wathaa nĩwo wovawa nginga.* **The hunting bow is decorated with animal hair.**
Kamba bows were embellished with elaborate decorations of animal hair and sinews.[50] From the Vascon era when many focused on commercial hunting, the proverb means people who execute their duties competently should be rewarded.

1730. *Ũa ũkagaasya mwene ĩlute ũmeasya makundo tene.* **A bowstring that will keep the hunter hungry overnight develops knots early.**
This proverb appears in traditional songs in northern Mwingi where it is varied in multiple ways. The word *ũkagaasya* appears as *ũkakaasya* in 'standard' Kĩkamba. Usage of the latter word would take out the proverbial flavour among the users. Drawn from a hunting context and dating from antiquity, this proverb indicates that signs of trouble in the near future can be easily detected.

1731. *Mũtwii wa mathoka tiwe ũtemaa namo.* **Whoever makes axes is not the one who cuts with them.**
With multiple variations employing arrows and bangles, this axiom reveals the contradictions of industrial productivity in Ũkamba. Smiths

---

(Long Beach: Safari Press, 1952), 170; Hardy, *Longbow*; Gordon Grimley, *The Book of the Bow* (New York: Putnams, 1958); Dennis Holman, *The Elephant People* (New York: Putnams, 1967); Classical International, *Psalms 19 in African Study Bible* (New York: Tyndale House Publishers, 2017).
[49] Mailu, *Kĩkyambonie*, 61, 73; Mwau, *Dictionary*, 669.
[50] Hunter, *Hunter*, 170.

did not keep the best of their products for themselves but produced for the market.

1732. *Mũtwii wa ngose nde yake mbaĩlu.*[51] **The one who makes tweezers does not have a fitting one for himself.**
Ngose was a small pincher-like instrument with which eyelashes and eyebrow hairs were plucked out. When elders had nothing to do they sat outside their houses and plucked their eyelashes one at a time very slowly until all the hairs were out. Although the pincher was so important, those who manufactured them did not make any for themselves.

1733. *Ũtwii ũte mũvuvĩi wĩvinya.* **Metal forging without a bellow blower is hard.**
This proverb means that single parenthood, especially for a father with little children, is hard. It points to the importance of cooperation in handling difficult tasks. The bellow blower (symbolizing wife) does not work with metals but is indispensable in ironworking. Thus, living without a wife and raising children without their mother is not easy for a man; it compares with blowing the fire and heating the metal at the same time. This was said among single fathers in the colonial period, when many women ran away to towns without sending remittances, leaving behind children in the care of men.

1734. *Vayĩ mũtwii ũtavĩtasya nzanga.* **There is no blacksmith who does not miss a line.**[52]
This proverb alludes to situations where smiths tried to be accurate in their art-making blades. No matter how precise they were, there were always some errors. The proverb emerged during the Monsoon era when Kamba metalworks intensified. It means anyone can make mistakes.

1735. *Maangi maingĩ mekĩaw'a mbĩtya.* **Multiple arrows are shot because of missing the target.**
The Kamba developed archery during the first millennium with a variety of projectiles usually translated as arrows. John Hunter lavishly described the excellent quality of Kamba arrows and the poison that was applied to them.[53] This ancient axiom means that one who aims at the target carefully should not miss it. Persistent attempts to achieve a desired goal are not in vain.

---

[51] Mwau, *Dictionary*, 660.
[52] Kimilu, *Mũkamba*, 119; Mutisya, *Proverbs*, 24.
[53] Hunter, *Hunter*, 176.

1736. *Yaangi īte nzyīma iaīlawa nyama.* **An arrow not in the hunt is not apportioned meat.**
As avid hunters, the Kamba organized hunting trips to places where animals were abundant. Once they killed an animal, each person was given a portion of the meat for his effort, but anyone absent was not given anything. This proverb means the benefit of a project is due only to participants.

1737. *Yaangi ya kīvīsī kīvavīaa mwelekana.* **A boy's arrow is feathered awkwardly.**
By the Vascon era the Kamba had developed the art of feathering arrows for speed and precision. Since this practice is evident by the 1300s, it is likely that it existed as far back as the first millennium and the proverb was in circulation during that period. Inexperienced boys placed the feathers facing each other so that the arrow flew zigzag. The maxim means careless people make embarrassing mistakes.

1738. *Yaangi ya Mūkamba yelekanasw'a na īngī.* **The arrow of a Mūkamba is compared with another.**
This maxim derives from hunting activities of the Islamic period. When the hunter shot his arrow he made marks on the ground with his feet where he stood. He then followed up where the arrow landed. If he could not find it, he returned to the marks and shot another arrow and, when it lands, there he will precisely find the first arrow. This proverb means certain things have to be compared in order to find a solution. A legal case, for example, is arbitrated using similar cases that had appeared previously. People often learn by example.

1739. *Kīmbithī kya thyaka kīsīwe nī mwene.* **Only the owner knows the secrets of his quiver.**
The contents of the quiver are concealed within it and only the owner knows what is inside. Kamba quiver carried not just arrows, but magic medicine, knives, 'trained bees', and other personal effects. For that reason, each quiver had personalized contents. The same with humans. Only a person knows what is in their mind; only the patriarch knows the secrets, weaknesses, and strengths of his household.

1740. *Thyaka nīwa syano ilūnda syīkaa ūthongwa.* **The quiver is for arrows, blade shafts are just stuck in.**
This ancient axiom talks about ranks and ranking people and objects. As mentioned in the previous entry, Kamba quivers contained weapons of diverse significance. It was primarily made for poisoned arrows in order to protect the poison from the elements and the hunter from poisonous accidental injury. Poisoned arrows were sealed with a soft-tanned skin wrap and then inserted into the quiver carefully, head first.

Other miscellaneous weapons were thrown in without any order. This hunter-derived maxim tracing back to the first millennium has multiple applications. It means people are to be treated according to their social, economic, and political status.

1741. *Mũndũ ũla ũvĩĩwe ndakũlasya ngĩĩtĩ.* **One whose house burnt down does not discriminate building material.**
Drawn from the architectural realm, this axiom has had different and changing applications since antiquity. The original houses were made of sticks and grass thatch. These structures often burnt down. In the event of emergency, to get shelter quickly, builders did not take time to choose the best material. By application, one who is desperate to accomplish a given goal does not care about the means to the end of that goal.

1742. *Mũthongole wetelasya mwene ĩtumo.* **Make do with the wooden lance until the iron spear is ready.**
This proverb alludes to the period when the Kamba used wooden implements and spears before the bow was adapted during the Islamic era. *Mũthongole* was a sharpened stick fashioned from hardwood, used in early days for hunting and trapping animals as well as for warfare.[54] Pegged where antelopes jumped over a fence the *mũthongole* pierced the animal's chest as it leaped, causing it to bleed to death. Apparently, this ancient proverb meant – in the remote past – that since spears were rare, trappers used *mũthongole* until they could procure spears. It teaches patience as one works systematically towards grander achievements.

1743. *Mũkumbũ wetelasya mwene kĩkuto.* **The red drawstring beckons a richer belt.**
Mũkumbũ, the drawstring (like a sash, or something thinner), was one of the most sought articles of Vascon-era trade. It was a piece of red cloth sold to Kamba traders by coastal merchants. It was a lavishly decorated belt surpassed by only another sash called *kĩkuto*. The proverb means an energetic innovator may well succeed more than a timid, lethargic, and unadventurous person. Coined during the Vascon era it reflects commercial engagements between Ũkamba and the coast, the consumers' desire for new goods eclipsing the old, while warning of the dangers of hastily abandoning the old.

1744. *Ĩvai iimanzawa akanĩ.* **One does not look for arrow poison among women.**
The Kamba, renowned for trade in arrow poison across East Africa before the Vascon era, produced several proverbs revealing their

---

[54] Kĩeti, *Barking*, 107; Mutisya, *Proverbs*, 71.

engagement with poison.[55] The proverbs therefore emerged during that period. Men often had to go around the villages to borrow or buy poison from fellow men rather than women, since women would never need such substances. The proverb, with some variations, plainly tells the listener: do not seek things in the wrong place.

1745. *Katemaa mbande kakengaa mwene.* **A double-edged knife deceives its owner.**
This adage from the Monsoon era came from a context of field-dressing game performed with a sword; an implement Lindblom noted was the most important tool.[56] A double-edged sword has an advantage but this proverb sees the opposite. When a large wild animal was killed near a village, for example, the villagers were free to run and chop as much meat as possible. Some worked systematically to cut as much as they could, but others, trusting the sharpness of their knives, cut randomly through tough, time-consuming bone and muscle. It emphasizes the significance of tact and strategy.

1746. *Ka kavyũ na nĩ kavyũ.* **Take the knife and it is hot.**
A literal translation, 'Take the hot one and it is hot!' makes no sense. The proverb was from antiquity presented as *Kaa nĩ kavyũ na nĩ kavyũ*, 'This is a knife and it is hot', to explain a complex matter to a novice who did not comprehend the magnitude of the matter. The speaker of this axiom means to say that the matter at hand is both serious and dangerous to handle at the same time.

1747. *Kavyũ ka mũsangasangi kenũkaa kate nyama.* **The knife of a wanderer returns home without meat.**
If a big animal was killed, everyone wanting meat brought his own knife to cut. Gluttons would move from one edge of the animal to another, jockeying for the best part. People who were systematic got their share while the glutton ended up with nothing. This refers to a man without a wife. He cannot build anything through promiscuity.

1748. *Kavyũ ka kũthinĩkĩwa ti kakwĩthinĩkia.* **A stored-up knife is different from a self-stored knife.**
This was not just about putting away a knife, but also safety, hygiene, and ritual. There was a special knife for circumcision called *kyenzi*, kept carefully hidden until circumcision day when armed confidants of the family carefully guarded the knife and its holder to make sure enemies

---

[55] Mwau, *Dictionary*, 658; Thomas Frasser and Joseph Tillie, 'Acokanthera Schimperi: Its Natural History, Chemistry, and Pharmacology', *The Royal Society* 58 (347–52) (January and March 1895).
[56] Lindblom, *Akamba*, 548.

did not gain access to the knife to secretly harm the child with lethal chemicals. This custom appears to have originated with the ascendancy of circumcision ceremonies in Kitui during the Islamic era.[57]

1749. *Kavyũ koĩva mũno katemaa o ũla ũkanoete.* **If a knife is too sharp, it cuts the sharpener.**
Braggarts make self-destructive decisions. A sharp blade was both good and so dangerous it could injure the owner. From the Monsoon era it advises against overambition and emphasizes tact and strategy.

1750. *Kuumwa kũitemanaa, na kuumana nĩ kũmantha maambo.*[58] **Mockery does not cut and mocking other people invites legal jeopardy.**
This is an ancient saying that unveils and encodes the history of Kamba conflict resolution. The maxim implies that insult does not inflict physical pain, so the offended party should reasonably endure it. The second part gives consolation to the offended, since the aggressive person will pay a fine (*mambo*) strictly imposed by elders.

1751. *Ndemangano ya mũnuka ti ya kavyũ.*[59] **The stabs of the mouth are not knife stabs.**
This adage calls for polite conversation since talking should not hurt. Individuals were encouraged to compose themselves in the process of debates, disputes, and disagreements. This emerged during the 1860s when fights with knives were common. This resembles the Western childhood chant, 'Sticks and stones may break my bones, but words will never hurt me.'

1752. *Mũsyĩmi mũlũmu nĩ welelasya maangi alea kũatha akenũkya maangi make.* **A strong hunter aims carefully so that, if he misses the target, he takes home his arrows.**
The manufacture of weapons was neither easy nor cheap so care was needed to maintain one's arms cache. This proverb means that one has to be careful that his solution to a problem will not become a problem itself. This is particularly advised of people who use proverbs (comparable to arrows) to not use them out of context.

---

[57] Lyn Thomas, '*Ngaitana* (I will circumcise myself)': The Gender and Generational Politics of the 1956 Ban on Clitoridectomy in Meru, Kenya', in *Female Circumcision in Africa: Culture, Controversy and Change*, ed. Bettina Shell-Duncann and Ylva Hernlund (Boulder: Lynne Reinner Publishers, 2000).
[58] Mailu, *Kĩkyambonie*, 55.
[59] Mwau, *Dictionary*, 663.

1753. *Mũsyĩmi woonthe akuaa maangi esĩ onthe nomowae avakĩĩla.* **Every hunter carries arrows knowing that each one can kill if he puts it on the bowstring.**
This proverb means that one should not underestimate what is at hand. Used as a device for commenting on social life this proverb demonstrates how the bow and arrow became symbolic and applicable to social life at the end of the first millennium.

1754. *Mũsyĩmi asyaa nĩwe wĩsĩ kũsyĩma.* **A hunter says he is the only one who knows hunting.**
This is about arrogance, ignorance, and pride. It emerged out of a hunting context where each hunter thought he was best at it until he met people who had greater capabilities.

1755. *Mũsyĩmi wĩ mbĩtya ndatiaa ĩkoto ĩsyaĩye ndakakome ĩlute.* **A hunter who cannot hit the target does not leave a hornbill lest he goes to bed starving.**
This proverb circulated mostly in the sparsely settled areas of eastern Kitui. Hunters had to be precise in their targets. If they missed, they lost their meal for that day. To guard against starvation, untrained hunters preyed on easy-to-get species such as the hornbill. Easy perhaps, but not honourable, since the meat was the least preferred. The hunter in this case stoops very low.

1756. *Mũsyĩmi e ndũũ na mũlaki.* **The hunter is a friend of the honey seeker.**
This is about complementarity and originated in eastern Kitui during the nineteenth and early twentieth centuries. Together with the previous proverb they were coined during a time when hunting was neither profitable nor easy. Hunters and honey seekers in distant lands where there was no food or water fused and formed alliances such that whoever struck on luck first helped the other starving groups. It was not easy for a person to combine the two professions – hunting and seeking honey. Here the need for cooperation and complementarity became important.

1757. *Mũsyĩmi nĩwe ũĩsaa ĩtema ĩte ĩlumu.* **The hunter eats fresh liver.**
This stresses the advantages of punctuality and proximity. The hunter is usually the first to taste the kill. Among the first parts of an animal Kamba hunters roasted and consumed after they killed it were the intestines, liver, kidneys, and spleen. The hunter had the advantage of eating fresh organ meat.

1758. *Ĩthoka yetu yĩsĩlaa mwakinĩ.* **A hard axe comes through the fire.**
The most common interpretation is that young people should accept hard discipline at school or home so they grow into responsible and respected adults. The axe, an anchor of life before the twentieth century, was the product of high heat and many days in the fire. This is to say that something of value comes through hard work.[60]

1759. *Mathoka me ngusunĩ ĩmwe mailea ũkũngũlanya.*[61] **Axes in the same bag do not fail to clatter and clang.**
Used to mend friendships and settle family feuds, it means close associates and family members are bound to disagree since they live in one place and share resources. When the Kamba carried axes, they threw them in a bag hung on one shoulder. As the person moves, the axes clang.

1760. *Kĩtew'aa amũkaw'a na mũtwethoka.* **A deaf person is awakened with an axe handle.**
First recorded without translation by Farnsworth in 1952, this proverb warns against arrogance and stubbornness.[62] The Kamba used the handle of an axe to beat enemies or kill an animal. The use of axe handles symbolized utter distaste for the individual. An arrogant person was therefore warned that he would be rewarded in this distasteful manner if he did not listen.

1761. *Mũtwethoka ũ wĩ kĩtheka ũmanthawa nĩ ũ wĩndavũnĩ.*[63] **The one in the sheath seeks an axe handle in the forest.**
Axe handles were valuable tools that were not only carved from specific hardwood species, but the wood had to be in a particular natural shape fit for an axe. To get one, a person needed to have an axe already in its handle, often hanging on the carver's belt. This axiom speaks to the importance of investment to gain profit. You have to own something to get something else. In other words, 'It takes money to make money.' This proverb emerged around the 1300s.

---

[60] Kimilu, *Mũkamba*, 115; Mbiti, *Weteelete*, 81.
[61] Mbiti, *Ngaeka*, 90.
[62] Farnsworth, *Grammar*, 71.
[63] Kimilu, *Mũkamba*, 117; Mutisya, *Proverbs*, 70.

1762. *Kathoka kanini kaitemaa mũtĩ mũnene.*[64] **A small axe does not cut a big tree.**
Tracing to the Islamic era, when the Kamba adopted axes, this proverb emphasizes the priority of the group above individual goals. It calls for social unity in families and communities. The more people, the more productivity, so to speak.

1763. *Ũĩ mũnene ũtũlĩaa mwene ĩthoka.*[65] **Too much sharpness breaks one's axe.**
Axes were extremely important from the fourteenth century on. Life was in many ways anchored around these implements. The axe cleared bushes to make farms, paths, and settlements, process big game meat, fight, and shape building materials. If these tools were damaged, it translated to substantial loss to the owner. If axes were too sharp, the blade would bend in the process of cutting hard material. The proverb admonished people to be careful in discerning what course of action to take in risky matters.

1764. *Kĩiva kĩtuaa kĩngĩ.*[66] **A hammer makes another hammer.**
Ironsmiths often made hammers, valued across East Africa. To make one the smith had to use an older hammer. It means positive traits can be passed on. Children benefit when their parents are educated and impart that knowledge to the young. Still, the old hammer can symbolize a good elder, teacher, leader, or trainer who will pass on skills to trainees.

1765. *Kĩiva kĩikũaa kĩtuaa kĩngĩ.* **A hammer does not last long making another hammer.**[67]
This proverb denotes the declining ability to do things that one did in his or her youth. It perfectly applies to modern retirement. People working beyond retirement age are told this proverb, meaning they are losing their energy and mental ability to work. It is also told to someone who has been dependent on his parents, meaning it is time to be on your own.

1766. *Ũvũnwa nzukũ nĩ ũmanzĩwa kailiva.* **Only a hammer can satisfy you with slander.**
The Kamba loath slander and condemn it harshly. In this axiom, which emerged after the Second World War when hammers began to appear in

---

[64] Joseph Mani, 'Cultural Patterns from Kamba Culture' (Nairobi: MA thesis, USIU 2014); John Makilya, *Life Lessons of an Immigrant: Sustainable Community-Owned Enterprises* (New York: Archway, 2017).
[65] Kimilu, *Mũkamba*, 119; Mbiti, *Weteelete*, 167.
[66] Kimilu, *Mũkamba*, 115.
[67] Kimilu, *Mũkamba*, 115.

Ũkamba, the speaker implies that habitual gossipers can only be satisfied with gossip when knocked with a hammer. That is a sarcastic way of saying the matter can be resolved only when the gossiper is killed or seriously injured.

1767. *Kyũma kĩkũnawa kĩkĩvyũ.*[68] **A metal is struck while it is hot.**
Opportunity should be seized at the right time. The Kamba were renowned ironworkers and worked different types of metals into implements, weapons, tools, and ornaments. The process involved securing iron ore and smelting it in furnaces into steel. The final product was further heated into a soft malleable substance, which was pounded into desired shapes and objects. To shape a metal, it had to be hit while hot. It was only in that near-molten state that the metal could be easily worked into shape. The deeper meaning is that certain matters are better dealt with at the opportune time.

1768. *Kyũma kĩtumbĩaa kĩngĩ ũito.* **A metal crushes another because of its weight.**
The deeper meaning of this Monsoon-era adage is that mishandling sensitive social and political matters is dangerous. Another interpretation is that the opinion of the rich, the learned, and the powerful prevails over that of the poor, the meek, and illiterate.[69]

1769. *Ĩlii yĩ mũsyĩ ĩyũwaa kya kwova.* **A string at home does not lack something to tie.**
Dating from antiquity, this proverb originated from circumstances where, after construction using strings, remnant fibres littered the compound. While other debris was burned, strings were spared.[70] It was usually applied in family situations to encourage members not to break up, stressing the importance of staying together.

1770. *Ĩlii yetelasya mwene mũkwa.* **A string keeps the owner waiting for a leather strap.**
The Kamba preferred leather straps for bearing burdens on their backs and for tethering animals. Until one killed an animal and extracted straps from the hide they had to make do with fibre. Thus, substitutes are as valuable as the object itself. Be patient with what you have as you work to achieve the most desirable object.

---

[68] Kituku, *Sukulu*, 53.
[69] Mutisya, *Proverbs*, 73.
[70] Kimilu, *Mũkamba*, 115; Mutisya, *Proverbs*, 47; Mwau, *Dictionary*, 669.

388 Part IV: Kamba Society

1771. *Athoni mayīkanīasya syondo theka.*[71] **In-laws do not throw away each other's baskets.**
This idiomatic statement points to the fact that, if the host was annoyed with a visitor on account of the latter's misconduct, the host picked up and threw the luggage to the guest instead of handing it over. This was symbolic of throwing the guest out of the house, and he would go his way and never come back. In contrast, since a marriage bond was the ultimate level of a good relationship, whenever in-laws visited, their luggage was kept in a special place and would never be thrown away.

1772. *Kīlinga kya kyondo kīimanzawa aūmenī.*[72] **Basket yarn is not sought among men.**
This proverb, drawn from a weaving context, represents a simple cultural truth: men do not weave, women do. The proverb, which dates back to the Vascon period, advises that it is prudent to know where to get certain things.

1773. *Mūkua nzūngī nene nīyake.* **Whoever carries a big basket, it's his own.**
The proverb means one cannot complain about a cause that he/she decided to take. Do not ask for help. This emerged in the early nineteenth century when women trading in foodstuff reached its zenith. The long-distance form of this trade in grains, legumes, and root crops was called *thūūī* or *kūthūūwa*. Baskets of varying sizes were the principal carriers of the food. Women used baskets that could carry what they needed, hence the literal meaning of the proverb.

1774. *Yokothaa ūndū yīanya ūtambī.* **The weaver twines according to her thigh size.**
Kamba weavers since the Vascon era have done twining on thighs. Two strings were moistened in the mouth and then rolled back and forth a few times on their thighs to form a thin twine called *ūnyenze*. The latter was then used for weaving. It was assumed that the bigger one's thigh, the better the weaver. The proverb implies that performance depends on the resources at the disposal of the performer.

1775. *Wetīkīla kasaū ndūkalee kamūkwa.*[73] **If you accept a gift calf, do not reject the tether.**
This expression dates to the Islamic era, when the Kamba developed leather straps for tethering cows. They were fastened around the base of the horns. By the end of the twentieth century, the strap was put

---

[71] Mwau, *Dictionary*, 645.
[72] Mwau, *Dictionary*, 650.
[73] Mwau, *Dictionary*, 672.

on the right front leg. This proverb points out that, if one has a calf, he will need the strap to secure it. Figuratively, anything good comes with responsibility. If you accept the goodies, accept the responsibility that comes with them.[74]

1776. *Wona Kasalũ kekya ũta mũongo noko kaĩkĩsye.*[75] **If you see the calf spit on its back, it spits for itself.**
This is about self-reliance. It warns that a young person should not bear responsibility before he matures – parents should.

1777. *Mĩiyo ndakua nĩlea ĩkwovwa.* **A heavy load that I cannot bear, I denounce it before it is piled up.**
This is a protest proverb said by someone opposed to a group's decision making. It was a polite way to say that the speaker was unable and unwilling to follow others' decisions as their proposal was unworkable and the speaker had no resources to bear the burden. The Kamba tied their burdens with ropes and leather straps to place on the shoulder or back to carry for long distances. This form of carrying burdens distinguished the Kamba from the surrounding communities and comes from the Islamic era.

1778. *Avai anini mavaa ũndũ meana.* **Few groomers groom according to their number.**
This proverb refers to family members sharing duties according to the strength of their labour force. It emerged during the Monsoon era and has since circulated in different variations. Within a small family, members offer as much labour as they can to meet family obligations. The term *avai* has two different meanings. First it means 'those who wear' and it is this meaning that Mutisya preferred: 'When a community with a small number of men is attacked, the women join in the defence. In an emergency all available personnel are deployed.' This interpretation is backed by oral traditions where girls and women using rocks and slingshots backed men who fought Kwavi with bows.

1779. *Avai ma mbũa mavaa ũndũ syaana.* **Those who dress in skins dress according to their availability.**
Emerging during the Monsoon era, before the above entry, this proverb alludes to the times when the precolonial Kamba predominantly used skins as clothes, beddings, and roofing material. The proverb means that one should live within his/her family's means; sharing is a communal virtue.

---

[74] Lindblom, *Akamba*, 480.
[75] Kimilu, *Mũkamba*, 119; Mutisya, *Proverbs*.

1780. *Vayĩ wokothwa ũkalea kumya mũthia.* **There is no thread that is twined without producing a tapered end.**
This axiom means that the indicator of educated people is not how long they have been in school, but their career at the end. Women obtained baobab fibres to be chewed soft as they went about their business. Softened fibre was then straightened and twined into a thread by pressing back and forth on the thighs. The final step was a pointed end to penetrate a needle. The proverb originated with the introduction of weaving during the Vascon era and means that every process must have a product.[76]

1781. *Kondo kene katitũngawa ke kathei.*[77] **Someone's basket is not returned empty.**
This maxim alludes to the Kamba sense of generosity and reciprocity. They delivered gifts to friends and relatives in baskets. However, with time, the parties involved developed a habit of returning the basket with a token, hence this proverb.

1782. *Mũũkwa nĩ kĩvyanyũ.* **The essence of the spring trap is in the trigger.**
The word *Mũũkwa* in this context means a trap, a combination of a long rope and a set of triggers. The best trap is that which can spring firmly and perfectly in a flash. The axiom further means a trap's worth is its ability to spring quickly to trap the creature. If it cannot do so, it is worthless. For humans, a man's worth is his deeds and the ability to honour his promises.[78]

1783. *Ũkya ndwalanĩlaw'a kĩthuma.* **One does not make a bed for poverty.**
Dating from the nineteenth century this axiom has multiple interpretations. One interpretation is that no one plans on poverty. It just happens and once it takes hold of someone it spreads its tendrils like a bottlegourd vine. Another noteworthy interpretation is that one must close all possible channels that poverty can use to entrench itself in a household.

1784. *Ka mũkati kaĩsaa mũkati mũkatĩthya ndeũndũ.* **The player's dice ruins only the player, not the salesman.**
This is a trade language of profit and loss coined during the late colonial era following the introduction of dice games for money in markets after the Second World War. Dice were instruments of pure chance, called

---

[76] Kimilu, *Mũkamba*, 119; Mutisya, *Proverbs*, 50.
[77] Mbiti, *Ngaeka*, 98.
[78] Mwau, *Dictionary*, 657.

karata in Swahili, a corruption for 'game cards'. The proverb emphasizes that the dice make facts in the world but never suffer from these facts: this could speak also to unintended outcomes in general. Dice are oblivious to the harm they cause (it says nothing about good rolls); dice can also make men rich, yet do not benefit from it. However, the proverb does not say this: it is about dice, and therefore chance, as intrinsically malevolent.

1785. *Ndŭkathaŭke kalata na ala maŭvundĩisye.* **Do not play card games with those who trained you.**
The axiom dates back to the Second World War when card games (*kalata*) emerged in Kenya. It warns juniors to distance themselves from their superiors who helped them rise in the ranks of political power. It is futile to compete with them.

1786. *Masaani elĩ matheu maikwatanya kĩko.* **Two clean plates cannot make each other dirty.**
This proverb was coined after kitchen plates became common in the 1930s. It means that gentlemen do not offend each other; walk in the right company. In marital, business, or romantic relationships choosing the right companion is rewarding.

1787. *Ndŭkandile ĩsaani.* **Do not cut me a plate.**
This postcolonial coinage is another way of saying do not blame me. Do not damage my reputation through slander. The plate in question is the music plate of a record player, used between the 1950s and 1980s.

1788. *Vaiingwa lelŭ ŭte ngulai.* **There is no road without corners.**
This emerged after the Second World War when winding country roads became common and automobiles began to ply them more frequently. There is no one without a fault. Sometimes people can contend with faulty alternatives.

1789. *Kameme kaisyokeaa.*[79] **The radio does not repeat.**
This proverb emerged between 1953 and 1963 because the first broadcast service carried programmes in Kĩkamba in 1953. By 1 July 1964, when Kenya Broadcasting Corporation was nationalized into Voice of Kenya, the Kamba had been exposed to radio enough to incorporate it into their proverbial lore. The proverb means that there are certain things that are said and done once. They cannot be repeated.

---

[79] Mwau, *Dictionary*, 648.

1790. *Kĩlũnda kĩyĩsĩ mbesa.* **The arrow does not know wealth.**
This emerged from the 1920s when money became common and the pice (Swahili *pesa*, Kĩkamba *mbesa*), began to circulate in Kenya. During the 1950s, prolonged court cases became prevalent between poor and rich. The poor who could not afford prolonged proceedings resorted to murdering the rich person with a bow. The proverb depicted conflict from lending and borrowing as merchants borrowed and refused to repay, once again with victims resorting to violence. Musicians popularized it in the 1980s to caution the wealthy to refrain from mistreating the poor lest they die.

1791. *Wenda kwongela kĩlilikano kovethya mũndũ mbesa.* **If you want to improve your memory, lend someone money.**
People like to do beneficial things that are unforgettable.[80] This teasing statement is a post-independence coinage, which points out that while borrowers may forget, lenders do not forget.

1792. *Yũa ya mbesa yĩyumawa.* **The money famine never ends.**
This statement emerged after independence as capitalism took hold and people began to rely on money for their livelihood. The lust for money never ends no matter how much one gets. This could be a variation of the next entry but their contexts differ.

1793. *Mbesa nĩ mathela ngwene.* **Money perishes as I watch.**
Money is a commodity that perishes quickly. This was created after independence when most Kamba began to invest in money. It warns the audience not to put their faith in money and instead to cherish family and interpersonal relationships. Together with the next entry this proverb shows attitudes towards money. For all it does in the economic realm, money is not a good commodity. It is unreliable and consistently fluctuates, leaving a void in the lives of those who deal with it.

1794. *Mbesa nĩ ndoi.* **Money is a witch.**
This reflects the view of money as an occult force that changes meanings, turns things upside down, is malevolent, and unpredictable. Emerging after the Second World War, the maxim unveils the Kamba's unfavourable view of money.

1795. *Ndũkakĩe ũnene wa ngalĩ manya wa ndeleva no ũla ũmwe.* **Do not fear the size of a vehicle for that of the driver is the same.**
This is an encouragement not to overestimate the task at hand. It emerged after the First World War when public transportation automo-

---

[80] Mutisya wa Ngai, 'Kyuo kya Ngoso, number 3'.

biles – called *gari* in Swahili and *ngalī* in Kīkamba – were introduced in Kenya.

1796. *Ngalī nthei yi maaū.* **An empty vehicle is faster.**
This axiom alludes to public transportation vehicles. They run faster when they are empty, but that is not what they are made for. They cannot make a profit if empty. This axiom emerged in the second half of the twentieth century when public service vehicles became very common. It is a figurative way of saying idle and irresponsible persons can do anything they want, whereas people with families to care about are not as free.

1797. *Satani akūne mbesa akwongelelaa ūthatu.* **When Satan gives you money, he adds anger.**
This is a recent coinage linked to the advent of Christianity and the money economy of the twentieth century. Satan is a Christian religious concept alien to pre-1900 Kamba cosmology, while money is an imperial commercial terminology of the interwar period. The proverb perpetuates the theme of money as evil and satanic. Because of the stressful way money in the modern economy is acquired, most rich people have a quick temper. This is interpreted as Satan's gift as payback for the money the rich person received.

1798. *Vaa syina ite īsaani.* **They will sing without a plate.**
This refers to a musical instrument common in the Kenyan music world from the 1940s to 1980s – the gramophone, locally known as *kīnanda*. The record player cannot produce music without the plate where the audio music is stored. So, this axiom is an idiomatic expression of impossibility. It emerged during the second half of the twentieth century.

1799. *Kūthi nesa ti kūlūka na ndeke.* **To fare well in life is not air travel.**
This emerged during the second half of the twentieth century when air travel became common in Kenya. It implies that there is no one formula to success.

1800. *Nīwakenia kūū ndekenī.* **You stuck your leg out of an airplane.**
This emerged after the Second World War as air travel increased. Ūkamba lies on the pathways of most local, regional, and international flights and for that reason planes of all kinds are seen flying from East to West. Such planes trigger imaginations as they fly low and make an unmistakable appearance and noise. The maxim means that you have made a terrible mistake.

1801. *Ũkoonw'a nĩ itho ta mũtwai wa ndeke.* **The eye will show you like a pilot.**
The Kamba prefer eye-witnessing to hearsay. Although their engagement with airplanes goes back to the First World War, this proverb is likely to have emerged after the Second World War when such airplanes became common and a fair number of Kamba worked in the aviation industry. Certainly, pilots rely on sight to do their job while flying and must have excellent vision, particularly normal colour vision. The proverb tells the doubting listeners that he/she will believe the story on the reckoning day.

1802. *Ũsũaa matinga ndwasũa ndeke ũkew'a.* **You hung on tractors; you have never tried an airplane.**
While tractors and airplanes appeared as early as the 1920s, the phrase 'hanging on tractors' refers to a late twentieth-century behaviour (among public transportation touts) of hanging on speeding buses, but certainly not on airplanes. This reflects how proverb creators imagine the objects they use. It also demonstrates that maxims do not always represent absolute truth. It means you have never tried the biggest challenge yet.

1803. *Mũtwai wa ĩtinga ndakĩaa kĩtoo.*[81] **A tractor's driver does not fear dust.**
This proverb originates from the late 1920s when tractors were introduced in Ũkambanĩ. As the tractor sped along it blew huge clouds of dust, leaving the driver dusty. One should not be afraid of risks involved in a good cause.

1804. *Ngwene mũkuthũ ta mbesa ya mũkoloni.* **I see through you like a colonial coin.**
This exemplifies the Kamba habit of comparing colonial and independence-era coins from the 1960s. The colonial-era coins had a hole in the centre, but the coins minted after independence were solid. It means that the speaker knows the tricks and secrets of the listener. The speaker asserts his/her supremacy in the conversation.

1805. *Wiingĩ mũseo nowa mbesa.* **The only good thing in excess is money.**
The only thing that is good in an excess amount is money. This was coined from the early years of independence when the majority of Kamba became money-minded and money came to redefine success and failure in life. This is one of a few proverbs that praises money, but praise with a hidden sinister tone. All other proverbs tend to condemn

---

[81] Kĩeti, *Barking*, 109.

money and depict money largely in a negative light. This proverb bends that perception a little bit by implying that, even though money is evil, possession of it is better than too many problems.

1806. *Mũtandĩthya ndekasya ngoo.*[82] **An investor never gives up.**
This emerged during the twentieth century as new models of investment appeared in commercial contexts. The axiom calls for persistence and pragmatism in dealing with challenging matters that are beneficial.

1807. *Kunini ndĩnywĩwaa mũyo ĩnywĩwaa kũmina ndetema.* **Quinine is taken for a cure of fever, not for pleasure.**
This appeared in a political song to persuade compatriots to stick with their political leader as candidate for a high electoral office. Some voters doubted the suitability of the candidate and this proverb suggested that people should not make easy choices but tough ones, just as taking bitter quinine pills brings recovery. This may trace back to the colonial era when quinine was introduced through imperial medicine.

1808. *Nondo ĩaniaw'a nĩ kũmĩthwa ndondo.* **The breast is made large by being bitten by a water beetle.**
Boys and girls craved for the moment their breasts would grow larger. In desperation, they used to pick up a species of water beetle called *ndondo* and place it on the nipple to bite so that the bite would swell like a mature breast. The actual meaning is that only rigorous efforts bear fruit, and without toil there is no enjoyment.

1809. *Kavaa kalĩnga kũte ngingo nthei.* **Better something than a naked neck.**
This adage emerged from the context of decoration of the body during the Monsoon era. The key word is *kalĩnga*, the diminutive version of *mũlĩnga*, referring to a piece of brass imported from the coast before 1900. The Kamba used to wear elaborate beads and copper ornaments. People without necklaces were encouraged to wear at least something on the neck, hence this proverb, dating to the Monsoon era in the context of long-distance trade in brass, copper, metal, and ornaments. The adage appears in literature.[83] It expresses satisfaction with a little gift.

---

[82] Mwau, *Dictionary*, 660.
[83] Kĩeti, *Barking*, 109; Mutisya, *Proverbs*, 46.

1810. *Kakũla ka ngũlĩlo kaĩlaa mũthenya ũmwe.* **A borrowed garment fits only one day.**
This proverb emerged during the twentieth century. Even though the Kamba had engaged in textile use and trade since the Monsoon era, the practice of borrowing clothes to wear for a given occasion began during the colonial era as colonial official pressure mounted on people to buy and wear modern clothes in public places. Those who did not have clothes borrowed their friends' and relatives' garments and returned them afterwards. The borrowed garment satisfied for that day only. The axiom stresses the importance of self-reliance.

1811. *Kyauma mũthenya kĩivwĩkawa ngũa.* **Once the termite hill produces flying ants in the daytime, it is not covered with clothes.**[84]
This alludes to flying ants that, during the rainy season, burst out and flood the area. Birds immediately attack these winged ants, called *kĩthwa*, while humans collect them for frying. Just as they cannot be concealed with clothes, open secrets are difficult to conceal. This axiom dates from the Vascon era when clothes became widespread.

1812. *Ũtatavaw'a aĩsaa chapati na nyunyi.* **One who cannot be told anything eats chapati with greens.**
This axiom dates from the 1890s, when Indian immigrants introduced chapati cuisine in Kenya. As the British colonial administration encouraged non-African cuisine as part of a desirable, modern lifestyle, chapati became a favourite dish among the Kamba. Even so, this maxim did not become popular until independence when chapati became common in Ũkamba. It is assumed unfortunate to consume chapati with greens instead of meat, chicken, or fish. The proverb emphasizes listening and taking advice from other people. Failure to listen to good counsel is tragic.

---

[84] Mwau, *Dictionary*, 653.

21

Politics, Conflict, and Peacemaking

1813. *Amaitha ma mũndũ no andũ amake.* **One's enemies are one's own people.**
From antiquity, this proverb warns people of the danger that lurks behind a sour relationship in a family or community. If misfortune happens, one is warned to search through divination first within the household before checking with a malevolent neighbour.

1814. *Atũi nĩmo matonyanaa nthongo.* **Neighbours prick each other's eyes.**
This ancient maxim first means neighbours are bound to take care of each other. Yet conflict is inevitable in a neighbourhood and neighbours often cause injury and loss to each other. The proverb persuades conflicting parties to reconcile.

1815. *Aũme monganasya na syĩngokoa.*[1] **Men suckle with elbows.**
This ancient proverb relates to conflict. While men–women relationships are soft and loving, men-to-men relationships are often rough and pitiless. Its purpose is simply descriptive of the character of men. It was used to serve diverse purposes.

1816. *Aũme nĩ nyamũ mbai.* **Men are fierce animals.**
Old women admonished teenage girls with this proverb, not to suggest that men were inhumane but to warn the girls that men's penchant for sex could ruin their lives. Playing with men would mean irresponsible conception, and most men would not be committed to the relationship after pregnancy occurred.

1817. *Aũme nĩ aũmani.* **Men are biters.**
This ancient truism assumes strong-willed men inevitably clash. It cautions that parents should separate their male children when they grow up by allocating land for them to settle a bit away from each other.

---

[1] Mwau, *Dictionary*, 646.

1818. *Aũme makĩtaa kũsama ti kũtha.* **Men only discuss matters; they do not gamble.**
Two words here (*kũsama* and *kũtha*) challenge comprehension if not spelt and translated properly. The word *kũsama* can mean 'to taste or discuss in consultation; to hold counsel'; the word *kũtha* may mean to gamble, but spelt with a double /a/ (*kũthaa*) means to compete for food on a plate. The axiom means men are better off consulting each other rather than gambling, which invites conflict. This becomes a warning not to lie to fellow men on serious matters involving resources or family affairs. In the second interpretation, with *kũsama* translated as 'to taste', it becomes a vehicle used seriously by older women to young girls as a caution against premarital pregnancy. It means in sex men have no long-term commitment but flatter women and move on. It may imply, however, that in table manners men just taste food but do not scramble for food.

1819. *Aũme nĩ ngũ syotanaa.* **Men are fire logs igniting each other.**
This ancient proverb reflects the Kamba engagement with the hearth as an exclusive space for male members of the family. It was a cultural fulcrum where young men were educated and judgements made. Men sitting at the hearth observed burning logs spreading flames to other logs and equated it with male conflict. It was a warning to minimize confrontation.[2]

1820. *Aũme mayuaa mbu.* **Men do not shriek.**
Men were dissuaded from crying or screaming when subjected to pain. Screaming was considered cowardice and a weak expression of who a man was. Sandra Newman tells us this distinction is a recent development in most cultures. In the past men routinely wept and no one saw it as feminine or shameful. When did Kamba men's tears dry up? Where did all the male tears go?[3] That question goes beyond the scope of this book. What is certain is that in challenging circumstances as far back as the Monsoon era, 'tearlessness' defined Kamba masculinity. The proverb encourages less complaint and more action and endurance.

1821. *Aũme nĩ kwonana kavii ke iko.* **Men are bound to see each other when the dik-dik is in the fire.**
This ancient adage is open to multiple interpretations. Mutisya saw it as saying 'superiority is best determined when there is something at stake'. It is from competition for meagre resources that a champion emerges. The Kamba organized hunting parties that killed and roasted

---

[2] Kimilu, *Mũkamba*, 115.
[3] Sarah Newman, 'Society Says That Men Aren't Supposed to Cry – But Why?', *The Reader's Digest*, 5 June 2018.

dik-diks. Since the animal was too small for everyone, the roasted meat was shared by casting lots, which were riddled with tricks. One person sat facing away from the meat, while the other would cut a portion, and then beat that chunk asking the other person to say whose lot that was. An unwise hunter could be tricked to have the worst share or no meat at all. Therefore, to reduce the impact of such tensions, whenever hunters killed a dik-dik and threw it into the bonfire, two aggrieved men tried to settle their disputes before the actual sharing of the meat.

1822. *Eka kũmbĩta kaa ta kavyũ mbĩte yĩĩ ta ĩthoka.* **Stop calling me 'this little one' like a knife, call me 'this big one' like an axe.**
This is an axiomatic objection of mockery and an assertion that the speaker is an expert on the matter. The axe was harder than the knife and could cut the hardest objects. A man of note was comparable to the hardened axe. The knife (symbolizing weakness in a person) is weaker than the axe, which could cut and crush anything the precolonial Mũkamba wanted to get rid of.

1823. *Eka kũmbĩta nganga kaswii.* **Stop calling me the chick of a guineafowl.**
The guineafowl's chick is stupid, does not know how to fly, and is even friendly to enemies.[4] To view someone as inexperienced is the worst mockery to them. Through this maxim the speaker asserts their ability to handle the matter at hand. This predates the colonial period and appears to have emerged when the Kamba developed sustained contacts with guineafowls.

1824. *Eka ũmuthatĩa mũathi, nĩ mbanga.* **Don't get angry at the archer; it is an accident.**[5]
This ancient axiom alludes to hunting and shooting a charging lion. As the lion jumped high, a Kamba archer shot the beast and rolled out of the way of its charge. Fellow archers were required to shoot at the lion within a fraction of a second to demobilize it. If the shooter did not roll away, he was rained on by arrows, hence the proverb. This is similar to 'do not play with a lion's tail'.

1825. *Mũtino ndwĩ nzamba.* **'The cock' is no match for fate.**
The cock (or rooster) in this ancient proverb symbolizes an invincible man. The proverb means no hero can outdo a misfortune; no one is an expert in avoiding danger. Accident can overtake anyone.

---

[4] Mwau, *Dictionary*, 646.
[5] Farnsworth, *Grammar*, 19.

1826. *Ngima ya mai ĩvokawa na maumoo.* **A mealiepap of poop is dinned with urine stew.**
This is used in a conflict context by the offended party, implying something like a brute for a brute. If someone does not apologize, he ought to be treated as rudely as he deserves. It emerged during the Islamic period when the Kamba adopted grains and processed them into mealiepap.

1827. *Nzamba ilĩ ityĩkalania kĩtutonĩ kĩmwe.*[6] **Two cockerels can never have harmony on the same threshing floor.**
The key to comprehending this proverb is the multiple meanings of *kĩtutonĩ*: a clearing for dancing or building; threshing ground; the cleared and cleaned section in front of a house also known as *nza nzeu*. Hens lived in such clearings during the day where cockerels often fought for dominance. It was hard for more than two cockerels to coexist in one clearing. Likewise, adults need space to avoid unnecessary competition and conflict.

1828. *Ndũũ ya Makaũ na Syokaũ ĩkaũ.* **The friendship of Makaũ and Syokaũ is violent.**
This proverb stresses the importance of maintaining good friendships and harmony within the family. The proverb emerged during the Vascon era. During that period the Kamba, Maasai, and Galla raided each other for livestock. Children born during this period were given such names as Makaũ for boys and Syokaũ for girls. These two names, significantly, mean war and suggest that such names can be traced to the beginning of external conflicts.

1829. *Ngũnga aikũngwa e mũkũngĩle.* **One hammered was already hammered.**
This common catchphrase in Machakos and Mwea appears in multiple variants with multiple interpretations. It derives from the act of sharpening hoes by hitting the sharp part with a hammer (*kũkũnga*) to sharpen it for weeding. The practice of sharpening hoes started in the late 1920s, which means the proverb emerged during the 1930s. It means people who usually excel have a propensity to do so, but those who fail in life are also predestined for such eventuality. The Kamba say that rumours are not always unreliable. If people accuse you of something, you have habitually done it for sure.

1830. *Kongo oowaiwe nĩ mũnuka.* **The mouth killed Kongo.**
This came out of a tale of a hunter named Kongo. He was in a group of warriors on a war mission when he went aside for nature's call. Coming upon a place of skulls he knocked one bleached skull to inspect it and

---

[6] Mwau, *Dictionary*, 667.

asked, 'Who killed these people?' The skull responded, 'Soon you will know!' Scared, he ran to tell the other warriors and the entire group trooped to the spot of the speaking skull. He asked the same question but no voice came out. The furious warriors killed him. As soon as he was dead the skull said, 'I told you that you will soon find out how we died. You are dead because of your mouth.' The maxim dates during the Vascon era when such expeditions became common.

1831. *Ĩkwani no ngewa.* **A court case is just a story.**
Someone with the courage to face prosecution would use this axiom to say that he/she was ready. It encourages the listener not to be scared by anything, for where there is a will there is way. This emerged during the twentieth century when court cases became common. Unlike traditional litigations, court cases involved arguments and stories on both sides.

1832. *Ilaũnĩ syĩkĩanaa.* **Crowns do not fear each other.**
In other words, equals have mutual respect in that they do not mock, harass, or look down upon each other. This emerged from the twentieth century, when, in the context of colonialism, political power rested on emblems worn on the head.

1833. *Kĩlaũnĩ kĩĩsawa kĩ mũtwe, kyaiwa nthĩ nĩ ĩsaaya.*[7] **A crown is eaten while on the head, when it is laid down it becomes a piece of aluminum.**
Emerging during the twentieth century, this axiom alludes to *kĩlaũnĩ*, 'crown', a colonial emblem worn on the head with an engraving of the monarch of England. *Kĩlaũnĩ* was a symbol of official status, power, authority, and resources that could benefit its holder. Colonial chiefs and police took advantage of the crown while they were on active duty by receiving gifts from civilians. Once they retired, resigned, or were fired, gifts ceased flowing. Therefore, it suggests people ought to take advantage of their privileged position while they have it.[8] At another level people say this proverb to infer that relatives and friends of a civil servant enjoy the benefits of his employment.

1834. *Kũnũva nthũ nĩ kũmyũaa.*[9] **To divest an enemy is to kill it.**
To destroy the property of a capable person who can rebuild is futile. You can succeed only if such a person is dead. As proof of the popularity of this maxim it has appeared in publications without explanatory notes since 1972.

---

[7] Mwau, *Dictionary*, 650; Mbiti, *Ngaeka*, XI.
[8] Mutisya, *Proverbs*, 2.
[9] Mailu, *Kĩkyambonie*, 16, 71; Mwau, *Dictionary*, 650.

1835. *Ĩtema yitĩaa kĩvũthya.*[10] **A liver chokes one because of pooh-pooh.**
Fat, liver, and liquids appear like easy things to swallow, but if one is not careful they can choke you. This ancient proverb was applied in the context of fighting. One was advised to think about the strength of the opponents before attacking them.

1836. *Ĩtina naumie ndisyokaa ĩngĩ.* **I do not return to a place I left.**
Similar to 'forward ever, backward never', this ancient axiom advises against repeating mistakes. It was also used in disagreement. If one sought reconciliation, the other, unwilling to reconcile, responded with this axiom.

1837. *Maela maamina aũme.* **Striving finished men.**
This has been in print since the 1960s but with unclear interpretations and translations. Mutisya made the best translation of all published variations, 'Attempts have always finished men.' Nevertheless, he did not link the proverb to its original context – *kũeela* or *kũelya*, 'to test' or 'to attempt'. To try what? To try a river or a deep pond at the risk of drowning – many daring swimmers have drowned while trying the deeper spots of a river or pond. The word was taken from that context – attempting, testing, or trying to compete with other men, and failing. The proverb warns against taking actions that endanger one's life.[11]

1838. *Mũndũ ndavuũlasya mũndũ wake mbee wa andũ.* **Do not expose your relatives naked to the public.**
Emerging after the First World War this alludes to the idea of exposing the nakedness of another person by lifting their skirts. This was an extreme insult and embarrassment. The maxim means people should not wash their dirty linen in public.

1839. *Mũndũũme ndomĩasya ĩkovi akwete kĩvanga.* **A man does not withstand a slap while holding a machete.**
Two Swahili words (*ikovi*, 'slap', and *kĩvanga*, derived from the Swahili word *panga*, 'machete'), which entered Kamba diction during the 1920s, serve as historical markers. The machete became widespread after the First World War. The axiom means people should not suffer while they have the ability to prevent the suffering. One's mind and knowledge are the symbolic machete, which can cut and resist suffering of any kind, even challenges from adversaries.[12]

---

[10] Mwau, *Dictionary*, 647.
[11] Farnsworth, *Grammar*, 56; Kimilu, *Mũkamba*, 116; Mwau, *Dictionary*, 656; Mutisya, *Proverbs*, 26.
[12] Mutisya wa Ngai, 'Kyuo kya Ngoso, number 7'.

1840. *Mwaĩki ũkwete kyenzi ndatheelawa.* **A circumciser holding the circumcising blade is not kicked.**
Circumcisers used a special knife called *kyenzi*. If someone lightly kicked them, severe injury to the initiate followed. Another interpretation is if one kicks the circumciser armed with such a sharp blade, the circumciser can quickly retaliate. The proverb means that one focusing on a given goal must concentrate on accomplishing that goal.

1841. *Mũndũũme ndaĩyaa ekaa ũthata.* **A man does not cry he just gets angry.**[13]
Men were trained to be tough and remorseless. Circumcision with a sharp knife was central to inculcating the belief that a man should endure all kinds of pain and hardship without groaning. As the household leader and the anchor of his family, the man had no room to show emotional weakness before his family.

1842. *Mũndũũme ndetaa methoi.* **A man does not shed tears.**
There are multiple variations of this maxim, which refers to restraint and self-control. For men, society's pressure to live self-controlled lives calls upon them to be strong and avoid emotions. For example, it is shameful for a man to cry. There is nothing that depicts this male stoic image more than the above proverb.[14]

1843. *Ndũkaavũthĩsye mũndũũme kũmũkĩlya kĩthũi.* **Do not underestimate a man if his chest is smaller than yours.**
This ancient axiom deals with honour. Strength was assumed to come from the size of the chest, not other muscles. When a big-chested person was defeated in wrestling, people used this and other proverbs to explain the abnormality. A big-chested person was expected to carry himself with humility and awareness that strength comes from different sources. Scorning a thinner person could be detrimental, so behave yourself in public.

1844. *Mũndũ ũkũkwĩka naĩ aũthekasya okĩla sua.* **Someone with ill intentions smiles at you daily.**
Tracing from antiquity this proverb warns against ill-intended companions who might use their closeness to cause harm. Enemies do not have to be openly hostile. Some pretend to be friends and cause damage using indirect means.

---

[13] Mutisya wa Ngai, 'Kyuo kya Ngoso, number 6'.
[14] Kaleli, 'Theoretical Foundations', 270.

1845. *Mūndū ūkakūvīvya ambaa kūkūmba muu.* **Someone who will burn you pours ash on you first.**
As men sat around the hearth to warm themselves in the morning and evening, those closer to the fire frequently stirred the embers, often flashing up the hot ash accidentally to other men. Some shrewd men used such opportunity to punish their opponents by first flashing ash towards the 'enemy' and eventually flashing up hot coals at him. The offender always claimed it was an accident. By extension, people who will hurt you may use unconventional means and fake it in a way that you will not suspect foul play. This proverb traces back to the Monsoon Exchange era.

1846. *Mūndū ūtesī nthimo athimawa na mūsyī.* **A person who does not know proverbs is tested with an arrow.**
This figurative statement means foolishness and that an inability to perceive or comprehend axiomatic language is dangerous. One can be killed for lack of this particular knowledge.

1847. *Mūndū mūnene aumawa na ūkewa.* **An adult or a senior person is mocked through a story.**
This ancient maxim reveals social power relations. Juniors had a way to challenge higher authority. You do not call in-laws by their names. You nickname them. A rich man is told off in proverbs. Do not say it directly to him.

1848. *Mūthaimwa nī mūtūi ndavītaa.* **One who is spied on by his neighbour never escapes.**
One's associates know his movements and secrets, so if they plot against him he is vulnerable and cannot escape. This is said about secrets that are in the hands of one's spouse, business partner, or leader after some disagreement. Since the two know each other's strengths, the only solution is reconciliation.[15]

1849. *Mūthanga ūvindasya ngūmbaū.* **The soil silences many champions.**
Appearing in popular music, this ancient axiom is a call for humility among men of valour. It means that mortals have limited strength against nature. It reminds audiences that at the end of life there is death and one cannot take material wealth to the grave. However, it is two proverbs in one. Grandfathers used it to admonish valiant grandsons to slow down and respect the meek, the old, the frail, and females. It refers to any kind of talent that makes one superior over others. One who brags about such talents is foolish when they fail to realize that it is all transitory.

---

[15] Muīmi, *Kīthyomo*, 36; Mutisya, *Proverbs*, 38; Mwau, *Dictionary*, 660.

1850. *Ũtaumwa nĩ mwana ndamũĩ.* **A person who cannot be mocked by a child does not have one.**
This proverb is less about insults and rebellious children and more about being gentle. It persuades parents to listen to children, consider their opinion, and bear with their faults.

1851. *Nasya nĩnou ndinasya ĩthĩnzwe.*[16] **When I said it is fat, I did not say skin it.**
This is an ancient axiomatic expression of the Kamba objection to people who drew conclusions from what other people said about their private matters. The proverb was used in two ways: to assert one's objection or to appease the offended person. In remorseful mood, the person drawing the wrong conclusion would say: 'What I said is not final. You can finalize the conversation, I am sorry.'

1852. *Nonie kwa kuma tyo kwa ũthi.* **I saw a point of departure; a destination is not a problem.**
This is a woman's protest proverb in a deteriorating marriage. In this context, the woman means at the time of the original wedding she knew clearly that she was leaving her parents' home and at the juncture of disagreement with her husband she clearly knows where to go. In application, men, particularly the poor, also used the proverb when they disagreed with the powerful. The maxim emerged during the Vascon era as a firm statement of disengagement.

1853. *Nzama nĩ ya elĩ wa katatũ nĩ mwĩlıcha.* **Secrets are for two, the third is an intruder.**
Emerging from antiquity, this speaks about the nature of secrets and confidentiality. It implies that two people can keep secrets between them. If one person revealed the secret, the other knew the partner's betrayal. If there was a third person, it was hard to determine who revealed the secret. It suggests two people can keep a secret if one of them is dead.

1854. *Ĩũma tiyo kyalya.* **A bite is not the pain.**
Snake-bite and scorpion-sting healers originally used this old saying. Their success is vaguely understood due to their secret *materia medica* and its occult–mystical nature. There are scores of well-known plants that Kamba healers used in snake-bite treatments.[17] Through the axiom healers meant that pain comes after the bite and results only come later. Outside this context, the axiom admonishes people to be patient for something to mature. Do not complain right away.

---

[16] Kĩeti, *Barking*, 111; Mwau, *Dictionary*, 663.
[17] Bethwell Owour and Daniels Kisangau, 'Kenyan Medicinal Plants used as Antivenin', *Journal of Ethnobiology and Ethnomedicine* 2(7) (2006), 1–8.

406   Part IV: Kamba Society

1855. *Mana yonwa nĩ ita ndyonwa nĩ athiani.*[18] **Spies cannot see a fortune that war bands can stumble on.**
This emerged from war and hunting expeditions of the Vascon era. Two important groups are alluded to – *ita*, a band of raiders or an army at war, and the rear guard composed of old men who waited to drive home the spoils. The second group is the *Athiani* (the spies and war chaplains) who were on the front line with the fighters and did not receive the best loot, as the rear guard did. This means that hardworking people are not always fairly compensated.[19]

1856. *Kaũ ndwakaa mũsyĩ.* **Squabbles do not build a family.**
Wife beating was common in precolonial Kamba. The proverb means such forms of discipline and conflict resolution were futile and only tore a family apart. The ancient axiom suggests that non-violent means are better in conflict management at all levels of society and state.

1857. *Kaũ ndwalanĩaw'a.* **No one prepares for war.**
This proverb means conflict is not planned for, it just happens. In another interpretation, it warns people to refrain from causing conflict.

1858. *Kaũ wĩkaa kũomboa.*[20] **Conflict only demolishes.**
This is among the oldest of Kamba proverbs. Kamba migration from Tanzania to eastern Kenya was undertaken in part as a result of tensions and conflict within their ancestral lands. The adage was coined as a means to dissuade people from engaging in conflict.

1859. *Kĩa kĩla wene.* **Fear what you see.**
This cautions against fear, fantasy, and hearsay. From ancient antiquity it reveals Kamba dogma of believing it when you see it but not when you hear it. Other entries in this book show the difference between the ear and the eye. Trust the eye more than the ear.

1860. *Ko nguĩvĩa kimba ũng'ethya?* **Am I paying blood money for staring at the corpse?**
This adage was used when the old admonished young people to refrain from matters that did not concern them. For instance, a person could be taken for a thief if they found stolen property and, out of curiosity, began examining the goods. If the owner found them at that moment, suspicion followed. If one found a dead person and stopped to look, he was suspected of murder.[21] In accidents, observers were victimized

---

[18] Kimilu, *Mũkamba*, 116.
[19] Mutisya, *Proverbs*, 13.
[20] Mailu, *Kĩkyambonie*, 55.
[21] Farnsworth, *Grammar*, 94; Watuma, *Syĩthĩo*, 52.

and accused of having killed the dead person, and at that moment would retort, 'Am I going to pay for just gazing at the corpse?'

1861. *Makĩaa ũta matesĩ kĩsasi kĩkaũ.* **They fear the bow, not knowing the bullet is superior.**
This emerged during the twentieth century when guns and bullets became common among the Kamba. The bow shoots but the bullet causes more damage. The statement means people fear what they do not know, yet what is on the way is a greater threat.

1862. *Kĩmũtwe kĩvotaa.* **A mere thought is not profitable.**
Mere thoughts cannot help settle a case unless they are spoken. This dates from the age of *asili* institutions (age of judges) during the Vascon era. Each village had its own judges (distinct and separate from a mere council of elders) who specialized in settling disputes.

1863. *Ndinda mũtwe ndĩsilaa.* **That which abides in the mind does not settle cases.**
This old maxim about settling disputes and cases encourages people to speak, as their thoughts alone cannot settle cases. It also discourages people from complaining later after judgement has been made. Some people complained after the case was settled that they thought they would be allowed more time to argue. Such arguments are too late to bear results.

1864. *Kĩtai kyumanasya nda na wĩtũũo.* **A tragedy upwells from the abdomen with diarrhoea.**
This is a figurative expression of how tragedy occurs due to both natural causes and reckless actions. Although an individual may play a part, this means tragedy is unpreventable.

1865. *Kĩtai nĩ kwĩmanzĩa, mbanga nĩ kũka.* **Tragedy is self-inflicted, but fate brings itself.**
This calls for people to avoid actions that cause self-injury, embarrassment, and tragedy. This adage warns that there are accidents that result from the reckless behaviour of victims. These proverbs originated from antiquity as social control measures.

1866. *Kĩtai nĩkĩsaa kwĩsa.* **The bare one often comes.**
This adage going back to antiquity means expectations often fail and advises to prepare for future uncertainties. One who is rich can be financially ruined or a pauper can in time become rich.[22]

---

[22] Kimilu, *Mũkamba*, 116; Kĩtukũ, *Folktales*, 68; Mutisya, *Proverbs*, 57.

1867. *Kĩtai kĩthethete kĩ syaa syĩ ngoto.*[23] **A predestined fate has claws.**
This means that once tragedy strikes it is hard to avoid. The doomed do not heed the warnings of the wise. The proverb denotes that persistent pursuit of bad habits draws one closer to tragedy. As many stories illustrate this proverb, it is clear that it points to natural causes of tragedy but tragedy that is linked to uncouth human habits.

1868. *Ngolya ya kĩtai ĩkolasya ngingo.* **A hook of tragedy, hooks the neck.**
Related to the above entry, this proverb concerns natural tragedies without human responsibility. As per Murphy's Law, anything that can go wrong will go wrong. It was said of people who defied warnings that they might jeopardize their safety.[24]

1869. *Mũndũ wa kĩtai avĩsaa nĩ ngima ĩkomie thome.* **An ill-fated person is scalded by a cold mealiepap left overnight at the hearth.**
Mealiepap was served hot, so fast eaters got scalded. The irony in this ancient proverb, which has multiple variations, is that the person scalded here is not just the glutton rushing to eat hot mealiepap, but a tragic fellow who is scalded even by cold mealiepap.[25] This statement means that ill-fated people have no escape from their tragic ends. They always take the riskiest path in life and end tragically.

1870. *Ndũkakootee nyamũ ya kĩtai ũta.* **Do not draw your bow against a fierce animal.**
This ancient adage from hunting contexts is often rendered in multiple variations. It warned that hunting lions, leopards, cheetahs, elephants, rhinos, and buffaloes was a risky endeavour that ought to be avoided whenever possible. It warns the audience to avoid conflict with people who are more resourceful or physically stronger. There is no chance of the listener prevailing in that conflict. While other variants have been left out, this is a variant of an older and important axiom that appears below.

1871. *Nyamũ mbai ndyoseawa ũta.* **One does not pick up a bow to shoot away a fierce animal.**
Unlike several other variations,[26] this axiom suggests that flight from danger is preferable to futile resistance. It admonishes people to respect

---

[23] Mutisya, *Proverbs*, 53; Mwau, *Dictionary*, 650; Muiu, *Cross-Cultural*, 97.
[24] Eric Partridge, *Dictionary of Catch Phrases* (New York: Scarborough House, 1992), 278.
[25] Mutisya, *Proverbs*, 53.
[26] Mwau, *Dictionary*, 670.

those who are more powerful. Although 'the beast' may cover different types of animals, this proverb alludes to a charging elephant and by extension buffalo, rhino, leopard, and lion.

1872. *Nyamũ ĩsu ũkwosea ũta ti ngũũe nĩ nzou nga na yew'a ngũngi iminaa mũndũ.* **The beast you are picking up the bow to shoot is not a pig; it is a female elephant and when it gets human scent, it tramples someone.**
This proverb refers to the power of women in precolonial Kamba. Female animals were the fiercest defenders of their young and hunters always refrained from hunting females. The Vascon-era proverb alludes to genderized thinking in hunting. Female beasts were rarely shot because they were both dangerous and producers of future game. The female elephant depended on scent and if it sensed the presence of humans, it charged. Hunters claimed a female elephant distinguished between the scent of a man and a woman, never attacking women. In modern political contexts, the axiom means that novices cannot compete with established politicians' money and charms.

1873. *Ndũkaaĩtae nũndũ kĩtae nĩkyũkaa.*[27] **Never boast because poverty does come.**
Many dangers threatened precolonial Kamba wealth, wiping it out instantaneously. Dating from the Vascon era, the axiom cautioned rich men to be both humble and vigilant.

1874. *Nĩkũkaa ngeni ĩtakũtũe.* **A stanger often intrudes.**
This cautions people to be prepared for contingencies. It emerged from the insecurity of the Vascon era, when the coast was enflamed and inland communities experienced tensions upon the arrival of Kwavi who raided the Kamba for cattle. As newcomers they were referred to as *ngeni ĩtakũtũe*, an unknown newcomer.

1875. *Kĩthethete kĩtiaa kyatuũla.* **A persistent fate eventually overwhelms.**[28]
This is the literal rather than free translation. The word *kĩthethete* or *kĩtheete*, depending on different dialects, refers to natural or self-inflicted tragic trends that leave trails of damage. It is said of someone who ignores warnings or signs of danger and persistently commits foolish acts that lead to injury.

---

[27] Mailu, *Kĩkyambonie*, 55.
[28] Kimilu, *Mũkamba*, 116.

1876. *Kĩya mwene nĩwe ũkĩmanzaa.* **The victim seeks his predator.**
This ancient axiom emerged out of observation on what drives people to tragedy. While some tragedies are natural, others result from careless and risky actions that lead to destruction. This is self-injury.

1877. *Kĩ kyambonie kĩkakwona.* **What befell me will befall you too.**
This ancient axiom was the title of a book written by David Mailu in 1972. It appeared in the text as *Kĩ kyambonie kĩkayo kĩna kwona asu ũkwĩw'a nĩ matuu makyo*, 'What happened to me will happen to you, and what you hear now are its rumbling feet.'[29] It is similar to 'The log in the pile does not laugh at the one in the fire.' The maxim was used in bitter contests and rivalries.

1878. *Kĩla kĩkaya mũndũ kĩmwaĩlaa ta ĩthaa.* **What will destroy someone fits him like an ornament.**
This is an ancient warning against potential tragedy: one must be careful to guard against falling prey to tragic incidences. Immorality and dangerous behaviour begins slow and eventually leads to addiction and ruin.

1879. *Kĩng'ei kĩkwatawa no kĩngĩ.* **Only a thief catches another thief.**
This ancient proverb is equivalent to 'Set a thief to catch a thief.' Because thieves have skills others do not, leaders began to employ reformed thieves to catch active thieves, hence the proverb. It means that people with similar traits know the secrets of each other.

1880. *Kĩng'ei kyakwatwa kyasyaa kĩmelaa muu.* **When a thief is caught he says he was eating the ash.**
The ancient Kamba differentiated between theft and petty larceny. The punishment for theft ranged from heavy fines to death. Less severe punishment was meted for larceny – stealing unessential and perishable items.[30] For the apprehended thief to make his case an excusable larceny, he would claim that he was eating ash, a totally worthless item – this was a lame excuse and denial of wrongdoing.

1881. *Kwaa mwĩkatha kũmaa mbaa matũ.* **The braggart's home hails delinquents.**
This exposes the underbelly of heroism and prowess. It means that from the home of those who boast about their upright morals hails delinquents; the mighty have their own share of weaknesses. Tracing back to the first millennium when the Kamba established durable villages

---

[29] Mailu, *Kĩkyambonie*, 64; Mwau, *Dictionary*, 649.
[30] Lindblom, *Akamba*.

and political units, this proverb persuaded families to be cautious in raising children.

1882. *Ngema kũvya ĩtũlaa kyano na ũtambĩ.*[31] **The 'uncookable' breaks the arrow with his thigh.**
This adage was drawn from the intersection of hunting and cooking legumes. In cooking, some peas were found hard to cook. These legumes represent humans who are impossible to admonish and teach. Because they are so stubborn, they could hardly pay attention to warnings. They were caught unaware by tragedy, the symbolic breaking of a poisoned arrowhead with a thigh, the softest part of the body and most vulnerable to poison. It means stupid actions end tragically. The adage is varied in different and important ways, and is akin to the next entry.

1883. *Ngema kũvya ndĩvĩsaa ona wa mĩtindya iko.* **The 'uncookable' is never done even if you keep it cooking forever.**
This axiom means those who cannot be advised will never learn their lessons. No amount of effort can rescue a stubborn person, who is comparable to peas that defy cooking.

1884. *Kyaũlũ kĩyĩ mwene.*[32] **That from above has no owner.**
This proverb emerged during the Vascon era. It was used by characters who shot arrows into the air in a public gathering comprised of disputing inter-ethnic parties. When the arrows hit members of the crowd who complained, the culprits responded with this proverb. No one can take responsibility of objects from the sky.

1885. *Kwene kũianaw'a too.* **One does not sleep sufficiently in alien places.**
Long-distance travellers have to lodge at some point, just as people with particular goals may have to make unpleasant but necessary choices. Emerging from the Monsoon era, this axiom points to the significance of home and self-reliance. Only personal home and, by extension, possessions, satisfy.

1886. *Kyathĩ kĩtwe kĩyĩ ũsũũ mũvyũ.* **An appointment knows no hot gruel.**
Porridge was the commonest delicacy shared in a gathering of people. When one made an appointment with such a gathering, he prepared porridge for them such that, by the time the gathering settled, the porridge was cool and ready for immediate consumption. The proverb means that decisions that have been made ought to be executed on time. One should not wait until the actual day to start preparations.

---

[31] Kimilu, *Mũkamba*, 117.
[32] Mwau, *Dictionary*, 653.

1887. *Kyathĩ kĩtwe kĩvuvĩwaa ngũli.* **A horn is not blown for a set appointment.**
The proverb emphasizes the need to keep appointments with prompt arrivals without reminders. When the Kamba agreed to meet at a particular place and time, they were generally quite prompt. However, on occasion of emergencies, a horn was blown and people rushed to the scene. A single continuous beat was meant to remind villagers that it was time to meet somewhere, from where all would go to help cultivate the farm for a colleague. While this proverb talks about political and military circumstances, the next variant talks about social circumstances on the home front.

1888. *Mĩlilo ĩliasya ĩtina.* **Regret comes last.**
This ancient adage warns that careless action can bring ruin, embarrassment, and regret.[33] This adage is used when unexpected outcomes arise. It talks about the results of accidental ignorance. It also cautions that ignorance cannot lead a person – study something carefully before you indulge in it.

1889. *Mauta makũũ mayiangaa nzaiko.* **Old perfume is not fit for a circumcision ceremony.**
This maxim alludes to important circumcision dances. Mealiepap seasoned with ghee was served to the dancers who were also anointed with fresh rather than aged ghee. With multiple variations and interpretations, this proverb was a reconciliation statement. If we disagreed in the past, we should not harbour grievances. It was also used to persuade listeners to change their way of doing something to something more nuanced.

1890. *Ũmĩĩsyo mũnene wetelaa mũuw'o.* **Perseverance anticipates peace.**
This old saying reflects struggles with life and has been around since the 1800s – most informants confirmed that the proverb emerged during the early years of that century. It encourages people in dire situations to persevere and they will eventually enjoy better times.

1891. *Mbanga ĩkalaa mokonĩ.* **Tragedy is handy.**
With multiple interpretations, this ancient axiom means tragedy lurks in every human action. That is, misfortunes are unpredictable and unstoppable.[34] It is used to rationalize sudden tragic incidences.

---

[33] Farnsworth, *Grammar*, 79; Mwau, *Dictionary*, 656.
[34] Mutisya, *Proverbs*, 54; Mwau, *Dictionary*, 654.

1892. *Mbanga ndĩsĩ mwene.* **Tragedy does not know the owner.**
Since antiquity this axiom has been used in various contexts. It means that accidents cannot be prevented, not even by the head of the family. He too can be a victim of it.

1893. *Mbanga ndĩvangaa mũtĩnĩ, ĩvangaa mũndũnĩ.* **Tragedy does not perch on a tree, but on a person.**
This encourages bereaved families that tragedy is part of life. In other words, there is no barrier against misfortune.[35] It has been used in this form since antiquity to console bereaved families and victims of accidents.

1894. *Mbuvaa ngũli ene maimba matau.* **I blow the horn when the owners' cheeks swell.**
The horn was used to communicate messages over long distances for events such as childbirth, invasion, fire, and others. There were experts in the task who put pressure on their cheeks and jaws. In occasional competitions, sly competitors waited until every expert was exhausted. Since horns were the business of hunters and pastoralists, and economic pursuits were already burgeoning by the fourteenth century, the proverb emerged around that period. The meaning and application are to be patient, be tactical, be observant, and act when others have tried their luck.

1895. *Mũkosewa ndesilĩaa.* **The plaintiff does not arbitrate for himself.**
This ancient proverb derives from a story of a historical character named Kyeela Ũkũne – one who measured the level of a laceration. It reflects the ways the Kamba handled conflict within their communities. The aggrieved party did not decide the fine or punishment to the offender but reported to the village head who then called a council of men to decide the case.

1896. *Mũndũ ngũmbaũ ndakĩaa kwendela kĩthekanĩ kĩthungu.*[36] **A courageous person does not fear going through a dense forest.**
In their migration from central Tanzania northward, the Kamba confronted dense forests and only courageous leaders could penetrate such forests infested with fierce animals. The ancient proverb means that courageous men do not fear to take risks if there is profit at the end.

---

[35] Mutisya, *Proverbs*, 54.
[36] Kimilu, *Mũkamba*, 118; Mbiti, *Weteelete*, 81.

1897. *Naũkwatĩa mbya ntheele syĩkaeme.* **If you hold the horns, the kicks should not overwhelm you.**
This cowboy-type maxim emerged during the Vascon era in the context of handling bulls that fought with their horns and hooves. It required a team of strong men to bring a bull down. The strongest man took hold of the bull by its horns, which helped subdue the animal. Those who handled the legs were responsible for less difficult tasks. This proverb was told to someone who needed help to tell him that the difficult task was done; so, he/she should deal with the lesser task.

1898. *Ndyaakw'a ngew'a.* **I have never died to taste it.**
An expression of defiance and protest since antiquity, this was used to protest decisions that pushed the speaker to an untenable obligation. It was a statement of despair close to saying, 'Let it be, I will not do it. Whatever the consequences, let it be.'

1899. *Mũndũ wĩ ngũlũ ndunianĩ aminaa naĩ.* **A proud person in the world ends miserably.**
This condemns pride and indicates the negative consequences of it. Pride is a vice within Kamba lore and a proud person has been observed to end in misery. Use of the Swahili word *ndunia*, 'world', indicates coinage in the twentieth century when Swahili became widespread.

1900. *Mũsyĩ wa ũtukũ ũtũngĩlawa vala wesĩla.*[37] **An arrow shot at night is sent back on its original path.**
This emerged during the Islamic era, when the Kamba adopted bows and arrows. The proverb is used both as an expression of revenge (where the speaker prefers a tit-for-tat response), and of gratitude as in 'One good turn deserves another.' The proverb calls for an appropriate response including retribution or reciprocity as necessary.

1901. *Mũtongoi wa kiita nĩwe ũũkitĩthasya.* **A war leader is the one who directs the battle.**
This emerged during the Islamic era when Kamba along the coast had such leaders. The word *kiita* refers to the bands of hunters or raiders, always under the command of one person, that emerged during that period. The proverb has multiple interpretations, one of which is that the responsibility of the matter at hand falls squarely in the hands of the listener.

---

[37] Kimilu, *Mũkamba*, 117; Kĩtukũ, *Folktales*, 39; Mutisya, *Proverbs*, 21; Watuma, *Syĩthĩo*, 56.

1902. *Mũtu wa mũndũũme aindaa kĩla ũkwenda.* **A man makes out of his flour whatever he desires.**
This proverb emerged with millet farming from which raw edible flour was ground by women and given to men to carry on their long-distance treks during the Vascon era. Beyond its context the maxim means decision lies with the person alluded to.

1903. *Kasũngĩa mwakinĩ kayaa malanga.* **One who dances by the fire does not lack scars.**
This ancient axiom means that it is prudent to learn what is harmful and avoid danger.[38] If one acts without judgement there are harmful consequences. This proverb is akin to the next entry.

1904. *Mwendi wa malanga ethongaa iko.* **The lover of scars plunges into the fire.**
With multiple variations, this talks about the self-infliction of pain. It means that aggressive people bring harm to themselves.

1905. *Ũtakũna ũngĩ amũkũnĩaa mwakonĩ.* **One who cannot beat another, beats him in the construction.**
This axiom speaks about strategy in conflict. Things that cannot be said or done directly and openly can still be accomplished through strategic methods. It speaks about strategies of getting around community norms. For example, if a man is upset with in-laws and cannot reprimand them because the norms forbid it, the offended invites the in-law to a building project, where he will pretend to cooperate in the project but let some of the building material strike on the in-law.

1906. *Ndũkawete malanga me andũnĩ.* **Do not mention scars when people have them.**
The truth hurts and it is often important not to speak certain facts in certain situations. For instance, talking about childlessness in the presence of a childless person was considered immoral among the precolonial Kamba.

1907. *Mũaani ndaawa.* **The divider is not divided.**
This alludes to ancient burial customs. When a household head died, elders appointed a man to divide up the deceased's estate. This man and the senior wife performed ritual sex called *kũaa*. This duty and office of *mũaani* was not attractive to ordinary men. So, whoever volunteered to do it often was usually a bad character. So, when he died, no one was willing to divide up his estate, hence the proverb. The benefactor benefits from no one.

---

[38] Mutisya, *Proverbs*, 27.

1908. *Mwĩkũla nĩwe wĩkaa ũla wai.* **The avenger is the destroyer.**
This ancient axiom, first recorded by Lindblom in 1911, means that in a physical fight, if a person is beaten, because of pain and anger he beats the man who just beat him hardest in revenge. The latecomer does better because of his experience.

1909. *Ndikĩaa kyũmbe nĩ kĩla kĩngĩ.* **I do not fear a creature while I am one.**
This protest axiom appeared in a song a woman from Kabati composed after she was incarcerated at Kinyangi prison, the first female inmate there. She composed the song after she prevailed in the court. She meant that a human being should never fear a human being no matter how strong and powerful they may be. I have found no precedents, so I assume she was the originator of that proverb in the 1950s.

1910. *Nditindĩaa vau va kũna ngwonie.* **I do not dwell on saying 'try me and I will show you fire'.**
In a fight, wise Kamba rarely struck first, for diverse reasons. At the peak of the altercation, they would tell opponents, 'try me and you will see fire'. Wise cowards then would make this threat, yet to their embarrassment have to flee before their opponents. Act forthrightly and do not indulge in empty boasts. According to oral accounts, this maxim emerged during the eighteenth-century era of Kamba duelling.

1911. *Ndongoi nĩyo ĩtusaa ũlũalũĩ.* **The leader breaks up the cobweb.**
In the precolonial era the Kamba often walked on narrow paths through forests where cobwebs stretched across their path. The first person passing along the trail cleared these webs with his body. The proverb suggests that great responsibility falls on the leader. The proverb was addressed to a person who had called for clan or group help and made his contribution towards the matter before the clan took responsibility.

1912. *Ndia ndĩekawa yanange mũsyĩ nĩ atĩ nĩyo ngũũ, nĩsyaawa ĩtina nayakombalya mbya.* **A fool is never allowed to spoil a household just because he is the oldest, he can be born last and still twist the horns.**
In its plain form this statement should be stated as 'A fool is never allowed to spoil a household just because he is the oldest, a bull can be born last and still twist its horns' – that is, live for a long time and do marvellous things. With multiple variations, this refers to conflict among siblings. After a patriarch died, leadership passed on to the eldest son. Even though the custom bestowed family responsibilities on the eldest son, there were checks and balances. This ancient proverb means that merit is paramount over formality. If the eldest son could

not lead, a more capable son took over, but maintained respect for the elder brother.

1913. *Syosya ndongosya ikomaa ngalĩko wa mũsyĩ.* **Livestock without a leader lodge outside the kraal.**
Emerging during the first millennium this proverb has variants in oral circulation and literature, commenting on how leadership was a highly revered institution. In every herd there was one that always led the way to pastures, watering points, and back home. If the herd lacked a leader, it arrived last at the watering point and found the water dirtied with mud, dung, and urine, and most importantly never made it home. Similarly, lack of leaders and role models leads to dislocation and failure in societies.[39]

1914. *Nĩ mauta ngũvaka ngakũa mbau.* **I am massaging you before I pull out your ribs.**
This was used as advice to politicians from the 1960s that in their career the present is the smooth part, the rough part is still ahead. The initial steps of the Kamba traditional massage were a very soothing application of oil on the belly and chest, but later followed by painful pulling of hands, pulling out of ribs, and pressing the chest.

1915. *Nĩmũvĩtu mũkambĩ.* **I survived measles.**
Measles reached East Africa through Monsoon Exchange commerce. It spread inland with trade and migration, and affected mainly children, such that the speaker of the proverb takes pride in his/her ability to survive that child-killer disease. It is an expression of confidence that the speaker is firmly grounded in the matter at hand and can beat any challenge.

1916. *Kelĩ kathũku nĩ ka ngundi.* **A bad double service is one with a punch.**
Boxing was one of the principal forms of traditional fighting in organized contests. Kamba fighters defended as far as possible from being hit on the chest. This proverb emerged during the Monsoon era.

1917. *Mũndũ wĩsĩ kaũ ndombaa ngundi.* **One who knows how to fight does not clench a fist.**
This ancient proverb is part of social control of those individuals who are strong in society not to use their energy for evil deeds. Second, the maxim challenges aggressive characters to desist from aggression for they will not win the conflict.

---

[39] Kimilu, *Mũkamba*, 118; Kituku, *Folktales*, 45.

1918. *Ngundi ya mbee nĩyo ĩminaa kaũ.* **The first punch determines the outcome of a fight.**
Boxing is an old culture whose styles vary with people and place. Kamba boxers punched the chest and with one solid blow a fighter could gain the victory. The ancient axiom points to the importance of laying a good foundation for everything in life.

1919. *Ngundi ya kĩvĩsĩ ndĩsĩ mũtwe wĩ mbuĩ.* **A boy's punch does not recognize a grey-haired head.**
Emerging after the Second World War this represents the lowest level of social degeneration of Kamba morals among youth. Colonialism brought young and old men into the same workplace and clubs where alcohol was served. Young men challenged elders in these social events. When questioned why they engaged in fights with elders in contravention of norms, the youth cited this proverb.

1920. *Watonywa nzongo ĩtonyee.* **An eye for an eye.**
Corresponding to tit-for-tat, this ancient axiom alludes to revenge. Retribution is a common phenomenon in world cultures such that the logic of tit-for-tat was not necessarily an invention of the ancient Babylonian King Hamurabi, who is credited for creating the law of an eye for an eye and tooth for a tooth – tit for tat.

1921. *Ngai aũnenga ũtongoi nũkũvataa mĩthato.* **When God gives you leadership, he withdraws your anger.**
Tracing back to antiquity this means that leadership requires patience and self-restraint. It implies that people who are quick to anger cannot lead.

1922. *Ng'ung'u na ng'ung'u maitinasya.* **No and No do not spend the day together.**
This ancient proverb means that quarrelsome parties do not coexist. Only agreeable people can live together.

1923. *'Kĩndũ kyoneku kĩkaekwe' ti wasya wa ngũmbaũ.* **It is not heroism to say, 'Do not spare anything that you have seen.'**
Emerging from the Vascon era this was an axiomatic condemnation of greed. It encouraged people to possess only what is necessary. It cautions against overambition in favour of moderation in capitalistic aspirations.

1924. *Ngũmbaũ ĩvalũkaw'a nĩ kĩsakwa.* **A maize cob topples a champion**
This axiom, tracing back to the Vascon era when maize reached East Africa, means that even men of valour have weaknesses. Insignificant

matters can present a challenge to the mighty. No one is all-knowing, self-sufficient, and invincible.

1925. *Ngũmbaũ yaũkĩwa ĩtelemaw'a nĩ mũnyĩlĩ.* **A mighty hero is scared by diarrhoea.**
This ancient axiom suggests that there are limits to almost everything. No matter how strong one is, he cannot challenge diarrhoea. Even champions succumb to it.

1926. *Ngũmbaũ ndĩkosaa malanga.* **A hero does not lack scars.**
This is about competition, conflict, aggression, and valour. This ancient proverb persuades listeners to refrain from trouble.

1927. *Ngũmbaũ ĩsyaa ngũmbaũ ĩngĩ.*[40] **A hero begets hero.**
A stable family will most likely produce stable children. Parents who have excelled in life nurture their children to excel. Success is often inherited from parents.

1928. *Ngũmbaũ ndĩtumĩaa.*[41] **A hero never matures. A hero never ages.**
Emerging from the Monsoon era, this implies that obsession with heroism does not allow one to upgrade relative to age and focus on adult matters. The second implication is that a hero is always a hero, and never ceases to be, regardless of changes in circumstances.

1929. *Ngwatanĩo nzeo no ya nzĩa.*[42] **The best union is of paths.**
This is an ancient axiom with multiple interpretations and meanings. First, it means when and where paths meet, they cause no trouble to each other. They only attract travellers. Second, when people meet along the way they make a more perfect union than if they live together. Conflict is inevitable in society.

1930. *Nguanĩo ya ndata ya mũtumĩa na kĩvĩsĩ ĩetae kĩumo.* **It is a curse for a young person to share a walking stick with an old man.**
Symbolically 'carrying' or 'sharing' means to date a girl – in fact, the Kamba word for dating is *kũkua*, to carry a girl. The girl is symbolically referred to as 'a walking stick'. If an old man approached a girl first, a lad was advised to find another lover. It was taboo for young and old men to date the same girl. The proverb calls for respect at different levels of the social order.

---

[40] Kimilu, *Mũkamba*, 118.
[41] Ngotho, *Mĩthimũkyo*, 7.
[42] Mwau, *Dictionary*, 666.

1931. *Wĩsĩ ũtesĩ.* **You know someone you really do not know.**
This is an accusing statement at the beginning of conflict. If these words involve two people, the speaker is telling the listener that he/she has no clue about imminent danger.

1932. *Thiĩ wa ĩtema wĩvanĩwaa ĩtemanĩ.* **The debt of a slashed bush is paid in a slashed field.**
Traditionally, men helped each other clear land for a farm using machetes. The recipient of such assistance later returned the favour in the same manner as repayment. The hidden meaning, however, signifies conflict. It means if you cut someone he will retaliate using a machete. If you offend someone, expect even bigger revenge than the original offence.

1933. *Ndũkaumange mũisikya ũtanamina masyaa.* **Do not insult the midwife before you are past child-bearing age.**
This originated with women during the Islamic period. As specialist midwives emerged in each village, young women developed and maintained good relationships with the specialists. The
maxim implies that if a young woman insulted midwives, she was endangering herself. The application of the axiom is clear from that context – respect all authorities.

1934. *Ũtheke ti wonze, mũkunzu wĩ nda.* **Leanness is not feebleness, wire is inside.**
Illustrated by the story of a little boy named Musau – the white one – who defeated an ogre that had vanquished all mighty men in the village, this proverb emerged after the First World War.[43] The word *mũkunzu* (wire) became widespread in the 1930s and became a symbol of stamina. The axiom encouraged strategy over muscle.

1935. *Ũtongoi wĩ wana ũmĩaa kĩla vandũ.* **Childish leadership defecates everywhere.**
Poor leaders often make careless blunders. This twentieth-century coinage equated political blunder with childish behaviour of defecating outside the toilet. It calls for civility and honour in politics.

1936. *Ũtongoi ti ng'ũndũ ya mũndũ.*[44] **Leadership is not a land of any particular person.**
This alludes to the significance of land ownership in Ũkamba. One's right to inherited land never lapses – the right is unconditional and

---

[43] Mũĩmi, *Kĩthyomo*, 19–21.
[44] KNA: DC/4/10 Machakos District Political Record Book 1930–1938; Mwau, *Dictionary*, 670.

timeless. However, the maxim, which emerged in the 1930s when debates about land tenure emerged, implies that leadership must be based on individual merit. There is no monopoly in political leadership.

1937. *Ũtongosya wĩ muuke, nũnyungaa wĩ na mũndũ akavikĩlwa nangĩ.*
Leadership has a fragrance that attracts people.
This reflects on the leadership in post-independence Kenya. The majority of those who agitated for independence were illiterate and semi-illiterate men, while postcolonial leadership was drawn from college-educated elites. From the 1970s, businessmen and/or their client-politicians took over leadership irrespective of ability. The proverb suggests that accumulation of wealth does not automatically qualify someone as a leader. Leadership is about skills to mobilize people for a progressive cause.

1938. *Vala nthũ ĩkaw'a tivo ĩvalũkaa.* **Where an enemy is thrown is not where he lands.**
This ancient proverb means that the bad wishes we accord to opponents do not always happen. In Kamba tradition, enemies were eliminated not only by physical force, but also through magic called *kwĩkaw'a/kwĩkya*, 'thrown/throw away'. Yet, the enemies 'thrown away' often flourished instead. The plans of the enemy are not the plans of God.[45]

1939. *Vala wĩona ũthei we vanda.* **Plant where you see a bare place.**
Although this proverb means one should make use of every opportunity, ironically, this ancient maxim was used in fighting. By these words, the speaker who was capably protecting himself from his opponent's blows meant, 'Hit me if you can.'[46]

1940. *Ũkongo ũkaya mũndũ ndaũkĩaa.* **A ravine that will eat a person is not feared by its victim.**
This talks about fate, foresight, complacency, and miscalculation in one's action. In the past, deep overgrown ravines were infested with poisonous snakes, fierce animals, and water-filled depressions that were dangerous to humans. People were warned to avoid crossing such ravines, but some habitually cut across them and eventually were killed. Injury and harm lurk more in familiar things than the unknown. Listen to good advice.

---

[45] Kimilu, *Mũkamba*, 117–18; Mũĩmi, *Kĩthyomo*, 10; Kĩeti, *Barking*, Kĩtukũ, *Folktales*, 37; Mwau, *Dictionary*, 670.
[46] Lindblom, *Riddles*, 37.

1941. *Ndaĩya ndyoneka na ngili.* **Respect cannot be purchased with one thousand shillings.**
This was culled from songs sung in the 1940s and 1950s in Kitui. The axiom posits a sharp distinction between the world of respect, kindness, and consideration (of interpersonal value and worth) and their rough analogues in the world of commerce and exchange (creditworthiness, patience, and reciprocity). However much reciprocity in commerce seems to rhyme with reciprocity between persons, there is an absolute wall between them: commercial debts and credits are temporary and negotiable; personal fault and honour are stains that require an altogether dissimilar process to fix, balance, and restore.

1942. *Mbĩngũ nĩ mũtethanio.* **Handcuffs are better exchanged.**
This emerged shortly after the establishment of a British colonial police force and the introduction of handcuffs. Before the First World War the colonial regime forced arrested men to collect money from villages and carry the money to 'money warehouses' in Kitui and Machakos towns. Carriers were handcuffed and, since the handcuffs were in short supply, one person was handcuffed while the other watched over him. After walking some distance, the handcuff was removed and exchanged to the other, hence the proverb.

1943. *Mũsikalĩ otaa na mbĩngũ.*[47] **A police officer dreams about handcuffs.**
This proverb, like the previous, is linked to the history of policing in Kenya beginning in 1896, when the first police station opened in Mombasa. In 1929, the colonial government created the Tribal Police to control native reserves. Many Kamba men enlisted in the force and used handcuffs to restrain culprits.[48] Emerging under such colonial circumstance, the axiom means that while pursuits become habits, the latter become part of one's character.

1944. *Mũndũ mũthei ndaũngamaa ta mũsikalĩ.* **A naked person does not stand to attention like a soldier.**
This emerged during the same period as the previous two entries, a period when Kamba men enlisted in the colonial army and police. A noticeable practice was regular drills and standing to attention with legs together and hands straight down. The axiom implies that a naked person cannot do that because his private parts will be exposed. This

---

[47] Mutisya, *Proverbs*, 28.
[48] Richard Waller, 'Towards a Contextualization of Policing in Colonial Kenya', *Journal of Eastern African Studies* 4(3) 2010: 525–41; Hans-Martin Sommer, 'The History of the Kenya Police 1885– 1960', a research report deposited at National Museums of Kenya, November 2007.

means one who cares about sensitive matters takes caution and thinks twice before speaking in public.

1945. *Wekya mavia volisi.* **You threw rocks at the police.**
This alludes to public confrontation with Kenya's police forces. For more than eighty years, defiance against the police was foolhardy. Stoning policemen who wielded guns, clubs, and shields was completely unthinkable until the 1980s. Anyone who dared was pursued and severely punished. The proverb, which emerged in the 1960s, points to the futility of certain endeavours. Do not play with fire.

1946. *Kĩamba nĩkĩsĩ vala ve mũisyo.* **The anklets know where there is danger.**
There are limits beyond which no one will dare go.[49] This reflects war practices in which Kamba warriors wore special war anklets. When people heard the jingling anklets, they knew danger was at hand and took appropriate actions. The maxim emerged during the Vascon era.

1947. *Wai ndwaa ndoelo.* **There is always a way out of each problem.**
Dating to the Vascon era this axiom has several interpretations. In any tragedy one cannot lack good counsel. Solutions to tragedy exist, they only need to be found.[50]

1948. *Mũumani ndaĩ kĩemo ngĩlana na mũumwa.*[51] **The insulter is not stronger than the insulted.**
This ancient maxim is about the degrading nature of engaging in insults. Both parties end unhappy. The proverb condemns aggression and calls upon community members to avoid insulting others.

1949. *Umaa nzounĩ ya Solo.* **Get out of Solo's elephant.**
This proverb originated with a singer from Ĩkũtha (Kitui) in the 1920s. The singer who had gone to work in Mombasa received news that the chief had taken his lover as wife. He travelled from Mombasa to Ĩkũtha. Near an old German mission station, he assembled a large dance troupe to entertain expatriates, then a common practice. Seizing the opportunity, he composed a song using this phrase, which at the same time praised a famous hunter named Solo, who never requested help in hunting and skinning elephants. Subsequently, the phrase became an axiomatic warning intruders to keep off.

---

[49] Mutisya, *Proverbs*, 73.
[50] Mutisya, *Proverbs*, 51.
[51] Mailu, *Kĩkyambonie*, 16.

1950. *Kamuu kayelw'a ĩkovi konaa ta kaũkũnangĩwa mbĩ.* **When a mosquito is being slapped, it thinks it is being applauded.**
This emerged during the twentieth century when clapping became a public practice and British slapping, called *ĩkovi*, a Swahili loanword, was introduced by the regime. Previously the Kamba were not keen on slapping, but had different ways of beating someone.

1951. *Nditindaa mwonzanĩ.* **I do not remain at seven.**
From antiquity three counting systems appear in Kĩkamba, reflecting changes in the Kamba language. This proverb was non-existent until the new form of counting emerged during the Vascon era. Number seven has been symbolically significant in all counting systems. The proverb means the speaker does not hesitate to call a spade a spade and will do important things immediately.[52]

1952. *Vayĩ kelĩ kangĩ.* **There is no second chance.**
This ancient maxim encouraged people to take advantage of opportunities as they appear. Luck knocks at one's door once in life.

1953. *Aũme mathaa mateuvĩtya kwoou ũlũkaa ũtekũvuĩla.* **Men shoot without missing so fly without perching.**
Chinua Achebe codified this African adage whose principal moral lesson is adaptability.[53] It reflects the pressure that African societies endured in the transition from traditional structures to 'the modern world'.

1954. *Kavii kaanawa ke iko.* **A dik-dik is shared while still roasting.**
This axiom has hidden meanings, perhaps meaning contested matters are sorted out in fights or such matters are resolved forthrightly when they emerge.

1955. *Aũme ndũngĩei ũta.* **Men return the bow to me.**
This war axiom was used an expression of distress in battle and call for reinforcement. It was a war cry uttered by a warrior finding himself encircled by enemies. He was in other words saying 'I am surrounded and need reinforcements.' Other fighters would then rush to the scene to clear the enemies. The axiom is used outside of a war context as an expression of exhaustion and call for help.

1956. *Mũndũũme nĩ kwĩkĩa ngotha ya kĩtenge.* **A man is to girdle in a *kitenge* fabric.**
This axiom encourages hard work with a goal to accumulate wealth and attain self-reliance. It emerged around the 1950s, when *kĩtenge* fabrics became common in Ũkamba as the attire for outdoor work.

---

[52] Lindblom, *Akamba*; Mwau, *Dictionary*, 675.
[53] Chinua Achebe, *Things Fall Apart* (New York: Anchor, 1994).

Politics, Conflict, and Peacemaking 425

1957. *Mbua ua mbola nyũmba ya sũsũ nĩ ya mbondo.* **Hey rain, slow down, my grandmother's house is sodden.**
This ancient proverb depicts the power of rain – its unstoppable ability to do good or evil. It is reputed to have come from a bird whose bowl-shaped nest of mud and grass received most of the rain water, spoiling its eggs and chicks. In distress the bird sang this line begging the rain to stop. It was used as a metaphoric statement telling powerful people not to harm the weak. It was also said in conflicts as a mockery to opponents, meaning the speaker will vanquish the opponent shortly, so be careful. It could also implore the powerful for leniency, just like the bird.

1958. *Ngũi ndĩkũaa.* **A singer never ages out.**
Singers are artists who maintain artistry almost to death. The second connotation of this ancient axiom is that a singer never sets himself above his age grade since he has to sing and dance with all ages.

1959. *Walea ũkũnia wĩ mũnini ndũlea ũkũnia wakũa.* **If you do not throw javelins in your youth, you will do so in your old age.**
This is common in central Kitui where youth played an erotic game called *kũkũnia*. The game involved making a javelin out of special wood. Groups of boys would gather as they tended livestock and throw their javelins in turn to see whose went the fuarthest. Those who reached the shortest distance were met with derision laced with erotic words. These games ceased after one attained adulthood.[54] The proverb means that certain things ought to be done during a specific period.

1960. *Kakuthu kau wĩvithĩte no kwĩaa sua matũ metĩke.* **That bush where you are hiding will shed its leaves when the sun shines.**
This ancient proverb tells someone he is standing on shaky ground. It tells a trickster his lies and secrets will be exposed.

1961. *Kakuthu kala mũtũĩe mwĩvithĩte nĩkasanziwe nĩ mbaa.* **The francolin trimmed the bush where you have been hiding.**
This precolonial proverb meant secrets of the listener have been exposed. Only thick bushes could hide someone but birds often reduced their leaves so that they could not shield anyone from view, just as the revelation of secrets expose conspirators.

1962. *Mũndũ wĩ mateng'e ndatambasya kĩthekanĩ.* **A bow-legged person does not walk in the bush.**
Bow legs resulting from malnutrition became prevalent during the nineteenth and twentieth centuries when the Kamba began to observe its

[54] Raphael Kĩthuka, 'The Traditional Games of the Akamba of Kenya' (MSC thesis, Kenyatta University, 2010), 51–3.

debilitating character and coined proverbs about it. It became a symbol of defectiveness. A bow-legged person walking in the bush confronts difficulties just as someone with weaknesses must refrain from certain chores.

1963. *Maeo aa mathekanasya nomo maũmanaa.* **The teeth that smile are the same that bite.**
Used to suggest that great friendships can break down, this ancient adage warns against hypocrisy and false friends. Do not be deceived by friendly looks. Friends today can be rivals tomorrow.

1964. *Ndũkakĩe lũma ũwĩta simba, lũma ndwĩmaayo ta ngunyũ.* **Do not fear an aardvark thinking it is a lion, it does not have teeth like claws.**
This originated with hunters who observed that while aardvarks have long and strong claws compared to lions, their teeth do not match. It means do not overestimate a task or its difficulty before attempting it.

1965. *Ĩtuvi ya ngũlũ nĩ kĩkw'ũ.* **The reward of pride is death.**
This is a warning that pride usually leads to blunders and self-destruction. It is similar to some biblical verses that condemn pride and praise humility. Nevertheless, this version is not a borrowing. Views about pride and humility were universal to world cultures.

1966. *Ĩtuvi ya naĩ nĩ kĩng'ole.* **The reward of sin is a gathering of condemnation by elders.**
This maxim alludes not to the Christian sense of sin, but to the practical actions the Kamba took against one who transgressed cultural norms. A public gathering called *kĩng'ole* either banished the transgressors from the village, torched their houses, or executed them by drowning or stoning. The maxim that emerged around the 1300s alongside *kĩng'ole* dissuades people from evil acts.

1967. *Isyĩmawa nĩ mũndũ na mũthoni wake.* **They are not hunted with an in-law.**
The Kamba took very seriously respect for in-laws. To maintain that respectability, they avoided working or even walking with in-laws. Any single error, even a reflex action like farting in the presence of an in-law, attracted a penalty of one goat. Hunting was the last thing a man could do with any member of his wife's family. This proverb comes from the Vascon era of immense hunting activities. It indicates that one must do things with the right people and stay in the right company.

1968. *Ĩsũvĩanei na kavalũkũ.* **Be cautious with the hare.**
The hare is depicted as cunning, slippery, and a sweet swindler. Oral tradition says this adage dates back to the first settlements in Ũkambanĩ. However, prudence leads historians to surmise that it specifically originated in Kamba encounters with hares in their habitat.

1969. *Mũndũ wĩ vinya ndakaw'a.* **A strong person is not helped to build.**
The Kamba adopted larger buildings during the Vascon era. Since construction consumed energy and time, construction became a social event rather than an individual affair. Men came with building materials and cordage. Women brought porridge to feed the builders and grass for thatch.

1970. *Mũndũ ũsu nĩ mũviku ta mbaa.* **That person is as hard as the francolin.**
Since the Monsoon era this proverb has circulated as a warning against underrating others. Do not try that person, he is as tough as francolin meat. The francolin was a symbol of stubbornness as it runs fast and waits for people to come close, then flies away. A stubborn person who played games with community members was compared to this bird.

1971. *Mũndũ ũsu e maiyũ maumbĩke.* **That fellow has buried bananas.**
An old catchphrase this illustrates proverbs' flexibility through its variants from the Monsoon to the Vascon era, following the introduction of sheep, bananas, and sweet potatoes – in that order – over many centuries. The axiom means that a person is mentally deficient.

1972. *Nĩwakĩkwata mũthia.* **You got it at the end of the tail.**
This ancient catchphrase warns the listener that they have made a terrible mistake. Pull back or you will perish.

1973. *Kĩtindo kĩ muma.* **Association or companionship has an oath.**
This comes from a circumcision song. It means that association breeds familiarity and creates firm bonds of friendship.[55]

1974. *Soo ndũvatawa kwaamba nĩ ĩko.* **A trumpet never ceases to make sound because of dirt.**
Imperial culture introduced metallic trumpets, which rapidly rusted and collected dust. However, Christian converts observed that dust and rust did not debilitate the functionality of the instrument. The maxim, therefore, means that it is the performance that matters, not the appearance.

---

[55] Mutisya, *Proverbs*, 34.

1975. *Wenda ũmanya ũka oou wũkĩtye.* **If you want to know me, keep coming.**
This warns an opponent that their words are provocative. The listener understands this as a red line and decides either to fight or retreat.

1976. *Wia ti ũkombo.*[56] **Reverence is not servitude.**
Honour often comes with humility. People who sought to be honoured often performed humbling deeds, to the shock of the proud. As the sages said, committing honourable duties was not submission to servitude. This proverb emerged during the Vascon era when Kamba trading with the coast learned about slavery and servitude. While the Kamba encouraged boldness, they discouraged excess aggression.

1977. *Uw'a mbu mana uw'a ũyuĩe.* **You scream in vain, screaming to yourself.**
Precolonial Kamba raised the alarm by making the repeated sounds: '*uuuii!*' '*uuuii ĩĩaüme küũĩ!*' Those who heard it rushed to the scene to help. If a horn was blown, only men armed for war responded. However, people never answered false alarms from characters noted for making false alarms. These customs began in the mid-seventeenth century when competition for resources led to interethnic warfare.[57]

1978. *Mũkoloni ndũlwa nĩwe.* **One cannot fail to identify a colonialist.**
From the second half of the twentieth century, this proverb appears in multiple songs and conversations, ironically not about European colonialists but of controlling, mean, and unreasonable people. This depiction reflects the actual experience and perception of colonial rule.

1979. *Waathya mavũa.* **You sought food during winnowing season.**
This proverb has various meanings. One, *mavũa* literally means the period when people thresh and winnow harvested crops. If one cries hunger then people can easily satisfy him with food. However, in a deeper sense *mavũa* may denote chaos or a situation where forces are beating one. In this sense the proverb warns someone his action might be inviting dispute and chaos.

1980. *Ndulani noyo ĩkĩlĩĩlasya nyeki nĩtomo.* **The gorer is the one that jumps over grass because of greed.**
This emerged among seventeenth-century herders grazing livestock on the plains with good grass. When starving cattle were driven to grass-rich niches, they browsed aggressively, often butting the weaker ones.

---

[56] Ngotho, *Mĩthimũkyo*, 46.
[57] Leslau, *Proverbs*, 35.

It was observed that the cow goring others in order to browse often misses the best grass. The axiom cautions people not to be greedy or they will miss the same opportunities they are fighting over.

1981. *Ngitī ngũmbaũ ndī matukũ maingĩ.* **A courageous dog does not live long.**
This maxim was propounded by a notable freedom fighter in the context of *nthenga* – a beer brawl – to admonish aggressive characters to calm down. He was comparing young men who thought they could fight anyone with courageous dogs that do not fear danger. In their eagerness to fight they would be killed.

1982. *Syavũa mwee na andũ syũlũkasya na angĩ.* **When they thresh millet with people, they winnow with others.**
Appearing in political songs, this maxim has a deeply hidden meaning requiring full content and contexts to fully understand. As one song goes, *Siasa syavũa mwee nandũ syũlũkasya na angĩ*, 'When politics thresh millet with people, they winnow with others', meaning that during the process of threshing, people talk of politics and politicians. However, during the ensuing winnowing, people change topic and speak about different political agendas and politicians. The whole discourse reflects the capricious nature of twenty-first-century politics, quickly changing imperceptibly. The singer is persuading those involved in politics to care more about permanent friendships than ephemeral politics.

1983. *Andũ matũanĩīe mailea kũtonyangana metho.* **Neighbours never fail to prick each other's eyes.**
Alluding to life in precolonial Kamba settlements this axiom promotes reconciliation when neighbours offend each other. The one seeking reconciliation through this axiom means that facts are facts, let us face reality in harmony.

1984. *Ĩtinĩawa nĩ kũthengeeya.* **It is gored for coming too close.**
Emerging from animal husbandry in the Monsoon era this alludes to bullfights. A bull is gored by coming too close to its opponent. Stay away from dangerous situations.[58]

1985. *Lisiki ya mũndũ yumaa yĩũlũ ĩmbange nĩ Ngai.* **One's fortune comes from heaven already reserved by God.**
This ancient axiom alludes to the Kamba belief in predestination. Good luck comes from the spiritual realm and cannot be manipulated to change. The axiom is also a condemnation of jealousy, informing those

[58] Mwau, *Dictionary*, 648.

who coveted other people's achievements to look inward to find their own God-given gifts for their own achievements.

1986. *Mũnyũ wa Ngai nduĩawa.* **God's salt is never rained on.**
This ancient axiom has multiple interpretations. First, it means God always protects the weak and the just. It also means God nurtures leaders from very humble backgrounds and protects them from evil until they mature to men of valour, virtue, and value. Salt symbolized the ideal taste and the best thing society could have. Women travelled long distances to dig and distil salt from salt licks. If it rained, the salt dissolved and lost its vitality. By implication even if 'the salt of God' is rained on, it will not dissolve. The whole concept suggests that God's grace is not seasonal, malleable, or subject to natural forces. It transcends all forces of nature and mankind's cruelty. The proverb expresses faith and hope even in hopeless situations.[59]

1987. *Ngai ndakomaa.*[60] **God never slumbers.**
This emerged from the twelfth century when *Ngai* replaced the old word *Mũlungu*. It was said by someone who escapes a tragedy implying God was their protector. This can refer to escape from economic hardship or physical insecurity.

1988. *Ngai wa mũndũ no mũndũ.* **The God of a person is another person.**
The significance of this axiom is that God is personalized, a development of the twentieth century. Before 1900, God was not personalized. Elders led in worship and gave blessings with prayers believed to be sufficient and long-lasting. The axiom suggests that a gift from God came through a person acting on behalf of God.

1989. *Mũndũ nĩ mũndũ nũndũ wa andũ.* **A person is a human being because of people.**
Since the first millennium the Kamba have lived in extended families, clans, and communities, giving rise to this proverb. It points out that a person was considered rich based on the number of friends, family members, and dependants they had. The ancient maxim encourages social behaviour, and tranquil communal unity.

1990. *Mwanake nĩ ĩvose.*[61] **A lad is arms-akimbo.**
Arms-akimbo is a stance signalling haughtiness, idleness, or arrogance. Women often use this phrase to show surprise, defiance, or pride. Preco-

---
[59] Kimilu, *Mũkamba*, 117; Kĩeti, *Barking*, 115; Kituku, *Sukulu*, 32; Mutisya, *Proverbs*, 56.
[60] Mwau, *Dictionary*, 664.
[61] Kimilu, *Mũkamba*, 74.

lonial Kamba generally saw it as an expression of inactivity and ignorance of the value of work. The proverb means if you want to appear clean but unproductive, hold on to your waist.

1991. *Mũndũ nde nywuĩĩa matumbĩ make.* **One does not drink the yoke of his own eggs.**
This ancient proverb condemns mean behaviour towards children such as incest. It compares a chicken consuming egg yolk to human self-destructive behaviour.

1992. *Ti kwenda kwa mũi kũminza moko, nĩ mũsandi kũvyũva.* **It is not the diner's choice to shake hands, it is because the mealiepap is hot.**
This axiom circulates in eastern Mwĩngĩ where the dish *mũsandi* is consumed, a meal unknown in other parts of Ũkamba. It is delicious and in the past people without spoons, but who could hardly wait for the meal to cool, scalded their hands and shook them in pain. It means people react in particular ways because of the stress they are under.

1993. *Nĩngolaa mũka ngenda indo.* **At times, I despise the wife and love livestock.**
Married men said this when their wives cheated or the in-laws became unreasonable. To demonstrate that a man loved a given woman, he had to give her father livestock. Nonetheless, if the marriage failed, the father had to return the cattle, justifying the maxim. It is used in any situation where one party fails to fulfil an agreement.

1994. *Ĩsoma yũkitaa na ũtee ũmwe na lelo.*[62] **A weak bull fights tactically.**
This proverb has featured in songs across Ũkamba for as long as there have been bullfights. After the animals had grazed, drunk, and rested, youths would drive the bulls against each other to make them fight. Soon they would fight without prodding. It advises listeners to be tactical and pragmatic when facing challenges, from political competition to job interviews.

1995. *Kyonze kĩyĩsaa kĩngĩ.* **A weakling does not eat another.**
This axiom means a weak person cannot help another weakling. Paupers seek help from the rich, not from other paupers.

1996. *Mũsumbĩ ũtauna ndaumasya moko ĩvose.* **An incompetent ruler never ceases [to have] arms akimbo.**
This encourages hard hands-on work as opposed to giving directives. A leader does the hard- hands-on work for his people. Rulers too can be

[62] Mwau, *Dictionary*, 647.

lazy, idle, and of no use to their subjects. This axiom appears to have originated from the diaspora when Kamba emigrants from Ũkamba formed centralized states during the Islamic period in parts of Tanzania.

1997. *Thinũa maangi maku vala ũthinĩkĩte.* **Retrieve your arrows where you dumped them.**
At day's end a man stored his unpoisoned arrows by driving them into his hut's thatch (*kũthinĩka*) with shafts facing up. A guest stored his arrows facing down by the compound fence before entering the homestead, and retrieved them as he left. This proverb was a way of telling an opponent 'mind your business and go away'.

1998. *Vandũ ndatia kaũ nditia maya.*[63] **A place I cannot leave a fight I cannot leave a feast.**
This refers to an offer of food signifying the relationship was for better or worse. Kĩtukũ says he coined this saying at Tala High School in the 1980s. It has since spread everywhere, which suggests either Tala people spread it or it predated his use.

1999. *Wakimwa ndwĩthiwa.* **If pounded, it will never be ground.**
This ancient axiom involves witchcraft-related conversation in which the speaker threatens that harm will come quickly. The rapacity of the harm is measured between pounding millet in a mortar and grinding it. It is also used in light moments to mean things have deteriorated.

2000. *Wĩkũma wĩlĩka.* **Despite your bark, you will be eaten.**
Like braggarts, cowardly dogs bark a lot, but prowling leopards capture and eat them. By application this means a baseless defence is futile, the truth will still come out. Used as a book title in 1990, this ancient axiom was used as a threatening axiom in conflicts and currently in political competitions.[64]

---

[63] Kĩtukũ, *Folktales*, 81.
[64] Kĩeti, *Barking*, 105.

Select Bibliography

Aardema, Verna. *Misoso: Once Upon a Time Tales from Africa*. New York: Scholastic, 1996.
Aardema, Verna, and Marcia Brown. *How the Ostrich Got Its Long Neck: A Tale from the Akamba of Kenya*. New York: Scholastic, 1995.
Adamson, Joy. *The Peoples of Kenya*. London: Collin & Harville Press, 1967.
Adeeko, Adeleke. *Proverbs, Texuality, and Nativism in African Literature*. Gainesville: University Press of Florida, 1998.
Adeleke, Durotoye. 'Yoruba Proverbs as Historical Records', *Proverbium* 26 (2009): 19–48.
Ademowo, Adeyemi Johnson, and Noah Balogun. 'Proverbs and Conflict Management in Africa: A Study of Selected Yoruba Proverbs and Proverbial Expressions', *International Journal of Literature, Language and Linguistics* 1(1) (2014): 39–44.
Adesoji, Abimbola. 'Yoruba Proverbs as a Veritable Source of History', *Proverbium: Yearbook of International Proverb Scholarship* 23 (2006): 1–15.
Al-Fida, Abu. *An Abridgment of the History at the Human Race*. Vols 1, 2. Constantinople, 1869.
Al-Masudi. In *The East African Coast: Selected Documents from the First Century to the Early Nineteenth Century*, ed. Stewart Parker Freeman-Grenville. Oxford: Oxford University Press, 1975.
Al-Masudi. *Meadows of Gold*. London: Routledge, 1989.
Ambler, Charles. *Kenyan Communities in the Age of Imperialism*. New Haven: Yale Press, 1988.
Anderson, David, and D. Johnson (eds). *Revealing Prophets*. London: James Currey, 1995.
Appiah, Peggy, et al. *Bu Me Bɛ: Proverbs of the Akan*. Oxfordshire: Ayebia Clarke Publishing, 2007.
Bailey, Clinton. *A Culture of Desert Survival: Bedouin Proverbs from Sinai and the Negev*. New Haven: Yale University Press, 2004.
Barendse, Rene. *Arabian Seas 1700–1763: Volume 1 The Western Indian Ocean in the Eighteenth Century*. Boston: Brill Publishers, 2009.

Barnes, A. *Seeing Through Self-Deception*. Cambridge: Cambridge University Press, 1997.

Baronov, David. *The African Transformation of Western Medicine and the Dynamics of Global Cultural Exchange*. Philadelphia: Temple University Press, 2008.

Bhebe, Ngwabi, and Advice Viriri (eds). *Shona Proverbs: Palm Oil with Which African Words are Eaten*. Harare: Booklove Publishers, 2012.

Boorstin, Daniel. *The Discoverers: A History of Man's Search to Know His World and Himself*. New York: Vintage, 1985.

Brenner, L. (ed.). *Muslim Identity and Social Change in Sub-Saharan Africa*. London: C. Hurst, 1993.

Brutzer, Ernst. *Der Geisterglaube bei den Kamba*. Leipzig: Evangelisch-Lutherische Mission, 1905.

Brutzer, Ernst. *Handbuch der Kambasprache*. Munich: Lincom Europa, 2012.

Brutzer, Herr. *A Kamba Grammar*. Berlin: Orientalische Seminar, 1905.

Bukenya, Austin, et al. (eds). *Understanding Oral Literature*. Nairobi: University of Nairobi Press, 1994.

Burton, Richard. *Wit and Wisdom from West Africa*. London: Tinsley Brothers, 1865.

Chami, F., G. Pwiti, and C. Radimilahy (eds). *People, Contact, and the Environment in the African Past*. Dar es Salaam: University of Dar es Salaam Press, 2001.

Chaudhuri, Kirti. *Trade and Civilization in the Indian Ocean: An Economic History from the Rise of Islam to 1750*. Cambridge: Cambridge University Press, 1985.

Chittick, Neville. *Manda*. Nairobi: The British Institute in Eastern Africa, 1984.

Clements, Jim. *The Clements Checklist of Birds of the World*. Ithaca: Cornell University Press, 2007.

Cotter, George, and Julius Nyerere. *Sukuma Proverbs*. Nairobi: Beezee Secretarial Services, 1965.

Cust, Rober. *A Sketch of the Modern Languages of Africa*. London: Trübner and Co., 1883.

Dalfavo, Albert. *Lugbara Wisdom*. Pretoria: University of South Africa Press, 1997.

d'Eeckenbrugge, Geo Coppens, et al. 'Worldwide Interconnections of Africa Using Crops as Historical and Cultural Markers', *East African Review* 52 (2019): 7–41.

Dunn, Rose. *The Adventures of ibn Battuta: A Muslim Traveler of the Fourteenth Century*. Berkeley: University of California Press, 1986.

Ehret, Christopher. *An African Classical Age: Eastern and Southern Africa in World History, 1000BC to A.D. 400*. Oxford: James Currey, 1998.

Elias, Taslim. *The Nature of African Customary Law*. Manchester: Manchester University Press, 1956.

Fabian, Johannes. *Language and Colonial Power: The Appropriation of Swahili in the Former Belgian Congo 1880 to 1938*. Cambridge: Cambridge University Press, 1986.

Farnsworth, Emma. *Akamba Grammar*. Nairobi: African Inland Mission, 1957.

Feierman, Steven. *The Shambaa Kingdom*. Madison: UW Press, 1974.

Flint, John. *The Cambridge History of Africa*. Vol. 5. Cambridge: Cambridge University Press, 1976.

Foeken, D., J. Hoorweg, and R. Obudho (eds). *The Kenya Coast: Problems and Perspectives*. Hamburg: Litverlag, 2000.

Fourshey, Catherine, Rhonda Gonzales, and Christine Saidi. *Bantu Africa 3500 BCE to the Present*. Oxford: Oxford University Press, 2018.

Freeman-Grenville, Stewart Parker. *The French in Kilwa Island*. London: Oxford University Press, 1965.

Freeman-Grenville, Stewart Parker. *The Medieval History of the Coast of Tanganyika*. London: Oxford University Press, 1962.

Gehman, Richard. *African Traditional Religion in Biblical Perspective*. Wheaton: Oasis International, 2012.

Gottlieb, Johann. *A Collection of 3,600 Tshi Proverbs in Use Among the Africans of the Gold Coast as Speaking the Asante and Fante Language, Collected, Together with their Variations, and Alphabetically Arranged*. Basel, 1879.

Gould, Francesca, and David Haviland. *Why Dogs Eat Poop, and Other Useless or Gross Information About the Animal Kingdom*. New York: Penguin Books, 2010.

Håkansson, Thomas. 'The Human Ecology of World Systems in East Africa: The Impact of the Ivory Trade', *Human Ecology* 32(5) (2004): 561–91.

Hamutyinei, Mordikai, and Albert Plangger. *Tsumo-Shumo: Shona Proverbial Lore and Wisdom*. Gweru: Mambo Press, 1987.

Hardy, Robert. *Longbow: A Social and Military History*. London: Bois d'Arc Press, 1992.

Hart, Henry. *Seven Hundred Chinese Proverbs*. Stanford: Stanford University Press, 1937.

Hatzel, Robert. *Snake, People and Spirits: Traditional Eastern Africa in its Broader Context*. Vol. 2. Newcastle: Cambridge Scholar Publishing, 2019.

Healey, Joseph (ed.). *Once Upon a Time in Africa: Stories of Wisdom and Joy*. Maryknoll: Orbis Books, 2004.

Hinde, Hildegarde. *Vocabularies of Kamba and Kĩkũyũ languages of East Africa*. Cambridge: Cambridge University Press, 1904.

Hobley, Charles. *Bantu Beliefs and Magic, with Particular Reference to the Kĩkũyũ and Kamba Tribes of Kenya Colony, Together with Some Reflections on East Africa After the War*. London: H.F. & G. Witherby, 1922.

Hobley, Charles. *Ethnology of Akamba and Other East African Tribes*. London: Frank Cass, 1910.
Hobsbawm, Erick, and Terence Ranger. *The Invention of Tradition*. Cambridge: Cambridge University Press, 2012.
Hofmann, Johannes. *Wörterbuch der Kamba-Sprache*. Leipzig: Leipziger Mission, 1901.
Humes, James. *Wit and Wisdom of Winston Churchill*. New York: Harper Perennial, 1995.
Huzii, Otoo. *Japanese Proverbs*. Vol. 33. Board of Tourist Industry, Japanese Government Railways, 1940.
Ibekwe, Patrick. *Wit & Wisdom of Africa: Proverbs from Africa & the Caribbean*. Trenton: Africa World Press, 1998.
Jackson, Kenell. 'Ngotho (The Ivory Armlet): An Emblem of Upper Tier Status Among the Nineteenth Century Akamba of Kenya ca. 1830–1880', *Kenya Historical Review* 5(1) (1977): 35–69.
Kaleli, Jeddy. 'Towards an Effective Christian Cross-Cultural Youth Training Model: A Youth Ministry International Case Study', DM thesis, Liberty Baptist Theological Seminary, 2004.
Kaleli, Jones. 'Theoretical Foundations of African and Western Worldviews and their Relationship to Christian Theologizing: An Akamba Case Study', PhD dissertation, World Mission, 1985.
Kavyu, Paul. *An Introduction to Kamba Music*. Kampala: East African Literature Bureau, 1977.
Kavyu, Paul. *Traditional Music Instruments of Kenya*. Nairobi: Kenya Literature Bureau, 1980.
Keter, Lucia, and Patrick Mutiso. 'Ethnobotanical Studies of Medicinal Plants Used by Traditional Health Practitioners in the Management of Diabetes in Lower Eastern Province, Kenya', *Journal of Ethnopharmacology* 139 (2012): 40–80.
Kibwaa, Joseph. *New Kikamba-English Dictionary*. NP: Book Venture Publishing, 2015.
Kibwana, Kivutha. *Law and the Status of Women in Kenya*. Nairobi: University of Nairobi Press, 1996.
Kĩeti, Mwĩkali. 'Myali Songs: Social Critique Among Kamba', MA thesis, University of Nairobi, 1988.
Kĩeti, Mwĩkali, and Peter Coughlin. *Barking, You'll be Eaten! The Wisdom of Kamba Oral Literature*. Nairobi: Phoenix Publishers, 1990.
Kimilike, Lechion. 'An African Perspective on Poverty Proverbs in the Book of Proverbs: An Analysis for Transformational Possibilities', PhD dissertation, University of South Africa, 2006.
Kimilu, David. *Mũkamba wa Wo*. Nairobi: Kenya Literature Bureau, 1962.
Kinyanjui, Sarah. 'Restorative Justice in Traditional Pre-Colonial Criminal Justice Systems in Kenya', *Tribal Law Journal* 10 (2009): 1–16.

Kituku, Vincent. *East African Folktales: From the Voice of Mũkamba*. Little Rock: August House Publishers, 1997.
Kituku, Vincent. *Sukulu Ĩte Ngũta: The School Without Walls Where Lessons Begin*. Boise: Vincent Kituku, 1997.
Kituku, Vincent, and Felisa Tyler. *Multicultural Folktales for All Ages: Traditional and Modern Folktales from Kamba (Kenya) and Tagloing (Philippines) Communities*. Newcastle: Arrowhead Classics, 1998.
Kĩtũnda, Jeremiah. 'Culture and Social Erosion in Ũkambanĩ: The Disintegration of African Culture and Environment, 1889–1989', MA thesis, Miami University, 1998.
Kĩtũnda, Jeremiah. 'Love is a Dunghill and I am the Cock that Gets on it to Crow', in *Hemingway and Africa*, ed. Miriam Mandel, 122–50. New York: Camden House, 2011.
Korosos, David. *Tugen Proverbs*. Nairobi: Phoenix Publishers, 1997.
Krapf, Johannes. *Travels, Researches, and Missionary Labours, During an Eighteen Years' Residence in Eastern Africa. Together with journeys to Jagga, Usambara, Ũkamba ni, Shoa*. London: Trübner and Co., 1860.
Lange, Kofi. *Three Thousand Six Hundred Ghanaian Proverbs*. Lewiston: E. Mellen Press, 1990.
Larby, Norman. *Kũsoma kwa mbee*. London: Longman, 1950.
Last, Joseph. *Grammar of Kamba Language, Eastern Equatorial Africa*. London: Society for Promoting Christian Knowledge, 1885.
Leslau, Charlotte, and Wolf Leslau. *African Proverbs*. New York: Peter Pauper Press, 1962.
Levtzion, N., and R. L. Pouwels (eds). *The History of Islam in Africa*. Athens: Ohio University Press, 2000.
Lindblom, Gerhard. *African Wanderings: Two Years of Ethnological Studies in British and German East Africa*. Stockholm: Bonnier Books, 1914.
Lindblom, Gerhard. *Kamba Folklore*. Vol. 3. Uppsala: Appelbergs Boktryckeri Aktiebolag, 1934.
Lindblom, Gerhard. *Kamba in British East Africa: An Ethnological Monograph*. Vol. 17. Uppsala: Appelbergs Boktryckeri Aktiebolag, 1920.
Lindblom, Gerhard. *Kamba Riddles, Proverbs and Songs*. Uppsala: Appelbergs Boktryckeri Aktiebolag, 1934.
Lindblom, Gerhard. *Notes on Kamba Grammar: With Two Appendices: Kamba Names of Persons, Places, Animals and Plants*. Uppsala: Appelbergs Boktrykeri Aktiebolag, 1926.
Lindfors, Bernth, and Okeyan Owomoyela. *Yoruba Proverbs: Translation and Annotation*. Athens: Ohio University Press, 1973.
Lonsdale, John. 'The Morale Economy of the Mau: Wealth, Poverty and Civil Virtue in Kĩkũyũ Political Thought', in *Unhappy Valley: Conflict in Kenya and Africa*, Vol. 2, ed. Bruce Berman and John Lonsdale, 315–504. London: James Currey, 1992.

Lonsdale, John. 'When Did the Gusii (Or Any Other Group) Become a "Tribe"?', *The Kenya Historical Review* 5(1) (1977): 122–33.

Maddox, Gregory. *Sub-Saharan Africa: An Environmental History*. Santa Barbara: ABC-CLIO, 2006.

Maher, Colin. 'Land Utilization as a National Problem With Special Reference to Kenya Colony', *East African Agricultural Journal* 2(2) (1936): 130–44.

Mailu, David. *Kaana Ngy'a*. Nairobi: Heinemann, 1983.

Mailu, David. *Kĩkyambonie: Kĩkamba Nthimo*. Nairobi: Combs Books, 1972.

Marriott, Joyce. *Ngewa (Stories)*. Nairobi: A.M. Publications, 1962.

Martin, Esmond. *Malindi: Past and Present*. Nairobi: National Museum of Kenya, 2009.

Marvin, Dwight. *The Antiquity of Proverbs: Fifty Familiar Proverbs and Folk Sayings with Annotations, and Lists of Connected Forms Found in all Parts of the World*. London: Wentworth Press, 2016.

Maundu, Patrick, et al. *Traditional Food Plants of Kenya*. Nairobi: National Museums of Kenya, 1999.

Mazrui, Ali. *The Africans: A Triple Heritage*. New York: Little Brown and Co., 1987.

Mbithi, Philip. *Self-Reliance in Kenya: The Case of Harambee*. Uppsala: Scandinavian Institute of African Studies, 1977.

Mbiti, John. *Akamba Stories*. Nairobi: Oxford University Press, 1983.

Mbiti, John. *English-Kamba Vocabulary*. Nairobi: Kenya Literature Bureau, 1981.

Mbiti, John. *Weteelete Ndakusaa: Kuetianisya na Ngewa Ya Mutunga na Syokau*. Nairobi: Vide- Muwa Publishers, 2012.

Mbiti, John, and Mutua Mulonzya (eds). *Ngaeka Waeka: Myali ya Kiikamba/ Kikamba Poems*. Nairobi: Akamba Cultural Trust, 2010.

Mbula, Judith. 'Penetration of Christianity into the Akamba Traditional Family', MA thesis, University of Nairobi, 1974.

Medhurst, Martin. *Eisenhower's War of Words: Rhetoric and Leadership*. East Lansing: Michigan State University Press, 1994.

Middleton, John (ed.). *Encyclopedia of Africa South of the Sahara*. New York: Charles Scribner's Sons, 1997.

Middleton, John. *The Kĩkũyũ and Kamba of Kenya*. London: International African Institute, 1953.

Middleton, John. *The World of the Swahili*. New Haven: Yale University Press, 1994.

Middleton, John, and Greet Kershaw. *The Central Tribes of the Northeastern Bantu*. London: International African Institute, 1965.

Mieder, Wolfgang. *African Proverb Scholarship: An Annotated Bibliography*. Colorado Springs: African Proverbs Project, 1994.

Mieder, Wolfgang. *The Politics of Proverbs: From Traditional Wisdom to Proverbial Stereotypes*. Madison: University of Wisconsin Press, 1997.

Mũĩmi, James. *Ngewa ya Syana*. Nairobi: Mowa Publishers, 1981.
Mũĩmi, James. *Nĩnendete Kĩthyomo Kitũ*. Nairobi: East Africa Publishing House, 1981.
Mũĩmi, James. *Nĩnendete kĩthyomo kitũ: Ũmaala Thome Ũtaawe*. Nairobi: East Africa Publishing House, 1980.
Muiu, Esther. *Cross-Cultural Religious Interaction of Kamba Community: The Culture and the Missionary Struggle*. Saarbrücken: Lambert Academic Publishing, 2012.
Munro, John (ed.). *Colonial Rule and Kamba: Social Change in the Kenya Highlands 1889–1939*. Oxford: Clarendon Press, 1975.
Muriuki, Godfrey. *A History of the Kĩkũyũ*. Nairobi: Oxford University Press, 1975.
Musila, David. *Seasons of Hope: Memoir of David Musila*. Nairobi: Maneeshmedia, 2019.
Musyoka, Stephen. *Against All Odds*. Nairobi: Peace Books, 2016.
Muthiani, Joseph. *Akamba from Within: Egalitarianism in Social Relations*. New York: Exposition Press, 1973.
Mutisya, Roy. *Kĩkamba Proverbs and Idioms: Nthimo Sya Kikamba na Myasyo*. Nairobi: Roma Publishers, 2002.
Mwandia, David. *Kilovoo*. London: Eagle Press, 1952.
Mwandia, David. *Kũsoma Kwa Kelĩ*. London: Macmillan, 1958.
Mwau, John. *Kĩkamba Dictionary: Kĩkamba–English, Kĩkamba–Kĩkamba, English–Kĩkamba*. Nairobi: Mwau, JH, 2006.
Mwiti, Edward. *1200 Kimeru Proverbs: Including Idiomatic Expressions and Similes*. Kenya: E.S. Mwiti, 2004.
Nagashima, Nobuhiro (ed.). *Themes in Socio-Cultural Ideas and Behaviour Among the Six Ethnic Groups of Kenya: The Visukha, the Iteso, the Gusii, the Kipsigis, the Luo, and Kamba*. Tokyo: Hitotsubashi University, 1981.
National Research Council. *Lost Crops of Africa, Volume 1–3*. Washington D.C.: National Academies Press, 1996–2008.
Ndeti, Kivuto. *Elements of Akamba Life*. Nairobi: East African Publishing House, 1972.
Ndisya, Joseph. 'An Analysis and Response to the Fear of Evil Spiritual Forces Among Kamba Christians in the Light of Biblical and Ellen White Teachings', PhD dissertation, Andrews University, 2015.
Newman, James. *The Peopling of Africa: A Geographical Interpretation*. New Haven: Yale University Press, 1995.
Ngotho, Thomas. *Kĩmena Kya Nzou na Mbũi*. Kampala: East African Literature Bureau, 1964.
Ngotho, Thomas. *Kũtheeyaa Kuma Yayanĩ*. Nairobi: East African Literature Bureau, 1962.
Ngotho, Thomas. *Mĩthimũkyo na Ngewa ingĩ*. Nairobi: Kenya Bureau, 1962.

Ngotho, Thomas. *Ngewa Nyanya na Moelyo*. Nairobi: East African Literature Bureau, 1962.

Northrup, David. 'Vasco da Gama and Africa: An Era of Mutual Discovery, 1497–1800', *Journal of World History* 9(2) (1998): 189–211.

Ng'weno, Hilary. *Makers of a Nation: Mulu Mutisya: The Men and Women in Kenya's History*. DVD. Nairobi: Kenya History & Biographies Co. Ltd, 2010.

Nsamenang, Bame, and Therese Tchombe, *Handbook of African Educational Theories and Practices: A Generative Teacher Education Curriculum*. Bamenda: Human Development Resource Centre, 2003.

Nyembezi, Sibusiso. *Zulu Proverbs*. Johannesburg: Witwatersrand University Press, 1957.

Nzioki, Sammy. *Kenya's People: Akamba*. London: Evans Brothers, 1982.

Obisakin, Lawrence Olufemi. *Proverbs in Communication: A Conflict Resolution Perspective*. New York: Triumph Publishing, 2010.

Ochieng', William, and Robert Maxon (eds). *An Economic History of Kenya*. Nairobi: East African Educational Publishers, 1992.

Oginga-Odinga, Jaramogi. *Not Yet Uhuru*. Nairobi: Heinemann, 1968.

Ogot, Bethwell (ed.). *Ecology and History in East Africa*. Nairobi: Heinemann, 1979.

Ogot, Bethwell (ed.). *Kenya Before 1900*. Nairobi: East Africa Publishing House, 1976.

Ogot, Bethwell (ed.). *Kenya in the 19th Century*. Hadith 8. Nairobi: Historical Association of Kenya, 1985.

Okesson, Gregg. *Re-Imaging Modernity: A Contextualized Theological Study of Power and Humanity within Akamba Christianity in Kenya*. Eugene: Pickwick Publications, 2012.

O'Leary, Michael. *The Kitui Akamba: Economic and Social Change in Semi-Arid Kenya*. Nairobi: Heinemann, 1984.

Oliver, Roland, and Gervase Mathew (eds). *History of East Africa*. Vol. 1. Oxford: Oxford University Press, 1963.

Omari, Cuthbert. *Methali na Misemo Toka Tanzania*. Nairobi: East African Literature Bureau, 1975.

Onyango, Peter. *African Customary Law: An Introduction*. Nairobi: Law Africa Publishing, 2013.

Opuku, Kofi. *Hearing and Keeping: Akan Proverbs*. Pretoria: University of South Africa Press, 1997.

Osborne, Myles. *Ethnicity and Empire in Kenya: Loyalty and Martial Race Among Kamba, C.1800 to the Present*. Cambridge: Cambridge University Press, 2014.

Owomoyela, Oyekan. *Yoruba Proverbs*. Lincoln: University of Nebraska Press, 2005.

Patel, D.L. *Ĩvuku ya Ngewa na Mbano: Kĩkamba*. Nairobi: D.L. Patel Press, 1956.

P'Bitek, Okot. *Acholi Proverbs*. Nairobi: Heinemann, 1985.

Penwill, Douglas. *Kamba Customary Law: Notes Taken in the Machakos District of Kenya Colony*. London: Macmillan, 1951.

Ranger, Terence, Ruth Marshall, and Olufemi Vaughan (eds). *Legitimacy and the State in Twentieth-Century Africa*. London: Palgrave Macmillan, 1993.

Robertson, Claire. *Trouble Showed the Way: Women, Men, and Trade in the Nairobi Area, 1890–1990*. Bloomington: Indiana University Press, 1997.

Russell-Wood, Anthony. *A World on the Move: The Portuguese in Africa, Asia and America, 1415–1808*. New York: Martin's Press, 1993.

Schmidt, Peter. *Iron Technology in East Africa: Symbolism, Science, and Archeology*. Bloomington: Indiana University Press, 1997.

Schmidt, Peter, et al. *The Tree of Iron*. Watertown: Documentary Educational Resources, 1988.

Shaw, Downes. *A Pocket Vocabulary of the Ki-Swahili, Ki-Nyika, Ki-Taita, and Ki-Kamba Languages*. London: C.M.S. Missionary in East-Africa, 1885.

Simiyu, Vincent. 'Land and Politics in Ũkambanĩ from the End of the Nineteenth Century Up To 1933', *Nouvelle série* 89 (1974): 101–46.

Somba, John. *Akamba Mirror: Some Notable Events in the Machakos District of Kenya, 1889– 1929 A.D*. Kijabe: Kesho Publications, 1979.

Somjee, Sultan. *Material Culture of Kenya*. Nairobi: East Africa Educational Publishers, 1993.

Spear, Thomas. 'Neo-Traditionalism and the Limit of Invention in British Colonial Africa', *Journal of African History* 44 (2003): 3–27.

Sperling, David. 'Survey of Islamic Manuscripts in Kenya', *International Survey of Islamic Manuscripts*, vol. 2. Leiden: E.J. Brill, 1993.

Stanner, William. 'The Kitui Kamba Market, 1938–39', *Ethnology* 8(2) (1969): 125–38.

Stevenson, Robert. *Kĩthamanĩ kya ũthwii*. Trans. John Mbiti. Nairobi: East African Literature Bureau, 1954.

Stevenson, Terry, and John Fanshawe. *The Birds of East Africa*. Princeton: Princeton University Press, 2002.

Subwa, Nyambe. *Zambian Proverbs*. Lusaka: Multimedia Zambia, 1993.

The Language Committee of the African Inland Mission in Ũkamba. *A Kĩkamba–English Dictionary*. Nairobi: Church Missionary Society Bookshop, 1949.

Thomas, Anthony. 'Adaptation to Modern Medicine in Lowland Machakos, Kenya: A Controlled Comparison of Two Kamba Communities', PhD dissertation, Stanford University, 1970.

Tignor, Robert. *Colonial Transformation of Kenya: Kamba, Kĩkũyũ, and Maasai from 1900–1939*. Princeton: Princeton University Press, 1976.

Titelman, Gregory. *The Random House Dictionary of Popular Proverbs and Sayings*. New York: Random House, 1996.

Tracey, Andrew. 'Kamba Carvers', *African Music Society Journal* 2(3) (1960): 55–8.
Trouillot, Michel-Rolph. *Silencing the Past: Power and the Production of History.* New York: Beacon Press, 1995.
Vail, Leroy (ed.) *The Creation of Tribalism in Southern Africa.* Berkeley: University of California Press, 1989.
Vail, Leroy, and Landeg White. *Power and the Praise Poem: Southern African Voices in History.* New York: James Currey, 1992.
Van Luijk, J.N. *Traditional Medicine Among Kamba of Machakos District, Kenya.* Amsterdam: Royal Tropical Institute, 1982.
Vansina, Jan. *Oral Traditions as History.* Madison: University of Wisconsin Press, 1985.
Walser, Ferdinand. *Luganda Proverbs.* Berlin: Reimer, 1982.
Wanjohi, Gerard. *Under One Roof: Kĩkũyũ Proverbs Consolidated.* Nairobi: Paulines Publications Africa, 2001.
Watt, Rachel. *African Inland Mission in Hearing and Doing.* New York: Hurlburt and McConkey Publishing, 1896.
Watt, Rachel, and Stuart Watt. *In The Heart of Savagedom: Reminiscences of Life and Adventure During a Quarter of a Century of Pioneering Missionary Labours in the Wilds of East Equatorial Africa.* New York: Marshall Brothers, 1892.
Watt, Stuart. *Vocabulary of the Kĩkamba Language.* Harrisburg: Keller Publishing, 1900.
Watuma, Blanche. *Mũkamba na Syĩthĩo Syake.* Nairobi: Sengani Publishers, 2011.
Weber, Katherine. *Objects in Mirror Are Closer Than They Appear.* New York: Broadway Books, 1995.
White, Luise. *The Comforts of Home: Prostitution in Colonial Nairobi.* Chicago: University of Chicago Press, 1990.
Whiteley, Wilfred. *Swahili: The Rise of a National Language.* London: Methuen Publishing, 1969.
Whiteley, Wilfred, and M.G. Muli. *Practical Introduction to Kamba.* London: Oxford University Press, 1962.
Wimmelbücker, Ludger. *Kilimanjaro: A Regional History.* Münster: Lit Verlag, 2002.
Yankah, Kwesi. *The Proverb in the Context of Akan Rhetoric: A Theory of Proverb Praxis.* New York: Peter Lang Publishers, 1989.
Zeleza, Tiyambe. *Akamba.* New York: The Rosen Publishing Group, 1995.
Zinnser, Hans. *Rats, Lice, and History.* Boston: Springer Press, 1935.

Index

aardvark, 51, 426
African Brotherhood church, 300
African Inland Mission, x, 7
Al-Masudi, xiii, 256, 433
antiquity, xiii, 14, 16–18, 25, 33, 37, 45, 47, 56–7, 62, 70, 76, 79, 84, 87, 89, 94, 98, 103, 105, 108–9, 111, 119, 124, 138, 140, 149, 177, 182, 192, 198, 203–4, 209, 211, 213–19, 221, 238, 240, 242, 248–9, 251, 254–8, 274–6, 296, 301, 316, 321, 327–8, 330–2, 337, 344–5, 349, 351, 353, 370, 372, 378, 481–2, 387, 397, 403–7, 413–14, 418, 424
    antiquity of a proverb, 5
    Kamba antiquity, v
apiculture, xiii, 96, 224, 313, 341, 365
    apicultural purpose, 28, 367
    Kamba apicultural norms, 93
Atwa, 284

bananas, xiii, 152, 427
    Zanzibar bananas, 289
Bantu, xiii, 318
buffalo, 47–8, 408–9
British, 162, 273, 279, 376, 422, 424
    British and French, xiv
    British administration, xiv, 212
    British colonial administration, 105, 396
    British Empire, 285, 354
    British farmers, 155
    British imperial army, xv
    British imperial builders, 96
    British planters, 152, 279

Cassava, xiv, 42–3, 163–4
cheetah, 54, 79, 408
Christianity, 7, 33, 97, 102, 114, 136, 152, 176, 248, 293, 300, 305, 321, 351, 393
    Christian converts, 84–5, 296, 426–7
    Christian missions, 355
colonial era, xiv, 63, 83, 89, 103, 106, 112, 147, 157, 213, 234, 262, 265, 286, 288, 313, 341, 351, 359, 368, 390, 394–6
    colonial coinage, 164
    postcolonial era, 125, 206, 231, 290–1
    precolonial era, 8, 33, 224, 416
Columbus, 155, 208
commerce, 3, 44, 74, 101, 146, 280, 417, 422
    imperial commerce, xiv, 106, 154, 159
community, 34, 39, 43–4, 49–50, 61, 74–5, 79, 83, 95, 102, 119, 121, 123, 125, 132, 142, 157–8, 161, 164, 167, 169, 178–81, 190, 194–5, 214–15, 222, 241–2, 256–8, 272–3, 279, 293, 296, 313, 321, 341, 343, 345, 347, 349, 371, 373, 386, 389, 397, 415, 423, 427
copper, 37, 280, 345, 395

death, 14, 18, 48–9, 61–3, 77, 80, 89, 103–4, 114, 143, 151, 160, 195, 211, 214, 220, 224, 253, 266, 287, 295–7, 302, 304, 321, 332, 337, 381, 340, 343, 348, 378, 381, 404, 410, 425–6

by stoning, 343
from poison, 237
of African pride, 248
of a patriarch, 124, 258, 284, 312, 416
of Kalekye, 247
Sting of death, 98

East Africa, xiii, 44, 61, 100, 124, 126, 134, 147, 152, 155, 158, 161, 165, 175, 197, 212, 237, 251, 285–6, 298, 339, 348, 366, 381, 386, 417–18
East African coast, xiv, 157
East African communities, 212
East African history, 3–4
East Africans, 17
East African cultures, 32
elephant, 24, 44–7, 97, 280–1, 372, 378, 408–9, 423
exchange, xiii, xiv, 41, 134, 158, 171, 179, 182, 193, 201, 216, 226, 254, 275, 280, 281, 358, 363, 375, 422
  Monsoon exchange, 3, 27, 101, 152, 165, 212, 237, 404, 417
  Vascon exchange, xiv, 3, 101, 137, 185, 215

family, 15, 27, 44, 49, 51, 73–4, 79, 95, 98, 100, 107, 120, 137, 143, 167, 177–8, 180, 185–6, 191, 194–5, 202, 208–9, 214–15, 220, 222, 230, 233, 235, 250, 253, 255–8, 261–3, 266, 274, 279–80, 284, 288, 292, 295–302, 307, 312, 317, 322, 340–1, 349, 355, 364, 382, 392, 397–8, 400, 403, 406, 413, 416, 419, 426
  family harmony, 32–9
  family head, 34, 56, 122–30
  family members, 16, 34, 102, 105, 124–5, 130, 169, 172, 225–6, 238–47, 297, 309–10, 315, 355, 369–74, 385, 389, 430
farming, xiii, 13, 15–16, 20–1, 29, 84–7, 90–1, 131, 168, 183, 201–3, 220, 225, 234, 304–9, 327, 373, 415

farm(s), 19, 30, 42, 44, 63–70, 91, 99, 127–39, 158, 163, 180–1, 193, 196, 207, 217, 265–7, 272, 291, 349, 386, 412, 420
farmer(s), 13, 15–16, 18–30, 67, 82, 84–7, 91, 94, 123, 155–9, 176, 187, 198, 214, 217, 340, 363
farming techniques, 30
farmlands, 128, 157, 207, 347
Farnsworth, Emma, 7–8, 38, 60, 66, 218, 332, 339, 385
flea, 99, 100, 102

Galla, 179–80, 278–9, 284, 400
Giriama, 146, 280–1

hare, 47, 111, 147, 154, 427
hearth, 9, 39, 119–26, 258, 306, 322–4, 330, 398, 404, 408
hippopotamus, 114–15
hunter(s), 38, 44–50, 52–9, 70, 74, 76–83, 86–7, 97, 111, 138, 176, 182–3, 217, 220, 254–5, 273, 276, 280, 288, 301, 324, 340, 367, 375, 378–81, 383–4, 399–400, 409, 413–14, 423, 426
hunting, xiii, 7, 28, 35, 48–50, 52–3, 56–7, 59–60, 72, 108, 114, 119, 140, 142–3, 255, 267, 292, 304, 335, 398–400
  hunting context(s), 55, 384, 408
  hunting expedition(s)/trips, 74, 280, 280 406
  hunting weapons, 370
    hunting bow, 378
    hunting dogs, 285
hyena, 23, 25, 51–3, 71–7, 83, 114, 140, 182, 208, 217, 257, 261–2, 284, 314

imperialism, xiv, 3, 113, 244
independence, xv, 3, 14, 20, 125, 127, 131, 134, 218, 223, 251, 265, 305, 316, 320, 332, 362, 392, 394, 396
  post-independence, 3, 8, 137, 234, 302, 392, 421
  pre-independence, 3, 8

iron, 191, 377, 387
  iron bar, 125
  iron blade, 365
  iron hoe, 222
  iron ore, 35, 387
  iron sheets, 228
  ironsmith, 386
  ironware, 212
  ironworking, 379
   workers, 387
Islam (Islamic era/period), xiii, 3, 17, 25, 27–30, 34–6, 61, 66–7, 78, 80, 83, 86, 91, 96, 122, 124, 131, 134, 136–7, 149, 151, 185, 236, 238, 240, 248, 255, 273, 284, 294, 297, 313, 315, 322, 335–6, 351–4, 377, 380–3, 386–9, 400, 414, 420, 432

Kenya, xvi, 7–9, 20, 26, 32, 53, 60, 74, 96, 105, 112–13, 137, 140, 142, 157, 161, 172, 179, 181, 212–13, 250, 266, 271, 278, 280, 285, 294, 314, 348, 354, 356, 359–61, 367, 421, 423
  coastal Kenya, x, 294
  development, 134
  eastern Kenya, ix, 3, 179, 406
  ethnic groups, 5
  government, 14
  Mount Kenya, xiii, 20, 283, 364
  politics, 234–5
Kikuyu, 281–3
Kilimanjaro, xiii, 96, 134, 152, 364, 377
Kitui, x, xii–xiii, 7–9, 15, 17, 35, 42, 58, 80, 83, 96–7, 135, 147, 162, 181, 222, 252, 271, 316–17, 353, 357, 383–4, 422–5
  Kitui dialect, x, 84, 284
  Kitui Kamba, x, 277, 284, 303
  Kitui County, 9, 218, 235
Krapf, xiv, 9, 44, 204, 238, 278
Kwavi, xiv, 122, 124, 179–80, 277–9, 283–4, 287, 314, 389, 409

leopard, 47, 96, 408–9
Lindblom, Gerhard, 6–7, 16, 53, 60, 65, 97, 177, 236, 265, 302, 304, 345, 382, 416

lion, xii, 48, 51, 76, 78–80, 87, 90, 96, 100, 399, 408–9, 426
loquats, xiii, 81, 152–4

Maasai (Masai, *see also* Kwavi), 122, 271, 277–9, 282, 400
Machakos, x–xiii, 7–8, 17, 32, 35, 84, 142, 158–9, 165, 176, 216, 218, 222, 231, 272, 284–90, 295, 300, 308, 330, 332, 339, 400, 422
maize, xiv, 84, 152, 196, 301, 317–18, 339, 366
marriage, 49, 85, 91, 123, 125, 129, 135, 141, 172, 175–9, 184, 188–9, 196, 207–11, 216–17, 222, 229–44, 247, 252–4, 262, 265–7, 300, 341, 351, 364, 388, 405, 431
Mbere, 283
Mboonĩ, 20, 48, 51, 236, 282, 367
Meru, 204
Mombasa (coins), xiv, 20, 212, 230, 422–3
monkey, 87, 90
Monsoon, 15, 18, 47, 142, 205, 222, 282, 313, 475, 528, 545

Nairobi, x–xiii, 142–3, 199, 271, 280, 290, 359

pawpaw, xiv, 134, 279, 298–9
potatoes (sweet, Irish), xiv, 155, 157–8, 427

raiding (cattle-raiding, raiders), xiv, 42, 50, 87, 91, 179–80, 220, 255, 277–9, 282, 284, 400, 406, 409, 414
rhino, 48–50, 365, 408–9

salt, 156, 191, 212, 218, 315, 320, 322, 430
Singũ, 288
snuff, 158–62, 212, 281, 311
social media, xii–xv, 3, 9–17, 348, 356
sugarcane, xiii, 136, 162–3, 237, 316
Syũkĩmau (prophetess), 283, 284

Tanzania, v, x, xiii, xiv, 34, 74, 96, 213, 236, 240, 271, 364, 406, 413, 432
Thaisũ, 284
tobacco, xiv, 120, 158–62, 186, 212, 251, 311
trade (Kĩng'ang'a/kĩnana trade system, long distance trade), xiii, 15, 16, 23, 58, 64, 69, 74, 89, 112, 127, 134, 148, 157, 195, 199, 212, 218, 235, 244, 253, 265, 266, 268, 273, 282, 286, 300, 307, 336, 356, 367–9, 376, 380, 384, 397, 400, 420

Vasco (da Gama, Vascon), xiv, 3, 7, 14, 21, 24–8, 35, 38–9, 42, 46, 51, 77–8, 80, 84, 93, 96, 101–7, 122, 124, 128–34, 137, 150, 152, 154–60, 164, 167, 169, 171, 175–6, 181–2, 185–6, 191–3, 203, 207–10, 215, 219–26, 230, 235, 238, 241, 244, 259, 277–9, 282–4, 287, 298, 301, 303–4, 310–12, 314, 317–21, 324, 326–8, 339, 346–7, 368, 375, 378, 380–1, 388, 390, 396, 400–1, 405–11, 414–18, 423–8

Witchcraft, 294, 296, 300–1, 432
Wizardry, 230, 301–2

Yatta, 50–1